Teaching Models

DESIGNING INSTRUCTION FOR 21ST CENTURY LEARNERS

Teaching Models

DESIGNING INSTRUCTION FOR 21ST CENTURY LEARNERS

Clare R. Kilbane, Ph.D.
Otterbein University

Natalie B. Milman, Ph.D.
George Washington University

PEARSON

Boston   Columbus   Indianapolis   New York   San Francisco   Upper Saddle River
Amsterdam   Cape Town   Dubai   London   Madrid   Milan   Munich   Paris   Montréal   Toronto
Delhi   Mexico City   São Paulo   Sydney   Hong Kong   Seoul   Singapore   Taipei   Tokyo

Vice President and Editorial Director: Jeffery Johnston
Executive Editor: Linda Ashe Bishop
Development Editor: Alicia Reilly
Editorial Assistant: Laura Marenghi
Senior Marketing Manager: Darcy Betts
Production Project Manager: Annette Joseph
Full-Service Project Management: Element LLC

Composition: Element LLC
Cover Images: 1, © Rob Marmion/Shutterstock; 2, © iofoto/Shutterstock; 3, © Monkey Business Images/Shutterstock; 4, © auremar /Shutterstock; 5, © karelnoppe/Fotolia.com; 6, © Monkey Business Images/Fotolia; 7, © goodluz/Fotolia; 8, © iofoto/Fotolia.com

Credits and acknowledgments borrowed from other sources and reproduced, with permission, in this textbook appear on the appropriate page within text.

Many of the designations by manufacturers and sellers to distinguish their products are claimed as trademarks. Where those designations appear in this book, and the publisher was aware of a trademark claim, the designations have been printed in initial caps or all caps.

Library of Congress cataloging-in-publication data not available at this time.

30 2022

ISBN 10:   0-205-60997-X
ISBN 13:   978-0-205-60997-0

To our teachers—who shared the art and soul of teaching with us.

About the Authors

Martha Ryan Cleary

Clare R. Kilbane, Ph.D., has worked with learners at all educational levels—from grad school to grade school—for more than 20 years. A former elementary educator and technology coordinator, Clare has a bachelor's degree from the University of Dayton, a master's degree in instructional design from Ohio State University, and a Ph.D. in educational evaluation from the Curry School at the University of Virginia. She has been on the faculty at the University of Massachusetts Amherst and Capital University, and she is currently a tenured associate professor of educational technology at Otterbein University. Clare has an active consulting practice with K–12 schools, is a frequent speaker at professional conferences, and has participated in numerous statewide grants and research projects involving technology integration and digital portfolios. She is the coauthor of the *Digital Teaching Portfolio Handbook* and *Digital Teaching Portfolio Workbook* with Natalie Milman and is currently coauthoring a text with Carol Ann Tomlinson for the Association for Supervision and Curriculum Development. She has also authored numerous articles, reviews, online courses, and multimedia materials. Clare lives with her husband, her daughter, and two Glen of Imaal terriers in Columbus, Ohio.

Stephen E. Milman

Natalie B. Milman, Ph.D., is associate professor of educational technology and coordinator of the Educational Technology Leadership Program in the Department of Educational Leadership at George Washington University's Graduate School of Education and Human Development. She earned her doctorate in instructional technology from the University of Virginia's Curry School of Education with a graduate specialization designed to prepare technology leaders. Natalie has taught at the elementary school level as a second-grade teacher, science specialist, mentor, and technology teacher in Los Angeles County, California. Her primary research interest is 21st century pedagogies. Her current research interests include one-to-one laptop and tablet initiatives, student engagement and learning through distance education, strategies and models for the effective integration of technology into the curriculum at all academic levels, and the use of digital portfolios for professional development. Natalie has published numerous articles and presented at many conferences. She has coauthored two books about digital portfolios with Clare Kilbane. She is the coeditor of the Current Practice Section of the journal *Contemporary Issues in Technology and Teacher Education* and serves on the American Educational Research Association's Technology Committee. Natalie lives in Virginia, outside of Washington, D.C., with her husband and two children.

Brief Contents

Contents

PART II Instructional Models

Foreword

To say that the beginning of my teaching career was inauspicious is to compliment it. I would like to think that some first-year teacher somewhere began with less awareness of the art and science of teaching than I did, but that may be a vain hope.

I began teaching high school students in a very rural K–12 school at the end of the first marking period as the result of a newspaper advertisement. I asked that I be allowed to observe the class for a day before I began teaching because I had no idea what content I would be expected to cover. In that day of observation, which was arguably at least a month long, I discovered that the students who were about to become mine not only did not listen to instructions but also did not remain in their seats as class progressed—and, in fact, could and did crawl out of the classroom's first-floor window to enjoy one another's company in the autumn air of the schoolyard. During that very long day, my thoughts never turned to the nature of the disciplines I would be teaching. Rather, I conducted an extended debate with myself about whether I really needed a job badly enough to return the next day. Reality won and I did return, armed with virtually no sense of what it meant to teach—let alone to teach well.

My first lesson plan for the two World History classes I taught consisted of a crossword puzzle. My instructional goal, had I known I should have one, was to see if I could use the puzzle to keep the students' attention—maybe to help them begin to work with me and to work with one another. In fact, I did keep their attention that day. They were completely absorbed with my lesson—because they had never seen a crossword puzzle and had no sense at all of how to answer #1 across which read, "Our country, abbr." There were two problems. They did not know the name of the country in which they lived, and they did not know the term *abbreviation* (which, of course, was abbreviated in the list of clues). The two class periods were incredibly diagnostic of the gap that existed between the prior experience of my students and the aspirations of the textbook.

My most promising "instructional innovation" that year came fairly early. As I tried to discover how I could help the tenth-graders connect with the content of World History, I discovered that religion was an important part of life for many of them. They were all Protestants, but they did not know that and were reluctant to take my word for it. So it seemed reasonable to begin our study with the Reformation. While it was not exactly at the front of the textbook, it felt important to help the kids see themselves and their world in the context of history. In talking with them about Protestantism, its roots, and their connection with those roots, I discovered that the students did not know any Catholics and had never heard of Judaism. So I planned a trip to a university town about 90 minutes away from the school and arranged for visits with a priest and a rabbi in their places of worship so that the two men could talk with the students a bit about the history of their faiths.

The trip was oddly successful. The students were thoughtful and respectful with the young priest and young rabbi. The trip itself spoke to the students of my interest in them, and they trusted me more for it. The small town we visited was vast to many of the students who had never traveled. One student said to me with some awe as we got on the bus to return to school, "You know what? I been looking as hard as I could all day long and I ain't seen the same person twice yet today." And the trip was helpful to me because it gave me the courage to reach outside the four walls of our classroom to a larger world as I taught.

The successes were modest, however. Students' learning suffered from their teacher's lack of clarity, precision, and finesse in teaching. Responding to a "throwaway" question on the unit test, one student told me that the most important thing on the trip for him was when we went to the "send-a-god" to see the "rabbit." There was some widespread confusion about possible connections between the word *Protestantism* and the word *prostitution.* And I think it is safe to say that the students never accepted that their brands of religion had anything to do with Martin Luther (whom they often referred to as Martin Luther King).

Over the decades that followed, I learned about designing instruction—slowly, awkwardly, and without the benefit of a framework or vocabulary to guide my thinking. I did some good things that would qualify as "sound pedagogy" and some embarrassing things that most certainly would not. I learned from both. But I wasted time and energy.

This book, *Teaching Models: Designing Instruction for 21st Century Learners*, creates in me a sense of longing to begin my work as a teacher again—armed with its insights. How much sharper might my thinking have been if I had known the vocabulary for four types of knowledge? How much more purposeful might my instructional choices have been if I had understood how and when to use 10 major instructional models? How many more students might I have reached if someone had illustrated for me how to attend to students' learning differences as I planned lessons? And how much more motivating might the learning opportunities I created for my students have been had there also been opportunity and guidance for using contemporary technologies to engage my students' thinking, and my own? I would sign up in an instant to go back to that first year and begin again if I could take that sort of knowledge with me.

The times we teach in are complex and challenging on every level, but we know so much more than we did just three decades ago about how the brain works, about how students learn, and about what teachers can do to maximize student potential. We understand the power of traditional models of teaching but cannot help recognizing that the skillful integration of 21st century technologies can enable more equitable learning opportunities for all. I am energized by the ways *Teaching Models* weaves together so many of the proven approaches and innovative strategies our profession has to offer. And I am excited for prospective and current educators who are willing to draw on this resource to become "educational designers" who can empower contemporary students to engage today and continue learning throughout their lives.

Carol Ann Tomlinson
William Clay Parrish, Jr. Professor & Chair
Educational Leadership, Foundations, & Policy
Curry School of Education
University of Virginia

PREFACE

Regardless of what you teach or where you teach, your success as an educator in the 21st century depends on your ability to design effective instruction for those you teach. Such instruction successfully addresses the individual and shared learning needs of a diverse population of students as they work to master content area learning and the skills required for life in a dynamic, fast-paced, technology-driven, global society. Contemporary educators find themselves surrounded by an unprecedented variety and quantity of powerful resources for teaching. However, these resources—whether they be materials, models, strategies, or technologies—are effective only to the extent that teachers know when and how to coordinate their use to prepare students for the increasing education and workforce demands they will face throughout their lives.

Designing effective educational experiences requires teachers to function as educational designers. An educational designer is a teacher who approaches instructional planning with purpose, uses knowledge of specialized systematic processes to identify and frame instructional challenges related to learners and content, and competently addresses these challenges through the skillful application of a broad repertoire of instructional models, strategies, and technologies. Educational designers approach the work of teaching with a new mind-set, a broadened skill set, and a high-quality tool set—all of which assist them in developing instruction that responds to their learners' needs. The new mind-set enables teachers to approach their work as empowered problem solvers who are aware of their ability to direct important dimensions of practice. The expanded skill set allows them mastery over systematic approaches to instructional planning and assessment processes. The high-quality tool set consists of a collection of models, strategies, and technologies for teaching that can make learning more efficient, effective, and engaging.

Text Organization

Part I of this text explains why functioning as an educational designer will lead to more successful teaching, and it proposes that this orientation supports optimal use of the models of teaching that are the focus of Part II. Chapter 1 frames the challenges of 21st century teaching, illustrates the influence of major trends on the profession, and highlights unique characteristics of 21st century learners. Chapter 2 introduces teachers to the field of instructional design and demonstrates how systematic processes used by instructional designers can support more effective teaching. Chapter 3 presents the different types of tools available for 21st century teaching and promotes the development of specialized knowledge for their implementation. Chapter 4 describes the three major types of assessment and their role in the assessment cycle. Knowledge of content in these chapters is critical for educational designers when deciding how to optimally use the instructional models in this book. Part I provides a foundational understanding that enables the reader to appreciate the enduring value of the instructional models in the context of 21st century teaching and to recognize how they can be made even more powerful when used in concert with the assessment cycle, differentiated instruction practices, and technology tools.

Part II of this text presents 10 powerful, proven models of teaching: Direct Instruction, Concept Attainment, Concept Development, Inductive, Vocabulary Acquisition, Inquiry, Problem-Based Learning, Cooperative Learning, Integrative, and Socratic Seminar. The presentation of these models demonstrates that they can be transformed for new relevance in the digital era and used to address the challenges of 21st century teaching through (1) the increased use of technology during planning, implementation, and assessment; (2) the integration of differentiated instruction principles and practices; and (3) their purposeful application by educational designers who apply systematic thinking and processes to design instruction for their students.

The 10 models selected for inclusion in this text support the development of skills and knowledge required for successful life, work, and learning in the 21st century, including the 4Cs—collaboration, communication, critical thinking, and creative thinking. They also address academic content across grade levels, are suitable for use in each content area, and can be used as specialized tools for addressing specific types of knowledge (i.e., factual, procedural, conceptual, and metacognitive).

In each chapter, we provide the history of the instructional model, relevant research, its steps, and practical information supporting its best use. Rich illustrations of the model in educational settings and detailed suggestions for differentiating the content of instruction, instructional processes, and evaluation of student learning are also integrated throughout. Each chapter utilizes a common structure for communicating chapter content—using recurring, descriptive section headings. This organization makes it easy for readers to locate information that corresponds with their particular interest in the model and their readiness for learning about it. Although each chapter is presented in a linear format, readers should feel free to read the various chapter sections in whatever order they choose and consider the various section headings as differentiated "entry points." The integration of technology as a tool to make the planning, implementation, and assessment that supports student learning more efficient, effective, and engaging is a major emphasis of each chapter. The integration of technology tools is intended to be treated as a standard practice—and not as an "add-on." Embedded in these chapters are field-tested lesson plans illustrating how differentiated practices and technology tools support all dimensions of the learning process.

Text Features

The following features have been included to promote the comprehension of those reading the text and to promote the application of content in the text to contemporary educational practice.

SCENARIOS These stories or "vignettes" illustrate each chapter's main ideas in practical classroom settings with diverse learners. Multiple scenarios are included in each chapter and referenced within chapter sections to connect the content to the "real world" of teaching in 21st century classrooms. These scenarios link chapter content to the reader's personal experiences while also raising questions and inspiring discussion. The opening scenario for each chapter connects to an in-depth lesson plan that illustrates the chapter's specific instructional model. Later, three scenarios present examples of how each model might be applied in practice at the elementary, middle school, and high school levels.

TECHNOLOGY TOOLS TABLE In each chapter from Chapter 5 through Chapter 14, a technology tools table provides readers an easy-to-navigate summary of specific tools that make implementation of the chapter's instructional model more efficient, effective, and engaging. Tools ranging from hardware like interactive whiteboards and student response systems to software and Web-based applications are included. The table highlights ideas that are embedded throughout the text and offers readers a concise guide promoting transfer to practice.

OPENING MATRIX This matrix appears at the beginning of each chapter from Chapter 5 through Chapter 14 to offer a short annotation of important ideas that are introduced. Readers can use the matrix to scan quickly through chapters and (1) view the matrix as an advanced organizer, (2) determine which models might be useful to them, (3) find models that can support specific instructional goals they have, (4) find models that might be made possible with technologies at their fingertips, or (5) jog their memory of what they have read.

LESSON PLAN/LESSON PLAN STEPS FIGURE These features, included in Chapters 5 through 14, provide in-depth illustrations of how each chapter's model can be practically applied to address specific curriculum objectives in a classroom context. Plans are intentionally varied by content area, standards, grade level, grouping, technology, and materials used. Each lesson plan illustrates how ideas about instructional models, differentiated instruction, and technology tools can be integrated within a practical setting. The lesson plan steps provide a concise summary of the major steps in the model lesson plan for quick reference. Content from both is referenced within the chapter text to provide examples that reinforce reader comprehension. Lesson plans can be used "as is" or modified by the reader in practice. Lesson plans link to current standards to demonstrate the match between models and standards.

DIFFERENTIATED INSTRUCTION AND DIFFERENTIATED INSTRUCTION EXAMPLES In this text, differentiated instruction is viewed as a standard practice that 21st century teachers should implement. It is an essential component of instruction and not simply an add-on. To communicate this view, this text integrates examples of differentiated instruction in practice throughout chapter content, lesson plans, and examples. It also features differentiated instruction in a special section of its own that provides concrete suggestions for how the content, process, and/or products associated with instruction at the elementary, middle, and high school levels might be adapted to make learning more productive for all students. Examples provide illustrations of how the steps of each instructional model inherently support differentiation and how additional modifications might make the model even more suited to diverse learners in elementary, middle, and high school settings.

CHAPTER SUMMARY Each chapter includes a summary that reviews major content in the chapter and serves as support for readers' comprehension and retention of main points.

APPLICATION ACTIVITIES These activities cultivate professional skills required for successful teaching and assessment with formal measures. In these activities, readers are challenged to consider how the processes of planning, teaching, and assessing in conjunction with the implementation of the instructional models can be optimized.

TECHNOLOGY INTEGRATION ACTIVITIES These activities help readers develop technological pedagogical content knowledge (TPACK) and the ability to integrate technology tools successfully.

JOURNAL ENTRY These prompts for reflection on the learning associated with each chapter promote thoughtful consideration of chapter contents and application to practice.

STEPS OF MODEL TABLE This table provides a short description of each step in the model introduced, including an outline of student and teacher roles. It acts as a reminder of key points and enables readers to scan chapters for relevance or refresh their memory of the chapter content.

CHAPTER OBJECTIVES/CHAPTER REVIEW QUESTIONS Each chapter begins with a list of targeted objectives that offer readers an advanced organizer of chapter content. Chapter review questions facilitate comprehension and retention.

Appendixes

The appendixes provide content relevant to all chapters in the text, conveniently located in one place.

APPENDIX A: THE ADDIE MODEL IN PRACTICE An illustration of how several educational innovations—the ADDIE model, the revised Bloom's taxonomy, and Understanding by Design—can be integrated to create high-quality instruction. The compatibility of these innovations is demonstrated in a practical example from classroom practice.

APPENDIX B: CONCEPT TEACHING ADVANCED MATERIALS Special support is provided for educators teaching concepts. This appendix provides a glossary of terms, graphics that illustrate key concepts, and black-line masters that will make teaching more productive.

APPENDIX C: WORKSHEETS Worksheets referenced throughout the text are gathered in one place for convenient access. The worksheets promote transfer of the book's contents to practice.

APPENDIX D: INSTRUCTIONAL MODELS MATRIX This graphic resource provides a quick visual for each of the instructional models. At a glance, teachers may access essential information about each model, including its steps, history, and support for the development of 21st century skills. The matrix makes it easy for readers to gain an overview of each model, compare them, and decide which are most relevant to their instructional goals.

APPENDIX E: LESSON PLAN FRAMEWORK Completion of this in-depth lesson plan framework supports a systematic approach to instructional decision making. The framework reflects major ideas in the text and is intended to cultivate more intentional practice and successful teaching.

Support Materials for Instructors

The following resources are available for instructors to download on www.pearsonhighered.com/educators. Instructors enter the author or title of this book, select this particular edition of the book, and then click on the **Resources** tab to log in and download textbook supplements.

INSTRUCTOR'S RESOURCE MANUAL AND TEST BANK (0133355128/9780133355123) The Instructor's Resource Manual and Test Bank include suggestions for learning activities, discussion topics, group activities, and a robust collection of test items. Some items (lower-level questions) simply ask students to identify or explain concepts and principles they have learned. But many others (higher-level questions) ask students to apply those same concepts and principles to specific classroom situations—that is, to actual student behaviors and teaching strategies.

TESTGEN (0133355128/9780133355123) TestGen is a powerful test generator that instructors install on a computer and use in conjunction with the TestGen test bank file for the text. Assessments, including equations, graphs, and scientific notation, may be created for both print and testing online.

TestGen is available exclusively from Pearson Education publishers. Instructors install TestGen on a personal computer (Windows or Macintosh) and create tests for classroom testing and for other specialized delivery options, such as over a local area network or on the Web. A test bank, which is also called a test item file (TIF), typically contains a large set of test items, organized by chapter and ready for use in creating a test, based on the associated textbook material.

The tests can be downloaded in the following formats:

TestGen Testbank file—PC	Angel Test Bank (zip)
TestGen Testbank file—MAC	D2L Test Bank (zip)
TestGen Testbank—Blackboard 9 TIF	Moodle Test Bank
TestGen Testbank—Blackboard CE/Vista (WebCT) TIF	Sakai Test Bank (zip)

Acknowledgments

This first edition text was in development for four years. During this time, many individuals contributed to supporting the authors and this project. We would like to gratefully acknowledge our husbands, Dennis and Doug, for believing in us and rearranging life to give us the time and support required to develop this book. We thank our children, Martha, Nadia, and Stevie, for their encouragement and hugs. We extend much gratitude to our former teachers and valued colleagues, Bob McNergney, Joanne Herbert McNergney, Carol Tomlinson, Dan Duke, Greta Morine-Dershimer, Portia Elliott, Sandy Paxton, Karen Robinson, Todd Kent, Kathy O'Reilly, Claire Parson, Glen Bull, Jim Cooper, and Walt Heinecke. These individuals provided us with opportunities, experiences, ideas, and insights that were instrumental in developing the text. We thank our former students—including those in Otterbein University's EDUC 610/6110, Denise Flint, Bette Roberts, and Shannon Prince—for providing motivation, practical examples, and valuable input on drafts of the text. We thank Niki Fayne, who gave us time, inspiration, and the gift of her informed insight while developing core ideas and introductory chapters.

We also thank our talented and hardworking editorial staff. Steve Dragin was the initial acquisitions editor who gets credit for initiating this project in the first place. Much appreciation also goes to Annalea Manalili and Barbara Strickland for their support at early development stages. We thank Kelly Villella Canton, our primary acquisitions editor, who provided the unparalleled expertise that kept us focused and ensured that this work would make a high-quality contribution to the field. We thank Alicia Reilly for her devoted and detailed work as our developmental editor and Linda Bishop, Karen Mason, Barbara Hawk, Annette Joseph, and countless others for their support in the production phase. Finally, we thank our reviewers, including Linda Behar-Horenstein, University of Florida; Donald W. Burwell, College of Idaho; John Cline, Wright State University; Mary L. Collins, NOVA Southeastern University; Becky J. Cox, University of Tennessee at Martin; Marie Lassmann, Texas A&M University–Kingsville; Marc Mahlios, University of Kansas; Colleen T. Sheehy, University of Indianapolis; Schrika Shell, University of Texas at El Paso; Lori K. Tanner, University of South Carolina Upstate; and Leslie Owen Wilson, University of Wisconsin–Stevens Point, for their important criticism and input on this work.

Teaching Models

DESIGNING INSTRUCTION FOR 21ST CENTURY LEARNERS

Teacher as Educational Designer

Clare Kilbane

t had been nearly three weeks since Franklin Elementary School had reopened after extensive renovations. In spite of the school board's original plan to demolish the school and construct a modern building in its place, public desire, funding, and a talented design team managed to save the cherished community landmark. Reconfiguring the historic building to ensure its function and relevance for another 100 years was not easy, but everyone knew that combining the best of old and new was the right thing to do.

Betty Roberts, a second-grade teacher, grinned while observing the organized chaos during her supervision of the morning rush. As she watched children spill out of the school buses, Betty reflected that students had changed during her tenure at Franklin. Although they still had the same boundless energy, joy, and wonder that had drawn her to work with them 22 years earlier, her students' interests, backgrounds, and learning needs had become more diverse. Thanks to the school's design team, important information about Franklin's students had been systematically identified through a needs assessment and was addressed in the building redesign. The faculty was amazed by the useful information that was discovered about its diverse student body when the right questions were asked. The end result—a well-functioning, renovated school—was proof that communicating with all stakeholders, including the students, was worth the effort.

Betty served on the building redesign committee alongside her principal, Dr. Angela Fayne. Betty knew that her leader was profoundly influenced by the design team's approach, so she was not surprised when Principal Fayne made a special announcement at the school's opening faculty meeting. "What our design team helped us learn about our students must not only *inform* the redesign of the building at Franklin Elementary, it should *transform* the instructional practices that go on within it," she said. "We serve all our students, and it is our responsibility to provide each one with the opportunity to fulfill his or her life's promise." She then proposed, "This year, we need to approach our work as 'educational designers.' Like the building design team, I want you to apply systematic thinking and processes when developing units and lessons. We need to become more skilled in using data from the assessment cycle and let it inform instructional decisions that coordinate knowledge and resources to provide equitable opportunities for all of our students." Workshops related to the topic began immediately and continued throughout the year.

Franklin's new learning environment offered more abundant resources for teaching than ever before. Upgraded electric and network infrastructures allowed for a video studio, new computers, mobile learning tools (e.g., tablets), and other high-tech equipment. Bigger classrooms with flexible seating, updated curriculum materials, and ample storage space for equipment enabled innovative teaching. In the renovated Franklin Elementary, access to adequate resources was no longer a barrier to effective teaching. Instead, the challenge became figuring out which resources to use, when to use them, and how to use them most effectively. Betty felt a deep professional responsibility to her students and community to give this challenge her best effort. But desire, hard work, and experience were not enough; she also needed to figure out how to integrate the new tools effectively and how to make optimal use of Franklin's resources to support her learners. Perhaps this is where her principal's new ideas about systematic processes and being an educational designer could prove helpful.

Betty had already used some systematic thinking when preparing for her new classroom space. Because the building renovation required teachers to move everything out of the building, she spent the summer organizing and "weeding" her instructional materials. As she carefully inventoried the boxes of books, manipulatives, software, and other resources she had used in the past, Betty was forced to decide what to keep, what to discard, and what to reinvent before returning to her classroom. As she examined the artifacts from her teaching, she considered which instructional practices had served her well and which might be outdated. She also identified areas where new techniques might be required to ensure her continued success and relevance with her new and future students.

Using the same deliberate and evidence-based practices employed by the building design team, Betty acquired important insights. She realized she would need to gain a better command of the assessment cycle and develop methods for integrating differentiation strategies and technology tools. The reflective process enabled Betty to develop both an improved understanding of her instructional resources and a more informed view of herself as a teacher.

As Betty followed her students into the school building, she laughed to herself when she realized that Franklin Elementary was not the only "historic landmark" that had experienced transformation during the renovation process. Moving into a new school building had not been easy, and Betty knew that it would prove even more challenging to move into a new educational era. Still, Betty knew, both moves would be entirely worthwhile. ■

CHAPTER OBJECTIVES

After reading this chapter, you will be able to:

- Describe the major trends influencing education in the 21st century.
- Explain some important characteristics of 21st century learners.
- Identify how the models of teaching can be transformed for increased relevance in the 21st century.
- Define what is meant by the idea of "teacher as educational designer."
- Articulate how being an educational designer can enable teachers to optimize their use of the models of teaching.

Introduction

Regardless of what you teach or where you teach, your success as an educator in the 21st century depends on your ability to design effective instruction for those you teach. Such instruction addresses the individual and shared learning needs of a diverse population of students as they work to master content area learning and the skills required for life in our fast-paced, technology-driven, global society. Contemporary educators find themselves surrounded by an unprecedented variety of powerful teaching resources. However, these resources—whether materials, models, strategies, or technologies—are effective only if teachers know when and how to use them.

In the opening scenario, we meet Betty, a second-grade teacher at Franklin Elementary School. Betty cares deeply about her students and wants to design instruction that is responsive to their needs. She has access to powerful resources and possesses extensive knowledge from experience. Yet in order to successfully prepare her diverse learners for the 21st century, she must reinvent her teaching practice. She must become, as Principal Fayne suggests, an "educational designer."

An **educational designer** is a teacher who approaches instruction with intention and clear goals. He or she applies specialized knowledge and skills to identify and frame instructional challenges and addresses them using a broad repertoire of instructional models, strategies, and technologies. Being an educational designer requires a new *mind-set*, a broad *skill set*, and a high-quality *tool set*. The new mind-set enables a teacher to approach his or her practice with increased control over important dimensions of the instructional process. The expanded skill set includes systematic approaches to instructional planning and assessment processes. The high-quality tool set consists of a collection of powerful models, strategies, and technologies for teaching.

With this design orientation, teachers like Betty can effectively support diverse learners as they work to meet the uniformly high standards for their learning. They can also make optimal use of the abundant resources for teaching in the digital era—especially the models of teaching that are the focus of this text. This design orientation gives teachers the flexible approach required for balancing the individual and shared needs of their students, adapting instruction, and coordinating the many resources available for teaching in contemporary classrooms.

Important trends shaping life and work in the 21st century and their influence on the field of education support the proposition that successful teachers will need to function as educational designers. We begin this chapter by highlighting these trends and explore their influence on the education of contemporary learners. Later, we explain why the traditional models of teaching presented in this text are more relevant than ever and describe how educational designers can maximize the potential of these models in the 21st century.

21st Century Trends and Their Impact on Education

What goes on inside of our nation's schools is increasingly influenced by what goes on outside of them. Five major trends—digital technologies, access to information, globalization, equity, and accountability—are changing the world in profound ways. As they do, they also affect preK-12 education and 21st century teaching through the ideas, movements, and reforms they inspire. An awareness of these trends and the ways they influence the field of education will help teachers better understand what is required to prepare 21st century learners for the future.

Digital Technologies

The development of powerful digital technologies and the pace of change associated with them are making an unprecedented impact on society around the globe. Digital technologies are distinct and different than the mechanical ones of the past. They are powered by electrical energy, perform functions that are not necessarily confined to a finite physical space, and are often connected to some type of data network. Their creation and integration into daily living has resulted in the "digital revolution."

Like the agricultural and industrial revolutions of the past, the digital revolution is influencing employment, education, citizenship, and most other aspects of daily living. The progress enabled by digital technologies and the processes these devices facilitate bring with it the same promise and peril of previous revolutions. Yet the digital revolution has two special features that characterize it. First, the product yielded from the use of digital technologies is quite often new information and ideas. As this "product" is processed, long-held assumptions about the most fundamental aspects of human existence are challenged. This means that the use of digital technologies not only changes the lives of individuals and communities but also the individual's understanding of the very concept of "life" and "community." Second, the pace of change associated with digital technology—including its development, functioning, and integration into daily living—is faster and more sustained than that associated with the mechanical technology of the past. This fact presents a challenge to human beings who are not always able to keep up with the pace of change dictated by the tools they create. These important characteristics associated with the development of digital technology are indeed revolutionary and suggest important implications for those who wish to prepare learners for the digital era.

Technology functions as both the fuel and the tool for educational change: Its importance in life and work necessitates a subsequent reform of curriculum and instruction, and technology itself can be a tool that facilitates this reform in classrooms and schools. Whether in a traditional classroom or a virtual one, students require both the foundations of academic knowledge and the real-life experiences that prepare them for citizenship in today's society. More and more, that means understanding and being able to use technology.

Reforms inspired by digital technology demand a transformation of what is taught and how it is taught in American schools. Such reforms are being championed by two different professional organizations—the Partnership for 21st Century Skills (P21) and the International Society for Technology in Education (ISTE). These organizations are influencing education at all levels through articulated standards for successful 21st century education. The P21 Framework and the ISTE's National Educational Technology Standards for Students (NETS•S) are structured guidelines that group and outline essential 21st century aptitudes. These two sets of standards provide guidance to states, schools, and educators alike. Teachers who approach instruction as educational designers need to know about the aptitudes these guidelines promote, and they must address them in their classroom practice.

THE P21 SKILLS FRAMEWORK. Formed in 2002, P21 (www.p21.org) is a U.S. organization composed of educational, governmental, and business leaders that advocates for the 21st century readiness of all learners. P21 has developed a comprehensive framework (see Figure 1-1) articulating the competencies that are required for successful employment and citizenship in the 21st century.

The P21 Framework acknowledges the continued role of traditional curricular subjects, or the "3Rs" (reading, writing, and arithmetic). However, this framework suggests that achievement in the digital era will require more than this curricular foundation. It highlights the importance of the "4Cs"—creativity, communication, collaboration, and critical thinking. It proposes that the 4Cs are as important as the 3Rs to college readiness and workforce success. The framework also promotes the development of lifelong learning skills

Figure 1-1   Framework for 21st Century Learning

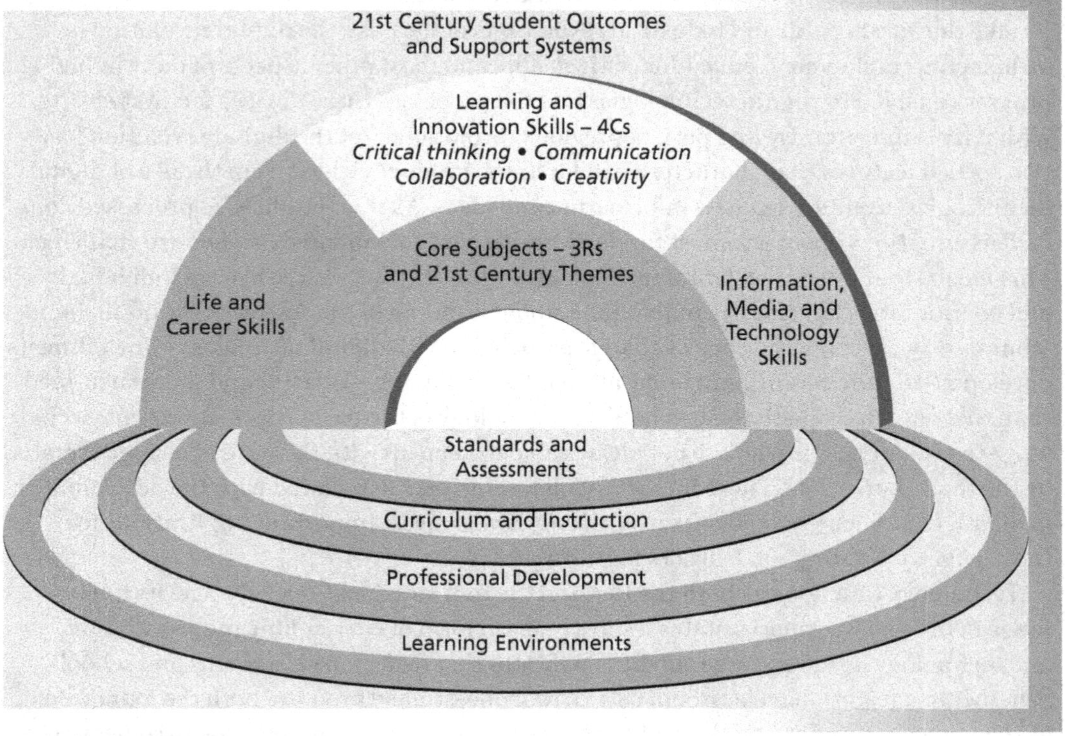

21st Century Student Outcomes
and Support Systems

Learning and
Innovation Skills – 4Cs
*Critical thinking • Communication
Collaboration • Creativity*

Core Subjects – 3Rs
and 21st Century Themes

Life and
Career Skills

Information,
Media, and
Technology
Skills

Standards and
Assessments

Curriculum and Instruction

Professional Development

Learning Environments

Partnership for 21st Skills, www.P21.org

that will be necessary for success in and beyond the imagined future. The P21 Framework communicates specific student outcomes educators should focus on when making decisions that affect curriculum and instruction. These indicators focus on four major areas:

1. Core Subjects and 21st Century Themes
2. Learning and Innovation Skills
3. Information, Media, and Technology Skills
4. Life and Career Skills

Formally and informally, the P21 framework is reforming what is taught and how it is taught in schools across the nation. In fact, nearly 20 states have committed to serving as P21 leadership states. These states have committed to design new standards, assessments, and professional development programs that correspond to the P21 framework. The framework is commonly integrated with grant initiatives at the state and federal levels, and P21 has even informed the development of national and international educational standards, such as the Common Core State Standards and ISTE's NETS•S.

ISTE'S NETS•S.[1]   The ISTE is a group of education leaders from around the globe who have worked for over 30 years to improve education through innovative and effective uses of technology. The group provides general information (via books, websites, and other resources) and support (via conferences, workshops, and other professional development tools) related to this goal. ISTE's NETS•S, originally developed in 1998 and later revised in

---

[1]National Educational Technology Standards for Students (NETS•S), Second Edition © 2007 ISTE ® (International Society for Technology in Education), www.iste.org. All rights reserved.

2008, describe in five domains what students must know and do for successful 21st century living and learning. These domains include the following:

1. Creativity and Innovation
2. Communication and Collaboration
3. Research and Information Fluency
4. Digital Citizenship
5. Technology Operations and Concepts

The NETS•S are used to develop educational offerings at all levels. They not only provide curriculum standards used in courses focused on the development of technology competencies but also help to integrate technology competency into traditional academic subject areas. The NETS•S have served as a blueprint for cultivating 21st century learning for more than a decade, and their impact is compounded when combined with the P21 Framework. Indeed, the P21 Framework and NETS•S illustrate the learning outcomes that will enable 21st century learners to be well prepared for an ever changing tomorrow.

Students do not develop technological competence without appropriate support from the adults who work with them. Anticipating this, ISTE developed additional sets of standards that assist in the preparation of school administrators (NETS•A), teachers (NETS•T), and coaches (NETS•C). Each set of standards expresses the knowledge, attitudes, habits, and skills adults must have to lead, teach, and support their students' development of technological competence.

Clearly, the P21 Framework and NETS•S are important for contemporary teachers to know about and utilize in their practice. These recommendations both inform and guide teachers who want their students to develop the skills, knowledge, and competencies necessary to live a productive, technologically competent life. Awareness of these standards and the reforms they inspire also helps teachers appreciate why a new mind-set, an expanded skill set, and a high-quality tool set are essential for effective teaching in the 21st century.

Access to Information

Anytime, anywhere access to information is one of the defining characteristics of the 21st century. Today, access to information is fast and convenient. It is also abundant. Although researchers are challenged to quantify the world's technological capacity, there is no question that the quantity of data stored, communicated, and computed is growing exponentially. This is not expected to change anytime soon, as access to advanced technological infrastructures (e.g., broadband technologies) increases around the world (Hilbert & Lopez, 2011). Although access to information still remains a challenge for some individuals and in some communities, a different challenge exists where it is plentiful: knowing how to evaluate, synthesize, apply, and benefit from information without being overwhelmed by it.

In most developed societies, information is accessible everywhere and anytime—including classrooms during the school day. Contemporary teachers can conveniently access digital text and multimedia resources that present content across the academic disciplines. Students' access to content is no longer limited to the hard-copy resources available in the school library or confined by the walls of the school. Lessons and activities may be made more relevant through the inclusion of "real-world" information from experts, researchers, and the media. Ideas, discoveries, and insights that expand students' understanding of academic content from around the world can now be accessed and discussed within classrooms. New information sources (e.g., blogs, online videos, wikis, and discussion boards) allow firsthand experiences and eyewitness accounts to be shared, complementing traditionally accepted sources. In short, the exponential growth and wide-reaching nature of information in most school environments creates many new opportunities for teaching and learning today.

As curriculum and instruction evolve in response to this trend, so does our understanding of the nature of knowledge and the methods required for its successful acquisition. Experts, such as those who study information processing, have refined their understanding of human cognition and the acquisition of knowledge in recent decades. These ideas are becoming more influential and mainstream in the field of education. An example of this trend is present in the recent revision of Bloom's taxonomy (Anderson et al., 2001). The taxonomy, originally published in 1956, was updated in 2001 to integrate new understandings gained from studies conducted over the last half century. Understanding what the taxonomy suggests about the types of knowledge and methods for promoting student learning will aid in the work of educational designers as well as the application of teaching models presented in this text.

REVISED BLOOM'S TAXONOMY: A NEW DESCRIPTION OF 21ST CENTURY KNOWLEDGE AND THINKING SKILLS.   For the last 50 years, Bloom's taxonomy has provided a useful understanding of the types of cognitive processes that humans are capable of demonstrating. It has also illuminated the skills that students must develop to be successful in life and work. The ideas expressed in the taxonomy and related works have been foundational for the development of existing curricula and instruction in U.S. schools. The revised taxonomy was developed to better support the "design and implementation of accountability programs, standards-based curriculums, and authentic assessments" (2001, p. xxii). The most obvious change, for those familiar with the taxonomy, is a shift from passive (original) to more active (revised) cognitive process categories. Figure 1-2 depicts the revised Bloom's taxonomy.

The most important change, however, is the addition of a "knowledge dimension" to the existing cognitive process categories, resulting in a multidimensional matrix. The change, intended to incorporate developments in cognitive psychology, brings to the mainstream education community an illustration of how cognitive processes relate to the formation

Figure 1-2   The Revised Bloom's Taxonomy

Knowledge Dimension	Cognitive Process Dimension					
	Remember	Understand	Apply	Analyze	Evaluate	Create
Factual						
Conceptual						
Procedural						
Metacognitive						

of different types of knowledge. It also describes how this knowledge must be supported through different categories of cognitive process dimensions.

The revised Bloom's taxonomy knowledge dimension suggests that there are four general knowledge types. Each has its own characteristics, which are described here briefly. For more in-depth information, read the Anderson et al. (2001) text, *A Taxonomy for Learning, Teaching, and Assessing*. **Factual knowledge** comprises the basic and essential elements a person must know (e.g., key vocabulary). **Conceptual knowledge** consists of knowledge of the relationship between classifications and categories. **Procedural knowledge** is knowledge about how to do something and when it is appropriate, and **metacognitive knowledge** comprises knowledge about cognitive tasks and one's own cognition. Each type of knowledge is distinct and important, and each can be gained through different cognitive processes. Deep understanding of knowledge is developed over time and through experiences that incorporate the varied types of cognition.

The revised taxonomy is highly practical and intended to be used as a tool in the design of curriculum, instruction, and assessment. It fosters systematic thinking about the analysis of content standards and the development of learning experiences that promote specific instructional objectives. Functionally, teachers can support their students' mastery of specific learning objectives by developing activities that integrate the different knowledge types and cognitive process categories. For example, a teacher might design a lesson targeting an objective related to a specified knowledge type and then orchestrate activities that incorporate varying levels of cognitive processes to promote student mastery. Using the taxonomy as a visual aid, teachers can ensure that students acquire knowledge of all types at graduated levels of complexity and understanding.

The description of the knowledge types presented in the revised taxonomy's "knowledge domain" challenges the profession's prevailing view that knowledge consists of only two types—declarative (i.e., knowledge about something) and procedural (i.e., knowledge about how to do something). In the information-abundant 21st century, the types of knowledge students must acquire and apply are not only more numerous but also more varied. Teachers approaching their work as educational designers will broaden and strengthen their skill set if they learn to use the revised taxonomy when developing lessons, activities, and units for their students.

Globalization

Globalization, the increasing interconnectedness of economies, communities, and individuals around the world, is another powerful trend in the 21st century. As globalization becomes more pervasive, a larger percentage of individuals have more of their existence affected by what goes on in the economies, environments, and governments of other countries. Technologies facilitate globalization because they make relocation, communication, and economic relationships easier, faster, and more productive. In particular, the rise of publicly accessible global communication channels like the Internet has enabled a faster, more egalitarian exchange of information resources among individuals and groups. As a result, our view of the world is broader than ever before—and is constantly changing.

Globalization has affected the lives of contemporary teachers in numerous ways. For one, it has resulted in increased ethnic and cultural diversity across student populations. Many classrooms across the United States have a greater representation of cultural, religious, and ethnic diversity than ever before. Changing immigration patterns in particular have resulted in more widespread occurrences of cultural and ethnic diversity across geographic areas and communities. Globalization has also affected job markets and the national economy. As a result, students and their families are more geographically mobile. It is not unusual for students to complete their educations across different borders—in multiple school districts, states, and, in some cases, even countries—or online.

Globalization—and the technologies that facilitate it—have affected the worldviews and long-term perspectives of teachers and learners alike. Google Earth® and satellite news broadcasts provide different views of our world's physical, cultural, and political environments. Social networks (e.g., Facebook® and Twitter®) and communication tools (e.g., Skype™ and Web conferencing) have enabled connections with people from all around the world. These new ties foster a mutual understanding that encourages citizens of the present to consider a shared destiny for the future.

Along with increased student diversity and geopolitical awareness, globalization has resulted in the development of more rigorous standards intended to ensure success of students in the globally competitive workplace. It has also necessitated pedagogical approaches that support diverse populations of learners in attaining these high standards. In the sections that follow, we will describe one set of standards developed to promote student preparedness for the global workplace—the Common Core State Standards. We will also share one popular approach for effectively embracing diversity, culturally responsive pedagogy.

THE COMMON CORE STATE STANDARDS INITIATIVE[2] (www.corestandards.org). The Common Core State Standards Initiative is a professional initiative that has resulted in the creation of a comprehensive curriculum framework for students in grades K-12. The "Common Core" articulates consistent national standards for student competence in Mathematics and English Language Arts. These rigorous standards acknowledge the importance of educational experiences in grades K-12, which prepare students for participation in a technology-driven, globally competitive workplace. In short, they promote educational reform that will

- better align college and work expectations with K-12 standards,
- demonstrate an increased awareness that K-12 experiences are important in workforce development,
- emphasize higher-order thinking skills required for contemporary living, and
- align U.S. standards with those of other top-performing countries.

The Common Core State Standards are intended to provide teachers with clear targets for developing instruction. They communicate the continued importance of strong educational foundations in the core subjects but also describe the additional knowledge and skills that will be required to excel in the future.

Recognizing the need for a consistent curriculum nationwide, 45 states and three U.S. territories have adopted the Common Core State Standards. Clearly, these standards will increasingly influence what is taught—and assessed—in U.S. schools. And as assessments connected to these standards are developed and implemented across grade levels, they will also provide teachers and students feedback that can be used to improve instruction.

CULTURALLY RESPONSIVE PEDAGOGY. In part because of globalization, the religions, cultures, and backgrounds of students in any given classroom are likely more diverse than ever before. As a result, teachers need to incorporate instructional strategies that capitalize on this diversity in order to teach effectively and promote good citizenship.

---

[2]© Copyright 2010. National Governors Association Center for Best Practices and Council of Chief State School Officers. All rights reserved.

Culturally responsive pedagogy (i.e., culturally responsive teaching) is teaching that incorporates, embraces, and fosters the academic success of all students by acknowledging students' cultural backgrounds and finds ways to integrate them into the curriculum. Students are members of communities and, as such, are likely to have cultural experiences, characteristics, and traits corresponding to those communities that an instructor can build on. Above all else, however, students are individuals. Any attempt to introduce culturally responsive pedagogy into the curriculum must first acknowledge this imperative.

According to Gay (2010, p. 36), culturally responsive pedagogy is characterized as follows:

1. Validating—Teachers should design instruction that both validates and affirms their students' backgrounds by acknowledging individual heritages and learning styles.
2. Comprehensive—Culturally responsive teaching should focus on the whole individual, not just the culture. Therefore, teachers should consider how instruction might affect students cognitively, socially, psychologically, and physically, among other dimensions.
3. Multidimensional—Teachers who employ culturally responsive teaching should plan instruction that provides students with multiple perspectives, media, and strategies for understanding the content.
4. Empowering—Culturally responsive teaching should help students achieve academic success, increase their self-confidence, and improve the world around them.
5. Transformative—Culturally responsive teaching builds on a student's cultural background and academic strengths, resulting in the positive transformation of his or her consciousness.
6. Emancipatory—Culturally responsive teaching liberates learners from the idea that there is only one truth or one way to do things. It offers a sense of freedom through "cooperation, community, and connectedness."

In practice, culturally responsive pedagogy involves using a variety of teaching strategies and resources that treat students' backgrounds as opportunities to enrich the curriculum. Teachers working as educational designers can incorporate different cultures and perspectives in many simple yet meaningful ways while also teaching students to think critically and become socially conscious. By applying culturally responsive pedagogy, teachers promote equity and mutual respect, acknowledge their students' differences, and celebrate students' identities through teaching, assignments, and curricular choices—all important classroom goals that promote the development of a more functional global society.

Equity

From local grassroots movements to large-scale initiatives involving national governments and multinational organizations, efforts are being made around the world to champion human rights and promote equity. Human rights movements have taken a variety of forms over time and in different communities. In some cases, equal rights are sought for those with different sexual orientations. In others, defending the rights of women or another marginalized group is the goal. Regardless of the focus, such movements assert that all human beings—regardless of birth, background, and circumstances—have rights that transcend these and other factors, including culture, government, geography, and education.

Promoting equity for all people and teaching all students equitably is a critical feature of education in the United States. The Elementary and Secondary Education Act (ESEA), the No Child Left Behind Act (NCLB), the Individuals with Disabilities Education Act (IDEA), and Title IX are examples of legislation that has promoted equity in recent decades. Each redefined—and continues to reshape—the laws and standards that ensure educational equity in the United States. Several tools that address the needs of students whose rights are promoted through this legislation have become expected modes for supporting equity in our nation's schools. In the following sections, we describe two of these tools: IDEA and differentiated instruction.

IDEA. Support for special needs learners has gained considerable momentum in the United States over the last half century. IDEA was originally signed into law as the Education for All Handicapped Children Act in 1975. The act was renamed the Individuals with Disabilities Education Act in 1990 and was newly amended (and extended) in 2004. IDEA mandates that all students receive a free, appropriate public education in the least restrictive environment. This means that students with special needs are legally protected in their right to be educated to the same extent as their peers without special needs. Over the years, the legislation and policies associated with IDEA have increased the accountability of services provided to students with special needs and streamlined the special education process. As a direct result of IDEA, the number of students with special needs who are mainstreamed (i.e., included) in classrooms with regular education students has steadily increased.

The specific support for each student with special needs is explained in an individualized education plan (IEP). An IEP is a legally binding document that provides a detailed accounting of a student's special education as well as the related services he or she will receive to address his or her individual needs. Students whose needs have not yet been identified or are less intensive are supported through the incorporation of response to intervention (RTI). RTI is a multitiered approach to instruction that monitors the progress of students who are experiencing academic challenges but who do not have IEPs. The RTI process involves scrutiny of a student's progress, documentation of his or her response to an intervention, and academic decisions based on that response. Because of IDEA, students receive equitable educational experiences and support through RTI and IEPs.

DIFFERENTIATED INSTRUCTION. One common method of supporting all learners, including those affected by IDEA, is differentiated instruction. Differentiated instruction is an approach to teaching that promotes equitable learning experiences for all students. It is teaching with planned responsiveness to the inherent diversity present in the population of a classroom. According to Tomlinson (2003), differentiated instruction occurs when "a teacher proactively plans varied approaches to what students need to learn, how they will learn it, and/or how they can express what they have learned in order to increase the likelihood that each student will learn as much as he or she can as efficiently as possible" (p. 151).

Although originally developed to address the needs of gifted students in regular education settings, differentiated instruction emphasizes considering the needs of all students, which is clearly an educational equity concern. Key principles of a differentiated classroom are the following:

- The teacher is clear about the subject matter's important concepts.
- The teacher understands, appreciates, and builds on student differences.
- Assessment and instruction are inseparable.
- The teacher adjusts content, process, and product in response to student readiness, interest, and learning profile.
- All students participate in respectful work.
- Students and teachers are collaborators in learning.

- Goals of a differentiated classroom are maximum growth and individual success.
- Flexibility is the hallmark of a differentiated classroom (Tomlinson, 1999, p. 48).

When differentiating instruction, teachers function as educational designers. They recognize and exercise control over various dimensions of the teaching, assessment, and learning processes. They use systematic approaches to identify learner needs and develop the instruction to address them. Teachers in a differentiated classroom regularly make decisions about the content that is learned, the processes by which students learn it, and the products created to demonstrate that learning. In practice, teachers who differentiate instruction might make modifications to one or more of these dimensions to enable individuals or groups to be more successful in meeting learning goals. These modifications might be made based on students' readiness, interests, or learning profiles (Tomlinson, 1999). Decisions made to foster the success of every student in a classroom promote equity.

There are many different strategies that can be utilized to differentiate instruction. Many are integrated throughout this text in the chapters that introduce the models of teaching (Chapters 5 through 14). In each, a special section highlights the way each model provides built-in support for differentiated instruction and suggests modifications that differentiate the content, process, and products associated with instruction. Additional examples of differentiation in practice are integrated throughout these chapters and chapter scenarios.

Accountability

In recent years, in an effort to attain popularly agreed-on goals and reach the ideals of equity, civility, and good citizenship, society has renewed its commitment to accountability. Accountability is the practice of holding an individual, organization, or group responsible for meeting expectations that are set for their actions. Stories that address accountability pepper the newspaper and media channels. When we read about a government leader who is investigated and praised for her consistent voting record on the issues, a doctor being sued for malpractice, or a school district being pressured to promote school safety through the creation of an antibullying policy, we notice society's attention to this important concept. Because teachers, schools, and school districts do such important work, it is reasonable that they are held accountable for this work. Although the term *accountability* often has a negative connotation, it is actually a neutral term. Accountability can result in recognition of good work performed as well as the opposite.

The pressure to hold states, districts, schools, and teachers accountable for student outcomes is significantly affecting the U.S. educational landscape. Although this pressure stems from a convergence of numerous influences, a significant contributor is the accountability required by NCLB. A provision of NCLB compels schools to report adequate yearly progress (AYP) to demonstrate student performance on standardized tests. As a result, states across the nation must demonstrate their schools are making AYP, which in turn compels districts, schools, teachers, and ultimately students to address and meet standards.

UNDERSTANDING BY DESIGN. Understanding by Design (UbD) is a curriculum design approach developed by Grant Wiggins and Jay McTighe (2005) that helps teachers develop more effective instruction by promoting the alignment of meaningful and clear curricular goals with the assessment of student learning. Inspired in part by the trend of accountability, schools and school districts across the United States are reforming educational experiences for students through the use of UbD. The idea behind UbD is that better curriculum planning will result in improved instruction which subsequently will produce higher student achievement across a larger portion of the student population. The goal of UbD is to teach for deep understanding of content. Deep understanding of content is characterized by six facets of understanding, which include the ability to (1) explain, (2) interpret, (3) apply, (4) have perspective, (5) empathize, and (6) have self-knowledge about a topic.

UbD relies on what Wiggins and McTighe call "backwards design," or the notion that planning is performed by working in reverse. Teachers first focus on the end results and desired evidence of student learning. Then they think backwards to determine what experiences are required to achieve these results. Development of **essential questions**—queries about the important ideas that will serve as the foundation for the instruction being designed—is also a critical component of UbD.

Using the UbD model, teachers examine the desired results of the instruction (i.e., outcomes) and the evidence (i.e., assessment) that they will use to demonstrate that students have achieved the desired results and then finally develop the learning plan (i.e., unit and lessons). UbD is a focused approach to curriculum design and, as such, requires the systematic thinking and design mind-set advocated in this text. It is also a positive approach through which teachers can develop the best learning opportunities for all of their students.

Making Sense of the Trends, Ideas, Movements, and Reforms

Five major trends—digital technologies, access to information, globalization, equity, and accountability—are influencing education in the 21st century. These trends affect the field of education directly—through the targeted ideas, movements, and reforms we have described—and indirectly—through their influence on students, teachers, and their environment. Because the students of today must function in the world of tomorrow, committed 21st century teachers need to acknowledge the influence these trends have on curriculum and instruction. They also need to recognize that keeping up with these shifts in the teaching and learning context requires approaching their work as educational designers.

This presentation of how trends affect education represents only one of many ways to frame the dynamic context of contemporary education. There are many other methods for interpreting what is going on in U.S. schools and society. Interpretation aside, however, it is clear that the trends influence one another and that the ideas, movements, and reforms they inspire are interconnected.

The interplay of these trends and education suggests that

1. preparation for life and work in a fast-paced, technology-driven, global society will require students and teachers to meet increasingly demanding standards;
2. learners' needs must be addressed for optimal learning;
3. teachers must balance learners' individual and shared needs;
4. the abundant resources available for teaching must be marshaled to meet this challenge; and
5. successful teaching requires a new mind-set, broad skill set, and high-quality tool set.

The following section examines important characteristics of 21st century learners that will require teachers to work as educational designers to be successful.

21st Century Learner Characteristics

Twenty-first century classrooms are characterized by an increasingly diverse student population. As Betty, the teacher in the opening scenario acknowledges, today's learners have more diverse backgrounds, interests, and learning needs than students from previous generations. Digital technologies, access to information, and globalization have contributed to this diversity. Efforts to promote equity and provide accountability will ensure it is valued and celebrated. In 21st century classrooms, teachers must be able to support a group of diverse learners as they work to meet the uniformly high expectations for their learning.

To provide equitable learning opportunities for all, teachers in 21st century classrooms must be able to identify the ways in which their student population is diverse and understand how this diversity affects learning and the

Today's Learners
(© Dawn Shearer-Simonetti/Shutterstock)

learning environment. Teachers then need to design learning experiences that balance students' individual and shared needs. That is, teachers need to use culturally responsive pedagogy and differentiated instruction strategies when developing standards-based instruction. To achieve this challenging balance, teachers in the 21st century classroom must be able to effectively integrate high-quality tools, such as instructional models, strategies, and technologies, so that their diverse population of students can meet uniformly rigorous standards.

Before they can design appropriate pedagogy, teachers need to understand the composition of their 21st century classroom. The following sections describe the important characteristics of 21st century learners. They explain how this generation's perception of themselves as individuals, as well as diverse cultural and linguistic backgrounds, exceptionalities, and experiences as digital learners, distinguish them.

21st Century Learners Are Individuals

The most important characteristic of 21st century learners is that they are individuals and identify themselves as such. American children today are growing up in a country and culture where personal freedom, self-expression, and individuality are not only accepted but also encouraged, valued, and celebrated. Twenty-first century learners not only have more unique experiences, values, and interests but also are growing up with a greater awareness of their own uniqueness. This does not mean that students no longer have shared characteristics with each other and their teacher. It *does* mean that it is more difficult to identify differences because there are more ways that individuals vary and greater differences occurring between these variations. The success of 21st century teachers in working with contemporary learners will be influenced by how well they can get to know their students as unique individuals and how effectively they can balance students' individual and shared learning needs. Teachers must identify the types of diversity their students bring to the classroom and address them through curriculum and instruction. The best way to learn about students' diversity is to use classroom-based assessment practices skillfully. Getting to know their students is the most practical way for teachers to design instruction that responds to their students' individual and group needs. We expand on these techniques in Chapter 4 and describe them in Part II of this text.

The trend in the profession today is shifting to the practice of applying a more flexible approach for identifying students and emphasizing a greater appreciation of the needs of individual students. However, in our profession, discussing and grouping students based on sets of shared characteristics (i.e., language, culture, and intellectual ability) is still a common practice. In the sections that follow, we will discuss some of the larger categories of diversity that are prevalent in schools throughout the United States. Part II of this book is devoted to sharing methods that help teachers address this diversity.

21st Century Learners Are More Culturally and Linguistically Diverse

Recent data suggest that students in our nation's schools speak more than 450 languages. Although language differences are most common among new and recent immigrants, linguistic and cultural diversity are also important factors to consider when working with students whose families have been in the United States for generations. Currently, more than 12% of all preK-12 students are considered to be English language learners (ELLs). Statistical forecasts indicate that by 2015, more than 50% of all students in K-12 public schools across the United States will not speak English as their first language (Gray & Fleishman, 2004, pp. 84–85). The number of multilingual and non-English-speaking households have also been rising steadily. For instance, "between 1979 and 2008, the number of school-age children (ages 5–17 years) who spoke a language other than English at home increased from 3.8 to 10.9 million, or from 9% to 21% of the population in this age range" (Aud et al., 2010, p. 32). Trend lines indicate the growth in cultural and linguistic diversity will continue, and, as it does, it will become more uniformly distributed across different geographic areas, socioeconomic levels, and communities (i.e., rural, urban, and suburban).

21st Century Learners Are More Commonly Identified with Exceptionalities

An increasing percentage of learners in contemporary U.S. classrooms have been identified as having special needs or exceptionalities. **Exceptionalities** are identified physical, cognitive, emotional, or behavioral characteristics that are significantly different from the societal norm. Students with exceptionalities have a range of differences, from specific learning disabilities to severe restrictions of movement or communication to giftedness. These needs must be met in order for students to have equitable learning opportunities.

Between 1976 and 2004, the number of youth served under IDEA (discussed in the previous section) increased from 3.7 million to 6.6 million, or from 8% to 14% of total public school enrollment (Hoffman & Sable, 2006). In 2007–2008, 13% of public school enrollment received special education services (Aud et al., 2010). These growth trends likely reflect the increased and improved identification of exceptionality as well as a federal mandate to provide the least restrictive environment for all learners.

The statistics also suggest that increasing numbers of learners with special needs are receiving better educational experiences and that a more diverse group of learners is spending more time in regular education classes. According to the National Center for Education Statistics (NCES), 96% of general education teachers have students with disabilities in their classrooms. On average, there are at least three to four students with IEPs integrated into each general-education class. Approximately 50% of all students with special needs in 2003–2004 spent 80% or more of their day in a regular classroom, up from 45% in 1994–1995 (NCES, 2005, p. viii). "About 95% of children and youth aged 6 to 21 served under IDEA in 2007–2008 were enrolled in regular schools" (Aud et al., 2010, p. 34). In the future, progress in the identification and possible medical interventions for those with exceptionalities will likely result in an increasing number of students with special needs as well as the methods for equitably supporting them. Teachers who can systematically identify learner's needs, develop modifications that address them, and apply powerful tools when doing so will be most successful.

21st Century Learners Are Growing Up in a Digital Era

No matter what their cultural, linguistic, socioeconomic, or academic backgrounds are, most 21st century learners are growing up in a digital, mobile, connected world characterized by constant and instant access to information. Continuous communication using digital tools is the norm, and the development of digital identities begins in early childhood and extends through adulthood.

Although the digital divide continues to exist, especially for those in certain demographic groups (Jansen, 2010), most learners are exposed to technology from infancy. Twenty-first century learners have had their birth photos taken digitally and posted online, played video games since toddlerhood, chronicled their lives by posting videos online using sites like YouTube, and interacted with friends using social networking sites such as Facebook® or applications like Facetime. Consequently, 21st century learners are digital natives—individuals who have grown up with "the digital language of computers, video games, and the Internet" (Prensky, 2001, p. 1). Twenty-first century teachers need to recognize that digital immersion and facility affects how their students think and learn and what motivates and engages them. The astute teacher will capitalize on students' digital lives and meaningfully incorporate similar technologies into their own teaching.

Making Sense of 21st Century Learner Characteristics

Clearly, addressing the individual needs of all learners while simultaneously attending to those shared by the whole group is challenging—and often impossible. Yet this is the challenge of teaching in the 21st century. Twenty-first century teachers simply cannot and should not use one-size-fits-all approaches when teaching today's diverse learners. They must acquire both powerful teaching strategies and strategic practices to function effectively. Today's learners need teachers who operate as educational designers—who get to know them well and can design effective, high-quality educational experiences based on their needs. They need teachers who know when and how to use standard, modified, and customized materials to help them achieve their highest potential. The following instructional models will assist teachers in designing the best pedagogy possible.

Models of Teaching for the 21st Century

The demands of 21st century teaching, as described in previous sections of this chapter, require teachers to respond with great effort, thought, and resources, including a variety of high-quality tools. The models of teaching that are the focus of this text represent some of the most valuable, time-tested tools that could be included in a teacher's repertoire. In the sections that follow, we explain what the models of teaching are and why they have increased relevance in the digital era. We then make recommendations for how these models might be transformed for optimal use in contemporary classrooms through the integration of differentiated instruction practices and digital technologies. Finally, we provide a brief rationale for the selection of instructional models in this text and share other information about our unique treatment of these models.

What Are the Models of Teaching?

The **models of teaching**, sometimes referred to as instructional models or models of learning, are specialized methods for facilitating learning. They are designed to promote specific learning outcomes related to required standards in the academic disciplines through the use of a specially orchestrated set of activities. In a lesson when an instructional model is used, learners progress through defined steps that intentionally structure and support their achievement of specific cognitive, psychomotor, and/or affective learning goals.

Instructional models are distinguished from other types of instructional approaches (e.g., strategies and simulations) because they have four critical attributes, including (1) syntax, (2) a social system, (3) principles of reaction, and (4) a support system (Joyce, Weil, & Calhoun, 2009). The way the attributes of each instructional model are manifested in the model are informed by theory about learning or learners and quantified with research. The development of the models through the years has paralleled innovations, discoveries, and trends in the fields of education and cognitive psychology.

Evidence of the development of the first instructional models initially appeared in educational literature during the 1960s. The first textbook on the topic was written in the early 1970s by Bruce Joyce, a teacher educator. Since this time, the number of instructional models has increased, and the variety has expanded. Most models have been developed to target a particular goal or set of goals determined by the individual or group who developed it. For example, the Concept Development model (see Chapter 7) was developed by Hilda Taba in the 1960s to expand students' understanding of concepts by challenging them to categorize, develop, extend, and refine their notions of concepts. Cooperative Learning models (see Chapter 12) were developed to promote the successful racial integration of schools.

Each instructional model provides not only a specialized way to address academic content but an added value as well (i.e., attainment of important goals that may not be stated in curriculum standards). Additional benefit is achieved through the specific structure of each model and the specialized activities through which students progress during their learning within the model. For example, in the Vocabulary Acquisition model (see Chapter 9), students not only learn targeted vocabulary words but also develop competencies for future vocabulary learning. In the Integrative model (see Chapter 13), students learn about important content materials in the academic disciplines and ways to work with data, analyze patterns, and make generalizations. The instructional models can be grouped into families consisting of multiple models that have similar goals and purposes. The social family of models promotes students' learning while also facilitating productive work in groups to prepare them for participation in democracy. Instructional models represent flexible, specialized tools that are time tested and based on educational research and theory. They represent some of the best ideas and approaches our profession has developed during the last century and have the promise to promote learning well into the next.

Instructional Models Included in This Text

From the many models of instruction available to teachers today, we have selected 10 for inclusion in this book. Those which appear have been chosen because they simultaneously address academic content while supporting contemporary learners' development of skills needed for life and work in the 21st century. In Figure 1-3, we list the models included in this text and provide a short summary that offers information about how these models respond to the demands of preparing learners for life and learning in the 21st century.

Figure 1-3   Models of Teaching in This Text

Chapter	Model	Summary	Support for 21st Century Learning
5	Direct Instruction model	A teacher-led instructional model that is useful for promoting understanding of procedures among students who gradually develop independence using new learning.	• Fosters logical, organized thinking • Fosters independent learning of procedures • Provides practice in and application of existing knowledge
6	Concept Attainment model	A teacher-guided instructional model through which students develop an understanding of a concept by examining examples and nonexamples and by analyzing their critical and noncritical attributes.	• Promotes discrimination and generalization • Fosters inquisitiveness
7	Concept Development model	A student-centered model that promotes understanding of concepts through inductive reasoning about examples for the purpose of grouping and classifying them.	• Supports ability to classify, think flexibly, and make generalizations • Fosters development of organizational skills • Encourages recognition of relationships and understanding of concepts
8	Inductive model	A teacher-guided model that challenges students to recognize patterns and details in content under investigation.	• Promotes inductive reasoning, skills of observation, and recognition of patterns and details • Allows practice with convergent and divergent thinking • Fosters interaction with and skills for making sense of content materials • Cultivates strategies for deep learning of content

continued

Figure 1-3 Models of Teaching in This Text
continued

Chapter	Model	Summary	Support for 21st Century Learning
9	Vocabulary Acquisition model	A teacher-guided model for teaching vocabulary in a procedural and inductive manner. The model helps students develop their own understanding of the meaning of a word(s) through analysis of the parts of the word and their meanings.	• Develops recognition of details, making of connections with prior knowledge, and creative thinking • Encourages development of skills for independent vocabulary learning
10	Inquiry model	A process-oriented instructional model that aims to teach students the skills, knowledge, and dispositions required for thinking systematically to answer important questions.	• Promotes problem-solving skills • Introduces students to scientific ways of knowing • Fosters skills and dispositions for learning to learn
11	Problem-Based Learning model	An active learning model that challenges students to learn and apply knowledge of content with problem-solving skills to meaningful problems in the academic disciplines.	• Cultivates application of knowledge to real-world contexts • Encourages learning of useful processes to solve problems
12	Cooperative Learning model	A model that capitalizes on students' inclination to learn socially and that promotes students' development of social skills and understanding of content.	• Promotes skills for productive collaboration and communication (listening and taking turns) • Teaches benefits of teamwork and cooperation
13	Integrative model	A teacher-guided model that supports students as they work to develop the ability to learn independently using various critical thinking skills. Students analyze an organized body of knowledge to develop new ideas and understandings while learning to think, analyze, and draw conclusions independently.	• Supports ability to draw conclusions, make connections, and formulate and generalizations • Encourages ability to examine, analyze, and make sense of large amounts of materials
14	Socratic Seminar model	A teacher-guided model that encourages development of thinking skills and exploration of ideas through the use of structured questioning with debate or dialogue.	• Fosters communication and collaboration skills (listening and questioning) • Develops thinking skills, including questioning, synthesis, and analysis

Instructional Models in the Past and Future

Like Franklin Elementary School, the instructional models could be considered a proud part of our community's past. Over the last half century, the models have provided educators with specialized tools that have enabled them to create more effective instructional experiences. They have been valuable because of their

- effectiveness in promoting student learning of academic content,
- focus on developing students in specific but different learning domains,
- usefulness in many settings,
- support for both individual and shared student needs, and
- ability to make learning more engaging.

Like Franklin Elementary School, reinventing the models would make them more effective for the 21st century learner and teacher alike.

The transformation of the instructional models can be achieved in three ways:

1. Through the increased use of technology to plan, implement, and conduct assessment
2. Through the integration of differentiated instruction principles and practices within the instructional models
3. Through the goal-directed application of the models by educational designers who apply systematic thinking and processes to design instruction for their students

Throughout the text, we approach the teaching models in light of these three methods of transformation. Through rich, descriptive scenarios and sample lesson plans, we demonstrate how technologies can make the models more efficient, effective, and engaging. We also explain how the models support differentiation either through the embedded strategies built into the models or through additional modifications that might be incorporated when desired. Finally, we present a reconceptualized view of how these models can empower teachers to work like educational designers and support 21st century learners in more focused and effective ways.

Teachers as Educational Designers

As we have illustrated in this chapter, successful 21st century teaching will require teachers to support diverse learners as they work to meet uniformly high standards. Because rapid, continuous change is the new norm, teachers need to constantly adapt as learners, standards, learning environments, and available tools change over the course of their careers. Operating as educational designers will allow teachers to flexibly adapt and experience continued success in the constantly evolving environment of 21st century teaching.

What Is a Designer?

If teachers are going to be educational designers, it helps to understand first what designers are. There are many kinds of designers who work in many different fields. Most of us are familiar with the work of fashion designers, graphic designers, industrial designers, and interior designers. Designers possess knowledge of their field and competence with specialized processes and thinking skills. They use these to identify, understand, and address problems or design challenges. For example, an interior designer has knowledge of aesthetics and architecture and the ability to communicate with homeowners to learn about their needs. He or she surveys existing resources, keeping in mind budget constraints, and then redesigns a room to make it both visually appealing and functional. Designers are highly skilled professionals who can work in dynamic, real-world settings to meet multiple goals simultaneously. They are people who not only enjoy their work but also perform it with a deep sense of commitment to their profession. Designers operate at the intersection of art and science, the abstract and concrete, and identify with both the theoretical and the practical. Functioning within these unique intersections is also necessary when teachers operate as educational designers.

An **educational designer** is a teacher who approaches instructional planning with purpose, possesses specialized knowledge, and utilizes systematic processes to identify instructional challenges. An educational designer addresses these challenges through the skillful application of a broad repertoire of tools. This complex statement benefits from a closer look. Educational designers are teachers who can do the following:

1. Approach instructional planning with purpose. By this we mean educational designers operate with the assumption that they have control over important dimensions of their work and are aware of their decision-making authority and responsibility. They are empowered. They know and understand the standards their students must attain and approach their work with focused goals and a clear sense of purpose.
2. Possess specialized knowledge. Teachers gain knowledge through experience, research, and study. Traditional knowledge teachers possess is often organized into different domains, including pedagogical knowledge, content knowledge, and pedagogical content knowledge. Teaching in the 21st century, however, also requires new knowledge—technological pedagogical content knowledge—discussed in Chapter 3.
3. Use systematic processes to identify instructional challenges. The challenges that educational designers must address are most often related to learners and content. Use of these processes is an outgrowth of an educational designer's goal-directed orientation to practice. Systematic processes teachers use include planning and assessment, but educational designers use these processes strategically. The revised Bloom's taxonomy, UbD, differentiated instruction, and instructional design approaches (e.g., ADDIE, introduced in Chapter 2) might also be considered systematic processes useful to educational designers.
4. Address these challenges through the skillful application of a broad repertoire of tools. Educational designers have many tools. Those addressed in this text include the instructional models, strategies, and technologies. An educational designer can use the elements in his or her repertoire individually and in an integrated fashion. An in-depth explanation of these tools is provided in Chapter 3.

Why Should Teachers Function as Educational Designers?

The role of a teacher is multifaceted. The most successful teachers are able to perform numerous roles simultaneously, including educator, motivator, social worker, salesperson, parent, therapist, and more, as required in their practice. As teachers develop into educational designers, they should not stop performing any of these important roles. Instead, they should approach their work with an awareness of their ability and the need to direct the important dimensions of their practice.

Teaching with this new mind-set still requires passion, dedication, hard work, talent, and drive, but it also operates with the assumption that these qualities must be focused in systematic ways to be most productive. As educational designers' work in the instructional domain of teaching becomes more purposeful, their use of the models of teaching that we present in Part II of this book will be more fruitful. When teachers work as educational designers, they are empowered in numerous ways, such as the following:

- **Educational designers know how to get to know their students.** Educational designers use their specialized skills and implement systematic approaches to gain deeper understanding of their students' individual and shared needs. These approaches also help them competently analyze learner needs (e.g., using tools like needs assessments) and address them in more strategic ways using approaches such as differentiated instruction and tools (e.g., technology).
- **Educational designers have a deep understanding of content.** The same systematic thinking and approaches that help educational designers get to know their students also aid them in analyzing their content. Educational designers employ tools such as UbD to create curriculum plans that enable deeper understanding of content.
- **Educational designers learn from practice.** When systematic approaches are used to design and implement instruction, teachers better understand what is going on in their practice. Such knowledge facilitates reflection and the learning that comes from it, which in turn improves their practice.
- **Educational designers experience a more rewarding practice.** More of their students are successful in attaining learning goals because it has been designed with their needs in mind. Students are better supported when working to attain standards and developing confidence—skills needed for their future life and learning. When student learning falls short of expectations, educational designers have the ability to figure out where the problem is and make improvements. As a result, teachers experience more ownership of the teaching process and higher satisfaction in their work.

The above-mentioned details result in more learners attaining high standards with increased frequency. This results in greater professional accomplishment and personal satisfaction as well.

In the remaining chapters of Part I of this text, we provide additional information to help teachers function more effectively as educational designers. In Chapter 2, we introduce the field of instructional design to emphasize the importance of adopting the design mind-set we advocate. We share one instructional design model and describe how the systematic thinking and processes used by instructional designers can benefit 21st educational designers. In Chapter 3, we introduce readers to the different types of tools that should be in an educational designer's tool set. Finally, in Chapter 4, we describe how the assessment cycle—something already in most teachers' skill sets—can be used more deliberately to promote learning for both teachers and students. The goal of Part I is to help teachers leverage the models discussed in Part II in ways that help them address the challenges of 21st century teaching.

Chapter Summary

This chapter explained that the successful preparation of 21st century learners for life and work in a fast-paced, rapidly changing, digital society will require teachers to approach their work with a new mind-set, a broad skill set, and a high-quality tool set. Digital technologies, access to information, globalization, equity, and accountability are important trends that have generated ideas, movements, and reforms that influence American schools. Rigorous standards, refined conceptions about learning, and the development of systematic approaches to curriculum and instruction promote and enable efforts to serve an increasingly diverse student population. Their readiness for life in and beyond the imagined future requires teachers to function as educational designers. An educational designer is a teacher who approaches instruction with intention and clear goals and applies specialized knowledge and skills to address instructional challenges with a broad repertoire of instructional models, strategies, and technologies. By functioning as an educational designer, teachers can optimize the instructional models presented in this text by integrating them with focused, systematic implementation; powerful educational technologies; and differentiated instruction practices.

Review Questions

1. What are some of the major trends shaping the world? How do they affect the field of education in the 21st century?

2. What are the most important characteristics of 21st century learners?

3. Why are traditional instructional models still relevant in contemporary classrooms? How might they be reinvented?

4. What is meant by the idea of "teachers as educational designers"? Define this idea.

5. Identify how being an educational designer can enable teachers to capitalize on the instructional models.

Resources

- Common Core State Standards Initiative—This site is the "official" website for this initiative: www.corestandards.org

- Differentiated Instruction 101—This screencast provides an overview of differentiated instruction: https://vimeo.com/51259497

- International Society for Technology in Education (ISTE)—ISTE is an international organization focusing on technology in education. It has been instrumental in establishing student, teacher, and school leader technology standards: www.iste.org/welcome.aspx

- Multicultural Education Pavilion—This site includes many resources addressing diversity in educational environments: www.edchange.org/multicultural

- National Center for Education Statistics (NCES)—NCES collects and analyzes national data related to education in the United States as well as other nations: http://nces.ed.gov/about

- Partnership for 21st Century Skills—This site houses the framework for 21st century learning: www.p21.org

- Universal Design for Learning (UDL), Center for Applied Special Technology (CAST)—This CAST site houses many resources about UDL: www.cast.org/udl/index.html

Instructional Design, Educational Design, and Designing Effective Instruction

© AVAVA/Shutterstock

Rich, a high school science teacher, expected to enjoy being a teacher representative for a National Aeronautics and Space Administration (NASA) Science, Technology, Engineering, and Math (STEM) curriculum project on 21st century careers. However, he did not expect that the experience would expand his skill set for designing instruction to better prepare his students for *their* 21st century careers. When his principal asked for a professional development summary, Rich shared, "Thanks to my NASA experiences, I have begun to approach my work like one of the NASA instructional designers. I am more scientific and strategic—especially when making instructional lesson plans and materials. Instead of developing activities around what materials are available, which standards I need to teach, or how much time I have, I now use more organized and logical ways to analyze learning goals, assess learner needs, and make lessons and materials that connect them. What I learned from this experience will help me become a more effective teacher."

The eye-opening experiences began when Rich met Kelsey and Kyle, the instructional designers for the NASA project. Because he had never even heard the term *instructional designer* before, Rich was surprised to learn that these two people and many others had full-time instructional design jobs at NASA creating plans for different training projects and instructional materials. Rich was a little jealous when he heard about the interesting things the instructional designers created, such as videos, software, and websites. However, Rich was less envious when he realized that the instructional designers did not work with or develop personal relationships with the learners for whom they designed instruction. Eventually, Rich discovered that instructional designers work in a variety of fields and locations, such as his local library, museums, and the public health department.

When Rich first heard the term *instructional designer,* he thought, "Hey, that is a fancy way of explaining what I do when preparing my unit and lesson plans." It did not take long for him to discover that there was a world of difference between the way that instructional designers approach the instructional process and his own. Rich discovered that instructional designers are deliberate and systematic and use specialized approaches. This allows them to create instruction that works for learners they do not know personally. It also helps them maintain uniform quality on the different types of projects they execute. Rich realized that his own effectiveness as a teacher could benefit by following this example.

During recent years, Rich had spent more and more energy developing custom-designed instructional videos, lesson plans, and lab experiments for his students. He had also made an increasing number of modifications to the lessons he used from teacher's manuals. Rich enjoyed this creative work, but his reasons for devoting additional time and energy to these tasks were rooted in necessity rather than pleasure. To ensure consistently high levels of success for his increasingly diverse learners, additional support and customization were required. Traditional methods of teaching and one-size-fits-all approaches were no longer sufficient. Rich had expected to learn a lot on the NASA project, but he did not expect to learn that his own professional skill set needed broadening to suit the expanding responsibilities of *his* 21st century career.

Rich discovered that he could design better instruction and materials in less time and with less effort by using the systematic thinking and specialized instructional design processes modeled by Kelsey and Kyle. He found the five-phase ADDIE instructional design model particularly helpful. It was easy to remember because it was named for its phases—**A**nalysis, **D**esign, **D**evelopment, **I**mplementation, and **E**valuation. Rich found ADDIE straightforward, easy to understand, and flexible enough that it could be used when creating both instruction and instructional materials. The phases in ADDIE were the same even if the learning goals, students, and available resources varied. The logical, disciplined thinking involved in using ADDIE was not totally foreign to Rich—it was similar to that used with other design approaches he knew about, including Understanding by Design (UbD). In fact, Rich often integrated the UbD curriculum planning model within the phases of ADDIE. ADDIE helped him make decisions about which technology to use, what information to look for during a pre assessment, and how to match objectives with learning activities to promote the "enduring understandings" that UbD helped him identify. Rich saw how thinking and working like a designer could improve his teaching and his students' preparation for life in the 21st century. His principal was so impressed with Rich's new skills that he gave Rich the job of leading an interdisciplinary team to redesign the ninth-grade research paper unit. Rich believed this was a great opportunity to apply what he learned. He could not wait to get started. ■

CHAPTER OBJECTIVES

After reading this chapter, you will be able to:

- Describe the field of instructional design and the instructional design process.
- Articulate how educational designers can benefit from systematic thinking and knowledge of instructional design.
- Distinguish between instructional design models and models of instruction.

- Describe the ADDIE instructional design model.
- Explain how teachers can use ADDIE to make better use of the instructional models and improve their ability to design instruction.

Introduction

Rich, the teacher in the opening scenario, discovered that logical thinking and specialized approaches could help him create more effective learning experiences for his students. Rich's students had become more diverse each year. Their increasingly varied needs were more challenging to meet using the traditional materials and instructional plans that had been successful in the past. Although he was already engaging in more careful instructional planning (using UbD) and modifying instructional materials (using differentiated instruction techniques), Rich realized his efforts would be more productive if they were tied to real data about students' needs and if they were more organized, systematic, and intentional. Many teachers, like Rich, are discovering that functioning as an educational designer with a new mind-set, a broadened skill set, and a high-quality tool set are necessary for continued success in the 21st century.

In this chapter, we share information about the field of instructional design and the instructional design process. The methods of instructional design have long been effective in other fields, and they offer great potential to improve the work of preK-12 teachers. Using instructional design approaches will empower teachers to work as educational designers as they decide how and when to use the instructional models in Part II of this text. First, we consider what is known about the existing approaches teachers use to design instruction. Next, we define what instructional design is, explore its origins, and consider its value to teachers. Then we provide a description of one popular instructional design approach called ADDIE and share how educational designers might apply ADDIE and systematic thinking to make decisions about the application of the instructional models in their own teaching. Finally, we illustrate how an educational designer's mind-set, skill set, and tool set enable more effective planning, teaching, and use of the instructional models of teaching described in Part II of this book.

Instructional Planning and Teaching

Most teachers enter the profession with an accurate understanding of what will be involved in teaching. Few teachers, however, have a realistic idea of what is required to plan for teaching. Planning for teaching or what is technically called "instructional planning" is the important work that maximizes learning opportunities for all students. Although it influences the success of the instruction implemented in the classroom, planning requires a different set of competencies than does instruction.

Researchers who study instructional planning have noted that several different activities are performed during the instructional planning process. Designing instruction is one. When designing instruction, teachers identify the standards that will be addressed, make choices about which instructional approaches to use, and select curriculum resources and sometimes develop their own. As the number and variety of instructional approaches and materials available for teaching have expanded and changed, so too must the mind-set and skill set of successful teachers. In the section that follows, we explore information about how teachers plan for instruction and explain why teachers might benefit from the adopting the perspectives and practices common among instructional designers.

Teachers' Approaches to Instructional Planning

In an era when the accountability that teachers have for student learning is constantly increasing, the most successful instruction is that which results in growth and achievement for all students. It would seem that using systematic processes to ensure that the identified needs of students direct all instructional decisions would be the most productive approach. Yet research on teacher planning suggests this is not the norm. Instead, it suggests that when making decisions during the instructional planning process, teachers draw on a wide range of knowledge but use it in unsystematic and nonlinear ways (Day, Calderhead, & Denicolo, 1993). It also contends that teachers plan instruction around materials, activities (Harris & Hofer, 2009a, 2009b; Harris, Mishra, & Koehler, 2009; Yinger & Clark, 1979; Zahorik, 1975), or objectives (Yinger, 1980). This implies that the process that teachers engage in when making crucial instructional decisions is dynamic and complex. However, it also indicates that choices about what to teach and how to teach it are often dictated by contextual factors besides those associated with students' identified needs. Greater success can be achieved if teachers develop facility with the systematic thinking and specialized approaches long used in the field of instructional design. These put data about learners at the center of all instructional decisions and have safeguards that ensure high-quality experiences for all learners. They also promote the best configuration of resources for instruction. In the sections that follow, we explain what instructional design is and elaborate on how knowledge of its processes will benefit 21st century teachers working as educational designers.

What Is Instructional Design?

Instructional design (sometimes called instructional systems design) is a systematic and scientific approach for designing instruction and creating instructional materials. Like the Internet, microwave ovens, and so many other useful innovations, the instructional design process was developed with funding from the U.S. Department of Defense. The origins of instructional design date back to World War II (Dick, 1987), when the military employed psychologists and educators to develop effective materials and methods for training personnel for numerous, varied, and essential military activities. Whether learning to build a tank, navigate a plane, or prepare military officers to move a battalion, the educational needs of military personnel were too important to attempt with anything other than a deliberate and systematic approach.

Instructional design approaches emerged as efforts were made to apply scientific principles and discoveries to promote learning. The instructional design process, which operationalizes the instructional design approach, involves five phases: (1) design, (2) development, (3) implementation, (4) evaluation, and (5) management. During the instructional design process, an instructional designer or design team works through each of these phases systematically. Each phase involves using specialized processes, structures, and tools.

The instructional design process uses both a systematic way of thinking about the world and instructional outcomes and a methodical one. Instructional designers use different instructional design models to work through the five basic phases of the instructional design process. All instructional design models progress through these same five phases, but each model uses different processes, structures, and tools to complete them.

Instructional Design Models versus Models of Instruction

Popular in intellectual circles, the term *model* is a simultaneously vague yet also specific word that expresses a mental construct for organizing a particular set of ideas important to those in the circle or community that uses the term. So, before going any further, we must distinguish between the concepts of an instructional design model and the models of instruction, which are the focus of this book.

Instructional design models emerge from the field of instructional design and are the practical expression of learning theory. Each instructional design model provides a different map for designers to follow through the five phases of the instructional design process, from creation of materials through delivery of instruction. Some popular instructional design models are ADDIE (Gustafson, 2002), ASSURE (Heinich, Molenda, Russell, & Smaldino, 1999), and the Dick and Carey model (Dick, Carey, & Carey, 2008).

Instructional models (i.e., models of teaching), however, are frameworks for implementing instruction in a classroom setting. They are research-based, proven procedures for teaching that support learners in achieving specific cognitive, affective and psychomotor outcomes, as described in Chapter 1. As Part II of this book illustrates, each instructional model has a particular set of steps or phases that teachers follow when planning and implementing a lesson. Like instructional design models, each instructional model has a unique theoretical basis (Joyce, Weil, & Calhoun, 2009) that informs its specialized structure and dictates the particular activities that occur during each of its step. An instructional model is a procedure for implementing a lesson or learning sequence; however, it is not a process for systematically developing learning experiences and materials. Instructional models work in limited settings, while instructional design models facilitate learning across most, if not all, educational contexts. Whereas models of teaching are the blueprints used to build a particular lesson, instructional design models are the processes used by those who develop such blueprints.

What Are the Applications and Uses of the Instructional Design Process?

Although military in its origins, the instructional design process is used in many different arenas today. It is commonly practiced by government agencies and in corporate training, higher education, and the educational publishing industry. The instructional design process is often central to the development and maintenance of museums and museum exhibits. It is used to develop different types of instruction, including courses, lessons, and modules offered through workshops, classes, and online sources. Instruction created using the instructional design process can address learning among students in a variety of groupings (e.g., individuals, small groups, and large groups) and over both short- and long-term time frames. The instructional design process is also applied in developing specific types of materials, including DVDs, videos, podcasts, and websites, using a variety of tools and delivery systems. Instructional design processes are useful when creating instruction that can be delivered in real time with an instructor or that which is "canned" and facilitated without an instructor. Instructional designers implement the instructional design process working alone and/or in groups. Because it provides support for collaboration, task delegation, and individual responsibilities, the instructional design process is especially useful to teams of subject matter and other experts as they coordinate and structure the development of instruction.

Instructional design is a process that emerges from a systematic way of thinking about the world and instructional outcomes. Instructional designers follow a procedural process for designing instruction. Different instructional design models also demonstrate, address, and perpetuate the philosophical views of different communities of designers. There are instructional design models that reflect the beliefs of constructivists (Willis, 2000) as well as those that are compatible with a more behaviorist perspective of learning (Dick et al. 2008). Therefore, although instructional designers employ instructional design principles that follow a specific process, they also choose approaches for the actual design of instruction and use resources based on their own educational philosophies.

Why Do Instructional Designers Use the Instructional Design Process?

The instructional design process benefits the designer and those who will use the instruction they develop. Instructional designers find that the instructional design process streamlines their work—saving time, energy, and money. In the dynamic, complex domain of learning, the methodical, step-by-step structure of the instructional design process focuses designers on their product's goals. The process creates order and logic through the systematic processes and thinking that it facilitates. The instructional design process also incorporates specialized instruments (i.e., flowcharts), processes (i.e., rapid prototyping), and tools (i.e., needs assessments) that make the creative experience easier, more enjoyable, and rewarding.

Both designers and learners benefit from the use of the instructional design process because its use results in high-quality instruction and instructional materials (sometimes referred to as a "product"). A high-quality product fulfills the goals for its creation and effectively supports the specified learning goals of its targeted audience. Numerous factors make products designed using the instructional design process more effective than those created without it. For one, the instructional design process ensures that the product is being created for specific and clear goals and purposes. Strategies for clarifying the purpose of the product are central to the instructional design process. Once these goals are identified, designers can more carefully and painstakingly attend to them during the design process. Clarity about specified product goals also informs interim checks and testing of the product during the development stages. Using instructional design processes, the designer can determine if the product will meet its goals while there is still plenty of time to adapt, change, and modify it as needed. The instructional design process delivers a more effective product because it strategically identifies the needs of the learners. When the needs of the eventual audience for the product are identified and understood, they can inform and influence all decisions related to the product. The end result is a product that is more tailored to the needs and goals of its target audience.

How Does Instructional Design Already Influence Classroom Practice?

Most teachers do not realize that instructional design and the instructional design process already affect most preK-12 classrooms—just indirectly. Early efforts to think about instruction in a uniform, scientific, and systematic way later influenced the development of some concepts that are largely influential in preK-12 classrooms, such as programmed instruction, the writing of behavioral objectives, criterion-referenced testing, and Gagné's (1965) conditions of learning. In addition, instructional design and its processes are also influential in classrooms through the materials and plans that educational publishers have developed using them. In fact, educational publishers who develop preK-12 textbooks and curriculum materials are some of the largest employers of instructional designers.

Despite the fact that research and common sense consistently suggest its value, the instructional design process per se is rarely, if ever, taught in teacher education programs. However, other systematic approaches for designing instruction, like UbD, are increasingly being taught in teacher education programs. Recall from Chapter 1 that, different from instructional design models, UbD is a curriculum planning model that promotes teachers' more effective instruction using systematic thinking and strategies similar to those used during the instructional design process. Differentiated instruction is another approach that promotes the use of logical, systematic thinking that is gaining popularity in contemporary classrooms. This approach involves thoughtful analysis of learners' needs and then modification of the content, learning process, and products expressing learning based on learner needs. Inherent in the practice of differentiated instruction is the notion that teachers are

Systematic Thinking Illustrated
(© marekuliasz/Shutterstock)

approaching their work as designers and making decisions based on data about learner needs to create more appropriate instruction. Neither UbD nor differentiated instruction is an instructional design model, but both approaches empower teachers to think in systematic ways about learners, curriculum, and their practice. They imply that teachers should approach instructional planning as educational designers.

How Might Teachers Benefit from Using the Instructional Design Process?

In the opening scenario, Rich discovered that his diverse learners have diverse needs, and the standards for their learning are increasing in rigor. At the same time, he noted that the resources for teaching are becoming more numerous, varied, and powerful. Rich wisely recognized that his existing approaches to designing instruction may not continue to achieve the same results. In other words, "Doing what he has always done may not allow him to get what he has always gotten!" Rich was right in thinking that more systematic thinking and specialized processes, like those used by the NASA designers, will be crucial to his ability to meet the challenges of teaching in the 21st century.

Use of the instructional design process will benefit teachers functioning as educational designers by helping them

- clarify the goals for instruction,
- identify and base instructional decisions on known learner needs,
- locate and choose resources that are most appropriate for learners and learning goals,
- frame the most important challenges for instruction,
- understand the effect of the instructional materials or methods they have created, and
- learn and grow through practice.

Later in this chapter, we describe how a teacher might apply the instructional design process—specifically the ADDIE model—when planning instruction. First, however, we will examine this model in detail.

■ The ADDIE Instructional Design Model

The ADDIE model is one of the most widely used instructional design models. ADDIE is simple and works flexibly in many different contexts to support the creation of instructional plans, experiences, and materials. Its memorable acronym describes the major activities in each of its phases—**A**nalysis, **D**esign, **D**evelopment, **I**mplementation, and **E**valuation.

Each ADDIE phase is purposeful and focused on the specific outcomes its name suggests. Use of ADDIE provides an organized, strategic plan for instructional design that ensures quality through consideration of all of the elements that influence learning. In practice, instructional designers work through the ADDIE phases in a progressive order, but they can repeat previous phases when necessary to fine-tune the instruction being developed. Figure 2-1 provides an illustration of the recursive nature of ADDIE's phases.

The following sections include a description of each of the ADDIE phases. Later we explain how using ADDIE in preK-12 settings might assist educational designers in deciding when and how to optimally apply the instructional models presented in Part II of this text.

Figure 2-1   ADDIE Model

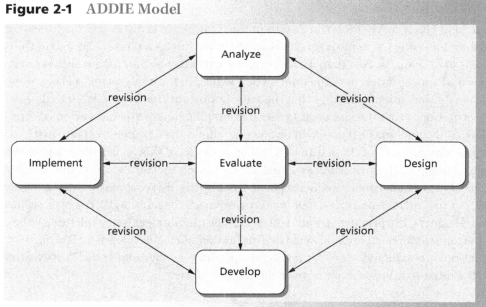

Created using Inspiration® Software.

The Analysis Phase

The first phase of ADDIE is the analysis phase. The four major goals in this phase are to (1) determine the instructional goals and objectives, (2) examine current and desired learner needs and characteristics, (3) identify contextual factors that might promote or hinder instruction (e.g., social and physical learning environment, available time, and so on), and (4) locate available resources. This clarifies the who, what, when, where, and how of instruction. During this phase, the designer engages in activities that challenge him or her to understand important dimensions of the learning context. The designer carefully considers the content and learning goals as they relate to characteristics of the specified audience. Typically, the analysis phase involves conducting a needs assessment (also called a needs analysis).

A **needs assessment** is a formal process implemented by a designer to identify information about the learning goals, the audience, the learning context, and available resources that will influence the design of instruction. A needs assessment requires a designer to (1) determine the desired status of the audience that will be achieved through interaction with the instruction to be designed, (2) determine the actual status of the audience before interaction with the instruction to be designed, and (3) analyze the gap between the two. This gap, or difference, between the desired and actual status represents the "need." In a classroom, the gap analysis might compare the learners at their present learning status (i.e., what they know related to targeted academic standards before instruction takes place) with the learners at their desired learning status (i.e., what students know related to the standards after learning takes place). Successful completion of this phase depends on how well aligned the desired status is with the instructional goals, how accurately the needs are identified, and how successfully the gap analysis is performed. The analysis phase is foundational for the rest of the design process. What is learned during this phase forms the basis for all activities that follow.

The Design Phase

The second phase in ADDIE is the **design** phase. This phase involves creating the actual plan for addressing the need or needs identified in the analysis phase. The goal in this phase is to develop the best plan for meeting these needs. The best plan is the one that most closely and appropriately uses the information gained in the analysis phase. For example, if the needs assessment identifies that the most important challenge related to designing instruction is that the audience speaks different languages and has various cultural backgrounds, then the best plan will be one that allows the designer to create instruction that provides support for these differences. For example, in this phase, the designer might plan to develop flash cards using an application to teach specialized academic vocabulary for the lesson before instruction takes place. During this phase, plans for evaluating the quality of the instruction in development are also made. Because ADDIE is used by instructional designers, the products created often include high-budget items intended to be used in a permanent form. Therefore, extensive evaluation during development (i.e., formative evaluation) is conducted. Plans for testing the product—sometimes called "beta testing"—with the intended audience are devised during this phase.

The Develop Phase

The third phase of ADDIE is called the **develop,** or "create," phase. In this phase, the instructional designer creates the instructional materials, sometimes called the "product," needed to support the goals identified in the analyze phase (through a needs assessment) and planned for in the design phase. If new information is discovered during the develop phase, it may be necessary to loop back and rework some (or all) of the previous phases of ADDIE. The develop phase is the "messy and applied" phase when abstract ideas are brought to life. Illustrations leave the designer's mind and appear on paper (or computer) in the form of assignments, assessments, or other instructional materials to foster learning. During the develop phase, instructional designers frequently work collaboratively with subject matter experts, graphic designers, and media technology experts. In some cases, these individuals are involved throughout all ADDIE phases. In others, they are brought in as needed to support the instructional designer's work.

The Implementation Phase

The fourth phase of the ADDIE model is the **implementation,** or "teaching/delivery of instruction," phase. This phase involves testing the product that has been created. It might involve testing the materials and/or implementing the instruction, unit, or lessons mapped out in the design phase. Implementation is often considered the teaching phase of the instructional design process. During this phase, designers have the opportunity to learn by applying their theoretical constructs in practical situations. For instance, they might examine the question, "Does the product work in practice?" The implementation phase is when designers find out. Formative evaluation is usually conducted as a part of this phase, merging the implementation and the next phase, evaluation.

The Evaluation Phase

The final phase in ADDIE is the **evaluation** phase. During this phase, instructional designers implement the plan for the evaluation of the instruction they have created. Even though the evaluation plan is typically created during the design phase, instructional designers can proceed with the full plan only after the instruction has been produced, created, and/or

Figure 2-2 Major Activities within Each ADDIE Model Phase

ADDIE Model Phase	Major Activities
Analyze	• Analyze academic standards and break into learning goals • Identify and examine learner needs • Consider important characteristics of the learning context • Conduct needs assessment • Inventory available materials and resources • Select appropriate instructional models of teaching
Design	• Review types of knowledge addressed in learning goals • Configure other instructional tools • Formulate plans for development of instructional plan and materials • Conceive evaluation plan • Devise sequence and plan pacing of unit
Develop	• Create lesson plans • Develop evaluation plan • Produce any instructional materials
Implement	• Teach unit • Implement use of instructional materials developed • Implement evaluation plan
Evaluate	• Analyze data generated from the evaluation plan • Determine levels of student growth, effort, and achievement • Examine quality of instructional plan and/or materials and make modifications as needed

delivered. During this phase, designers implement their evaluation and then use the information gained from it—such as anecdotal data and student feedback and questions—and from their own observation and judgment to modify the instruction as needed. Keep in mind that this phase does not involve evaluating the effort, learning, and growth that the target audience experiences when interacting with the instruction. Rather, the focus of activities during this phase is the evaluation of the instruction that has been developed.

Each of the five phases in the ADDIE model is unique and important. Each involves activities that contribute to making the instructional design process more efficient and the product resulting from it more effective. Figure 2-2 provides a listing of the ADDIE phases and a short description of the important activities performed within each phase.

How Can Teachers Use ADDIE?

Teachers can use ADDIE phases in whole or in part to help them develop more effective lessons, units, and instructional materials. The focused, organized thinking guided by the various ADDIE phases can increase instructional effectiveness when concentrating on large instructional challenges, such as determining the best way to meet curriculum standards in a unit of instruction, or small ones, such as selecting the best model of teaching to address a standard dealing with conceptual knowledge. Teachers can use just one ADDIE phase, such as the analysis phase to help them better understand the learning context, or apply them all when the situation warrants. ADDIE can be used as often as a teacher deems it useful. It might be applied on a regular basis for weekly lesson planning or when designing a more challenging unit. The systematic, focused thinking employed when using the ADDIE model is the same regardless of the context of its use.

ADDIE promotes goal-driven and rewarding practice in an era during which unprecedented opportunities for creative teaching exist but are subject to increased accountability measures. ADDIE empowers educators to make the most of the abundant resources available for teaching and promotes the optimal configurations of professional knowledge and tools. It is especially helpful in supporting teachers who are functioning as educational designers. Implementation of the phases within ADDIE can help them integrate their skill set and tool set effectively. Appendix A provides an in-depth illustration of how Rich, the teacher in the opening scenario, implements the ADDIE model when leading an interdisciplinary team in redesigning a ninth-grade research paper unit. The scenario illustrates how high-quality instruction can be developed by using data about students when making instructional decisions, integrating ideas from the revised Bloom's taxonomy (Anderson et al., 2001), and practicing UbD (Wiggins & McTighe, 2005) within ADDIE's phases. The following sections introduce specific ways that the phases of the ADDIE model and the systematic thinking that it promotes might empower teachers working as educational designers. As we describe each phase of the ADDIE model, we provide specific applications for classroom teachers.

Analyze

During the analysis phase, teachers work to (1) identify instructional goals, (2) understand learner needs, (3) consider the learning context, and (4) locate available resources. Although educators often perform some of these activities during regular instructional planning, they do not usually address all four of these goals with intention. Working through the analysis phase focuses teachers' attention on these four goals and establishes a structure for applying systematic thinking to design instruction and instructional materials.

ADDIE AND CONTENT STANDARDS. The analysis phase provides support for aligning instruction with recognized standards. Whether curriculum standards come from the Common Core State Standards, an individual state, a professional association (e.g., International Reading Association, National Council of Teachers of Math, and so on), or a school district, when teachers engage in the analysis phase, they actively connect the instruction being designed with the "officially" designated content. During the identification of standards, teachers target specific standards and consider how they are connected to the scope and sequence of the larger curriculum and discipline.

The analysis phase also provides support for teachers' as they work to translate the targeted standards into learning goals or objectives. Although the terms *learning goals* and *objectives* mean different things to different people, here they refer to a written expression of what students are expected to know and be able to do as the result of instruction. These learning goals are easiest to work with when they are (1) focused, or deal with only one type of knowledge that will be targeted through instruction (i.e., factual, procedural, conceptual, or metacognitive); (2) stated as learning outcomes; and (3) clear.

The learning goals should be appropriate to the readiness of the learners, significant enough to justify their efforts to learn, and aligned with state and national standards. Through analysis of the learning goals, teachers who are designing instructional experiences and materials gain clarity of purpose and deeper understanding of the targeted standards. This understanding informs the choices made in the subsequent ADDIE phases about how to design instruction that addresses the unique nature of the learning goals. That deeper understanding also creates the space for insights related to selecting the most appropriate approaches and materials to use in the development process. Figure 2-3 provides an example of how the learning goals for Rich's research paper unit might be considered in light of these suggestions.

Figure 2-3 Example: A Systematic Method for Analyzing Standards, Developing Learning Goals, and Considering Student Readiness

Standard	Ohio Academic Content Standards: English Language Arts, Research, Grade 9	Standard Broken into Discrete Learning Goals	Student Readiness: Foundational/Prior Knowledge, Skills, and Experiences Necessary for Learning
	Compose open-ended questions for research, assigned or personal interest, and modify questions as necessary during inquiry and investigation to narrow the focus or extend the investigation.		
Conceptual knowledge: Are there concepts associated with this standard?	The general concepts to understand here are "What are questions?" and "What is research?" The specific concept on which to focus is the concept of "What is a research question?"	**Learning Goal #1:** Students will understand what a research question is. *I CAN statements:* • I can describe what a research question is and how one is different from a general question. • I can describe what a high-quality research question is.	Students must know what a question is. Students must know what research is and how research questions and their quality affect the productivity of research.
Factual knowledge: Are there facts associated with this standard?	There are some general "facts" that students will have exposure to and need to understand by the end of this learning sequence, such as the following: Not all questions are research questions. Not all research questions are high-quality ones. The characteristics of high-quality research questions are (1) they are of interest to the researcher, (2) they are important/worth pursuing, (3) they can be answered (in general), (4) they can be answered with the skills/knowledge/resources available to the researcher, and (5) they are manageable—they are focused (neither too broad nor too narrow). Other facts: Research questions guide all research. High-quality research questions result in more successful research processes and more useful results.	**Learning Goal #2:** Students can name the critical attributes/characteristics of research questions in general and high-quality research questions in particular. *I CAN statements:* • I can name the attributes of a research question. • I can distinguish between a research question and other types of questions. • I can identify a high-quality research question from a list.	Student must have a sense of what research questions are used for in school and real-world contexts. Students must understand the concept of quality in ideas, objects, and processes. Students must be able to understand what a critical attribute is. It will help if students are able to discriminate, differentiate, and think critically about abstract ideas like research questions.

continued

Figure 2-3   Example: A Systematic Method for Analyzing Standards,
continued   Developing Learning Goals, and Considering Student Readiness

Standard	Ohio Academic Content Standards: English Language Arts, Research, Grade 9	Standard Broken into Discrete Learning Goals	Student Readiness: Foundational/Prior Knowledge, Skills, and Experiences Necessary for Learning
	Compose open-ended questions for research, assigned or personal interest, and modify questions as necessary during inquiry and investigation to narrow the focus or extend the investigation.		
	High-quality research questions often lead a researcher to ask other research questions.		
Procedural: Are there procedures associated with the standard?	It will be useful if students can "inventory" their own interests and identify areas of personal interest that might lead them to topics for possible research. It will be useful to be able to apply a set of criteria to evaluate the quality of a research question.	**Learning Goal #3:** Students will be able to identify some areas that interest them that they might want to learn more about. **Learning Goal #4:** Students will be able to apply a set of criteria to evaluate the quality of a research question. *I CAN statements:* • I can examine my interests and brainstorm a list of things that I would like to learn more about. • I can determine the quality of a research question by comparing and contrasting examples of research questions to the critical attributes for a high-quality research question.	Students will need to have prior experiences with topics connected to research that direct their interests. It will help if students have experience applying criteria to evaluate an object, idea, or thing. It will help if students are able to think logically and procedurally.
Meta cognitive: Are there any metacognitive ideas associated with the standard?	Can I formulate research questions? Can I formulate a research question that works for me?	**Learning Goal #5:** Students will be able to develop a research question based on their own interests and refine this question to make it a high-quality one. *I CAN statement:* • I can develop a high-quality, open-ended research question based on my own interests.	Students will need to be able to apply prior learning experiences in this unit when attempting to accomplish this learning goal.

During the process of analyzing learning goals, teachers also need to consider how students' attainment of the learning goals will be influenced by the students' own readiness. Teachers determine students' readiness for learning by considering what prior or foundational knowledge, skills, and experiences students will need for each learning goal—and if the students possess them. Figure 2-3 highlights some of the knowledge, skills, and experiences students would need to be successful with the learning goals in a research paper unit. Pre-assessments that attempt to identify student readiness can be created during future ADDIE phases. More on pre-assessment is presented in Chapter 4.

When teachers engage in a systematic analysis of the learning goals, they design instruction and instructional materials that are more purposeful, focused, and connected to learner's needs. Systematic approaches such as UbD and the revised Bloom's taxonomy can be integrated into ADDIE's analysis phase to clarify what students should learn. Appendix A illustrates this. After drafting learning goals, teachers can use the revised Bloom's taxonomy (see Chapter 1, Figure 1-2) to plot different types of knowledge and cognitive process categories. By doing so, they better understand which types of knowledge (i.e., factual, procedural, conceptual, metacognitive) the goals involve and what type of cognitive processes will be required to attain them.

In addition to supporting an inventory of learner readiness, the analysis phase encourages an inventory of which resources might be used to support the learners, enhance the attainment of standards, and address contextual factors. See Figure 2-4 for some useful questions to consider during the analysis phase.

Design

Strategic and systematic thinking is also prevalent during the design phase. At this stage, teachers make a conscious choice about the priorities of instruction rather than letting factors such as time, available resources, and potential interruptions dictate the activities they will use in the classroom. Teachers should let their stated priorities—the content and the known needs of their learners—direct the selection of activities that will facilitate learning. Focusing on identified priorities helps teachers frame the challenges in designing instruction and use strategic efforts to address them.

The design phase encourages teachers to think purposefully about the specialized tools available for teaching—such as the models of teaching presented in Part II of this text—and how they might be best matched with the challenges associated with connecting learners with specific content. For example, the teacher might make choices about which instructional model would be most appropriate to address a specific learning goal and/or which technologies might best support learners' needs. Instruction is more efficient and effective when the types of knowledge addressed by various learning goals are matched with the right instructional model.

For example, consider Rich, the teacher in the scenario at the beginning of this chapter. If Rich is redesigning the ninth-grade research paper unit and wants his students to understand the characteristics of a good research question, his efforts are made more productive using the strategic thinking supported by the design phase. First, Rich will acknowledge that his learning goal deals with conceptual knowledge and that a model for teaching concepts is required. Then he will consider the nature of the concept he is teaching and select the best instructional model for teaching concepts from the three available—Concept Attainment (Chapter 6),

Figure 2-4 Analysis Phase—Questions to Consider

Instructional Needs

- What must I teach to fulfill state, district, and/or local standards?
- What type of knowledge does the content represent (e.g., factual, procedural, conceptual, metacognitive)?
- Why am I teaching this content?
- What are the goals and objectives?
- How do the standards connect with previous or future learning?
- How can I differentiate the unit/content to address learner needs?

Learner Needs

- What are the students' *current* knowledge, attitudes, skills, and habits?
- What are the students' *desired* knowledge, attitudes, skills, and habits?
- How will I know students have learned the content?
- What measures should I use for pre-assessment, formative assessment, and summative assessment?
- What are my students' interests, needs, motivations, and learning styles?
- How does this lesson relate to the real world? (e.g., What skills are students learning that they will need later in life?)

Contextual Needs

- Where will I teach this unit/lesson (e.g., face-to-face, inside/outside of classroom/lab, online/hybrid, computer lab, and so on)?
- How much time (hours/days/weeks/months) should I plan to teach this unit/each lesson?
- What are the social dynamics of the class/group?

Resource Needs

- What resources are available (e.g., interactive whiteboard, computers, books, list of websites, realia, people, and so on)?
- What resources will I need to purchase/locate/borrow?
- What other resources will I need?
- What skills/knowledge are needed to use these resources?

Concept Development (Chapter 7), and the Inductive model (Chapter 8). Rich selects the Concept Attainment model to support students' mastery of this learning goal because it offers unparalleled support for teaching concepts with clearly defined attributes, such as the concept of a "good research question."

Appendix D offers a matrix that describes the various characteristics of the instructional models presented in Part II of this book. This matrix can support teachers as they systematically progress through the design stage and decide which instructional models to use to support specific and distinct learning goals.

During the design phase, it helps to employ organizational techniques and tools. Brainstorming, creating checklists, and using goal/task planners, graphic organizers, flowcharts, and webs can also support the formulation and conceptualization of the design that will be used in the next ADDIE phase. See Figure 2-5 for an example of a graphic organizer that can be helpful at this stage. Also, see Figure 2-6 for useful questions to consider during the ADDIE design phase. Appendix E offers a lesson plan framework that structures

Figure 2-5 Goal and Task Organizer

Goal	Task Required to Accomplish the Goal

Figure 2-6 Design Phase—Questions to Consider

- What knowledge, attitudes, skills, and habits do I want students to develop by the end of instruction?
- What are the standards, goals, and objectives I will use to design the unit/lesson?
- What instructional delivery method(s) or model of teaching (e.g., Concept Attainment model, Integrative model, and so on) will be most effective in meeting the standards, goals, and objectives? (After choosing a model of teaching, it will be helpful to review the sections on "Planning for Teaching With" the different models in their corresponding chapters.)
- What specific measures will I use for pre-assessment, formative assessment, and summative assessment? (See Chapter 4 for more about these types of assessment.)
- How will I ensure that students learn content at different levels of the revised Bloom's taxonomy?
- How will I differentiate content, process, and product?
- How will I sequence and scaffold instructional activities?
- How should I group students to teach the content (e.g., whole class, small group, pairs, and so on)?
- Which specific resources will I use?

the systematic thinking and decision making. The lesson plan framework is a useful tool during numerous ADDIE phases.

Develop

During the develop phase, teachers creatively connect learner needs with appropriate experiences and materials. They also make plans to differentiate materials and instructional approaches. During this phase, teachers can improve the quality of their materials by reflecting on some simple questions to make sure they are faithful to the original analysis performed during the first phase of ADDIE. Some questions teachers should ask themselves during the develop phase are included in Figure 2-7.

During the develop phase, teachers who are planning a lesson or unit that uses an instructional model should refer to the chapters in Part II that describe each model. Within these chapters, we describe each instructional model's steps and the ways the model might be modified to support learners with different needs. These chapters also provide illustrations of the ways digital tools might make learning more efficient, effective, or engaging when using each instructional model. There is also a description of each model presented in Appendix D.

Implementation/Evaluation

The implementation phase is the "teaching" or "doing" phase of the ADDIE model. Ideally, those using ADDIE will discover that they have created the best possible instructional experiences and materials for their learners. In most cases, the implementation phase will reveal the positive impact of decisions made in previous ADDIE phases. However, this phase can also reveal how poor-quality decisions made in earlier phases produce negative effects on student learning. When that occurs, teachers experience the implementation phase as a learning experience and an opportunity to build their professional knowledge and improve their practice for the future.

When attempting to understand student learning, it is useful to analyze students' (1) effort, (2) achievement of learning goals, and (3) growth over the instructional experience. Examining each of these—both separately and in connection with each other—is important. Considering them separately is necessary because each provides unique information about the specific dimension of student learning (e.g., "How well did 'Student X' master the learning goal?"). Considering them together is also necessary because the information is complementary and suggests the interplay of more than one dimension of learning (e.g., "'Student X' did not quite master the learning goal but grew a great deal during the learning process."). Teasing out information about each dimension of learning can be challenging. For example, how much students learn is sometimes related to how

Figure 2-7 Develop Phase—Questions to Consider

- Are the learning materials and activities I am developing appropriate for the types of knowledge I am addressing in the learning goals and this lesson?
- Are the learning materials and activities I am developing responsive to the identified needs of my learners?
- Are there choices learners might be given about learning activities and materials that would support differentiation and individual learning needs?

Figure 2-8 Implement/Evaluate Phase—Questions to Consider

- Effort: How much effort did students expend? How did instruction influence student motivation and effort? What evidence is there of their effort?
- Achievement: How much learning occurred? How many learning goals did students achieve? How well did students address these goals? What evidence do I have of student learning?
- Growth: How much growth occurred from the beginning to the end of instruction?
- Quality of Instruction: How instrumental was the instruction in promoting student growth? How instrumental was the instruction in supporting student achievement? How instrumental was the instruction in encouraging student motivation and effort? What evidence is there of the quality of the instruction?

much effort they put forth—but not always. A well-designed lesson might result in great learning and growth without a lot of effort. The best understanding of student learning occurs when information about all three dimensions of learning are known.

Measuring each of these dimensions of learning presents unique challenges. For example, measuring the amount of growth students experience as a result of instruction requires a comparison with their prior knowledge and skills. This comparison can take place only when students' prior knowledge and skills are known, so pre-assessment information is required to determine this and should be collected before instruction occurs. Questions that might be asked to improve efforts during these phases are provided in Figure 2-8.

The instructional models presented in Part II of this book can be more fully utilized with the application of the ADDIE model. Knowledge of the instructional design process and the purposeful use of this process can allow teachers to be more than just people who make choices that help students learn. It can help them function as designers who make the most effective choices to support learning of all types of content and for all learners.

Chapter Summary

Traditional methods of designing instruction are no longer adequate in supporting diverse 21st century learners as they work to meet uniformly rigorous standards. To address these challenges, in this chapter we suggested the use of systematic thinking about instructional planning and introduced readers to the field of instructional design and the instructional design process. We showed how teachers can, by using the mind-set of a designer and adding specialized processes to their skill sets, determine the best use of instructional tools in a time of abundant resources for teaching. We also explained and illustrated the benefits teachers might experience if they function like educational designers and use a design approach to instructional planning. Instructional design is a systematic approach for designing instruction and creating instructional materials. Although developed initially for the military, instructional design is now used in a variety of settings.

One popular instructional design model is the ADDIE model. It involves careful and strategic analysis of learners, the instructional context, and the learning environment. It is a practical, flexible process for developing effective instruction. Teachers can apply the ADDIE phases when designing simple instruction, such as lessons study guides. They can also use the model when working individually or to coordinate work among groups of teachers. Instructional design approaches like ADDIE allow teachers to optimize their use of the instructional models presented in Part II of this book and promote more rewarding, productive practice.

Review Questions

1. What is instructional design? What are its origins? What does an instructional designer do?

2. Describe the benefits of using instructional design in several different fields. What are the benefits for teachers and the field of education?

3. What are the differences between *instructional design models* and *models of instruction*?

4. What are the benefits of systematic thinking and the instructional design process for classroom teachers?

5. Describe the phases of the ADDIE model.

6. Explain how approaches like UbD are compatible with and can be integrated within the ADDIE phases.

7. Explain how the instructional design process and systematic thinking can help educational designers capitalize on the instructional models.

Resources

- A Brief History of Instructional System Design—This site provides a history of instructional system design: www.nwlink.com/~donclark/history_isd/isdhistory.html

- Instructional Design Central—This site is a good resource for instructional design. For example, the following provides a timeline for instructional design: www.instructionaldesigncentral.com/htm/IDC_instructionaltechnologytimeline.htm

- Instructional Design Models—This site provides a compilation and description of the many models of instructional design: http://carbon.cudenver.edu/~mryder/itc/idmodels.html

- Instructional Design Lessons—The purpose of this site is to support faculty teaching, student learning, and practitioners in the field using instructional design: www.itma.vt.edu/modules/spring03/instrdes/assignments.htm

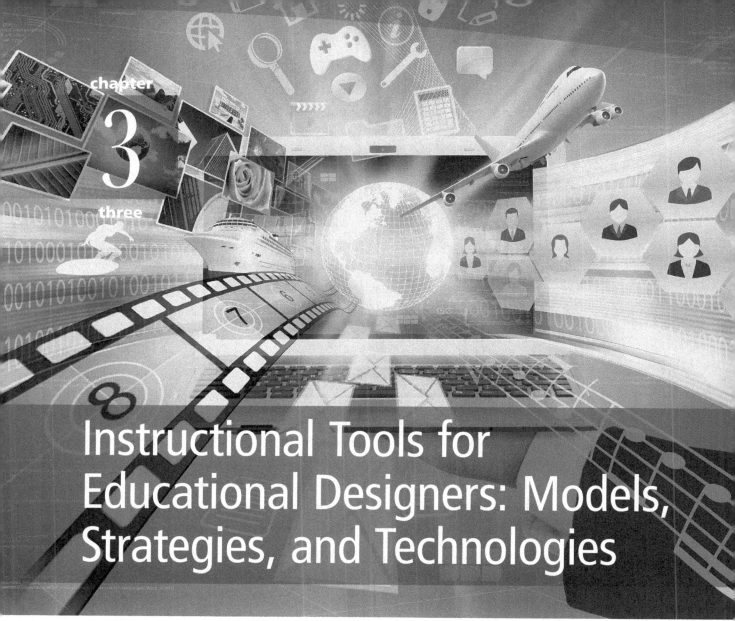

Instructional Tools for Educational Designers: Models, Strategies, and Technologies

© nmedia/Shutterstock

Jerry O'Shea bent over a collection of cardboard boxes. School would start next week, and before it did, he wanted to unpack the woodworking tools he had stored during the renovation to his basement workshop. As a master woodworker, Jerry had accumulated a huge collection of tools over the years. Earlier that day, while he was unpacking them, his wife had asked if he really needed so many. Jerry assured her that certain tools were re-

quired for certain tasks—they were not usually interchangeable, which was why there were so many. "Have you ever tried driving a nail with a screwdriver?" he asked.

Jerry could not help reflecting that this same principle also applied to the large collection of instructional tools he had acquired throughout his career as a teacher. Instructional models including Problem-Based Learning, strategies such as graphic organizers, and even technologies like clickers could all be considered tools. Each could make the accomplishment of a particular task more efficient and effective. In his basement workshop and in the classroom, Jerry had learned great things were possible when the right tool was paired with its skilled use.

This knowledge did not make developing the first-quarter curriculum plans for his first-grade class any easier. At his computer the evening before, he had been overwhelmed thinking about all the ways he might address the curriculum standards. Jerry had years of experience teaching fourth grade, but for the coming year, he was reassigned to first grade because his experience and talents were needed to address various challenges in that cohort of students. To help Jerry work effectively with his students, his principal had promised him a new set of tablet computers and an allowance for apps. The classroom already had an interactive whiteboard and desktop computer. His principal was sure Jerry would be glad to have so many different tools to use with his young learners. Jerry, however, was not. In the past, he had always been frustrated by his lack of tools, but now he felt pressure to make good use of them.

Over the years in his basement workshop, Jerry had learned how and when to use each tool. He had built his competence through regular practice and experimentation. Taking classes and working with other enthusiasts had helped accelerate his learning, but the most powerful lessons had come from his own experiences—both successes and mistakes. Jerry had learned that some tools were more complex than others, but all made certain tasks simpler, saved time and energy, or aided his capabilities in some important way. Some tools made his work more precise, others more aesthetic. All were needed—or so he convinced his wife.

When it came to woodworking, Jerry knew not only how and when to use each of his tools but also how to integrate multiple tools to complete the most challenging woodworking tasks. When it came to the new tools in his teaching tool kit, Jerry was not as confident. How should he start planning to optimize their use? Surely there must be support for helping him understand the tools better and learn how to make the best use of them. "By bringing the same passion to teaching as I do my woodworking," he thought, "I should be able to master the new tools and rise to the challenges of the incoming first-graders." ■

After reading this chapter, you will be able to:

- Define what technological pedagogical content knowledge is (TPACK).
- Explain how teachers can use, benefit from, and develop TPACK.
- List the different types of tools available for teaching.
- Describe characteristics of high-quality tools.
- Explain the three "Es" for choosing and using tools for teaching and learning.

Introduction

A craftsman is only as good as the type, variety, number, and quality of his tools, yet tools alone cannot produce the best product. A craftsman must have the skills required to use a broad and varied set of tools together and alone, and he must also know when and how to apply these tools for their most productive use.

Teachers who approach their work as educational designers operate like craftsmen who help students build a firm foundation that supports their future life and learning. Teachers, like Jerry, address challenging tasks related to this goal on a daily basis. Some challenges are big (i.e., developing units that target factual, procedural, conceptual, and metacognitive knowledge in ways that are meaningful to groups of diverse learners), and other challenges are small (i.e., developing new content for a demonstration in an individual lesson using a particular instructional model). All challenges require the careful coordination of knowledge, skills, and tools to overcome obstacles that impede student learning and growth.

The 21st century teacher's tool set must include high-quality instructional models, strategies, and technologies. To apply these tools optimally in real-world settings, teachers need to possess the mind-set and skill set of an educational designer. Doing so will help them discern if, when, how, and why to use their tools to address the specific learning challenges related to students' attainment of instructional goals.

In Chapter 2, we introduced a popular instructional design model called ADDIE to demonstrate the utility of systematic thinking and processes in an educational designer's skill set. In this chapter, we introduce the concept of technological pedagogical content knowledge, or "TPACK," which is a concept that informs an educational designer's mind-set, defines needed skills in a designer's skill set, and informs the best selection and application of tools in a designer's tool set. We define TPACK and then explain how teachers can develop it and benefit from it. We finish the chapter by highlighting three types of 21st century instructional tools—instructional models, instructional strategies, and technologies—valuable to teachers as they support diverse learners in achieving high standards. The information in this chapter lays the foundation required for using technology to make the instructional models presented in Part II of this text more efficient, effective, and engaging.

TPACK

TPACK is a model for organizing the different knowledge domains that teachers must develop and integrate to teach effectively in the 21st century. Fully understanding the foundational ideas related to TPACK is critical for teachers like Jerry who are making decisions about how to get the most out of their tools for teaching. To that end, we share a brief history of the ideas that underpin TPACK. Then we describe TPACK in detail by exploring the different ways teachers can develop and benefit from it.

Origins of TPACK

In the 20th century, Lee Shulman, a leading educational researcher and then president of the Carnegie Foundation for the Advancement of Teaching, articulated what he believed teachers should know to be successful. Shulman proposed that teachers required (1) knowledge of their content—content knowledge, (2) knowledge of how to teach—pedagogical knowledge, and (3) an integrated understanding of the two—pedagogical content knowledge (Shulman, 1986, 1987). The concept of pedagogical content knowledge implies a commingling of content knowledge with pedagogical knowledge. Teachers need to know *how to teach* subject matter and *how to make it comprehensible* to students with different backgrounds, conceptions, and preconceptions. The resultant integrated knowledge is derived from both "research" and "wisdom of practice" (Shulman, 1986, p. 9). Figure 3-1 depicts these knowledge domains and their relationships.

Though Shulman's ideas are still relevant today, the introduction and integration of technology in our society and classrooms has forced an evolution in thinking about teachers' knowledge domains and teaching competence. Mishra and Koehler (2006), two teacher educators, were the first to publish an expanded view of Shulman's categories of teacher knowledge that included technology as a domain. Originally expressing the idea as "TPCK" (2008) and later as "TPACK," they acknowledged in their model the complex interplay of

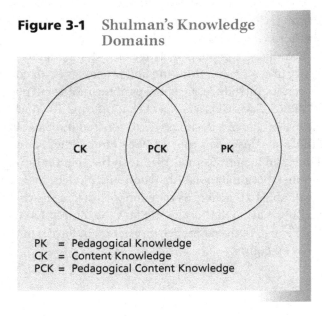

Figure 3-1   Shulman's Knowledge Domains

PK = Pedagogical Knowledge
CK = Content Knowledge
PCK = Pedagogical Content Knowledge

Figure 3-2   TPACK

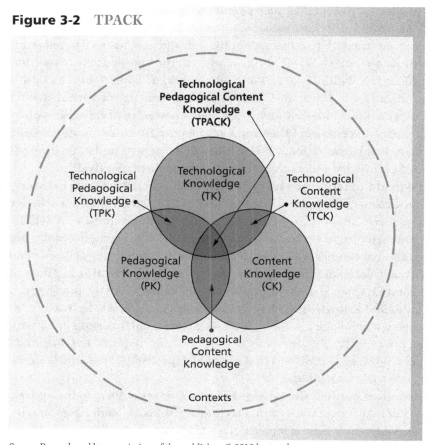

Source: Reproduced by permission of the publisher, © 2012 by tpack.org

a teacher's knowledge of content, pedagogy, and technology in creating successful learning experiences, as Figure 3-2 illustrates. As such, Mishra and Koehler's revised model increased both in theory and in practice the complexity of Shulman's original model. Even quickly comparing the models as depicted in Figure 3-1 and Figure 3-2 makes apparent the expansion of knowledge and competence required for teachers.

TPACK DEFINED. TPACK represents the integration of traditional and new knowledge domains required for teaching in a digital age, as Koehler and Mishra's (2008) definition shows:

> [TPACK] is the basis of effective teaching with technology and requires an understanding of the representation of concepts using technologies; pedagogical techniques that use technologies in constructive ways to teach content; knowledge of what makes concepts difficult or easy to learn and how technology can help redress some of the problems that students face; knowledge of students' prior knowledge and theories of epistemology; and knowledge of how technologies can be used to build on existing knowledge and to develop new epistemologies or strengthen old ones. (pp. 17–18)

These 21st century knowledge domains consist of the following:

- **Pedagogical Knowledge (PK)**—The term *pedagogy* refers to the specialized knowledge required for effective instruction. Pedagogical knowledge, then, within the context of classroom teaching, involves all the understanding a teacher possesses that leads to effective instruction, such as comprehension of the instructional planning process, knowledge of classroom management, instructional time use, instructional theories, and students' psychological, physical, and psychosocial development.

- **Content Knowledge (CK)**—This term refers to the knowledge teachers must have to teach effectively within a particular content area, such as science, social studies, or music. According to Shulman, CK includes the knowledge of central facts, concepts, theories, and procedures within a given field; knowledge of explanatory frameworks that organize and connect ideas; and knowledge of the rules of evidence and proof (Shulman, 1986). In addition, CK also refers to a teacher's understanding of the nature of knowledge and methods of inquiry in a particular field.

- **Pedagogical Content Knowledge (PCK)**—This specialized knowledge occurs at the intersection of PK and CK. It is that knowledge that informs a teacher's decision-making process about appropriate methods for teaching specific content in his or her subject area. It also refers to the specialized knowledge teachers develop about the organization of content within a discipline. For example, a science teacher might use PCK to make decisions about the best way to teach the scientific method—opting for a hands-on experience over reading about and memorizing the process from a text.

- **Technological Knowledge (TK)**—This term refers to knowledge teachers have about educational technologies (both high-tech and low-tech) that support classroom teaching and productivity. TK also refers to the knowledge required to set up and operate this technology, solve problems that might occur during its use, and communicate about such tools with others.

- **Technological Content Knowledge (TCK)**—This term refers to the understanding teachers develop about the way that technology supports understanding the content area that they teach. For example, in science a tool like a microscope allows students to explore the crystals in table salt. The technology tool enables understanding of the subject matter through support for student discovery.

- **Technological Pedagogical Knowledge (TPK)**—This term refers to the knowledge a teacher has about the technologies that exist for instruction, their capabilities, and their suitability for combining them with instructional models and strategies. Teachers use TPK to make decisions about how technology might best support a particular instructional model, instructional strategy, or activity type in a lesson. This type of knowledge also refers to a teacher's understanding of productivity tools that might enhance his or her practice, such as newsletter applications, online survey tools, attendance, and grading.

- **Technological Pedagogical Content Knowledge (TPCK)**—This term refers to the interplay and integration of knowledge a teacher possesses in different professional knowledge domains as he or she makes decisions about educational technology that affect his or her classroom practice. This idea suggests that true and effective technology integration requires a foundational knowledge in all teaching domains and a specialized knowledge of their integration. TPCK involves knowing when and when not to use technology to support teaching and learning in the content areas as well as how to do so most effectively.

TPACK is the first formalized and popularly accepted conceptual framework building on Shulman's professional knowledge domains. It expands the knowledge domains to include competencies for teaching in a digital age. The TPACK framework has been instrumental to understanding the contextual and complex nature of teaching with technology—and the kind of knowledge that teachers must cultivate to teach 21st century learners effectively.

Technology, learner needs, and curriculum are constantly changing; therefore, teachers will need to expand their TPACK throughout their careers to respond to these changes. Certainly, teaching today's diverse learners can be a daunting task. Teachers need not only quality tools in their tool set but also the skill set to plan for the best use of those tools and the ability to use them effectively and appropriately. In other words, teachers need the mind-set to direct their understanding about their role in addressing specific challenges in practice. As this text shows, technologies can support high-quality teaching in numerous ways. They can support the design of instruction and its implementation using instructional models and strategies and promote use of the assessment cycle to inform both of these—but only if teachers apply their TPACK.

How Can Teachers Use and Benefit from TPACK?

Teachers can use and benefit from TPACK in several ways. First, TPACK offers teachers a mental framework for visualizing the complex relationships between the different domains of their knowledge. It provides them with strategies for leveraging specialized knowledge when planning and implementing educational technologies. Using systematic processes, such as a resource inventory implemented during the steps of ADDIE, teachers can identify the tools they have to support instruction and then make intentional decisions about which tools are most appropriate for addressing the particular instructional challenges they face. Like Jerry in the opening scenario, teachers might need to understand technology better before they can design and implement instruction that is responsive to their learners' needs—and also before using it to develop content or to facilitate student expression of learning.

Second, TPACK can serve as a tool enabling an analysis of a teacher's knowledge and for planning future professional development he or she requires for optimal use of educational technology. Teachers can examine their competence in each of the TPACK knowledge domains and in their integration, identify areas of strength and weakness, and then plan professional development experiences (i.e., classes, workshops, seminars, readings, and so on) in the most critical areas. For example, Jerry might feel he is proficient in using and applying technology tools (TK) but acknowledges that he needs help figuring out how these tools can be used to teach specific content standards (TCK).

Third, TPACK can provide teachers a language or common vocabulary for communicating with each other about activities related to technology integration. Teachers familiar with TPACK can share ideas more effectively because they understand the same vocabulary, ideas, and concepts indicated in the TPACK framework. For example, one teacher might ask a colleague for advice on what TCK might be useful when helping students analyze primary source documents in social studies. Sharing the same vocabulary, they can work together more easily as they make plans to integrate technology in purposeful and meaningful ways in their classrooms. In addition, understanding TPACK can help teams of teachers plan professional development opportunities, create technology plans, and purchase technology equipment. Having TPACK as a common frame of reference streamlines collaboration and communication about technology.

How Do Teachers Develop TPACK?

There are many ways teachers can develop TPACK. First, they can become familiar with what TPACK is. Some ways are to participate in technology-focused learning opportunities such as graduate-level education, workshops, conferences, and learning communities focused on helping them develop in the various TPACK knowledge domains. Second, teachers can develop TPACK by applying instructional design to the integration of technology in the teaching and learning process. Finally, teachers can research their own applications of TPACK within the instructional models in this text and other learning designs. We elaborate on these in the following sections.

TEACHERS DEVELOP TPACK BY LEARNING ABOUT IT. Essential to developing TPACK is understanding what it is in the first place. Learning about the general idea of TPACK and its various knowledge domains and applying it to practice are wonderful learning opportunities for teachers. The end of this chapter has several resources that teachers might explore to learn even more about TPACK.

Because technology and students are constantly changing, developing TPACK can—and should be—a continuous part of teachers' preparation and professional development. One way to cultivate TPACK is for teachers to conduct a self-assessment of their knowledge and competence in the specific domains (see Figure 3-2) and then identify professional development goals in areas where growth is needed. For example, in the opening scenario, Jerry might set a goal of expanding his TK with tablet computers and then increase his TPK by learning how to use them with first-graders.

Another way to learn about TPACK is to participate in formal and informal postsecondary education and professional development offerings focused on implementing technology. Additional education provides teachers with opportunities to learn about, plan for, and implement technology in their teaching. Teachers develop TPACK by reading blogs written by tech-savvy teachers and other experts and working in learning communities focused on technology. Learning communities are groups of people interested in learning about and sharing resources related to a particular topic or area. Because people often learn best from their own peers, connecting with a group of people with similar professional development interests provides support for exploring and experimenting with technology. Tapping into online learning communities is particularly beneficial when learning to use technology. It exposes teachers to new technologies and modes of learning as well as to ideas about technology. Learning communities of teachers who work together face-to-face, at a distance, or both are able to learn from and with one another and help each other identify skills that might be worth developing.

TEACHERS CAN DEVELOP TPACK BY APPLYING INSTRUCTIONAL DESIGN TO THE INTEGRATION OF TECHNOLOGY IN THE TEACHING AND LEARNING PROCESS. Teachers develop TPACK by applying instructional design approaches, such as the ADDIE model (see Chapter 2), to the planning, design, development, implementation, and evaluation of instruction. This is the case because when teachers use ADDIE, they follow procedures that require purposeful attention to all domains of knowledge. Moving through the steps of ADDIE, teachers develop TPACK and gain important professional knowledge from experience.

Teachers also need to apply the systematic thinking of instructional design to the meaningful, transformative use of technology in teaching. The goal is to use technology to make learning more efficient, effective, and/or engaging (see Figure 3-3). We call these criteria for meaningful, transformative use of technology the "3Es." These ideas are elaborated on later in this chapter.

We recommend that teachers ask themselves three simple questions during the analysis phase of the ADDIE model or any other time they integrate technology with teaching:

Figure 3-3   Attributes of Technology for Meaningful,
Transformative Learning

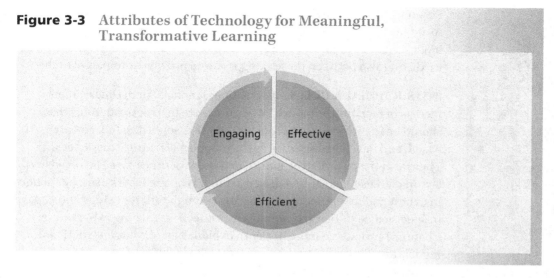

1. How can technology be used to make the teaching and learning process more efficient?
2. How can technology be used to make the teaching and learning process more effective?
3. How can technology be used to make the teaching and learning process more engaging?

TEACHERS DEVELOP TPACK BY RESEARCHING THEIR OWN USES OF TECHNOLOGY. Implementing
TPACK and learning from its impact on student learning can also help teachers further
develop TPACK. For example, Jerry, the teacher in the opening scenario, might use an app
designed by an occupational therapist to help his students develop the fine motor skills
required for holding a pencil. He can ask students for their reactions to this innovation and conduct more formal research into student motivation and time on task to understand the impact of
time spent on such activities. Effective use of assessment (addressed in Chapter 4) can also help
teachers learn more about their uses of technology and potential impact on student learning.

21st Century Instructional Tools

In today's kitchens, garages, offices, laboratories, workshops, and classrooms, a seemingly limitless supply of tools make our work easier and more effective than ever before.
Any object that makes our work or life more productive, saves time and energy, or extends
human capacity in any way is considered a tool. The designation of a tool extends beyond
the mechanical and digital to include ideas and processes that make human work more
productive and meaningful. In this discussion, we use the term *tool* to refer to instructional
models, instructional strategies, and technologies.

Types of Instructional Tools

There are many different types of instructional tools teachers might choose from when planning, implementing, or evaluating learning. Instructional tools differ from one another in
their origins, purposes, ease of use, and complexity. For instance, simple ideas, such as mnemonic devices (e.g., "Please excuse my dear Aunt Sally" for remembering the order of operations: **p**arentheses, **e**xponents, **m**ultiplication and **d**ivision, and **a**ddition and **s**ubtraction), or
more complicated ones, such as the SQ3R study-skills method (i.e., Survey, Question, Read,

21st Century Technology Tools
(© Gladskikh Tatiana/Shutterstock)

Respond, Review), might all be considered instructional tools. Tools used to aid teaching can be categorized into one of three groups—instructional models, instructional strategies, or technologies. In the following sections, we distinguish between these categories and provide examples of each.

INSTRUCTIONAL MODELS. Instructional models, sometimes called models of teaching or models of learning, are instructional tools that should be in every teacher's tool kit. They are sophisticated, research-based, and developed structures that support learning experiences. They form the basis for the nature and order of procedures involved in a lesson plan used in content area learning. When teachers use a particular instructional model, learners progress through different steps and engage in specified cognitive, psychomotor, or affective learning experiences. Chapter 1 provides a more in-depth explanation of what instructional models are. Figure 1-3 and Appendix D also include a description of all of the models of teaching included in this book.

INSTRUCTIONAL STRATEGIES. Instructional strategies are simple, powerful ideas and devices that help teachers accomplish instructional goals in efficient, effective, and/or engaging ways. They are easy to explain and implement while being useful and relevant in many settings. They are often informally shared via word of mouth (i.e., without being written down). Instructional strategies may be referred to by different names in different settings. For example, what is called Sustained Silent Reading (SSR) by some teachers might be DARE (Drop Everything and Read) by others. The same strategy might also be implemented in slightly different ways by individual teachers with the same degree of effectiveness.

Instructional strategies have many benefits. Because they are easy to incorporate, they can scaffold student learning in numerous and practical ways. Often, they save time and energy and facilitate the learning of abstract ideas (e.g., sentence diagramming). The focused nature of instructional strategies provides support for learners with visual, auditory, or kinesthetic learning preferences or any of the nine multiple intelligences (i.e., spatial, linguistic, logical-mathematical, bodily-kinesthetic, musical, interpersonal, intrapersonal, naturalistic, or existential). Some examples of instructional strategies commonly implemented for these purposes are the use of a flowchart (visual), incorporation of a song (auditory), and jumping on a giant map to locate different states (kinesthetic). Instructional strategies tend to be easy for teachers to implement and for students to learn. As such, they are most often implemented as activities students complete or do as part of a larger goal. Even though instructional strategies can be used alone or easily integrated into existing lessons and the models of teaching, they are not themselves models of teaching. As tools, instructional strategies can accomplish specific instructional tasks that might not be achieved in the same way or at all without them. See Figure 3-4 for a list of several instructional strategies.

TECHNOLOGIES. Technologies of relevance to educational designers are software, hardware, and other devices that have value for instruction. The sheer number of technologies—particularly digital technologies—available to support teachers and learners is overwhelming. Planning for and using technology is not an easy task. A benefit and challenge for 21st century teachers, as Jerry notes in the opening scenario, is that there are more technologies available and emerging than ever before. It is impossible to keep up with

Figure 3-4   Examples of Instructional Strategies

- **3-2-1**—Students write three, two, and one idea(s) based on a prompt (e.g., write/draw/act *three* major ideas you learned, write/draw/act *two* questions you still have, and write/draw/act *one* major idea that summarizes what you learned) (see Figure 4-1 for an example).
- **Brainstorming**—Students list, draw, or record in some way their ideas about a particular topic without worrying about what is right or wrong.
- **Exit cards**—Teacher asks students to write or illustrate an answer to a query as a requirement for leaving the class (sometimes called a "ticket to leave" or "exit ticket").
- **Graphic organizers**—Charts used to organize or present ideas (see Figure 4-1 and Figure 4-3 for examples).
- **One-minute-paper**—Students write everything they know about a topic or respond to a question in one minute.
- **Story maps**—Students develop a "map" about a story that examines the who, what, where, when, and why of a story.
- **Think-pair-share**—After a teacher poses a question, students pair up with a partner to describe their responses. Then they share their ideas with the larger group.

the continuous and rapid development of new technologies and the innovative ways they might be integrated in P-12 classrooms. Yet 21st century teachers must learn to harness the potential of technology to make learning more efficient, effective, and engaging for all students. Therefore, teachers must make informed, purposeful instructional choices as to which technologies best support their learners' needs.

The teacher's role in selecting technologies for learning is absolutely critical. Many technologies have been specifically designed for educational environments (e.g., educational software, "clickers," interactive whiteboards, and so on); others have been developed primarily for environments such as business and adapted for classroom use (e.g., Microsoft Office Suite). Some of these technologies are objects that students physically interact with or manipulate (e.g., computer hardware and peripherals). Other tools must be loaded or installed on another device to allow interaction (e.g., computer software or Web-based applications).

An important challenge that 21st century teachers—especially those who function as educational designers—face is selecting the right tool or combination of tools to address the challenges they experience in teaching. The instructional design process can help teachers meet this challenge. The systematic approach applied in instructional design encourages teachers to make an inventory of available tools and existing challenges. It forces them to focus and specify their goals by asking questions like "What is my goal?" and "What can I draw on to achieve it?" By functioning as educational designers, teachers become empowered to make the best use of their available tools and can make decisions about the types of technologies best suited to get them there.

The Use of Instructional Tools

The three primary goals for using tools (whether they be models, strategies, or technologies) to support instruction are to make learning more

1. efficient,
2. effective, and/or
3. engaging for all learners.

Creating instruction that attains these 3Es is one important goal for teachers working as intentional, focused educational designers. The starting point for making decisions about tools should be the students' needs as determined through assessment (described indepth in Chapter 4). Once those needs are identified, teachers need to consider how their choice of tools will foster efficient, effective, and engaging learning.

TOOLS MAKE LEARNING MORE EFFICIENT. Tools should support instruction in ways that save time, energy, money, or any combination of the three. Because these three resources are precious commodities, this presents many opportunities for improved efficiency. For example, instructional time is saved when a teacher is able to tailor multimedia materials created for the whole class to target specific learner needs. Students' energy is conserved when they are able to access an organized selection of research materials via a website their teacher has created. Money is saved when free online services are used to create more powerful learning opportunities.

TOOLS MAKE LEARNING MORE EFFECTIVE. Tools that make student learning more successful are considered more effective. Success can be measured through improved student learning outcomes for individuals or the whole class. More effective learning might also be that which results in greater amounts of learning, deeper learning, or learning that is more rewarding for students and their teacher. Examples of effective technology implementation abound. Take, for example, the use of digital texts, which are used by students with dyslexia. They provide these students equitable access to critical ideas in the content areas. Or consider the use of visualization tools—they can make abstract ideas more comprehensible for many students who struggle with concepts until they represent them in a more concrete manner.

TOOLS MAKE LEARNING MORE ENGAGING. Tools that evoke cognitive, affective, and psychomotor interest make learning more engaging. Skilled teachers know how to design instruction using technology to make it more novel, entertaining, and sensory rich. Consider the use of audience response systems, or clickers. Use of these interactive tools has the power to transform even the most mundane learning experiences—improving students' attention spans, invoking curiosity, and increasing enjoyment in the learning process.

Optimal use of any tool requires that it is paired with skilled use and appropriate goals. Teachers functioning as educational designers will use systematic thinking informed by TPACK as they work to make decisions about the best applications of their available tools. The 3Es provide educational designers simple-to-remember goals for technology integration and criteria that can help them determine success and learn from practice.

Characteristics of High-Quality Tools

Not all tools are created equal. Some, when integrated, are more likely to to result in a successful transformation of the learning process than others. Although a teacher's TPACK will largely influence the success of his or her efforts to integrate technology for specific instructional goals, the quality of the tool itself is also highly influential in its instructional impact. In the sections that follow, we identify several characteristics of high-quality tools. High quality tools can be characterized as follows.

POWERFUL. A powerful tool makes the efforts of the person using it better or greater than those without. A powerful tool might enhance, amplify, or magnify the nature of the impact made by the user. Take, for example, the use of a digital camera, which might be used by students recording the emergence of a caterpillar from its chrysallis. The camera enables students to share an uploaded video of the experience and watch it in wonder with their parents and caregivers. A powerful tool might also improve the quality of the work done by individuals. For example, consider a multimedia software program that enables learners to add transitions, titles, graphics, and other professional elements to make a more compelling video-recorded persuasive speech. Or a powerful tool can reduce the effort required and also aid or supplement the skills needed to accomplish a particular task. Consider the use of word prediction software, which supports learners in the writing process so their ideas can be more fully and accurately expressed. It goes without saying that a powerful tool should address the 3Es, and its degree of power is correlated with how much it makes learning more efficient, effective, and engaging.

DEPENDABLE. High-quality tools are dependable and have high odds of working—especially when the right conditions are in place. They might have few breakable parts, figurative parts (i.e., instruction), or literal parts (i.e., disk drives, ports, and so on). For example, a Venn diagram is a robust tool for helping learners compare ideas. It has relatively few parts that can be confused in a learning setting. More sophisticated high-tech tools can also be dependable. For example, a tablet computer has few parts to confuse and break. These tools (and those like them) are dependable when they are well made, well maintained, and carefully used.

PRACTICAL. Such tools do a job that the user and other experts would consider worth doing. Practical tools surround us in our classrooms. Unfortunately, so do impractical ones. An example of a practical tool is an interactive whiteboard that might be used to demonstrate sentence diagramming during a grammar lesson. A teacher with an interactive whiteboard can develop and preload sentences in advance to save time that would otherwise be spent writing them on the board. During the lesson, the teacher can use the pen feature to edit the sentences as necessary to illustrate key learning points. Impractical tools are those that waste students' (and teachers') time or detract from the instructional task at hand. For example, websites or software programs that have a lot of bells and whistles to accomplish tasks that can be accomplished as effectively but more simply are impractical. Practical tools and their uses align well with the goals of the teacher and support learning of the required content. Practical tools enhance rather than distract from the learning experience.

FLEXIBLE. High-quality tools are flexible enough to perform a number of different tasks. In an educational context, a flexible tool is one that works with many different learners and subject areas. It is also able to be used by individuals or groups and to support various learning goals and activities. A flexible tool can be used with proficiency by learners of all ages and ability. An example of a flexible technology is a concept mapping tool. It can be used to manipulate data and draw conclusions related to content standards in social studies. The same tool can be used to demonstrate learning in a biology class on a completely different topic, such as respiration.

ENDURING. Fads come and go, but the use and appeal of high-quality tools endure. When a tool meets the attributes of quality articulated previously (i.e., it is powerful, dependable, practical, and flexible), it will have long-standing appeal and utility. While many tools are upgraded continuously, the main aspects of the tool remain the same (e.g., database tools might be upgraded but still function to organize data).

As anyone who has attempted to use a tool knows, the risk of a tool's failure is positively correlated with its potential impact. In other words, the greater the tool's promise, the greater its chance of malfunctioning. Such risk should not deter educational designers from attempting to use tools, but it should encourage them to ensure that they (1) have specific and appropriate goals for the use of the tool, (2) are able to implement the tool skillfully, and (3) have selected high-quality tools. In this way, educational designers can achieve the 3Es and transform learning with greater frequency and less frustration.

Chapter Summary

In this chapter, we described that the required professional knowledge for effective teaching has expanded as the available resources for teaching have increased. We explained the idea of TPACK, which expands traditional conceptions of essential teacher knowledge. This powerful mental framework articulates what teachers must know and integrate to meet the needs of 21st century learners. Teachers can use, benefit from, and develop TPACK. Development of TPACK enables them to design more effective instruction and increases the value of the instructional models explored in Part II of this book. The powerful resources that teachers have for teaching today include instructional models, instructional strategies, and technologies. Instructional models are sophisticated and developed structures for learning experiences that support attainment of specific cognitive, psychomotor, and affective learning outcomes. Instructional strategies are simple, easy, and powerful ideas or devices that support student learning. Technologies are digital tools that support academic learning in educational settings. These tools should make learning more efficient, effective, and engaging. Instructional models, instructional strategies, and technologies are considered high quality if they are powerful, dependable, flexible, practical, and enduring.

Review Questions

1. How would you define TPACK?

2. How might teachers use, benefit from, and develop TPACK?

3. Name and describe the different types of instructional tools available for teaching.

4. What are the characteristics of high-quality tools?

5. Explain the 3 for choosing and using tools for teaching and learning.

Resources

- AACTE Committee on Innovation and Technology. (Ed.). (2008). *Handbook of Technological Pedagogical Content Knowledge (TPCK) for Educators*. New York: Routledge/ Taylor & Francis Group for the American Association of Colleges of Teacher Education— This is a book written about TPACK.

- All Things TPACK—This site aggregates information from various sources (e.g., GoogleScholar and blogs) about TPACK: http:// mkoehler.educ.msu.edu/TPACK/?cat=6

- Technological Pedagogical Content Knowledge wiki—This wiki includes information about the history of TPACK, TPACK by content areas, a reference library, and more: www.tpck.org

- SITE TPACK Special Interest Group—This group brings together researchers, developers, and teacher educators interested in exploring TPACK: http://site.aace.org/sigs/tpack-sig.htm

- TPACK Activity Types Wiki—This site provides activities for integrating technology according to content area: http://activitytypes.wmwikis .net

- TPACK Google Group—This is an online Google discussion group for those interested in exploring TPACK: http://groups.google.com/ group/tpack

- TPACK 101—This video provides a short, multimedia explanation of TPACK: http://vimeo .com/16291486

Classroom-Based Assessment in the 21st Century

Charlie Jackson would be the first to admit that using the "clickers" was a desperate attempt to get her students' attention. Charlie, a high school Spanish teacher, figured using the audience response system tools, (aka "clickers") was worth a try because her students were far more interested in "talking tech" than "speaking Spanish." The clickers worked as she had anticipated. What pleasantly surprised her was that using this technology to facilitate assessment practices would affect not only her students' learning but also her own. Using this tool allowed her to hone her assessment skills and communicate better with her students. In turn, knowledge of her students enabled her to design more responsive, effective instruction—instruction that resulted in a larger number of students achieving anticipated learning goals a greater percent of the time.

Using the clickers allowed Charlie to collect assessment information about her students efficiently and effectively at each point of the learning process. Before instruction occurred, she could find out whether students were ready for new learning and take that important information into account during her planning. While teaching, Charlie could check students' understanding, provide additional support when needed, and gauge the effectiveness of her instructional implementation. At the end of a learning sequence, students could confirm their attainment of learning goals by taking an online quiz that linked their responses directly to her gradebook. Though Charlie would never have imagined it, effective assessment practices, aided by the clickers and other technologies, had made her a better teacher. Being able to obtain accurate information about student learning when she needed it enabled her to learn immediately and constantly about the ways her instructional decisions affected her students. The more she understood the influence of her instructional decisions on students' learning, the better instructional decisions she could make. It also did not hurt that the clickers made her students more interested in class and less difficult to manage.

The communication channel opened up by the clickers made Charlie feel like she had finally learned to speak the students' language. She no longer had to guess what students understood based on their body language or expressions. Clickers helped Charlie understand what types of learning challenged her class in general and specific students in particular. Although formative assessment played a significant role in her new assessment program, over time Charlie began relying more on pre-assessments. She learned that the process of designing instruction could be streamlined if important information about student readiness was known. Determining whether students lacked the foundational understanding of vocabulary, grammar, and pronunciation uncovered important information that influenced development of her unit. For instance, when studying verb conjugations, she quickly pre-assessed students' understanding of how to conjugate verbs based on tense and person, discovering information that she used to tailor learning experiences. In time, Charlie found she was always starting her planning for new lessons with an audit of "entry-level" understanding. To use class time more efficiently, Charlie put the pre-assessment online and asked students to complete them outside of class. Students enjoyed using a cell phone or Web browser to indicate their mastery of the content.

Before long, Charlie discovered she was changing her methods of summative assessment as well. Her increasing comfort with technology helped her embrace alternative ways to document and communicate student learning. She encouraged students to use digital audio recorders to capture their competence with Spanish-speaking skills and gave them the option of using multimedia technology to create podcasts for their classmates on topics of their own choosing related to Spanish culture. Improved assessment practices connected Charlie with her learners in powerful and productive ways. Technology in different forms facilitated this connection by making it more efficient, effective, and engaging. Charlie had always believed that improved communication could change the world—this was one of the reasons she became a Spanish teacher in the first place. She just never dreamed that better communication using her assessment skills could also change her classroom. ■

CHAPTER OBJECTIVES

After reading this chapter, you will be able to:

- Explain what Classroom-Based assessment is and how it supports high-quality instruction for teachers working as educational designers.
- Describe the three types of Classroom-Based assessment—pre-assessment, formative

assessment, and summative assessment—and their benefits for teachers and students.
- List some of the ways technology supports and poses challenges when used for assessment.

Introduction

Effective assessment practices support better communication about learning between students and teachers. Better communication between students and teachers leads to richer, more productive relationships; more appropriate instruction; and transformative learning. As Charlie, the teacher in the opening scenario, discovers, the information gained from Classroom-Based assessment throughout the instructional process can be used to design more efficient, effective, and engaging learning experiences for her students. Charlie learns that frequent use of pre-assessment and formative assessment can provide unique insights about her learners' needs that help her make better instructional decisions before and during the learning process. Her experience with assessment also heightens her awareness of how improved communication with learners can influence instructional decisions and student learning. Each type of assessment—pre-assessment, formative assessment, and summative assessment—supports the learning process in distinct and powerful ways. As Charlie masters each assessment type, she is empowered to make learning experiences better for her students and more rewarding for herself.

Every educational designer's skill set must include proficiency with Classroom-Based assessment. This chapter will deepen your understanding of Classroom-Based assessment and help you increase your competence with this important component of practice.

Assessment has always been an important part of effective teaching, and it is even more important given the diverse needs of today's learners and the high standards of 21st century teaching. For educational designers, the first step in mastering assessment practices is using pre-assessment with a greater sense of purpose and focus. Pre-assessment promotes efficient use of time and energy. It grounds instructional decisions in real information about students' needs. It also ensures that instruction is responsive to the unique needs that learners have and promotes the best combination of instructional models, strategies, and tools.

This chapter begins by explaining what Classroom-Based assessment is and how it supports effective instructional design. It shares insights about the special role assessment plays for teachers approaching their work as educational designers. Next, it describes pre-assessment, formative assessment, and summative assessment and explains how each benefits teachers and students. The chapter closes by suggesting how technology can aid the implementation of assessment practices and support the analysis of the information assessments generate.

Classroom-Based Assessment

Classroom-Based assessment is focused and purposeful communication with students about important dimensions of the learning process at distinct stages of that process. Classroom-Based assessment is distinguished from other forms of assessment (i.e., standardized assessment) because its primary purpose is to promote students' learning within the classroom in the academic content areas. Teachers typically develop Classroom-Based assessments, such as quizzes and tests, or use those already developed by educational publishers to complement textbooks. Teachers are increasingly using alternative assessments that capture evidence of student learning in nonwritten modes. Authentic assessments—that are measures of student learning that have meaning to and are motivational for learners—are also gaining popularity as a means of Classroom-Based assessment.

Other forms of assessment, such as standardized assessments, compare student achievement against "norms" or measure students' proficiency against grade-level expectations. What distinguishes Classroom-Based assessment is its potential to improve instructional experiences rapidly. Classroom-Based assessment aims to gain information about student learning and then empower students and teachers with that knowledge as a means to promote increased achievement related to curriculum standards. That means that classroom assessment not only occurs within classrooms but also supports the learning that happens there. Classroom-Based assessment may be conducted formally (i.e., in ways that are premeditated, planned, or scripted) or informally (i.e., through more natural, unpremeditated, or unplanned interactions). It may be graded or ungraded. All well-crafted that Classroom-Based assessments communicate information about student learning that helps teachers deepen their understanding of student effort, growth, and achievement.

Classroom-Based assessment should occur throughout the entire instructional process and not only at the end of a lesson or unit. Likewise, it should occur throughout an academic term and not just at its closure. Conceptually, Classroom-Based assessment can be classified into three major types:

1. Pre-assessment
2. Formative assessment
3. Summative assessment

Each type has its own distinct purposes, and the name of each corresponds with when, during the instructional process, it takes place. Later in this chapter, we describe in greater detail these types of Classroom-Based assessment and their benefits.

How Do Educational Designers Use Classroom-Based Assessment?

Teachers functioning as educational designers are guided by the assumption that instruction is more effective when it has been intentionally tailored in response to the unique needs of their learners as they relate to targeted learning goals. An educational designer's mind-set also acknowledges that skilled use of assessment can establish and develop a supportive relationship with students that will positively influence learning. In the hands of an educational designer, assessment practices are powerful—especially when incorporated throughout all stages of the instructional process. These practices can improve teachers' ability to (1) identify educational challenges that might affect student learning, (2) understand the nature of these challenges, and (3) modify instructional approaches to address these challenges. We elaborate on these ideas in the sections that follow.

Effective assessment practices allow educational designers to ground their instructional decisions in actual data collected about what students know as opposed to basing them on conjecture or assumption. They enable teachers to design instruction based on the students they are teaching—not the students they think they are teaching, the students they taught previously, or the students they wish they were teaching. Information gleaned through the different types of assessment helps teachers understand

- the extent to which students are ready for new learning,
- the extent to which individual students' needs differ from one another,
- what motivates/interests students,
- students' attitudes about learning,
- characteristics that groups of students have in common,
- the appropriateness of instructional methods for learners,
- student growth,
- the extent of mastery related to learning goals, and
- students' proficiency with targeted skills and knowledge addressed in the lesson.

It is easy to see how information gained through assessment affects the quality and impact of instructional decisions made by educational designers. Skilled use of assessment throughout the learning process provides an important mechanism for planning, responding, and measuring how well instructional decisions support student learning. It also supports a teacher's ability to learn from practice by providing information about the effects of instructional decisions and their implementation. This information fuels reflection about future iterations of the instructional design.

Assessment is an essential tool for educational designers because it helps them learn about the following:

1. What the real needs of learners are as they relate to targeted learning goals before instruction takes place.
2. How instructional decisions are working to support learner needs during instruction.
3. How many and how well learners are able to attain targeted learning goals during the learning process.

Because educational designers are intentional and deliberate decision makers, they realize that the information they gain about students through assessment is critical to making instructional decisions. Educational designers simply cannot do their work as effectively without information from all three types.

Strong relationships between teachers and students are critical to promoting student learning. If used effectively, each type of assessment in the assessment cycle can support and enhance those relationships. Successful teachers use assessment as a two-way communication channel that allows them to ask students to share important information about themselves. Students appreciate and learn to take advantage of this opportunity to communicate questions, concerns, and information about their learning. These exchanges foster better learning and create strong, supportive learning communities.

Knowing when and how to utilize each type of assessment and understanding which technology, technique, or strategy to use when collecting assessment information are vital for the effective use of the instructional models included in Part II of this book. Information gained from assessment can help educational designers determine which model to use, when to use the model, and how to best differentiate instruction within the implementation of the model to support their particular learners.

Pre-assessment information can help a teacher understand the compatibility of a model of teaching for targeted learning goals and with a specific group of learners. For example, the Concept Development model presented in Chapter 7 requires that students have a basic understanding of a concept. Therefore, that model may not be appropriate to use when learners lack foundational knowledge about the concept. Conducting a targeted pre-assessment can reveal whether learners will be successful with the chosen model of teaching. If the model is found unsuitable, the teacher can replace it with a different model. In our example, the Concept Attainment model (which is presented in Chapter 6) might be a better choice for students lacking foundational knowledge and skills because lessons using this model supplement students' knowledge by exposing them to examples that illustrate the concept.

Formative assessment can also promote effective use of the models of teaching. Through formative assessment, teachers can verify that a model's implementation is supporting student learning during the process of instruction. Most—but not all—models of teaching presented in this text embed formative assessment within their steps and design. After determining if and how a certain model of teaching includes formative assessment techniques, a teacher can incorporate additional techniques as needed.

Effective use of summative assessment practices is also instrumental for educational designers who want to optimize their use of the instructional models. Knowledge gained from summative assessment enables educational designers to understand more clearly (1) what students have learned, (2) how the model influenced learning, and (3) what effect, if any, the lesson implementation had on student learning.

Types of Assessment

Each type of assessment provides important and distinct information to teachers functioning as educational designers. In the sections that follow, we describe pre-assessment, formative assessment, and summative assessment in more detail. We also share their benefits for teachers and students.

Pre-assessment

Pre-assessment is communication, questioning, or another investigation that occurs *before* a learning sequence (i.e., an activity, lesson, or unit) takes place. Its primary purpose is to ascertain students' readiness for the learning experiences to come. In the introductory scenario, Charlie uses a pre-assessment to discover whether students have the foundational knowledge and skills required for new learning. As illustrated in that scenario, teachers use pre-assessment to gather information about student readiness so they can make instructional decisions that are better aligned with identified student needs. Such decisions might include (1) which instructional model might be most appropriate for learners to use, (2) how much time will be needed for implementation, (3) what type of grouping will support known learners' needs, (4) which tools or materials would facilitate completion of learning activities, (5) how formative assessment could be efficiently

Assessment for Learning
© iQoncept/Shutterstock

implemented, and (6) which forms of summative assessment could best illustrate student achievement.

Student readiness is determined by many factors, including students' possession of foundational knowledge and skills required for learning, their current level of proficiency with targeted learning goals, and their motivation for new learning. The knowledge about learners gained from pre-assessment practices supports proactive planning for individual and shared student differences and promotes instructional efficacy for the teacher. When teachers gather, analyze, and use information from pre-assessment, they can design lessons that better challenge, support, motivate, and scaffold student learning.

Another goal of pre-assessment is to establish baseline data regarding students' current level of knowledge and skills (i.e., mastery of targeted learning goals before instruction takes place). Once the instruction occurs, teachers can compare baseline data to student achievement as a means to quantify and evaluate the learning. Without baseline data, teachers cannot arrive at a complete understanding of individual and group attainment of targeted standards, goals, or objectives. By comparing outcomes to pre-assessment information, teachers can see how the instructional decisions they made with regard to planning and implementing the lesson influenced student learning. For example, Charlie uses clickers to pre-assess and formatively assess students' knowledge of verb conjugations. Doing so shows her whether the lessons she designed and the support she provided had an impact. By effectively implementing pre-assessment techniques and analyzing their outcomes, Charlie is able to determine the impact of her instructional efforts and decisions both on individuals and the group.

The single most important purpose of pre-assessment is to capture and communicate important information about students' entry-level knowledge and skills before a learning sequence, but that is not its sole purpose. Much like a movie trailer provides a quick, advanced look at a movie, a pre-assessment tool can give students a preview of the content

Figure 4-1 K-W-L Chart

K: What do you know about the topic?	W: What do you want to learn about the topic?	L: What did you learn about the topic?

they will learn. In that way, pre-assessment serves as an advanced organizer for the unfamiliar content. Pre-assessment can also motivate learners and excite them about the new skills and knowledge they will gain through the upcoming learning process (Stiggins, 2005). In those situations, pre-assessment facilitates self-discovery and empowers students to take ownership of the learning process.

Pre-assessments can take many shapes and forms. They might consist of specific tools, such as a K-W-L graphic organizer (see Figure 4-1 for an example), or involve more general strategies, such as questioning (e.g., asking students to explain how they would solve a problem).

The use of graphic organizers, checklists, and quizzes that determine what students already know about concepts are common pre-assessment practices. Frequently used strategies include having students create drawings or diagrams, write journal responses in response to a prompt, or share ideas using "think-pair-share." (Think-pair-share is a discussion-based activity during which students think about a question/topic, partner with another student, and then share their ideas/thoughts about the question or topic.) Some of the models of teaching presented in Part II of this book include a pre-assessment step. These are highlighted in a section titled "Planning for Teaching with . . ." in each of the models' chapters.

Teachers may use one or many pre-assessments simultaneously, depending on their particular goal(s). Although the rationale for conducting pre-assessment is strong, the time and energy that teachers have to devote to the process is often limited. Focusing and prioritizing the goals one has for conducting pre-assessment makes it more purposeful. When possible, pre-assessment should attempt to document students' understanding so that both teachers and students can refer back to these results. Documentation should provide a visible comparison of what students know before and after instruction as well as a record of the student's learning at a particular point and time. Benefits of comparative documentation extend also to students. Evidence of student learning provides the impetus for students to reflect on their own learning. Seeing such evidence can help them understand their strengths and weaknesses and motivate them to develop their own goals for learning.

Figure 4-2   Benefits of Pre-Assessment

For Teachers:	For Learners:
• Helps teachers plan better lessons • Increases likelihood of instructional effectiveness • Helps teachers understand their impact • Provides teachers baseline information about what students already know about a topic	• Gives students input regarding what will be learned • Provides introduction to anticipated learning (can serve as an advanced organizer) • Promotes awareness of the boundaries of existing knowledge and skills

WHY CONDUCT PRE-ASSESSMENT? When used effectively, pre-assessment provides teachers accurate information about learners. That feedback should inform decisions that make instruction more responsive to individual and shared needs. Pre-assessments typically allow teachers to (1) determine whether students possess foundational knowledge and skills required for new learning, (2) appraise students' existing knowledge of the content that will be addressed, (3) discover the attitudes (e.g., motivation and interest) and habits (e.g., learning style) of learners toward learning, (4) gather real data for needs assessments, (5) promote metacognitive awareness of learning, and (6) foster students' ownership of their learning. Each of these reasons for conducting pre-assessments is associated with benefits for students and teachers alike. Figure 4-2 summarizes other benefits.

Pre-assess the foundational knowledge and skills required for learning. To be successful in any learning sequence, students require a firm foundation on which to build new understandings. One of the purposes of pre-assessment is to determine whether students have this foundation. Logically, the targeted standards for a lesson or learning sequence dictate what foundational knowledge and skills are required. For example, in the opening scenario, Charlie wants her students to be able to conjugate verbs in Spanish. In this case, she wants to discover whether students know and can use verb tense and person. Without this foundational knowledge, students will have great difficulty attaining the desired learning goals.

Before designing a pre-assessment that examines foundational knowledge and skills, teachers must first identify and understand what foundational knowledge and skills provide the basis for a specific learning goal. For example, Charlie might create a pre-assessment for determining how well students understand the building blocks for conjugating irregular present tense verbs. Her pre-assessment might elicit information on how well students know subject pronouns, verb stems, and regular verb endings in the present tense.

Depending on the content standard or learning goal a learning sequence addresses, teachers should ask, test, and examine the following:

- What students must already know to be successful in the anticipated learning sequence (What knowledge or vocabulary must they know before starting the new unit or lesson?)
- What students must be able to do to be successful in the anticipated learning sequence (What specific skills do they need to be able to do before starting this unit or lesson?)

Pre-assess for existing knowledge and skills. Teachers might also conduct pre-assessment to determine the extent to which students already possess mastery of the targeted knowledge and skills that will be introduced in a learning sequence. In other words, teachers will want to know if students already know and can do new learning before it is formally taught. Students might have already developed mastery of the new content during a prior grade level, another course, at another school, or through other educational experiences unknown to the teacher. For example, a teacher teaching a unit on multiplying decimals might want to pre-assess students to determine if they can already multiply decimals. Likewise, this teacher would benefit from knowing how many and which students have already mastered this learning goal.

There are many ways to preassess students' existing knowledge of content. One simple approach is to ask students to complete the final evaluation (e.g., an ungraded test) that will be used at the end of the learning sequence. This method allows students to demonstrate any knowledge they have and introduces them to what they will be expected to learn during the upcoming learning sequence. Another approach for establishing students' existing knowledge of targeted learning standards is to ask students to document what they know about a topic by completing a graphic organizer, such as the empty-head organizer in Figure 4-3.

By measuring pre-existing mastery of learning goals or the knowledge and skills that are associated with them, teachers gain insight about what students know, what they do not know, and what misconceptions they might have related to the learning content. In some cases, teachers may find that most students (or a particular student) have already mastered the content. In such instances, the teacher can proactively plan methods so that existing mastery of the content might be strengthened, deepened, or expanded. In this way, when students exhibit aptitude with the anticipated standards before instruction takes place, the teacher can plan to implement differentiation strategies that challenge all students appropriately. More often, pre-assessment of existing knowledge and skills reveals that a subset of students has some mastery of targeted learning goals, but this mastery might be inconsistent across the entire class. In this situation, data from pre-assessment can help a teacher identify which dimensions of the standards have been mastered, how well, and by whom. Such information can suggest that individuals or groups of students might need special interventions or be suited for sharing knowledge as peer teachers.

Pre-assessment often reveals which aspects of content might be understood incorrectly and by whom. Pre-assessing for existing knowledge and skills allows teachers to identify and then address potentially problematic misconceptions students have before entering a learning sequence. Misconceptions and misunderstandings that are not recognized early can cause significant problems as students encounter new learning. For example, a common misconception for primary-age children is that a dime is worth less than a penny because it is a smaller coin. When erroneous understandings such as this are discovered at the beginning of a learning sequence, teachers can correct them. They can teach students the appropriate understandings and support their learning from the beginning of the lesson rather than trying to correct it in progress or after the fact, when it has already created an obstacle to comprehending new content.

Pre-assessment of existing content knowledge is also important because it identifies what students already know before teachers introduce a learning sequence. Without this baseline information, teachers cannot determine the impact or the value their instruction adds to the learning process. Unless a teacher measures what students know before teaching a learning sequence, it is practically impossible to determine how much the teacher's instruction affected students' learning at its close. For instance, if

Figure 4-3 Empty Head Graphic Organizer

Fill this head with everything you know about: _____
(include intended topic here)

there is no pre-assessment conducted at the beginning of a unit (i.e., no baseline data about what students already know or do not know) and a student earns an "A" on a final exam, how will a teacher know if the student's performance had anything to do with the teacher's instruction during the unit? Comparison of pre-assessment and summative assessment data can also show the impact of teachers' instructional planning and implementation on a particular student or group of students. Those comparisons serve as useful references for response to intervention and other efforts to support students' special learning needs.

Pre-assess to gain information about student interests and learning style. Pre-assessment is particularly useful in identifying information about students' diverse interests and learning styles. In a differentiated classroom (see Chapter 1 for an explanation of differentiated instruction) and in classrooms that implement culturally responsive pedagogy (see Chapter 1 for an explanation of culturally responsive pedagogy), teachers often give students pre-assessments to collect information about their attitudes, interests, and individual learning styles or profiles as they relate to the anticipated learning. By doing so, teachers can learn valuable information that can be used to ensure the best match with the types of instructional strategies available to engage and motivate learners. Focused efforts to determine specific information from students through pre-assessment are similar to processes used for instructional decision making during the Analysis phase of the ADDIE Model presented in Chapter 2.

Although the term *pre-assessment* is often used to describe assessment performed before a particular unit or lesson, it is can also refer to information gathered outside the context of a particular learning sequence (i.e., at the beginning of the school year). More general types of pre-assessments are conducted to identify information about student interests and learning styles. Regardless of when during the school year they are administered, general pre-assessments can help teachers understand their students' status as it compares to a larger set of standards or expectations. Teachers can create their own questionnaires or surveys to identify student interests or learning styles, or they can use resources available online. Figure 4-4 provides a short list of learning style inventories. Many more inventory tools can be found by searching online. Students are not the only ones able to provide relevant information about themselves. Parents, caregivers, and others (e.g., speech therapists, occupational therapists, and so on) who interact with learners can also provide useful information when asked to do so. Figure 4-5 is a pre-assessment summary chart that teachers can use when conducting pre-assessments.

Pre-assess as a part of the needs analysis to help design instruction. Although pre-assessment helps teachers better understand learner needs, another important use for data gained from a pre-assessment is to design more effective instruction. The systematic analysis conducted during classroom assessment is similar to the Analysis phase in the ADDIE model. There are many instructional, learner, contextual, and resource

Figure 4-4 Learning Style Inventories

- Edutopia's What's Your Learning Style?: www.edutopia.org/multiple-intelligences-learning-styles-quiz
- Scholastic:
  - Do You Know Your Middle Schooler's Learning Style?: www.scholastic.com/familymatters/parentguides/middleschool/quiz_learningstyles/index.htm
  - Multiple Intelligences Questionnaire (PDF), Grades 1–6: http://printables.scholastic.com/printables/detail/?id=36447
- New Jersey Education Association: www.njea.org/pdfs/LearningStyleInventory.pdf

Figure 4-5 Summary of Pre-assessment Information

Purpose	What to Do with This Information	Examples of Pre-Assessment Strategies
• To identify competence or deficits with relation to foundational knowledge • To identify competence or deficits with relation to foundational skills	• Acknowledge competence and make plans to build on this or otherwise leverage it • Reteach or otherwise address deficits before a learning sequence • Plan to support diversity among students within a learning sequence	• Surveys • Inventories • Checklists
• To discover existing mastery of content standards • To identify existing knowledge (nonmastery level) of content standards	• Identify mastery if it exists and make plans for differentiation • Identify misconceptions and faulty knowledge and make plans to address it within a learning sequence • Consider grouping to support various a levels of prior knowledge • Create choices to allow students to self-differentiate standards-based learning • Develop a plan for using time wisely	• End-of-unit or chapter test • Concept maps • Journal entries
• To discover information about individual differences among students in interest or learning profile • To identify information that can be used to consider how student characteristics overlap	• Use information to devise ways to interest students in learning • Identify areas of interest that might be incorporated or accentuated in the learning sequence • Identify ways to provide learning through "channels" that are most appropriate	• Learning style inventories • IQ testing • Myers-Briggs tests

factors to consider when designing instruction (see Figure 2-4 in Chapter 2 for several important questions to consider). Without doing some kind of pre-assessment, teachers might design instruction that fails to address learner needs. For instance, a teacher might design instruction based on their *assumptions* of students' knowledge, attitudes, skills, and/or habits and not on their *actual* knowledge, attitudes, skills, and/or habits. Like Charlie in the opening scenario, a Spanish teacher might assume that her Level 2 students already know how to conjugate *–ir* verbs but then learn that they actually do not.

Pre-assessment allows teachers to collect information about what their students know so that they can make the best educational design decisions about the

1. degree of support required for some or all learners during the instructional process,
2. best instructional configurations or groupings to use for teaching (e.g., whole group, flexible grouping, or pairs),
3. instructional models that might be most beneficial (e.g., direct instruction model, concept development model, and so on),
4. instructional media and tools that might be most beneficial (e.g., high-tech/low-tech, overhead, video, and so on),

5. instructional strategies that might be best to use (e.g., graphic organizers, note taking, and so on),
6. strategies that allow optimal pacing of instruction,
7. estimated time required for instruction,
8. appropriate scaffolding, and
9. best methods for formative and summative assessment.

Pre-assess to promote metacognitive awareness of learning. Pre-assessment serves as a road map for learning. That is, pre-assessment introduces learners to concepts, facts, skills, and principles that will be learned in the forthcoming lessons. Having a road map helps students think more deeply about their own learning and provides needed structures for this thinking. When pre-assessment examines students' interests and learning styles, students have a means for reflecting on their individual learning needs. That reflection is a form of metacognition. Students learn about themselves when they are asked to inventory what they know and reflect on how they learn.

Pre-assess to foster students' ownership of their learning. Metacognitive awareness creates a platform for students to take ownership of their own learning. Students who are able to think about their own learning make better educational choices, positioning them to figure out how to advocate for it. This broader understanding and deeper self-awareness (also known as self-knowledge) enables students to become better self-advocates. Self-advocacy is an individual's ability to communicate, convey, negotiate, or assert his or her own interests, desires, and needs effectively. Students who are confident self-advocates are better learners—both inside and outside the classroom. Teachers approaching instruction as educational designers realize that self-advocates can become partners in the design and delivery of more effective instruction, and such a partnership produces instruction that is more fulfilling for students and teachers alike.

Formative Assessment

Formative assessment is assessment conducted at various points during the implementation of a learning sequence. As such, formative assessments collect information about student progress and the effectiveness of instruction. The main goals of formative assessment are to (1) determine whether and how parts of the instructional process can be modified to address the needs of learners better, (2) check for understanding, (3) verify procedures, (4) correct misconceptions, and (5) reinforce concepts. Formative assessment also supports the development of student self-awareness, fosters student–teacher relationships, and enhances satisfaction in the learning process for teachers and their students. Charlie, the teacher in the opening scenario of this chapter, uses formative assessment to engage students in learning and understand the instructional process from the learner's perspective.

Information or data gained through formative assessment helps teachers working as educational designers modify pacing, strategies, grouping, grading procedures, and the content materials used to teach lesson objectives. Therefore, formative assessment enables calibration of the learning process. Several formative assessment strategies are included in Figure 4-6. Figure 4-7 illustrates the "3-2-1" activity, which can be used as a formative assessment.

Figure 4-6 Formative Assessment Strategies

- Observation (with and without checklists)
- Conferencing
- Responses to spontaneous or planned student and/or teacher questions
- Answers to classroom response systems
- Homework
- Reflective journaling
- Anecdotal notes recorded by the teacher of student performance
- Completion of graphic organizers (e.g., see Figures 4-1 and 4-3)
- Checklists
- Quizzes
- One-minute summary paper
- Freewriting
- 3-2-1 activity (see Figure 4-7)

WHY CONDUCT FORMATIVE ASSESSMENT? Common sense suggests that it is a good idea to check in with students during the learning process to make sure that instruction is being experienced as anticipated. Research confirms the value of checking in on learning in progress. Well-designed formative assessments have been shown to improve student learning (Black & William, 1998a, 1998b). Not surprisingly, formative assessment helps educational designers find out if the decisions they made work, for whom, and how well. An important benefit of formative assessment is that it provides this information when there is still time to make instructional changes to improve student learning outcomes.

There are many reasons to use formative assessments, as the following section describes. Teachers can deepen their understanding of students' development along the knowledge and cognitive process dimensions. They can ascertain how well students are developing procedural knowledge about a topic. They can also gauge students' thinking and interest as it develops throughout a learning sequence. Using data from formative assessment, teachers can modify instruction to meet learners' needs as learning takes place. Formative assessment also serves as self assessment and peer assessment tools that inform both students and teachers alike about learning.

Conduct formative assessment to examine students' developing understanding across the knowledge and cognitive process dimensions. As discussed in Chapter 1 and illustrated in Chapter 2, the application of the revised Bloom's taxonomy in the design of learning

Figure 4-7 3-2-1 Activity

3	What are three facts you learned about _____?
2	What are two facts that surprised you about _____?
1	What is one question you still have about _____?

experiences enables more focused, intentional and effective instruction. It does so by facilitating better matches between the types of knowledge targeted in learning goals and cognitive process categories. Therefore, formative assessment designed with this taxonomy in mind promotes student learning across the various cognitive process dimensions. For example, if a teacher is trying to teach verb conjugation, using the taxonomy might push her to challenge students to learn this procedural knowledge by remembering, understanding, applying, analyzing, evaluating, and creating. Formative assessments conducted after the completion of various learning activities, including homework, lessons, viewing a video, and so on, might reveal how successful students are in each of these cognitive process categories.

Development in each of the distinct knowledge and cognitive process dimensions requires special support for different types of learners. According to Anderson et al. (2001), the knowledge dimensions are factual, conceptual, procedural, and metacognitive knowledge. The cognitive process dimensions are remembering, understanding, applying, analyzing, evaluating, and creating. Formative assessment can improve instructional efficacy by revealing how well instruction is addressing the development of individuals and groups of students along these knowledge and cognitive process dimensions. Assessments conducted for this purpose identify what students know and do not know, what instructional approaches are working and for which students, and what challenges exist. Formative assessment also helps teachers ensure that students reach beyond basic levels of learning (e.g., remembering) to more challenging levels of learning (e.g., creating). For instance, an elementary-level social studies teacher might use formative questioning to gauge students' learning about finding coordinates on a map. By using formative assessment to emphasize development of targeted knowledge and cognitive process dimensions, as shown in Figure 4-8, the teacher ensures that students master learning at increasingly complex levels. Their knowledge is applied with growing sophistication.

Conduct formative assessment to examine students' developing procedural knowledge about a topic. Formative assessments can help teachers gain information about students' mastery of procedural knowledge (i.e., what students know and can do related to a particular task). Often, such knowledge is demonstrated with a physical activity that students perform with their hands or the rest of their bodies. For example, teachers might ask students to demonstrate how to create an angle using a protractor or how to find coordinates of a location on a map, as in the example in Figure 4-8. Observing students performing such tasks helps teachers correct any procedural errors that might result in even more mistakes when working on advanced problems for which this information will later be foundational knowledge.

Conduct formative assessment to examine students' developing thinking about a topic. When formative assessments are designed to demonstrate "what's going on" in a student's head, they can provide a teacher with insight about a student's ability to work independently through the problem-solving process, revealing how the student processes ideas and information. For example, teachers might ask students to "think aloud," a strategy to verbalize and explain their ideas about a reading passage, vocabulary word, or a problem. As the student narrates his or her thinking process aloud, the teacher can interject to make any necessary corrections or ask questions to deepen students' learning. Consequently, students become metacognitively aware of their learning.

Figure 4-8   Sample Formative Assessment across Knowledge and Cognitive Process Dimensions

Knowledge Dimension	Cognitive Process Dimension					
	Remember	**Understand**	**Apply**	**Analyze**	**Evaluate**	**Create**
Factual	Define latitude and longitude.					
Conceptual		Describe the relationship between latitude and longitude regarding parallelism and perpendicularity.				
Procedural			Find the latitude and longitude for the following U.S. cities: Los Angeles, Miami, New Orleans, and Washington, D.C.			Create a map of an imaginary country that includes its latitude, longitude, and a compass rose.
Metacognitive				Analyze how the co-ordinates of these cities were found. Think aloud how they were located with a partner. Use a digital recorder to record the think aloud about how one of these four cities was located.		

Conduct formative assessment to examine students' developing interests about a topic. Formative assessment can help students and their teachers examine students' choices during the learning process. Assessments that allow students to express opinions and make choices affecting their learning provide information to teachers about what motivates their students. To gather this type of information, teachers might ask students to explain what they like about a topic, for example, by asking students a question like "What interests you about this topic?" Although teachers cannot always incorporate students' interests in every topic studied, they can certainly try.

Conduct formative assessment to modify instruction to meet diverse learner needs. What teachers learn about their students through formative assessment can be made immediately useful by applying it to adjust and modify instruction as it occurs. For instance, in the opening scenario, Charlie might learn that, before giving a unit test, she has to reteach how to conjugate verbs because students have not fully grasped the concept. If she neglects to conduct formative assessment, she might give a unit test and discover that the majority (or a small group) of students do not understand how to conjugate verbs. It is better for Charlie to use formative assessment as a "preemptive strike" to uncover the emerging needs of struggling students before precious time is wasted. Insights acquired from formative assessment can also be recorded and used for future planning.

Conduct formative assessment for self-assessment. Formative assessment can serve as a self-assessment tool that allows students to examine their own learning. In fact, Black and William (1998b) see it as an essential and necessary component of effective formative assessment. Both teachers and students should take responsibility for learning from formative assessment. Self-assessments can consist of checklists students complete about their own learning or journal or blog entries they write in response to reflective questions, such as "What did you learn today? What was the most useful/meaningful thing you learned today? What are some questions or concerns you still have regarding the topic we are studying?" Encouraging students to select their method of self-assessment empowers them to direct the type of information they share with their teacher. Self-assessment opportunities give students an important voice during the learning process and make them more self-aware (metacognitive). Both agency and metacognition promote students' effective future learning.

Conduct formative assessment for peer assessment. Peers can play an important and constructive role in the process of formative assessment. When appropriately orchestrated, peer involvement in assessment can affect learning and also create community among learners. Before undertaking peer assessment in the classroom, teachers need to give guidance on how to provide such meaningful feedback to peers. Educating students about the purpose of the peer assessment—to give feedback on their peer's knowledge about a topic—is critical. Formative assessments conducted by peers can be as simple as putting a sticky note on another student's essay describing key strengths and areas needing improvement or completing more formalized checklists and open-ended questionnaires developed by students and/or teachers.

HOW DO LEARNERS BENEFIT FROM FORMATIVE ASSESSMENT? Formative assessment allows learners to express themselves as they are learning and growing—or in some cases as they are learning and groaning! Formative assessments serve the practical purpose of allowing students to express feelings during the learning process and receive support as they need it. These assessments also provide a means for students to communicate to their teacher that they require additional, specialized help to achieve the learning goals. Formative assessments let students praise their teacher's planning or provide critical feedback. The greatest benefit of formative assessment for students is that it communicates needs "just in time," so teachers can intervene and support student learning when it is most valuable. Figure 4-9 provides a summary of several ways that formative assessment benefits students and teachers.

Figure 4-9   Benefits of Formative Assessment

Formative Assessment	
For Teachers:	**For Learners:**
• Offers opportunity to affirm lesson implementation • Provides feedback on effectiveness of instruction • Suggests ways to make instruction more appropriate • Increases likelihood of instructional effectiveness • Supports communication with learners and nurturing	• Enables students to suggest necessary instructional changes • Affirms student progress • Provides important information about students' learning to teacher • Fosters opportunity for self-monitoring and self-awareness

Summative Assessment

Summative assessment is considered a formal measure of what students know and can do as a result of instruction. By "formal," we mean that the assessment is planned, intentional, and focused. In the opening scenario, Charlie uses summative assessment to find out whether her students have mastered the targeted learning goals. She does so using traditional assessments (e.g., tests and quizzes) and alternative assessments (e.g., audio recording of conversations), and authentic assessments (e.g., podcasts). We will discuss these types more thoroughly later in this section.

Each type of summative assessment is unique, but all share the primary goal of gathering information about student learning to make some type of judgment. Teachers routinely make appraisals about student learning based on a finished product, exam, or other expression observed at the end of a unit or learning sequence. Information gained through these summative assessments provides students, their parents/guardians, teachers, and schools with an appraisal of students' achievement, growth, and effort.

Summative assessments typically serve as the basis for students' formal grades. Often, they ask students to make or do something with the knowledge and skills gained through instruction. Traditionally, this form of assessment has measured the breadth and depth of student learning related to curriculum standards, but student progress might also be measured in relation to other outcomes, such as behavior and attitude.

As its name suggests, summative assessment involves determining the sum total of student learning after a particular unit of instruction. It occurs post facto. That chronology means that teachers administer summative assessment after fully delivering instruction. In that way, summative assessment provides teachers a forensic look at student learning and the unit of instruction. The results of the summative assessment reveal what and how deeply students learned from the instruction. The results also reflect instructional choices made by the teacher while designing instruction or implementing it.

TYPES OF SUMMATIVE ASSESSMENT.   Three main types of summative assessment are traditional, alternative, and authentic. Figure 4-10 distinguishes between these different types of summative assessment.

Figure 4-10   Comparison of Traditional, Alternative, and Authentic Assessment

Assessment Type	Modes	Characteristics	Examples
Traditional	Written	• Uses written modes to gain information about student learning • Meaningful to teacher but not student • Are usually indirect measures of learning	Tests, quizzes, reports
Alternative	Verbal, physical	• Uses alternative modes to gain information about student learning • Student may or may not be granted choice over modes. • May be direct or indirect measures of learning	Audio-recorded evidence, physical demonstration, pictorial product
Authentic	Written, verbal, physical	• Students have choice about the task used to gain information about student learning • The tasks of assessment have meaning to student • Are direct measures of learning	Skits, podcasts, creation of real-world materials such as brochures

Traditional assessments consist of some type of written work, such as a paper, essay, report, or test. These assessments may be available from educational publishers to complement instructional materials, or teachers may construct their own. Construction of high-quality assessments, those that are both valid and reliable, may require specialized training.

Alternative assessments are those that enable students to demonstrate learning through one or more nonwritten modes (e.g., verbal, physical, and so on). A physical demonstration (e.g., hands-on activity) or pictorial product (e.g., diagram, graph, chart, and so on) is an example of an alternative assessment. Alternative assessments are widely considered more supportive modes of assessment for 21st century diverse learners. Those that allow learners to use technology are growing in popularity as a way to support today's digital learners.

Alternative assessments are becoming increasingly popular options because they provide rich information about students' learning and match the most effective assessment mode with individual students. For students who understand content but have difficulty communicating it in the structure of a formal assessment, demonstrating their comprehension with alternative assessments can be more effective. For example, a student who has difficulty with spelling and written expression may not provide accurate information about his or her learning about Spanish culture on a written test. That student might provide more accurate information about her mastery if allowed to submit an audio report. Advocates of alternative assessment favor it because it can promote matching the best mode of expression to the individual learner. The flexibility and variety inherent in alternative assessment increase the odds that students have access to a mode of expression that matches their strengths. Students engage in making choices about the best way to communicate their learning (Wiggins, 1998; Wiggins & McTighe, 2005).

The use of **authentic assessments** as a method of summative assessment is also becoming more popular in contemporary classrooms. Authentic assessments are those that are meaningful to students—the tasks involved in assessment relate to students' lives in real ways. They demonstrate student learning through the completion of tasks that are relevant and important to the learner. They afford opportunities to apply and demonstrate knowledge and skills in a practical context. Authentic assessments might be performed using alternative modes of expression similar to those used in alternative assessments. However, the key distinction between these assessment types is the nature of the tasks the assessment involves, not the mode used to present learning. The tasks that demonstrate learning must be meaningful to students in authentic assessment. Often this means the mode of expression is an alternative one but not always. For example, an alternative assessment like a podcast could also be authentic if it involved the student doing something meaningful to demonstrate mastery of targeted standards, such as creating a recorded conversation with a peer about the important elements of Spanish culture. This would be authentic and use an alternative mode of communication. Sometimes the words *alternative* and *authentic* are used interchangeably in the field of education, but they are different. Each type of assessment has special critical attributes, as has been illustrated.

DIRECT VERSUS INDIRECT MEASURES.   As much as possible, summative assessments should be direct measures of student learning. **Direct measures** are those that ask students to demonstrate what has been learned (i.e., skills and knowledge) for a practical purpose. Because they challenge learners to apply new learning, direct measures are more accurate indications of the breadth and depth of student learning. They also illustrate whether students can transfer their learning to a real-world setting. For example, an art teacher might measure her students' knowledge of the principles of graphic design by asking students to use these principles to create an effective newsletter. Students would apply what they had learned (e.g., the principles of contrast, alignment, repetition, and proximity) to create a print publication for a particular audience. The teacher might also ask learners to include an explanation of each of the principles and their value in the newsletter as a way of making sure students could articulate the principles as well as apply them.

Indirect measures are assessments and/or products that measure only students' possession of knowledge and skill—not their application of it—and only at a superficial level. If the same art teacher wanted to measure her students' knowledge indirectly, she might ask them to name each of the principles of design and explain each in a traditional pencil/ paper test. By doing so, she would learn if they could recall and comprehend this content. However, she would have limited understanding of how well students could apply this knowledge. We can see from this illustration the different levels of quality in these learning products and also the varying levels of difficulty involved.

WHY CONDUCT SUMMATIVE ASSESSMENT?   Teachers should conduct summative assessment to discover information about student achievement, growth, and effort because it informs learners and the others who care about them about students' academic performance. This form of assessment provides students with information about their own achievements. It can also impact the design of instruction for future students when interpreted by the teacher. High-quality summative assessments are linked directly to standards, goals, and objectives. Summative assessment has many benefits. See Figure 4-11 for several of them.

Figure 4-11   Benefits of Summative Assessment

Summative Assessment	
For Teachers:	**For Learners:**
• Provides information on student progress • Provides opportunity for reflection on quality of lesson, planning, and implementation • Confirms or refutes teacher's perception of student learning	• Provides acknowledgment of success • Identifies areas for future growth • Can result in additional learning about content • Acts as a launching pad for future learning • Provides input resulting in greater self-awareness

Conduct summative assessment to inform students of their end-of-unit/course achievement. Most teachers must evaluate students' achievement and performance at some point in time but typically during certain academic intervals (e.g., quarters, semesters, and so on). Therefore, one goal of summative assessment is to collect data for determining a student's grade at the end of a unit, time period, or course. The best summative assessments provide information that illustrates what students know as well as how well they know and apply it.

Conduct summative assessment to inform future practice/instructional design. Information gleaned from summative assessments can help educational designers learn from practice. By analyzing assessment data, teachers can understand how their instructional decisions influenced student learning. They can learn whether instructional models were well matched with content, whether differentiations were effective, and whether tools were properly configured. Insights gained from an analysis of which students achieve, at what levels, and how consistently can promote a teachers' instructional efficacy.

Technology Support for 21st Century Classroom-Based Assessment

As Charlie learns through experience, technology tools can be supportive of good teaching throughout the assessment process. Charlie benefits from using clickers, digital recorders, and multimedia software. These technologies allow her to improve her instructional efficacy, measure student learning, and understand how her instructional decisions have affected her students. She discovers that the right technologies, effectively implemented, can make her assessment efforts more efficient, effective, and engaging.

Clickers prove to be a tool that greatly improve Charlie's efficiency with many tasks. Instructional time is saved when student responses are instantaneously received. Record-keeping time is also reduced because Charlie has configured the clicker software to record student assessment data directly in her gradebook. Analysis time, that time spent

identifying individual and shared needs that are uncovered in pre-assessment and formative assessment data, is also reduced. The process involved in making sense of student
performance data is greatly streamlined because the clicker software easily creates graphs
and charts ready for interpretation. To summarize, appropriate integration of technology
makes the assessment process more efficient by

- providing rapid access to information,
- making the recording of student learning less time consuming, and
- aiding in the analysis of individual and shared needs.

The use of technology can also makes assessment more effective. Rather than retro-
fitting the lesson to meet students' needs as they arise, Charlie is able to use clickers to
gain accurate information that enables her to plan proactively for potential problems and
circumvent them through decisions she makes in her planning. Charlie's use of the clickers also enables her to gain varied and broad information about student learning during
the process of instruction that enables just-in-time support should problems arise. Use of
special tools for summative assessment enables Charlie to support her students' expression
of learning in modes that will allow the most powerful demonstration of student learning.
It also records evidence of student learning that can be used to promote reflection.

To summarize, the use of technology for assessment can make assessment more effective by

- letting students share up-to-the moment information about their learning,
- quickly measuring a broad and varied set of learning goals,
- providing evidence of student learning in the most effective mode (i.e., written, verbal
  and physical),
- capturing evidence in a format that can be reviewed at another time and in greater
  depth, and
- recording direct evidence of student learning in a meaningful real-world context.

It goes without saying that Charlie's use of technology can improve effectiveness only
when certain conditions are in place. The clickers must work correctly, and students
must use them with integrity (giving honest answers and not "goofing off"), or their use
will be meaningless. If Charlie has created high-quality, valid, and reliable assessment
questions that cover all learning objectives under investigation, she will receive up-to-
the moment information about the extent of her students' learning over a broad and
varied set of learning goals.

It must also be noted that tools like clickers are inappropriate for measuring all types of
learning. Clicker-type tools work well for assessing procedural and factual knowledge, but
they are less effective in measuring conceptual and metacognitive knowledge. Other measures are required for these more complex and multifaceted knowledge types. For example,
in the alternative assessment Charlie has implemented—an audio recording of students
meeting standards related to their learning of conceptual and metacognitive knowledge—
she can actually hear students using their Spanish knowledge and skills in speaking the language. The alternative audio assessment has also allowed Charlie to capture data illustrating student learning in a format that she and her students can review later. Both she and her
students can return to the audio files and do more in-depth analysis when time permits.

The use of technology can also make assessment practices engaging. Charlie finds that
her students are more motivated to learn when they can share what they learn in school

using technologies that are important to them outside of school. The clickers are different, novel, and exciting. Classes are more active when students have the chance to share information about their understanding before, during, and after learning takes place. Students indicate that they are emotionally, intellectually, and psychologically engaged in learning when they can use tools that are valuable to them—whether these be clickers, cell phones, or the Internet. Technology tools also facilitate and make more enjoyable students' communication with their teacher and peers. The result is the creation of a learning community that is important to digital learners.

To summarize, technology makes assessment more engaging by

- adding novelty and excitement,
- making what happens in school more relevant to what happens outside of it,
- integrating all stages of the learning process, and
- allowing students to participate in a community with their teacher and each other.

Specific suggestions for the transformative integration of technology within the assessment cycle used when implementing the models of teaching are presented in Part II of this book.

Challenges Associated with the Implementation of Technology

Any suggestion that technology can positively influence any dimension of teaching and learning (including assessment) should come with a caveat: technology can have a negative impact if it is not used appropriately, meaningfully, proficiently, or purposefully. For example, if Charlie were not able to design quizzes that used clickers effectively and in ways that gave students appropriate items to respond to or if she could not correctly integrate the clicker software with her gradebook, the use of such powerful tools would backfire. To be successful using technology to support assessment, teachers need to have mastery of and integrate several different domains of professional knowledge when designing assessments using technology, as described in Chapter 3.

First, teachers must possess technological knowledge, or skill in using a particular technology tool (e.g., computer, tablet, or clicker) or application (e.g., software or Web application). Second, the teacher needs to have technological pedagogical knowledge. This type of knowledge informs a teacher about the appropriate way to use a technology to support pedagogy. Finally, a teacher needs TPACK, or technological pedagogical content knowledge (see Chapter 3 for a thorough explanation of TPACK), the ability to integrate the various technology tools for pedagogical purposes and to understand if, when, and how to best leverage technology to achieve instructional goals.

When selecting technology to incorporate in any type of Classroom-Based assessment, teachers need to consider more than just whether technology is available and whether it adds value. They should also consider whether students have the ability to use the technology to communicate information effectively about their learning. If not, then there is a chance that inaccurate information about student learning will be collected through the assessment and thereby negate its impact. For example, if Charlie's students do not know how to use a digital recorder or multimedia software program needed to make a podcast, they might not be able to communicate to Charlie that they mastered the intended learning goals. When selecting technology tools for the support of the instructional process, teachers should consider students' skill with the mechanics of a tool (i.e., how to make it work) as well as their ability to use it effectively to demonstrate assessment-related information with this tool (i.e., how to make it work for a purpose).

Chapter Summary

In this chapter, we provided an explanation of what Classroom-Based assessment is and why it is important to teachers who approach instruction as educational designers. We explained that the effective use of assessment practices can help teachers in multiple ways. Assessment practices can enable teachers to identify educational problems that might affect student learning, understand better the nature of these problems, and modify appropriately their instructional approaches. Such competencies aid educational designers in using the models of teaching in Part II of this text.

We then explained the three types of Classroom-Based assessment—(1) pre-assessment, (2) formative assessment, and (3) summative assessment—to emphasize their role in the teaching and learning process. Pre-assessment is communication with students to determine their readiness for learning before learning takes place. Formative assessment is communication with students that determines the appropriateness of instruction while learning is taking place. Summative assessment enables teachers to appraise student learning and provides information about the quality of instructional design and delivery.

Each type of assessment has distinct purposes and is named for the point in the instructional process during which it is implemented. When implemented successfully, the process of assessment, as well as the information that is generated from it (i.e., the product of assessment), can benefit teachers and learners alike.

Review Questions

1. What is Classroom-Based assessment? How is it important to educational designers?

2. How does Classroom-Based assessment support high-quality instruction?

3. List the three types of Classroom-Based assessment and describe their benefits for teachers and students.

4. How does technology make assessment more efficient, effective, and engaging?

5. What are some challenges associated with using technology for assessment?

Resources

- Adequate Yearly Progress—This site, developed by the U.S. Department of Education, provides several resources on adequate yearly progress: www2.ed.gov/nclb/accountability/ayp/edpicks.jhtml

- Edutopia (Assessment)—This site is a comprehensive site about educational assessment, ranging from standardized to alternative assessments: www.edutopia.org/assessment

- Kathy Schrock's Guide to Educators: Assessment Rubrics—This site has a lot of examples of rubrics that can be downloaded and modified: www.schrockguide.net/assessment-and-rubrics.html
- National Center for Research on Evaluation, Standards, and Student Testing (CRESST)—CRESST conducts research related to assessment, evaluation, technology, and learning: www.cse.ucla.edu/about.html

- North Central Regional Library (Assessment)—This site provides resources for ensuring educational equity with alternative assessments, rethinking the role of assessment, integrating assessment to support student learning, reporting assessment results, and assessing young children's progress: www.ncrel.org/sdrs/areas/as0cont.htm

Model	Direct Instruction Model
Knowledge Supported	Factual and conceptual, but especially powerful in supporting development of procedural knowledge.
Added Value	Teaches specific content while allowing students to develop knowledge and skills that can be practiced independently. Also promotes students' development of linear thinking and problem-solving skills.
Technologies to Integrate	• Online reference tools and multimedia content services to aid presentation
	• Screen capture or use of digital and audio recording equipment to record presentation or provide support for guided practice
	• Interactive whiteboards to aid presentation or practice
	• Audience response systems and online quiz tools to support assessment
	• Multimedia discussion tools to extend learning

The Direct Instruction Model

ajt/Shutterstock

Terence Thatcher, a third grade teacher, was excited to be working in a school with a site license for concept-mapping software. Better access to high-tech teaching tools was one of the motivations that led Terence to transfer to Lockborne Elementary. Here, technology resources and a half-time technology coach were made available through a federal grant intended to turn around failing schools. Lockborne had a high population of English Language Learners (ELLs) and students in difficult economic circumstances. Terence knew the use of technology could do more than just educate these learners—it might also emancipate them from a life in poverty. Terence had not lost his determination or idealism after seven years of teaching. He was a charismatic, innovative and highly successful teacher. And now, with appropriate tools at his fingertips, the year ahead held great promise!

Terence knew there were lots of ways the concept-mapping program could support his learners, especially the ones who were struggling, but he was uncertain how to introduce it to his students. Concept mapping in general was unfamiliar to them, and he strongly suspected that trying to teach the new software in addition to the new technique would overwhelm his students. Then he realized he did not have to face this challenge on his own. "Now," he thought, "It's time to take advantage of having a technology coach!"

Heidi was Lockborne's technology coach. She had 25 years of experience in business and corporate training and was now the technology support specialist for two elementary schools in the district.

When Terence found Heidi in the media center, he asked, "Hey Heidi. Quick question for you: If I'm introducing a new instructional strategy—concept mapping—and a new technology—the concept-mapping program—what's the best way to do it? I don't have a lot of time, and my students struggle with English fluency."

She replied, "Glad to hear you're not wasting any time getting started with new technologies, and techniques, Terence! If I were trying to introduce two new things at the same time, I'd use a tried-and-true method like the Direct Instruction model. Follow model that old adage, 'If you're learning a new task, use familiar tools; if you're learning new tools, use a familiar task.'"

"Whoa," replied Terence. "Isn't that old fashioned? I haven't heard the term 'direct instruction' since I was a student teacher."

Laughing, Heidi replied, "Sometimes oldies but goodies are the way to go! The model will allow you to tap into students' prior knowledge first and present new ideas with multiple means like an explanation *and* a demonstration—which will be a great benefit to the ELL students in your class. Then you can let students try out the new learning—the concept mapping—along with you as guided practice. When they're ready for it, you can give the students opportunities for independent practice. You can gradually remove support as students gain proficiency. In the business where I worked previously, we used this approach all the time to teach new processes in our training sessions, especially those involving technology. It's fast and effective, even if it isn't as sophisticated as some of those other techniques I've heard your students raving about. Why not give it a try?"

A grinning Terence replied, "Perhaps I can put my innovative reputation at stake and test drive the Direct Instruction model. That is, as long as I make sure people know it was your idea! I wouldn't want anyone around here to think I was getting stuffy!" ■

CHAPTER OBJECTIVES

After reading this chapter, you will be able to:

- Describe the Direct Instruction model, including its history and steps.

- Communicate the applications and benefits of the Direct Instruction model and share what it might look like in a classroom.

- Explain how the Direct Instruction model is implemented and how to plan for teaching with it.

- Identify how the model enables differentiated instruction and supports diverse learners.

- Describe how technology can enhance teaching with the Direct Instruction model.

Introduction

The Direct Instruction model is a popular instructional method in all types of educational environments. From preschool to high school and beyond, teachers favor it because its implementation yields positive and measurable student learning outcomes through an efficient use of time and resources. Students like it because it provides clear targets, a supportive structure for their learning, and feedback at important stages of the learning process. Teachers like it because, when matched with appropriate learning goals, lessons designed with the Direct Instruction model have a proportionately large impact on student learning when compared with the amount of time and energy required for planning and implementation. Few models offer "so much bang for the buck."

In this chapter's opening scenario, teacher Terence Thatcher has embraced innovative strategies and technologies for instruction, but he still finds a need for the Direct Instruction model. Using this model, Terence is able to address his students' needs for foundational skills and knowledge. As a result, he has time to devote to the deeper learning he will facilitate with more sophisticated instructional practices. In an era of increasingly elaborate models for teaching, the Direct Instruction model endures because it is practical, useful, and complements newer, more innovative approaches. This chapter provides an overview of the Direct Instruction model, the different steps in the model, and the types of content best taught using it. The chapter closes with the benefits of the Direct Instruction model and suggestions for its implementation.

What Is the Direct Instruction Model?

The Direct Instruction model is a popular, teacher-directed approach for addressing factual, procedural, and conceptual knowledge in all content areas and grade levels. In this model, the teacher's role is to understand and introduce new content in a prescriptive way to students. The teacher provides students with "expert" guidance by sharing with them knowledge and insights gained from experience and study. The student's role is to listen, learn, practice, and apply the knowledge, skills, or procedures he or she is taught. The Direct Instruction model, sometimes referred to as "I do it, we do it, you do it," or "model, lead, and test," can be used to address a variety of knowledge types (see Chapter 1 for information about types of knowledge). See Figure 5-1 for examples of sample content to address with the model. The Direct Instruction model is most efficacious when used to teach procedures or procedural knowledge but can also be used to teach factual and conceptual knowledge.

The implementation of the model begins with the introduction of new content by the teacher. This introduction might consist of a simple description of the lesson objectives (e.g., "Today you will learn how to classify animals using concept-mapping software.") or a more elaborate expression of learning goals and outcomes. The next step involves the teacher's presentation of the actual facts, procedures, or concepts to be learned using a lecture or demonstration (e.g., the teacher shows students how to create a simple concept map). Following this, the teacher guides students in practicing the new content. As students become more experienced and competent as a result of their guided practice, the teacher gradually reduces the support he or she provides. During the last stage of the model's implementation, students demonstrate their learning through independent practice and apply their newfound mastery of the content to novel situations without help from their teacher.

The Direct Instruction model is so frequently and widely used in schools that it has influenced our cultural ideas of what teaching and learning should look like—including what a teacher's role is (e.g., demonstrating and directing student practice) and how students should behave (e.g., listening, applying, and practicing). The idea that "teaching is telling, and learning is listening" is influenced by the widespread use of this model. Although the Direct Instruction model is sometimes criticized for its rigidity and emphasis on teacher direction, this model produces positive learning outcomes for many different groups of learners when it is matched with appropriate instructional goals.

Despite its popularity and ubiquity, the Direct Instruction model is still subject to some misconceptions and misunderstandings that are worth addressing. First, it is important to clarify that the Direct Instruction model is not the same as the Lecture model. Although both models are teacher directed and represent behaviorist views of teaching and learning, the Direct Instruction model is different in that it offers the students an opportunity to do something—practice the new content learned with their teacher's guidance. In the Lecture model, students take a more passive, listening role. (This difference is likely why the Lecture model is less effective than the Direct Instruction model. When Lecture is the sole method of instruction, it does not provide guided practice of new content.) In contrast, the Direct Instruction model is characterized by a significant amount of guided and independent practice for students.

Another important misconception held by some is that the Direct Instruction *model* is the same as the Direct Instruction *method*. The Direct Instruction method, sometimes called "big DI" (to refer to its name as a proper noun) or "DISTAR" (Direct Instruction System for Teaching Arithmetic and Reading), is an instructional method that involves systematic curriculum design and implementation of a prescribed verbal and behavioral script. It was developed to support disadvantaged elementary school students by Siegfried Engelmann and Wesley Becker in the 1960s and incorporates the principles of applied behavioral analysis. Big DI is a programmed instruction similar to a "pre-packaged product" involving intensive teacher training and scripted teaching. Although their names suggest great similarity, the Direct Instruction model and Direct Instruction method are quite different in practice.

Figure 5-1 Sample Content to Explore Using the
Direct Instruction Model

Subject	Concepts
Art	• How to use a brayer and ink pad. • How to glaze pottery. • How to properly use various types of watercolor tools. • How to put materials away properly. • How to critique a piece of art work.
Health/Physical Education	• How to skip. • How to wash hands properly. • How to play a game. • How to create a healthy menu. • How to resolve a conflict successfully. • How to use a condom.
Language Arts	• How to print the letter "a." • How to summarize a paragraph. • How to write a persuasive essay. • How to write a haiku poem. • How to diagram a sentence. • How to write a thesis paper.
Mathematics	• How to add two-digit numbers. • How to use base-10 blocks. • How to add fractions. • How to determine the area of a triangle. • How to use a protractor. • How to solve a proof.
Music	• How to ring a hand bell properly. • How to hold a bow correctly. • How to read a line of music. • How to determine the musical key of a composition. • How to breathe properly for optimal voice support.
Social Studies	• How to create a family tree. • How to use historical artifacts to answer questions. • How to compare two historical time periods. • How to analyze primary source materials. • How to draw a political cartoon.
Science	• How to read a Fahrenheit thermometer. • How to classify animals. • How to test a hypothesis. • How to make an observation. • How to maintain a log. • How to handle chemicals safely.

What Are the History and Origins of the Direct Instruction Model?

The Direct Instruction model emerged from a behaviorist view of the teaching and learning process. B. F. Skinner's (1953) theory of operant conditioning was highly influential in its development, and informed much research on the model's efficacy. The model is consistent with Skinner's theory proposing that all behavior results from external stimuli. In the Direct Instruction model, an individual's response or voluntary behavior (i.e., learning) is directly related to a stimulus (i.e., instruction) in the environment. Research on teacher-effectiveness and observational learning shows that the steps within the Direct Instruction model influence learning in many positive ways (Kauchak & Eggen, 2012)—especially when used to teach content that can be broken into discrete segments with outcomes that can be observed and measured.

There are several other variations of the Direct Instruction model. The most commonly referred to and implemented are Slavin's model (2006), the Huitt model (2008), and Madeline Hunter's model (1982). Each of these instructional models relies on the same general teacher-directed approach to presenting content and supporting student learning but uses different terminology to express various steps in the model and utilizes special strategies to support student learning.

When Should the Direct Instruction Model Be Applied and Why?

The Direct Instruction model is a highly effective model of instruction for teaching procedural and conceptual knowledge with clearly defined steps and attributes. It is also helpful when introducing new topics and reinforcing the foundational knowledge and skills students require to understand more complex topics or perform more intricate tasks. It has additional use for teaching content that can be easily replicated and practiced by students. We describe these applications of the model in the following sections to promote the use of the model when it will yield the most benefit. Teachers should use the Direct Instruction model to:

Teach Procedural Knowledge That Has Clearly Defined Steps and Concepts with Clear Attributes

Not all procedures have steps that can be clearly defined. Some involve steps that are difficult to articulate or describe. Clearly defined procedures are those that can be easily described, identified, copied, and practiced. Some examples of procedures that might be taught with the Direct Instruction model include tying a sheepshank knot or adding decimals. When tasks such as these can be accomplished by performing a specific set of procedures in sequence, then the Direct Instruction model works well.

Teaching concepts with clearly defined attributes is also a productive application of the model. **Concepts** are ideas that provide learners necessary mental constructs that support the organization and comprehension of facts and other information. (See Chapter 6, Chapter 7, Chapter 8 for more information about models to support concept teaching, and Appendix B for detailed information about concepts.) Though ubiquitous in the academic curriculum and everyday life, concepts often require reinforcement from experiences in different settings over time to promote deep learning. The Direct Instruction model can be used to teach some concepts and speed the learning curve. Concepts with characteristics or critical attributes that are widely recognized and can be articulated to others work well with the model. The model is also effective when teaching concepts with concrete, simple, and visible attributes. The concept of visual symmetry, for example, is appropriate for the model and has clearly defined attributes. The characteristics of a symmetrical object are commonly accepted and easy to understand when examining concrete examples. Those qualities allow the concept of visual symmetry to be taught at a basic level with the Direct Instruction model. Symmetry as a general concept however, including manifestations of the concept in music or motion, might require a different model to teach fully.

Introduce New Topics

The Direct Instruction model is a natural fit for introducing vocabulary, skills, processes, or techniques at the beginning of a new unit. For example, Scenario 5-3 later in the chapter, describes students learning to apply the order of operations at the beginning of a math unit. The model might be effectively used to generate interest in the topic of study, communicate learning goals to students, or provide students with an opportunity to develop basic skills required for future learning. Basic reading (e.g., phonics) and mathematical skills (e.g., addition) are often taught using the Direct Instruction model.

Reinforce Foundational Knowledge and Skills

To be successful building new understandings, students must have a strong foundation upon which to build. Most objectives or learning goals require basic understanding of concepts, facts, or procedures as the basis for new learning. For example, learning the procedures for telling time on an analog clock requires mastery of associated factual knowledge. Before students can be successful telling time, they must be able to identify the hour and minute hands and understand what the teacher means by these terms. The Direct Instruction model is often an appropriate method for reviewing or re-teaching such content. Even if students should already be familiar with such content, pre-assessment might reveal that they are not. The Direct Instruction model offers an efficient and quick way to address any areas where foundational knowledge might be lacking. For example, before teaching how to tell time on an analog clock, the teacher might want to use the Direct Instruction model to teach students the terminology she will use in the lesson and ensure they can identify and name relevant clock parts.

Teach Procedures, Skills, or Techniques That Students Can Replicate

Teachers should choose the Direct Instruction model when students need to learn content, procedures, skills, or techniques that they can replicate and practice. For instance, Scenario 5-1 presented later in the chapter describes students learning to do jumping jacks, an exercise that they need to execute correctly. With the teacher's guidance, students learn and practice how to perform jumping jacks.

What Are the Steps in the Direct Instruction Model?

The Direct Instruction model has four major steps: (1) Introduction, (2) Presentation, (3) Guided Practice, and (4) Independent Practice. These steps are described in the following sections. Figure 5-2 provides an overview of teacher and student roles when using the Direct Instruction model.

Figure 5-2   Teacher and Student Roles in the Direct Instruction Model

Direct Instruction Model Steps	Teacher's Role	Student's Role
Introduction	Teacher describes lesson objectives and what students will do. **Teaching Tip:** Write on the board or project on a screen the objectives and overview of the lesson.	Students listen and watch the teacher.
Presentation	Teacher presents and demonstrates the new content. Often the teacher thinks aloud while demonstrating the new content. The teacher should incorporate mechanisms to check for understanding. **Teaching Tip:** Record the presentation using a video camera so students can review the presentation, especially if a think-aloud is used.	Students listen and watch the teacher. The teacher may choose to ask students to take notes or engage them in some question and answering.
Guided Practice	Teacher demonstrates the new content with novel or different examples while students follow along and practice the new content. In this phase, the teacher may stop and start the practice often and ask for students to participate in the practice of the new content. The teacher should incorporate mechanisms to check for understanding. **Teaching Tip:** Build-in many opportunities for the students to practice the new content and ask questions. Also check that all students are understanding the content. Incorporate technology for recording success when students gain mastery of new content.	Students are engaged in practicing the new content. They might also be called upon to demonstrate the new content to the class or in other pairs or groupings.
Independent Practice	Teacher now acts more as a facilitator and monitor of students' independent practice. If the independent practice occurs in class, the teacher should circulate the room to assist students as needed. **Teaching Tip:** Clearly articulate how students will demonstrate their mastery of new knowledge. Using video or audio recording tools will enable learners to capture their understanding and can help students demonstrate their learning. These recordings can be used for peer teaching, as well.	Students practice new content independently.

Step One—Introduction

The goal of the introduction step is to prepare students for new learning. During this step, the teacher communicates the purpose for the lesson. The teacher also motivates students and gains their attention.

There are several ways to establish the purpose for learning. One method is for the teacher to share the objectives written in his or her lesson plan with the students. These objectives, or "learning goals," express what will be learned, how it will be learned, and how new learning will be demonstrated. Displaying objectives on a blackboard, interactive whiteboard, or handout is an effective way to introduce them. Introduction to the objectives provides students an advanced organizer, as well. Advanced organizers aid learning and retention. The sharing of "I can" statements—statements that express the learning objectives in student-friendly language—is another effective way for establishing the lesson purpose. "I can" statements clearly connect the curriculum standards with learning experiences. They are considered easier for students to comprehend than lesson objectives. An example of an "I can" statement from the Direct Instruction Model Lesson at the end of this chapter is, "I can create a simple concept map that demonstrates my understanding of animal classifications."

The purpose for learning is further established by providing the students with a general and specific rationale for their learning. The general rationale communicates why the learning is important to students in their lives. The specific rationale explains how new learning will contribute to their success in the unit of study or academic discipline. In Scenario 5-1, which appears later in this chapter, a PE teacher demonstrates this practice. She tells her kindergarteners that learning to do jumping jacks will promote their cardiovascular health and increase their coordination—making them more proficient in other physical activities, such as soccer.

Although establishing the purpose for a lesson by communicating to learners the objectives, "I can" statements and rationales may suffice, additional strategies may be needed. Asking a question during this step can increase student understanding of the purpose and objectives. For example, in the Direct Instruction Model Lesson at the end of the chapter, the teacher might ask, "Is there a visual way to organize our understanding of concepts?" Posing a question can help capture students' attention. In Scenario 5-2, a Science teacher might pique students' interest in learning to record scientific observations by asking, "I wonder what will happen if each of us records observations in a different manner?"

Step Two—Presentation

In this step, the teacher presents to the students the facts, procedures, or concept(s) addressed in the lesson. Depending on the content addressed in the lesson, the teacher might demonstrate a procedure, share the critical attributes for a concept, or teach factual knowledge during the presentation. Approaches for the presentation vary depending on the unique nature of the content being addressed. For example, procedural knowledge of how to do something might be demonstrated by the teacher with accompanying explanations. A concept's critical attributes might be illustrated using physical or digital photos. Facts might be taught through simple explanation and sharing or with additional resources. In the Direct Instruction Model Lesson at the end of this chapter, for example, the teacher simultaneously describes and demonstrates how to create a concept map.

Often, the presentation takes the form of a think-aloud. A **think-aloud** is a strategy where teachers share their thoughts out loud for the students to make their mental activity explicit. For instance, a teacher may present and simultaneously describe out loud how to solve a quadratic equation by explaining verbally the steps undertaken to solve the equation as well as the thinking involved about how to solve the equation.

Step Three—Guided Practice

In the guided practice step of the model, the teacher further addresses the content with an additional example, scenario, or problem. In this step, however, the students work along with the teacher, and the teacher provides guidance and feedback to students as they work. This practice challenges learners to transfer the knowledge they have been introduced to in Step One to a novel situation. By providing content information in small increments, the teacher supports the students and makes it easier for them to follow along. The Direct Instruction Model Lesson at the end of this chapter shows how a teacher guides students in the creation of a concept map.

Teachers can use various types of support during guided practice. The think-aloud strategy is a useful practice. It can also be beneficial to record the procedural steps that were demonstrated in short, written form where all students can see them. Many teachers find the use of a mnemonic device helps students during guided practice. A **mnemonic device** is a learning aid that provides a method of memorizing ideas and their order in a memorable sentence or word. The letters in the mnemonic corresponds in order with the first letter in each word of the sentence or each letter in a word. For example, in Scenario 5-3, the teacher provides students with the sentence, "**P**lease **e**xcuse **m**y **d**ear **A**unt **S**ally," to help students remember the mathematical order of operations—**P**arentheses, **E**xponents, **M**ultiplication, **D**ivision, **A**ddition, **S**ubtraction. Similarly, the word "FACE" might help learners remember the identity and order of notes read on the treble clef when learning music.

During the guided practice step, the teacher typically provides corrective feedback about a student's progress to address any mistakes or misunderstandings. This feedback should not be graded. Students must feel they can practice without the risk of being penalized for their failure. However, informally, recording some evidence of students' responses and behaviors is appropriate. This can provide a valuable forensic tool enabling analysis of students' learning process, struggles and successes.

During the guided practice step, teachers must observe their students' progress to confirm their students understand and are all progressing through their practice. Checking the rate of student progress is also a good idea. In the Direct Instruction Model Lesson at the end of this chapter, the teacher tells students that in this step she will be stopping to check how students are doing. Intermediate checks allow the teacher to determine if students comprehend the content and are working at the same pace. The hallmark of the guided practice step is the supportive interaction between the teacher and student. The teacher provides guidance required as needed to support the learner's acquisition of the new content. The support is gradually withdrawn as the learner becomes more independent.

Step Four—Independent Practice

During independent practice, students should work on their own and practice activities that are similar to those the teacher presented. Independent practice activities might involve additional problems or scenarios that are identical to those already completed or ones that apply learning in a new and novel context. As illustrated in the Direct Instruction Model Lesson Plan at the end of this chapter, students are given a lot of leeway for independently creating another concept map—provided they address the minimal requirements for the number of concepts and subordinate concepts in the concept map they are asked to create.

Depending on their objectives and the needs of their students, teachers may provide independent practice opportunities at varying levels of difficulty. For instance, a teacher who senses that her students need additional practice for reinforcement will likely assign problems or tasks at the same level of difficulty used in the guided practice step. However, a teacher who wants students to stretch their skills or apply them in a slightly more challenging context might provide a more rigorous level of independent practice. For example, using the Direct Instruction Model Lesson at the end of this chapter, the teacher might ask some students to include a larger number of subordinate concepts than other students. Regardless of the level of difficulty, it is important during the independent practice step that students practice the same content that the teacher introduced in the presentation and guided practice steps.

Students should only be asked to practice the content independently when they have had sufficient guided practice to create a solid foundation for their successful independent work. In this phase, evidence of student learning is often formally collected and evaluated to assess student understanding. The information the teacher gathers about student performance should also inform future lesson design. For example, in the Direct Instruction Model Lesson, the teacher asks students to submit their final concept maps created with the concept-mapping tool. Grading these concept maps provides information about which students have mastered the concept, and which ones need additional support or remediation.

What Does the Direct Instruction Model Look Like in the Classroom?

In the sections that follow, three scenarios illustrate possible ways that the Direct Instruction model might be applied in various classroom contexts. The scenarios demonstrate the model's suitability for teaching in different subject areas and grade levels. They also illustrate variations in how the model might be implemented. They depict different ways to share instructional goals, various means for presenting new information, and the integration of numerous teaching tools.

Scenario 5-1

In Patty Bilson's physical education class, 25 eager kindergarten students surround her. They are waiting attentively for her to teach them how to do jumping jacks. First she explains why they are going to learn to do jumping jacks—to promote their heart health and improve their coordination (which helps in other sports they will learn to play). Next, she explains the steps of the lesson and the lesson's progression. She says, "During this lesson, you will learn what a jumping jack is. Then you will learn to describe the correct way to do a jumping jack with words. Finally, you will do a jumping jack and practice it until you can do several correctly."

Thereafter, Patty demonstrates how to do jumping jacks correctly, with arms and feet moving in the correct position with the right timing. As she does so, her tablet computer records and projects her moves onto a large screen in the gym for all of the students to see.

After the demonstration, she plays the recording while also describing the attributes of a correctly performed jumping jack, which include: (1) jumping in place, (2) a two-part jump with an out/ up move and together/down move, (3) legs and feet moving outward and up, and (4) synchronizing the timing of hands and feet correctly.

Once students understand the attributes of correctly performed jumping jacks, they are asked to pair up and describe them to one another. She asks students to distinguish between the characteristics of a jumping jack done correctly from one done incorrectly. Then she asks her students to try doing jumping jacks with her. Afterwards she asks them to practice in pairs, videotape one another using their tablet computers, replay the video and discuss. Finally, as her students practice independently, Patty assesses their progress. She will repeat the assessment in other kindergarten PE classes until all of the students have mastered this skill.

Scenario 5-2

Students in Diane Stone's sixth-grade science class are learning about sustainable development. They have learned that butterflies are a key indicator species for the impact of land development in their California town. As part of a state-wide project, they are tracking data related to the types, numbers, and behaviors of butterflies they see in their schoolyard during a three-month time period. Later, they will share their data online with the project directors who will then combine it with that collected by other students throughout the state.

Their teacher will use the Direct Instruction model to teach her students how to conduct their observations. First, she will inform students that in this lesson they will learn the importance of consistency in scientific record keeping. She will outline methods to increase consistency across different "scientists" participating in their study, and ways they will record data about butterflies they see in their schoolyard. Diane decides to use the DVD video she received from the butterfly project to present the concept of "observation" and the importance of "consistency" in science. After this introduction, Diane will demonstrate how to (1) identify different types of butterflies, (2) recognize the behaviors of butterflies, (3) record an observation in a log book, and (4) enter this information into the online database.

She starts her presentation by showing a video of a butterfly she recorded using a digital camera. Then she demonstrates how to use a log book to record its behavior from a range of options they have already studied (including puddling, feeding, and basking) and identify its species by using a guidebook. Next, she takes the log book to a classroom computer and demonstrates how to enter the data from this observation in the butterfly project's online database. When she is finished presenting the procedures for observation, research, and recording of information, she asks questions to clarify understanding of this process.

The class then follows the process together. They watch another butterfly video and then collectively record the observation on the board so all can see how it is done. Then, they enter this information into the project database. They repeat this process two more times using two other videos. When all of the students feel fairly comfortable with this process, Diane asks them to try it on their own. At this point, those who are still feeling a little unsure of the order of steps can ask for a handout that lists and summarizes the steps in a table. Once the students demonstrate that they have mastered the observation process, they will be able to conduct and record observations in the school's butterfly garden.

Butterflies for Classification
© velora/Shutterstock

Scenario 5-3

Larry Karanfilov stands in front of his ninth-grade algebra 1 class and places on his overhead projector a transparency stating the learning goal, "Students will learn to evaluate
and simplify expressions by applying the order of operations and the properties of rational numbers." He explains to students that they must master this foundational content
before advancing to more complex algebra problems. After sharing this rationale, Larry
explains that they are going to review a procedure for solving complicated math problems that will make their work easier and more successful. The students mumble that
they already know how to do this, but Larry counters by explaining that over 85% of the
class got the process wrong on the pre-test. So, he is going to review this to ensure they
all know it. He realizes that sometimes math "academic vocabulary" complicates the
learning, so he takes a few moments to ensure all students understand the terms "simplify" and "expression" the way he intends to use them.

   After his explanation, Larry writes "$3 + 1^2 \times 5 \div 2 - 3$" and also the mnemonic "Please
Excuse My Dear Aunt Sally" on the board. He explains to his students that this is a way of
remembering the order in which mathematical operations must be performed when solving complex problems. Several students cry out, "I remember now!"

Next, Larry writes the words "parentheses," "exponents," "multiplication," "division," "addition," and "subtraction" vertically under each letter of the mnemonic. Then, he rewrites the expression to include parentheses, such as "$(3 + 1)^2 \times (5 \div 2) - 3$" and models how to reevaluate the expression using the mnemonic. He models and explains how to solve the problem using the order of operations.

Next the class tries guided practice. During this step of the lesson, Larry asks each student to use a marker and small dry-erase board to write the expression $9 - x + 1 + 3x$. Larry then asks students to use the mnemonic to help them simplify it using the order of operations—together. This is accomplished simultaneously with Larry asking students what to do next and him modeling, explaining, and correcting them as they make suggestions to solve the problem. Even though each student has his or her own dry-erase board, the class works through the same problem at the same time. The practice is collective, not individual.

After Larry has guided students in solving three different problems, Larry asks them to try a few problems in pairs. Circulating around the room while they work, he can see who is struggling and provide one-on-one guidance and support. For the next round of problems, he asks the students to use the digital video cameras to record their answers. He asks students to share their videos with their peers to check their procedures for solving the problems. At the end of the class, Larry asks students to complete a practice problem on an exit card independently. He collects these cards as students leave the classroom. He will review them before they return the next day and be prepared to provide appropriate follow-up based on evidence of their understanding from this lesson.

What Do These Scenarios Illustrate?

These scenarios show just some of the varied contexts in which the Direct Instruction model can be used. The teachers in the three scenarios use different tools and techniques, and work with learners in various subjects and grade levels, yet each implementation of the model progresses through the same basic steps in a predictable order. In each scenario, teachers established the purpose for learning, presented new information, and then provided their students opportunities for guided and independent practice. Students were actively involved when the teacher presented new information. They were also engaged during the guided practice, even as the teacher gradually withdrew support in response to their growing proficiency. Nonetheless, in each circumstance instruction was teacher led and directed.

Despite the uniform application of the process, each teacher incorporated different technology tools in his or her lesson. The support that each teacher gave his or her students varied, as did the strategies each teacher proposed for practicing the new content. These variations accommodated teacher style, the unique nature of the content being addressed, and needs of the learners involved. The Direct Instruction model promotes quality implementation through consistently used and ordered steps, and it is flexible enough to work with various types of content and settings.

REFLECT: Take a moment to examine each of these scenarios and the types of technologies utilized. What other variations did you notice? Describe how you might modify the Direct Instruction model based on your own teaching style. How might those modifications benefit your particular student population?

Planning for Teaching with the Direct Instruction Model

Success with the Direct Instruction model requires that it be used to address content that has clearly defined attributes or steps. The selection of appropriate content is one important consideration to address when planning to teach with the model. Other measures teachers should take are to (1) develop clear goals and expectations, (2) review the knowledge/skills being taught, and (3) select appropriate problems and examples to use. These are described in the sections that follow.

Choose Factual, Conceptual, or Procedural Knowledge That Has Clearly Defined Attributes or Steps

As previously addressed, the Direct Instruction model is most effective when teaching factual, conceptual, or procedural knowledge that has clearly identified attributes or steps. Knowledge that has vague, complex, or inconsistently defined characteristics is not well-suited for teaching with the Direct Instruction model. Not only will it be difficult to break down such content into steps or easily identified attributes for presentation and practice, it will also be difficult to articulate and measure successful learning demonstrated by students.

Develop Clear Goals and Expectations

All lessons should have clear goals and expectations. For the Direct Instruction model, clear goals and expectations also need to be developed for each individual step. Otherwise, progression from the guided practice step to independent practice step is not possible. If the lesson goals and expectations are not known, a teacher cannot identify when students are capable of moving on to work independently.

Sometimes the effort to develop goals and expectations is helped by imagining what students will be able to know or be able to do at the end of the lesson. For example, in Scenario 5-1, Patty has thought through what it looks like for students to perform a jumping jack successfully and knows what students must be able to do before independent practice takes place. She has identified that a correct jumping jack must involve (1) jumping in place, (2) a two-part jump with one move out/ up and another together/down, (3) legs and feet moving outward and up, and (4) synchronizing the timing of hands and feet correctly. Patty's advance identification of these expectations allows her to consider what foundational knowledge or skills students might need for success. This awareness puts Patty in a position of knowing how better to coach and support her students as they work in the guided practice step. The result is more successful learning for all.

Review the Knowledge and Skills to Be Taught

During the planning stage for the Direct Instruction model lesson, teachers should review the content they will address to ensure that they do not overlook an important detail that students need to know or step they must perform. Because teachers have mastery of the content they will teach, they are often disconnected with the experiences and understandings of their students. As teachers spend time working through the facts, concepts, or procedures to be taught, they also need to think creatively about how learners might experience the learning in the lesson. Visualizing the lesson from the students' point of view gives teachers perspective about areas where additional clarification or other support might be needed. For example, in Scenario 5-3, Larry Karanfilov identifies that some academic vocabulary demands related to his lesson might present problems for some learners. As a result, he makes sure to clarify what he means when he uses the terms "simplify" and "expression" in his lesson. He thereby increases the chances that his students will actually comprehend his demonstrations and be able to practice the order of operations successfully.

Select Appropriate Problems, Examples, or Models

Student success during the various steps of the model is influenced by the quality of problems, examples, or models used when presenting the content. The best items for use in guided practice and independent practice are those which relate directly to the content that has been presented and are chosen to represent different and increasing levels of difficulty. In Scenario 5-2, Diane uses several different video recordings of butterflies to present the procedure for making and recording scientific observations. Each video recording she chooses should demonstrate one or more of the behaviors she is asking students to observe. As a collection, the recordings should cover observations at various levels of difficulty, and Diane should allow students to experience those behaviors in increasing levels of difficulty during the guided practice and independent practice. In this way, students can get support doing more difficult work with their teacher and also experience success working independently.

Differentiating Instruction with the Direct Instruction Model

The Direct Instruction model is popular because it works across content areas and grade levels, and with learners of varying abilities. The model has inherent features that support learners with different interests, readiness, and learning profiles, yet it can be modified according to the content of instruction, learning process, and methods for evaluation of student learning. In the sections that follow, we address some possible methods for differentiating the Direct Instruction model. Additional examples for differentiating instruction can be found in the Direct Instruction Model Lesson at the end of this chapter.

Content

Teachers who differentiate instruction hold high expectations for all learners and do not differentiate the content that is learned (the curriculum standards) by expecting less of some learners. Instead, they attempt to support the differentiation of content by differentiating how their students access or experience the content.

Traditionally, a teacher would use real-time demonstrations in front of a whole class or small group to present new content and provide opportunities for guided practice. One simple way to differentiate the presentation of content is allowing students to access the demonstration in recorded format after they have already experienced it in person. A recorded presentation has two distinct advantages: it can be replayed multiple times and also manipulated (i.e., sped up, paused, or slowed down) as needed. For example, while teaching the order of operations in Scenario 5-3, Larry might record a video demonstration of his lesson on the order of operations. The video would capture his demonstration and enable it to be posted and shared in the class online course management system. This would provide students the opportunity to review different parts of the demonstration, if needed, using the play, pause, and stop features of the video. Larry could also create a screencast or Khan Academy-like video (see www.khanacademy.org) demonstration using a computer screencast tool modeling the procedure and then sharing it in a similar fashion.

Differentiated access to the content can also be achieved by creating alternatives to a teacher demonstration. Some options for the presentation of new content could be a pre-recorded video, audio recording, animation, or simulation. These materials, if presented in multimedia format provide some obvious advantages over traditional, real-time demonstrations. In addition to the advantages of recorded demonstrations mentioned previously, they also allow for presentation of (1) more varied information, (2) more voluminous information, (3) information that comes from a context outside the classroom, or (4) more engaging information. The importance of these additional advantages will depend on the goals for instruction.

Process

The very design of the Direct Instruction model supports the needs of diverse learners during the learning process. The model's steps include a straightforward and logical process for presenting new information that supports students who benefit from structured learning experiences (e.g., students with attention difficulties). The model also helps students such as English Language Learners who benefit from initial direct teacher support that gradually decreases as their student proficiency develops.

Teachers using the Direct Instruction model can differentiate the process by infusing variety in student groupings and offering different choices for practicing the content. Instead of moving through each model step as a whole class, students can be divided into pairs or small groups during any step of the model. Working with a partner or group might particularly benefit students with interpersonal strengths and allow them to receive more peer-to-peer support and scaffolding. Students might also benefit by participating in a think-pair-share, an activity where they can discuss their understanding of the content with a partner. This activity enables students to consider what they know and enables interactions in a nonthreatening manner before ideas are shared with teachers or other classmates. Likewise, students might have the opportunity to work in small pairs during guided practice and in small groups for independent practice.

Teachers might also differentiate the learning process by giving students a choice from several different graphic organizers to use for recording their understanding of the content. For instance, a teacher might give students the choice of a KWLH chart (see Worksheet 5-1), a two-column notes page, or the "empty bucket" organizer (see Worksheet 5-2) for scaffolding the content. All worksheets appear in Appendix C.

Product

In the Direct Instruction model, differentiating the learning product involves providing multiple ways for students to demonstrate their learning during the independent practice step. Students might be assigned a specific option for expression of learning or they might be allowed to make their own choice from a reasonable range of options. In some cases, this means allowing students to select a topic of their own interest to demonstrate their learning. In other cases, choice involves giving students a menu of assessment options from which to choose.

For example, in the Direct Instruction Model Lesson at the end of this chapter, the teacher demonstrates how to develop a concept map using a concept-mapping tool. Students need to indicate that they know what a concept map entails and understand how to develop one using the tool. For their independent practice, students might be allowed to create a concept map representing any content they choose provided they meet their teacher's requirement for performance—including one main concept, five subordinate concepts, and linking words. Or, the teacher could provide a menu of options for students to apply the content addressed in the lesson. Some options could be creating a concept map on the different classes of animals (e.g., vertebrates or mammals), drawing an original concept map on a concept of their own choosing, or developing a partially completed concept map with an answer key for other students to solve. Wise teachers use choice to motivate students for learning tasks.

What Are the Benefits of Applying the Direct Instruction Model?

The Direct Instruction model has decades of research demonstrating its effectiveness. It helps teach students how to think, fosters independence, and develops automaticity. Teachers functioning as educational designers will want to consider these benefits as they match tools, such as the instructional models in this text, with the standards they must teach and their students' varied needs. The Direct Instruction Model:

Helps to Develop Thinking Skills

The Direct Instruction model is an excellent model for teaching linear thinking and problem solving. It is logical, sequential, and detailed. Students observe teachers modeling and presenting the content to be learned and then work with this content through guided and independent practice. Through the structure of guided and independent practice in the model, students learn to think in a disciplined and organized manner. The process prepares them for experiences that involve more detailed and sophisticated logical patterns such as the scientific method and the SQ3R (survey, question, read, recite, review) reading method. For instance, in Scenario 5-2, students learn how to identify butterflies and record their observations. Their teacher, Diane, demonstrates how each part of this process is performed and then facilitates students' coordination of each detailed step in a logical order. This experience prepares students to apply thinking skills in a procedural manner and perform more complex scientific observations in the future.

Helps to Develop Automaticity

The Direct Instruction model develops **automaticity**, the ability to complete a task automatically. The ability to multiply two numbers without deep thought is an example of automaticity. The Direct Instruction model helps develop automaticity through practice, both guided and independent. For instance, in Scenario 5-3, ninth-graders review the order of operations. After sufficient guided and independent practice, the students should have learned the order of operations and be able to implement it with accuracy—and without having to expend much energy on thinking. This automaticity will save them time and energy as they progress in their mathematical studies, and allow them to problem solve with more ease.

Fosters Independent Learning

A major benefit of the Direct Instructional model is that it promotes content mastery and develops students' ability to complete a task independently. The Direct Instruction model encourages and supports students, as they learn and work to become independent when practicing skills. It provides clear learning targets with guidance and feedback that is gradually reduced as learning occurs.

Promotes Knowledge of Self

As students participate in the Direct Instruction model, they have the opportunity to learn about themselves, as well as about the content. They can learn about their ability to think procedurally, pay attention, attend to details, and work carefully. Because this model involves interactions with the teacher during the guided practice stage, students can receive corrective feedback about their learning and the skills they are learning. This is evident in Scenario 5-1. As kindergarteners learn how to do jumping jacks, they receive supportive input from their teacher and their peers.

What Value Does Technology Add to the Direct Instruction Model?

Technology may be utilized in many different ways to enhance the experience of students and teachers in the Direct Instruction model. The examples that follow demonstrate how technology might make the model more efficient, effective, and engaging while planning, implementing, and developing assessments in the model. Figure 5-3 lists and describes numerous technologies introduced in this chapter that support teaching using the Direct Instruction model.

Planning

Technology can serve as an excellent tool for teachers when planning a Direct Instruction model lesson. Use of web-based search engines such as Google can make it easy to find useful teaching resources. Multimedia encyclopedias available online and as apps continue to be an excellent resource for factual, procedural, and conceptual content. The use of these tools can yield many ideas for the development of lesson plans and resources for teaching. Teachers can also find videos, animations, and other resources that are beneficial during the introduction step. Some teachers rely on free resources, such as "TeacherTube," a video sharing website with an education focus, to get ideas for how to demonstrate content, for example "How to write a DBQ (document based question)" or "How to do long division." Other teachers and school districts subscribe to web-based multimedia services like BrainPop.com (www.brainpop.com) and Discovery Education Streaming (http://streaming.discoveryeducation.com) that provide access to extensive databases of multimedia teaching materials. Khan Academy (www.khanacademy.org)

Figure 5-3 Technology Tools for the Direct Instruction Model

Use	Tools
Planning	
Checking procedures, getting ideas for demonstrations, recording practice	Tools for developing content demonstrations • Encyclopedias • Internet Search Engine Tools providing content demonstrations • Discovery Education Streaming: http://streaming.discoveryeducation.com • BrainPop: www.brainpop.com Tools for recording content demonstrations • Tape Recorders • Digital Cameras • Digital Audio Recorders
Implementing	
Supporting guided practice and independent practice	Tools for screen recording • SMART Notebook Recorder tool: www.smarttech.com • Camtasia: www.camtasiasoftware.com Tools for demonstrating content • TeacherTube: www.teachertube.com
Assessing	
Demonstrating knowledge during assessment	Creating assessment tools • Quizstar: http://quizstar.4teachers.org • Quia: www.quia.com Audience response systems (clickers) • SMART Response interactive response systems: http://www2.smarttech.com/st/en-US/Products/SMART+Response • Turning Technologies: www.turningtechnologies.com/studentresponsesystem Demonstrating student learning • PowerPoint • Prezi: www.prezi.com • Digital video camera • Smartphone or tablet computer camera Sound recording • Audacity: http://audacity.sourceforge.net • Digital audio recorder • Portable media player (e.g., iPod, MP3 players) • VoiceThread: http://voicethread.com/#home

is another popular resource for materials that could be used during planning or during the implementation of the model. This resource could be a helpful tool if teachers need to refresh their understanding of the procedures, concepts, or other content they are teaching.

Another way technology facilitates planning is by allowing teachers to practice their lessons before delivering them. Because the success of a lesson based on the Direct

Instruction model is largely determined by how well a teacher plans and demonstrates the content the lesson addresses, it often helps to practice the lesson before actually teaching it in front of a class. Setting up a video camera, or audio recorder, and practicing the demonstration is helpful in a few ways. First, it gives the teacher a chance to think through the various steps of the procedure and consider how these might be received by (or pose problems) for their students. Insights gained during this practice can make a teacher more aware of how to convey important details to students. Second, recording a dry run provides the teacher a way to practice and check for misstatements or mistakes that might be made during the real presentation with students. Even the simplest of stumbles can cause confusion or introduce errors in students' learning. By reviewing a recorded practice run, a teacher can ensure he or she will correctly perform the demonstration in the lesson. Third, providing a record of the demonstration provides students the opportunity to refer to it later and as many times as they desire. In some cases, students who need to see the demonstration a second or third time might watch or listen to the demonstration as a refresher or to provide additional reinforcement.

Implementation

Various technologies can be useful during the steps of the Direct Instruction model. During the introduction phase, various tools might be incorporated to enhance the presentation of new information. Archives of past learning or a preview of what will be introduced in the lesson might be presented using video or audio clips of the procedure to be taught. In the presentation step, a multimedia demonstration that includes slides with graphics, audio, and/or simulations might provide a more accurate and information-rich explanation of a process. For example, when teaching how to create a concept map (see the Direct Instruction Model Lesson), the various steps involved could be recorded so that students can repeat these steps as needed. Using technology in this manner provides more and different information for students. Technology allows teachers to connect with experts in the field even when there are none close by. For example, instead of presenting the content herself, a teacher could use a video presentation featuring an expert to introduce the content. Such videos are often available using an online service like Discovery Education Streaming (http://streaming.discoveryeducation.com) or TeacherTube (www.teachertube.com). Sometimes experts can even present the new information in a Direct Instruction model lesson using live videoconferencing tools and a webcam. In this way, the teacher provides students with a different presentation of content that might be more credible or reliable than that which he or she might be able to provide. If experts are used, the teacher should make sure the expert understands how to present content in ways that are appropriate for the students.

Technology might also assist in the guided practice step of the model. A teacher might make use of technology to give students additional opportunities or different opportunities for guided practice. For example, a teacher might use recording tools, available in most interactive whiteboards, to make a video and audio recording of additional examples for reducing a fraction. Camtasia is another commercially available software tool for making, editing, and combining video and audio with screen shots. Students who need more practice before working on their own might watch recordings tailored for extra reinforcement. Also, students who are absent can watch how to solve a problem when reviewing this video.

Depending on the content being addressed, technology might also be used in the independent practice step of the Direct Instruction model. Technology gives students the opportunity to choose the medium they would like to use for practicing the content they need to learn. For example, if a teacher is teaching how to diagram sentences, students might choose between practicing this skill with pencil and paper (see Figure 5-4), a word processor (see Figure 5-5), or stylus and tablet

Figure 5-4   Example of a Paper/Pencil Sentence Diagram

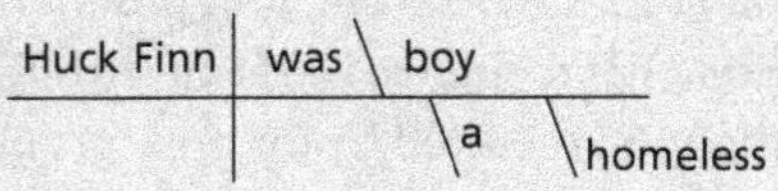

Huck Finn | was \ boy
            \a \homeless

Figure 5-5   Example of a Word-Processed Sentence Diagram

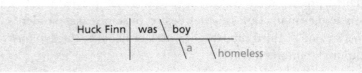

Huck Finn | was \ boy
            \a \homeless

computer. Students might be responsible for creating a simple presentation using a tool like PowerPoint or Prezi (www.prezi.com), that demonstrates each step and its significance in order. Another option might be for students to record themselves demonstrating new content using previously mentioned tools, share it, and invite comments using an online tool such as VoiceThread (http://voicethread.com).

Assessment

Various technology tools can support the assessment cycle throughout the steps of the Direct Instruction model, but technology is particularly useful during the guided practice and independent practice steps.

During both of these steps, audio and video technologies can be useful tools that allow information about students' learning as it happens and after it happens to be captured. Audio can be recorded using simple tape recorders (which many schools still have and function reliably), digital voice recorders, certain cell phones or mp3 players, and free, open-source tools such as Audacity (http://audacity.sourceforge.net). Video can be recorded using many smartphones, tablet computers, webcams, and digital video cameras. When these tools are used to record student learning, it is possible to closely analyze and gain insight into students' learning. When teachers and students use audio and video tools to record, play, replay, and watch video in slow motion, it is possible to see how various procedures are learned and how well they are accomplished. VoiceThread, a multimedia-centered discussion tool (www.voicethread.com), supports additional communication related to student learning. Students using VoiceThread can upload video and audio materials that demonstrate their learning and share them using VoiceThread's web-based environment. Tools like VoiceThread increase student motivation by easily expanding the learners' audience—allowing them to present their attainment of procedures learned with the Direct Instruction model to their peers and others online, ideally in secure environments. As shown in Scenario 5-3, students who learn to apply the order of operations can demonstrate their competence by recording it with a digital video camera. They might be encouraged to share their videos using the VoiceThread website, where classmates and the teacher can view and comment on this student's degree of success. (Any time students are photographed, recorded, or videotaped, teachers need to secure permission from students and their parents or guardians, as well as make appropriate provisions for protecting student privacy.)

Technology-supported quizzes presented using software or online applications, such as Quizstar (http://quizstar.4teachers.org) and Quia (www.quia.com), can also be helpful during the guided practice and independent practice steps. These tools make it easy to assess students' learning of the content being addressed using the model. Audience response systems, or "clickers," present another high-tech way to conduct formative and summative assessment during the Direct Instruction model. As these tools rely heavily on multiple choice and True/False questions, teachers need to take particular care to craft questions that assess students' understanding of various procedures. For example, in the Direct Instruction Model Lesson at the end of the chapter, the teacher might develop some scenarios of how to create a concept map, some of which are wrong and some of which are correct. Then, the teacher could ask students to click on their answer. Within seconds, the teacher and the students can see the number correct and incorrect. If many students select the wrong answer, the teacher will know to review the procedures through guided practice or choose another way to introduce the material. Because displaying class results is optional, teachers can use audience response systems to deliver traditional summative assessment, as well.

Direct Instruction Model Lesson Plan Example

The Direct Instruction Model Lesson serves as an illustration of how the Direct Instruction model might be implemented using simple technologies found in most classrooms. See Figure 5-6 for a breakdown of the steps as they would occur in the lesson.

Figure 5-6   Outline of the Direct Instruction Model Lesson Steps

Direct Instruction Model Steps	Direct Instruction Model Lesson
Introduction	Teacher describes lesson objectives to students. Students watch and listen to the teacher.
Presentation	Teacher presents new content and demonstrates concept mapping. Teacher shows how to create a concept map using a concept-mapping tool. The teacher explains each step in creating a concept map as he or she creates it. Students watch and listen.
Guided Practice	Teacher demonstrates how to create a concept map using concept-mapping tool, as students create their own concept map too. Teacher watches and advises students as they practice and stops to ensure that all students are creating their own concept maps at the same pace.
Independent Practice	Students create their own concept maps independently using a concept-mapping tool. As students create their concept maps, the teacher circulates around the room to provide assistance as needed. This work will be assessed later to ensure understanding of the new content.

LESSON CONTEXT

GRADE LEVEL(S): Third to high school levels

CONTENT AREA: Language arts—but can be modified for any subject area and grade level

PHYSICAL TEACHING ENVIRONMENT: This lesson will be taught in a computer lab with one computer per student with computers facing the projector in the front.

APPLICATION OF REVISED BLOOM'S TAXONOMY: This lesson requires students to use the remembering and creating levels of the revised Bloom's taxonomy because students apply their knowledge about creating concept maps independently.

Lesson Plan

GOAL: Students will learn about concept mapping.

Standard(s) Addressed:

ISTE NETS For Students 2007 #3[1]

OBJECTIVES:

1. Students will describe what they know about concept maps by illustrating what they have learned about concept maps on a sheet of paper.
2. Students will be able to develop a basic concept map using concept-mapping tool with 100% accuracy.

ESTIMATED TIME: approximately 30 minutes

MATERIALS NEEDED:

- PowerPoint lesson on graphic organizers (provide both hard and digital copies for each student)
- Concept-mapping tool (software such as Gliffy: www.gliffy.com, Inspiration: www.inspiration.com, SmartDraw: www.smartdraw.com, or Visio: http://office.microsoft.com/en-us/visio/default.aspx)
- Teacher workstation connected to a projector

PREREQUISITE SKILLS: Learners should have experience working on a computer.

NOTE: (1) Items that are in italics are to be spoken by the teacher. (2) Specific instructions for using your choice of concept-mapping tool may be different.

LESSON PROCEDURES (Text in italics is suggested teacher dialogue.)

Anticipatory Set (Introduction): [4 minutes]

Motivation *Have you ever had trouble understanding how topics or concepts were related in any of the classes you have taken? Do you think it would have helped if your teacher had given you an outline or visual representation of what you were to learn before he or she taught the unit?*

---

[1]National Educational Technology Standards for Students (NETS·S), Second Edition © 2007 ISTE ® (International Society for Technology in Education), www.iste.org. All rights reserved.

Information   *I imagine some type of visual representation would have helped you learn some topics better. Today you are going to learn what graphic organizers are. Also, you will learn how to create a specific type of graphic organizer called a concept map. You will create a basic concept map by following along as I show you how to create one using a concept-mapping tool.*

Connection   *What do you know about graphic organizers? Fold a piece of paper in half and then in half again (so you have four squares). Draw a line to divide the paper into four squares. On the left side, write everything you know or think you know about graphic organizers and concept maps. Do not write anything on the right side. You will write what you learned about graphic organizers and concept maps at the end of this lesson.*

EXAMPLE:

What I know about graphic organizers	What I learned about graphic organizers
What I know about concept maps	What I learned about concept maps

Presentation: [5 minutes]
Now I will demonstrate how to create a concept map. As I demonstrate each step, I will explain it using a "think-aloud strategy" where I will explain what I am doing, as well as share my thinking, while I do it. I will also record this using the video camera, so you can review how to make a concept map later on.

The teacher now models the creation of a concept map (see Figure 5-7 Concept Map) while students watch, using a computer, projector, and the concept mapping tool.

Guided Practice: [10 minutes]

The teacher explains the various steps required to create the concept map, as she and the class create one together about invertebrates.

Figure 5-7 Concept Map

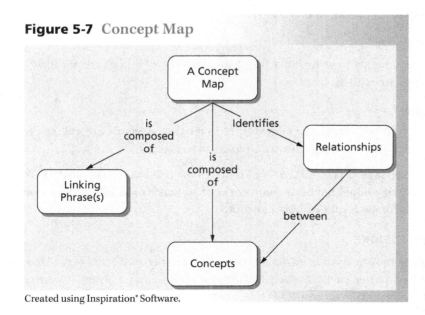

Created using Inspiration® Software.

Ask students to open concept-mapping tool on their computers.

Explain and show the different "views" in the concept-mapping tool (e.g., in Inspiration: Diagram & Outline).

Explain: *We are going to create a concept map about invertebrates together—The purpose of this exercise is to learn how to create a simple concept map using a concept-mapping tool—it is not for you to explore. You will have time to do that later.*

Ask students to click in the box that says "main idea" and type "Invertebrates."

There are a number of ways in which you can create the subordinate concept. The way I will show you now is by first clicking on the "main idea" oval so that you see little tiny boxes around it. Now you can create a linked subordinate concept by clicking on the appropriate "create" item on the menu. Since we are going to have five different "parts," let's create five subordinate ovals. Watch how I do it, and create these yourself too. Please raise your hand if I go too fast. Also, I will be stopping and walking around to ensure you are all creating concept maps at the same pace. Please do not move ahead.

Now, let's reorganize these ovals so they appear in a hierarchy.

Type the word "are" as the "linking verb" between the main concept and the subcategories.

Let's change the links to make them angled rather than straight. Press down on the mouse over the entire concept map. Now go to the word "Link" at the top of the menu and release the mouse on "Auto 90".

Let's add the following items for each sub-category: Phylum Mollusca, Phylum Echinodermata, Phylum Arthropoda.

Under each subcategory, add one subcategory and type "such as." The teacher then demonstrates how to add graphics, change color, font, links, etc.

Independent Practice: [10 minutes]

Students work independently to create a similar concept map based on an example given to them such as "vertebrates." (For this example, see Figure 5-8.)

They should create a concept map that consists of one main concept and three subordinate concepts. They should also include linking words to demonstrate relationships, as they saw in the presentation and did in the guided practice. Figure 5-8 is an example of a concept map students might create.

Closure: [2 minutes]

Teacher asks students to write what they learned in their "K-L" charts (or use 3-2-1 type activity to restate student learning).

ASSESSMENT

Formative assessment Teacher walks around to see that students are able to create a sample concept map based on the example given to them.

Summative assessment The unit concept map will be used as the summative assessment. The concept map should have one main concept, at least three subordinate concepts, and linking words for each subordinate concept.

LESSON EXTENSIONS

Concept maps may be used in various subject areas to help students organize and compare subject matter. To demonstrate their learning, students can be given concept maps with incomplete information or be asked to create them from scratch.

Figure 5-8   Vertebrates Concept Map

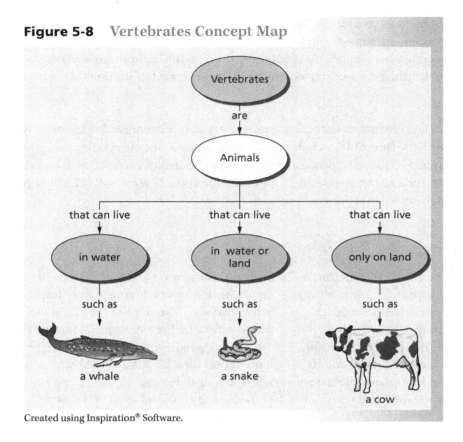

Created using Inspiration® Software.

Differentiation Strategies for the Direct Instruction Model Lesson

Below are some strategies one might apply to differentiate instruction in the Direct Instruction Model Lesson.

Content

Although the content of instruction usually cannot be differentiated, it is possible to differentiate the materials used to present that content information. Simple possibilities include varying who or what presents the information (i.e., a person, video, computer program, another student, etc.). In this lesson, information about graphic organizers could be presented in several ways. First, students might experience a recorded and narrated PowerPoint presentation delivered by their teacher made using a screen-capture tool (such as Camtasia). Another way to vary the content presentation would be to provide support for hearing-impaired students by having the teacher wear an augmentative device. By amplifying the teacher's voice, students who have auditory difficulties are better able to receive important information. The information in PowerPoint could also be provided in a printed outline format to all students or just those who need it.

Process

The Direct Instruction model always follows the steps indicated; however, the grouping of students and the tools used to support learning (i.e., manipulatives, instructional handouts, kinds of instructions provided in these handouts) may be varied. Intentional homogeneous and heterogeneous groupings can be used. For example, the students might be asked to work together in groups to complete the graphic organizer at the beginning of the lesson or to scaffold student learning more effectively during the guided practice portions of the model.

Product

The type of final product expected from students may be differentiated in several ways. For instance, with the Direct Instruction Model Lesson students may use concept-mapping tools (e.g., Inspiration software) or pencil and paper. Offering students a choice as to how they might demonstrate their learning—as long as they show mastery of the content presented and practiced through guided practice—is beneficial.

Chapter Summary

This chapter introduced the Direct Instruction model— a teacher-directed approach for teaching factual, procedural, and conceptual knowledge across subject areas and grade levels. Though perceived as a "traditional" model of instruction, it has become a perennial favorite in classrooms because it is highly efficient in its use of instructional time and effective when matched with appropriate content.

In this model, the teacher's role is to introduce the content in a direct or prescriptive way. The student's role is to learn and repeat the procedures taught and apply the same procedures to novel situations. Teacher direction and guidance provided in the model are gradually decreased as students become more independent, skilled, and capable practicing and applying the new procedures, skills, and knowledge. Participation in the model fosters students' ability to think in linear, logical,

and procedural ways and to function independently while also developing their automaticity and self-knowledge. The steps of the model include (1) Introduction, (2) Presentation, (3) Guided Practice, and (4) Independent Practice. Each step provides less support for students as their competence with new learning develops.

Technology is useful in all of the model's steps. It is particularly helpful for recording the teacher's presentation of content and capturing student practice for formative and summative assessment. Differentiation can be incorporated in the model through the support provided by the teacher. Additional methods of differentiation include varying the presentation of content and demonstration of student learning. The model is a traditional one but as important as ever to 21st century learners who must learn factual, procedural, and conceptual knowledge in efficient ways.

Review Questions

1. What is the history of the Direct Instruction model?

2. What are the steps of the Direct Instruction model?

3. What type of content is best to teach when applying the Direct Instruction model? Provide and explain examples of content that would be appropriate and inappropriate.

4. What are the benefits of applying the Direct Instruction model? What are some of the challenges?

5. How can the Direct Instruction model be used to differentiate instruction and support diverse learners' needs?

6. How can technology be used to implement the Direct Instruction model?

Application Exercises

To promote your ability to apply the learning you gained in studying this chapter, please complete the following exercises that challenge you to analyze a lesson plan you have written using the Direct Instruction model OR using the lesson plan example included at the end of this chapter. These exercises are designed to help you to (1) develop and build your Technological Pedagogical Content Knowledge, (2) increase your ability to integrate technology more effectively into the model, (3) expand the skills, knowledge, and dispositions required to learn from practice, and (4) become a more intentional teacher and a better educational designer.

TECHNOLOGY INTEGRATION ACTIVITY

1. Consider the following and discuss with a partner or reflect independently.
   a) In the lesson plan you are analyzing, how does (or could) the integration of technology tools make learning more efficient, effective, and engaging? Can you explain and indicate how the impact on student learning might be measured?
   b) Will all learners be aided through the integration of technology? Are there some who might need special support to gain full benefit from technology tools? How might you support this? Is there a way to leverage your students' strengths in technology to the benefit of this lesson? How?
   c) What plans could you put in place to promote more successful use of technology and minimize (or eliminate) risk of failure? What proactive plan could you put in place ahead of lesson implementation to ensure technology works smoothly and for all learners? What reactive approach could you take to ensure desired learning still occurs if technology malfunctions during the lesson?

TEACHER PERFORMANCE ACTIVITIES

2. **Academic Vocabulary and Language Demands:** Academic vocabulary is the vocabulary that students must be able to understand to be successful performing content area learning.

Language demands involve the ways language is used in speaking, writing, listening, and reading in the learning tasks of a lesson and expressions of student learning. In the context of the lesson plan you are working with (your own or the one provided in the chapter), consider the following questions and discuss them with a partner or reflect on them alone.
   a) What academic vocabulary and language demands exist in the lesson? Make a list of the academic vocabulary students must comprehend and language demands of the Direct Instruction model or learning experiences in the lesson plan.
   b) How would you determine whether and which students have mastery of the academic language before the lesson begins?
   c) How might students be supported in developing proficiency with academic language in this lesson context?

3. **Planning:** In the context of the lesson plan that you are analyzing, discuss the following with a partner or reflect independently.
   a) Explain how the steps of the Direct Instruction model build on each other to lead students to make clear and meaningful connections among identified learning goals or objectives.
   b) Consider how you have addressed or might address a variety of learning needs.
   c) What research or theory supports the use of this model for instruction in your learning context?

4. **Implementation:** In the context of the lesson plan that you are analyzing, discuss the following with a partner or consider these independently:
   a) Explain how the steps of the Direct Instruction model and the activities that students will perform in the lesson you are reviewing will result in engaged learning. What indicators would you look for during the implementation of your lesson to measure who is engaged and how much?
   b) How well does your lesson challenge learners to apply their learning in meaningful contexts? Explain.

5. **Assessment:** Consider the following and discuss with a partner or reflect independently.

a) Does the plan you are reviewing make use of information gained through pre-assessment to inform the design of the lesson? Would consideration of students' backgrounds, prior learning, and experiences as they relate to learning goals/objectives help you design a more effective lesson? How?

b) How does or could the lesson plan you are reviewing use formative assessment to direct the more successful implementation of instruction? Is there a way to make it more intentional or improve it to address students' strengths or learning needs?

c) How does the plan you are reviewing support students' expression of learning? Are there multiple forms of evidence of student learning? How might students learn through an analysis of their performance?

6. **Analyzing Teaching:** Consider the following issues, and discuss them with a partner or reflect independently.

a) Now that you have created and/or analyzed a lesson plan using the Direct Instruction model, consider how the model supports effective teaching. Can you cite specific evidence or references that support your claim? Be specific in expressing your ideas.

b) What did you learn from this activity that might inform your future practice?

Discussion Question

The Direct Instruction model is often described as a teacher-centered model of teaching. However, it is a very effective model for teaching procedural skills. Describe how you have used or plan to use the Direct Instruction model in your own teaching. Explain why. What are the benefits and challenges of using this model in your teaching?

Journal Entry

Describe a lesson when you learned *how to do* something new in one of your courses. Write down the different steps that helped you learn most and explain why. Explain how these steps relate to the steps in the Direct Instruction model.

Resources

- National Institute for Direct Instruction—This site provides information about the Direct Instruction model developed by Siegfried Engelmann and Wesley Becker: www.nifdi.org

- Procedural Tasks—This resource provides an excellent description of what procedural tasks are: www.indiana.edu/~idtheory/methods/m4b.html

- Think-Aloud Strategy—This resource offers a description of the think-aloud strategy, including why it is an important strategy: www.teachervision.fen.com/skill-builder/problem-solving/48546.html

Model	Concept Attainment Model
Knowledge Supported	Conceptual Knowledge
Added Value	Supports development of critical-thinking skills—specifically deductive reasoning, discrimination, and generalization
Technologies to Integrate	• Online reference tools for planning
	• Concept-mapping tools for thinking through concepts
	• Image and multimedia search tools for generating examples and nonexamples
	• Multimedia presentation tools for sharing examples and nonexamples
	• Digital projection, interactive whiteboards, and creativity tools to aid presentation
	• Web 2.0 tools to facilitate sharing
	• Audience response systems to aid assessment
	• Screen recording for review
	• Smartpen and tablet computers to support differentiation

The Concept Attainment Model

ajt/Shutterstock

Suzy Robertson-Christoff, a middle-school art teacher, had been teaching the concept of "symmetry" to her seventh-graders for the last five years. She was aware that students had to learn the concept to meet the state standards, but she also recognized that they needed it as a foundation for other key concepts in art, as well as in subjects such as biology and mathematics. Before they could relate to art in more sophisticated ways (e.g., understand and interpret the work of artists like M.C. Escher), her students would need to develop foundational knowledge of symmetry and the ability to transfer this knowledge to other contexts (e.g., the analysis of artistic composition). But while Suzy was certain of her reasons for teaching symmetry, she was uncertain of the best way to teach it! Making her students memorize the definition rarely enabled them to use their understanding in any meaningful way. Surely, there must be a better approach!

Fortunately, Suzy ran into Juan Ramos, a fellow seventh-grade art teacher, in the Central Office parking lot before a district-wide art curriculum committee meeting. He noticed her look of defeat and asked, "Is anything wrong?"

"Ugh, it's this lesson on symmetry I'm planning," she replied. "I've been teaching it for five years and it just never goes right." She went on to explain the different approaches she had used, the lessons learned from her mistakes, and her frustration that after many years of teaching she still had not figured out the best way to teach this concept.

Juan listened sympathetically. "You know, I sometimes feel frustrated teaching concepts like symmetry, too—but less so after I learned about the models of teaching in a graduate class I took. I think your problem with last year's lesson was your instructional approach. The approach you described sounds better suited for learning simple facts. What you need is a specialized model for teaching concepts."

Suzy listened with interest. "What do you mean by 'concept'?" she asked.

"Concepts are the 'big ideas' that students gradually come to understand through various encounters," Juan explained. "Students form a more complete understanding of the concept of symmetry by experiencing it in different contexts. Each of these experiences is called an 'instance.' Keep in mind that our understanding about a concept is formed as we recognize that various examples of a concept have things in common. These 'things' are called 'critical attributes.'"

"So tell me, when you teach symmetry, how do you teach it?" asked Suzy.

"I use the Concept Attainment model to structure the lesson because it is a model designed for concept teaching," Juan said. He continued, "Although there are other models for teaching concepts, this one works well for symmetry because symmetry is a concept with clear critical attributes. I come up with really good pictures that relate to the concept and introduce them to the class one-by-one. Students have to analyze the items and discriminate between them to identify the concept's critical attributes. In case you couldn't tell, it's a model that takes more study and preparation—but it's worth it!"

Suzy could not wait to read about and try out the Concept Attainment model. She was eager to learn this approach to teaching concepts and wondered if it would help her students learn the concept of symmetry more deeply. ■

CHAPTER OBJECTIVES

After reading this chapter, you will be able to:

- Describe the Concept Attainment model, including its history and steps.

- Communicate the applications and benefits of the Concept Attainment model, and learn what it might look like in a classroom.

- Explain how the Concept Attainment model is implemented and how to plan for teaching with it.

- Articulate how the Concept Attainment model might enable differentiated instruction and support diverse learners.

- Describe how technology can enhance teaching with the Concept Attainment model.

Introduction

As an art teacher, Suzy understands that some tasks are difficult, if not impossible, to accomplish without the right tool. Creating a sturdy and waterproof ceramic pot without a working kiln, making a print without ink, and putting together a weaving without a loom are equally challenging. Suzy's success in teaching symmetry was limited because she lacked the right tool—that is, the right teaching tool—to teach concepts. No amount of hard work, desire, and ingenuity can substitute for the power of having the right tool for the job. In this chapter, we present one tool useful for teaching concepts—the Concept Attainment model.

Using the Concept Attainment model, educators can create effective lessons for teaching concepts and capitalize on students' natural inclination to think deductively. (Deduction involves drawing conclusions about specific instances by examining general ideas, concepts, or characteristics already known to be true.) They can build on learners' natural capacity of comparing and categorizing new ideas. The format of lessons designed with the Concept Attainment model is enjoyable and engaging for students and teachers alike—feeling more like a game than a traditional lesson. Using the Concept Attainment model requires careful planning and preparation, but its use provides incomparable support for teaching certain concepts. It benefits students by helping them develop the mental framework necessary for understanding concepts and the thinking skills useful in their classroom and beyond.

What Is the Concept Attainment Model?

The **Concept Attainment model** is a dynamic, interactive, teaching model that supports students' deep understanding of concepts and development of conceptual knowledge. As discussed in Chapter 1, conceptual knowledge includes knowledge of the relationships between big ideas such as classifications and categories. Development of conceptual knowledge hinges upon the comprehension of specific concepts (e.g., days, weeks, and years) that together form bigger ideas (e.g., the measurement of time). Concepts are addressed in all academic subject areas and grade levels. For some examples of concepts typically taught in various subject areas, see Figure 6-1.

Figure 6-1 Example Concepts by Academic Subject Area

Subject	Concepts
Art	Color wheel, creative medium (e.g., oil), sculpture, bathos, performance art, artistic inspiration
Language Arts	Academic rules, capital letters, adjectives, genre, irony, poetic justice
Mathematics	Bar graphs, geometric shapes (e.g., cube), volume, abstract math, fraction, Pythagorean theorem
Music	Musical notes (e.g., C), wind instruments, meter, composition, tone
Health/Physical Education	Body systems (e.g., skeletal), game rules (e.g., foul ball), wellness, self-esteem, "safe sex"
Social Studies	Land formations (e.g., atoll), farming, map, flag, ancient class systems (e.g., plebian), representative democracy, imperialism, cardinal directions
Science	Circuits, properties of matter, sources of energy, exothermic reaction, animal classification (e.g., vertebrate), distance, sound waves

Specifically, the Concept Attainment model is a teacher-guided model through which students develop an understanding of a concept through the examination of examples and nonexamples of the concept and the analysis of their critical and noncritical attributes. **Examples** are instances that illustrate or exemplify a concept. **Nonexamples** are instances that *do not*. Examples and nonexamples may consist of realia (i.e., real objects such as a ball to represent a sphere), pictures, text, video clips, animations, sounds, songs, poems, articles, words, mathematical computations, sentences, etc. In the process of comparing examples and nonexamples, students identify the critical and noncritical, or variable, attributes of the concept. **Critical attributes** are common, essential, fixed, and specific characteristics unique to a concept. **Noncritical**, or **variable, attributes** are any features of a concept that vary and are not necessary characteristics of the concept. For example, a critical attribute of the concept "insect" is that an insect has three body parts (i.e., the head, thorax, and abdomen), whereas wings are a noncritical attribute of an insect because only some insects have wings (e.g., ants and bees are insects each consisting of three body parts—all bees have wings, but only some ants do). For more in-depth information about concepts and concept vocabulary, please refer to Appendix B.

The Concept Attainment model has a long history of use in education. Although originally designed to support the development of students' conceptual knowledge, the model simultaneously supports their acquisition of strategies for reasoning and critical thinking. The model builds upon and expands students' prior knowledge of a concept to the point of mastery—allowing them to "attain" the concept under study.

Some of the benefits of this model suggested by research are that it supports student learning by (1) promoting retention, (2) engaging students in active learning, (3) supporting higher-order thinking (a.k.a. critical thinking), and (4) capitalizing on students' prior knowledge. These and other benefits are discussed in greater depth later in this chapter. In addition to being grounded in research, this model is embraced by teachers because it acknowledges and expands upon students' lived experiences during the learning process, promotes student ownership of learning, and helps students explore relationships among specific concepts and big ideas in their discipline.

What Are the History and Origins of the Concept Attainment Model?

The study of concepts has roots in cognitive science, philosophy, and psychology. Jerome Bruner, a notable cognitive psychologist, studied how humans think and learn about concepts. Over half a century ago, Bruner and two colleagues—Goodnow and Austin—developed the Concept Attainment model based on research they conducted and documented in their book, *A Study of Thinking* (Bruner, Goodnow, & Austin, 1956). Bruner believed that almost all cognitive activity involves categorizing. The Concept Attainment model promotes categorizing by challenging learners to look for critical attributes that enable them to distinguish between examples and nonexamples. Bruner's research serves as the foundation for how we teach concepts today, and it is now more relevant than ever given the proliferation of information in the "information age" and our need to process, synthesize, categorize, and apply it.

A great deal of research and several variations of this model have emerged since the model's inception. One of its biggest proponents was Hilda Taba (1967), an influential curriculum theorist, reformer, and teacher whose work emphasized the need for students to develop, understand, and make generalizations about concepts. She wrote about the Concept Attainment model as a component of the Taba Curriculum Development Project. Taba was an advocate for teaching concepts and reasoning, and this model exemplified her ideas. Taba also promoted the use of this model because of its ability to support the needs of diverse student populations (Taba & Elkins, 1966). Other scholars, such as Merrill and Tennyson (1977), Tennyson and Cocchiarella, (1986), and Tennyson and Park (1980), studied and applied the model extensively, too. Their work further developed our understanding of the Concept Attainment model as we apply it today.

When Should the Concept Attainment Model Be Applied and Why?

The Concept Attainment model is recommended for teaching conceptual knowledge, promoting students' thinking skills—specifically the ability to discriminate and generalize—and introducing or assessing concepts. It is most effective when used to teach concepts with clear critical attributes and when high-quality examples of the concept can be identified and shared. Teachers should use the Concept Attainment model to:

Teach Conceptual Knowledge

Teachers should choose the Concept Attainment model when teaching conceptual knowledge. Concepts are the building blocks of conceptual knowledge that take the forms of categories and classifications of information. That is, concepts are the basis for conceptual understanding and the Concept Attainment model. As stated previously (see Chapter 1), conceptual knowledge is knowledge about

1. classifications and categories,
2. principles and generalizations, and
3. theories and models and structures (Anderson et al., 2001).

Concepts are the foundation for classifications, principles, and theories. The Concept Attainment model supports students' understanding of general concepts, as well as specific ones related to curriculum standards.

In addition to directly supporting the development of conceptual knowledge, the Concept Attainment model also promotes development of learning related to other types of knowledge. For example, to the extent that learning to work through steps in the Concept Attainment model can be considered learning a "procedure," students develop procedural knowledge when they engage in it (Anderson et al., 2001). Through the Concept Attainment model, students also learn how to test their hypotheses and analyze them based on the examples and nonexamples presented. When students learn the vocabulary for understanding concepts, they develop factual knowledge, too. Metacognitive knowledge is developed when students reflect on the thinking performed while analyzing examples and nonexamples.

Develop Students' Generalization and Discrimination Skills

The Concept Attainment model is an ideal model for promoting deductive reasoning. The model offers students the opportunity to learn and practice generalization and discrimination. **Generalization** refers to a person's *ability to identify critical attributes in an example* and associate them with a concept. For instance, after being presented with a series of examples of numbers with only two factors (e.g., prime numbers) and another set of nonexamples with more than two factors (e.g., composite numbers), students might generalize that the concept has to do with numbers that only have two factors, which are prime numbers. Inherent in the practice of correct generalization is disregarding features that are not attributes of the concept. For example, in a second-grade math classroom, a donut might be considered an example of the concept "circle," but the frosting and sprinkles on the donut would not. **Discrimination** refers to a person's *ability to identify critical attributes in a nonexample* and recognize them as not being associated with a concept. Nonexamples vary in the degree of relatedness to the concept. Some are considered *close in* and others *far out*. **Close in nonexamples** exhibit some but not all the characteristics of the concept; **far out nonexamples** demonstrate fewer or none of the characteristics. Take, for instance, a giraffe and a donkey. A giraffe is a *far out* nonexample of a horse, whereas a donkey is a *closer in* nonexample. Similarly, as illustrated in the Concept Attainment Model Lesson at the end of the chapter, an image of a coiled snake is a *far out* nonexample of symmetry, and a profile of a tiger's face is a *closer in* nonexample.

Introduce or Assess Concepts

The Concept Attainment model is a useful tool when introducing or ending a unit of instruction. Many teachers find it is an excellent assessment tool—providing information about students' prior knowledge, aptitude, and the growth of their knowledge and skills over time. Information generated from pre-assessment can be used to make better instructional decisions (e.g., how differentiating instruction might be most effective for a particular learner or group of learners). Post-assessment data can help a teacher ascertain the effectiveness of a learning sequence (e.g., a lesson or unit). For example, consider a middle-school science teacher teaching a unit on kinetic and potential energy. The teacher might first use a Concept Attainment model lesson as a form of pre-assessment to examine students' background knowledge of the concept "energy" by introducing examples and nonexamples of energy. Students who have prior experience with the concept will likely be able to list its critical attributes or form a definition of it more quickly and accurately than those who do not. Teachers can use this information to make decisions about how to address the different learning needs in the classroom and plan differentiated instruction strategies such as flexible grouping (i.e., grouping students in various configurations—pairs, small groups, whole class—to maximize their learning), tiered instruction (i.e., creating a unit with varied activities that are more suitably matched with students' readiness for learning), and multiple levels of questions (i.e., the teacher adjusts the types of questions and the ways in which they are presented based on what is needed to advance problem-solving skills and responses). All of these techniques better support learners.

By the end of the unit on kinetic and potential energy, the teacher might use a Concept Attainment model lesson again, but this time as a post-assessment of students' understanding of the concept using more complex examples and nonexamples. Students should provide evidence that they can apply their conceptual knowledge accurately and in novel situations to illustrate full mastery. For example, students might share examples of potential and kinetic energy in the world around them—making sure to also share a list of the critical attributes of the concept. Use of the Concept Attainment model may be a good method for supporting a differentiated summative assessment. For example, students might be given the option of taking a traditional assessment (e.g., a written test) or challenged to develop their own Concept Attainment model lessons to "test" their peers' conceptual knowledge. Both approaches allow students to demonstrate their mastery of the concept. The Concept Attainment model is powerful because it offers support for the assessment process in so many ways.

Teach Concepts with Clear Critical Attributes

The Concept Attainment model is a specialized tool whose value is unsurpassed for teaching difficult concepts as Juan, the teacher in the opening scenario suggests. However, it is not a model well-suited for teaching *all* concepts. Knowing which concepts to teach with this model leads to greater instructional efficacy. The Concept Attainment model is best used to teach concepts with critical attributes that are clear. Clear critical attributes are those that (1) possess concrete critical attributes, (2) have widely accepted critical attributes, (3) may be categorized, (4) are easily identified in examples, and (5) can be presented in a classroom.

Although most of the traits of clear critical attributes do not need explanation, several do. Concrete critical attributes are those that one can see, touch, hear, smell, or feel in some way (e.g., one can see, touch, hear, and smell a dog). Note, these are different from critical attributes that are abstract and exist only in the mind (e.g., democracy, success, and community). Widely accepted critical attributes are attributes of concepts that are consistent and commonly established, recognized, and accepted.

To illustrate the traits of clear attributes, consider the following examples. The concept of "a mammal" is well-suited for teaching with the Concept Attainment model because it has clear critical attributes. We can see, feel, hear, and even smell mammals. Mammals' critical attributes are also widely recognized. Although they were established by the scientific community, most people know or have been taught the same critical attributes. The critical attributes of mammals include that they are warm-blooded vertebrates that bear live young, have four-chambered hearts, have bodies covered with hair, and glands that secrete milk. Mammals are able to be categorized. In fact, the need to classify them resulted in the development of this concept in the first place. Lastly the concept of mammals can be illustrated in a classroom using pictures, videos, or even realia (although being at a zoo while teaching the lesson might make presentation through realia easier!).

The concept "democracy" would be a concept not well-suited for teaching with the Concept Attainment model because it is not concrete. Although one can see the effects of democracy, one cannot see, smell, hear, feel, or touch democracy in a physical way. Although some might agree that it has some widely accepted attributes (such as being a government created by the people), this concept's attributes are not consistent across historical periods or geographical locations. Even though historical documents and current news stories might be used to illustrate democracy, it would be difficult to illustrate *all* of decomcracy's critical attributes in pictures, video, and realia.

These examples are just a simple introduction into the unique challenges experienced when teaching concepts. They make a case for the importance of teaching concepts and doing so with the most effective instructional model available.

Use When High-Quality Examples and Nonexamples Can Be Created

Because this instructional model requires the use of examples and nonexamples that accurately represent concepts (or in the case of nonexamples, serve for contrast), it is critical that teachers only choose the Concept Attainment model when they are able to create a rational set that effectively illustrates the intended concept. A **rational set** is a purposefully selected and organized group of examples and nonexamples that stimulate students' thinking (e.g., discrimination and generalization) in the Concept Attainment model.

Use of a rational set, rather than a set selected at random, ensures that students have appropriate structure and challenge for their learning. Sharing a rational set alleviates students' tendencies to overgeneralize (i.e., students might think nonexamples are examples), undergeneralize (i.e., students might believe nonexamples are examples), and misconceptualize (i.e., students might confuse examples with nonexamples and vice versa) (Markle & Tiemann, 1970). Note, however, that in building a rational set, research has shown that there is no absolute or prescribed number of examples and nonexamples that should be used. Rather, the ideal number of examples and nonexamples varies based on the characteristics of the concept—including how many attributes the concept has, how concrete the concept is, and what students' learning needs are (Tennyson & Park, 1980). The selection, ordering, and quantity of examples and nonexamples in the rational set should be informed by the unique characteristics of one's students. This is when being an educational designer can be helpful. Using a designer's mindset and skill set, a teacher can identify important information about students—such as which students may require more examples and nonexamples compared to others—and tailor a lesson so it is more responsive to specific learner needs.

What Are the Steps in the Concept Attainment Model?

The Concept Attainment model has four major steps:

1. Presentation of examples
2. Formation and analysis of hypotheses
3. Closure
4. Application

These steps are described below, and also presented in Figure 6-2, Teacher and Student Roles in the Concept Attainment Model.

Step One—Presentation of Examples

In this step, the teacher challenges students to observe and analyze items that relate to the concept and begin distinguishing between them. He or she presents a group of labeled examples and nonexamples to the students. These items may be introduced in several ways. These items might be gradually sorted into two columns (one entitled, "examples," and another, "nonexamples"), or the teacher may simply state and/or write that the item presented is an "example" or a "nonexample" on the board. Some teachers prefer to use the terms "yes" and "no," "positive" and "negative," or "☺" and "☹" labels instead. During this step, students should record the critical attributes they identify in the examples. The selection and presentation of examples plays an important role in the teacher's success in fostering critical thinking and analysis of the critical attributes of the concept to be learned.

The teacher has a great deal of freedom when presenting the examples and nonexamples. For instance, the teacher may present the examples and nonexamples to the class as a whole, students individually, or small groups. Similarly, the teacher may wish to share all of the examples and nonexamples at once as in Scenario 6-3 or the teacher may wish to share them one at a time via a prepared presentation as in the Concept Attainment Model Lesson. Software programs such as Keynote®, PowerPoint®, Inspiration®, and SMART Notebook™ are useful for presenting examples and nonexamples. Drawing pictures on a chalkboard or whiteboard also works, as does showing students different photo flash cards.

Regardless of the technology used during the presentation, the fundamental technique for classifying the items is the same. For example, a teacher who wants to introduce the concept of symmetry to her students might use a PowerPoint presentation she created in advance. She would introduce one example of a symmetrical picture saying, "This is an example," and then when she presents a nonexample, saying, "This is not an example." (See the Concept Attainment Model Lesson at the end of this chapter.) She would gradually introduce examples and nonexamples while simultaneously asking students to list critical attributes and form a hypothesis as explained in step two, "formation and analysis of hypotheses."

Step Two—Formation and Analysis of Hypotheses

During the presentation step, students are also forming and analyzing hypotheses. Steps one and two, therefore, occur concurrently. In this step, as the teacher introduces examples and/or nonexamples of a concept one by one, he or she asks students to analyze their attributes for the purpose of forming a **hypothesis,** or educated guess about what the concept is.

Figure 6-2 Teacher and Student Roles in the Concept Attainment Model

Concept Attainment Model Steps	Teacher Role	Student Role
Presentation of examples	The teacher presents examples and nonexamples and then asks students to form a hypothesis of the concept. **Teaching tip:** Explain and provide practice of the "rules" of the concept attainment model prior to presenting examples and nonexamples. Be sure to inform students how they are to record the attributes or provide a form for recording this information.	The students record attributes of examples and nonexamples.
Formation and analysis of hypotheses	The teacher asks students to examine their hypotheses, verify or refute their hypotheses, and then challenges students to support their hypotheses with data (attributes). **Teaching tip:** Scaffold students' analyses by asking questions as examples and nonexamples are presented. Be sure to require that students record the critical attributes they identify, so they are prepared to substantiate their hypotheses with this data.	The students form and record hypotheses about the concept. They must also substantiate their hypotheses with data from examples and nonexamples.
Closure	The teacher asks students to summarize the critical attributes of the concept, formulate a definition of the concept, and then reflect on the entire concept attainment process. **Teaching tip:** Ensure that students have the correct hypothesis and that they have substantiated their hypothesis by referring to the data (examples and nonexamples) presented.	The students develop a definition of the concept based on its critical attributes. They then reflect on the Concept Attainment process—recording ideas about what and how it was learned.
Application	The teacher asks students to apply their knowledge in novel situations. **Teaching tip:** Provide students with multiple opportunities to demonstrate their learning.	The students apply their knowledge by locating, changing, or creating other examples and nonexamples.

Forming a hypothesis requires students to discriminate and generalize. First they must distinguish between the examples and nonexamples—carefully analyzing their differences and similarities to arrive at the concept's critical attributes. Then they must make a generalization by proposing the concept that is exemplified by the critical attributes that have been identified. For example, in the Concept Attainment Model Lesson, the teacher introduces examples and nonexamples of symmetry, and students form educated guesses proposing the concept based on their analysis of the attributes they notice in the examples and nonexamples presented in a PowerPoint demonstrated by their teacher. A student might hypothesize that "Symmetry is when at least two sides or parts of an object are exactly the same size, shape, and color," or "This concept is something that has a mirror image."

During this step, the teacher should provide a sufficient amount of time for students to develop and analyze their hypotheses. Critical-thinking processes like discrimination and generalization can take some time and mental energy. The teacher may need to provide guidance that helps students identify common attributes among the examples presented. Asking probing questions is helpful. Finally, the teacher should help students form a working definition of the concept. It may be necessary to remind students that nonexamples may have some attributes of examples but are nonexamples because they do not have *all* of the critical attributes. A working definition consists of students' description of the concept based on its critical attributes. Students should also be prepared to justify their hypotheses based on the *data* (i.e., the attributes of the examples and nonexamples presented).

Step Three—Closure

In this step, the teacher guides students in forming a formal definition of the concept being addressed. At this point, the teacher also challenges students to analyze and reflect on their learning process. The first task is accomplished by helping students synthesize a definition of the concept based on their individual hypotheses and analysis of the concept's critical attributes. For example, in the Concept Attainment Model Lesson, the teacher would summarize students' definitions of symmetry. Then, she would challenge the class to reach consensus about a definition such as "a symmetrical object is one that demonstrates the property that both sides of the object reflect each other across a vertical and horizontal line or surface (a line of symmetry)." As the students craft a definition, the teacher must also ensure that they have an appropriate, correct, and complete understanding of the concept. Teachers should also make certain to correct any misconceptions about the concept or its attributes.

The second task in the closure step requires teachers to ask students to reflect on the experiences that occurred during the learning process that resulted in attaining the concept. Linking students' understanding with a definition of the concept occurs at this time and helps students analyze their thinking process and learning experience. Through this reflection, students expand their metacognitive knowledge—that is, their ability to think about, become aware of, and analyze their own thinking. For instance, to help students reflect on their thinking in the Concept Attainment Model Lesson at the end of this chapter, the teacher asks students to think about the lesson and consider, "What did you learn about 'symmetry'? What did you learn about analyzing the examples and nonexamples? Were you surprised at your initial hypotheses? How long did it take to comprehend what 'symmetry' is?" After students record what they have learned, the teacher should give them the opportunity to share the lessons learned with their peers and benefit from the insights that might be shared.

Step Four—Application

In this step, the teacher asks students to take their understanding to the next level by applying it in a more challenging way. He or she provides students with additional examples and nonexamples to analyze and asks them to change nonexamples into examples (if possible). The teacher then conducts assessment of students' learning by asking them to create or locate their own examples demonstrating the critical attributes of the concept. The teacher may also ask students to transfer their knowledge to new situations and use it in a meaningful way. It is important for the teacher to provide students with multiple and varied opportunities to demonstrate their mastery of the concept. For example, in the Concept Attainment Model Lesson, the teacher provides students a worksheet (see Worksheet 6-4 in Appendix C) with objects drawn on it. Then, she asks them to determine whether any of the objects are nonexamples that can be changed into examples. She prompts them to explain in writing or verbally *why* or *why not* by using words and vocabulary learned during the closure step of the lesson.

What Does the Concept Attainment Model Look Like in the Classroom?

If you were to walk into any classroom, in any school, at any grade level, and in any subject area, you might see the Concept Attainment model in action—and yet, its various implementations might look quite different. The model is incredibly versatile and suitable for varied teaching settings. Likewise, it is flexible enough to adapt to personal teaching styles, student needs, and even available resources.

In the sections that follow, we provide three scenarios to illustrate how the Concept Attainment model might be applied in different classroom settings. We distinguish between the essential components of the model—what must be done for a teacher to exercise fidelity to the model of Concept Attainment—and adaptations that can be made to the model to meet the distinct needs of a particular classroom setting. Each scenario demonstrates specific differences in the ways teachers might implement this model.

Scenario 6-1

Teacher Euronda Johnson is hovering over a small group of fourth-grade, language-arts students at a large rectangular table. Elsewhere in the room, students are typing on computers, reading, and doing other activities. Students working with Euronda are watching with great interest as she "deals" file cards on the table in front of them one by one. As she flips the cards over in front of the eager students, they wait to see which of two columns, labeled "Examples" and "Nonexamples", she will sort them into. On the first card the word "carrot" is written. She sorts it into the column that says "Example." The next card says "radish" (nonexample). The next card, an example, has the word "caret" written on it. The remaining examples "dealt" to the students are "fare, fair, meet, meat, tee, tea, weak," and "week." Some of the nonexamples include "unfair, vegetables, coffee," and "month." After each card is dealt, students will turn away from the table and quickly write ideas of the attributes of the example on a notepad—taking care to cover their answers. With each new card presented, they return to their notes and add or eliminate attributes from their list.

Using their notes, students take stock of the critical attributes of the concept and begin to form a hypothesis of what the concept might be. Their hypothesis will consist of, at the very least, the concept's critical attributes. It might also include a name for the concept or a working definition. One student writes down "words that sound the same but are spelled differently—homophones," and another has written "words that sound the same but are written differently." These students raise their hands and the teacher reviews their guesses and nods. These students smile and continue to watch quietly while their classmates finish playing the "game."

After the last card has been dealt, Euronda asks the students to record their final guesses and turn in their notes. She will review their attribute lists and hypotheses to better understand the thinking processes they used during the lesson. Students may receive credit for their efforts and thinking even if they did not arrive at the correct concept definition. The concept definition is shared with the group, and she asks each student to write a few examples of homophones they know. Then, she checks to see if these are correct. If students understand the concept, they are challenged to write a limerick using a set of homophones. If they do not understand, she works with them individually until they master the concept.

Scenario 6-2

During a seventh-grade unit on energy, teacher Candice DiLorenzo wants to address the science content standard, "Students will be able to distinguish between renewable and nonrenewable energy sources and understand the advantages and disadvantages of both types." To meet this standard, Candice has decided that she will teach students the concept of "nonrenewable energy" first, because once they understand this concept, it will be relatively simple to teach renewable energy sources and then compare the two.

She first reviews her textbook and curriculum guide to ensure her definition of a nonrenewable energy source is accurate (i.e., an energy source that cannot be replenished in a short period of time). Then she develops a list of the critical attributes of nonrenewable energy sources which include that they are

1. found in the natural world,
2. obtained in some way that affects the physical environment,
3. not replenished, and
4. valued for its use by human individuals, communities, and nations.

She then thoughtfully selects examples and nonexamples of nonrenewable energy sources she believes all students will recognize, especially considering some are photos she has taken of such sources in their community. She creates a PowerPoint presentation.

Each of the slides that exemplify examples includes two pictures linked together with a line indicating their relatedness. These include: A picture of an oil refinery linked to a picture of a car (see Figure 6-3), a picture of a coal mine linked to a picture of an electric plant, a picture of a wood-burning fireplace linked to children warming their hands, and a picture of a nuclear reactor linked to a glowing lamp with children reading under it. The slides showing nonexamples are formatted in a similar way. Her nonexamples include a picture of a windmill linked to someone drawing water from a well, a picture of a solar panel next to a picture of a house lit up at night, and a picture of a hydroelectric dam linked to a glowing television.

When Candice introduces the Concept Attainment model lesson the next day, she explains that she wants students to understand an important energy concept. To do so they will play a game to see if they can guess the concept. The game involves three important science skills—discriminating, generalizing, and hypothesizing. To practice these skills, they will examine examples and nonexamples together. Students will write down what qualities the examples have in common (generalizing) and that are not shared by the nonexamples (discriminating). Students will develop a hypothesis about what the concept is

Figure 6-3 Examples of the Concept

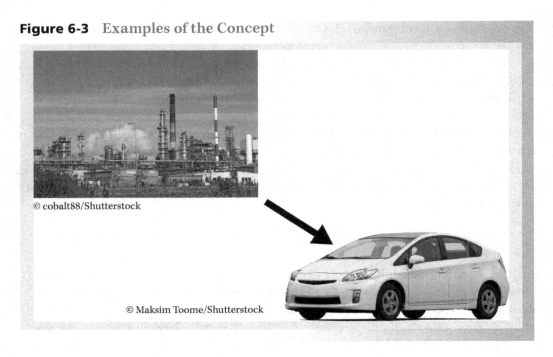

© cobalt88/Shutterstock

© Maksim Toome/Shutterstock

and describe its critical attributes (hypothesizing). As a class, the hypotheses will be shared and a definition of the concept formalized. Finally, students will apply their conceptual knowledge of the concept by suggesting other examples and nonexamples of nonrenewable energy sources.

Scenario 6-3

Doug Crawford is a high school library media specialist who regularly uses the Concept Attainment model with his ninth-grade students. Today, he has checked out and set up the school's portable lab in the media center. The goal for this lesson is to pre-assess what students already know about the concept of a "credible Internet resource," because it is important for students to understand that not all websites are equally trustworthy. He wants to teach them to review websites for credibility, accuracy, and reasonableness.

Doug has set up a website that shows a table consisting of two columns headed with the words "Examples" and "Nonexamples." In each column, there is a selection of websites. In the examples column he has included "The White House Web Page" (www.whitehouse.gov) and "The Weather Channel's Web Page" (www.weather.com). In the nonexamples column he includes references to two different news parody sites, "The Onion" (www.theonion.com) and "The Daily News" (www.the-daily-news.co.uk).

Before students begin this lesson, he tells them that their job will be to review the websites one by one—paying attention to the characteristics that the examples have in common with one another and that are not characteristics shared by the nonexamples. He further instructs them that the websites in the examples column illustrate a concept he wants to teach them. Students are then asked to craft a hypothesis of what the concept is and what its critical attributes are. Doug provides students with a worksheet that reiterates these instructions and also a graphic organizer for recording the elements of their hypotheses. Because Doug often uses the Concept Attainment model, students are comfortable with these instructions. Most students are able to work independently—freeing Doug up to work with the three students who have IEPs.

When students have completed their review of the examples and nonexamples, they are asked to turn in their worksheet. He indicates that he will review their work that evening as a form of pre-assessment. With this information, he will have a better idea of how much time is needed to cover this unit and whether students should be taught in a whole group or work in smaller groups according to readiness and prior knowledge.

On the following day, students will share their hypotheses in small groups to formulate a shared definition of the concept. At the conclusion of this unit, students will create their own websites in which they will briefly describe the concept of reliable internet sources and list their own examples and nonexamples that might provide information for their term paper. These pages will be linked to the library home page to educate other students, their parents, and community members.

What Do These Scenarios Illustrate?

These scenarios illustrate just some of the modifications that can be made to the Concept Attainment model. The Concept Attainment model was used in different grade levels (i.e., fourth-, seventh-, and ninth-grades) and content areas (i.e., language arts, science, and library/research). Also, the teachers presented the content in varied ways. Euronda used flash cards in Scenario 6-1, and Candice and Doug employed computer technologies in Scenarios 6-2 and 6-3. In each scenario, teachers selected rational sets of examples and nonexamples to demonstrate the concept. Yet, how students analyzed the examples and nonexamples and the questions the teachers asked for prompting their analysis varied.

REFLECT: Take a moment to examine each of these scenarios as variations of the Concept Attainment model. How did they vary at each step; for example, how did each teacher bring closure? Examine how you might modify the Concept Attainment model and how it might benefit your current or future students.

Although there are many ways to apply the Concept Attainment model in practice, we advise against making changes to the ordering of steps or goals of the Concept Attainment model because these research-based steps have been found to promote learning using the sequence shared. If the Concept Attainment model does not meet your needs, we recommend exploration of other models in this text that support concept teaching, such as Concept Development (Chapter 7) and the Inductive Model (Chapter 8).

Planning for Teaching with the Concept Attainment Model

There are several planning considerations teachers take into account *before* teaching with the Concept Attainment model. These measures include (1) carefully analyzing the concept, (2) teaching students the rules for learning with the Concept Attainment model, and (3) scaffolding students' learning and metacognition through questioning and application activities in the Concept Attainment model. When teaching with the Concept Attainment model, educational designers:

Analyze the Concepts

Mastery of a concept occurs gradually through numerous and varied experiences with examples and nonexamples of a concept. Knowledge of concepts is developed over a lifetime. Adults and teachers, by virtue of having had more life experience than their students, possess sophisticated understandings of most concepts. They are often not consciously aware that their knowledge has become internalized.

Teaching successfully with the Concept Attainment model requires teachers to bring these internalized understandings to the surface and examine them with a fresh perspective. A teacher needs to develop a deep understanding of the concept he or she will teach through reflection on his or her definition of it and awareness of the experiences that might have been instrumental in his or her acquisition of knowledge about it. The teacher's analysis of the concept should include the

1. formation of a definition of the concept,
2. identification of its critical and variable attributes, and
3. selection and ordering of quality examples and nonexamples into a rational set.

FORM A DEFINITION OF THE CONCEPT. The first step in the process of analyzing a concept is forming a definition of the concept. Although teachers might review a dictionary or textbook definition of the concept, it is also useful for teachers to write the definition in their own words first and then examine the published definition for comparison. Teachers may choose to use either definition or a combination of the two, whichever best meets their students' needs for learning the concept. Teachers often feel challenged writing down a succinct yet accurate definition—it is harder than it seems!

IDENTIFY A CONCEPT'S CRITICAL AND VARIABLE ATTRIBUTES. Another recommended step for analyzing concepts is identifying and articulating the concept's critical and variable attributes. A complete definition of the concept will include these attributes. Creating a concept map can be useful at this time. A **concept map** is a visual diagram that graphically represents ideas and their relationships. In a concept map, key concepts are often connected by links that have descriptive words on them explaining the relationship(s) between the concepts. Each subordinate concept is more specific and less general than the concept drawn from it. A concept map shows the relationships between ideas and attributes of a concept. Ideas can be listed in the form of words, phrases, pictures, drawings, questions, or statements. Creating a concept map allows a teacher to define a concept and list its attributes and related concepts. Concept maps also enable teachers to organize, reorganize, classify, and label items related to the overarching concept. Because elements of a concept map are connected by lines, linking word(s), or prepositions, the relationships among concepts is quickly apparent.

Four popular types of concept maps include:

- **Flowchart**—This chart uses connecting lines to organize information in a procedural manner. It shows the sequence or order for completing a task, solving a problem, or implementing some other systematic process of events.
- **Hierarchical**—This type of concept map organizes concepts in a hierarchical manner with the most important concept (the superordinate concept) on the top. Coordinate and subordinate concepts fall under the main, superordinate concept.
- **Pictorial**—This concept map displays items using graphics, pictures, or drawings. The emphasis is on the pictorial representation of the concepts.

Figure 6-4 Example of a Combination Concept Map

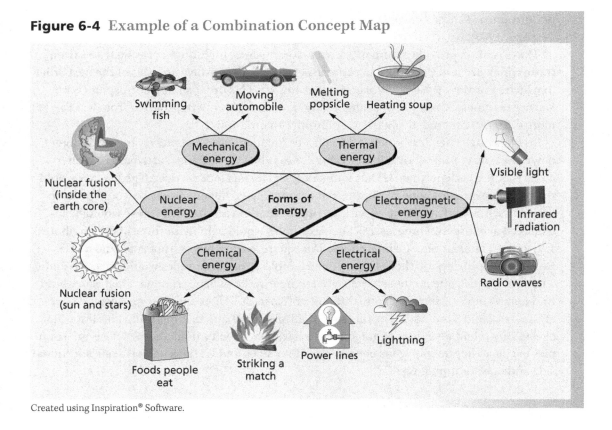

Created using Inspiration® Software.

- **Web, spider, bubble, or cluster**—Although their appearance is different, these concept maps all organize information around an important, central concept and position all of the subordinate concepts surrounding it.

A concept map created by a teacher during the planning process can later be shared with students to help them visualize the concepts and the relationships between them. Combinations of concept map types can also be effective. For instance, Figure 6-4 is a combination of two different kinds of concept maps—it shows a bubble concept map that also incorporates clip art (pictorial).

Other tools can help in conducting an analysis of a concept. One is presented in Worksheet 6-1. This planning tool helps teachers examine the targeted concept, as well as list and order selected examples and nonexamples. Worksheet 6-2 provides an example of a completed worksheet for the concept of symmetry. Both worksheets are available in Appendix C.

SELECT AND ORDER QUALITY EXAMPLES AND NONEXAMPLES INTO A RATIONAL SET.
The goal of the Concept Attainment model is to clarify and enable students to attain concepts—not create confusion about them. Using high-quality examples and nonexamples will promote comprehension and minimize confusion. This is accomplished when a teacher creates a rational set of carefully selected examples and nonexamples. Such rational sets (1) are divergent enough to facilitate discrimination but test generalization, (2) have matched nonexamples that differ only slightly from the examples (*close in* nonexamples), and (3) differ in difficulty as evidenced by previous students' classification

performance of these concepts (Tennyson, Woolley, and Merrill as cited in Driscoll & Tessmer, 1985).

These criteria provide a framework for distinguishing high-quality rational sets from those which are not. Creation of a rational set should also involve analysis of the best order in which to present the examples and nonexamples. This order should correspond with learner readiness. Ordering of examples and nonexamples might progress from less to more difficult, concrete to abstract, or familiar to unfamiliar.

To illustrate, when introducing the concept "quadrilateral," a teacher might first break down the concept into its attributes. This concept has three critical attributes which include that it (1) is a polygon, (2) has four sides, and (3) has four vertices. The teacher would then locate examples with attributes that are obvious to introduce (these would be introduced first), as well as examples with attributes that are more subtle (these would be introduced as the lesson progresses). Such examples would exhibit all three of the attributes: 1, 2, and 3. For example, she might include a square, a rhombus, a trapezoid, and a kite. Next, she would develop the very easy nonexamples. These examples would have attribute 1 but not 2 and 3. She might select a right triangle and a scalene triangle. Then, she would find nonexamples which are more difficult or "close-in." These nonexamples would have attributes 2 and 3 but not 1. For this she might select a shape that has four sides but is not closed. She might also list a pentagon and a hexagon, which would also be "close-in" examples because they are polygons consisting of four sides and vertices but have one additional side and one additional vertex.

Teach Students the Rules of the Concept Attainment Model

The introduction of a concept using the Concept Attainment model will work more smoothly if teachers share some ground rules for how the model works. Students must do the following:

- Remember that BOTH examples and nonexamples of the concept will be shared.
- Concentrate on what the examples have in common (the critical attributes, especially).
- Remember that nonexamples may have some critical attributes of examples.
- List all the attributes of the concept as examples and nonexamples are presented.
- Eliminate (cross out) attributes that do not apply to new examples when introduced.
- Write down their hypotheses as the teacher presents examples and nonexamples— What do they believe the concept is and what do they think its critical attributes are?
- Form a working definition of the concept as examples and nonexamples are presented.
- Keep hypotheses private—students should not shout out or share hypotheses unless they are working in groups or pairs.
- Be prepared to discuss their hypotheses and their rationale based on the data presented (examples and nonexamples).
- Substantiate hypotheses based on the data presented in the examples and nonexamples.
- Reflect on the progression of their thinking and the turning point of their learning experience (i.e., the moment when they recognized their hypothesis of the concept was correct).

Establishing rules or standards for behavior at the lesson's outset will increase the likelihood of success when implementing the model.

Scaffold Students' Learning and Metacognition

Teachers we know who have taught concepts using the Concept Attainment model can attest that the model requires thoughtful scaffolding of students' learning and metacognition through questioning and application activities. Although the model offers built-in support through its various steps, teachers need to plan questions proactively to guide students' thinking and actions during each step of the Concept Attainment model. Teachers should craft questions that help students form hypotheses based on their analysis of critical attributes identified in the examples and nonexamples. For example, in the Concept Attainment Model Lesson, the teacher asks explicit questions during each step of the model, such as the following:

1. Presentation of examples: *What attributes does 'X' example have that are similar to 'Y' example?*
2. Formation and analysis of hypotheses: *What is your hypothesis about what this concept (symmetry) is?*
3. Closure: *How would you define "symmetry"? How would you explain what it means to someone else?*
4. Application: *Are there any nonexamples that can be changed into examples? Why or why not?*

Planning activities that are performed to proactively support learning will not only improve students' understanding of the concept, it will also support students' development of metacognitive skills. These skills are essential to continued reflection which promotes independent learning and growth beyond the duration of the lesson. In addition to determining which questions to ask before implementing a Concept Attainment model lesson, teachers should plan *what students should do* during each step. Worksheet 6-3 in Appendix C presents a planning tool teachers might use to help them plan for scaffolding students' learning with the Concept Attainment model lesson.

Differentiating Instruction with the Concept Attainment Model

There are many modifications that can be made during the implementation of this model to support diverse learners. Typically, teachers differentiate the content, process, or product based on learners' interest, readiness, and learning style. Additional examples for differentiating instruction can be found in the Concept Attainment Model Lesson.

Content

Differentiating content in a Concept Attainment model lesson involves modifying the types of materials students interact with to learn about content. Materials that communicate the critical and variable attributes in examples and nonexamples are easiest to differentiate. Choices about the materials used to present the content in the Concept Attainment model should be based on the characteristics of a particular concept and the needs of individuals or groups of students.

A teacher may choose from many types of materials for the presentation of content—magazines, newspaper articles, photographs, digital text, animations, sounds, videos, and realia. Care should be taken to consider the relative difficulty or ease of use of each type of material for various groups of learners. Visual learners in a geometry lesson might understand the pictorial representation of a concept (e.g., a picture of a sphere) better, while kinesthetic learners may only be successful in grasping the critical attributes of "sphere" after manipulating it in three dimensions (e.g., a ball). Materials presented in digital format might also offer an advantage for learners with special needs. A student with visual impairment reviewing examples and nonexamples of narrative poetry during an English class would be able to function more independently listening to examples read aloud with a text-to-speech program than interacting with traditional printed materials.

When selecting examples and nonexamples, it is also important to consider students' prior knowledge with the particular examples and nonexamples chosen. Students with limited prior knowledge of musical notation might understand a concept like "music in a minor key" more quickly by listening to audio examples than by reviewing sheet music. Especially in cases when students may come from diverse cultural and socioeconomic backgrounds, efforts should be made to consider what students might already know about examples and how they might react to these examples. A second-grade child newly emigrated from Mogadishu might not have the same knowledge of a penguin (presented as a nonexample in a lesson on mammals) as his peers. And a Hindu student might think of different critical attributes when viewing a picture of a cow (in this same lesson) than his Christian classmates. Although it is impossible to consider all of the possible ways students will associate with and experience various examples and nonexamples, *all* students will be more likely to learn if their teachers think carefully through the selection of materials used to present critical attributes and the examples in the rational set.

Process

The process of instruction might be differentiated in several ways to support the needs of learners in a differentiated classroom when the Concept Attainment model is used. During the presentation of examples (Step One), students might be allowed to make a choice to work individually or in pairs, as they record the critical attributes of examples and nonexamples. This would support learners who might be slower or quicker to recognize attributes. A helpful modification to make while students are working with examples and forming their hypotheses (Steps One and Two), might be to allow students to make a choice about how they go about recording ideas related to the development of their hypothesis. Some students might prefer a structured graphic organizer (see Worksheet 6-3 for an example), yet others could be equally successful recording their ideas in a less defined way on a blank sheet of paper. Still other students might benefit from a very structured worksheet that prompts them to respond to specific questions about each example and nonexample. Incorporating differentiated techniques in the closure step (Step Three) could be as simple as providing reflection prompts that guide students through the thinking process. It might also involve recording their reflections in an audio file.

Product

Differentiation can also occur with the method students use to demonstrate their learning during the application step (Step Four). Depending on the concept being learned, it might be appropriate for students to choose from a menu of different assessment options to display their mastery of a concept. One student might opt to create a song about mammals that articulates each of the critical attributes of the concept. Another might want to write a newspaper article reporting on a discovery of a new animal found in the wild and classified as a mammal because of its characteristics. An English Language Learner (ELL) might choose to create a collage that illustrates these attributes and then describe them with the help of his or her ELL teacher. Other students may decide to present their understanding using phrases and bullet points.

Although modifications during individual steps in the implementation of this model support differentiation, it is also important to note that this model offers built-in support through its design. First, it supports students in building their experiential knowledge of a concept through the introduction of examples and nonexamples. When students see the illustration of critical attributes, their understanding of concepts expands whether they have prior knowledge of the concept being studied or not. This helps "level the playing field" between learners with experience and those without. The design of the Concept Attainment model also supports differentiation by providing teachers with information about students' thinking processes—which the model makes visible during its distinct steps. The information that becomes apparent when the learning process is broken into distinct steps that reveal student learning in-progress can strengthen relationships and promote better instructional decision making. For example, if a teacher learns that one of his students is inclined to "jump to conclusions" without thoughtful analysis of examples and nonexamples when forming hypotheses, this teacher can help the student become aware of this problem and correct it.

What Are the Benefits of Applying the Concept Attainment Model?

The Concept Attainment model has many benefits. It builds on students' prior knowledge, promotes exploration of different perspectives, examination of relationships among concepts, and development of critical-thinking skills, as well as engages students' curiosity. The Concept Attainment model:

Builds on Students' Prior Knowledge

This model helps students build on their prior knowledge and make connections between what they already know and what they will be learning. In the Concept Attainment model, students seek to understand the relationships between examples and nonexamples, which requires them to reflect on their prior knowledge. For example, students studying polygons in math might recognize that many polygons are symmetrical—which was a concept learned in art at an earlier point that year.

Enables Examination of Content from Different Perspectives

The Concept Attainment model promotes the examination of concepts in a number of different ways and from different perspectives. Students are able and even encouraged to bring their own unique background knowledge and experiences to the learning task. For example, students might look at an empty soda can as an example of a cylindrical-shaped object, an item that could be recycled, or an object made from a metal alloy. When students review and classify examples and nonexamples, they also learn to sort out relevant information—a skill increasingly important in our information-rich and knowledge-poor society. With its emphasis on forming hypotheses, the model encourages multiple ideas, viewpoints, and experiences of diverse learners.

Promotes Exploration of the Relationships Among Concepts

Learning about a particular concept raises students' awareness of what concepts are. Once students start to see concepts, they begin to recognize them everywhere. From this awareness, students develop the capacity to acknowledge and explore the interrelatedness of concepts, distinguish between them, and make generalizations about them. As Merrill and Tennyson (1977) contend, it is not enough to list the attributes of a concept; students must also distinguish the relationships among the critical attributes of a concept to understand its meaning and connection to other concepts.

This model helps students fully comprehend a concept's attributes resulting in enhanced retention of the concept. Retention is positively influenced when students are challenged to go beyond memorizing the definition, which represents factual knowledge of a particular concept, to understanding fully the concept's critical attributes.

Promotes Critical Thinking

The Concept Attainment model promotes critical thinking and analysis in each of its distinct steps. Students must examine critically the examples and nonexamples presented, record the critical attributes, compare their commonalities and differences, and form and test hypotheses about the concept in question. As students gradually progress through each step, they learn and practice discrimination and generalization with a purpose—to make a hypothesis that results in new learning.

Engages Students' Curiosity

Another benefit of the Concept Attainment model is that it engages students' curiosity. This is particularly true when the ground rules are spelled out and high-quality examples and nonexamples are chosen. In many ways, this model is like a game students might play or a mystery they might want to solve. Technology that provides visual representations of the concept can be used to capitalize on students' natural interest. Many teachers incorporate special effects and animations during their presentation of examples to increase suspense during the learning process.

What Value Does Technology Add to the Concept Attainment Model?

Technology offers many benefits during the different stages of the Concept Attainment model. Technology can aid teacher productivity as planning occurs, assist in the presentation of the concept, promote student practice of a concept, and facilitate the assessment of student learning. These benefits are described in the sections that follow. Figure 6-5 summarizes a variety of technology tools that support the planning and teaching of concepts using the Concept Attainment model.

Figure 6-5   Technology Tools for the Concept Attainment Model

Use	Technology Tools
Planning	

Use digital resources to help define concepts	Reference tools available online
	• Dictionaries
	  • Dictionary.com: http://dictionary.reference.com
	  • Merriam-Webster (click on "dictionary"): www.merriam-webster.com
	  • Shahi (a visual dictionary that combines Wiktionary content with Flickr images, and more!): http://blachan.com/shahi
	  • Visual dictionary: http://visual.merriam-webster.com
	  • Visuwords (online graphical dictionary): www.visuwords.com
	• Thesaurus
	  • Dictionary.com's thesaurus: http://thesaurus.reference.com
	  • Merriam-Webster (click on "thesaurus"): www.merriam-webster.com
	  • Visual thesaurus: www.visualthesaurus.com
	• Quotation database
	  • Bartlett's Familiar Quotations: www.bartleby.com/quotations
	• Search engines
	  • Clusty: http://clusty.com
	  • Google: www.google.com
	  • Mooter: www.mooter.com.au

Use concept-mapping tools to portray concepts visually	Concept-mapping tools • Freemind: http://freemind.sourceforge.net/wiki/index.php/Main_Page • Gliffy: www.gliffy.com • Inspiration: www.inspiration.com • Kidspiration: www.kidspiration.com • Mindmanager: www.mindjet.com/default.aspx • Mindview: www.matchware.com/en/products/mindview/default.htm • SmartDraw: www.smartdraw.com • Visio: http://office.microsoft.com/en-us/visio/default.aspx
Search for media demonstrating examples and nonexamples	Image search tools • Google Image: http://images.google.com • Picsearch: www.picsearch.com • Creative Commons: http://creativecommons.org Media search tools • YouTube: www.youtube.com • TeacherTube: www.teachertube.com • Blinx: www.blinkx.com
Implementing	
Present (and order) examples and nonexamples digitally	Multimedia presentation tools • PowerPoint: http://office.microsoft.com/en-us/powerpoint/default.aspx • Keynote: www.apple.com/iwork/keynote Creativity tools • HyperStudio: www.mackiev.com/hyperstudio/index.html • SMART Notebook: www2.smarttech.com/st/en-US/Support/Downloads/default.htm • Kidpix: www.kidpix.com • Pixie 2: www.tech4learning.com/pixie

continued

Figure 6-5 Technology Tools for the Concept Attainment Model
continued

Use	Technology Tools
Implementing (continued)	

Project examples and nonexamples to small and large groups of students	Interactive whiteboards
	 • Panabord: www.panaboard.com
	 • SMART Board: http://smarttech.com
	 • Promethean: www.prometheanworld.com
	
	 Interactive pen displays
	 • SMART Podium: http://smarttech.com/Support/Browse+Support/Product+Index/ Hardware+Products/SMART+Podium+Interactive+Pen+Display/ID350
	 • Mimio: www.mimio.com/products/mimio_pad/index.asp
	 • Smartpen: www.livescribe.com
	
	 Basic digital projection tools
	 • Document camera/visual presenter
	    • Elmo: www.elmousa.com
	    • Dukane: www.dukcorp.com
	    • LCD Panel
	 • In Focus Video Projector: www.infocus.com
	
	 Low-tech projection tools
	 • Overhead projector
	 • Opaque projector

Form and analyze hypotheses	Interactive whiteboards (see above) Interactive pen displays (see above) Tablet computers, convertible notebooks, and slates—several companies sell these specialized computers. We recommend doing a search online to find the latest, best products.
Assessing (Application & Closure)	
Demonstrate understanding in digital format before and after learning	Any digital tool may be used for demonstrating understanding. Students could use the Web 2.0 tools listed below, as well as a word-processing program. Some interactive tools that could be used with a whole class or a small group include the following: Audience response systems • TurningPoint: www.turningtechnologies.com Interactive whiteboards (see above)
Reflect and share learning in digital format	Digital audio recording devices: • iPod with iTalk: www.griffintechnology.com/products/italk • Olympus: www.olympusamerica.com/cpg_section/cpg_vr_digitalrecorders.asp Screen recording (screencasting) • Camtasia: www.techsmith.com/camtasia.asp • Captivate: www.adobe.com/products/captivate • Jing: www.jingproject.com • Screencast-O-Matic: www.screencast-o-matic.com • Smartpen: www.livescribe.com Web 2.0 Tools • VoiceThread: www.voicethread.com • Wikispaces: www.wikispaces.com • PBWiki: www.pbwiki.com • Moodle: www.moodle.com • Blogger: www.blogger.com • Wordpress: www.wordpress.com

Planning

Technology can make assembling sets of examples and nonexamples more efficient because the examples and nonexamples can be rearranged quickly and easily in many different ways. Also, technology allows teachers to locate examples and nonexamples easily using image search engine tools like Google™ Images (http://images.google.com), Picsearch® (www.picsearch.com), and Creative Commons (http://creativecommons.org). They can also search video repositories, such as YouTube™, (www.youtube.com), TeacherTube®, (www.teachertube.com), Blinkx (www.blinkx.com), and Truveo® (www.truveo.com). Many search engines also include advanced search features that enable users to locate audio examples such as music clips or animal sounds.

Teachers can use digital search tools in the planning stage to determine the critical and noncritical attributes of a concept and the relationships among its critical attributes. For example, Doug, the teacher in Scenario 6-3, might want to teach the concept of "primary source." He might examine online entries for the concept in Merriam-Webster's dictionary, Roget's thesaurus, Wikipedia®, the Library of Congress Learning Page, Encyclopedia Britannica, and the National Council of Social Studies. Likewise, a cluster search using a tool like Yippy® (http://yippy.com) or Mooter (www.mooter.com.au) might yield interesting ideas previously unconsidered about attributes of the topic, as well as suggestions for examples and nonexamples.

Concept-mapping tools such as Inspiration, Kidspiration®, MindManager™, Openmind, and SmartDraw® are also useful during planning. Teachers can create visual representations of concepts to use during instruction. Such visual representations can be used during the presentation step, and they may also be shared with students as a graphic organizer to record what was learned or used as a study guide later. Teacher-created concept maps can also be used to assess student understanding. Many teachers create these as a part of the planning process for a Concept Attainment lesson, as well.

Implementation

Many technologies can make the presentation of examples and nonexamples more engaging and effective. Using digital examples and nonexamples is practical because it

1. minimizes costs for purchasing realia (i.e., real, physical examples and nonexamples);
2. reduces the physical space needed to store materials;
3. facilitates sharing and display of examples and nonexamples (e.g., through a website or digital presentation), and
4. simplifies organization and reorganization of examples and nonexamples.

Multimedia presentation tools (e.g., PowerPoint, Keynote, Kid Pix®, SMART Notebook, etc.) encompass all of those practical aspects of using technology to implement a Concept Attainment lesson. Many kinds of examples and nonexamples (e.g., clip art, images, animations, audio, video, graphs, and charts) can be shared using multimedia presentation tools. Such tools also streamline the process of organizing the concepts in the presentation. With the click of a mouse, a teacher using presentation software can reorder her examples easily and quickly—even between classes—if she discovers the current ordering of examples and nonexamples is confusing her students.

More complex resources such as charts, graphs, and websites can be organized and presented using a webpage or even a word-processed document with links (see Scenario 6-3). Some teachers appreciate the interactivity of interactive whiteboards or tablet computers for presenting examples and nonexamples. As they are introduced, students are encouraged to select items with their fingers and drag them to the appropriate column (example or nonexample).

In addition to enhancing a presentation by making it a rich, multimedia experience, technology tools also allow all students in the class to interact with the material at the same time. By projecting examples and nonexamples on a screen or interactive whiteboard, teachers make the lesson a shared experience. Demonstrations of the concept can be seen by all and experienced in a group setting. The shared experience of the Concept Attainment model creates an engaging atmosphere in the classroom. Methods for projecting the examples and nonexamples include interactive whiteboards (e.g., SMART Board™, Promethean, Panabord™, Mimio®), multimedia projector, document camera, or a simple overhead or opaque projector. New apps make it possible to display the whiteboard files simultaneously on a tablet computer for students who benefit from a close view of the presentation.

Assessment

There are numerous ways to use digital tools in the assessment process. As students' understanding of concepts grows over time, digital tools are particularly useful for archiving and capturing learning at the various stages of their development. In other words, digital tools do a good job of creating snapshots which illustrate student understanding at a particular time which can then be reviewed, compared, and assessed. If a teacher wants students to demonstrate their understanding of a concept in digital format at the beginning of a lesson, he or she might provide the student with an unsorted set of examples and nonexamples in a digital file that can be manipulated and reviewed over and over again. After sorting the concepts, the student can save the file with his or her name and the date in the file name to indicate his or her understanding of the concept at that point in time. Later in the unit, after experiencing opportunities to build understanding of the concept, the student might be asked to open the unsorted file again and demonstrate his or her growing understanding. Once again, the teacher might instruct the student to save the file with his or her name and the date. At the close of this unit, all of the files can be compared and the student can be asked to review, analyze, reflect on, and express the growth of his or her knowledge over time.

Digital tools support reflection in many ways. Web 2.0 technologies enable and facilitate the sharing of this reflection. The quality of students' reflections are often improved when students know they will be sharing their ideas with others. Blogging platforms such as Blogger (www.blogger.com) and Wordpress (www.wordpress.com) are excellent tools for recording learning experiences and reflecting on them. Teachers can also encourage students to post reflections to online discussion boards using tools such as Moodle (www.moodle.com) or some other content management system. Multimedia discussions like those possible in VoiceThread (www.voicethread.com) and on wikis (e.g. PBWiki: www.pbwiki.com, Wikispaces: www.wikispaces.com) might further support student reflections and conversations about their learning. Such tools allow students to share their understandings with their peers and potentially other students around the world studying the same concept.

Concept Attainment Model Lesson Plan Example

The Concept Attainment Model Lesson is an example of how this model might be implemented in practice. Figure 6-6 provides an outline of the model's steps as they might occur in the lesson.

Figure 6-6   Outline of the Concept Attainment Model Lesson Steps

Concept Attainment Model Steps	Concept Attainment Model Lesson
Presentation of examples	Teacher presents examples and nonexamples that illustrate symmetry. Teacher asks students to list the attributes of the examples and nonexamples presented and examine commonalities among the examples and nonexamples.
Formation and analysis of hypotheses	Teacher asks students to form a hypothesis of the concept through critical analyses of the examples and nonexamples. Students "test" and substantiate their hypotheses as examples and nonexamples are presented. The teacher verifies or refutes their hypotheses.
Closure	Teacher asks students to summarize the critical attributes essential to the concept "symmetry." They are also asked to formulate a definition of "symmetry" and reflect on their learning during the lesson.
Application	The teacher asks students to change nonexamples into examples of symmetry (see Worksheet 6-4), then asks them to formulate their own examples of symmetry in nature.

LESSON CONTEXT

GRADE LEVEL(S): This is a lesson suitable for all educational levels. However, the targeted audience for this lesson is a seventh-grade art class.

CONTENT AREA: Art—but can be modified for other subject areas such as science.

PHYSICAL TEACHING ENVIRONMENT: This lesson will be taught in a regular classroom with a computer and projector for the PowerPoint presentation.

APPLICATION OF REVISED BLOOM'S TAXONOMY: This lesson requires students to use the *remembering* level of the revised Bloom's taxonomy by explaining what they have learned about symmetry, as well as the *applying* level of Bloom's taxonomy, because students are to apply their knowledge about symmetry in changing nonexamples to examples and providing new examples of symmetry.

Lesson Plan

GOAL(S): Students will learn what symmetry is.

Standard(s) Addressed:

ISTE NETS for Students 2007 #4[1]

---

[1]National Educational Technology Standards for Students (NETS•S), Second Edition © 2007 ISTE ® (International Society for Technology in Education), www.iste.org. All rights reserved.

OBJECTIVE(S): Students will be able to form hypotheses about the definition of "symmetry" by examining examples and nonexamples of this concept with 100% accuracy.

ESTIMATED TIME: 20–30 minutes depending on how much time students need to analyze examples and nonexamples.

MATERIALS NEEDED: Symmetry PowerPoint, paper, pencil

PREREQUISITE SKILLS: Students should understand the following vocabulary: attributes, concept, characteristics, and hypothesis.

LESSON PROCEDURES (Text in italics is suggested teacher dialogue.)

Anticipatory Set (Introduction): *Today, we are going to play a game to learn a new concept. I will share different examples and nonexamples of the concept. As I share these examples, please write down the different attributes, or characteristics, of these examples and nonexamples. You will need to figure out the common characteristics among the examples and hypothesize about what the concept is. Keep in mind that there may be some attributes common to both examples and nonexamples. The objective is to determine the critical attributes of the concept.*
Before we get started, here are some ground rules for our game:

1. *Keep your hypotheses private. Do not shout out or share your hypotheses with anyone.*
2. *Write down your hypotheses as I present the examples and nonexamples to you.*
3. *Concentrate on what the examples have in common.*
4. *List the attributes of the concept as examples and nonexamples are presented.*
5. *Eliminate (cross out) attributes that are not represented in examples.*
6. *Form working definitions of the concept as examples and nonexamples are presented by writing down your definition. Remember: Nonexamples may have some attributes of examples.*
7. *Be prepared to discuss your hypotheses and support it with data (examples and nonexamples).*

Presentation: The teacher presents examples and nonexamples of symmetry using the PowerPoint presentation. Students generate hypotheses as the teacher presents examples one by one. NOTE: The teacher may wish to provide students with a printout of the presentation to facilitate recording of ideas. As the teacher presents examples and nonexamples, she asks the following:

1. *What attributes does 'X' example have that is similar to 'Y' example?*
2. *How are the attributes different from those presented in the nonexamples? Explain and justify your reply with data from the examples/nonexamples.*
3. *What similarities and differences have you noticed between the examples and nonexamples? Explain and justify your reply with data from the examples/nonexamples.*

Analysis of Hypotheses: Students analyze (or test) their hypotheses based on the examples and nonexamples presented in the presentation. During this step, teachers should ask probing questions as needed, such as the following:

1. *What is your hypothesis about what this concept is?*
2. *What is your definition of the concept? (Write it down).*
3. *How do data presented (examples and nonexamples) support your hypothesis?*
4. *Why do you believe you are correct?*

5. *Share your hypothesis with a partner. Discuss why you believe your definition of the concept is correct.*

At some point, students need to be told that the concept of the lesson is "symmetry." This may become apparent as students share their hypotheses. If not, the teacher should make sure students understand that symmetry is the concept illustrated by the examples and nonexamples.

Closure: Teacher asks students to think about their own definition of "symmetry" based on the presentation. Then, students pair up with a partner and share their ideas with one another, then with the whole class, to develop a class definition of symmetry. Teacher says: *With your partner, modify your definition of the concept based on your analyses. Then, we will share your definitions with the class as a whole to form a class definition of the concept.* After students have developed a consensus about the definition and attributes of "symmetry," the teacher asks students to reflect on their learning by asking them: *Now I would like for you to think about the lesson. What did you learn? How did you learn it? What did you learn about "symmetry"? What did you learn about analyzing the examples and nonexamples? Were you surprised at your initial hypotheses? How long did it take to comprehend what "symmetry" is? Please write down your ideas on a blank sheet of paper. Be specific, too.* After students write down what they learned, the teacher should give them the opportunity to share their lessons learned with their peers.

Application: Teacher gives students additional examples/nonexamples to analyze, asks students to change nonexamples into examples, or asks students to create several examples that have the attributes of the concept. Use Worksheet 6-4. Students could also ponder the question: *Are there any nonexamples that can be changed into examples? Why or why not?*

ASSESSMENT

Formative assessment Throughout the lesson the teacher should be assessing whether students grasp what the critical attributes of the concept are by asking probing questions, examining students' notes, and learning about their hypotheses.

Summative assessment Include a question on a final unit exam related to the concept, its definition, and/or its attributes.

LESSON EXTENSIONS AND MODIFICATIONS

- Students may learn about three different types of symmetry: reflection, rotation, and translation.
- Students may explore their school, home, or art museum to find other examples of symmetry around them.
- Examine Escher's art: www.mcescher.com/Gallery/gallery-symmetry.htm
- Watch Learning Links presentation online: www.linkslearning.org/Kids/1_Math/2_Illustrated_Lessons/4_Line_Symmetry/index.html
- Assign or incorporate additional online activities:
  - National Council of Teachers of Mathematics, mirror tool: http://illuminations.nctm.org/ActivityDetail.aspx?ID=24
  - National Council of Teachers of Mathematics, translations and bilateral/rotational symmetry: http://illuminations.nctm.org/LessonDetail.aspx?ID=L474

- Java activity, Welcome to Our Introduction to Symmetry: www.geom.uiuc. edu/~demo5337/s97a/java.html
- Symmetry activity, Hael Media Website: www.haelmedia.com/OnlineActivities_txh/ mc_txh4_001.html

Differentiation Strategies for the Concept Attainment Model Lesson

Below are some strategies one might apply to differentiate instruction in the Concept Attainment Model Lesson.

Content

Students might experience the content in this lesson in different ways. The content in this Concept Attainment Model Lesson consists of the examples and nonexamples of symmetry. The teacher may use realia (e.g., real symmetrical items) to demonstrate symmetry, such as fruit, butterfly, pocket folder, etc. The use of realia or images rather than written text would support the needs of English Language Learners (ELLs) who might find it difficult to read textual prompts. To promote inclusion of all students' backgrounds, a teacher might want to take special care when selecting examples to ensure that those selected are culturally significant to his or her students. To illustrate, he or she might decide to use the Indonesian and Jamaican flags as examples of symmetry and the American and Brazilian flags as nonexamples of symmetry. The lesson might be taught in groups that correspond to ability level so that students who catch on easily might be challenged with more difficult examples and nonexamples (e.g., words or sentences that are symmetrical such as palindromes). Those who struggle might be supported with more numerous and concrete examples. Those who have mastered visual symmetry might be challenged to consider the concept in music or movement.

Process

The process of instruction might be varied in numerous ways to support the needs of learners in the class. First, to assist the ELLs, the teacher might provide instructions for the lesson in advance to her students in their native language translated by a translation tool (software or App). Further, she might allow them to write their notes in their native language and later provide a summary of thinking in English. Teaching this lesson in a succession of small groups rather than a whole class might enable the teacher to support students who have difficulty focusing in whole-class activities. She could also provide all of the examples and nonexamples at once using flash cards. Alternatively, students could work in pairs or small mixed-ability groups from the onset.

Product

A quality assessment of students' understanding of the critical attributes of symmetry might be gained through an examination of student expressions given a range of tools and options. Students might demonstrate their understanding by drawing symmetrical objects using their choice of a computer, pencil, or other tool, and then by describing what makes them symmetrical orally or in a written paragraph. These options would support those who struggle with written expression. They may also allow gifted learners to choose an appropriate challenge.

Chapter Summary

This chapter introduced the Concept Attainment model, an instructional model for teaching concepts and supporting students' acquisition of conceptual knowledge. Teachers using this model introduce examples and nonexamples to students who then analyze them and form hypotheses. At the end of this fluid, cyclical process, students will have developed a definition of the concept, reflected on their own learning, and applied their newfound knowledge to novel situations. The model is beneficial in that it builds on students' prior knowledge, promotes critical-thinking skills (specifically discrimination and generalization), and engages curiosity. Technology can support this model by facilitating the presentation of items related to the concept, capturing a record of student learning, and supporting expression of the learning process.

Review Questions

1. What is the history of the Concept Attainment model? Why was it developed?

2. What are the steps of the Concept Attainment model?

3. What type of content is best to teach when applying the Concept Attainment model? Provide and explain examples of content that would be appropriate and inappropriate.

4. What are the benefits of applying the Concept Attainment model? What are some of the challenges?

5. How can the Concept Attainment model be used to differentiate instruction and support diverse learners' needs?

6. How can technology be used to implement the Concept Attainment model?

Application Exercises

To promote your ability to apply the learning you gained in studying this chapter, please complete the following exercises that challenge you to analyze a lesson plan you have written using the Concept Attainment model OR using the lesson plan included in this chapter. These exercises are designed to help you to (1) develop and build your Technological Pedagogical Content Knowledge, (2) increase your ability to integrate technology more effectively into the model, (3) expand the skills, knowledge, and dispositions required to learn from practice, and (4) become a more intentional teacher and a better educational designer.

TECHNOLOGY INTEGRATION ACTIVITY

1. Consider the following and discuss with a partner or reflect independently.

   a) In the lesson plan you are analyzing, how does (or could) the integration of technology tools make learning more efficient, effective, and engaging? Can you explain and indicate how to measure the impact on student learning?

   b) Will all learners be aided through the integration of technology? Are there some who might need special support to gain full benefit from technology tools? How might you support this? Is there a way to leverage your students' strengths in technology to the benefit of this lesson? How?

   c) What plans could you put in place to promote a more successful use of technology and minimize (or eliminate) risk of failure? What proactive plan could you put in place ahead of lesson implementation to ensure technology works smoothly and for all learners? What reactive approach could you take to ensure desired learning still occurs if technology malfunctions during the lesson?

TEACHER PERFORMANCE ACTIVITIES

2. **Academic Vocabulary and Language Demands:** Academic vocabulary is the vocabulary that students must be able to understand to be successful performing content area learning. Language demands involve the ways language is used in speaking, writing, listening, and reading in the learning tasks of a lesson and in the expressions of student learning. In the context of the lesson plan you are working with (your own or the one provided in the chapter), consider the following questions and discuss them with a partner or reflect on them alone:

   a) What academic vocabulary and language demands exist in any lesson designed with the Concept Attainment model? What are the words associated with learning concepts and using the model that pose a challenge to the plan's targeted learners?

   b) Make a list of the academic vocabulary students must comprehend and language demands of the Concept Attainment model lesson plan you are reviewing. How might students' backgrounds, lived experiences, and prior learning experiences affect their prior knowledge of these terms?

   c) How would you determine whether and which students have mastery of the academic language before the lesson begins?

   d) How might students be supported in developing proficiency with academic language in this lesson context? What visual or other resources might you use?

3. **Planning:** In the context of a lesson plan that you are analyzing, discuss the following with a partner or reflect independently:

   a) Explain how the steps of the Concept Attainment model build on each other to lead students to make clear and meaningful connections among identified learning goals or objectives.

   b) Consider how a variety of learning needs have been addressed in the lesson.

   c) Anticipate any misconceptions students might have coming into the lesson related to

the concept. Describe any misunderstanding students might develop related to the concept during the lesson.

   d) What research or theory supports the use of this model for instruction in your learning context?

4. **Implementation:** In the context of the lesson plan that you are analyzing, discuss the following with a partner or consider these independently:

   a) Explain how the steps of the Concept Attainment model and the activities that students will perform in the lesson you are reviewing will result in engaged learning. What indicators would you look for during the implementation of your lesson to measure who is engaged and how much?

   b) How well does your lesson challenge learners to apply their learning in meaningful contexts? Explain.

   c) What thinking skills can be learned and applied by students in future learning through participation in this lesson? Can you describe another context where the thinking skills might be utilized?

5. **Assessment:** Consider the following and discuss with a partner or reflect independently:

   a) Would consideration of students' backgrounds and prior learning and experiences as they relate to learning goals/objectives help you design a more effective lesson? How?

   b) How does or could the lesson plan you are reviewing use formative assessment to direct the more successful implementation of instruction? Is there a way to make it more intentional or improve it to address students' strengths or learning needs? What type of feedback would or could students be provided?

   c) How does the plan you are reviewing support students' expression of learning? Are there multiple forms of evidence of student learning? How might students learn through an analysis of their performance? What specific indicators would you look for as evidence of student learning to determine how deeply and well they understand the targeted concept?

6. **Analyzing Teaching:** Consider the following and discuss with a partner or reflect independently:

a) Now that you have created and/or analyzed a lesson plan using the Concept Attainment model, consider how the model supports effective teaching. Can you cite specific evidence or references that support your claim? Be specific in expressing your ideas.

b) What did you learn from this activity that might inform your future practice?

Discussion Question

One of the benefits of the Concept Attainment model is that it helps students develop critical-thinking skills. First, discuss how the Concept Attainment model promotes critical-thinking skills and metacognition. Then, talk about how you will foster students' critical thinking and metacognition when you teach with this model (i.e., what will you do or say?).

Journal Entry

Examine the Concept Attainment Model Lesson included in this chapter or another Concept attainment lesson. List other examples and nonexamples you might use for teaching the concept of symmetry, and determine other ways for introducing and ordering these examples and nonexamples into a rational set. How did you make these decisions? Explain why.

Resources

- EDUCAUSE Clickers Response Systems—This site contains a number of resources pertaining to audience response systems. Resources ranging from recommended reading to a research study report are posted here. See http://www.educause.edu/library/clickers

- Hilda Taba—Here you will find a brief autobiography of Hilda Taba: www.answers.com/topic/hilda-taba

- Instructional Strategies Online—This site provides a definition, purpose, and resources for understanding the Concept Attainment Model. See http://olc.spsd.sk.ca/DE/PD/instr/strats/cattain/index.html

- Audience Response Systems
  - Senteo™: http://www2.smarttech.com/st/en-US/Products/Senteo

- TurningPoint: www.turningtechnologies.com

- Jerome Bruner—This page describes Bruner's constructivist learning theory. See http://tip.psychology.org/bruner.html

- NSDL Science Literacy Maps—This site houses the National Science Digital Library (NSDL) consisting of many different Science Literacy concept maps which may be used as students explore various science concepts. See http://strandmaps.nsdl.org

- Science and Technology Concepts for Middle Schools—STC/MS™ is an inquiry-based middle-school science curriculum developed by the National Science Resources Center. See www.stcms.si.edu

Model	Concept Development Model
Knowledge Supported	Conceptual Knowledge
Added Value	Supports development of critical-thinking skills—specifically inductive reasoning, categorizing, classifying, comparing, contrasting, interpreting data, and generalizing
	Supports development of creative-thinking skills—such as divergent thinking and generation of ideas
Technologies to Integrate	• Online reference tools to assist teacher comprehension of concepts
	• Concept-mapping tools to facilitate learner listing, grouping, and labeling
	• Image and multimedia search tools to promote development of items for analysis
	• Multimedia and creativity tools to support listing, grouping, and labeling
	• Basic digital production tools and interactive whiteboards to support presentation and social learning
	• Audience response systems for assessment
	• Screen recording to support documentation of learning
	• Smartpen and tablet computers to support differentiation

The Concept Development Model

ajt/Shutterstock

Upon entering the school office, third-grade teacher Tameka Jackson noticed a note from the new principal in her mailbox. She quickly read its contents, "Tameka, I would like to schedule your yearly observation on Thursday, October 17, from 10:00 a.m. to 11:15 a.m. I'm looking forward to seeing you in action. Cecilia Nguyen." Tameka took a deep breath and thought, "An hour and fifteen minutes to prove my competence . . . what can I do to show how skilled I am? How can I demonstrate my understanding of content and my mastery of the best method for teaching it? How can I show Principal Nguyen that I respect the diverse backgrounds and experiences of my students and challenge them to think critically about their existing knowledge? I want her to see that I can use technology in ways that make learning more efficient, effective, and engaging. What and how should I teach?"

Although Tameka had over 12 years of teaching experience, she wanted to be sure to impress Dr. Nguyen with a top-notch lesson. Tameka had just finished applying for a district-level mentor teacher position and was hoping to share some of her hard-earned expertise with others during her next career stage. A positive evaluation from Dr. Nguyen was crucial. Tameka consulted with a trusted colleague and decided she would teach a Concept Development lesson about the concept of fiction. She had taught this lesson the previous year with great success—the students enjoyed the active, creative nature of the model. They also liked building new learning on previous knowledge and experiences as they worked to understand the concept of fiction at a higher level. What Tameka liked about this instructional model was that once her planning for the lesson was done, she could become a facilitator of learning. This allowed her to "step back," observe her students, and learn about their understanding of content and individual approaches to learning. She thought the lesson would be particularly impressive to Dr. Nguyen because this year's instructional focus was on critical thinking. Her lesson exercised a good deal of that! It also would not hurt that the model supported English language learners well by acknowledging their varied backgrounds and cultural experiences.

"Yes. This lesson would be perfect," she thought.

October 17 arrived quickly, but Tameka was prepared. When Dr. Nguyen entered the classroom, her students politely acknowledged her but quickly became absorbed in the lesson. Everything went off without a hitch, and before she knew it, the time was up. Dr. Nguyen caught her attention, waved, and slipped out of the room. So, she was surprised when she noticed a note on her desk from Dr. Nguyen that said, "Interesting lesson! Let's talk after our staff meeting today—I have a few questions."

"What questions does she have?" Tameka wondered. She thought back over the steps of her lesson. First she asked students to make a class list of some examples of fiction stories. Eager to share the titles of stories that were important to them, they responded sharing such stories as *Little Red Riding Hood*, *James and the Giant Peach*, *Little Oh*, *Mufaro's Beautiful Daughters*, and *Abuela's Weave*. Once the students had made a list of stories that were important to them, she handed out laptops to previously assigned pairs of students. Then she explained that all fiction stories had special characteristics and that by working together in this lesson, they would discover these and bring their understanding of fiction stories to a new level.

The students revved up their laptops and started working with the concept-mapping software program called Kidspiration. They first picked one story from the class list. Then they recorded ideas they remembered about the story. They found it easier to work with a particular story of their own choosing than one she might assign. One group selected *Little Red Riding Hood* and recorded their ideas in a list. (An illustration of their work was saved and entered into Worksheet 7-1 in Appendix C.)

In the next step of the lesson, she asked students to consider how the ideas listed as items could be grouped together. Then she challenged them to label each group and explain these groupings to another pair of students. If they wanted, they could also regroup them if it made sense after they explained their ideas to others.

After running through the lesson in her mind, Tameka thought, "Yes. It had gone smoothly." She was uncertain what questions Dr. Nguyen might have for her.

The rest of the afternoon went by slowly. As soon as the staff meeting was over, she headed straight to Dr. Nguyen's office. Displaying some reservations, she asked Dr. Nguyen, "So, what questions do you have about my lesson? Was something wrong?" Dr. Nguyen realized her vague note had worried Tameka. She said, "I'm so sorry if I worried you. Actually, I thought everything was great. I just wanted to compliment you on a successful lesson and find out more about that intriguing 'approach' you used. I've been in education a while, but I've never seen a lesson like that before, so I want to know more about your teaching method. Is it a critical-thinking strategy? Do you use it for other lessons?"

What a surprise! Tameka realized Dr. Nguyen was interested in learning from her—not critiquing her! She sat down and excitedly began to tell Dr. Nguyen how and where she learned the Concept Development model and how it might be applied in content areas other than language arts. By the end of the meeting, Dr. Nguyen had signed Tameka up to provide an overview and mini-lesson of the Concept Development model at the next staff meeting. Leaving Dr. Nguyen's office, Tameka had a feeling that she was already on her way to being a mentor teacher! ■

CHAPTER OBJECTIVES

After reading this chapter, you will be able to:

- Describe the Concept Development model, including its history and steps.
- Communicate the applications and benefits of the Concept Development model and share what it might look like in a classroom.
- Explain how the Concept Development model is implemented and how to plan for teaching with it.
- Articulate how the Concept Development model might enable differentiated instruction and support diverse learners.
- List ways technology can enhance teaching with the Concept Development model.

Introduction

Novice and expert teachers differ in the number and variety of instructional approaches they use on a regular basis. Expert teachers not only have a larger repertoire to pull from, but they can also match instructional models and strategies appropriately with the needs of their learners and the standards they must learn. In the opening scenario, Tameka reveals her expertise by using the Concept Development model for teaching the concept of fiction to her third-graders. She knows that, while there might be other ways to teach this content, she realizes that the Concept Development model is a specialized tool that acknowledges the diverse backgrounds of her learners and promotes their critical thinking while also stretching their knowledge of content to new levels. Dr. Nguyen is rightfully impressed by Tameka's competence.

In this chapter, we present another model that might be added to a teacher's repertoire for teaching concepts. Like the Concept Attainment model (Chapter 6) and the Inductive model (Chapter 8), the Concept Development model offers a refined method for promoting students' understanding of certain concepts. Because there are different types of concepts and reasons for teaching them, a competent teacher needs a variety of concept models in his or her tool kit and knowledge about how to implement each.

The Concept Development model allows students to build on existing knowledge of and experiences with a concept to refine and extend their knowledge. It is well-suited for teaching abstract and complex concepts that are more difficult to grasp, teach, and represent. With its emphasis on developing students' conceptual knowledge, the Concept Development model is similar to other models for teaching concepts. It is, however, distinct from these other models in that it (1) is appropriate for teaching concepts that are abstract and complex, (2) promotes understanding of the relationships between concepts, (3) challenges students to deepen and extend existing understanding of a concept, and (4) pushes students to exercise a distinct set of thinking skills (i.e., interpreting data, organizing, classifying, comparing, synthesizing, and generalizing).

What Is the Concept Development Model?

The **Concept Development model** is an interactive, engaging instructional model that challenges learners to expand and refine their understanding of concepts through various cognitive processes. It capitalizes on students' natural inclination to acquire new knowledge and situate new concepts and their characteristics into existing conceptual frameworks. When practicing this model, learners identify, analyze, organize, and classify examples of a concept and use this experience to make generalizations about it. They analyze what they know and have experienced about a concept and look for and compare patterns to deepen their understanding of a specific concept and its relationship to other concepts. When participating in the Concept Development model, students simultaneously practice critical-thinking skills, learn about the specific concept being studied, and develop conceptual knowledge. Conceptual knowledge, as is explained in Chapter 1, is knowledge of the relationships between classifications and categories.

Figure 7-1 Sample Concepts to Explore with the Concept Development Model

Subject	Concepts
Art	artistic media (watercolor, acrylic, oil, pastel), principles of graphic design, artistic movements
Language Arts	literary themes, types of poetry, elements of character development
Mathematics	place value, fractions/decimals/integers, geometric shapes
Music	families of instruments, musical genre
Health/Physical Education	food groups, body systems, emotions, teamwork
Social Studies	types of government, geographic regions, responsibilities of citizenship
Science	types of seeds, food web, habitats, types of clouds

The Concept Development model is best used when a teacher wants students to build on their existing knowledge about a concept and refine their understanding of it. For example, in the opening scenario, students are asked to consider the concept of fiction by analyzing what they know about fiction from specific stories they have read that are considered part of the concept of "fiction." Students consider details about specific fiction stories in particular and make and evaluate generalizations about such literature in general.

Benefits of this model include that it teaches critical-thinking skills, helps students retain and gain content knowledge, and acknowledges students' diverse backgrounds and prior knowledge. Other benefits include that it promotes the recognition of similarities and differences, challenges students to identify patterns, engages students in active learning and hands-on activities, and helps teachers learn about students' prior knowledge. Figure 7-1 provides several examples of different concepts that might be explored using the Concept Development model.

What Are the History and Origins of the Concept Development Model?

Hilda Taba (1967) developed the Concept Development model to expand students' understanding of concepts by challenging them to categorize, develop, extend, and refine their notions of concepts. It was conceived through her work on a U.S. Department of Education grant to develop a K-8 social studies curriculum known as the "Taba Curriculum Development Project" (TCDP). The TCDP involved the development, testing, and evaluation of social studies curriculum over a 10-year period with students in Contra Costa County Schools in California. It was completed in 1969. During her work on the project, Taba also conducted research on children's thinking. She used the findings from this research to improve the TCDP curriculum and to fine-tune the steps and questions used in the Concept Development model. She discovered that each child's experiences with and competence for thinking varied considerably and asserted that all children should be taught thinking skills systematically, actively, and incrementally. Taba's ideas were revolutionary at the time—and are still relevant today.

The Concept Development model provides a formal instructional opportunity for students to grapple with concepts and develop their thinking skills. In this model, the teacher structures instruction for students and supports their growth and development by asking probing questions that build on their prior knowledge, stimulate their thinking, and foster deeper understanding of concepts.

The Concept Development model reflects many of Taba's beliefs about teaching and learning, including the notion that (1) students should construct their own understanding of concepts, (2) teachers should teach students to think by structuring meaningful learning experiences for them, and (3) curriculum should consist of "three blocks of knowledge—key concepts, organizing facts, and specific facts" (Fraenkel, 1992, p. 172). The model also reflects Taba's work as a teacher educator, curriculum theorist and designer, and researcher who was influenced by the progressive education movement. Taba studied with John Dewey and William Kilpatrick and worked with Ralph Tyler. Taba is also credited with developing other instructional models including the Inductive model (see Chapter 8).

When Should the Concept Development Model Be Applied and Why?

The Concept Development model is a powerful model of teaching. It develops students' conceptual knowledge, allows teachers to introduce or assess new concepts, teaches thinking skills, and builds on students' prior knowledge and lived experiences. Ways in which teachers should use the Concept Development model are discussed in the following sections.

Develop Conceptual Knowledge

To achieve academic success, students must understand what concepts are in general and also comprehend the particular concepts embedded within the curriculum. The nature, variety, and difficulty of concepts that are addressed within the academic subject areas differ considerably. A concept's complexity, attributes, and level of concreteness can make it more or less challenging for learners to grasp. Because there are so many contexts in which concepts need to be taught—and so many individual concepts—it is not surprising that there are numerous models for teaching them. The Concept Development model is so named because it is an appropriate model to use when a teacher intends to develop students' understanding of a concept with which they already have some familiarity. If no familiarity exists, the Inductive model (Chapter 8) might be a better choice.

The Concept Development model is useful for addressing abstract concepts. Abstract concepts often have attributes which cannot be experienced easily or concretely through the senses—such as the concept of good nutrition (in Scenario 7-3) or fiction literature (in the opening scenario). The Concept Development model works to promote students' understanding of abstract concepts because it enables learners to draw from prior experiences they have had with the concept being explored. Such experiences may have occurred over a long period of time in numerous settings, and the Concept Development model allows students to revisit these experiences. The model provides a vehicle for students to structure their analysis as they look for patterns and compare and generalize about them.

The Concept Development model is also useful in helping students understand complex concepts. Complex concepts are challenging for learners because their mastery often requires understanding of the relationship between the concept being explored and its relation to other concepts. The Concept Development model provides appropriate structure for helping students learn about the main concept in a lesson (i.e., fiction) while also learning other related concepts (i.e., nonfiction and literary genre). As students grapple with complex concepts, they can ask questions to help them form generalizations about these concepts. Often, the generalization represents a main idea or broader, unifying concept for a unit of instruction. For example, learning about fiction enhances understanding during a yearlong study of literary genres. The Concept Development model is especially suited for students to develop an understanding of how the elemental concepts that comprise a larger concept relate, including the hierarchy of their relationship. For example, students would learn that the terms *fiction* and *nonfiction* are used when discussing literature to express whether a piece of writing is factual. Writings in various literary genres may be fiction or nonfiction. Students explore the relationship between concepts by grouping, regrouping, labeling, and forming a synthesis (generalization) of the items listed.

Introduce or Assess New Concepts

Although teachers typically use the Concept Development model to develop students' conceptual knowledge, the model can also be effectively used as a pre- and/or post-assessment tool. For example, a teacher might use a Concept Development model lesson at the beginning of a unit and then engage students in a similar Concept Development lesson at the end of the unit. In this way, it is possible for the teacher and students to compare the students' knowledge about a concept at the beginning of a unit with the knowledge they demonstrate of the concept at the end. For example, students might list all of the animals they can think of and group them by where they live at the beginning of a science unit. By the end, they might group them into mammals, fish, reptiles, amphibians, and birds. Students' analysis of their own learning and growth might round out the assessment by providing an opportunity to examine learning and think metacognitively. Students might be prompted to write a reflective piece examining "what I knew about this concept at the beginning of the unit" and "what I learned about this concept by the end of the unit." Such evidence is an excellent example of alternative assessment and might make a compelling artifact for inclusion in a learning portfolio.

Teach Thinking Skills

Over 50 years ago, Hilda Taba was one of the first proponents of formally teaching critical-thinking skills to children in schools. One of her most influential beliefs was that children should be taught these skills incrementally, developmentally, and systematically. Today, Taba's ideas endure as evidenced by the continued importance of critical-thinking skills in the Common Core Standards and P21 Framework (see Chapter 1). The Concept Development model provides students an appropriate structure for learning and practicing the skills needed for examining a concept through listing, grouping, labeling, and regrouping ideas for the purpose of refining and extending their knowledge of it.

Concept formation, interpretation of data, and generalizing are thinking skills that students learn in the process of a Concept Development model lesson. Concept formation occurs when students list and group the items related to a concept. Interpretation of "data" occurs when students examine their existing knowledge of a concept through listing, grouping, and regrouping. Generalizing involves the application of complex understandings gained in one context (e.g., one step) to another related concept or context. Generalizations extend a known relationship, such as an academic rule, law, understanding, or hypotheses, to another example, instance, or concept. For example, students who learn to identify characteristics of fiction can also generalize the critical attributes of historical fiction. Though all of these critical-thinking skills are considered thought processes that most people are capable of performing, variation exists in each student's natural proficiency with each—not all learners are equally capable of practicing them. All students can benefit from structured opportunities to practice and refine these thought processes while they learn concepts and academic content.

Figure 7-2 provides an illustration of some of the critical-thinking skills students develop in each of the steps of the Concept Development model.

Figure 7-2   Concept Development and Student Thinking Skills

Concept Development Model Step	Thinking Fostered
Listing	• Activating prior knowledge • Recalling • Interpreting
Grouping	• Classifying • Comparing • Categorizing • Identifying attributes • Interpreting data • Recognizing patterns
Regrouping	• Analyzing • Generalizing • Restructuring • Verifying
Labeling	• Articulating • Expressing • Summarizing
Synthesizing	• Generalizing • Composing

Build on Students' Prior Knowledge

Even the youngest learners come to school with significant and important lived experiences. Research (Bransford, Brown, & Cocking, 1999) suggests that students' prior knowledge plays an important role in their ability to learn, recall, and make connections with (and sometimes corrections to) and among concepts. It also suggests that when students' background and lived experiences are acknowledged they feel included and learn more successfully. The Concept Development model acknowledges this. Students begin sharing their prior knowledge by listing their ideas related to a concept through open-ended questioning (i.e., questioning with no "correct" answer). Then students proceed to group, label, and regroup their ideas. Teachers should therefore choose this model when they wish to learn what students already know about a concept and when they are sure they already have relevant experiences. For instance, in the Concept Development Model Lesson at the end of this chapter, students have already read fictional stories. The teacher's job is to build on students' prior knowledge and experience by reading fictional stories, progressing through the steps of the Concept Development model, and helping them develop a deeper understanding of the concept "fiction story."

What Are the Steps in the Concept Development Model?

There are two major inductive thinking tasks performed through the five steps in the Concept Development model, as Figure 7-3 shows. The inductive thinking tasks are concept formation and interpretation of data. These tasks are embedded in the five steps of the model and initiated by teacher questioning:

1. Listing
2. Grouping
3. Labeling
4. Regrouping
5. Synthesizing

Figure 7-3 Inductive Thinking Tasks Embedded in Concept Development Model

Concept Development Model Steps	Inductive Thinking Task
1. Listing	Concept formation
2. Grouping	
3. Labeling	Interpretation of data
4. Regrouping	
5. Synthesizing	

Step One—Listing

In the first step of the Concept Development model, students examine their prior knowledge of a concept by creating a mental inventory of their existing knowledge of the concept. This step usually begins with the teacher asking, "What do you know about *x* concept? Can you think about some examples or items related to this concept?" For instance, in the Concept Development Model Lesson at the end of this chapter, the teacher asks, "What do you know about the characteristics of a fiction story? Can you explore these by listing some examples of fiction stories and thinking about them?" The students' role is to recall items from their own experience related to the concept—all of which should be devised openly by students and not the teacher. Depending on the concept being explored, the "items" recalled and listed might include (1) ideas related to a concept, (2) attributes of a specific concept, (3) concrete or abstract examples of a concept, or (4) nonexamples related to the concept. This step of the model is intended to be very open ended, and at this point, the teacher *should not* intervene by pointing out that certain items are "wrong" or do not "fit" with the concept in question—even if they are incorrect. Any erroneous items listed will be dealt with in later steps of the model. It is also important for this step to be a "low-stakes" activity so that all students are encouraged to participate. If students are evaluated in this step, it should be done informally and only after students have completed listing their ideas. The resultant inventory of items will then be reconsidered and restructured in subsequent steps of the Concept Development model.

The listing performed in this step is simply brainstorming ideas related to a concept. Brainstorming should enable students to develop a deeper understanding of the concept by exploring their prior knowledge. As such, it is important for students to generate as many ideas related to the concept as possible. Several strategies may help students generate a more extensive list of ideas. The teacher may have students work independently to list items and pool their answers with each other. Alternatively, the teacher might provide students with pictures or other cues to stimulate students' prior knowledge. Teacher questioning can also help students list and learn from considering more complicated and complex examples. Encouraging students to consider what they see and notice—details related to these items as they list them—can be helpful. Often, such observations spark additional ideas.

Note that students who have greater prior knowledge of a concept and greater confidence may find this step easier than those who do no not. While some students may race to the task, others will drag their feet. Nonetheless, all students should be encouraged to continue generating ideas even if they seem to exhaust all possibilities.

During this step, teachers should allow students to work in whatever way it is easiest for them. Some students may want to begin listing items that are simple examples or ideas related to the concept and then expand later to more complicated examples and ideas. With more abstract concepts, it might be easier to select one example of a concept and then explore as many ideas and attributes of that concept as possible during the listing step. For example, in Scenario 7-3, students list as many foods as they possibly could remember eating over the period of a week.

Step Two—Grouping

The goal of this step is to challenge students to interpret the items they have listed (i.e., think more carefully about what these items suggest about their existing knowledge), analyze these items (i.e., compare items by assigning them to groups that indicate their relatedness), and represent their thinking about how items are related. Once students have developed a comprehensive list of items associated with the concept (in the listing step), the teacher then asks students to organize the listed items into groups to show how they relate to one another. During this step, a teacher might ask students, "Examine the items you listed. How can these be grouped together?" Similarly, in Scenario 7-2, the teacher asks students to consider how instruments might be grouped together into families.

As students do this categorization, their thinking processes should shift from open-ended brainstorming to more focused interpretation and analysis of the ideas or "data" they have listed. During this shift, the teacher challenges students to think about their existing knowledge in new ways. Data interpretation involves identification of characteristics for the purpose of comparing and grouping. The process involved in the organization of ideas and the thinking that occurs during this step is as important as the actual groupings devised. Focusing on the process, the teacher may learn about students' conceptual knowledge and thinking skills. Consequently, the student will develop a baseline understanding of his or her knowledge and thinking skills as they evolve. Frequently, students categorize the items they have listed based on their similarities, but in some cases, they might group together items that do not seem to fit other categories. Questions a teacher might ask during this step include "Do any of these items belong together?" and "Are all items in your groups alike in all of the same ways or are some more alike than others?" Refer to the Concept Development Model Lesson for an example of how students might organize the items they previously listed into groups.

As much as possible, the teacher wants to help students become aware of their content knowledge, thinking skills, and the rationale for their actions. The teacher might ask questions such as "In this case, why did you group the items in the way they were grouped?" It is helpful if students are required to share this thinking aloud or record it in written or audio form so they can reflect on it at a later time. For example, in the Concept Development Model Lesson the teacher says, "Remember, what you just shared with me about why you grouped these items this way—you will want to think about this later." The teacher may also want students make a record of their groupings (i.e., take photographs, save copies of computer files, or record group names) and archive their thinking about the groupings (i.e., keep written anecdotal records, use a digital voice recorder, or take photographs).

Step Three—Labeling

The purpose of this step is for students to articulate and formalize their thinking about their grouping decisions. After students group the listed items, they should analyze their reasons for grouping the items in a particular way. That is, they should become aware of their rationale. One way to help them crystallize their reasoning is by creating a "label" for each of the groupings in the form of a simple word or phrase that describes the items in the group. This step takes the interpretation and analysis of data to a more intentional and formal level as the teachers asks students to articulate their thinking behind the groupings they made in Step Two. For example, in Scenario 7-1, the teacher challenges his students to devise the labels of "living things" and "nonliving things" after analyzing photographs of objects in their classroom that fit these categories.

The teacher's role in this step is to assist students with the challenging tasks of articulating and recording the rationale for their labels. To help students think more deeply about the labels for their groupings, the teacher might ask students to explain their groupings and the labels they created for them. The teacher might say, "How do these items relate to one another?" "What are the common characteristics of items (within and among groupings)? What is one word or phrase for each group that describes it?" This step challenges students to become metacognitive, to articulate their thinking to themselves and others, and to justify their groupings and rationale for them.

Step Four—Regrouping

The goal of this step is to consider and recognize alternative patterns existing in the items that have been listed or to correct and/or to reorganize any items that might be grouped more appropriately after labeling. This step challenges students to reconsider their previous thinking and the labels they devised in Step Three. Often during Step Three, new insights emerge, as students articulate their ideas by generating labels. These insights extend or deepen students' learning of a concept and prompt them to consider new or different groupings of their items. Students take their thinking and their awareness of it "to the next level" of the cognitive process dimension when they re-examine every item, its grouping, and its label. Students should justify their groupings, regroupings, and any new or revised labels by explaining how the items in the various groups relate or do not.

As students revisit the items, they may (1) reclassify some items into existing groups, (2) change the labels of their groups to represent more accurately the items contained within them, or (3) revise or generate additional labels for new groups and reclassify existing items.

In any case, students should be able to explain why they made such changes. A teacher might ask, "Why did you group your items under X category?" "Is there another way you could have classified these items?" "Why have you relabeled your items?" "What new ideas have you had during this process?" "What explanation do you have for your groupings?" These questions stimulate a student to engage in more complex thinking and advanced cognitive processes.

A teacher can learn a lot about his or her students by watching how they react when they are asked to regroup their items. Some students balk at this step, not wanting to repeat a task they have already completed. In most cases, their unwillingness to regroup items stems from more fixed and less flexible thinking habits. In other cases, students are reluctant to engage in regrouping because they do not understand the purpose of doing so. Our world, however, is not fixed and finite. The teacher may need to communicate the fact that flexible and fluid thinking patterns are necessary in our world—a world where ideas and our perception of them evolve and change. Helping students recognize that concepts change, including how we think about them, and that fluid thinking has a purpose will promote their success in this model and in future learning.

Step Five—Synthesizing

The purpose of this step is to help students synthesize their understanding of the concept by creating a generalization about it based on their thinking. In this step, the teacher asks students to examine all of the groups and their labels. Then students are asked to make a connection between them by providing a summary statement that describes their relationship. For instance, the teacher might ask, "What is one sentence that summarizes the connection between the items you organized into groups with different labels?" to help students develop a generalization in the form of a phrase or sentence that represents the relationship between the items listed, grouped, labeled, and regrouped. Here students must be challenged to make a generalization based on the evidence (i.e., items that have been grouped and regrouped into categories and labeled) they have examined. Teachers should define what a generalization is and model how to develop one with students. It often helps to do this before using the Concept Development model. A teacher might assist students by providing them a definition of a generalization, such as "a generalization is making an all-purpose conclusion based on the examination and analysis of particular examples—the items listed and grouped." Some examples of generalizations are "All birds are animals," "All fiction stories consist of made-up characters, settings, and/or plots," and "Schools function to prepare students to live fully, work effectively, and participate in a democracy."

What Does the Concept Development Model Look Like in the Classroom?

Although the Concept Development model was developed to teach social studies, it may be used in any subject area because categorizing concepts and understanding their relationships are essential aspects of learning in any subject area. In the sections that follow, we provide three scenarios that illustrate what the Concept Development model might look like if you were to observe it being applied in different classroom settings for concept teaching. The model's use is illustrated in different subject areas and grade levels and using different teaching techniques and resources. While reading the scenarios, pay special attention to the ways teachers customize the model in their own teaching contexts. Also make note of how the steps of the Concept Development model are consistently implemented yet still flexible enough to enable the unique instructional decisions made by the teachers. At the end of these scenarios, you will be asked to compare the various implementations of this model.

Scenario 7-1

Joe Justice, a first-grade teacher, is busy facilitating science learning centers in his classroom. The first two centers have students reviewing content from the unit just finished on the water cycle. The third has students preparing for a lesson on living and non living things. In this center, students work with Joe to take photos with the digital camera of living and non living things that will be used for a Concept Development model lesson the following day.

Interest is highest at the photography center. Mr. Justice explains to the students in his instructions, "In this center, you will be using our digital camera to take pictures of everyday objects we see so that tomorrow we can consider what we know about these things." One student in this group snaps a few shots of the class pets—a lizard, a bullfrog, a guinea pig, and a hermit crab. Another takes pictures of the contents of her desk. When Mr. Justice rings the bell, the students switch groups.

Mr. Justice repeats the same instructions for the new group at the photography center, and the group begins taking pictures of desks, light fixtures, the pencil sharpener, classroom computer, chairs, blackboards, pencil cup, books, and the third-graders at recess they see through the window. The bell rings again, and the final group takes its photos. These students snap photos of one another, a box of crayons, and the sprouts growing in paper cups on the windowsill from last week's science experiment.

On the following day during their science block, students will be placed into centers again. Each group will participate in one center activity that involves using an interactive whiteboard with a file Mr. Justice created from the collection of classroom images taken at the photography center. Students will be encouraged to group images into categories based on their similarities—again working in their assigned, small groups guided by their teacher. Students will be encouraged to label these groups and explain the reasons for their groupings. Mr. Justice will facilitate this process by asking questions that challenge students to compare items, identify patterns, and examine what they know about the objects they have photographed. Mr. Justice will also archive this process using an audiovisual recording software application that comes with the interactive whiteboard and by saving a copy of the file once students have sorted the photographs. Mr. Justice will use this information to help him understand his students' existing concept of living and non living things.

Student taking picture with digital camera
© wavebreakmedia Shutterstock

By the end of the unit, he anticipates that his students will be able to do this activity again and group images independently. He expects that by this time, students will be able to explain some of the differences between living and non-living things in their classroom and bring in examples from home for both categories. He hopes that when they review the work he has captured at the beginning of the unit, they will understand how much they have learned and see how their understanding of the concept of living and nonliving things has grown.

Scenario 7-2

Tamara Ryan, a middle school music teacher, stands in front of her class projecting her laptop on a large screen. She begins her lesson by asking her students what they know about the characteristics of various musical instruments. They volunteer some simple responses, such as "They make different kinds of noises" and "They are made of different materials." Then she asks her students to name all of the musical instruments they can think of.

As they share their responses, Tamara enters their answers into a concept-mapping program on her laptop. When she types on the keyboard the individual instrument names, a shape appears on the computer screen with an outline around it, allowing her to manipulate and move it. Once students have listed a fair number of instruments, Ms. Ryan asks them to consider how these items might be put into groups.

One student named Sylvia volunteers to come up to the front of the classroom and group the items she thinks belong together on the interactive whiteboard. Sylvia moves the shapes containing the names of the various instruments into five groups in different areas of the whiteboard. The first grouping includes a snare drum, a bass drum, and a tambourine; the second includes a clarinet, a flute, and a recorder; the third includes a trumpet, a trombone, a xylophone, and a saxophone; the fourth includes a violin, a cello, and a guitar; and the fifth includes a piano and a tuba. Next, Ms. Ryan asks Sylvia to explain her reasons for grouping these items as she did. She says, "I put all the round instruments in one group, all the long straight instruments in another. In the third group I put all metal instruments. The fourth group has all the instruments that have strings, and the fifth has really big instruments. Next, Ms. Ryan asks Sylvia to give each group a name or label. Her labels include the following:

- Group 1: Round instruments
- Group 2: Long straight instruments
- Group 3: Metal instruments
- Group 4: Instruments with strings
- Group 5: Instruments that are really big

Ms. Ryan uses a feature in the concept-mapping program to label each group. She inserts a graphic that contains each group's name in the center of each group's items. Next, Ms. Ryan asks if there are any other students who would like to demonstrate on the whiteboard how they would regroup the items and name their groups. Charles comes to the front of the classroom and moves the items into three groups and labels them as follows:

- Group 1: "Instruments that make noise when struck or hit": bass drum, tambourine, xylophone, and piano
- Group 2: "Instruments that make noise when blown": clarinet, flute, recorder, trumpet, trombone, tuba, and saxophone
- Group 3: "Instruments that make noise when being plucked": violin, cello, and guitar

Ms. Ryan looks over his groupings and then asks other students if they want to comment on what Charles and Sylvia did or add anything they learned by watching. Phoung raises her hand and responds, "I think they both did a good job using the whiteboard and doing their grouping. It was kind of like seeing what was going on in their brains when they moved the instruments around the screen and labeled them. It also made me remember learning about the different musical instrument families last year. We had to memorize 'Wind, Strings, and Percussion.' These were kind of like the groupings Charles made. But what I learned in this activity that was different was *why* these different instruments are in these families, and I began thinking about what we learned in science earlier this year when we learned about vibration and sound."

Ms. Ryan replied, "Good. I was hoping you would be making connections with what you had learned already in music and also with other subjects like science. I was also hoping that you would think about some similarities and differences. Did anyone do that?"

Owen's hand popped up, "Yeah. I was thinking that there are a lot of 'right ways' to group the instruments if you do it by what they have in common. For example, some instruments have what they are made of in common, others have their sounds in common, some have their physical size in common, and some have the types of feeling they make you feel in common. I could not help thinking that people writing music . . . er . . . composers, have a lot of different kinds of instruments to choose from when they're thinking about how to choose and use instruments to create different types of moods with their music."

Ms. Ryan responded, "Nice addition, Owen. I was hoping you would develop some deeper understandings like this from the activity. You are right: We can group the different instruments in lots of different ways. There are many ways to group instruments—for example, in ancient China, instruments could be grouped by the materials they were made of—stone, silk, wood, etcetera. And we could group them by their pitch—soprano, alto, tenor, bass (just like we group people in a choir). Today, however, we are going to think about how they make sound. Given this emphasis, I am wondering if anyone can make a general statement about musical instrument families based on what you learned in this lesson from the last set of groupings that Charles completed."

Katrina raised her hand and volunteered, "How about musical instruments make sounds of different types based on the materials they are made of and how we interact with these materials. They can be grouped into families based on how they make sounds and music." "Very good generalization," Ms. Ryan responded.

Scenario 7-3

Maria Garcia's tenth-grade health classroom is very quiet. Students are hunched over and recopying items from their food diaries for the week on yellow sticky notes. Next, they write their names on a piece of 11" × 7" paper and begin to stick these notes to the paper in groups of their own choosing. Then Ms. Garcia asks them to describe their reasons for grouping the foods into various groups as well as to examine how the items grouped together are similar. For instance, one student, Ousman, creates the following groups: "junk food" and "healthy food," "food eaten at home or at school," and "food eaten for breakfast, lunch, or dinner." He then sorts the items he recorded from his daily diary onto the sticky notes into these various categories and writes a summary of his work on the back of the page. Ms. Garcia expects that by the end of the unit on nutrition, students will be able to group items from a typical week in their food diaries in a couple of different ways, such as by (1) nutrient density, (2) food group, (3) level of fiber, and (4) type of fat (e.g., trans fat). Then students will be asked to comment on the amount of food items they eat in each group in a reflection that should propose some lifestyle/diet goals and changes for the future.

What Do These Scenarios Illustrate?

These scenarios illustrate some of the benefits of the Concept Development model. For one, the learning in the model is meaningful to students because what is studied is based on what students already know. Lists of items might come from students' prior knowledge (e.g., musical instruments they have seen and played, as in Scenario 7-2) or from their environment (e.g., living and non living things from their classroom, as in Scenario 7-1) or personal experiences (food diary items, as in Scenario 7-3). The model promotes different types of thinking skills—listing, comparing, classifying, synthesizing, and generalizing. The model also promotes deeper understanding of concepts by challenging students to revisit their prior knowledge and extend it to new levels. These scenarios also illustrate that some modifications can be made to the Concept Development model to make it better suited for a particular setting. As you noticed, the model worked effectively in first-grade science, middle school music, and a tenth-grade high school health class to challenge students to reconsider and explore concepts with which they were already familiar more deeply. This model can also be taught using various materials (e.g., index cards, digital cameras, and sticky notes) and media (e.g., text, audio, and photographs). Moreover, the model was conducted with a small group amidst other activities and in whole group settings.

REFLECT: Take a moment to examine each of these scenarios and the variations of the Concept Development model. Consider how you might modify the Concept Development model to make it work in the context of your subject area and grade level. How might it benefit your students?

◼ Planning for Teaching with the Concept Development Model

In general, when planning to use any model for concept teaching—whether the Concept Attainment model (Chapter 6), the Concept Development model, or the Inductive model (Chapter 8), teachers will need to clarify their understanding of and purpose for addressing the concept. Appendix B has resources for clarifying concepts before teaching with these models. When planning to use the Concept Development model in particular, teachers should (1) carefully analyze the concept, (2) teach students the steps for learning with the Concept Development model, (3) scaffold students' learning and metacognition through questioning and application activities. The things that educational designers do when teaching with the Concept Development model are discussed in the following sections.

Analyze the Concepts

Before the teacher can effectively teach a concept, he or she must be clear about what the concept is, why it is being addressed in the content area curriculum, and at what developmental level it should be taught.

True mastery of a concept requires development and refinement of one's understanding through multiple experiences and varied interactions with the concept over time. Teachers who consider their own "journey" of understanding about a concept are better able to help their students as they make their own journey. For example, Maria, the teacher in Scenario 7-3, might reflect on her struggles to learn about good nutrition. She might remember the challenges she faced when trying to understand that different foods have different nutritional values and how difficult it was to understand how seemingly similar foods might have entirely different nutrients. She might also remember that the food plate relevant to students only after they understand these foundational concepts.

Teach Students about the Concept Development Model

Although many students proceed through the Concept Development model steps without any problems (as long as the teacher provides guidance and good questioning), teachers should first practice the Concept Development model with students before teaching concepts with it. Alternatively, teachers could provide their students with an outline of the steps of the model and questions to consider for each step. Worksheet 7-1 provides an example of how a pair of students working together in the Concept Development Model Lesson completed the worksheet. Worksheet 7-2 is a blank worksheet teachers might wish to use with their students. These worksheets are available in Appendix C.

One way to introduce the Concept Development model is to explore a common concept—the concept of "our class." Teachers might use individual students as "items" that are listed. She would write each student's name on a sticky note. Without making her grouping explicit, she would organize the notes into two groupings—one of boys and one of girls (by gender). As they watch their teacher grouping, students are challenged to identify the reason for grouping and suggest labels for the groups. Then the teacher might regroup the notes with the students' names by age and challenge students to make a generalization based on these groupings. A statement like "Our class consists of boys and girls who are ages 8 and 9" would be a generalization that describes the concept of "our class."

Scaffold Students' Learning and Metacognition

Although the Concept Development model is an open-ended model of teaching, it will be successful only if teachers provide the appropriate amount of time required for learning and sufficient scaffolding of students through questioning and application activities, as the following sections describe:

TIME: THE AMOUNT OF TIME DEVOTED TO IMPLEMENTING A CONCEPT DEVELOPMENT MODEL LESSON WILL STRONGLY INFLUENCE ITS SUCCESS. Teachers who use the Concept Development model must recognize that teaching thinking and practicing thinking takes time. A Concept Development model lesson might take several class periods or a whole scheduled block to complete. Concepts being explored should be of significant importance to justify these time requirements. Additional considerations should be made to ensure that the lesson does not take up too much time—that it is not overkill. Otherwise, students will lose interest or become fatigued. Determining the right amount of time required for a lesson may take some trial and error. It also requires paying close attention to how students work through the lesson. If students start to lose interest during the lesson, it may be best to move to another lesson or activity and return to the Concept Development model lesson another day.

QUESTIONING: TEACHERS SHOULD PLAN WHICH QUESTIONS THEY WILL ASK DURING EACH STEP OF THE CONCEPT DEVELOPMENT MODEL IN ADVANCE. Although they will also likely ask other questions, during the lesson, developing a list of probing questions related to each step's purpose will better facilitate student thinking during each step. Taba et al. (1971) crafted generic questions for each step that teachers should ask:

1. Listing: "What do you see (notice, find) here?"
2. Grouping: "Do any of these items seem to belong together? Why would you group them together?"
3. Labeling: "What would you call these groups you have formed?"
4. Regrouping: "Could some of these belong in more than one group? Can we put these same items in different groups? Why would you group them that way?"
5. Synthesizing: "Can someone say in one sentence something about all these groups?" (p. 67)

For an example of questions a teacher might ask students during each step, review the Concept Development Model Lesson.

APPLICATION ACTIVITIES. Taba explicitly developed the Concept Development model to include support for student thinking through its five steps. Even so, how these steps are implemented is open ended. The three main considerations teachers must make related to scaffolding students' learning is to determine (1) which tool(s) students will use to list, group, regroup, and label their items related to the concept being studied; (2) how students will be grouped during all of the steps (e.g., whole group, pairs, heterogeneous, and so on); and (3) how teachers will structure students' analysis of the items listed, grouped, labeled, and regrouped. In the Concept Development Model Lesson, for instance, the teacher asks students to list their ideas in pairs using Kidspiration, a concept-mapping program. However, students can also list their ideas individually, in pairs, or in small groups using a piece of paper, a dry-erase board, or technology tools (see the section on "What Value Does Technology Add" later in this chapter for examples of technology tools a teacher might use).

A teacher might provide structure for students' analysis by asking them to number the items they list on a piece of paper—1 to 20—and then compare the first item, number one, with all the other ideas listed. This challenges students to note their ideas on a piece of paper and list all the numbers of ideas that go together on one line of notebook paper. Then they would be asked to compare idea number two to all the remaining ideas and make a note of these items on one line of notebook paper and so on until they will have examined all of the items listed in this systematic manner. Scaffolding provided through detailed instructions can support all learners, but it is particularly helpful to students who might have trouble focusing on the activity or even starting it in the first place, such as one with attention-deficit hyperactivity disorder.

Differentiating Instruction with the Concept Development Model

Typically, teachers differentiate the content, process, or product associated with instruction based on learners' interest, readiness, and learning style. Below we describe suggestions for differentiating the Concept Development model along these lines to meet the needs of diverse learners. Additional examples for differentiating instruction can be found following the Concept Development Model Lesson.

Content

The Concept Development model has wonderful built-in support for learner differences. In its very design, it acknowledge and builds on learners' prior knowledge and lived experiences—validating these and capitalizing on them in the learning process. However, additional modifications can be made within the implementation of the model to enable greater support for individual learners. For instance, differentiating content in a Concept Development model lesson often involves modifying the materials students work with as they manipulate ideas related to the content—the concept being studied. There are several ways to to accomplish this. Because students express their ideas when progressing through the various steps of the Concept Development model through listing, grouping, labeling, re-grouping, and synthesizing their ideas, this can be differentiated by offering students different options for expressing these themselves. The content can be differentiated by providing students access to a broad range of tools that may be used. Some options include file cards, sticky notes, a concept-mapping application (i.e., software such as Inspiration or an online tool like Gliffy), photographs, realia, and other manipulatives.

Providing students with choices about the tools and methods they use to express and organize their ideas will motivate them to articulate their thinking and facilitate their manipulation of ideas—empowering them to take charge of their own learning. For example, young children with limited writing skills and English language learners may find that listing their ideas in written format slows down their learning. In this case, students might use voice recognition software to convert their ideas into something that can be manipulated physically. Alternatively, another student, their teacher, or a classroom aide might assist them to record their ideas. Visual learners might prefer to use symbols or clip art in lieu of words. Therefore, the teacher could allow them to cut examples from magazines or other print media. If technology is available, a teacher might work with a small group of students to locate clip art that represents their ideas and then use an interactive whiteboard to display the images to the whole class. Kinesthetic-tactile learners could then manipulate the pictures into groups, regroup them, and even label them with the teacher's assistance.

When selecting the concepts to be explored in a Concept Development model lesson, teachers must consider the breadth and depth of students' prior knowledge with those concepts. Some students' knowledge may be extensive and others' experiences quite limited. The variation among students in a classroom might be significant or fairly uniform. Organizing students into heterogeneous groups might support this variation, as discussed in the next section. In cases when it does not, however, some concepts may not be able to be explored using this model. Teachers must also be careful to consider how their students' different cultures affect their understanding of a concept. For instance, the concept "evolution" has different meanings for different groups of people.

Process

The two primary ways a teacher might differentiate the process of instruction within the steps of the Concept Development model are through use of flexible student groupings and the scaffolding of activities within the different steps. Flexible grouping involves the use of different kinds of grouping of students for different purposes in the differentiated classroom. Sometimes groups will be homogeneous for a specific characteristic (i.e., prior knowledge), and sometimes they might be heterogeneous. Whether the groups are homogeneous or heterogeneous depends on the teacher's reason for grouping. If a teacher's goal is to support a student with limited prior knowledge of the concept to be learned, the most supportive grouping would be a heterogeneous one that brings that student together with those students who have more extensive prior knowledge. If the goal for grouping is to support slow starters, then mixing those students with faster starters in heterogeneous groupings would be most supportive. Grouping learners of varying prior knowledge and with different start times together is most likely to result in success. The teacher may also prefer to conduct the listing step with the class as a whole and subsequent steps individually.

The steps in this model are, by their very design, a form of scaffolding. Even so, a teacher may wish to provide step-by-step instructions for students who need such scaffolding and less direction for those who do not. A teacher might even give students a choice of using such instructions or not. The section "Planning for Teaching with the Concept Development Model" provides concrete planning suggestions for scaffolding instruction using this model.

Another way to differentiate the learning process is to provide students with opportunities to share their work with one another. Sharing their work and the rationale for their actions (e.g., why they grouped items in a certain way) provides students practice articulating their ideas. It also affords them the opportunity to experience different points of view that may help expand their understanding of a concept.

Product

Choice is a powerful motivator. When possible, give students the opportunity to decide how they will apply their knowledge to capitalize on their different strengths (some teachers even design activities that address students' multiple intelligences). This differentiation helps to address diverse learners' needs and strengths, and it provides teachers varied opportunities to evaluate their learning. For example, students who have completed a

Concept Development lesson on the nutritional density of foods in their diet might be given a choice between (1) developing a week's menu of nutritionally dense meals, (2) creating a video tour of a grocery store that showcases foods that would be nutritionally dense, (3) planning and designing a newsletter that might be sent home to explain nutritional density to parents of their classmates, or (4) creating a radio-style audio recording of an interview with an expert about nutritionally dense foods.

When providing choices for the demonstration of student learning, teachers must be careful to make sure that the same standards can be assessed through each assessment option presented.

What Are the Benefits of Applying the Concept Development Model?

Some of the benefits of the Concept Development model include that it teaches thinking skills; helps students retain content understanding; helps students see similarities, differences, and identify patterns; challenges students to exercise creative thinking; is active and hands on; promotes student expression, and helps a teacher learn more about his or her students. What the Concept Development model should do is discussed in the following sections.

Teaches Students Thinking Skills

Taba believed that students could learn thinking skills and that it was imperative for them to do so. Therefore, she developed the Concept Development model for students to cultivate and practice applying thinking skills in a systematic way. In this model, students have the opportunity to learn through their own practice, through a variety of thinking skills, and by working with and watching others work through the thinking process.

Helps Students Retain Content Understanding

Throughout the steps of the Concept Development model, students are engaged in making connections between the various items they have listed and in justifying their groupings and labels. Student involvement in this way promotes greater retention of content (Bredderman, 1978; Worthen, 1968) than other, less engaging explorations, such as reading or listening. What students remember is also broader. That is, the model helps students see similarities and differences and identify patterns.

Helps Students to See Similarities and Differences and to Identify Patterns

Following the steps of grouping, labeling, regrouping, and synthesizing, students actually work with the concept instead of simply reading about it or listening to a teacher lecture on it. The identification of patterns, themes, similarities, and differences is important across subject areas and relates to such academic standards as recognizing themes in literature, classifying living organisms, comparing various forms of governments, and more. In that way, the skills developed by the Concept Development model are highly transferable to other contexts.

Challenges Students to Exercise Creative Thinking

In addition to promoting critical-thinking skills, the Concept Development model requires and makes possible the practice of creative thinking (a different kind of thinking than critical thinking). Jonassen (2000) defines creative thinking as thinking that "uses more personal and subjective skills in the creation of new knowledge, not the analysis of existing knowledge . . . major components of creative thinking are synthesizing, imagining, and elaborating" (p. 28). When students generate novel groupings and labels to describe these groupings, students think creatively and construct new ideas based on old ones. This synthesis and creation are easy for some learners and showcase their talents. These thinking activities challenge others and provide them with practice and opportunities to develop. Subsequently, different types of learners have opportunities to grow and stretch intellectually.

Promotes Active Hands-On Learning

For a model focused on teaching concepts, it is perhaps surprising that the Concept Development model is active and hands on. It can involve the manipulation of physical objects, physical movement, and activity. This type of learning is enjoyable and energizing to students—especially those who are often disinterested in academic learning.

Acknowledges and Builds on Students' Prior Knowledge

Throughout all of the steps of the Concept Development model, students relate their prior knowledge and experience with the concept. From the initial stage, where they list items related to the concept through the final stage and demonstrate the expansion in their understanding that results from the lesson, students have the opportunity to access and build on their lived experiences and knowledge to build deeper understandings of the concept.

Aids Student Expression

This benefit is a considerable one for both teachers and students. Because this model involves taking what is in one's mind and expressing it on paper or a computer screen, it enables those engaged in it—and those watching—to visualize what students know and how they think about it. For instance, in the scenarios in this chapter, students have a variety of opportunities for expressing their learning and using different media.

Helps Teachers Learn More about Their Students

The final benefit of the Concept Development model is that it helps teachers learn more about the students they teach. The more a teacher knows about his or her students, the more he or she can teach them. The model allows teachers to observe students as they think systematically through a process. This is helpful in several ways. Because students can work through this process independently (after learning how it works), teachers can observe and analyze students' thinking as it unfolds. While students are working, teachers can observe and make anecdotal records that help them better identify and understand ways they might support student learning. Also, because the processes students apply through this model illustrate their competence in critical-thinking skills, teachers can better identify areas of strength and weakness. Observing students during a Concept Development model lesson can illustrate the amount of prior knowledge students have and the command they have over that prior knowledge. Also revealed is their ability to organize ideas, think flexibly, and, in some cases, interact with others.

What Value Does Technology Add to the Concept Development Model?

This section describes several unique ways in which technology might be utilized for the planning, implementation, and assessment of learning when using the Concept Development model. Figure 7-4 summarizes a variety of technology tools presented in this chapter that can support the planning and teaching of concepts using the Concept Development model.

Note that many of the same value-added benefits found in the Concept Attainment model (Chapter 6) are also relevant for the Concept Development model. However, several technology tools that help teachers capitalize on the Concept Development model in particular are described below.

Figure 7-4   Technology Tools for the Concept Development Model

Use	Tools
Planning	

Use digital resources to help define concepts	Reference tools available online
	• Visualization tools
	  • Shahi (a visual dictionary that combines Wiktionary content with Flickr images, and more!): http://blachan.com/shahi
	  • Visual dictionary: http://visual.merriam-webster.com
	  • Visuwords (online graphical dictionary): www.visuwords.com

Implementing	
Listing Grouping Labeling Regrouping Synthesizing	Concept-mapping tools • Freemind: http://freemind.sourceforge.net/wiki/index.php/Main_Page • Gliffy: www.gliffy.com • Inspiration: www.inspiration.com • Kidspiration: www.kidspiration.com • MindManager: www.mindjet.com/default.aspx • Mindview: www.matchware.com/en/products/mindview/default.htm • SmartDraw: www.smartdraw.com • Visio: http://office.microsoft.com/en-us/visio/default.aspx

continued

Figure 7-4   Technology Tools for the Concept Development Model
continued

Use	Tools
Implementing (continued)	

	Word cloud tools
	• Wordle: www.wordle.net
	• Tagcrowd: http://tagcrowd.com
	• TextTagCloud generator: www.artviper.net/texttagcloud
	
	Multimedia presentation tools
	• Keynote
	• Microsoft PowerPoint
	
	Interactive pen displays
	• Mimio: www.mimio.com/products/mimio_pad/index.asp
	• Wacom: http://wacom.com/en/store/interactive-pen-displays.apx
	
	Basic digital projection tools
	• Document camera/visual presenter
	  • Elmo: www.elmousa.com
	  • Dukane: www.dukcorp.com/av/audiovisual.htm
	• LCD Panel
	• In Focus Video Projector: www.infocus.com
	
	Low-tech projection tools
	• Overhead projector
	• Opaque projector
	
	Other
	• Smartpen: www.livescribe.com
	• Tablet computers, convertible notebooks, netbooks, slates, and ultrabooks: Several companies sell these specialized computers. We recommend doing a search online to find the latest, best products.
	• Touchscreen: www.hp.com/united-states/campaigns/touchsmart

Assessing	
Archiving growth in conceptual understanding and thinking skills throughout the lesson	Interactive whiteboards • Panabord: www.panaboard.com • SMART Board: http://smarttech.com • Promethean: www.prometheanworld.com Screen/interactive whiteboard recording • CamStudio (open source): http://camstudio.org • Camtasia: www.techsmith.com/camtasia.asp • Captivate: www.adobe.com/products/captivate • SMART Notebook: www.smarttech.com/st/en-US/Products/SMART+Board+software Sound recording • Audacity: http://audacity.sourceforge.net • Portable media player (e.g., iPod, MP3 players) • VoiceThread: http://voicethread.com/#home

Planning

Technology can be helpful in the planning phase of the Concept Development model. Tools that help a teacher think through the concept are particularly helpful. For instance, teachers can use visualization tools available online to examine concepts they might like to teach before creating lesson plans using the Concept Development model. Seeing how the tools work is a way to simulate or forecast related concepts and to identify any key vocabulary students might need to learn beforehand. For instance, after examining the concept "communism" using the online graphical dictionary Visuwords™ (www .visuwords.com), a world history high school teacher might realize that a lesson on "collectivism" would likely benefit students before teaching a Concept Development model lesson on communism. Figure 7-5 is a snapshot of the concept "communism" using an online graphical dictionary.

Figure 7-5   Snapshot of Communism Using Online Graphical Dictionary

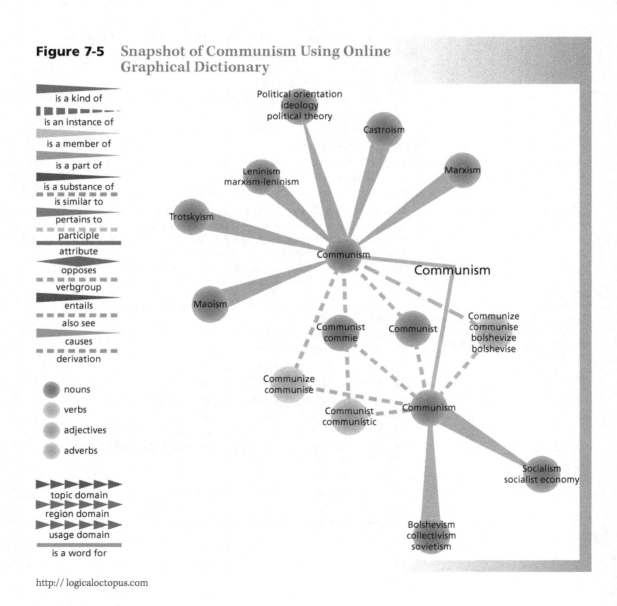

http:// logicaloctopus.com

Implementation

Several different technology tools can be very beneficial to the implementation of the Concept Development model, such as concept-mapping tools, word cloud tools, and tablet computers, interactive whiteboards, or touch screens.

USE CONCEPT-MAPPING TOOLS FOR LISTING, GROUPING, LABELING, AND RE-GROUPING. Concept-mapping tools such as Kidspiration, Inspiration, SmartDraw, and Visio®—to name just a few—are useful for helping students list, group, label, and regroup their ideas related to a concept. Using concept-mapping tools, students can easily list their ideas related to a concept, then sort their ideas in thought bubbles or nodes around the screen by physically moving them or making groups appear similar visually. They can also change colors and other graphic attributes to label the ideas or even group or regroup them. As their thinking progresses, they can show linkages of items and relationships in ways that are highly descriptive and easy to change. For instance, the Concept Development Model Lesson and Scenario 7-2 describe how a teacher might use the Kidspiration concept-mapping tool software program for students to list, group, label, and regroup ideas related to fiction.

USE WORD CLOUD TOOLS TO HELP STUDENTS VISUALIZE DIFFERENT GROUPINGS.
A word cloud, also known as a text cloud or a tag cloud, is a visual representation of a group of words that illustrates some kind of a relationship (e.g., they can be organized alphabetically or range in font size based on the frequency in which a word appears). Word clouds can help students visualize the items they have listed in different ways and compare their items with those selected by other students. For instance, teachers might ask students to create word clouds and then compare their results with one another to help them conceptualize different ways to group and label their items. Figure 7-6 contains a word cloud of the items listed in the introductory scenario and available in Worksheet 7-1 in the listing step of the model.

USE TOUCH SCREEN COMPUTERS OR WHITEBOARDS FOR STUDENTS TO LIST, GROUP, LABEL, AND REGROUP ITEMS. Students can use tablet computers, interactive whiteboards, or touchscreen computers to manipulate physically the items they list into groups using a stylus pen (digital pen) or their fingertips. These tools also allow them to label and regroup these items easily. Such physical manipulation is especially useful for learners whose ability to pay attention is improved through tactile and visual stimuli and those who might find it physically difficult to communicate with pencil and paper or a computer mouse. Some students with fine motor skills challenges use these tools with assistive devices or even interact with interactive whiteboards using everyday objects like a tennis ball. Holding such objects in their hands gives students with physical impairments or gross motor difficulties the ability to access and fully interact with digital equipment.

Assessment

Assessment of learning in the Concept Development model usually focuses on gathering information about a student's understanding of the concept being studied and his or her ability to exercise thinking about this concept. In both cases, the focus of the assessment should

Figure 7-6   Word Cloud of Items Listed in Worksheet 7-1

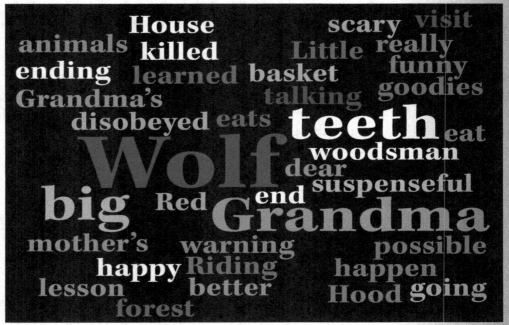

wordle.net

Source: This word cloud was created through the online tool Wordle™, available at http://www.wordle.net

be to measure the growth in each student's learning from the start to the end of the lesson. Technology that facilitates the archiving of student learning is particularly helpful because it enables deeper analysis and reflection. Interactive whiteboards are just one technology that can be used to do this. Interactive whiteboards allow teachers and students to take archiving of the thinking process a step farther. Students can use a screen recording tool (which comes free with most interactive whiteboard hardware) or a screen capture program to capture evidence of how they group, regroup, and label their items. A video file including audio can be created with the click of only three buttons. Students can then compare their recordings with those of others to further deepen their understanding of the concept. Their teacher can view these files to examine what went on, what went right, and what went wrong while students were engaged in the learning process.

Concept Development Model Lesson Plan Example

The Concept Development Model Lesson serves as an illustration of how the Concept Development model might be implemented using simple technologies found in most classrooms. Figure 7-7 provides an outline of the Concept Development model steps as they would occur in the lesson.

Figure 7-7   Outline of the Concept Development Model Lesson Steps

Concept Development Model Steps	Concept Development Model Lesson
Listing	Students list all of the ideas/traits/characteristics they can think of that are related to the concept "fiction" based on personal experience or examples presented to them.
Grouping	Students group the ideas that are similar together.
Labeling	Students label the different groups of ideas about "fiction" based on their similarities.
Regrouping	Students examine their groups related to "fiction" and determine whether there are alternative ways to group the ideas.
Synthesizing	Students analyze the groupings related to "fiction" to form a summary of the "data" and to develop generalizations about it.

LESSON CONTEXT

GRADE LEVEL: Third

CONTENT AREA: Language Arts

PHYSICAL TEACHING ENVIRONMENT: This lesson will be taught in a regular classroom with laptops from a rolling cart, but it could also be taught in a computer lab if laptops were not available for classroom use. Students will have the option of working alone or in pairs for this lesson. They might move their desks together if they work in pairs.

APPLICATION OF REVISED BLOOM'S TAXONOMY: This lesson involves various levels of cognitive processing according to the revised Bloom's taxonomy (presented in Chapter 1). It addresses the *remember* and *understand* categories when students are asked to list and group. It involves *analyze* when students are asked to group, regroup, and define the critical attributes of the concept.

Lesson Plan

GOAL(S): Students will be able to identify and explain the defining characteristics of fiction stories.

Standard(s) Addressed (English Language Arts):

- Common Core State Standard Grade 3 #2: Recount stories, including fables, folktales, and myths from diverse cultures; determine the central message, lesson, or moral and explain how it is conveyed through key details in the text.[1]

---

[1] © Copyright 2010. National Governors Association Center for Best Practices and Council of Chief State School Officers. All rights reserved.

- NCTE/IRA 3: Students apply a wide range of strategies to comprehend, interpret, evaluate, and appreciate texts.[2]
- NCTE/IRA 10: Students' whose first language is not English make use of their first language to develop competency in the English language arts.
  For a complete list of the standards, go to http://www.ncte.org/standards.
- ISTE NETS for Students 2007 #4 and #6.[3]

OBJECTIVE(S):

1. Students will be able to make some generalizations about the characteristics of fiction stories based on personal experiences or examples presented.
2. Students will be able to correctly create a definition of fiction stories after exploring the generalizations they make.
3. Students will be able to use a concept-mapping tool, such as Kidspiration software, to express and explore their ideas.

ESTIMATED TIME: Approximately 45 minutes

MATERIALS NEEDED:

- Adequate desktop or laptop computers for students working alone or in pairs.
- The software program Kidspiration or another concept-mapping tool.
- Pencil and paper.
- A pre-created Kidspiration file including some of the characteristics of fiction stories for students who might struggle generating a list on their own. Alternatively, an example of the activity using nonfiction stories might be useful as scaffolding.

PREREQUISITE SKILLS: Students will know how to use the software program Kidspiration (or another concept-mapping tool of your choice) and be familiar with using this tool to create concept maps.

LESSON PROCEDURES (Text in italics is suggested teacher dialogue.)

Anticipatory Set (Introduction): [5 minutes]

The teacher asks students to name some examples of fiction stories. *Based on what you know, what are some examples of stories that we have read in class that we would consider fiction?* The teacher records students' replies on the board. *For the next few days, you will work in pairs to examine what you know about these stories and then use these ideas to summarize the elements of fiction stories. You will be asked to list everything you know about a fiction story, group your ideas, label these ideas, regroup them, and summarize (synthesize) your ideas into a generalization.*

---

[2] Standards for the English Language Arts, by the International Reading Association and the National Council of Teachers of English, Copyright 1996 by the International Reading Association and the National Council of Teachers of English. Reprinted with permission.

[3] National Educational Technology Standards for Students (NETS•S), Second Edition © 2007 ISTE ® (International-al Society for Technology in Education), www.iste.org. All rights reserved.

Listing: [10 minutes]

The teacher gives students an opportunity to work in pairs or alone on a computer based on students' individual preferences or his or her perception of their needs. He or she asks them to pick a story from the list of those shared by class members and then allows them to use the concept-mapping program Kidspiration to list everything they remember from this story. They might include the names of characters, events that happen, places involved, objects in the story, and other elements. *Try to use the computer program to list what you remember about one of the fiction stories we listed. You do not need to use complete sentences—fragments of ideas are okay to include. As you write specific ideas you remember about your story, think about how it might be similar to other ideas you have already listed. Later we will examine how your ideas can be grouped and how these groups of ideas might provide information about the characteristics of fiction stories.*

Students brainstorm phrases and terms associated with the fiction stories they have selected. For example, the pair that selected *Little Red Riding Hood* listed "Grandma's house, Little Red Riding Hood, Wolf, basket of goodies, going to visit Grandma, forest, disobeyed her mother's warning, wolf eats Grandma, could not really happen, suspenseful, happy ending, big teeth, talking animals not possible, scary, wolf is killed in the end, woodsman, 'My, what big teeth you have 'a lesson is learned, funny, and' "All the better to eat you with my dear!'"

For an example of what this work would look like, refer to Worksheet 7-1. The students will use the program Kidspiration to do their brainstorming. This program allows them to type the ideas into nodes or thought bubbles of information that appear as typing in different-shaped boxes. As the teacher circulates among the students, he or she might want to help students recall and record their ideas or use the program more efficiently if necessary. He or she might also help students remember ideas associated with specific stories. Students might benefit from seeing one another's work. The teacher might want to encourage them to take turns walking around the room to look at the ideas of their peers. The teacher would then say, *"Once you have made your list with your story, you may look at what other groups have done and see if you want to add any of their ideas to your own."*

Grouping: [5 minutes]

The teacher encourages students to consider how the various ideas they listed are similar. *Now that you have listed all the characteristics you can think of related to the fiction story you chose, consider whether any items are similar. Can you group these characteristics together?* The students will use the program Kidspiration to click the mouse on each node and move these characteristics into groups on the computer screen. The students may want to number each group to help them keep track of their thinking. The teacher may help students get started with grouping or facilitate appropriate grouping of items if needed.

The pair of students who selected *Little Red Riding Hood* came up with the following grouping:

- Group 1: Grandma's house, forest
- Group 2: forest, Grandma's house
- Group 3: talking animals, couldn't really happen
- Group 4: basket of goodies, axe
- Group 5: Little Red Riding Hood, Wolf, woodsman, Grandma
- Group 6: happy ending, wolf eats Grandma, disobeyed her mother's warning, wolf is killed in the end, going to visit Grandma
- Group 7: "My, what big teeth you have," "All the better to eat you with my dear!"

- Group 8: a lesson is learned, happy ending
- Group 9: wolf is killed in the end, going to visit Grandma, wolf eats grandma

Labeling: [5 minutes]

The teacher asks students to label each group of characteristics. *Now that you have grouped items together that are alike in some way, see if you can come up with a label that describes all of the characteristics in each group.* The students will use the program Kidspiration to label the groups. They may even indicate group membership by changing the shapes around each node in a group so that they appear with the same shaped outline. For example, nodes dealing with "characters" might be square, those dealing with "setting" might be made diamond shaped, and so on.

The pair working with *Little Red Riding Hood* labeled its groups this way:

- Places in the story: Grandma's house, forest
- Things in the story: basket of goodies, axe
- Characters: Little Red Riding Hood, Wolf, woodsman, Grandma
- Things that happen/action: happy ending, wolf eats Grandma, disobeyed her mother's warning, wolf is killed in the end, going to visit Grandma
- Things about the characters/characterization: wolf has big teeth, Red Riding Hood is disobedient, and Grandma is in bed
- Fairy tale things: a lesson is learned, happy ending
- Not real things: couldn't really happen, talking animals not possible
- Things characters say: "My, what big teeth you have," "All the better to eat you with my dear!"
- What we think about this story: scary, suspenseful, funny

In this step, the teacher circulates and reviews students' labels. In some instances, the teacher may want to help students by providing or reminding them of a more appropriate name for some groups. For example, she might suggest students to use the word *setting* for the phrase "places things happen" or *dialogue* for "Things characters say."

Regrouping: [5 minutes]

The teacher challenges students to look at the characteristics/ideas they have listed again and consider whether the ideas should be grouped differently. *Once you have made your first groups, look at them again and consider whether they could be grouped differently. Could some of these belong to more than one group? Can we put these same items into different groups? Why would you group them that way?* The students will group their characteristics together and reexamine them.

The *Little Red Riding Hood* pair decided to combine two groups (i.e., characters and descriptions of characters) into a larger group called "characters names and descriptions."

The teacher might want to ask students to explain their reasons for regrouping and provide evidence of their conceptual understanding and growth.

Synthesizing: [5 minutes]

The teacher encourages students to examine their groups and the labels assigned to these groups. Then she asks them to use what they learned about the story they chose to explore to make a generalization about all fiction stories. She asks them to see if they can connect all the groups together in a sentence that explains what fiction stories are. *Can you say in one sentence something about all of the groups?* Students might say, *Fiction stories are make-believe stories that tell things that happen to characters in certain settings—sometimes using dialogue.*

Evaluating the Process: [10 minutes]

The teacher asks students to write down the sentence that explains their ideas about fiction stories. She asks students to share these with another person or group. *First share your generalization with someone else. Combine any ideas that you have in common and decide whether ideas that are different should be included.* Then students share their combined generalizations with the class, and a class definition is developed. For example, *Fiction stories relate different events that happen to a group of characters imagined by the author. They use elements including dialogue, characterization, plot, and conflict to develop the story. Some types of fiction stories include fairy tales, fables, myths, and legends.* To evaluate student performance, the teacher might examine student work as explained below.

ASSESSMENT

Formative assessment Possible factors to evaluate include a student's growth in the understanding of the concept of characteristics of fiction stories, and the ability to think critically and exercise thinking skills.

Summative assessment Ask students to list the critical attributes of fiction stories and give some examples.

LESSON EXTENSIONS AND MODIFICATIONS

Students could do the following:

- Create a chart comparing fiction with non fiction
- Compare one type of fiction with another (i.e., folktales and fairy tales)
- Keep a list of all the fiction stories they read and make notes of the fiction characteristics in these stories
- Create a matrix containing the story name, main characters, plot details, and setting of fiction stories they read

Differentiation Strategies for the Concept Development Model Lesson

The following sections have suggestions that could be applied to differentiate instruction in the Concept Development Model Lesson.

Content

Although the content standards must be attained by all students, those who have already mastered the understanding of what fiction is might be challenged to go deeper with this exploration of the concept of fiction stories. They might be asked to think about different genres within the category of fiction, such as folktales, fairy tales, short stories, science fiction, fantasy, and so on. They might work individually or in groups to investigate and make generalizations about these concepts.

Process

Several differentiations for individual interest, readiness, and learning profile might be made in the process of learning.

To differentiate for physical ability, cognitive style, learning modality, and comfort with technology, students might be given an option to use any of the following:

a) a software program or computer,
b) a touchscreen computer interface or interactive whiteboard (i.e., SMART Board or touchscreen),
c) assistive devices,
d) augmentative devices, or
e) pencil and paper and file cards.

Unless learning to use a specific technology is one of the objectives, some flexibility with the means of expression will support students without compromising the learning objectives.

There are numerous ways to support English language learners in this learning process. For example, a group of students who are from the same foreign country and in the same class might be encouraged to work together on this in their first language. Then they would be supported as they summarized their results in English. A teacher of English language learning might assist these students with the assignment. In addition, this group of learners might be given some help with the generation of characteristics of fiction and then left to group and label them on their own. Fiction stories from their own culture might be presented as examples to explore.

An additional way to support these learners, if their ability to comprehend spoken English is better than their ability to read it, would be to use the text-to-speech feature in Kidspiration. This feature would allow students to have the program read the text in different thought bubbles aloud. With the computer reading for these students, they might be better able do the grouping portion of this lesson independently.

Product

The product students create (i.e., the evidence of their thinking and comprehension of the concept) would be differentiated depending on the media they chose to work with in the learning process. For instance, one way to support students who are English language learners might be to encourage students to make their generalization in a bulleted list if that is easier for them than writing a sentence. They could work on making these ideas into sentences during a follow-up session with their teacher.

Chapter Summary

This chapter introduces the Concept Development model, an instructional model for developing students' conceptual knowledge and critical-thinking skills. The model uses a procedural process that supports students as they work to build on existing knowledge of a concept and refine it. Students learn to analyze, look for patterns, make generalizations, and deepen their knowledge of concepts being studied, as they work through the model's steps of listing, grouping, labeling, regrouping, and synthesizing. The model can be used to teach abstract and complex concepts as well as those that are concrete and simple. Some of the benefits of the Concept Development model include that it teaches thinking skills, helps students retain content understanding, helps students see similarities and differences and to identify patterns, challenges students to exercise creative thinking, is active and hands on, and helps a teacher learn more about his or her students. The Concept Development model is particularly useful in contemporary classrooms. It validates and builds on students' unique background and experiences. It also enables the integration of a wide variety of technologies that are meaningful to digital learners.

Review Questions

1. What is the history of the Concept Development model?

2. What are the steps of the Concept Development model?

3. What type of content is best to teach when applying the Concept Development model? Provide and explain examples of content that would be appropriate and inappropriate.

4. What are the benefits of applying the Concept Development model? What are some of the challenges?

5. How can the Concept Development model be used to differentiate instruction and support diverse learners' needs?

6. How can technology be used to implement the Concept Development model?

Application Exercises

To promote your ability to apply the learning you gained in studying this chapter, complete the following exercises that challenge you to analyze a lesson plan you have written using the Concept Development model *or* using the lesson plan example included in this chapter.

TECHNOLOGY INTEGRATION ACTIVITY

1. Consider the following and discuss with a partner or reflect independently:

   a) In the lesson plan you are analyzing, how does (or could) the integration of technology tools make learning more efficient, effective, and engaging? Can you explain and indicate how the impact on student learning might be measured?

   b) Will all learners be aided through the integration of technology? Are there some who might need special support to gain full benefit from technology tools? How might you support this? Is there a way to build on strengths students bring to this lesson related to technology? How?

   c) What plans could you put in place to promote a more successful use of technology and less risk of failure? What proactive plan could a teacher put in place ahead of lesson implementation to ensure technology works smoothly and for all learners? What reactive approach could a teacher take if technology malfunctions during the lesson to ensure desired learning still occurs?

TEACHER PERFORMANCE ACTIVITIES

2. **Academic Vocabulary and Language Demands:** Academic vocabulary is the vocabulary that students must be able to understand to be successful performing content area learning. Language demands involve the ways language is used in speaking, writing, listening, and reading in the learning tasks of a lesson and in the expressions of student learning. In the lesson plan you are working with (your own or the one provided in the chapter), consider the following questions and discuss them with a partner or reflect on them alone:

   a) What academic vocabulary and language demands exist in any lesson designed with the Concept Development model? What words associated with learning concepts and using the model might pose challenges for the plan's targeted learners?

   b) Make a list of the academic vocabulary students must comprehend and language demands of the Concept Development model lesson plan you are reviewing. How might students' prior knowledge of these terms be affected by their backgrounds, lived experiences, and prior learning experiences?

   c) How you would determine whether and which students have mastery with academic language before the lesson begins?

   d) How might students be supported in developing proficiency with academic language in this lesson context? What visual or other resources might you use?

3. **Planning:** In the lesson plan that you are analyzing, discuss the following with a partner or reflect independently:

   a) Explain how the steps of the Concept Development model build on existing knowledge students have gained from their prior schooling or lived experiences. How could teachers build on student strengths or weaknesses as they work through the Concept Development model?

   b) Consider how a variety of learning needs have been addressed in the lesson. What are the ways that this model differentiates instruction within its steps? What other strategies for differentiation might be supportive to integrate?

   c) Anticipate any misconceptions students might have coming into the lesson related to the concept. Describe any misunderstanding students might develop related to the concept during the lesson.

   d) Identify research or theories that you are familiar with that support the use of this model for instruction in your learning context. If so, how?

4. **Implementation:** In the lesson plan that you are analyzing, discuss the following with a partner or consider independently:

   a) Explain how the steps of the Concept Development model and the activities that students will perform in the lesson you are reviewing will result in engaged learning. What indicators would you look for during the implementation of your lesson to measure who is engaged and how much?

   b) How well does your lesson challenge learners to apply their learning in meaningful contexts? Explain.

   c) What thinking skills can be applied by students in future learning through participation in this lesson? Can you describe another context where the thinking skills might be utilized?

5. **Assessment:** Consider the following and discuss with a partner or reflect independently:

   a) Would consideration of students' backgrounds and prior learning and experiences as they relate to learning goals/objectives help you design a more effective lesson? How?

   b) How does or could the lesson plan you are reviewing use formative assessment to direct the more successful implementation of instruction? Is there a way to make it more intentional or improve it to address students' strengths or learning needs? What type of feedback would or could students be provided?

   c) How does the plan you are reviewing support students' expression of learning? Are there multiple forms of evidence of student learning? How might students learn through an analysis of their performance? What specific indicators would you look for as evidence of student learning to determine how deeply and well they understand the targeted concept?

6. **Analyzing Teaching:** Consider the following and discuss with a partner or reflect independently:

   a) Now that you have created and/or analyzed a lesson plan using the Concept Development model, consider how the model supports effective teaching. Can you cite specific evidence or references that support your claim? Be specific in expressing your ideas.

   b) What did you learn from this activity that might inform your future practice?

Discussion Question

Consider the differences between the Concept Attainment and Concept Development models. Is one of these models easier for students and teachers to understand and engage in than the other? Why do you think so?

Journal Entry

Explain the advantages and challenges of using the Concept Development model for teaching concepts in your subject area. Why would you or why would you not use this model? Are there certain concepts that would be particularly appropriate to teach using this model?

Resources

- Hilda Taba
  - The University of South Carolina Museum of Education provides a "Voices from the Past" biography of Hilda Taba that includes an audio clip: www.ed.sc.edu/museum/past-taba.html

- Here you will find a brief autobiography about Hilda Taba: www.answers.com/topic/hilda-taba

Model	Inductive Model
Knowledge Supported	• Factual Knowledge
	• Conceptual Knowledge
Added Value	• Supports development of critical-thinking skills—specifically inductive reasoning and convergent thinking
	• Supports development of creative thinking—specifically divergent and generative thinking
Technologies to Integrate	• Visual presentation tools to share examples and nonexamples
	• Digital video and audio tools to demonstrate examples and nonexamples
	• Assessment tools and audience response systems to assess learning of the concept

The Inductive Model

ajt/Shutterstock

The news delivered by the assistant superintendent for instruction at the districtwide back to school teacher in-service meeting was a bit concerning. It was hard to know which message caused more worry among the members of the English department at Wilson High: that the new state proficiency tests had been redesigned to emphasize critical-thinking skills and deep understanding of content standards or that this year's merit pay would be determined by their students' pass rates on these tests. Fortunately, Martha Ann Richards, a tenth-grade English teacher, had too much to do to spend time worrying. Besides, she found it more productive to work smart and hard rather than worry long and hard.

Today, Martha Ann was working through her first quarter's unit plans with the goal of identifying and improving existing lessons that emphasized deep learning. She had decided to begin improving the learning outcomes for *all* of her students by accentuating the positive and revising successful plans to make them work better for a larger percentage of her learners. Because her students were increasingly diverse, this was a good strategy for her. In this year's fourth-period tenth-grade English class alone, there were students representing eight different nationalities from five different continents. There were students from Africa (Egypt and Gambia), Central America (El Salvador), South America (Peru and Venezuela), Asia, (Korea), and the United States. She could not help chuckling to herself as she recalled the days when she used to see diversity as a "black and white" issue. Today, it was so much more challenging to address the needs of diverse learners in the classroom, but she was up to the challenge!

The first plan Martha Ann identified for improvement was one on sonnets that she designed with the Inductive model. She had used this model with success in the past for many different lessons. In this model, students were challenged to analyze real examples of literature by searching for and comparing patterns in an effort to achieve deep understanding. Fortunately, the model asked them to apply the same critical-thinking skills the new proficiency tests emphasized.

Last year, Martha Ann had given students Shakespearian sonnets printed on paper and asked them to examine these examples while they answered the questions that would lead them to understanding the characteristics of a sonnet, such as "How many stanzas? How many lines? What is the rhyme scheme? What meter is used?" Afterward, she had asked them to develop their own definition of a sonnet. This year she would improve the plan by developing better questions and asking students to document their learning. If she succeeded in getting more students to develop a deeper understanding of sonnets, she was sure they would pass the items on the proficiency exam related to sonnets and those asking them to demonstrate critical-thinking skills as well. ■

CHAPTER OBJECTIVES

After reading this chapter, you will be able to:

- Describe the Inductive model, including its history and steps.
- Communicate the applications and benefits of the Inductive model and learn what it might look like in a classroom.
- Explain how the Inductive model is implemented and how to plan for teaching with this model.
- Name ways the Inductive model might enable differentiated instruction and support diverse learners.
- List how technology can enhance teaching with the Inductive model.

Introduction

In the chapter's opening scenario, Martha Ann works to improve her students' critical-thinking skills by revising a lesson designed with the Inductive model. The plan she has designed with this model challenges learners to analyze, look for patterns, and connect what they learn to real examples in English literature. Students must examine examples of sonnets to answer the bigger question "What are sonnets?" In doing so, students are actively involved in thinking, considering, and constructing their own ideas about literature and required content standards. Martha Ann's use of the Inductive model will help her students achieve deep understanding of content standards as well as transferrable skills that will help them be successful on proficiency tests and throughout their lives.

In this chapter, you will learn about the Inductive model. The Inductive model uses inductive reasoning to challenge learners to draw general conclusions about a concept through examination of particular instances of this concept. It draws on natural patterns of thinking or sense making—providing students with an opportunity to practice, refine, and understand the usefulness of inductive reasoning. The chapter begins with a detailed explanation of what the model is and how it was developed. Then it shares specific strategies for its implementation and offers methods for supporting diverse learners. Finally, the chapter describes how various types of technology add value to the model and its implementation.

What Is the Inductive Model?

The Inductive model is an active, engaging model of instruction that encourages students' development of critical-thinking skills as they explore and learn concepts in the academic content areas and the facts associated with these concepts. Lessons planned with the Inductive model challenge learners to make full use of their senses to observe and recognize details and patterns in materials related to the content under investigation. Such activity promotes understanding of a topic. According to Wiggins and McTighe (2005), **understanding** entails more than factual knowledge. It consists of six different facets. When students truly understand, they "(1) can explain what they know, (2) can interpret what they have learned, (3) can apply their learning to novel situations, (4) have perspective about the big picture and other points of view, (5) can empathize by valuing others' points of views, and (6) have self-knowledge by demonstrating metacognitive awareness" (p. 84). This idea of understanding is very similar to notions about deep learning (Bereiter, 2002).

Figure 8-1 Example Concepts in the Academic Subject Areas

Subject	Concepts
Art	column types, Romanesque paintings, purposes for using various creative media
Language Arts	iambic pentameter, onomatopoeia, subject-verb agreement
Mathematics	fractions, geometric shapes (e.g., triangle), number patterns
Music	meaning of musical language (e.g., forte, pianissimo), tempo, rhythm
Health/Physical Education	relationship between heart rate and breathing rate, characteristics of healthy fats
Social Studies	concept of culture, geographic features (e.g., mountain ranges), concept of feudalism
Science	laws and principles (e.g., Bernoulli's Principle), non-Newtonian fluid, requirements for seed germination

The Inductive model is so named because of its reliance on inductive reasoning. **Inductive reasoning**, a kind of thinking that involves making generalizations through examination and analysis of particular examples, is commonly associated with the teaching of math and science and is integral to learning in all disciplines (see Figure 8-1 for Example Concepts that might be taught with the Inductive model). The model is exceptional in its ability to teach students to identify similarities and differences in written materials and those presented in other media formats (e.g., audio or video), give students opportunities to practice both convergent and divergent thinking (defined later in this chapter), and develop skills and dispositions for lifelong learning.

What Are the History and Origins of the Inductive Model?

The roots of inductive reasoning can be traced to the works of Sir Francis Bacon. Sir Francis Bacon (1620/1855) trained as a lawyer but was also considered a philosopher. He challenged the centuries-old, common philosophy of deductive reasoning, developed by Aristotle, for scientific analyses in his work *Novum Organum*. In this work, Bacon promoted inductive reasoning as a form of scientific inquiry that should occur through observation, analysis of facts, and the drawing of conclusions. Of note is that, contrary to deductive reasoning where conclusions are considered the "truth," in inductive reasoning, conclusions are not considered "truth." Instead, the conclusions may not be true even though the premises leading to the conclusion seem to be true because an example that one is unaware of might exist that refutes the conclusion. Inductive reasoning begins as an open-ended, exploratory process; deductive reasoning is a focused, procedural process that involves the testing of what is known or hypothesized. Although Bacon's works may not be studied much today, his influence on modern thinking and reasoning cannot be underestimated.

More direct influences on the Inductive model are found in the work of Taba (1967), who is also credited with influencing or developing other instructional models, such as the

Concept Attainment (Chapter 6), Concept Development (Chapter 7), Inquiry (Chapter 10), and Integrative (Chapter 13) models. Fraenkel (1992) considers Taba to be "the first to advocate the development and use of inductively organized teaching strategies" (p. 175). Yet, the inductive model also displays characteristics of Bruner's (1960) discovery learning, which builds on students' prior knowledge and relies on a teacher's guided inquiry.

What Are Convergent and Divergent Thinking?

Before examining the phases in the Inductive model, it is important to explore two types of thinking that shape this and several other instructional models—convergent and divergent thinking. The terms *convergent* and *divergent*, when associated with thinking, were coined by Guilford (1950) based on studies he conducted on creativity. Comprehension of these terms is necessary to understanding fully the Inductive model due to the essential role they play in the model's various phases: the open-ended phase (which involves divergent thinking) and the convergent phase (which involves the focusing of thinking). The word **divergent** means "from each other" or "relating to or being an infinite sequence that does not have a limit or an infinite series whose partial sums do not have a limit"[1] ("divergent," n.d.). The term **convergent** means "tending to move toward one point or to approach each other"[2] ("convergent," n.d.). In educational terms, we might consider divergent thinking as "a search that uncovers several answers" and convergent thinking as "thinking through to one correct answer" (Glover, Ronning, & Reynolds, 1989, p. 256). Guilford associated divergent thinking with creativity and convergent thinking with the type of thinking tested in IQ tests. Further, he considered both types of thinking as essential to intellectual ability (Guilford, 1956b, as cited in Glover, et al., 1989). An awareness of these two types of thinking and their relevance in the learning process has persisted ever since. The Inductive model supports both types of thinking through its progressive steps that promote the exploration of ideas, meaning making, and deep learning.

▮ When Should the Inductive Model Be Applied and Why?

The Inductive model may be used when teaching content from any of the academic disciplines. This model has long been used in science and math but is an incredibly valuable tool in any subject area. It can be effectively used to (1) teach concepts, (2) encourage students to develop critical-thinking skills, (3) develop pattern recognition and detail identification, and (4) assess understanding of concepts. The following sections elaborate on these ideas.

Teach Concepts

As with the Concept Attainment (Chapter 6) and Concept Development (Chapter 7) models, the Inductive model is best applied when teaching concepts and the facts associated with these concepts. It is particularly suited to teaching concepts with clearly identifiable attributes. (The model also works with abstract concepts but the examples used must be carefully selected.) The quality of examples and nonexamples is critical to the success of this model because students' examination of the similarities, differences, and patterns observed in

---

[1,2] By permission. From Merriam-Webster's Collegiate® Dictionary, 11th Edition © 2012 by Merriam-Webster, Incorporated (www.Merriam-Webster.com).

these items will form the basis of their comprehension of a concept. If weak examples are selected (e.g., those with attributes difficult to identify), students will not successfully understand the concept they are supposed to be learning.

Note that the Inductive model is unlike the Concept Attainment model in that it makes use of fewer examples and nonexamples. The Inductive model also differs from the Concept Development model because materials for analysis are provided by the teacher. Also, although having some prior knowledge is beneficial, it is not required. For example, in the Inductive Model Lesson at the end of this chapter, after the lesson introduction, students are asked to examine a Shakespearean sonnet provided by their teacher. No prior knowledge about sonnets is needed. Students must only come to the Inductive model lesson ready to use their thinking skills to understand better the concept based on what they observe in the resources before them.

Develop Critical-Thinking Skills

The Inductive model develops students' critical thinking by requiring them to practice observation, recognition of patterns, and identification of details through their examination of examples and nonexamples. This means that students use many thinking skills in a purposeful and motivational way when using the Inductive model. While implementing the model, teachers can promote students' recognition of detail and promote keen observation by modeling it themselves or highlighting the efforts of students who are already proficient.

Assess Students' Understanding of a Concept

The Inductive model is well suited for assessing how well students have mastered a concept they have already learned. Scenario 8-1 shows techniques for using the Inductive model to accomplish some of the goals of assessment. In this scenario, a class is learning about geometric shapes. The teacher uses the model to determine how well students understand rectangles. After introducing the objectives of the assessment, the teacher asks students to share their observations about the rectangles she presents. She then questions them about the specific attributes inherent in rectangles. After this process of divergent and convergent questioning, the teacher invites students to define what a rectangle is and then find or create other examples of rectangles in their homes, communities, or classrooms. In this way, the teacher identifies what students have come to know and understand about geometric shapes—specifically rectangles.

What Are the Steps in the Inductive Model?

The Inductive model consists of five major phases, or steps: (1) lesson introduction, (2) divergent phase, (3) convergent phase, (4) closure, and (5) application. These are described below. Figure 8-2 outlines the teacher's and students' roles at each point in the model.

Step One—Lesson Introduction

During this phase, the teacher introduces the main objectives and procedures for the lesson. As the Inductive Model Lesson shows, during this phase, the teacher typically explains that students will examine various materials that will help them think about the content

Figure 8-2 Teacher and Student Roles in the Inductive Model

Inductive Model Steps	Teacher Role	Student Role
Lesson introduction	The teacher explains that students will examine various examples (and possibly nonexamples) representing the content to be learned. The teacher also lets students know that they are to look for patterns and differences among the examples and nonexamples.	Students listen and become interested in the lesson.
Divergent phase	The teacher presents students with examples and nonexamples. The teacher asks open-ended questions that stimulate student exploration and support careful analysis of examples and nonexamples.	Students examine and compare the example(s) and nonexample(s) presented in a divergent manner with guidance from their teacher.
Convergent phase	The teacher asks questions or provides other materials that challenge students to consider observations related to the examples and nonexamples and arrive at the desired learning goals.	Students examine and compare the example(s) and nonexample(s) presented in a more convergent manner with guidance from their teacher.
Closure	The teacher presents opportunities for students to demonstrate their learning of the content or concept using their own words, drawings, or actions. The teacher provides support for learners who may need it.	Students demonstrate their learning of the content or concept using their own words, drawings, or actions.
Application	The teacher challenges learners to apply their learning to real-life scenarios.	Students apply their learning to real-life scenarios.

that is being explored. The materials may include examples of a concept, nonexamples of the concept, or a combination of the two. The teacher will also want to explain that the content being studied will be a concept and the factual knowledge related to that concept. The teacher may refer to the concept being learned by a name (i.e., "In this lesson, we will be exploring sonnets.") or by expressing that students will be exploring curriculum content and that they will understand what the content is and what to call it as the lesson progresses. At this time, the teacher also tells students that they will need to look for patterns and differences among the example(s) and nonexample(s) that are shared to promote thinking about the concept. This overview is critical to establishing the road map for what students will learn to do as well as piquing students' interest in the lesson.

Step Two—Divergent Phase

During this divergent, or "open-ended," phase, students examine and compare the example(s) and nonexample(s) introduced to them. They make observations about them and attempt to recognize characteristics and patterns in what they see. These may be presented in a variety of formats including but not limited to photos, simulations, videos, experiments, and much more. Teachers can facilitate learning during this phase by asking questions that require students to justify any conclusions they draw about the patterns identified in the examples. All questioning should be divergent and *open ended* (not able to be answered with a simple "yes" or "no" answer, or a single word). Examples of open-ended questions related to the lesson example and scenarios that appear later in this chapter include the following: "In what ways are these poems similar? In what ways are they different?" "What do you notice about these columns?" "What do the following rectangles have in common?" "What do you notice about these examples of plagiarism?" Divergent questions typically have more than one "right" answer. They serve the purpose of helping students generate a variety of ideas about a topic while also promoting their creative or divergent thinking.

Step Three—Convergent Phase

The convergent, or "closed," phase of the Inductive model involves challenging students to focus their thinking on the concept that is being examined. Here again, teacher questioning is critical to ensuring that students are performing the type of thinking that will help them attain desired understanding of the content being studied. During this phase, teacher questioning should be convergent. That is, the questioning should help learners connect or combine information gleaned through examination of the content to form a precise understanding of the content. Questions should be asked with the goal of helping students discover the concept's specific attributes. For instance, a teacher might ask students to relate the new content to that previously learned. Or a teacher might provide some type of scaffolding in the form of a handout that has questions relating to the various characteristics or ideas students should focus on and learn. Convergent questions that relate to the lesson plan and scenarios in this chapter might include "How many stanzas do the example poems use?" "Which column style is most ornate?" "What differences exist in the measurement of angles in these triangles?" or "What characteristics do all of the examples of plagiarism have in common?" Depending on the lesson's learning goals, teachers might choose to highlight key features of the content that students should compare, or they might wait until the closure phase.

Step Four—Closure

One of the main goals of the Inductive model is to challenge students to develop their own definition and understanding of the content being studied. The closure phase of this model provides students with the opportunity to demonstrate their understanding of the content and concept in any number of ways. For example, teachers might ask students to record an aural definition of the content or concept, draw a picture of it, or even act it out. Teachers might also want students to compare their understandings with each other to form a shared definition of the content. Again, the important goal of this phase is for students to determine their definition of the content and not for the teacher to provide it. Teachers should ensure that students have an appropriate and correct understanding of the content/concept being studied. The approach for closure might be simple, as in Scenario 8-1 when Ms. Kim asks students to define a rectangle, or more complex, as in Scenario 8-3 when Mr. Higgins asks students to complete a graphic organizer that lists critical and variable attributes of plagiarism.

Step Five—Application

As with many other models that include an application phase (e.g., see Chapter 6, Concept Attainment model), the purpose of this phase is twofold. Students need to demonstrate the knowledge they gained as well as apply it in novel ways or situations. For the application phase in the Inductive Model Lesson at the end of this chapter, students are asked to write their own Shakespearean or English sonnets, then post them to a wiki.

Ideally, students will apply their learning in real-life scenarios. However, it is not always possible for students to do so. In such instances, teachers might ask students to find examples or create them, as in Scenario 8-1 where students are asked to locate examples of rectangles in their community, find them online, or create them.

What Does the Inductive Model Look Like in the Classroom?

The Inductive model may be implemented in a variety of ways and during various points of study within a unit. As stated previously, this model is best applied when introducing a concept, although it may certainly be used for assessing comprehension of a concept, too. Teachers may choose to use just one or two examples or nonexamples or more. They may present them to students all at once or one at a time. Likewise, the format and complexity of examples and nonexamples may be varied, making the model robust and flexible for many different teaching situations. The following three scenarios show some of the different contexts in which teachers can effectively use this model. Although the teachers' goal for using the model (i.e., for learning or assessment) and other implementation details vary from scenario to scenario, the phases of the model, their order, and the use of questioning remain the same.

Scenario 8-1

Miss Kim's third-grade class is studying geometric shapes. She uses the Inductive model to assess students' comprehension of the different types of rectangles by providing different examples of rectangles (see Figure 8-3) in varying sizes and orientations. After introducing the objectives of the assessment (lesson introduction), Miss Kim puts students in pairs and provides each team with a digital audio recorder that will capture student input that she can review later. She is interested in understanding each student's proficiency responding to convergent and divergent thinking tasks. She will use this information to design future unit plans and provide differentiated support later within this unit.

Figure 8-3 Rectangle Examples

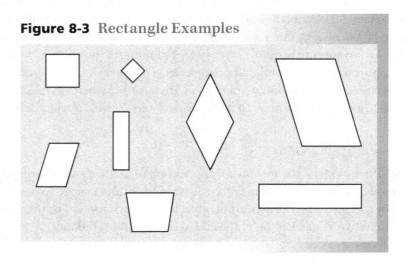

First, Miss Kim asks students to take turns sharing their observations of the various rectangles (open-ended phase) while also recording their responses on the digital recorder. Questions such as "What do you notice about these objects? What similarities do you see? What differences?" are posed. Later Miss Kim questions students about specific attributes inherent in rectangles (convergent phase) by asking them questions like "How many sides does each geometric shape have? How many corners?" After this process of divergent and convergent questioning, Miss Kim closes by challenging students to define what a rectangle is by using the online tool VoiceThread™. For the application phase, she asks them to find other examples of rectangles found in their homes, communities, or classrooms by posting a picture, drawing, or graphic of the rectangle with an accompanying verbal or written explanation to their VoiceThread. If they are unable to find examples, she allows them to create their own.

Scenario 8-2

In Lelia Bobbit's sixth-grade art class, students are studying ancient Greek architecture and three orders of Greek columns: Corinthian, Doric, and Ionic. In the first phase of the Inductive model (introduction), Mrs. Bobbit explains that, by the end of the lesson, students will examine the orders of Greek columns and, through their analyses, arrive at a definition for each. Mrs. Bobbit shares that they will work in different groupings and examine materials providing information about the three types of columns.

In the open-ended phase, Mrs. Bobbit clusters students into heterogeneous groups of four. She has intentionally grouped learners so that those who struggle answering open-ended questions are clustered with at least one other student who is proficient at this type of questioning. She gives each student a number from one to four and each group a color photo of each type of column. Mrs. Bobbit stresses that no answer is incorrect during this phase, and then she asks the first question: "What do you notice about the columns?"

Student #1 from each group is asked to respond first to the question, thus modeling open-ended responses for the other students in their group. Mrs. Bobbit continues asking the second question: "What similarities and differences do you see?" Student #2 is asked to respond first this time. Students #3 and #4 get their chances later in the lesson.

Throughout the question-and-answer period, a designated group member serves as the recorder of the group's discussion and, using a laptop, records the group's observations of the columns in the class wiki in a posting called "Observations during the open-ended phase." At the end of this phase, each group has an opportunity to review the ideas that other groups posted in the wiki. They share and compare contributions, leading all the groups to a better understanding of the concept, Greek columns, before they move to the next phase.

In the convergent phase, Mrs. Bobbit keeps the students in groups but asks them to stop what they are doing and pay attention to her at the front of the class. She asks students to focus on the characteristics of the different orders of Greek columns, particularly characteristics they have not yet noted. As students reexamine the same photos of columns used earlier in the lesson, Mrs. Bobbit then asks more specific questions, such as "What does the capital look like?" and "Does each column have a base?" While Mrs. Bobbit asks these questions, she also points to the different parts of the column (e.g., base, capital) on an interactive whiteboard. During this questioning and display of columns, students post their ideas to the class wiki using their tablet computers.

For the closure phase, Mrs. Bobbit asks students to develop a working definition of each of these columns in their small groups and post it to the class wiki in a section called, "Closure—Definition of Greek column types." To apply what they have learned, students must find in their neighborhoods images that reflect their definitions of the different orders of columns. They are asked to take digital photos of their discoveries and upload them to the wiki. If they are unable to find examples in their neighborhoods, students must use reference books or online resources (such a museum website) to find examples of the orders of Greek columns. The final activity for the application phase is to create a real column displaying all of its respective critical attributes using a creative medium of their own choosing—salt dough, modeling clay, papier-mâché, computer drawing tool, or something else.

Scenario 8-3

As a middle school library media specialist, Mr. Higgins needs all of his eighth-graders to understand the characteristics of plagiarism before they begin work on their class research paper. He uses the Inductive model to expose learners to examples of plagiarism, including (1) a term paper purchased online to be intentionally submitted as a student's original, creative work about a book; (2) a paper containing a copied passage and phrase that was not correctly attributed; (3) a paper containing verbatim plagiarism (an unacknowledged direct quotation); and (4) an example of plagiarism paraphrasing passages from the book while maintaining the basic paragraph and sentence structure. He uses a multimedia presentation tool to share the examples of plagiarism so that students can easily read, review, and navigate the various examples and explanations of this type of academic dishonesty. In the divergent phase, as he introduces the examples, he asks students to discuss with a partner the characteristics they see and notice about these examples. He asks them to consider the characteristics of each example and its similarities and differences from the other examples. Mr. Higgins also asks them to record their ideas using the laptops. The next day, for the convergent phase of the Inductive model lesson, he begins asking more specific questions as students review each example again: "Did the author reference the ideas of others correctly? How did the author reference other works?"

During the closure phase, students are asked to define plagiarism in written format and list critical attributes and variable attributes of plagiarism in a two-columned graphic organizer.

Finally, for the application phase, Mr. Higgins asks students to write a paragraph that has instances of plagiarism. Then he asks students to trade their papers to find these instances, explaining how they know they are examples of plagiarism.

What Do These Scenarios Illustrate?

These scenarios show three different ways in which the Inductive model might be implemented, using various student groupings (e.g., whole group and small group as in Scenario 8-2), technology, scaffolding of students' learning (e.g., using graphic organizers in Scenario 8-3), and questioning (all three

Mr. Higgins helping a student
© Alexander Raths/Shutterstock

scenarios). It shows that the steps, questioning techniques, and roles of the students and teachers stay the same while most all other aspects of the model can be modified to suit a particular set of learning goals and teaching contexts.

REFLECT: After you have read these scenarios, consider the variations in how each teacher implements the Inductive model. Think about the different reasons each of the profiled teachers had for selecting the model to teach their particular content. Reflect on the variation in the materials used, the subject areas covered, and the teachers' different teaching styles. Consider how you might modify the Inductive model to teach academic content and how it might benefit your students. Also, consider the questions you might need to ask to scaffold their learning during the different phases of the Inductive model.

Planning for Teaching with the Inductive Model

Teachers who carefully plan their use of the Inductive model will enjoy its implementation all the more. They will be better able to respond to unanticipated student needs as they arise. Prior planning for teaching with this model should involve (1) selecting and organizing access to source materials, (2) conducting assessment, (3) developing divergent and convergent questions, and (4) planning for closure and application. The following sections discuss what educational designers should do when teaching with the Inductive model.

Select and Organize the Source Materials

Teachers using the Inductive model in contemporary classrooms have a vast array of materials available to support and enrich their implementation. As with other models that promote comprehension of concepts (i.e., Concept Attainment in Chapter 6 and Concept Development in Chapter 7), the quality of examples used has a dramatic influence on students' success mastering the content. Before selecting examples, teachers should list the critical and variable attributes of the content presented (for information about critical and variable attributes, see Chapter 6). Once these attributes are noted, teachers should select materials that have these attributes, taking care to incorporate as many different types of examples as would be helpful—written, video, audio, and even physical.

In the opening scenario, for instance, Martha Ann Richards selects sonnets that have the attributes of Shakespearean sonnets (e.g., they consist of 14 lines organized into four stanzas, quatrains that adhere to their appropriate purposes and rhyme scheme, and are written in iambic pentameter). Similarly, in Scenario 8-2, Lelia Bobbit chooses to share photographs of Greek columns that vividly display for study the specific attributes of these architectural features.

If a teacher picks examples in formats other than text (e.g., audio), he or she will need to check that these materials can be efficiently and effectively accessed by learners; for example, teachers might need to test uploading and posting materials to a class wiki or website.

Conduct Assessment

Teachers should consider how they will conduct pre-assessment, formative assessment, and summative assessment of students' learning. Pre-assessment can help teachers capture baseline information about students' prior knowledge, readiness, and interests related to the concept. Having that information before instruction occurs can help teachers proactively plan for students' learning differences and differentiate instruction. Pre-assessment can also reveal the level to which students are comfortable with thinking in a convergent and divergent manner and help teachers plan for scaffolding instruction based on learner needs (e.g., if students have difficulty with convergent thinking, the teacher might pair a student who struggles with convergent thinking with a student who is more proficient at this type of thinking).

Teachers should also consider how they will assess their students' learning formatively as they progress through the phases of the Inductive model. This might involve giving students quizzes, reviewing any assignments students might complete to document their learning (e.g., a graphic organizer, as in Scenario 8-3, that students create to show their understanding of plagiarism), or informal checks with students to ensure they are learning the content. The particular strategy selected for gauging students' learning in progress is not as important as the fact that progress is checked during each phase of the model to ensure that students grasp the content that is being studied.

Finally, teachers will need to explore ways to conduct summative assessment that determines whether all students have achieved deep understanding of the concept. Therefore, the closure and application phases might incorporate ways to assess students' understanding of the concept(s) on both an individual and differentiated basis (e.g., some students might define what a rectangle is while others might find examples in their communities, as in Scenario 8-1). Readministering the pre-assessment at this stage can show the extent to which student mastery has increased.

Develop Divergent and Convergent Questions

Quality questions, those that will lead students to engage in divergent and convergent thinking effectively, are critical to the model's success. A teacher must be both familiar with the concept under investigation and clear about the goals for student mastery when developing questions. Keep in mind that divergent questions are open-ended and do not have one right answer. Convergent questions (or "closed" questions) have specific answers that are either right or wrong. For example, the Inductive Model Lesson at the end of this chapter provides examples of specific questions the teacher might ask students during the divergent and convergent phases. In the divergent phase, the teacher asks open-ended questions, such as "What do you notice about these two poems? What do they have in common?" Then, in the convergent phase, the teacher asks closed questions that require specific answers, such as "How many lines does the poem have? How many stanzas does the poem have? How many lines are in each stanza? What is the rhyme scheme? What is the meter?" The divergent questions should focus students' attention on the critical attributes of the concept, as the Inductive Model Lesson also shows.

Plan for Closure and Application

Plans for closure and application are important to devise before implementing an Inductive model lesson. Figuring out appropriate activities for these two phases will not only help teachers plan instruction for all of the Inductive model's phases but also enable the teacher to ensure that the implementation effectively meets anticipated learning goals.

The teacher should consider whether adequate closure can be provided by asking students to write a textual definition of the concept or whether students would benefit from more elaborate or varied opportunities to demonstrate their understanding of the concept. For instance, a teacher might determine that, for closure, students should be able to write out or speak (record) their definition. This was the case in Scenario 8-1 where students could record an explanation of what a rectangle is rather than defining it in writing. Depending on the nature of the concept being defined, it might be necessary to allow students to share their understanding using a technological tool (as in Scenario 8-1) or graphic organizer (as in Scenario 8-3).

Thinking through opportunities for students to apply their learning in the application phase is important, as well. Prior planning allows teachers to think creatively about the best method to enable student expression of knowledge and gives them time to collect resources that might be useful. In this phase, teachers can also incorporate differentiation by allowing students to apply their knowledge using different tools and through different applications. For example, one student or group might be able to draw geometric shapes with pencils, whereas another might be able to find examples in their communities and photograph them with a digital camera.

Differentiating Instruction with the Inductive Model

The Inductive model, like most models in this text, is ambitious in its very design and includes plans to develop students' capabilities in ways that are both broad and deep. However, achieving this in actual practice can be challenging. Also, such challenges can be counteractive if there is no support to address learner differences or if the support is inappropriately matched with learner needs. For the Inductive model to be beneficial, consideration must be paid to learner differences and how they might be bolstered. The sections that follow explain how the model effectively develops the potential of learners with different needs when they are supported and guided in responsive ways.

Content

Built into the Inductive model is an opportunity to provide learners with rich content materials. The authentic nature of materials used in the Inductive model makes them more meaningful than those that might be presented in typical instructional materials (e.g., texts, charts, and so on). The rich format of these materials—audio, visual, and other forms—also makes them more motivational and engaging. Sometimes, however, use of rich materials can backfire because they can be difficult to read, interpret, and use. To promote maximum usability of materials, it is important to choose examples and nonexamples carefully and support their use in the classroom. When selecting materials for exploration, teachers might consider the following questions:

1. Which materials will best support the needs of different learners in my classroom? (e.g., could the needs of visual, auditory, and/or kinesthetic learners be addressed using these materials?)

2. Are the materials I selected relevant to all learners? Will any learners need additional explanation of materials (i.e., their context, their interpretation, and so on) to understand them?
3. Have I provided materials in an appropriate format for my learners? Would materials in a wider or narrower variety be better to include? Can all learners access the materials I have chosen?
4. What challenges might my learners experience while examining these materials to learn about the concept? What supports can I provide to help all learners be successful?

The teachers in this chapter's scenarios have made intentional choices about the types of materials to include in their lessons. They have also provided appropriate supports for differentiation. For example, in the Inductive Model Lesson at the end of this chapter, the teacher uses sonnets in written and audio-recorded formats. By doing so, she provides both visual and auditory learners with the opportunity to access the material in ways that best align with their learning modality—and her English language learners also benefit by reading and listening to the sonnets. Her selection of materials motivates her students *and* supports their comprehension. By having access to materials illustrating the concept in multiple modalities, her students are able to attain higher levels of performance as they move through the progressively more challenging phases of the model.

Process

The Inductive model's greatest strength is also one of its greatest challenges: It situates practice of two completely different types of thinking—divergent and convergent thinking—in a back-to-back manner. After using the model even once, teachers will recognize that some learners have a natural strength practicing convergent thinking and that others have greater aptitude with divergent thinking. Some students will find both types of thinking to be challenging. Pre-assessment of learner readiness (discussed previously in the "Planning for Teaching with the Inductive Model" section) before introducing the lesson using the Inductive model may yield information about students' capabilities that could support effective use of heterogeneous grouping or peer modeling. For example, in Scenario 8-2, Mrs. Bobbit has created heterogeneous groups of students who have varying abilities applying divergent and convergent thinking. Another way to support learners throughout the Inductive model is to provide materials that aid students in performing various phases of the model, as in the use of the graphic organizer in Scenario 8-3.

Product

In the Inductive model, teachers tend to use the application and closure steps to gain information about student learning for assessment. Differentiating assessment in this model involves providing students options for expressing their learning. Offering choices of how and which tools students might use for demonstrating their learning allows students to select the product best suited to showcase their learning. For example, to support English language learners in the Inductive Model Lesson at the end of this chapter, students are asked to write their own sonnet. To differentiate the product, teachers might give students the option of writing their own sonnet songs, provided that they accurately include the attributes of sonnets, such as length, rhyme scheme, meter, and number of stanzas.

What Are the Benefits of Applying the Inductive Model?

There are many benefits to this model—several overlap with those of other concept models (i.e., Concept Attainment model in Chapter 6 and Concept Development model in Chapter 7). Benefits specific to this model are discussed in the following sections.

Fosters and Scaffolds Inductive and Critical-Thinking Skills

Through divergent and convergent questioning, teachers scaffold and develop students' inductive and critical thinking. This is accomplished by guiding students in an analysis of materials (examples) that begins as an open-ended and broad examination of a concept and then ends as a specific, generalization or summation of the concept.

Engages Learners in Identifying Patterns and Differences

A goal of the Inductive model is for students to learn concepts inductively—that is, through their own experiences and analysis of examples representing the concept(s). This process involves identifying the similarities and differences in the example(s) to help them formulate their own understanding of the concept.

Supports Numerous Thinking Styles

Each of us may practice various types of thinking but it is likely that one will be more natural and comfortable to us. Because this model exercises both divergent and convergent thinking, it provides different types of thinkers with opportunities to exercise and develop these two thinking types.

Promotes Deep Learning

Throughout the Inductive model, teachers ask students to examine the examples, identify patterns and relationships, and form generalizations or definitions. All of these activities are characteristic of deep learning of content resulting in understanding (Wiggins & McTighe, 2005).

Allows Students to Demonstrate Their Own Learning

The Inductive model promotes students' demonstration of their own learning, particularly in the closure and application phases of the model during which students develop generalizations, definitions, or summaries of the concept and then apply their understanding in novel, real-world ways.

Provides Students the Opportunity to Apply Their Learning

One of the best ways to emphasize the value of learning is to give students an opportunity to put their knowledge into practice. The Inductive model requires students to apply their learning in the final, application phase of the model. In this phase, students practice using new knowledge for practical purposes and become aware of the importance of recently mastered concepts through firsthand experiences.

What Value Does Technology Add to the Inductive Model?

Technology can make learning more efficient, effective, or engaging in many different ways when implementing the Inductive model. Below are just a few examples. Also, Figure 8-4 provides a summary of the tools introduced in this section.

Planning

FIND EXAMPLES AND NONEXAMPLES. Search engines and online databases are excellent tools for identifying rich, meaningful examples and nonexamples. This offers students motivational materials to analyze and observe, such as the audio recording of a sonnet in the Inductive Model Lesson at the end of the chapter or examples of Greek columns online for Scenario 8-2. Efforts should be made to go beyond text-based materials. Using advanced search engine features can make finding files of particular types, such as audio, video, simulations, and animations, much easier.

Figure 8-4 Technology Tools for the Inductive Model

Use	Tools
Planning	
	Locate content materials, such as videos, simulations, and audio, using search engines and online databases • Google: www.google.com Resources organizing access to content materials and/or presenting assignments • Weebly: www.weebly.com • Prezi: www.prezi.com • Posterous Spaces: https://posterous.com
Implementing	
	Visual presentation of questions or sharing of examples and nonexamples • Keynote: www.apple.com/iwork/keynote • SMART Notebook: www.smarttech.com • PowerPoint: www.microsoft.com Word processor • Weebly: www.weebly.com • Wikispaces: www.wikispaces.com • Animoto: www.animoto.com
Assessing	
	Online survey tools • Flisti: http:// flisti.com • Google Forms: www.google.com/google-d-s/forms • Survey Monkey: www.surveymonkey.com Audience response system tools • Turningpoint "clickers": www.turningpoint.com Audio and digital recording • Digital audio recorder, tape recorder, digital video • VoiceThread: http://voicethread.com

ORGANIZE MATERIALS AND PROVIDE STUDENTS WITH ACCESS TO THEM. Technology tools allow teachers an effective means for organizing and sharing examples and non-examples. Consider using a tool like Prezi (www.prezi.com) to create a presentation that allows students to explore examples and nonexamples or a website development tool such as Weebly (www.weebly.com) to present the examples using hyperlinks to various online locations. Other notable tools are Keynote, PowerPoint, and Posterous Spaces.

Implementation

The use of technology can aid a teacher in each of the different phases of the Inductive model. Specific suggestions are included in the sections that follow for implementing technology.

LESSON INTRODUCTION. Teachers can provide a more efficient overview of the lesson by using presentation tools to share the lesson objectives and the tasks students will complete. With a computer and projector or an interactive whiteboard, display the major points of the lesson using software such as Keynote (www.apple.com/iwork/keynote), PowerPoint (http://microsoft.com), Word, or some other word-processing tool.

In the introduction, the teacher could outline the major phases of the model and alert students to the amount of time they will have to work during each phase. The presentation could also include a few questions to scaffold their learning. The presentation of even dull information like instructional objectives may be made more engaging through the incorporation of animations, color, and other media. Using a digital avatar of a former President like George Washington to explain the purpose of an assignment makes the presentation novel and commands student attention. One tool, called Voki (www.voki.com), makes it easy for teachers to create such avatars.

DIVERGENT PHASE. Technology is useful in this step because a teacher can introduce the example(s) and/or nonexample(s) using various media, such as photos, text, or movies collected into a digital folder for viewing; a website that displays examples; a simulation; or a podcast. Animoto is a Web-based tool (www.animoto.com) that makes it very simple for teachers to compile video, photo, and/or music examples and/or nonexamples illustrating a concept into engaging video slide shows. More simply, examples can be pasted into a word-processed document and projected for all of the students to see, as in Figure 8-6 from the Inductive Model Lesson that involves display of a sonnet.

In some instances, using technology to present examples and/or nonexamples will do more than enhance student interest—it will provide additional information that might not be possible to communicate using text-based presentations. For example, providing a video of various instruments being played will enable students to understand more about these instruments (e.g., how they sound and how they are played) and ways they might be classified (e.g., into a family such as woodwind, brass, or percussion) than if they saw only photos of the instruments. Interactive whiteboards make it particularly easy to display such media to students in a size they can see from anywhere in the classroom. Using features such as the "screen shade" and "spotlight tool," which are available with some interactive whiteboard software packages, allows a teacher to add visual interest and even suspense to this phase, as various examples are more dramatically unveiled.

CONVERGENT PHASE. During this phase, the teacher asks students more specific questions about the attributes of the concept. Technology may assist by highlighting key attributes that may not be apparent to students. For instance, using the Inductive Model Lesson at the end of this chapter, a teacher might use a projector to display sonnets that have the rhyme scheme already noted and color coded for visual learners. Font styles and sizes can also be changed to make viewing attributes easier, or the teacher might simply write out the rhyme scheme as he or she points it out to students—directly on the whiteboard. Similarly, students may use a tablet computer equipped with a touch screen to code sonnets for easy understanding. Many students benefit from having visuals up close for viewing.

When using video examples and/or nonexamples, editing tools can help students see and, therefore, understand them better. For example, a teacher might use a digital video camera to record the "egg in a bottle" experiment about changes in air pressure. The experiment involves placing a hard-boiled egg in the opening of a bottle after placing paper on fire inside of the bottle. Students can stop, speed up, slow down, and rewind the experiment to see what happens with their own eyes (even though the egg is bigger than the mouth of the bottle, a change in air pressure causes the egg to be pushed through the opening). Because they can review the video as often and as slowly/quickly as they like, students develop a better understanding of why the egg falls into the bottle. The recording enables students to manipulate the video of the experiment to understand better this scientific demonstration of a concept.

CLOSURE. Teachers could ask students to record their definition or understanding of the concept using a variety of media. For example, students might be asked to create a short podcast using free software for recording audio on a computer or other device such as a smartphone, and then upload their podcast to the web. Students might use a blog, such as Class Blogmeister (http://classblogmeister.com), or a wiki, such as Wikispaces (www.wikispaces.com) to log what they learned through their explorations in this Inductive model lesson.

APPLICATION. There are many ways to apply technology during the application phase. For instance, in Scenario 8-1, students can download examples of geometric shapes from the Internet, take pictures in their community using digital cameras, or design 3-D versions using graphic software. Students can use different technology tools to apply their learning (e.g., by creating an example of the concept learned) or by recording their understand via video or audio.

Assessment

As noted previously in the "Planning for Teaching with the Inductive Model" section, teachers should incorporate pre-assessment, formative assessment, and summative assessment in their plans for implementing the Inductive model. Technology can assist teachers in these three different types of assessment. Three major types of technology tools that could be used are the following:

1. Audience response systems and survey/quiz tools can be used for conducting all three types of assessment. For instance, teachers might provide some convergent questions using a student response system to learn in a formative manner whether students comprehend the attributes under study. Student response systems and survey tools (especially polls) can be used for the application and closure phases as well. For example, teachers could pose a variety of convergent questions about sonnets in the Inductive Model Lesson at the end of the chapter and find out immediately the percentage of students who answer correctly.

2. Graphic organizers and multimedia tools are helpful in facilitating student expression of learning. For example, in Scenario 8-3, Mr. Higgins provides students a graphic organizer

that helps them distinguish the critical attributes from variable attributes associated with plagiarism. The novelty of these tools often motivates learners, but the tools also enable student expression during the closure and application phases. For example, for students who have difficulty drawing or creating a diagram that demonstrates their understanding of geometric shapes (as in Scenario 8-1) with pencil and paper, teachers might allow or encourage the use of electronic illustration tools (e.g., Kidspiration, a drawing application, or the Paint accessory available in Windows computers).

3. Video or audio recording can assist with documentation of critical-thinking skills. The Inductive model promotes critical-thinking skills. By assessing these skills, teachers can make informed modifications to their instruction in ways that support differentiation. Video and audio recorders are practical tools for capturing student learning. As in Scenario 8-1, use of these tools allows a teacher to gain information about individual student performance in a whole-class setting that can be reviewed at a later time or shared with a student during a private learning conference. Teachers might also use a tool like VoiceThread (http://voicethread.com) to document students' thinking around the concept learned.

Inductive Model Lesson Plan Example

The following lesson is an example of how a lesson might be designed using the Inductive model. Figure 8-5 provides an outline of the lesson's different phases.

UNDERSTANDING SONNETS LESSON PLAN

LESSON CONTEXT

GRADE LEVEL(S): Tenth

CONTENT AREA: English

PHYSICAL TEACHING ENVIRONMENT: This lesson will be taught in a rectangular-shaped high school classroom with desks and chairs. No special equipment is necessary. Seats should be in a U shape, facing the chalkboard in the front of the room.

Figure 8-5 Outline of Inductive Model Lesson Steps

Inductive Model Steps	Inductive Model Lesson
Lesson introduction	Provide an overview of the lesson by explaining that students will examine a type of poem. Students are to observe patterns and differences.
Divergent phase	During this divergent stage, students examine various Shakespearean sonnets. They are to examine and note any interesting points or patterns. The teacher should ask students open-ended questions.
Convergent phase	This is the "closed" phase of the model where the teacher asks probing questions that are more specific about sonnets (e.g., "What is the rhyme scheme?")
Closure	Students make conclusions or form a definition about what a sonnet is.
Application	Students apply their knowledge by writing their own sonnets.

APPLICATION OF REVISED BLOOM'S TAXONOMY: Students work from the *understand* (by becoming aware of what a sonnet is) to the *create* levels (by writing their own sonnet).

Lesson Plan

GOAL(S): Students will learn about the English/Shakespearean sonnet.

Standard(s) Addressed:

National Council for Teachers of English/International Reading Association (NCTE/IRA) Standards for the English Language Arts: [3]

1. Students read a wide range of print and nonprint texts to build an understanding of texts, of themselves, and of the cultures of the United States and the world; to acquire new information; to respond to the needs and demands of society and the workplace; and for personal fulfillment. Among these texts are fiction and nonfiction, classic and contemporary works.

2. Students read a wide range of literature from many periods in many genres to build an understanding of the many dimensions (e.g., philosophical, ethical, aesthetic) of human experience.

3. Students apply a wide range of strategies to comprehend, interpret, evaluate, and appreciate texts. They draw on their prior experience, their interactions with other readers and writers, their knowledge of word meaning and of other texts, their word identification strategies, and their understanding of textual features (e.g., sound-letter correspondence, sentence structure, context, graphics).

4. Students apply knowledge of language structure, language conventions (e.g., spelling and punctuation), media techniques, figurative language, and genre to create, critique, and discuss print and nonprint texts.

5. Students use a variety of technological and information resources (e.g., libraries, databases, computer networks, video) to gather and synthesize information and to create and communicate knowledge.

   For a complete list of the standards, go to http://www.ncte.org/standards.

Common Core Standards: [4]

RL.9-10.10. By the end of grade 9, read and comprehend literature, including stories, dramas, and poems, in the grades 9–10 text complexity band proficiently, with scaffolding as needed at the high end of the range.

OBJECTIVE(S):

1. Students will be able to describe the major characteristics (e.g., rhyme scheme of abab cdcd efef gg, 14 lines, meter, content) of an English/Shakespearean sonnet by analyzing several examples of English/Shakespearean sonnets.

2. SWBAT write an English/Shakespearean sonnet that correctly includes all of its major components/characteristics.

---

[3] Standards for the English Language Arts, by the International Reading Association and the National Council of Teachers of English, Copyright 1996 by the International Reading Association and the National Council of Teachers of English. Reprinted with permission.

[4] © Copyright 2010. National Governors Association Center for Best Practices and Council of Chief State School Officers. All rights reserved.

ESTIMATED TIME: 20–40 minutes

MATERIALS NEEDED:
- Optional: Computer with speakers and Internet connection
- Sonnets handout page with several sonnets (see Figure 8-6). You may print Shakespeare's sonnets from many sources; one free source provides the sonnets in their 1609 published form: http://etext.lib.virginia.edu/toc/modeng/public/ShaSonQ.html

  Suggested sonnets to examine:
- Shakespeare's Sonnet #18—"Shall I Compare Thee to a Summer's Day?" (recording in RealPlayer: www.swisseduc.ch/english/readinglist/shakespeare_william/sonnets/index2.html#18

Figure 8-6 Sonnets for Inductive Model Lesson

Poem #1

Shall I compare thee to a summer's day?
Thou art more lovely and more temperate:
Rough winds do shake the darling buds of May,
And summer's lease hath all too short a date:
Sometime too hot the eye of heaven shines,
And often is his gold complexion dimm'd;
And every fair from fair sometime declines,
By chance, or nature's changing course untrimm'd;
But thy eternal summer shall not fade,
Nor lose possession of that fair thou ow'st,
Nor shall death brag thou wander'st in his shade,
When in eternal lines to time thou grow'st;
So long as men can breathe, or eyes can see,
So long lives this, and this gives life to thee.

Poem #2

When in disgrace with fortune and men's eyes
I all alone beweep my outcast state,
And trouble deaf heaven with my bootless cries,
And look upon myself, and curse my fate,
Wishing me like to one more rich in hope,
Featur'd like him, like him with friends possess'd,
Desiring this man's art, and that man's scope,
With what I most enjoy contented least;
Yet in these thoughts myself almost despising,
Haply I think on thee,—and then my state,
Like to the lark at break of day arising
From sullen earth, sings hymns at heaven's gate;
For thy sweet love remember'd such wealth brings
That then I scorn to change my state with kings.

- Shakespeare's Sonnet #29—"When in disgrace with fortune and men's eyes" (mp3 and RealPlayer recording: www.swisseduc.ch/english/readinglist/shakespeare_william/sonnets/index2.html#29
- Shakespeare's Sonnet #116—"Let me not to the marriage of true minds," (mp3 and RealPlayer recordings: www.swisseduc.ch/english/readinglist/shakespeare_william/sonnets/index5.html#116
- Shakespeare's Sonnet #147—"My love is as a fever, longing still"

PREREQUISITE SKILLS: Students should be able to read and comprehend text at the tenth-grade level, as well as understand what rhyme, rhythm, meter, and iambic pentameter mean.

LESSON PROCEDURES (Text in italics is suggested teacher dialogue.)

Lesson Introduction: [2 minutes]

Did you know that April is National Poetry month? To celebrate and to address our standards, we are going to examine some poems written by an author whose work you are familiar with (I will tell you who it is later). We will listen to, read, and examine a few poems written by this author, you will need to look for patterns and differences among the poems to determine the characteristics of this type of poem.

Open-Ended Phase: [8 minutes]

Introduce lesson by providing students with two English/Shakespearean sonnets (see Figure 8-6) and asking two students to read the poems (sonnets) aloud (or play a recording of them), then asking the following:

1. *What do you notice about these two poems?*
2. *What do they have in common? (answers could be: number of lines, rhyming scheme)*

Convergent Phase: [8 minutes]

Ask more probing questions (see questions below) to draw out the major characteristics of English/Shakespearean sonnets and record students' responses on an overhead, chalkboard, or computer connected to a projector. Teacher shares Figure 8-6 to point out the rhyme scheme. Teachers may also wish to provide students with a handout (see www.readwritethink.org/lesson_images/lesson830/SonnetChart.pdf) or the "Interactive Sonnets Characteristics" chart available online (see http://interactives.mped.org/view_interactive.aspx?id=580) that scaffold this phase.

Think about what we have been studying with regards to poetry (rhyme, meter, and so on). What characteristics of poems do these two poems have in common?

1. *How many lines does the poem have?*
2. *How many stanzas does the poem have?*
3. *How many lines are in each stanza?*
4. *What is the rhyme scheme?*
5. *What is the meter?*

Closure: [5 minutes]

Ask students to summarize their definition of an English/Shakespearean sonnet based on the characteristics discussed today:

Based on your examination of the poems, write your definition of an English/Shakespearean sonnet in your personal class blog.

Application Phase: [15 minutes]

Ask students to write their own English/Shakespearean sonnet:

In our class wiki about sonnets, write your own sonnet, and read a sonnet written by at least two other students. Critique the sonnet of your assigned partner and make suggestions for improvement.

ASSESSMENT

Formative assessment Gauge students' responses and review students' journals/learning logs/blogs to check for understanding.

Summative assessment Students individually write their English/Shakespearean sonnet, which is evaluated using a rubric that assesses whether they have the correct syllabic meter, line lengths, rhyme, rhyme scheme, rhythm, and expressive content.

LESSON EXTENSIONS

Extensions:

1. Ask students to complete a different lesson on sonnets:
   a) www.readwritethink.org/lessons/lesson_view.asp?id=830 (This resource is a lesson for discovering various sonnet forms)
   b) http://interactives.mped.org/view_interactive.aspx?id=580
   c) http://edsitement.neh.gov/view_lesson_plan.asp?id=365
2. Ask students to explore other sonnets at:
   a) www.bartleby.com/70/index1.html (has all of Shakespeare's sonnets online)
   b) Sonnet Central: www.sonnets.org
3. Ask students to explore the Academy of American Poets' website: www.poets.org/npm
4. Have students rewrite the poems in contemporary English and compare old English with contemporary English.
5. Have students sign up to receive Shakespeare's Sonnet of the Day at http://killdevilhill.com/shakespeare.shtml
6. Have students publish their sonnets at www.poetry.com
7. Introduce Elizabeth Barrett Browning's sonnet, *How do I love thee? Let me count the ways.*
8. Have students examine Italian/Petrarchan sonnets and compare/contrast to English/Shakespearean sonnets.

Differentiation Strategies for the Inductive Model Lesson

The following sections provide ideas for differentiating instruction using the Inductive Model Lesson.

Content

Teachers may differentiate student access to content by providing both print and recorded versions of the sonnets. By listening to recorded version of the sonnets, students will be able to stop and replay portions of the sonnet if they desire as well as hear how different people might read the same sonnet. The teacher might also wish to choose sonnets of varying levels of complexity. English language learners may need additional support for understanding vocabulary.

Students who have a basic understanding of sonnets might locate and further explore "global sonnets" (those from countries other than England) and identify similarities and differences in the themes, number of lines per poem, number of lines per stanza, meter, and rhyme scheme. Further, academic vocabulary should be addressed for all students.

Process

To differentiate the learning process, teachers could introduce examples and nonexamples in different groupings. For instance, teachers could move from whole-group instruction in the introduction phase, to small groups examining the different examples in the divergent and convergent phases, back to whole-group instruction in the closure, then finally to independent work in the application phase. Further, teachers can also provide instructions in spoken and written formats or even translated into various languages. Easy translation of instructions can be made with free Web-based translation tools like Google Translate (http://translate.google.com); however, it is important to point out that such translation tools do not provide translations with 100% accuracy.

Product

Students will create their own sonnets—but they might do this in a variety of ways. For instance, students could write their sonnets using word-processing software and then present them by acting them out, using presentation software, or creating a class wiki of sonnets. This very task allows for differentiation by making it possible for students to express themselves and their ideas creatively. They might choose different themes for their sonnets.

Chapter Summary

In this chapter, you read about the Inductive model—an active, engaging model of instruction that encourages students' development of critical-thinking skills as they explore and learn concepts in the academic content areas. The Inductive model promotes inductive reasoning—advocated historically by Francis Bacon and more recently Hilda Taba. Lessons planned with the Inductive model challenge learners to make full use of their senses to observe and recognize details and patterns in materials related to the content under investigation. Such action promotes understanding of a topic. The Inductive model allows learners to develop and refine knowledge of a concept even when they do not already possess prior knowledge of it. It scaffolds learners by providing them with examples of a concept (similar to Concept Attainment) but does so in an inductive way (similar to Concept Development). Among the benefits of the Inductive model are that it fosters and scaffolds inductive and critical-thinking skills, engages learners in identifying patterns and differences, supports numerous thinking styles, promotes deep learning, allows students to demonstrate their own learning, and provides students the opportunity to apply their learning.

Review Questions

1. What is the history of the Inductive model?

2. What are the steps in the Inductive model?

3. What type of content is best to teach when applying the Inductive model? Provide and explain examples of content that would be appropriate and inappropriate.

4. What are the benefits of applying the Inductive model? What are some of the challenges?

5. How can the Inductive model be used to differentiate instruction and support diverse learners' needs?

6. How can technology be used to implement the Inductive model?

Application Exercises

To promote your ability to apply the learning you gained in studying this chapter, complete the following exercises that challenge you to analyze a lesson plan you have written using the Inductive model *or* use the lesson plan example included in this chapter.

TECHNOLOGY INTEGRATION ACTIVITY

1. Consider the following and discuss with a partner or reflect independently:
   a) In the lesson plan you are analyzing, how does (or could) the integration of technology tools make learning more efficient, effective, and engaging? Can you explain and indicate how you will measure its impact on student learning?
   b) Will all learners be aided through the integration of technology? Are there some who might need special support to gain full benefit from technology tools? How might you support this? Is there a way to build on strengths students bring to this lesson related to technology? How?
   c) What plans could you put in place to promote a more successful use of technology and minimize (or eliminate) risk of failure? What proactive plan could you put in place ahead of lesson implementation to ensure technology works smoothly and for all learners? What reactive approach could you take to ensure desired learning still occurs if technology malfunctions during the lesson?

TEACHER PERFORMANCE ACTIVITIES

2. **Academic Vocabulary and Language Demands:** Academic vocabulary is the vocabulary that students must be able to understand to be successful performing content area learning. Language demands involve the ways language is used in speaking, writing, listening, and reading in the learning tasks of a lesson and in the expressions of student learning. For the lesson plan you are working with (your own or the one provided in the chapter), consider the following questions and discuss them with a partner or reflect on them alone:
   a) What academic vocabulary and language demands exist in any lesson designed with the Inductive model? What words are associated with learning concepts and using the model that might challenge learners?
   b) Make a list of the academic vocabulary students must comprehend and the language demands of the Inductive model lesson plan you are reviewing. How might students' prior knowledge of these terms be affected by their backgrounds, lived experiences, and prior learning experiences?
   c) How would you determine whether and which students have mastery of the academic language before the lesson begins?
   d) How might students be supported in developing proficiency with academic language in this lesson context? What visual or other resources might you use?

3. **Planning:** In the context of the lesson plan that you are analyzing, discuss the following with a partner or reflect independently:
   a) Explain how the phases of the Inductive model build on existing knowledge students have gained from their prior schooling or lived experiences? How could teachers build on student strengths or weaknesses with relation to existing knowledge they must build on in the Inductive model?

b) Consider how a variety of learning needs have been addressed in the lesson. What are the ways that this model differentiates instruction within its steps? What other strategies for differentiation might be supportive to integrate?

c) Anticipate any misconceptions students might have or experience about the concept as they come into the lesson. Describe any misunderstanding students might develop related to the concept during the lesson.

d) What research or theory supports the use of this model for instruction in your learning context? Does the work of any theorists you may have studied support the use of this model?

4. **Implementation:** In the context of the lesson plan that you are analyzing, discuss the following questions with a partner or consider independently:

a) Explain how the phases of the Inductive model and the activities that students will perform in the lesson you are reviewing will result in engaged learning. What indicators would you look for during the implementation of the lesson to measure who is engaged and how much?

b) How well does your lesson challenge learners to apply their learning in meaningful contexts? Explain.

c) What thinking skills will students gain in this lesson that they can apply to future learning? Can you describe another context where those thinking skills might be utilized?

5. **Assessment:** Consider the following and discuss with a partner or reflect independently:

a) Would consideration of students' backgrounds and prior learning and experiences as they relate to learning goals and objectives help you design a more effective lesson? How?

b) How does or could the lesson plan you are reviewing use formative assessment to

direct the more successful implementation of instruction? Is there a way to make it more intentional or improve it to address students' strengths or learning needs? What type of feedback would or could students be provided?

c) How does the plan you are reviewing support students' expression of learning? Are there multiple forms of evidence of student learning? How might students learn through an analysis of their performance? What specific indicators would you look for in evidence of student learning to determine how deeply and well they understand the targeted concept.

6. **Analyzing Teaching:** Consider the following issues and discuss them with a partner or reflect independently:

a) Now that you have created and/or analyzed a lesson plan using the Inductive model, consider how the model supports effective teaching. Can you cite specific evidence or references that support your claim? Be specific in expressing your ideas.

b) What did you learn from this activity that might inform your future practice?

Discussion Question

Based on the application exercise, explain the pros and cons of the Concept Attainment, Concept Development, and Inductive models of teaching. Describe a concept you would teach using each model. Also, discuss whether the same concept(s) could/should be taught using all three models.

Journal Entry

The Inductive model is one that fosters students' application of critical-thinking skills in the divergent and convergent phases of the model. What types of questions are best used for each phase? Explain why.

Resources

- Sir Francis Bacon's *The Advancement of Learning*—www.gutenberg.org/etext/5500

- Winpossible video, Inductive vs Deductive Reasoning—www.winpossible.com/lessons/Algebra_I_Inductive_vs._Deductive_reasoning.html

chapter

9

nine

Model	Vocabulary Acquisition Model
Knowledge Supported	• Factual Knowledge
	• Conceptual Knowledge
Added Value	• Provides students with scaffolds for learning about vocabulary
	• Promotes research-based strategies for effective vocabulary instruction
Technologies to Integrate	• Online dictionaries and tools for learning the morphology and etymology of vocabulary
	• Concept-mapping and drawing/paint tools to record and demonstrate learning of vocabulary
	• Search tools to locate examples of vocabulary in varied and multiple contexts and media

The Vocabulary Acquisition Model

ajt/Shutterstock

An Li knew the challenges of learning a new language firsthand. His family had emigrated from China to Philadelphia, Pennsylvania, when he was 12 years old. At the time, he spoke no English, but through hard work and study, he mastered English well enough to join the high school debate team. An had graduated at the top of his class and received scholarship offers to several colleges. Later, he graduated from law school magna cum laude. An understood that his mastery of English had been crucial to these successes. However, he also knew the skills he had developed while learning to understand a new culture, language, and vocabulary had been equally important to his success. After 20 years working as a lawyer, An had decided to become a teacher so that he could help students from circumstances like his own and share his love for his adopted country and its empowering democracy.

The desire to become more skilled at supporting English language learners in his high school social studies classroom had led An to attend today's workshop on "Academic Language." The workshop taught An some powerful new strategies that he could use to help his students master important words related to content area learning, but he was surprised that the workshop instructor did not suggest that students be encouraged to learn the etymology of words. Learning prefixes, suffixes, and root-word meanings had been instrumental to An's learning and achievement at every educational level. Such knowledge had enabled him to achieve high scores on standardized college entrance exams and be successful as a law student. He still used the decoding and inquiry strategies he had learned in his daily life when learning new forms of communication—like texting.

After the workshop, An approached the workshop instructor, Sabina Rogers, and asked, "Sabina, your strategies today were useful, but I am interested in knowing if teaching the etymology of words is something you would recommend. In my educational experiences as an English language learner, this has been quite empowering. I believe the study of words might help my students, too. Is there a formal method for teaching students to study words in the academic subjects? As you indicated in your workshop today, vocabulary is not just something that must be studied and learned in language arts."

Nodding, Sabina replied, "Yes. Studying words is very important, and there is a model for doing it. I'm glad you asked me about it. I had planned to introduce a model called the "Vocabulary Acquisition model" in the workshop, but the teachers in our group today had so many good questions that I ran out of time."

An chuckled and responded, "People saw such relevance in your topic that they could not help but have more interest and questions. I am glad you answered them. I learned a lot."

Sabina responded by telling An how to get hold of a book from the district resource library that had detailed information about the model she had mentioned. Then she offered to give him a crash course on the model so that he would know whether to make the trip downtown for the book. The two sat down.

"Now An," Sabina started, "you teach social studies, right? There are so many great words you can use to facilitate students' understanding of language and ability to learn about new words. To encourage this, you can use what is called the Vocabulary Acquisition model. First select a word that has significance to your subject and is one that is unfamiliar to your students—like 'democracy.' Then pretest students to learn what they already know about it. Next, have students examine their responses to the pretest. They can review their spellings and definitions of the word and explain to one another why they spelled the word and defined it as they did. In doing so, they will have an experience that promotes deep analysis of the word. This will prepare them for expanding their knowledge of the word as they explore its meaning by examining its synonyms, antonyms, prefix, suffix, and so on. At this next phase in the Vocabulary Acquisition model, students will use references to stretch their learning and make sure they gain an accurate understanding of the word in question. Then students will see and practice using the new word in context and take a posttest to evaluate their learning. That is the shorthand explanation of the model, but you can see that one of its greatest strengths is that it provides students multiple ways to access and learn important vocabulary. In the model, learning goes beyond memorizing and teaches words in a meaningful context. It also enables students to develop skills for future vocabulary learning. Of course, before you introduce the Vocabulary Acquisition model, you have to do your homework by learning about the model and, most importantly, knowing which word or words you want to teach. The chapter I mentioned will provide good ideas for how to choose those words, but it is common sense that the word has to be important to the content you are teaching and one whose understanding is essential for building new understandings and comprehension."

An thanked Sabina for her time. He had already decided it was worth picking up the book—even if it meant heading downtown at rush hour. Experience had taught him that some learning was worth the extra effort. As he drove, he could see Philadelphia City Hall in the distance; he thought about what it represented (democracy, revolution, and so on), and that was it—he knew he would start the American Revolution unit with a Vocabulary Acquisition model lesson using the word *revolution*. After all, how could his students study this important event in their hometown's history without having a deep understanding of what the word *revolution* means? If his students also learned strategies to expand their vocabulary in future learning—so much the better! ∎

CHAPTER OBJECTIVES

After reading this chapter, you will be able to:

- Describe the Vocabulary Acquisition model, including its history and steps.
- Communicate the applications and benefits of the Vocabulary Acquisition model and learn what it might look like in a classroom.
- Explain how to implement and plan for teaching with the Vocabulary Acquisition model.

- Articulate how the Vocabulary Acquisition model might enable differentiated instruction and support diverse learners.
- Describe how technology can enhance teaching with the Vocabulary Acquisition model.

Introduction

The more words you know, the more you *can* know. Vocabulary functions like a key that unlocks doors of understanding. Words allow us to comprehend our world and express our thinking about it. Comprehension of words is essential to learning and correlated with school success or failure. Even though the development of vocabulary is of recognized importance, all too often it is only formally addressed in English and language arts classes. Successful learning across the academic content areas is influenced by students' mastery of "academic vocabulary" and the language of instruction or "academic language" (Anstrom, et al., 2010; Scarcella, 2008). Students' comprehension of the content they read and hear and their ability to express their knowledge are correlated with the breadth and depth of their vocabulary. Attention to vocabulary development must occur not only in the language arts but also in every subject area. Models and strategies that facilitate vocabulary development—emphasizing understanding and retention—are important tools in every teacher's tool kit. They improve learning for all students, from native English speakers to English language learners (ELLs) to students with learning disabilities. In this chapter, we introduce the Vocabulary Acquisition model—an effective way of teaching vocabulary. You will also learn the steps of this model, when and why to apply it, and how it benefits learners in academic and lifelong learning.

What Is the Vocabulary Acquisition Model?

The Vocabulary Acquisition model is a teacher-guided instructional model that facilitates students' development of vocabulary in a procedural and inductive manner. The model enables students to attain deep understanding of key vocabulary in each academic discipline. It also allows them to develop skills useful for independent vocabulary learning and cultivates students' appreciation for the complexity of language. In the Vocabulary Acquisition model, students engage in carefully orchestrated experiences that enable them to study words and apply them in context. After being assigned words carefully selected by their teacher, students examine their prior knowledge of the word and hypothesize about its meaning and spelling. Then they work to extend this understanding of the word's meaning by analyzing the parts of the word and the meanings of these parts. They study the word's synonym and antonyms as well as its etymology and morphology—actively engaging in the identification of patterns that naturally occur in both words and language. Figure 9-1 includes some examples of possible words across different content areas that might be studied using the Vocabulary Acquisition model.

The Vocabulary Acquisition model can be utilized when teaching factual or conceptual knowledge types (Anderson, et al., 2001) and stretches student thinking beyond basic levels of the cognitive process dimension. It encourages them to go beyond remembering and understanding vocabulary—challenging them to achieve deep understanding as they apply the word within context and to analyze its structure. When reflection about one's learning is incorporated within the model, it also promotes the development of procedural knowledge.

Figure 9-1   Words to Explore with the Vocabulary
Acquisition Model

Subject	Words
Art	concave, impressionism
Language Arts	prefix, cinquain
Mathematics	circumference, vector
Music	harmony, orchestra
Health/Physical Education	aerobic, triceps
Social Studies	civilization, democracy
Science	energy, system

What Are the History and Origins of the Vocabulary Acquisition Model?

Although teachers have traditionally used methods for word study and some of the activities in the Vocabulary Acquisition model, Thomas Estes was the first to coin the model's
title and formalize its steps (Gunter, Estes, & Schwab, 2007). The model addresses the need
for students to develop a deep understanding of words by exploring the etymology, meanings, and patterns inherent in words. Deep understanding of vocabulary—the comprehension of a word's complexity and its relationship to other concepts—is at the core of the
model. The Vocabulary Acquisition model builds on students' prior knowledge and asks
students to make connections to other usages and related words—all cornerstones of effective vocabulary instruction (Baker, Simmons, & Kameenui, 1995).

WHAT IS DEEP UNDERSTANDING?   Students acquire deep understanding through active
engagement in the learning process, especially when they exercise the higher-level cognitive processes enumerated in the revised Bloom's taxonomy (Anderson et al., 2001). Deep
understanding results when students appreciate new learning in relation to that which
is already known and can be known. According to Bereiter (2002), "To have deep understanding means one is attuned to nonobvious structural or causal properties of the thing
and to that thing's relations to other things" (p. 104). During the learning experiences
that the Vocabulary Acquisition model fosters, students do not passively accept their
teacher's definition of a word. Instead, they craft their own deep understanding of the
word when considering its complexity and relationship to other words and concepts.

WHAT IS DEEP UNDERSTANDING OF VOCABULARY?   Deep understanding of vocabulary
consists of three different activities: association, comprehension, and generation (Stahl
& Fairbanks, 1986). **Association** involves students' ability to make connections between
a word, its definition, or context. **Comprehension** refers to how students demonstrate
their knowledge of vocabulary by using the word in a sentence or classifying it with related

Figure 9-2   Definition of *Morphology*

> **Morphology \mȯr-ˈfä-lə-jē**
>
> Function: noun
>
> Etymology: German *Morphologie*, from *morph-* + *-logie* -logy
>
> First Known Use: 1830
>
> 1 a: a branch of biology that deals with the form and structure of animals and plants
>   b: the form and structure of an organism or any of its parts
> 2 a: a study and description of word formation (as inflection, derivation, and compounding) in language
>   b: the system of word-forming elements and processes in a language
> 3 a: a study of structure or form
>   b: structure, form
> 4: the external structure of rocks in relation to the development of erosional forms or topographic features

By permission. From Merriam-Webster's Collegiate® Dictionary, 11th Edition © 2012 by Merriam-Webster, Incorporated (www.Merriam-Webster.com).

words, such as antonyms and synonyms. **Generation** includes students' application of the word in a novel situation or sentence or by defining the word in their own words. Teaching vocabulary for deep understanding involves students' participation in these distinct types of mental processes around important words they must know.

Let us examine the entries for *morphology* (see Figure 9-2) and *etymology* (see Figure 9-3) found in the *Merriam-Webster Dictionary*. These two words are essential for understanding the vocabulary acquisition process, and their exploration here will allow an opportunity to practice learning for deep understanding. Note that these entries provide the pronunciation of these words, and they also share the etymology and definition, too. Consider how often you ask students to examine the morphology or etymology of a word. If you are like most teachers, you probably do it very infrequently. Yet, by examining this information, students retain and understand more information about the word. Deep exploration catalyzes deep understanding, whereas surface exploration results in surface understanding.

The Vocabulary Acquisition model helps students in numerous ways. The most important are that it teaches students a deep understanding of the words studied and enables them to achieve greater success in exploring words in the future. When students learn and

Figure 9-3   Definition of *Etymology*

> **Etymology \ĕt'ə-mŏl'ə-jē**
>
> Etymology: Middle English *ethimologie*, from Anglo-French, from Latin *etymologia*, from Greek, from *etymon* + *-logia* -logy
>
> First Known Use: 14th century
>
> 1: the history of a linguistic form (as a word) shown by tracing its development since its earliest recorded occurrence in the language where it is found, by tracing its transmission from one language to another, by analyzing it into its component parts, by identifying its cognates in other languages, or by tracing it and its cognates to a common ancestral form in an ancestral language
> 2: a branch of linguistics concerned with etymologies

By permission. From Merriam-Webster's Collegiate® Dictionary, 11th Edition © 2012 by Merriam-Webster, Incorporated (www.Merriam-Webster.com).

apply strategies for examining the morphology and etymology of vocabulary, they understand critical components for comprehending the meanings and spellings of words. This helps them function more successfully and independently in other learning experiences. For these reasons, the Vocabulary Acquisition model is important for 21st century learners who will be expected to learn and use new words throughout their lives.

Research on Vocabulary Acquisition

The importance of vocabulary acquisition is supported by research on reading. Studies suggest that reading comprehension is highly correlated with vocabulary knowledge, whether learners are native English speakers or those learning a second language. Francis et al. (2006) contend that "mastery of academic language is arguably the single most important determinant of academic success for individual students" (p. 7). However, methods for vocabulary development must be appropriate to the age and ability of the reader to be successful (National Reading Panel, 2000).

Although a great body of research supports the significance of vocabulary for comprehension, there is little research on the best approaches or combinations of approaches for vocabulary instruction and the measurement of vocabulary growth. Moreover, research further suggests that teachers do not have much interest in teaching vocabulary (Cassiday & Wenrich, 1997, 1998); this is likely due to the inability of traditional vocabulary development approaches to result in authentic, meaningful, and integrated learning. In spite of this limited research, a number of strategies have been shown to support students' vocabulary development, such as direct instruction of academic vocabulary or language (Marzano, 2004), multiple exposures to vocabulary in meaningful contexts (Beck, McKeown, & Kucan, 2002), and opportunities to make connections between the vocabulary studied with other words (Baker, Simmons, & Kameenui, 1995). The Vocabulary Acquisition model provides a meaningful and authentic way to learn vocabulary.

Several challenges are associated with word development, and teachers who recognize them can be more supportive of their students as they learn new vocabulary. In the *Handbook of Reading Research*, Nagy and Scott (2000) point out five factors that foster word knowledge and illustrate the complexity of such knowledge:

1. **Incrementality**—Word learning takes place in many steps. Students might first learn a word with a first-grade understanding, but incrementally come to a full understanding of this word as they experience it throughout their schooling experiences. For example, the understanding we have of the word "school" is different and not as complex in first grade as it is after we finish college.
2. **Polysemy**—Words have more than one meaning, and the more frequently a word occurs in a language, the more meanings it is likely to have. Words can have two or more related meanings. For example, the word "bear" refers to the animal and also means to "carry."
3. **Multidimensionality**—Knowledge of words involves knowledge of a word's various dimensions including its connotation and denotation. Connotation is the emotional and imaginative association surrounding a word. Denotation is the strict dictionary meaning of a word. Word knowledge involves grasping both. The degree of difficulty involved in understanding a particular word is determined in part by how many dimensions a word has and whether and how well these multiple dimensions correspond with each student's unique cultural background and experiences.

4. **Interrelatedness**—Words depend on other words and ideas for meaning. We cannot fully understand certain words without understanding others. For example, the word "platypus" can only be fully understood by understanding the word "mammal."

5. **Heterogeneity**—A word's heterogeneity is based on its inherent qualities and complexity. Words vary in many ways. Some are more difficult to learn than others and require more support. For example, learning prepositions like "around," "in," and "by" require different support than learning words like "parallelogram" or "rhombus." (pp. 271–273)

These factors often pose difficulty as children strive to attain knowledge of new words in various contexts. Being aware of them will help teachers interact with and provide support for diverse learners in their classroom.

Vocabulary acquisition is particularly challenging for students who are ELLs. Their limited academic vocabulary leads to diminished academic success when they reach middle and high school where academic language and its complexity become more common (Francis et al., 2006). In addition to being aware of the five factors described above, teachers who work with ELLs might benefit from the findings of the Vocabulary Improvement Project (Carlo, et al., 2004), a project designed to improve the English vocabulary of native Spanish speakers. The findings were as follows:

- Words to be studied should be encountered in several different contexts to display semantic breadth.
- The study of the spelling of words is important because it helps develop clear phonological representations and builds orthographic knowledge.
- Instruction should focus on powerful mechanisms for learning about words rather than long lists of target words.
- Morphological analysis and knowledge of key derivational morphemes should be taught explicitly.
- Information about multiple meanings and practice in recognizing these should be an explicit part of instruction.
- Possibilities for inferring meaning from context and limitations on those possibilities should be taught explicitly.

The Vocabulary Acquisition model addresses each of these principles in its various steps—making it an excellent model for ELLs and native speakers of English alike.

When Should the Vocabulary Acquisition Model Be Applied and Why?

The Vocabulary Acquisition model is best applied to teach vocabulary words in any content area—but not just any vocabulary words. Selection of words should be strategic and intentional. That is, the best use of the model is for teaching words whose comprehension is foundational for other learning, words that have morphology and etymology useful for understanding other words, and words whose meanings vary by context. The following sections discuss what teachers should use the Vocabulary Acquisition model for.

Teach the Etymology and/or Morphology of Words

Two of the main purposes of the Vocabulary Acquisition model are for students to analyze the etymology and morphology of particular words and gain an appreciation for the etymology and morphology of all words. Teachers should choose this model when they want their students to understand a word's parts and meanings as a way to enhance their overall comprehension of the word. The teaching of the meanings of word parts, such as prefixes, suffixes, and root words, can enhance students' factual and conceptual knowledge, which can later help them with deciphering other, related words. Much academic vocabulary consists of Greek or Latin language roots, so students benefit in the short and long term by learning these roots. For instance, if students know that the morpheme *cent* derives from the Latin, *centum,* which means "hundred," they will probably find it easier to grasp other words consisting of the same morpheme—for example, *centigrade, centimeter,* and *percent.* Likewise, in social studies, students may then understand better what *century* and *centennial* mean. When a root for one word is understood, it becomes foundational for future learning of related words with the same root. The more connections students find between words, the more patterns they see in language, and the more independent they become learning new words.

Teach Academic Vocabulary and Language

Every discipline has vocabulary and language that enables clear and consistent communication with others about facts, procedures, and concepts of shared importance. Artists, attorneys, historians, mathematicians, musicians, scientists, and teachers, for example, all use terms and language distinctive of their disciplines. The same is true within individual academic content areas; each content area—whether it be social studies, physical education, foreign language, or mathematics—has unique vocabulary and language that serves as "background knowledge" (Marzano, 2004), or information critical to understanding various topics. Words of importance in one content area can often have specialized meanings that might vary when the word is used in other content areas. Take, for example, the word *ruler,* which means something quite different in math (a tool for measurement) than it does in social studies (an individual who governs).

Sound understanding of vocabulary is important for comprehending content. If students lack understanding a particular word, they may struggle to develop higher and deeper levels of conceptual understanding about the content they are studying. For instance, to understand more fully a unit on the American Revolution, students need to understand what *revolution* means, as illustrated in the Vocabulary Acquisition Model Lesson Plan at the end of the chapter.

Foster a Deep Understanding of Vocabulary

Mastery of academic language is critical to students' academic success in any content area (Francis et al., 2006). Such mastery involves attaining a deep understanding of vocabulary in general and certain vocabulary words in particular. The Vocabulary Acquisition model fosters students' deep understanding of vocabulary because it requires them to use cognitive processes. While analyzing vocabulary introduced with this model, students conduct an inductive study of the explicit meanings of words, their etymology and morphology, and ways in which the words relate to other words. Moreover, they examine multiple instances of the vocabulary through engagement with texts and other media that use this vocabulary.

The instruction of academic vocabulary is not a novel practice. It has long been a critical aspect of student understanding in many different disciplines. However, most strategies that address vocabulary instruction, such as highlighting important words in textbooks or requiring students to write definitions for all of the words introduced in a new chapter, do not support deep learning of these words, nor do they cultivate an appreciation for word patterns and language the way the Vocabulary Acquisition model does.

What Are the Steps in the Vocabulary Acquisition Model?

The Vocabulary Acquisition model has five major steps: (1) pretest knowledge of words critical to content, (2) elaborate on and discuss invented spellings and hypothesized meanings, (3) explore patterns of meaning, (4) read and study, and (5) evaluate and posttest, as described below. Figure 9-4 outlines the roles of students and the teacher while employing these steps.

Step One—Pretest Knowledge of Words Critical to Content

During this step, the teacher tests students' knowledge of the critical vocabulary that he or she has identified that students need to learn. One way to test that knowledge is by using a

Figure 9-4   Teacher and Student Roles in the Vocabulary Acquisition Model

Vocabulary Acquisition Model Steps	Teacher Role	Student Role
Pretest knowledge of academic vocabulary	Teacher asks students to spell and define the vocabulary to examine their prior knowledge.	Students attempt to spell and define the vocabulary.
Elaborate on and discuss invented spellings and hypothesized meanings	Teacher asks students to explain their spellings and hypothesized meanings of the vocabulary.	Students explain their spellings and hypothesized meanings of the vocabulary.
Explore patterns of meanings	Teacher asks students to examine the patterns and meanings inherent in the vocabulary. Teacher asks students to determine (or helps them, if needed) the etymology of the vocabulary and related words, such as antonyms and synonyms.	Students examine the patterns and meanings of the vocabulary by learning or figuring out the etymology of the vocabulary and related words, such as antonyms and synonyms.
Read and study	Teacher designs and scaffolds opportunities for students to read and study the vocabulary in meaningful and as varied contexts as possible.	Students read and study the vocabulary in meaningful and varied contexts, as possible.
Evaluate and posttest	Teacher designs assessment(s) to evaluate students' mastery of the vocabulary.	Students demonstrate learning of vocabulary by completing a test.

"vocabulary word map," a type of graphic organizer. Another way is to administer a simple multiple-choice test that measures students' prior knowledge about the vocabulary word. Scenarios 9-1, 9-2, and 9-3 illustrate a variety of ways a teacher might pretest students.

Whatever the type of pre-assessment used, students need to feel that they can hypothesize about the word's definition and spelling freely without any concern about the correct way to define and spell it. At this stage, performance anxiety about accuracy can interfere with the progression of the model, as information gained in this step will be used to develop learning activities for the student in the other steps of the model. Special efforts should be made to ensure that students understand the role of the pretest is to prepare them for what will be learned and help their teacher understand their current level of readiness for new learning. This step builds on research that suggests the value of developing and expanding students' prior knowledge (Piaget, 1923/1926). This step also serves to dispel any misconceptions students might have by examining what they already know about a topic, whether it is correct or incorrect.

Step Two—Elaborate on and Discuss Invented Spellings and Hypothesized Meanings

During this step, students engage with the word being studied, deepen their understanding of it, and develop experiences with it. In short, students "play with" the word being studied in various ways to deepen their understanding of it. In this step, the students describe and discuss the spellings and meanings of the word(s) on the pretest. It is best to offer students the opportunity to discuss, share, and examine one another's hypotheses so that they can learn from one another. Students might initially work in pairs and later in small learning groups, as in Scenario 9-3, or in small groups, as in Scenario 9-1.

Step Three—Explore Patterns of Meanings

In this step, students examine spelling patterns by reviewing the various spellings of the words. Also, they interrogate the meaning of the words by determining related words, antonyms, and synonyms. Through this type of activity, students also begin to see the different patterns and relationships between the vocabulary words and other words. For instance, in Scenario 9-1, students begin to see the similarities and differences between the different types of polygons by examining the words, their meanings, and examples.

Step Four—Read and Study

Simply put, this step capitalizes on studying and using the vocabulary word(s) *in context*, which is integral to vocabulary comprehension. Students should experience words in context and discuss the word placement and usage. Emphasis should also be placed on giving students an opportunity to apply the vocabulary words in context. In this way, they can practice a meaningful exchange about ideas—communicating like experts. For example, in science, it is important to understand and use the lingua franca or vernacular language of scientists. Words such as *conductor* and *equilibrium* have different meanings in different contexts. In one context, a conductor is a person who leads a symphony or a train, but in physics it is "a material capable of transmitting another form of energy" ("conductor," 2012). Similarly, equilibrium refers to "a state of intellectual or emotional balance" ("equilibrium," 2012), yet, in the context of physics, it means "a state of balance between opposing forces or actions that is either static (as in a body acted on by forces whose resultant is zero) or dynamic" ("equilibrium," 2012).

There are many approaches teachers might use to facilitate students' reading and studying of vocabulary. Students might be asked to read and study the words in context and then practice their understanding by

- creating and acting out an imaginary dialogue between two experts that uses the words;
- drawing or creating pictorial representations using various media (including digital media);
- bringing in real examples of the vocabulary (see Scenario 9-1);
- writing a classified ad or short newspaper article that uses these words;
- writing the obituary of an important figure in the content area that makes use of these words;
- creating a poem or song that uses these words;
- creating a crossword puzzle;
- using pantomime, charades games, or another physical activity to demonstrate the meaning of words;
- performing the vocabulary (see Scenario 9-2, where students perform different types of tempo); or
- writing a letter to someone else explaining their understanding of these words.

Step Five—Evaluate and Posttest

The purpose of this step is to assess students' understanding of the vocabulary after implementing the previous steps of the Vocabulary Acquisition model. How teachers go about testing students' understanding may vary. For instance, whereas many teachers will likely want to test their students' knowledge as part of a larger test on the unit of study, others will prefer to test the vocabulary words more explicitly via a vocabulary test. The assessment should gauge students' deep—not merely their superficial—understanding of the vocabulary words. To accomplish that, teachers may ask students to use the vocabulary in novel contexts, such as those listed above in Step Four, only this time they would perform these tasks for assessment rather than practice. Students might also be asked for assessment purposes to define the vocabulary in their own words, create pictorial representations or posters (as in Scenario 9-3), or share related words, such as synonyms and antonyms.

What Does the Vocabulary Acquisition Model Look Like in the Classroom?

There are a variety of ways in which the Vocabulary Acquisition model might be implemented, such as by varying the time allotted to lessons conducted with the model, the selection of distinct activities within each step, and the number of words a lesson addresses. Variations like those enable the model to function effectively in most educational settings across content areas and grade levels. The model can be used formally for specific lessons, or it can be made a regular daily or weekly feature in classrooms, too. In the following section, we illustrate several different examples of the model being used to indicate the flexibility and power of the model.

Scenario 9-1

Rich Malouf's second-graders were going to be working on a unit on polygons for the next week. They would be doing a lot of hands-on activities to support their learning, but they would also be adding daily to their math vocabulary journals. Rich had been using these journals for several years to promote students' understanding of academic vocabulary, especially in math, science, and social studies. He began using the journal the year his school was emphasizing students' ability to write across the content areas, and the journal worked so well that he kept using it. Rich found that by asking his students to maintain journals, they tended to experience better retention of the vocabulary used in math. He noticed that his students were better able to decipher other words that were new to them—especially those with similar roots or affixes. His students also used their journals as reference tools—if they forgot a definition, they often flipped back to their journals and remembered it!

Rich introduced today's lesson by explaining to the class that they would be learning about polygons. He reminded them that, just as with other new vocabulary they had learned previously, they would soon be able to add this new word to their math vocabulary journal. Rich wanted to start the unit with a Vocabulary Acquisition model using the word *polygon* because he knew that once students learned what one was and meant, they would be able to create their own polygons and also learn new ones more quickly! He began by asking students to write and define *polygon* in their journal using the "New Word Graphic Organizer" (see Figure 9-5 for an example). The graphic organizer prompted students to attempt spelling the word, hypothesize its meaning, list related words, and develop a definition.

Rich walked around the room, looking over students' shoulders to review their work in their graphic organizer to gain pre-assessment information about their understanding of the word and concept of polygons. He reminded them that the pretest would not be graded and that they could revise their ideas anytime. He told them, "I know the word *polygon* is a big math word, and many of you may not know what it means or how to spell it. That is okay. Just remember, by the end of the lesson, you will be able to use your knowledge about this word to identify and draw different types of polygons."

Figure 9-5   Vocabulary Journal—New Word Graphic
Organizer Example

My Vocabulary Journal	
I believe the word is spelled like this: Pollygone (sounds like: polly-gawn)	My spelling is correct: ☑ Yes or ☑ No. The correct spelling is: polygon
I believe the word means: I do not know!	Here is our shared definition: A shape made up of straight lines that have more than one side.
☑ Synonym(s) or ☒ Related Words: ~~Antonym(s):~~ Triangle, rectangle, pentagon, hexagon, octagon	Example(s):

Most students made attempts at spelling the word *polygon* in the graphic organizer; however, few even attempted to define it. So, Rich showed them a hexagon as an example of a polygon, saying, "This is a polygon. Now try to define it." Students' eyes lit up with a sense of reassurance as they jotted down their ideas about the definition of a polygon. Obviously they knew it was some kind of shape—and they had all seen this shape before.

For the next step, Rich grouped students in pairs and asked students to compare and contrast their spellings and definitions they had recorded in the graphic organizer. As they discussed, Rich observed students to ensure they were on task and comparing notes. He encouraged them to probe one another for further explanations, ask questions for clarification, and make revisions to their original definitions.

Then Rich set to work ensuring that all students revised the content in their graphic organizers to include correct information about polygons. To do so, Rich projected an empty "New Word Graphic Organizer" on the interactive whiteboard and worked with the students to complete it with what they had determined was the correct information.

After completing the graphic organizer, students moved to the third phase of the lesson and explored patterns in meaning by sharing names of other words that might be considered polygons based on the definition. One student stated a triangle is a polygon. Rich confirmed that a triangle is a type of polygon. Then students shared more examples (e.g., square, diamond, rectangle) that they recorded in their math vocabulary journals. When one student stated that a circle is a polygon, a few students looked very confused. Rich then asked the class to discuss with their partners whether a circle is a polygon by first reviewing the definition and then deciding if a circle fits that definition. After reviewing the definition, most of the students figured out this was a trick question. A circle is not a polygon since it does not have any straight sides. To be sure everyone understood, Rich asked his students to give him a quick thumbs up or down to show whether they agreed or disagreed that a circle is a polygon. The majority chose thumbs down. Then he asked a couple of students who got this correct to explain why they chose thumbs down.

The next, fourth phase involved reading and studying about polygons in several different ways: they read books about polygons, made patterns with mosaics of polygons cut from construction paper, and completed homework that required that they bring photos, clippings from magazines, or real examples of polygons to the class all that week. Each day, students piled their examples onto different tables: one table had triangles, another squares, and another polygons consisting of more than four sides. At this point, Rich asked students to discuss patterns they noticed in the meanings for the polygons they had not named (i.e., those with more than four sides, such as a pentagon, octagon, or decagon). He also recorded the names and characteristics of polygons on a piece of chart paper while discussing the meanings of the different word parts (see Figure 9-6). Finally, at the end of the two weeks studying polygons, the students had a post test that involved all of the different types of polygons they had studied.

Scenario 9-2

Anjali Gupta knew better than to take for granted that students knew music terminology—even considering how strong the music program was in her school district. She was not surprised that her sixth-graders did so poorly on a listening pretest of the different types of tempo.

She had played five different songs representing different types of tempo and asked students to use a musical word to describe each. She had not originally planned on teaching her students the tempo vocabulary explicitly. The unsatisfactory results of the

Figure 9-6   Graphic Organizer Example—Polygons

Polygons		
Type of Polygon	Number of Sides	Example
Triangle	3	
Rectangle	4	
Pentagon	5	
Hexagon	6	
Septagon	7	
Octagon	8	
Nonagon	9	
Decagon	10	

pre-assessment, however, prompted her to incorporate a Vocabulary Acquisition model lesson that would build on their prior knowledge about tempo but also ensure her students comprehended fully what tempo meant. After all, how were they going to perform in the midyear concert if they did not have a solid grasp of tempo?

Students had already finished the first phase of the model with the pretest in which she had asked them to spell and define *tempo* and five of the major terms for tempo: *adagio, andante, moderato, allegro*, and *presto*. Anjali knew it was not necessary for students to know *all* of the tempo terms, but understanding these five was critical. So, as she passed out the pretests (without corrections), she began planning the lesson in her head to use on the fly. The lesson would not take long and would hold students' interest. Plus, they would *know* these terms after this lesson.

For the second phase of the lesson, Anjali asked students to discuss their spellings and definitions of tempo in general and the five types of tempo in particular. They worked first in pairs (for 10 minutes) and then in groups of four (for 10 minutes); however, they were not allowed to look up the definitions and spellings yet. She wanted them to interrogate what they already knew and come to a group consensus about the definitions and spellings. Some got it right but most confused the terms resulting in some interesting debates!

After coming to a small group consensus, she shifted to the third phase of the Vocabulary Acquisition model, which involved their examination of patterns of meanings of the words. Anjali now allowed students to look up the words to ensure they had the correct information and background. She wanted them to learn what the word meant and how it had been derived so that they could comprehend the words more fully as well as learn about the words' origins. Students recorded this information in the class "wiktionary," an online wiki of terms they would add to and refer to throughout the year, by including the spellings and definitions of the words. Before allowing them to post to the wiktionary, however, she asked them to keep track of the words using a graphic organizer (see Figure 9-7 for an example of

Figure 9-7   Template for Tempo Terms—Wiktionary

Term	My Pronunciation	Pronunciation	Origin	Means
Tempo				
Adagio				
Andante				
Moderato				
Allegro				
Presto				

the template). Each group of four would be responsible for adding to the wiktionary, but all students would need to discuss the patterns and meanings in their small groups.

Once it was clear they had finished the task, Anjali began the fourth phase. She shared that they would begin the most fun part by reading and studying about the words with more depth—first, they would go to the San Francisco Symphony's SFS kids online Music Lab to explore the five types of tempo (see www.sfskids.org/templates/musicLab .asp?pageid=11). By clicking on the online metronome, students would be able to see how the metronome moves and hear how the tempo sounds for all five tempo terms. Then they would read more about tempo in their music textbooks. She emphasized that tempos are not merely about speed—they are associated with different moods, too. She knew that this knowledge would help them understand tempo better. Therefore, they would listen to different songs representing different types of tempo. After that, as a class, they would practice playing music at different tempos using their instruments.

Finally, for the fifth phase of the Vocabulary Acquisition model lesson, Anjali would test the students on their understanding of tempo. The test would be part in-class and part take-home. For the in-class portion, students would be asked to spell and define the tempo words on a traditional test. Then, for the take-home portion, they would be asked to create an online glogster "poster" (www.glogster.com) that incorporated images and sound and post it to the wiktionary.

Scenario 9-3

Susanna Newton, a high school journalism teacher (tenth- through twelfth-graders), was going to be "flipping" her classroom using a Vocabulary Acquisition lesson plan to teach about ethics. She would ask her students to do what might normally be required for homework at school (i.e., studying) and do what was normally done in school (i.e., listening to lectures and demonstrations) at home. Susanna's strategy would provide students support developing skills and habits that would allow them to be more productive studying and doing homework after school when they were alone and many without the support of grown-ups.

The Vocabulary Acquisition model lesson would work perfectly to help students learn how to study vocabulary words—especially considering they were on a block schedule. Although they did not meet every day, they had 90-minute periods where they could dig into the lesson with depth. Susanna explained to her students that, for the next two weeks, they would watch her lectures at home to prepare for in-class learning. In class, they would learn how to study words and expand their academic vocabulary.

For the first phase, the students would complete in class an ungraded pretest where they would spell and define the word *ethics* without looking it up anywhere or discussing it with their peers. She explained that this would gauge their background understanding of this concept, one of the most important and challenging concepts journalists encounter. Then, for the second phase, she would ask students to elaborate on and discuss their spellings and definitions of *ethics* in small groups during the same class session.

© Yuri Arcurs/Dreamstime

During the third phase, they would examine and discuss the similarities and differences noted in their spellings and definitions as well as determine any antonyms, synonyms, or other related words. The fourth phase would be completed with work done at home and also in class. Outside of class, students would have to complete several activities, including reading one of the ethics codes listed on the American Society of News Editors site (http://asne.org/key_initiatives/ethics/ethics_codes.aspx) or the Professional Journalists Code of Ethics (www.spj.org/ethicscode.asp), watching *Absence of Malice* or *Shattered Glass* (movies that dealt with the ethics of journalists), and reading the National Scholastic Press Association's *Model Code of Ethics for High School Journalists* (http://nspa.studentpress.org/pdf/wheel_modelcodeofethics.pdf). In class, students would debate at least five scenarios from the PBS Online NewsHour interactive website, "Making the Ethical Choice" (www.pbs.org/newshour/media/media_ethics/quiz.php). (These are online cases about ethics choices that journalists need to make.)

For the fifth and final phase, students would work in small groups of four to develop their own tests for assessing their peers' understanding about what ethics means and its importance to the field of journalism. Each group would need to develop two test items. They could create traditional case scenarios or find or develop a short video, role play, or multimedia presentation to use as the basis of their items. Each test item would have to include a brief synopsis of the ethical issue at stake and one possible resolution to the problem. From these items, she would choose the best five items for their test.

What Do These Scenarios Illustrate?

These scenarios show how the Vocabulary Acquisition model can be modified to challenge students to develop deep learning of words and language in a variety of settings. Teachers might implement the Vocabulary Acquisition model as a regular part of classroom instruction (as in Scenario 9-1, where students maintain a math vocabulary journal), when introducing new units (see Scenario 9-3), or as needed when students need to learn vocabulary with depth (see Scenario 9-2). The number of words studied, the specific activities stimulating learning in its steps, and the amount of time can all be varied based on content area demands, teacher style, and learner needs.

REFLECT: Review the different implementations of the Vocabulary Acquisition model in the scenarios. Reflect on how, in each one, the teacher guided students through the different phases of the model. What approaches might you employ when using this model? For instance, would you use a more inductive approach to learn other vocabulary, as in Scenario 9-1 about polygons, or would the lesson be more structured, as in Scenario 9-2 or 9-3?

Planning for Teaching with the Vocabulary Acquisition Model

Planning to teach the Vocabulary Acquisition model involves choosing essential academic vocabulary, learning the morphology and etymology of the vocabulary selected, and choosing varied, meaningful resources in which the vocabulary is found. What educational designers do when teaching with the Vocabulary Acquisition model is discussed in the following sections.

Choose Vocabulary That Is Essential to Student Understanding of Content

Clearly, vocabulary comprehension is critical to students' academic success. Not all vocabulary, however, is equally important. Some words are foundational for other learning and more essential. Without deep comprehension of some words, students will not be able to understand the material as quickly or deeply. Teachers can use vocabulary lists found in textbooks as starting points for determining essential vocabulary. Although deciding which vocabulary is essential, teachers will also need to consider how many words to introduce. This choice is informed by a teacher's knowledge of content, allotted time, and learners' needs. For example, in Scenario 9-2, there are several more types of tempo Anjali could have introduced, but she decides that her students need to learn only five major types.

Learn the Morphology and Etymology of Vocabulary Selected

Prior to introducing the vocabulary to be studied, teachers should have a solid understanding of the morphology and etymology of the selected words so that they can guide students in better comprehending the vocabulary. In many cases, the teacher will be the one who first explains to the students the morphological and etymological components of the vocabulary. For example, in Scenario 9-1, after being provided an example of a polygon, the second-graders are able to share several other examples, but they do not know the morphology or etymology of the words *triangle* or *pentagon* until the teacher explains them.

Select Resources in Which the Vocabulary Occurs in Varied, Meaningful Contexts

One advantage to the Vocabulary Acquisition model over more traditional approaches to vocabulary instruction is that it provides students the ability to explore the word or words being studied in a meaningful context. Therefore, the quality of students' learning and the model's implementation is tied in part to the quality of the resources that help students discover word meanings. These resources should present accurate information about the words and how they are being used within a unit or academic discipline. Resources should also be selected that demonstrate multiple, interesting, and meaningful use of the word being studied.

The type and variety of resources used are also important to consider. Print resources such as encyclopedias, textbooks, and newspapers are useful and readily available in most classrooms but should not be relied on solely. Using print resources exclusively for instruction of new words can present a double challenge to students who cannot read well. If print is used exclusively, ELLs and students with reading challenges, for example, will struggle with both understanding the new word and reading. Varying the resources used to present information about words—for example, by including multimedia, audio, and video—is valuable for all learners and especially for those who find navigating print more challenging.

In Scenario 9-3, students read and study about instances of ethics in several different contexts and using a variety of types of media (e.g., print, code of ethics, movie, case scenarios). Seeing ethical dilemmas in different contexts helps students understand how the concept of ethics relates to others as well as in the case of ethics in journalism, where there are many areas that are not cut and dried and have simple solutions. Examining the code of ethics from different organizations also helps students understand ethics as a multidimensional concept, influenced by many societal conditions.

Determine How to Scaffold the Lesson

After making the prior decisions, teachers will then need to determine how to scaffold the lesson. Although the Vocabulary Acquisition model has distinct phases that serve to scaffold student learning of vocabulary, Scenarios 9-1, 9-2, and 9-3 show that these phases are not prescriptive—there are many ways in which teachers might scaffold the model's different phases. For instance, in Scenario 9-1, the teacher shares an example of a polygon since the word *polygon* is new to the students. However, once he introduces an example, students have no trouble sharing other examples of polygons (e.g., triangle) even though they do not know the word's etymology. Later, the teacher introduces students to the etymology of several types of polygons (and the word *polygon*, too). His goal at that point is for his students to gain a deeper understanding and ultimately be able to interpret other words with similar morphological features.

Differentiating Instruction with the Vocabulary Acquisition Model

There are multiple ways in which a teacher might differentiate instruction while using the Vocabulary Acquisition model to teach vocabulary. Use of the model itself acknowledges that all learners can benefit by direct teaching of study skills, but the model also supports differentiation of the content of learning, the learning process, and the product that students create to demonstrate their learning.

Content

Differentiating the content of instruction in this model involves providing students access to resources related to the word being studied that are different in their authenticity, levels of complexity, and format. (These are the resources that students "read and study" during the fourth phase of the Vocabulary Acquisition model.) Students might consult newspapers, magazines, and radio broadcasts (more authentic) or textbooks or nonfiction books (less authentic). The complexity of materials might be varied according to students' reading level and calibrated to individual student needs as students access materials in different formats ranging from video and audio to experiential demonstrations. The students in Scenario 9-2 learn about tempo by listening to and selecting different types of tempo on a virtual metronome using the San Francisco Symphony's Music Lab. They also experiment with different types of tempo using real instruments. In Scenario 9-3, students examine different representations of ethics as codes or standards followed by professional organizations, and they also investigate the concept of ethics by working with the scenarios on the PBS NewsHour website.

Process

Teachers can differentiate instruction within the process of the five phases of the Vocabulary Acquisition model as well. Each of the scenarios in this chapter shows not only a different way the teacher might apply the different phases of the model (e.g., in Scenario 9-3 the teacher "flips" instruction by having students complete most work in class and individual work at home during the fourth read and study phase, and in Scenario 9-2 the teacher first introduces the vocabulary using music) but also how teachers can have students work through the model with different groupings (e.g., individually, pairs, small groups, whole group). Teachers can allow students to self-select groupings based on interest, or they can assign students to ability-level groups to read and study. Finally, teachers can have students complete different graphic organizers, as in Worksheet 9-1, 9-2, or 9-3 (available in Appendix C), to read and study the vocabulary.

Product

The product of instruction, or the means that students use to demonstrate their learning, can be differentiated in various ways in the final phase of the Vocabulary Acquisition model. This phase involves an evaluation and posttest of the vocabulary learned. Teachers can choose the method for assessment or allow students to choose how to demonstrate their learning. The assessment can be closed, as in a traditional test, or more open, as in a performance (e.g., performing different types of tempo using an instrument, as in Scenario 9-2) or a type of multimedia output (e.g., Scenario 9-3).

What Are the Benefits of Applying the Vocabulary Acquisition Model?

A clear benefit of the Vocabulary Acquisition model is that it helps improve students' understanding of vocabulary, which is essential to their academic success. Yet the model also has several other benefits, discussed in the following sections.

Fosters Deeper Understanding of Words

This model fosters deeper understanding of specific vocabulary and the complexity and composition of words in general. For instance, in Scenario 9-3, students examine what *ethics* means in a variety of contexts—they learn, through the use of cognitive processes at the higher levels of the revised Bloom's taxonomy (e.g., analyze), that *ethics* is not a cut-and-dried word. Its implications in context, especially given the cases examined, show how complex the word is. This also helps students develop a deeper understanding beyond the definition of the vocabulary.

Teaches Students to Examine Words' Morphology and Etymology

Simply studying lists of words or being able to spell them correctly does not serve students well if those actions fail to result in retention. By learning the morphology and etymology of words, students are more likely to maintain their learning and develop strategies for deciphering and understanding word parts in other situations. Students can make inferences about a word's definition by breaking a word down into its various parts, as in Scenario 9-1, where students learn about different types of polygons. Knowing the morphemes of the words help students understand better word meanings, knowledge that students can apply to other contexts. The students studying polygons will learn the morpheme *penta-* when they cover pentagons, and then they will probably be able to apply it years later in English class when studying iambic *penta*meter. Additionally, studying morphology and etymology helps with spelling and enhances students' ability to decode and comprehend other words using morphemes they learn.

Link to Prior Knowledge

The Vocabulary Attainment model builds on students' prior knowledge of vocabulary from the first step—pretesting. This connection to prior knowledge is consistent with theories on cognition and helps to dispel any misconceptions the student might already have about a word. Moreover, the practice of openly acknowledging students' prior knowledge and either building on or revising these understandings scaffolds learning. This is most evident in Steps One and Two of the model, during which students must first spell and define the vocabulary and then elaborate on and discuss the invented spellings and hypothesized definitions.

Addresses Various Learners' Needs

This model accommodates variation in the way students demonstrate their prior knowledge of vocabulary words, how they explore the use of words, practice meaning, and demonstrate their understanding of words. As such, it provides many ways for the needs of learners to be addressed. For example, using graphic organizers supports visual learners as they attempt to comprehend the meaning of the word, its parts, and ways in which it relates to other words. Opportunities to study and to explore patterns and meanings can be varied for individuals and groups. Students can be grouped in different ways as well.

Provides Practice in Different Contexts

Step Four of this model provides students the opportunity to learn more about the vocabulary by experiencing these words in multiple and different contexts. This step also allows students to apply their knowledge. In Scenario 9-1, students read and study by finding examples of different polygons in magazines or elsewhere.

Promotes Transfer of Knowledge

Knowledge transfer is the ability to apply the understanding of concepts, facts, procedures, and principles in another context. In this model, students can read and study the vocabulary through various contexts and media and then share this knowledge—also in a variety of contexts. Students gain a deep understanding of the vocabulary, in turn promoting their retention of the vocabulary. Deep understanding can transfer to other contexts and other uses of the vocabulary or its morphemes.

What Value Does Technology Add to the Vocabulary Acquisition Model?

A meta-analysis conducted by the National Reading Panel (2000) indicates that the use of computers in vocabulary instruction is more effective than some traditional methods. More research is needed, however, to explore the various roles computer technology might play in supporting student development of vocabulary, the use of computer-aided instruction, Web-supported learning of other types, and computer software mind tools (Jonassen, Beissner, & Yacci, 1993). This section covers a variety of technology tools teachers might consider using for planning, implementing, and assessing student learning when using the Vocabulary Acquisition model. Figure 9-9 provides a summary of the different technology tools that might be helpful for the planning, implementation, and assessment of the Vocabulary Acquisition model.

Planning

There are many technology resources teachers can use to plan a lesson using the Vocabulary Acquisition model. Numerous tools are available online for teachers to learn the morphology and etymology of words. Several are dictionaries (e.g., Visual Dictionary: http://visual.merriam-webster.com), thesauruses (e.g., http://thesaurus.com), and etymology tools (e.g., www.etymonline.com). An Internet search of vocabulary using a nonlinear search tool might reveal the various practical meanings and provide students context for situating correct applications of the term. For example, searching the word *etymology* using a tool like Yippy (http://yippy.com) might result in a cluster that indicates use of the word as it relates to (1) the dictionary, (2) the origins of words, (3) history and linguistics, (4) history of words, (5) pictures, and (6) Latin (see Figure 9-8 for an example).

Teachers might also wish to develop graphic organizers to help students visualize their learning better. For instance, in Scenario 9-1, the teacher developed a graphic organizer for students to use when recording their learning, and in Scenario 9-2, students developed one to add to a class wiktionary. Note that a graphic organizer tool can be used for planning, implementation, or assessment of student learning.

Implementation

Not only is technology beneficial in the planning of lessons with this model, but it is also very useful in the model's implementation. Students and teachers can use search engines and directories to find and learn

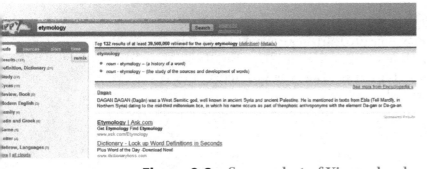

Figure 9-8   Screenshot of Yippy clouds
Courtesy of Yippy Inc.

Figure 9-9   Technology Tools for the Vocabulary Acquisition Model

Use	Technology Tools
Planning	
	Etymology and morphology of words
	• Dictionary.com: http://dictionary.reference.com
	• EtymApp: www.etymapp.com
	• Merriam Webster Online Dictionary: www.merriam-webster.com
	• Online Etymology Dictionary: www.etymonline.com/?term=etymology
	• Thesaurus.com: http://thesaurus.com
	• Visual Dictionary: http://visual.merriam-webster.com
	• Visual Thesaurus: www.visualthesaurus.com
	• Vocabulary.com: www.vocabulary.com
	Graphic organizers or tools
	• Bubbl: http://bubbl.us
	• Gliffy: www.gliffy.com
	• Inspiration: www.inspiration.com
	• Kidspiration: www.inspiration.com/Kidspiration
	• Popplet: http://popplet.com
	• SpicyNodes: www.spicynodes.org/index.html
Implementing	
	Search directories and engines
	• Google: www.google.com
	Audio recording
	• Digital audio recorder or tape recorder
	Digital video
	• Digital video recorder or camera on computer
	Drawing/Painting tools
	• ArtPad: http://artpad.art.com/artpad/painter
	• KidPix: www.mackiev.com/kidpix/index.html
	• SumoPaint: www.sumopaint.com/app
Assessing	
	Online survey tools/SMS Polling Tools
	• Surveymonkey: www.surveymonkey.com
	• Poll Everywhere www.polleverywhere.com
	Test creation tools
	• Quibblo: www.quibblo.com
	• QuizStar: http://quizstar.4teachers.org
	Other tools
	• Glogster: www.glogster.com
	• VoiceThread: http://voicethread.com

more about the vocabulary in different contexts and media. Students may create a word-processed document (or use a graphic organizer) in the first stage that they can modify later as
they learn the correct spellings and meanings of the words in Steps 1 through 4 of the model.
Finally, teachers might also ask students to use audio or video to record their understanding

of vocabulary. For example, in Scenario 9-1, students create a video-recorded "walking tour" showing them explaining the different polygons found in the classroom. Students can also use drawing and paint tools to illustrate their understanding of vocabulary. Paint programs (i.e., KidPix) and free online paint tools can help students document their learning of the vocabulary. Note that drawing and paint tools can also be used for assessment.

Assessment

Assessment is a critical aspect of the Vocabulary Acquisition model. Teachers may use online tools, games, or templates to test students' knowledge of the targeted vocabulary in the first and/or last step of the model. For instance, teachers may use online puzzle-making tools (e.g., www.readwritethink.org/materials/crossword), an online quiz tool (e.g., QuizStar http://quizstar.4teachers.org), or games such as Science Vocabulary Hangman (http://education.jlab.org/vocabhangman). Numerous templates in PowerPoint make it easy for students and teachers to play Jeopardy with vocabulary as part of the pre- or posttesting process. Finally, creative online tools like Glogster (www.glogster.com) and VoiceThread (http://voicethread.com) provide creative ways to incorporate multimedia and sharing.

Vocabulary Acquisition Model Lesson Plan Example

The following lesson plan is an example of the Vocabulary Acquisition model. Figure 9-10 provides an outline of the lesson's different steps. When first introducing this model, we recommend presenting one word at a time. This may seem time consuming, but it is important for students to learn the strategy for deciphering words, a strategy that students will

Figure 9-10   Outline of the Vocabulary Acquisition Model Lesson Steps

Vocabulary Acquisition Model Steps	Vocabulary Acquisition Model Lesson
Pretest knowledge of words critical to content	Teacher asks students to spell and define *revolution*.
Elaborate upon and discuss invented spellings and hypothesized meanings	Students share and explain their definitions and spellings of *revolution*.
Explore patterns of meanings	Teacher asks students to brainstorm synonyms and an antonym for *revolution* and develop an exemplary sentence using this word.
Read and study	Students read and study songs that use the word *revolution*, as well as study the word in a historical context.
Evaluate and posttest	Teacher tests students on the spelling, definition, synonyms, and etymology of *revolution*.

be able to implement later on their own. After students become comfortable with this model, a teacher may use several pertinent vocabulary words instead of just one. Finally, this model can be combined with other models. For instance during the "read and study" step, teachers may wish to use other models, such as the Inquiry (see Chapter 10) or Integrative (see Chapter 13) model, to "read and study" the vocabulary.

LESSON CONTEXT

GRADE LEVEL(S): High school

CONTENT AREA: History

PHYSICAL TEACHING ENVIRONMENT: This lesson will be taught in a regular classroom. Blackboard, dry-erase board, or an interactive whiteboard is needed, as well as a computer and projector.

APPLICATION OF REVISED BLOOM'S TAXONOMY: Students work from the *understand* level (by spelling and defining *revolution*) to the *apply* level of the revised Bloom's taxonomy (by writing a sentence that uses this word) to the *analyze* level (by brainstorming synonyms for *revolution*).

Lesson Plan

GOAL(S): Students will understand the factors that led to the French Revolution.

Standard(s) Addressed:

IRA/NCTE: 3:[1] Students apply a wide range of strategies to comprehend, interpret, evaluate, and appreciate texts. They draw on their prior experience, their interactions with other readers and writers, their knowledge of word meaning and of other texts, their word identification strategies, and their understanding of textual features (e.g., sound-letter correspondence, sentence structure, context, graphics).

NCSS VI: Power, Authority, & Governance: Social studies programs should include experiences that provide for the study of how people create and change structures of power, authority, and governance

For a complete list of the standards, go to http://www.ncte.org/standards.

Common Core Standards Language Standards[2]

- Determine or clarify the meaning of unknown and multiple-meaning words and phrases based on grades 9–10 reading and content, choosing flexibly from a range of strategies.
  a) Use context (e.g., the overall meaning of a sentence, paragraph, or text; a word's position or function in a sentence) as a clue to the meaning of a word or phrase.
  b) Identify and correctly use patterns of word changes that indicate different meanings or parts of speech (e.g., analyze, analysis, analytical; advocate, advocacy).
  c) Consult general and specialized reference materials (e.g., dictionaries, glossaries, thesauruses), both print and digital, to find the pronunciation of a word or determine or clarify its precise meaning, its part of speech, or its etymology.

---

[1] Standards for the English Language Arts, by the International Reading Association and the National Council of Teachers of English, Copyright 1996 by the International Reading Association and the National Council of Teachers of English. Reprinted with permission.

[2] © Copyright 2010. National Governors Association Center for Best Practices and Council of Chief State School Officers. All rights reserved.

    d) Verify the preliminary determination of the meaning of a word or phrase (e.g., by checking the inferred meaning in context or in a dictionary).

- Demonstrate understanding of figurative language, word relationships, and nuances in word meanings.
  - **a)** Interpret figures of speech (e.g., euphemism, oxymoron) in context and analyze their role in the text.
  - **b)** Analyze nuances in the meaning of words with similar denotations.
- Acquire and use accurately general academic and domain-specific words and phrases, sufficient for reading, writing, speaking, and listening at the college and career readiness level; demonstrate independence in gathering vocabulary knowledge when considering a word or phrase important to comprehension or expression.

COMMON CORE READING STANDARDS FOR LITERACY IN HISTORY/SOCIAL STUDIES 6–12, GRADES 9–12, CRAFT AND STRUCTURE: Determine the meaning of words and phrases as they are used in a text, including vocabulary describing political, social, or economic aspects of history/social studies.

OBJECTIVE(S): Students will do the following:

1. Define the word *revolution* by comparing and contrasting different spellings and definitions of the word *revolution*
2. Develop synonyms for the word *revolution* by brainstorming in pairs
3. Write an exemplary sentence using the word *revolution* by working in small groups

ESTIMATED TIME: 25 minutes

MATERIALS NEEDED:
- Chalkboard/dry-erase board
- Vocabulary Acquisition model graphic organizer (see Worksheet 9-4 in Appendix C)
- Computer with speakers and projector to show *one* of the following videos:
  - Beatles' "Revolution" (3:17 min): www.youtube.com/watch?v=87yq372R4Ts
  - Tracy Chapman's "Revolution" (2:52 minutes): www.youtube.com/watch?v=7rZbvi6Tj6E

PREREQUISITE SKILLS: Students should know and understand the following vocabulary: prefix, suffix, and synonym.

LESSON PROCEDURES (Text in italics is suggested teacher dialogue.)

Pretest Knowledge of Words Critical to Content: [2 minutes]
Teacher asks students to spell and define *revolution*. *On the handout I provided you, spell and define the word* revolution.

Elaborate on and Discuss Invented Spellings and Hypothesized Meanings: [5 minutes]
Teacher asks students to share their definitions/spellings in pairs and to decide on one definition/spelling. *Now I'd like you to pair up with your partner. Share your hypothesis—your definition and spelling of the word* revolution. *Decide which is correct.* Teacher then asks students to share their spellings and definitions with the class. Teacher writes these on the board and then tells students which spellings are correct and which definition(s) is correct.

Explore Patterns of Meaning: [4 minutes]

Teacher asks students to brainstorm synonyms and antonyms for the word and to develop an exemplary sentence using the targeted words. *Continue working in your pairs by brainstorming at least three synonyms and one antonym for* revolution. *Write these down in your "Word Study" booklet.*

Read and Study: [7 minutes]

Teacher provides the words to the song "Revolution" by the Beatles and Tracy Chapman and plays these songs, too. She guides students in focusing on how the words are used in these songs. Note: Teachers may engage students in this step in a variety of ways. For instance, they may wish to implement a different model in this step (e.g., apply the Integrative model). The key is for teachers to provide meaningful opportunities for students to read and study about the vocabulary in context.

Evaluate and Posttest: [5 minutes]

Teacher quizzes students on the spelling, definition, synonym, and etymology of *revolution* by asking students to record their ideas on a blank vocabulary word map. Note: Some students may need more time to complete this quiz.

Closure: [2 minutes]

Teacher brings closure by reviewing student findings, generalizations, conclusions, and analyses. *Today, we explored the spellings, definitions, and synonyms for the word* revolution. *Revolution—with regards to our unit of study—is (1) a sudden, radical, or complete change, (2) a fundamental change in political organization, especially the overthrow or renunciation of one government or ruler and the substitution of another by the governed; (3) activity or movement designed to effect fundamental changes in the socioeconomic situation; (4) a fundamental change in the way of thinking about or visualizing something, as in a change of paradigm (the Copernican revolution); or (5) a changeover in use or preference, especially in technology.*

Differentiation Strategies for the Vocabulary Acquisition Model Lesson

In the sections that follow are some suggestions one might apply to differentiate instruction in the Vocabulary Acquisition Model Lesson.

Content

Differentiating content means differentiating the students' access to materials that presents content. In this lesson, students access information about the word *revolution* through a variety of media that communicate the meaning of the word *revolution*. The students experience this word in both visual and auditory formats. The word appears in print written on the board and other materials. Students also experience it presented in the songs by the Beatles or Tracy Chapman. The approach of introducing the word in various modalities is beneficial to all students but especially supports students with special needs. Another option for differentiating access to content in this lesson might be to allow students the use of print and/or electronic dictionaries during the "Explore Patterns of Meaning" step of the lesson. ELLs might benefit from the opportunity to explore the word in a dictionary that is written in their first language as well as in English.

Process

There are many ways to differentiate the learning process in this lesson. Doing so might mean using flexible groupings to encourage interactions among students of various ability levels or using more homogeneous groupings to provide interactions that are less varied. Either approach might be appealing to a teacher, depending on the composition and nature of his or her class.

If a classroom has two or more ELLs who speak the same language, a teacher might differentiate the learning process by simply allowing them to discuss the meaning of the word in their first language during Step Two. Then these students would be asked to share the results from their discussion with the group in English.

To further differentiate, the teacher might consider providing instructions for each step of the Vocabulary Acquisition model in a written format rather than just providing them orally. Some students will need visual reinforcement. Others may learn better if they understand the complete progression of the lesson before starting.

The teacher could provide students a range of options for exploring the word in greater depth during "Step Four." Options might include the following:

- Working individually, search three history books and find the word *revolution* in the index. Explore the use of this word in the chapters and write a brief explanation of what you find.
- Listen to the songs "Revolution" by Tracy Chapman and the Beatles. Working in a small group, write about the similarities and differences between the concept of revolution in both songs.
- Working with the classroom aide, explore a passage that uses the word *revolution* and more deeply explore how this word is used in context.

Product

The product that demonstrates student learning in this lesson must present evidence of each student's comprehension of the word *revolution* along multiple lines—spelling, definition, synonyms, and etymology. To differentiate the product demonstrating this learning, students could be provided a menu of options to choose from to demonstrate their knowledge of *revolution*. This range of options might recur each time the Vocabulary Acquisition model is used. The options might include the following:

- Complete a word map that includes the spelling, definition, synonym, and etymology of the word.
- Draw an artistic representation of the word. Be sure to include a brief explanation of the drawing and the proper spelling, definition, synonyms, and etymology.
- Provide verbal evidence of understanding of this word, including the proper spelling, definition, synonym, and etymology. You might present a skit, interview, or poem in real time or record it for your teacher.
- Simply write out the spelling, definition, synonym, and etymology of the word on a lined piece of paper.

Chapter Summary

This chapter introduced the Vocabulary Acquisition model, an effective model for teaching students vocabulary important to learning. The model allows students to develop skills that enable them to continue developing their vocabulary independently. The Vocabulary Acquisition model is helpful to all learners but particularly useful to ELLs because it helps them build competencies required for learning English and gain critical understanding of essential words in the academic content areas. The model is best utilized when teachers explicitly want to teach the etymology and/or morphology of words, academic vocabulary and language, and a deep understanding of the same. The Vocabulary Acquisition model has five major steps: (1) pretest knowledge of words critical to content, (2) elaborate on and discuss invented spellings and hypothesized meanings, (3) explore patterns of meaning, (4) read and study, and (5) evaluate and posttest. It is a robust model that works well in all educational contexts. The model's many benefits include that it fosters deep understanding of words, links to prior knowledge, provides students with practice using words in different contexts, and promotes the transfer of knowledge.

Review Questions

1. What is the history of the Vocabulary Acquisition model?

2. What are the steps in the Vocabulary Acquisition model?

3. What type of content is best to teach when applying the Vocabulary Acquisition model? Provide and explain examples of content that would be appropriate and inappropriate.

4. What are the benefits of applying the Vocabulary Acquisition model? What are some of the challenges?

5. How can the Vocabulary Acquisition model be used to differentiate instruction and support diverse learners' needs?

6. How can technology be used to implement the Vocabulary Acquisition model?

Application Exercises

To promote your ability to apply the learning you gained in studying this chapter, complete the following exercises that challenge you to analyze a lesson plan you have written using the Vocabulary Acquisition model *or* the lesson plan example included in this chapter.

TECHNOLOGY INTEGRATION ACTIVITY

1. Consider the following and discuss with a partner or reflect independently:
   a) In the lesson plan you are analyzing, how does (or could) the integration of technology tools make learning more efficient, effective, and engaging? Can you explain and indicate how you will measure its impact on student learning?
   b) Will all learners be aided through the integration of technology? Are there some who might need special support to gain full benefit from technology tools? How might you support this? Is there a way to build on strengths students bring to this lesson related to technology? How?
   c) What plans could you put in place to promote a more successful use of technology and minimize (or eliminate) failure? What proactive plan could you put in place ahead of lesson implementation to ensure that technology works

smoothly and for all learners? What reactive approach could you take to ensure that desired learning still occurs if technology malfunctions during the lesson?

TEACHER PERFORMANCE ACTIVITIES

2. **Academic Vocabulary and Language Demands:** Academic vocabulary is the vocabulary that students must be able to understand to be successful performing content area learning. Language demands involve the ways language is used in speaking, writing, listening, and reading in the learning tasks of a lesson and in the expressions of student learning. For the lesson plan you are working with (your own or the one provided in the chapter), consider the following questions and discuss them with a partner or reflect on them alone:

   a) Even though lessons with the Vocabulary Acquisition model promote the learning of new words, there may be words associated with the language of instruction that must be understood for students to participate fully in the Vocabulary Acquisition model. What academic vocabulary and language demands exist in the lesson being analyzed? Make a list of the academic vocabulary that students must comprehend to succeed in the learning experiences described in the lesson plan.

   b) How would you determine whether and which students have mastery of the academic language that is not the main focus of the lesson before it begins?

3. **Planning:** In the context of the lesson plan that you are analyzing, discuss the following with a partner or reflect independently:

   a) Consider how students' backgrounds and experiences outside of school might affect their understanding of the word(s) that are the focus of the lesson. How might the students benefit from the learning experiences in the plan? How might students' cultural or family assets be built into the plan?

   b) Explain how the steps of the Vocabulary Acquisition model build on students' prior knowledge to support new learning.

   c) Explain how this lesson and use of the Vocabulary Acquisition model helps students develop literacy. Give specific examples from

the plan that "pinpoint" specific learning experiences and skills learners develop as they work to become more literate in precise, professional language.

   d) Describe any misunderstandings you anticipate students will have about the words being studied in the Vocabulary Acquisition model lesson you are analyzing. Why is it important for students to acknowledge these and correct them as they learn?

   e) Explain the logic of the sequencing of the steps in this model. Draw on theory or research to explain your reasoning.

4. **Implementation:** In the context of the lesson plan that you are analyzing, discuss the following questions with a partner or consider independently:

   a) Explain how the steps of the Vocabulary Acquisition model and the activities that students will perform in the lesson you are reviewing will result in engaged learning. What indicators would you look for during the implementation of your lesson to measure who is engaged and how much?

   b) How well does your lesson challenge learners to apply their learning in meaningful contexts? Explain.

5. **Assessment:** Consider the following and discuss with a partner or reflect independently:

   a) Does the plan you are reviewing make use of information gained through pre-assessment to inform the design of the lesson? How?

   b) How does or could the lesson plan you are reviewing use formative assessment to direct the more successful implementation of instruction? What type of feedback would you provide? Explain. Is there a way to make the implementation of instruction more intentional or improve it to address students' strengths or learning needs?

   c) How does the plan you are reviewing support students' expression of learning? Are there multiple forms of evidence of student learning? How might students learn through an analysis of their performance?

   d) What criterion will be used to measure students' success mastering the words being studied in the Vocabulary Acquisition model lesson you reviewed? What would you expect to see in a student work sample related to this lesson? Can you describe how the criteria would be demonstrated?

6. **Analyzing Teaching:** Consider the following questions and discuss with a partner or reflect independently:

   a) Now that you have created and/or analyzed a lesson plan using the Vocabulary Acquisition model, consider how the model supports effective teaching. Can you cite specific evidence or references that support your claim? Be specific in expressing your ideas.

   b) What did you learn from this activity that might inform your future practice?

Discussion Question

Review the Vocabulary Acquisition Model Lesson on the word *revolution*. What are the advantages and disadvantages to using the music videos? What other ways could you teach this vocabulary word?

Journal Entry

Explain the advantages and challenges to using the Vocabulary Acquisition model for teaching key vocabulary. Would you use this model? Why or why not?

Resources

- Academic Vocabulary—This site, developed by the State of Tennessee, provides several resources and word lists for teaching academic vocabulary: http://jc-schools.net/tutorials/vocab/TN.html

- Oklahoma Academic Vocabulary—This site, developed by the State of Oklahoma, provides lists of academic vocabulary for schools to use: http://sde.state.ok.us/curriculum/BAV/default.html

- Teaching Vocabulary in the Content Areas— This resource covers teaching vocabulary in the content areas: www.pgcps.pg.k12.md.us/~elc/readingacross2.html

- High School Academic Vocabulary—This site provides lists of academic vocabulary frequently taught at the high school level: www.u-46.org/roadmap/dyncat.cfm?catid=746Online

- Science Vocabulary Hangman—Game of Hangman about science vocabulary: http://education.jlab.org/vocabhangman

- Word Journal Template—This is another format for a word journal that teachers might wish to use: www.readwritethink.org/lessons/lesson_view.asp?id=20

- Venn Diagram—The Venn diagram is a tool developed by Jacob Venn in the late 1800s for comparing ideas. It can be used for comparing vocabulary as well as for comparing ideas in many other different subject areas. The Venn diagram has at least two overlapping circles but may have more. In the area(s) that overlap, one records the similarities between the two vocabulary words, and where the circles do not overlap is where one writes the unique characteristics of that word. Tools for creating Venn diagrams online are the International Reading Association's Interactive Venn Diagram: www.readwritethink.org/materials/venn (two overlapping circles), http://interactives.mped.org/view_interactive.aspx?id=28&title= (three overlapping circles), or Teach-nology's Venn Diagram Worksheet maker: www.teach-nology.com/web_tools/graphic_org/venn_diagrams. Other tools are available for purchase, such as Inspiration (www.inspiration.com), as well as many of the same tools for creating different types of graphic organizers or concept maps.

Model	Inquiry Model
Knowledge Supported	• Procedural Knowledge
	• Conceptual Knowledge
	• Metacognitive Knowledge
Added Value	Teaches thinking skills—specifically how to solve a problem, explore a question, or gain more information for understanding
Technologies to Integrate	• Online quiz/survey tools for pre-assessment
	• Collaboration tools to facilitate inquiry process or collaborative learning
	• Assignment tracking tools to facilitate formative assessment
	• Rubrics to promote summative assessment
	• Online assessment tools
	• Simulations to facilitate inquiry process
	• Audience response system tools to capture data for inquiry or assessment
	• Digital video/audio recording to present or capture data or express learning
	• Online posters or website creation tools to present evidence and demonstrate learning

The Inquiry Model

ajt/Shutterstock

Gina Mitchell's best teaching brainstorms seemed to come when she least expected them. This time the brainstorm hit at the grocery store between aisles 12 and 13. She was shopping with her 8-year-old son, Dominic, and their goal was to buy snacks for a Cub Scout meeting they were hosting.

Dominic had been saving his allowance for a few weeks, and now he needed to purchase snacks that were a good value. And then the brainstorm hit. She was giving her son the same lesson her students needed about consumer education!

She could use Dominic's "good-value" snack challenge to help her students learn consumer math skills and also address a content standard: "In grades 6–8 all students should develop and use strategies to estimate the results of rational-number computations and judge the reasonableness of the results" within a meaningful context. Using what she would call the good-value snack challenge, Gina would help her students learn the content identified in the standard while simultaneously facilitating their development of an important life skill.

As Dominic tried to decide which brand of raisins to purchase, she could not help asking him, "Which brand do you think is a better value—the generic/store brand or the name brand? How do you think we can figure this out?"

He responded, "Mom, what do you mean by value?" Gina realized that was a good question for an 8-year-old—and one that would need to be answered before moving on with this purchase *and* her lesson. After all, value might mean quality (i.e., taste) or quantity (i.e., the number of raisins, the weight of the raisins), and it is something that can be quite subjective.

She explained this to her son, adding that because the raisins would be part of the snack trail mix they would make, the raisins would not be the focus of the snack, and therefore he should consider the number of raisins per box as the indicator for whether it was a good "value." So, she asked him, using the number of raisins per box as the value factor, "Which do you think is a better value?"

Dominic replied, "Well, I'd say the store brand. If I could get the same number of name-brand raisins as the store brand, why would I pay more for the store brand?"

"Good point," Gina replied. "Is there a way you could find out whether you are right or not?"

Dominic replied, "I could buy both and count how many are in all of the boxes of each type and then compare them."

"Good idea," she replied, "but that is a lot of counting—there is a faster way to do it, and I will show you how tonight when I work on one of my lesson plans for this week's upcoming unit on estimation. Now let's buy the rest of the ingredients for your trail mix." Gina was clearly going to enjoy this educational conversation and teaching a meaningful math lesson, too. ▪

CHAPTER OBJECTIVES

After reading this chapter, you will be able to:

- Describe the Inquiry model, including its history and steps.
- Communicate the applications and benefits of the Inquiry model and learn what it might look like in a classroom.
- Explain how the Inquiry model is implemented and how to plan for teaching with it.
- Articulate how the Inquiry model might enable differentiated instruction and support diverse learners.
- Describe how technology can enhance teaching with the Inquiry model.

Introduction

There is no doubt that we live in the information age where it is common to experience information overload, find data so plentiful that it has to be warehoused, and even conclude there is "nothing new under the sun." As a result, learners in contemporary classrooms run the risk of believing that there is enough information already available, that their active engagement in the creation of new knowledge is unnecessary, and that their personal quest for discovery and understanding is without benefit.

On the contrary, students' involvement in inquiry and discovery is all the more important because it helps them develop critical-thinking skills. Such skills are especially important for students to develop because they need to learn how to interrogate the information many have instantaneously and perpetually available to them. When engaging in the Inquiry model, students benefit from involvement in the process of inquiry and also from the product (e.g., a solution) of this inquiry. In the opening scenario, Gina becomes excited thinking about how the Inquiry model lesson will benefit her math students by learning to use a systematic process to answer the question "What brand of raisins is the better value?" Her students will learn to ask good questions, develop and carry out a systematic process to answer their questions, and assess their own learning. They will also gain specific learning about math, including rational-number computations, averages, and other statistical concepts.

Students at all educational levels can benefit from direct involvement in the inquiry process—whether one is a kindergarten student learning about objects that sink or float, a high school student learning about the Civil War (see Scenario 10-3), or a middle school student determining how many calories she consumes daily (see Scenario 10-2). Regardless of level, learning to pose questions and work systematically to find their answers allows students to gain an appreciation for the discoveries of the past and teaches them the techniques required for finding new insights in the future. It can also introduce them to the joy and thrill of the discovery process.

Moreover, what is learned in the inquiry process can help students more deeply understand, retain, apply, and transfer knowledge of facts, principles, and concepts in every subject area. The skills, knowledge, and dispositions learned in the inquiry process will help learners solve problems and function productively in their future work and life. In addition, the emotional and intellectual interest students experience while they engage in inquiry can get them hooked on this type of learning, resulting in more engaged learning.

This chapter introduces the Inquiry model. It is a model that builds on natural curiosity to provide students the opportunity to learn a systematic approach that leads to discovery and deeper understanding of the world and the processes involved in comprehending it.

What Is the Inquiry Model?

The Inquiry model is a process-oriented instructional model that aims to teach students the skills, knowledge, and dispositions required for thinking systematically to answer important questions. Through participation in the Inquiry model, students also develop knowledge of academic content that includes understanding of facts, principles, and concepts within a meaningful context—the solving of a problem. The Inquiry model is engaging, active, and often collaborative. It approximates the same systematic processes used in various real-world occupations (i.e., science, engineering, medicine, design, and so on) and often results in authentic learning experiences for students. Students become actively involved in the creation of new knowledge and learn the inquiry process as well as how much time, creativity, and energy it takes to create new knowledge. Using the Inquiry model's structured approach, students investigate a phenomenon by examining or posing a problem, forming hypotheses, analyzing data, and testing their hypotheses. They then draw conclusions about their hypotheses and findings and communicate their results. The Inquiry model originated in the sciences but can be applied in any subject area or grade level. See Figure 10-1 for sample topics appropriate to explore with the Inquiry model.

The Inquiry model can be applied when teaching content from any of the knowledge dimensions—factual, conceptual, procedural, and metacognitive knowledge (Anderson, et al., 2001)—as long as it involves learning how to form hypotheses, conduct investigations, analyze data, and solve problems. More about how this model supports the various knowledge types is provided in the section titled "When Should the Inquiry Model Be Applied and Why?"

What Are the History and Origins of the Inquiry Model?

The long history of inquiry methods in education and the sciences is a testament to their perennial importance. Two major strengths of the Inquiry model are that it provides a systematic approach for discovery and introduces those participating in the model to the processes involved in scientific ways of knowing. The scientific method, perhaps the most well-known form of scientific inquiry, was documented in the *Book of Optics* by Ibn al-Haytham in the 11th

Figure 10-1   Sample Topics to Explore with the Inquiry Model

Art	What is realism?	What art was characteristic during the Renaissance?
Language Arts	What is plagiarism?	What purpose do poetic conventions serve in poetry?
Mathematics	What is pi?	What is the most commonly occurring color of M&Ms?
Music	How does the length of an instrument affect its pitch?	What characteristics do folk instruments around the world have in common?
Health/Physical Education	How does physical activity affect one's heart rate?	What are the characteristics of bullies?
Social Studies	How was propaganda used during World War I?	What are the predominant beliefs that influence government in the Middle East?
Science	Which items float or sink?	How does air temperature affect air pressure?

century (known as Alhazen in Europe and considered by many as the first scientist) (Saud, 1990). This method introduces a structured approach for conducting inquiry about scientific phenomenon. Its steps include defining or posing a problem, forming and testing hypotheses, analyzing data, drawing conclusions, and communicating results ("scientific method flowchart," n.d.). In the 20th century, largely due to funding from the National Defense Education Act (NDEA) of 1958—a reaction to the launching of the Soviet Union's *Sputnik* satellite—other Inquiry models, including the Biological Science Inquiry model (Schwab, 1963), the Learning Cycle (Karplus, 1977), and the Suchman Inquiry Training Model (1962), were developed. More recently, the proliferation of information sources and a need to teach the synthesis and appropriate management of these resources fostered the development of the BSCS 5E Instructional Model (BSCS, 1989, 2008) and the WebQuest Model (Dodge, 2007).

Why do so many Inquiry models exist? Are they all really necessary? The answer to both questions is "yes." Each model of inquiry is a product of the community that has created it and emanates from that community's need to solve perceived problems. A particular community's methods for solving problems are influenced by (1) what specific problems confront the community, (2) how the community perceives these problems, (3) which tools the community has access to when solving the problem, and (4) what methods individuals in this community deem are best to address these problems. Close analysis of the different models shows many similarities between them, yet each approach represents a unique manner of solving specific types of problems. A good example of this phenomenon is the WebQuest model (see www.webquest.org/index.php), which originated in the educational technology community. The WebQuest model emerged from a need that members of this community saw for structuring the exploration of information resources available on the Internet for the academic purposes of students at all academic levels, ranging from elementary to postsecondary levels. Figure 10-2 provides information about the WebQuest model.

Exploration of the steps of various Inquiry models suggests that they share common goals but have different methods for accomplishing them. Although inquiry has its roots in the scientific community, inquiry is fundamental to all disciplines. Each of these Inquiry models, no matter the discipline from which it originated, involves (1) students who are

Figure 10-2 WebQuest Model

The WebQuest model was created by Bernie Dodge and Tom March in 1995 (Dodge, 1995, 1997). They describe this inquiry approach as "an inquiry-oriented activity in which some or all of the information that learners interact with comes from resources on the Internet, optionally supplemented with videoconferencing" (Dodge, 1995, 1997) and other technology tools, such as spreadsheets, digital media, databases, and so on. It is important to note that most WebQuests (to search for examples, see www.webquest.org/search/index.php) have characteristics of other models discussed in this text, such as problem-based or cooperative learning. Yet all WebQuests apply inquiry and consist of the same "building blocks" or steps, as outlined in Figure 10-3. Teachers who wish to use this Inquiry model have different options for getting started. They may use a WebQuest that has been created and shared on the Internet by its creator (usually a teacher), or they may create their own using a template from the WebQuest website, QuestGarden, a Web-based WebQuest authoring tool (see http://questgarden.com), or some other website authoring tool. Sometimes teachers modify WebQuests created by others to meet the individual needs of their own students. The electronic presentation of these inquiry-based learning experiences makes them easy to modify and change—one of their many appeals. WebQuests are an excellent way to integrate technology into the inquiry process.

Bernie Dodge, PhD, San Diego State University.

active in the discovery process, (2) the use of higher-order thinking skills (cognitive processes that fall in the higher levels of the revised Bloom's taxonomy), (3) emphasis on the importance of both the learning process and the product of learning, and (4) discovery through a specific, systematic process or structured set of steps and procedures.

In this chapter, we provide a general model of inquiry that is useful in many different contexts and content areas rather than an in-depth treatment of the different Inquiry models referred to above. Figure 10-3 provides a summary and the major steps of several Inquiry models for general information purposes and to pique your interest in learning more about these models. In addition, this table communicates the power of the general model we present and highlights its distinction from the other variations of inquiry.

WHAT IS INQUIRY? The concept of inquiry, like so many concepts, is both broad and deep. Its definition varies, depending on the context and community in which it is used. Levstik and Barton (2001) suggest a broad definition for inquiry as "the process of asking meaningful questions, finding information, drawing conclusions, and reflecting on possible solutions" (p. 13). However, the amount of detail describing what inquiry is corresponds with the community that provides the description.

Figure 10-3 Steps in Different Inquiry Models

Biological Science Inquiry Model	Learning Cycle	Suchman Inquiry Training Model	BSCS 5E Instructional Model	The WebQuest Model	General Inquiry Model
Area of investigation is posed to students	Engage	Select a problem and conduct research	Engage	Introduction	Identifying a problem or question
Students structure the problem	Explore	Gather data	Explore	Task	Making hypotheses
Students identify the problem in the investigation	Extend	Develop a theory and verify	Explain	Process	Gathering data
Students speculate on ways to clear up the difficulty	Evaluate	Explain the theory and state the rules associated with it	Elaborate	Evaluation	Assessing hypotheses (analyzing data)
		Analyze the process	Evaluate	Conclusion	Generalizing about findings
		Evaluate			Analyzing the process

Figure 10-4 Definition of *Inquiry*

in·qui·ry

Pronunciation: \in-ˈkwī(-ə)r-ē, ˈin-,; ˈin-kwə-rē, ˈiṇ-; ˈin-,kwir-ē\

Function: noun

Date: 15th century

1: examination into facts or principles: research

2: a request for information

3: a systematic investigation often of a matter of public interest

By permission. From Merriam-Webster's Collegiate® Dictionary, 11th Edition © 2012 by Merriam-Webster, Incorporated (www.Merriam-Webster.com).

In most groups, inquiry is defined as an active process that involves examination and research, as Figure 10-4 shows. Yet for the science community, inquiry involves even more than these basic practices, as Figure 10-5 shows. In the National Science Teachers Association's (NSTA's) standard that addresses inquiry, competence with specific sub skills associated with inquiry is required—such as collecting, interpreting, and observing. The NSTA notion is that students should perform the very same actions scientists perform when "doing science" (e.g., conducting observations, questioning, data analyses). These processes and those involved in inquiry fall within the cognitive process dimension. The cognitive process dimension consists of "understanding," "analyzing," and "evaluating" information (Anderson et al., 2001, p. 30). Moreover, references to inquiry or inquiry-type processes or actions can be found in some shape or form in most other content area standards.

WHAT ARE THE LEVELS OF INQUIRY? Although exploration and discovery are inherent goals for all inquiry lessons, the purpose for exploration and discovery is not always similar in every inquiry lesson. Because the purpose for inquiry differs, the procedures and outcomes for inquiry lessons may differ as well. As a result, few inquiry lessons have identical procedures or outcomes—and lessons using the inquiry model may in fact be carried out quite differently. Some explorations are more open ended, inductive, and student led. Others are more focused, deductive, and teacher directed. Others will fall somewhere in between a structured and an open-ended investigation.

Figure 10-5 NSTA Standard 3—Inquiry

NSTA Standard 3—Inquiry

Teachers of science engage students both in studies of various methods of scientific inquiry and in active learning through scientific inquiry. They encourage students, individually and collaboratively, to observe, ask questions, design inquiries, and collect and interpret data in order to develop concepts and relationships from empirical experiences. To show that they are prepared to teach through inquiry, teachers of science must demonstrate that they:

    a. Understand the processes, tenets, and assumptions of multiple methods of inquiry leading to scientific knowledge.

    b. Engage students successfully in developmentally appropriate inquiries that require them to develop concepts and relationships from their observations, data, and inferences in a scientific manner.

The purpose for exploration and discovery in an inquiry lesson corresponds directly with the different "levels of inquiry." The term *levels*, described in more detail in this section, refers to how much guidance and structure teachers provide for students to complete an Inquiry model lesson or other inquiry investigation. The term also refers to the nature of the inquiry (e.g., teacher directed or student directed). Examination of the level of inquiry helps teachers make better decisions when planning and teaching inquiry-based lessons.

Teachers' awareness of the purpose for using the Inquiry model helps them decide how to best adapt and modify a lesson based on students' needs. Increased awareness also improves their ability to match objectives and outcomes with curriculum standards. In addition, they can perfect how they articulate their goals, procedures, and intended learning to students, leading to clearer communication about the inquiry. See Worksheet 10-1 in Appendix C for an example of some of the questions a teacher might ask him- or herself before planning an Inquiry model lesson.

This increased and better communication fosters students' partnership in the learning process. This active involvement is one of the strengths of the Inquiry model. Some academic content corresponds better with lessons that involve more structured approaches (e.g., confirmatory inquiry) and others more open-ended ones (e.g., open inquiry). Therefore, it helps to comprehend the four levels of inquiry, which fall on a "continuum" (Banchi & Bell, 2008, p. 26).

Schwab (1963) and later Herron (1971) were the first to conceptualize inquiry as having levels, although it was Rezba, Auldridge, and Rhea (1999) who formalized inquiry into a continuum of four different levels, based on these predecessors' work (Bell, Smetana, & Binns, 2005). The four different levels of inquiry, including examples, are as follows:

1. **Confirmation/Verification**—Students confirm a principle through a prescribed activity when the results are known in advance. "In this investigation you will determine whether common household goods are acids or bases using red cabbage juice. You will test apple juice, cream of tartar, salsa, and vinegar. Using the procedure outlined, you will record the results using the PDF saved on your laptops and answer the questions at the end of this inquiry."
2. **Structured Inquiry**—Students investigate a teacher-presented question through a prescribed procedure. "Today you will analyze the question, 'What are the effects of acids and bases?' You will examine the effects by testing what happens to red-cabbage-juice extract when mixed with vinegar and household ammonia. Then you will complete your examination based on the different steps outlined, record your results, and answer questions related to this investigation."
3. **Guided Inquiry**—Students investigate a teacher-presented question using student designed/selected procedures. "Design an investigation using common household acids and bases to answer the following question: What effects do acids and bases have when mixed with red-cabbage-juice extract? Determine the different steps of your investigation, including developing a hypothesis, procedures, materials, data tables, graphs, and conclusions. Proceed with your investigation on approval."
4. **Open Inquiry**—Students investigate topic-related questions that are student formulated through student-designed/selected procedures. "Develop an investigation that explores acids and bases. Proceed with your investigation on approval" (modified from Rezba et al., 1999).

Although these four levels of inquiry were developed with science instruction in mind—they certainly apply to *any* subject area. Figure 10-6 shows the different levels of inquiry

Figure 10-6   Levels of Inquiry and Information Provided to Students

	Question	Procedure	Solution
1. Confirmatory Inquiry	√	√	√
2. Structured Inquiry	√	√	
3. Guided Inquiry	√		
4. Open Inquiry			

Source: Banchi and Bell (2008, p. 27).

and the amount and type of information provided to students. For instance, in a lesson that utilizes confirmatory inquiry, the teacher would provide the question, outline the procedures students would follow, and know the solution to the problem/question. On the other end of the inquiry continuum, in open inquiry, students would generate their own problem or question and procedures for investigating it; there would be no predetermined solution, and, in some cases, there may not even be a correct answer.

RESEARCH ON INQUIRY.   Inquiry has been the subject of research in many different subject areas and contexts in education, from preschool to higher education. Yet research on inquiry has been most prevalent and documented in the sciences, most notably starting in the 1960s as a result of the NDEA-funded curriculum projects described earlier in this chapter (e.g., Biological Sciences Curriculum Study). One can debate the applicability of this research to other content areas, yet research on science inquiry shows some interesting findings. Not only do these findings support more recent understandings about how people learn (Bransford et al., 1999), but they also show that inquiry has a variety of positive outcomes on student learning in science, such as improvement in "scientific literacy, familiarity with science processes, vocabulary knowledge, conceptual understanding, critical thinking, and positive attitudes toward science" (Haury, 1993, as cited in Olson & Loucks-Horsely, 2000, pp. 125–126). More current research on inquiry in the sciences, funded by the National Sciences Foundation, has been conducted by the EDC Center for Science Education (see http://cse.edc.org/products/inquirysynth). These findings also build on previous research and show similar results.

Research on the use of inquiry in education was also conducted by Hansler (1985) in a three-year study examining the effectiveness of using inquiry in the third through the seventh grade. He found that inquiry "(1) is a potentially highly effective method of teaching cognitive skills, (2) appears to be appropriate for use with elementary level to college level students, and (3) can be used with almost any subject matter" (p. 1).

Although these results appear quite general, their merit is in the finding that inquiry is an effective method for nearly every subject area and grade level. It should be noted, however, that simply using inquiry methods is not always effective. This is particularly true if the model is not applied well or the methods do not match the assessment, as was the case in a study by Friedman and Heafner (2007). Friedman and Heafner found that for inquiry to be most powerful, students must learn and develop skills for conducting inquiry over time, and teachers must assess students in ways that adequately match the methods in which they learned. For example, the researchers suggest that the learning assessed in a multiple-choice test does not correspond with the learning gained through an inquiry lesson.

When Should the Inquiry Model Be Applied and Why?

The general Inquiry model may be used when teaching content from any of the knowledge dimensions—factual, conceptual, procedural, and metacognitive knowledge (Anderson et al., 2001); however, it is a particularly strong model to use when teaching students the procedural knowledge of problem-solving and cognitive process skills. The Inquiry model is also useful for developing students' metacognitive thinking. This section describes when the Inquiry model should be used and why. The following sections discuss what teachers should use the Inquiry model to do.

Teach the Procedural Knowledge of Problem Solving

Problem solving is a complex mental process that involves cognitive processes to (1) identify or frame a problem(s), (2) apply knowledge or skills in an effort to better understand the problem, (3) initiate action(s) to address or solve the problem through the application of knowledge and skills, and (4) consider the impact of actions taken. That process is very useful in the academic disciplines and increasingly important for productive functioning in the world. Not only does the Inquiry model incorporate problem solving, but it is also an excellent means for teaching how to problem solve.

In many subject areas, teaching **problem solving** is part of the content standards or incorporated in the framework for the corresponding standards for that content area. For example, the National Council of Teachers of English (2009) *Framework for 21st Century Curriculum and Assessment* states, "Twenty-first Century readers and writers must . . . Build relationships with others to pose and solve problems collaboratively and cross-culturally" (para. 2). In all subject areas, problem solving or participation in the inquiry process can be used to promote understanding of content standards as well. For instance, in the Inquiry Model Lesson at the end of the chapter, students can learn and apply statistical mathematics terminology and computation, such as mean, median, and mode, while also figuring out the better value when buying raisins (i.e., using a generic/store brand versus a name brand).

It is important to note that problem solving is a skill that should be taught and practiced frequently. It is not a skill that students know or acquire because they are innately curious, nor is it a skill they learn after being exposed to it only once. It is a procedural process that requires repeated exposure, modeling, guidance, and practice. Problem solving is a skill that some students have more natural aptitude for than others, but it is one that all students can and should learn.

Develop Students' Cognitive Process Skills

Cognitive process skills are those that fall within the various knowledge dimensions of the revised Bloom's taxonomy table (Anderson et al., 2001). The six major categories of

Figure 10-7   Inquiry Model Steps and Cognitive Process Skills

Inquiry Model Steps	Revised Bloom's Taxonomy Cognitive Process Category
1. Presenting/posing question	• Create: Generating (if using guided or open-ended inquiry where students devise their own questions)
2. Making hypotheses	• Understand: Inferring
3. Gathering data	• Create: Planning (if using guided or open-ended inquiry where students develop their own methods for the inquiry) • Apply: Executing, Implementing
4. Assessing hypotheses (analyzing data)	• Understand: Interpreting, Classifying, Inferring, Comparing • Analyze: Differentiating, Organizing, Attributing • Evaluate: Checking, Critiquing/Judging
5. Generalizing about findings	• Understand: Explaining • Evaluate: Checking, Critiquing/Judging
6. Analyzing the process	• Understand: Interpreting, Summarizing, Comparing, Explaining • Analyze: Attributing • Evaluate: Checking, Critiquing

cognitive processes are (1) remember, (2) understand, (3) apply, (4) analyze, (5) evaluate, and (6) create. Each category has several other cognitive process verbs associated with it that describe distinct types of thinking that human beings are capable of practicing. Although the Inquiry model involves many different cognitive processes, it is especially valuable in providing real and relevant ways for students to exercise the processes in the higher levels of the taxonomy (e.g., those in the "analyze" or "evaluate" category). Figure 10-7 illustrates the six steps of the Inquiry model and associated cognitive process skills.

Teach Metacognitive Thinking

Metacognitive thinking (thinking about thinking) is an important component of the Inquiry model and to learning in general. The ability to reflect on and examine one's own thinking carefully leads to greater self-awareness and promotes growth and development. This is a skill required for successful life and work in the 21st century. Just as problem solving is a skill that should be taught, modeled, and practiced, so should metacognitive thinking. The Inquiry model incorporates metacognitive thinking in its last step (described more thoroughly in the section "What Are the Steps in the Inquiry Model"). As a conclusion to using the model, students analyze their inquiry process by scrutinizing their actions, the rationale and plan for them, and their consequences or outcomes.

What Are the Steps in the Inquiry Model?

The general Inquiry model consists of six major steps: (1) identify or present/pose question, (2) make hypotheses, (3) gather data, (4) assess hypotheses, (5) generalize, and (6) analyze inquiry process. These steps are described below, and Figure 10-8 shows the major steps as well as teacher and student roles in this model. (Note that the roles will vary depending on the level of inquiry employed in the Inquiry model lesson.)

Figure 10-8   Teacher and Student Roles in the Inquiry Model (Guided Inquiry)

Inquiry Model Steps	Teacher Role	Student Role
Present/pose question	The teacher poses a question. **Teaching tip:** Ensure that the question or problem posed is interesting, open ended, reasonable, researchable, and justifiable.	The students read and/or listen to the question or problem posed by the teacher.
Make hypotheses	The teacher asks students to make hypotheses. **Teaching tip:** Help students form hypotheses by asking probing questions, if necessary.	The students develop hypotheses individually or in small groups.
Gather data	The teacher helps students find, gather, and organize data for analyzing their hypotheses. **Teaching tip:** Students may need help organizing their data for analysis.	The students organize data that they will examine.
Assess hypotheses (analyzing data)	The teacher asks students to analyze their hypotheses. **Teaching tip:** Encourage students to assess how the data supports or refutes their hypotheses.	The students assess their hypotheses by analyzing their data.
Generalize about findings	The teacher asks students to summarize and generalize their findings. **Teaching tip:** Help students make connections between other content they have studied with what they learned in the Inquiry model.	The students summarize their findings and make generalizations about their findings to other areas.
Analyze the process	The teacher asks students to analyze the inquiry process they completed by reflecting on what they did and what they learned. **Teaching tip:** Ask students to review every step of the Inquiry model as well as to examine and think about what they did.	The students reflect on the inquiry process as a whole, including what they did and what they learned.

Step One—Identify or Present/Pose a Problem or Question

The first step in the Inquiry model is the identification (or presentation) of a problem or question. The Inquiry Model Lesson at the end of the chapter poses the problem, "What factors make a brand of raisins a better value?" Depending on the objectives of the lesson and the level of inquiry desired by the teacher (see the previous section on the levels of inquiry), the teacher might provide the question (e.g., in confirmatory, structured, or guided inquiry), or the students may determine it themselves (e.g., in open inquiry). The problem or question will serve as the focus of investigation for the lesson. It can be displayed using a computer and projector or written in a student's inquiry notebook. Sometimes the comprehension of particular academic vocabulary or other information is necessary to understand the problem or question. For example, the term *value* might have different meanings that should be explored or addressed before students can effectively explore the question driving the inquiry. Making sure that students have the prerequisite knowledge and skills for the task of the inquiry before introducing the Inquiry model and this step will improve the potential success of the lesson.

Step Two—Make Hypotheses

During this step, students should make hypotheses before gathering or analyzing any data. Hypotheses are assertions, proposed explanations, or educated guesses that will be analyzed using data or a process. Sometimes they are called inferences. A hypothesis is usually expressed in a sentence format, such as "The store brand of raisins will be the best value because it has more raisins for the price per unit." Students develop hypotheses based on their past experiences and knowledge (including their prior observations, content area learning, peer conversations, and review of knowledge sources, such as websites and other reference materials). Students unfamiliar with the Inquiry model or who have limited background experience or knowledge about the inquiry topic may need guidance in forming hypotheses. A teacher might ask the question "Which brand of raisins will be the better value?" to elicit hypotheses about which box of raisins will be the better value. The teacher might then guide students in developing their hypotheses by having students brainstorm a list of hypotheses as a whole group or in small groups, share their hypotheses with a group of peers, and then determine the best hypotheses to investigate. Whatever approach teachers use, it is important for students to record their hypotheses in some way, such as writing or typing them or posting them on a wiki.

Step Three—Gather Data

During this step, students gather data related to the problem or question. Depending on the level of inquiry, students may need to develop a strategy for gathering data for themselves (such as in Scenario 10-2) or utilize data provided by their teacher and organize it themselves. In the structured inquiry demonstrated in Scenario 10-3, students need to become familiar with the data in the "Valley of the Shadow" project and figure out how to make sense of it. In the Inquiry Model Lesson at the end of the chapter, students need to gather data by counting the number of raisins in each box and then combine their data as a class. In a confirmation/verification inquiry, such as in Scenario 10-1, students who build geometric shapes with drinking straws and clay will need to reflect on their experiences and then determine how to organize their data about the strength of various shapes.

No matter the level of inquiry, during this step in the Inquiry model, it is imperative that teachers provide **scaffolding**, an instructional technique where a teacher models the learning task for students and structures it so that students learn gradually. Other support—in the form of teacher-designed worksheets, spreadsheets, and other tools—is also helpful. The teacher might demonstrate how to organize the data, if necessary. For instance, in the Inquiry Model Lesson at the end of the chapter, the teacher may need to provide some students with data worksheets or access to a spreadsheet that provides support for calculating averages as well as organization of their data. Teachers should not take for granted that students will know how to organize the data—this is why the level of experience and understanding of the different levels of inquiry is important.

Step Four—Assess Hypotheses (Analyze Data)

During the assessing hypotheses step, students analyze the data they have gathered to determine whether it supports or refutes their hypotheses. This step is challenging because it requires students to make sense of what they have discovered and make connections between what they thought they would find (their hypothesis) and what they actually did find (the data). Students should revisit their hypotheses, examine the data they gathered, and determine how and why their hypotheses are correct or incorrect. As they document their analyses, they should describe how they made their conclusions about their hypotheses.

In the Inquiry Model Lesson, students are challenged to determine the better value of raisins based on the number of raisins per box. Once students have determined the average number of raisins per box, they will need to connect that data to their hypothesis to determine which brand had the most raisins per box and was the better value. Drawing direct connections between the hypothesis and the data can be a challenging task. During some inquiries, students might generate more data than is useful. When that occurs, students will need to discern which data is valuable and which is extraneous—and in many cases, teachers will have to assist them in this process, too.

Step Five—Generalize about Findings

Generalizing findings involves making conclusions about the insights identified through discovery and exploration. Making generalizations about the problem or question should go beyond simply answering the problem or question to include a rationale for the generalization. The explanation should also connect the process of analysis with the data.

In the Inquiry Model Lesson at the end of the chapter, based on the generalizations made about the best value of raisins, students might consider whether their findings are applicable to other products, such as potato chips or cereal. Similarly, they might also deliberate whether this experiment would enable them to generalize about what the better value is when purchasing clothing, for instance, determining the better value between a generic/store-brand or designer/name-brand sport shirt.

Step Six—Analyze the Process

A critical characteristic of the Inquiry model is analyzing the inquiry process and its procedures. This involves metacognitively reflecting on the entire process starting with the question or problem posed (or initiated by students if open inquiry was the level of inquiry desired). Sometimes this process involves self-analysis or a personal determination of the quality of one's thinking and activities during the inquiry. Of particular interest to the students should be the effectiveness of various procedures in and approaches to the exploration. This is also a time for students to reflect on what was learned and how both their knowledge and their skills grew through the process. In the Inquiry Model Lesson at the end of the chapter, students might reflect on how they determined the best value of raisins and what the best approach might be for making this determination. They could decide if the quality of raisins is important or if using a multifactorial approach in their investigation might yield a different result.

What Does the Inquiry Model Look Like in the Classroom?

When participating in an Inquiry model lesson, students are actively involved in learning content through exploration and discovery. Although the process of discovery might be similar, there are significant differences in (1) the materials, (2) the way inquiry is structured, (3) the degree of open-endedness, and (4) intended outcomes—just to name a few. The following scenarios illustrate different levels of inquiry, including confirmation/verification, guided inquiry, and structured inquiry. They also show the power of the Inquiry model to engage learners in asking good questions and taking responsibility for learning the inquiry process. The scenarios demonstrate varying levels of teacher support and direction while also showing how students can be empowered to learn and use important life skills that they can apply beyond the scope of the Inquiry model lesson.

Scenario 10-1

Students are working in groups in a fourth-grade science class. Each has 30 drinking straws and clay. Their teacher has presented them with this challenge: "You will compete to see which group can build the tallest and the strongest bridge. We will test the strength of your bridge by stacking 20 pennies on each bridge."

Students will apply what they have learned about the strength of different geometric objects and their combinations. They will confirm or refute prior learning with this active, hands-on experience. The teacher explains that before getting started, students must form and record their hypotheses about how they will build and test their bridges. Then they will have the rest of the class period to build and test their bridges. As they test their bridges by stacking pennies, students must also keep track of where pennies are placed and how many pennies their bridges support without falling. Students must also record their tests using the video camera on their tablet computers. This way, they can see exactly when and where their bridges might collapse. Finally, the teacher asks students to answer the following questions at the end of their exploration and share their answers with other groups:

- Why did you design the bridge this way?
- How many times did your group have to start over?
- What steps did your group take to design this bridge?
- How many pennies was your bridge able to support?
- How might you change the design of your bridge to support even more pennies?
- What did other groups do with their designs that worked well in this challenge?
- How did the construction and testing of your bridge confirm or refute what we learned about the strength of different geometric structures?

Through this process, students have the opportunity to confirm or refute scientific principles. Of course, to do this, they first need to be able to remember and recall these principles and then demonstrate that they can apply them in real situations when they build their bridge. Their understanding of these principles is challenged and finally concretized when students articulate their understanding to their teacher and other groups orally at the end of the lesson.

Scenario 10-2

While learning about healthy nutrition and eating habits in physical education, seventh-graders become interested in learning some of the different ways to monitor and manage their own diets. The teacher helps the students formalize their interest into a question (e.g., "How many calories do I consume on a daily basis on average?" or "How healthy are the foods I eat?"), form hypotheses, and determine how they will gather and analyze data to answer the question. Although the teacher offers to help them figure out how to answer their question, it is the students who determine their course of action—not the teacher. In this guided Inquiry model lesson, students have the opportunity to pursue questions that interest them. As a result, their motivation is strong, and they are more actively engaged. Students also learn how to articulate a question of interest and figure out how it might be answered. Students work with materials they need based on their questions. Some decide to use online tools, such as the U.S. Department of Agriculture's SuperTracker (www.choosemyplate.gov/SuperTracker), to assess their caloric and nutritional intake. Others opt to keep a food diary using spreadsheets or word-processing software or specialized apps on their smartphones. In some cases, students select the best tool available, and in others they choose based on comfort, familiarity, skill, or their own habits.

Students have the option of working alone or in groups depending on what makes the most sense to answer their question—learning dictates the investigation rather than arbitrary classroom rules or conventions. Throughout the process, the teacher monitors the students' plans for the inquiry, including their hypotheses, their ideas for testing their question, the data they propose to collect, analysis of their hypotheses, and generalizations. Students respond positively to the purpose and focus of this Inquiry model lesson.

When the inquiry is over, students share with one another the results of their learning as well as their analysis of the entire inquiry process. They quickly learn that there are many different ways to monitor one's diet and that the variety of approaches provides different information that can lead to more informed eating and living and ultimately better health. As one student described it, "It is like we all took different snapshots of the same thing—we just see different details depending on where we are standing when we captured them." Students also learn that multiple and varied tools exist for monitoring one's diet and that some work better, more easily, and with less cost than others.

Scenario 10-3

Students in an eleventh-grade history class are working in small groups using wireless laptops in their classroom to explore primary source materials that have been collected and archived in a Web-based digital repository called "The Valley of the Shadow: Two Communities in the American Civil War" (http://valley.vcdh.virginia.edu). In this structured Inquiry model lesson, students are tasked with answering the question "What happened to slaves when their owners died?" based on a lesson their teacher located online

© auremar/Shutterstock

(www2.vcdh.virginia.edu/teaching/vclass-room/slavewillsinst.html). Because the teacher provides students the question to investigate and the procedures for answering the question, the lesson is considered a structured inquiry.

First the teacher asks students to form hypotheses about the question. Then she tells them that they will find the answer to the question by examining the wills of several slave owners, newspaper articles, slave owners' diaries, and the slave owner census. As students gather and explore these materials, they learn about the Civil War as it was experienced by the people of two communities in the United States. During and after examining the data, the teacher often stops the class to ask students to assess their hypotheses, thinking, and justifications by asking, "As you examine the data, be sure to think about how the data supports or refutes your hypotheses. And, remember, you will need to justify your conclusions."

Finally, he or she asks them to make generalizations about their findings and to reflect on the entire inquiry process in which they participated to solve the question. Not only do students learn the social studies content standards that relate to content knowledge and historical processes, but they also learn the process by which historians "do history." Reconstructing history is, itself, an inquiry process that involves gathering documents, verifying their authenticity, analyzing them, creating and testing hypotheses, and making conclusions. Students discover several challenges associated with historical research and communication—misinterpretation, bias, and reliance on inauthentic data.

What Do These Scenarios Illustrate?

The process of asking good questions and working to answer them is an interesting and rewarding one. Perhaps the most striking feature of these scenarios is that students are engaged in meaningful and purposeful work. Students do not ask questions like "What are we supposed to be learning?" or "Why is this relevant?" or "Are we finished yet?" Instead, students care enough to work through the rigors of the Inquiry model lesson. In the scenarios above, they strive to find out what happened to slaves when their owners died, whether what they have learned about building bridges is true, and how to monitor their own nutritional intake. As illustrated, inquiry actively engages students, supports content area learning, and teaches students thinking processes that are valuable for continued learning. They also show flexibility in the use of the Inquiry model in different grade levels and subject areas and that explorations designed to support varying levels of inquiry can serve different purposes.

Planning for Teaching with the Inquiry Model

Before teaching with the Inquiry model, teachers should (1) determine the level of inquiry they will use to teach; (2) craft a good question or problem if conducting a confirmatory, structured, or guided Inquiry model lesson; (3) establish that the content is a good match for the Inquiry model; and (4) determine the accessibility of the data needed for analysis. (Note: Data are essential for the Inquiry model. If data that will enable students to answer the problem through inquiry activities are not available, then another model is more appropriate.) The following sections discuss what educational designers do when teaching with the Inquiry model:

Determine the Level of Inquiry

Prior to teaching a lesson or unit using the Inquiry model, teachers should determine the level of inquiry they wish to incorporate. This determination will serve as a guide for designing instruction. Before making any decisions about the "right type" of inquiry to use, the teacher must be clear about the purpose of the inquiry. For example, if an objective of the Inquiry model lesson is to encourage students to learn about the inquiry process, then the teacher might decide that a structured inquiry (one in which he or she articulates the steps) is the best approach. Alternatively, if the Inquiry model lesson is to empower students to develop their own methods for the inquiry, then an open inquiry would be appropriate. In all cases, however, the level of inquiry selected should match the purpose of the inquiry as well as the experience level of the teacher and students with conducting inquiry. Once the level of inquiry has been determined, the teacher can plan accordingly.

Craft (or Help Students to Craft) a Good Inquiry Question or Problem

If teachers choose to plan an Inquiry model lesson or unit that falls in one of the first three levels of inquiry (i.e., confirmatory, structured, or guided), they will need to craft a good question or problem. Good inquiry questions are those that are interesting, open ended, reasonable, researchable or testable, and justifiable. It goes without saying that good questions are also those that will result in students learning intended curriculum standards. Interesting questions are those that will hold the attention of the target audience for the duration of the Inquiry model lesson. Open-ended ones often start with a "why," "what," or "how" question. These types of questions typically have more than one correct answer. A reasonable question is also one that can be researched and justified. For example, a reasonable question to explore in the Inquiry Model Lesson at the end of the chapter is "Which type of raisins, generic/store brand or name brand, is the best value of raisins to buy?" Students can investigate and compare store- and name-brand raisins to make a decision about which is the best value. Also, they can provide a rationale for their conclusions. Finally, some of the best inquiry questions have more than one correct answer.

Establish That the Content Is a Good Match for the Inquiry Model

An essential component to the success of instruction that incorporates the Inquiry model is that the content be a good match for the type of learning that it fosters. Specifically, the Inquiry model requires students to apply a systematic process for exploring a question or problem through the analysis of data. Content that is best taught using a discovery-driven or problem-based approach is a good match for the Inquiry model. For example, in the Inquiry Model Lesson at the end of the chapter, a purpose of the lesson is for students to determine what a good value for raisins is. In this lesson, there is no right or wrong answer per se—the point is for students to explore and test their hypotheses and justify their conclusions. In this lesson example, the process of discovery is more important than the final product or conclusion.

Determine the Accessibility of the Data Needed for Analysis

Before choosing the Inquiry model, teachers need to find out if they have access to data that will allow students to examine the predetermined (if it is a confirmatory, structured, or guided inquiry) or yet-to-be-determined (as is the case in open-ended inquiry) question or problem. Although this is common sense, it is important to make this determination before choosing the Inquiry model because it is essential for student learning: How can students attempt to answer or make conclusions about a question or problem if they cannot analyze the data necessary to do so?

This is one reason that good, reasonable questions are essential. In the case of the Inquiry Model Lesson at the end of the chapter, students should have access to actual boxes of generic/store- and name-brand raisins to compare them. Clearly, an expense is required. If a teacher has no budget to purchase the raisins for students to examine, then obviously this lesson cannot be done, unless students bring in the raisins or the teacher can pay for them. Similarly, in Scenario 10-3, students must have access to the data housed on the Valley of the Shadow website; therefore, students must have access to a reliable computer and Internet connection and have the necessary skills and knowledge to navigate the website.

Differentiating Instruction with the Inquiry Model

The Inquiry model challenges students to learn content standards through active engagement in the discovery process. Its very design includes some ready-made opportunities to integrate differentiation strategies with the model. For example, flexible grouping, which involves asking students to work together in various configurations, is a common feature of the Inquiry model that can be used to support student learning. Depending on need, students can work in heterogeneous or homogeneous groups to gather and analyze data.

The rich and meaningful learning that takes place in the Inquiry model is the perfect foundation on which to build supportive strategies for a broad range of student learners.

Content

In the Inquiry model, there are a variety of ways a teacher might differentiate the content associated with instruction according to the level of inquiry being applied in the lesson. In a confirmatory or structured Inquiry model lesson, teachers will provide the students with the framework for conducting the inquiry as well as the content for investigating it. Here, teachers can differentiate content through the use of different media sources (e.g., digital text, podcasts, videos, and so on) geared towards students' reading levels or interests. For instance, in Scenario 10-2, a teacher could use diverse media for students to learn about nutritions such as watching a video, reading materials in print or online (including the health section of a newspaper).

Using a variety of media changes the nature of student interactions with content. Working with the content becomes a multisensory experience and provides access to ideas in ways that are arguably richer and potentially more interactive. Digital materials can also provide greater accessibility to content for English Language Learners (ELLs) and those with special needs. For example, free text-to-speech tools, such as Natural Reader (www.naturalreaders.com), convert any digital text (e.g., Microsoft Word files, Web pages, e-mails) into a natural-sounding voice. Such tools provide audio support for students who struggle reading text-based materials that are less challenging for other students. With reading challenges removed from the task, those students are better able to focus on exploring the ideas related to the content in the Inquiry model lesson. This differentiation might also be useful for students who experience difficulty reading in general or across academic content areas. Figure 10-9 provides an effective tool for helping teachers determine the readability level of text.

Another way to differentiate content might be to provide students different materials to work with during the Inquiry model. For example, in Scenario 10-3, the teacher might assign specific resources in the website's primary-source archives for different groups of students to review rather than have them sift through the full range of materials that might be too complicated or sophisticated to understand and read.

Process

One simple way to differentiate the process of any lesson to respond better to students' levels of readiness is to vary the amount of student and teacher involvement and decision making

Figure 10-9 Microsoft Word Readability Tool

When written materials are used extensively as a data source in an Inquiry model lesson, their complexity should be considered and matched with student readiness for learning. Care should be taken to ensure that the readability level of written materials is appropriate and matches the skill level of the learner. Microsoft Word has a feature in its "Spelling and Grammar" settings that will determine the readability of any text copied into the program. A teacher who plans to incorporate digital text (i.e., various websites) as data sources might copy several paragraphs of this text into Word, run a readability check on it, and determine which students might have the reading skills to benefit from it.

in the inquiry process. The Inquiry model is well suited for this task because each level of inquiry provides a different type of structure (see Figure 10-6) that can be incorporated into the lesson for various groups of students as they explore the same content. For example, a teacher might ask several groups of high-achieving students to explore a question through a guided Inquiry model lesson. In the Inquiry Model Lesson at the end of the chapter, this group of students might be given this challenge: "Your job is to determine the best value of raisins for our trail mix. First, you will define the term *best value*, and then you will determine the different steps of your investigation, including developing a hypothesis, procedures, materials, data tables, graphs, and conclusions. Next, you will proceed with your investigation, on my approval of your plan." A different group of students might participate in a structured Inquiry model lesson where they would be grouped heterogeneously by ability level and told, "Today you will analyze the value of boxes of raisins based on the average number of raisins per box. You will first determine the number of raisins in your own boxes and then calculate the average across the class. You will complete your examination based on the different steps outlined, record your results, and answer questions related to this investigation." Figure 10-6 demonstrates how the four levels of inquiry vary depending on the amount of information provided to students.

Another method for differentiating the learning process during an Inquiry model lesson is to provide different levels of scaffolding for students during its different steps. One form of support might involve providing detailed instructions for completing the steps of the Inquiry model lesson. For example, if the whole class is conducting the inquiry in Scenario 10-3, then the teacher might provide targeted instructional supports to guide students through the structured inquiry process using data on the Valley of the Shadow website. Some students might use a worksheet that guides them through all of the steps of the Inquiry model, while other students may function quite well without one.

Product

When differentiating the product of any lesson, choice is a powerful motivator. If assessment goals can be achieved through multiple methods, then create a "menu" of possible assessment methods to give learners the opportunity to consider the best means to express what they have discovered through the Inquiry model. A multimedia presentation, worksheet, podcast, lab report, e-mail, video, or journal entry might be equally good methods for communicating what was done and learned during an Inquiry model lesson. The requisite skills, talents showcased, time needed, and resources required for each of these products differ. Allowing students to make their own best choice can increase their ownership of and elicit their best work.

■ What Are the Benefits of Applying the Inquiry Model?

The Inquiry model has many benefits that are described in the section that follows, including that it may develop different types of knowledge; promote active, engaged learning; develop students' cognitive process skills; improve students' attitudes about content areas; facilitate student understanding; encourage students to serve as partners in the learning process; help students appreciate intellectual property; and support lifewide and lifelong learning. The following sections discuss what the Inquiry model does.

Develops Factual, Conceptual, Procedural, and Metacognitive Knowledge

Through the Inquiry model, students develop knowledge within all of the different knowledge dimensions: factual, conceptual, procedural, and metacognitive. For example, in the Inquiry Model Lesson at the end of the chapter, students learn the factual knowledge of what an average is, the procedure for determining the price-per-unit value of items that can be counted (and averaged), and the conceptual knowledge of "value" and how this might change depending on the context of the investigation and the metacognitive skills of reflection on their thinking process.

Promotes Active, Engaged Learning

Active learning is generally defined as any instructional method that gets students intellectually, physically, or emotionally involved in the learning process. In engaged learning environments, students perform meaningful tasks where they are expected to think about what they are doing. In the Inquiry model, students' natural curiosity is activated, and they participate in discovering the answers to meaningful questions rather than simply absorbing information passively. They learn to answer their own questions about the process of discovery, which can be challenging and also exhilarating.

Develops Cognitive Process Skills

The Inquiry model develops students' cognitive processes across all of the different levels of the cognitive process dimension. Figure 10-7 illustrates the different cognitive processes developed through the different steps of the Inquiry model.

Facilitates Student Understanding

Active engagement in the learning process is positively correlated with student understanding. When students have the opportunity to inquire and explore, learning becomes personal, novel, and memorable. In this way, what is learned is more important, valued, and effective.

Encourages Students to Serve as Partners in the Learning Process

Various characteristics of the Inquiry model make students active partners in the learning process. Particularly when conducting a guided or open inquiry, students ask their own questions, are responsible for discovering the answers, and are accountable to their teacher and peers for their efforts. All of this promotes students' ownership of their learning.

Helps Students Learn to Appreciate Intellectual Property

After creating their own knowledge and forming their own conclusions through the Inquiry model, students are more likely to appreciate existing knowledge in each discipline and the work involved in creating it. They also understand that new facts and principles are the product of someone's (or some group's) effort to inquire and better understand the world. Students' understanding of intellectual property and plagiarism increases through the experience of owning their own ideas. Inherent in the appreciation for knowledge is that students learn to value the contributions of those who devote their lives to scientific progress and humankind's quest for understanding the universe.

Supports Lifelong, Lifewide Learning

Students today must participate in learning throughout their lifetime. Those who practice the Inquiry model while in school will be able to continue practicing it outside of the school environment, too. The facts and principles they learn, along with process and thinking skills, can easily transfer to real-world settings—enabling them to be more autonomous and independent and allowing them to practice learning "just in time" as life requires.

What Value Does Technology Add to the Inquiry Model?

This section describes several unique ways in which technology might be utilized for the planning, implementation, and assessment of learning when using the Inquiry model. Figure 10-10 provides numerous technologies introduced in this chapter for supporting the teaching of the Inquiry model.

Figure 10-10 Technology Tools for the Inquiry Model

Use	Technology Tools
Planning	
	Online quiz, survey tools, or SMS Polling • Quiz Center: http://school.discoveryeducation.com/quizcenter/quizcenter.html • QuizStar: http://quizstar.4teachers.org • SurveyMonkey: www.surveymonkey.com • Poll Everywhere: www.polleverywhere.com Ask an expert • Center for Innovation in Engineering and Science Education: www.ciese.org/askanexpert.html Collaboration • Curriki: www.curriki.org/xwiki/bin/view/Main/WebHome Tracking or online organization of assignments • Assign-A-Day: http://assignaday.4teachers.org • Weebly: www.weebly.com • Intel's Showing Evidence Tool: http://educate.intel.com/en/ThinkingTools/ShowingEvidence

continued

Figure 10-10   Technology Tools for the Inquiry Model
continued

Use	Technology Tools
Implementing	

Presenting/posing question
 	
Making hypotheses
 	
Gathering data
 	
Generalizing about findings
	Simulations
	• National Council of Teachers of Mathematics (simulation on distance, speed, and time relationships): www.nctm.org/standards/content.aspx?id=25037
	• BrainPop: www.brainpop.com
	• Discovery Streaming: http://streaming.discoveryeducation.com
	Collaboration
	• Google Docs: http://docs.google.com
	• Wikis (two possibilities)
	  • http://pbworks.com
	  • www.wikispaces.com
	• University of Virginia's Center for Technology and Teacher Education: www.teacherlink.org/content/math/relatedlinks/datacollection.html
	Illustration
	• Intel's Seeing Reason Tool: http://educate.intel.com/en/ThinkingTools/SeeingReason/
	• Bubbl: http://bubbl.us)
	• Wordle:www.wordle.net

Assessing	

Analyzing the process	Creating assessment tools
	• Rubrics (see also quizzes and surveys in the "Planning" section of this table),
	  • Rubistar: http://rubistar.4teachers.org
	  • QuizStar: http://quizstar.4teachers.org
	• Audience response systems (clickers)
	  • SMART Response interactive response systems: http://www2.smarttech.com/st/en-US/Products/SMART+Response
	  • Turning Technologies: www.turningtechnologies.com/studentresponsesystem
	Students demonstrating their learning
	• Digital video recording (mini camcorder)
	  • smartphone
	  • tablet computer
	• Online posters
	  • http://poster.4teachers.com
	Sound recording
	• Audacity: http://audacity.sourceforge.net
	• Digital audio recorders
	• Portable media players (e.g., iPod, MP3 players)
	• VoiceThread: http://voicethread.com/#home
	Website creation
	• Wikis: www.wikispaces.com
	• Weebly: www.weebly.com

Planning

Tools of particular use at this stage are those that help teachers understand their students' readiness for learning before the lesson, become better prepared to support students during the Inquiry model, and create materials that will scaffold students' learning throughout the lesson.

Figure 10-11   Pre-Assessment Example

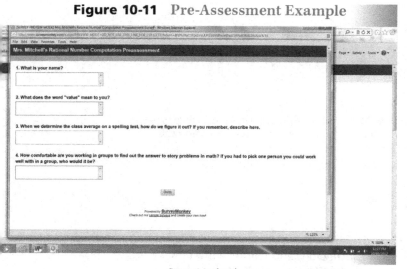

SurveyMonkey (www.surveymonkey.com)

CONDUCT PRE-ASSESSMENT. Pre-assessment is always an important part of the learning process and a cornerstone of differentiated instruction. It offers teachers and students a necessary channel of communication before instruction begins that can give students input into the learning process. It also provides teachers with important information about students' prior knowledge of content (including their existing misconceptions and false assumptions), prerequisite knowledge and skills, and other factors that contribute to the planning of a lesson.

An online survey tool (e.g., SurveyMonkey) is useful for pre-assessment purposes. A teacher might use this tool to create a short questionnaire assessing these factors. Figure 10-11 shows a simple pre-assessment that a teacher might use before implementing an Inquiry model lesson. This short pre-assessment can provide a teacher with information about students' existing understanding of the concept "value," their prerequisite knowledge of how to figure an average, and practical information about whom this student might work best with in a small group. Each bit of information will enable the teacher to plan the lesson better. Online survey tools are easy to use. While they do require that students complete them using a device (e.g., computer), which can be a barrier for some teachers, they also provide results instantaneously and in a summarized form that facilitates analysis.

CONNECT OR COLLABORATE WITH OTHER TEACHERS. Although teachers typically know a great deal about a topic to be studied, in many cases, connecting or collaborating with others might benefit teachers and their students. Teachers and students can learn a great deal from other students who have different perspectives as well as from experts found via Internet user groups or an "ask an expert" website. Collaborating with other educators is easy via sites like Curriki. Alternatively, teachers might also subscribe to a listserv or blog in a content area. Teachers can find listservs and blogs through national professional associations (i.e., National Council for Teachers of Math) or an online search.

SUPPORT STUDENTS DURING THE LEARNING PROCESS. Technology can assist teachers in supporting students in a variety of ways. First, teachers can create documents, such as worksheets, that scaffold the inquiry process (e.g., see Worksheet 10-2 in Appendix C). Second, teachers might require students to use technology to collect, organize, record, analyze, and share their findings. For instance, in the Inquiry model lesson, a teacher might require students to use spreadsheets for collecting, recording, organizing, and analyzing their data and also for creating visual representations (e.g., charts) that illustrate their findings. Working with the spreadsheets in those different ways can support students when they begin to form conclusions.

SCAFFOLD STUDENTS DURING THE LEARNING PROCESS. Teachers can take advantage of technology tools during the planning process by using them to create materials that can scaffold students' learning during the Inquiry model lesson. Although worksheets and other hard copies might be useful, examples of other types of useful tools are online website-building tools to develop and share student instructions side by side with Web-based links they might want to use during the discovery process. One free, open-ended tool is Weebly. This tool can be used to build a simple website. Another useful tool for this purpose is "Assign-A-Day," which allows teachers to create a calendar and link Web-based assignments to various days in the calendar. Yet a another tool is Intel's "Showing Evidence," which allows students to form hypotheses, identify and evaluate data, form conclusions, and reflect on them. By doing these activities, a teacher might structure a lesson so that instructions and resources appear in the same place to promote organized and focused learning experiences and minimize errors and complications from typing Web URLs into a Web browser.

Implementation

Technology can be utilized at all stages of the Inquiry model—from presenting or posing a problem to analyzing the process—and in ways that emulate how professionals in the related field use it during their real-life inquiry process. For example, meteorological scientists use various instruments for recording weather conditions and then enter those data into software before making predictions. Likewise, students could use gauges, thermometers, and other weather instrumentation to record weather conditions. They could then record and analyze the data using a spreadsheet. Similarly, students in Scenario 10-3 can use the plethora of data sets (e.g., census data from the 1800s) and digital primary sources (e.g., letters written by Thomas Jefferson) available on the Internet to conduct historical analyses—just as historians do. Below are a few ways in which technology might be used to enhance the various aspects of the Inquiry model and possibly also make learning more efficient, effective, and engaging.

PRESENT/POSE A PROBLEM OR QUESTION. Videos, photos, simulations, and other media may be used to present or pose a question or problem in any subject area. For instance, the National Council of Teachers of Mathematics has a simulation for understanding distance, speed, and time relationships. Discovery Streaming and Brain Pop are two subscription-based websites that provide multimedia resources that might stimulate student interest and learning in an Inquiry model lesson that can be used for posing questions or problems.

MAKE HYPOTHESES. Students may record their hypotheses using audio or video, a word-processing program, wikis, or Intel's "Showing Evidence" tool. Wikis, for example, are quite useful when conducting inquiry with classes in other locations (e.g., with students in another country or state). Recording student hypotheses using a digital whiteboard can provide a way to refer back to and revise at a later time as new information is gained through the Inquiry model.

GATHER SOURCES. Because it is a treasure trove of data, the Internet can play an integral role in the "Gather Data" step of the Inquiry model. Students can collect data from many different sources by conducting online searches and downloading data sets for analysis. The University of Virginia's Center for Technology and Teacher Education has a list of websites for collecting data, maps, and charts. Below are some examples in various content areas:

- Art—Examine art from the National Gallery of Art (www.nga.gov)
- English—Explore free texts via Project Gutenberg (www.gutenberg.org)

- Music—Explore music from a genre from the Library of Congress (http://memory.loc .gov/ammem/browse/ListSome.php?category=Performing%20Arts,%20Music)
- Social Studies—U.S. Census Bureau (www.census.gov/schools/for_teachers/index .html) site to gather census data to gather data about the U.S. population
- Science—Collect data about seismic activity from the U.S. Geological Survey (http://earthquake.usgs.gov/eqcenter/recenteqsww)

Students might also view the Internet as a database that can be used to study phenomenon such as information sharing on Wikipedia, a social phenomenon.

ORGANIZE (AND PRESENT) DATA. Historians, scientists, and other professionals use databases, spreadsheets, visual displays of information, and word-processed reports to organize data, among many other examples. Students can emulate those practices by organizing their resources on websites or by using social bookmarking and other Web-based tools, including Google Docs. Students can use these tools not only to organize data but also to learn how to organize data for analysis—another important aspect of the Inquiry model. Students can use visualization tools, such as Intel's "Seeing Reason" tool, or concept-mapping tools, such as bubbl or Wordle, to create visual representations of their understanding.

ASSESS HYPOTHESES (ANALYZE DATA). Students may conduct queries, using databases, spreadsheets, and video (replay), and they can develop reports using those same tools. Again, the Intel "Showing Evidence" tool can be helpful for this. Visual displays of their analysis (e.g., in the form of charts or diagrams created using spreadsheet or graphic-organizer software) can help students compare and assess their hypotheses.

GENERALIZE ABOUT FINDINGS. Technology offers learners the opportunity to edit and revise their understandings and to demonstrate and share them using multimedia. For instance, students can create a multimedia presentation (e.g., using Keynote or PowerPoint), jointly develop a wiki that records their findings, create a video on YouTube, and share a video presentation using VoiceThread. These representations of their learning can extend to include generalizations that may apply to other areas as well.

ANALYZE THE PROCESS. There are many technology tools that students might use to help them analyze the inquiry process. They can use video or audio (e.g., podcasts) to replay the steps completed in the Inquiry model as well as word-processing software or other technology tools for reflecting about their learning (e.g., using Keynote, PowerPoint, VoiceThread, and so on). Students can use all of these different technology tools to analyze the inquiry process they completed.

Assessment

Assessment in the inquiry process attempts to get at (1) what students know and (2) what students can do. Technology helps with both, as the following sections explain.

CREATE ASSESSMENT TOOLS. Various tools, including online quiz tools and audience response system tools or "clickers," might be suitable for measuring what students know. These tools make it easy to track student learning during and at the conclusion of an Inquiry model lesson. For example, in the Inquiry model lesson, the teacher might ask students to answer questions during the "Gather Data" step and then later gauge their progress by asking them to respond to oral questions regarding their discovery process. Students might respond to their teacher's questions using clickers, starting with a simple nonacademic question, such as "Is your group successfully executing its strategy for answering the Inquiry question?" or something more academic, such as "Of the options written on the board right now—a, b, c, and d—what is the best method for calculating the average number of raisins per box?"

Online quiz tools can also be used to measure what students know. Sites like Quizstar (http://quizstar.4teachers.org) make it easy to create, assign, and grade basic assessments. Likewise, tools like Rubistar (http://rubistar.4teachers.org) facilitate the creation of rubrics that might be used for evaluating (and communicating expectations for) student work on papers, projects, and other less traditional assessments.

ENABLE STUDENTS TO PRESENT THEIR LEARNING. Technology is also a tool that shows in rich and descriptive ways what skills and understandings students gained during the Inquiry model lesson. Digital cameras, video cameras, mini camcorders, and podcasts can be used to present a "report" from the lesson. Tools such as VoiceThread (www.voicethread.com) enable digital lab reports and sharing. Other possibilities include presenting discoveries in online posters or posting them to free websites or wikis. The deep and broad learning students experience can be detailed and examined repeatedly—and even in slow motion.

Inquiry Model Lesson Plan Example

Planning lessons using the Inquiry model presents a unique challenge. Depending on the level of inquiry desired, the teacher or the students will have more involvement in determining what happens and how during each step of the Inquiry model. So, for example, if a teacher wants students to complete an open Inquiry model, then the students will establish the question(s), procedure, and solution—not the teacher. That makes it nearly impossible to write an open Inquiry model lesson plan with much detail. Teachers can and should, however, develop lessons for confirmatory, structured, and guided Inquiry model lessons. The level of detail will vary, but each lesson type should include questions and scaffolding. The lesson plan shared in this section is considered a guided Inquiry model lesson because the teacher determines the question, but the students determine the procedures for answering the question posed. Figure 10-12 provides an outline of the steps of the Inquiry model lesson.

GRADE LEVEL(S): Sixth

CONTENT AREA: Math and/or language arts

PHYSICAL TEACHING ENVIRONMENT: This lesson will be taught in a regular classroom that also has a computer, projector, and whiteboard.

APPLICATION OF REVISED BLOOM'S TAXONOMY: This lesson primarily addresses the *analyzing* level of the revised Bloom's taxonomy since it requires students to analyze data (the raisins) to form conclusions.

Figure 10-12   Outline of Inquiry Model Lesson Steps

Inquiry Model Steps	Inquiry Model Lesson
Presenting/posing question	The teacher poses the question "Which brand/type of raisins offers the better value?"
Making hypotheses	The teacher asks students to hypothesize which is the best value of raisins.
Gathering data	Students gather and organize their data.
Assessing hypotheses (analyzing data)	Students analyze the data by counting the number of raisins per box. They record this information in their spreadsheet. Then they calculate and analyze the data.
Generalizing about findings	Students summarize their findings, form conclusions, and make generalizations about their findings.
Analyzing the process	Students reflect on the inquiry process they completed in this lesson. They examine what they did in the lesson and what they learned.

Lesson Plan

GOAL(S): Students will learn that they may use mathematics for making sound purchasing decisions.

Standard(s) Addressed (MATH):

Common Core State Standard Statistics and Probability: 6.SP: Summarize and describe distributions.[1]

- 4. Display numerical data in plots on a number line, including dot plots, histograms, and box plots.
- 5. Summarize numerical data sets in relation to their context, such as by: a. Reporting the number of observations. b. Describing the nature of the attribute under investigation, including how it was measured and its units of measurement. c. Giving quantitative measures of center (median and/or mean) and variability (interquartile range and/or mean absolute deviation), as well as describing any overall pattern and any striking deviations from the overall pattern with reference to the context in which the data were gathered. d. Relating the choice of measures of center and variability to the shape of the data distribution and the context in which the data were gathered.

National Council of Teachers of Mathematics: In grades 6–8 all students should develop and use strategies to estimate the results of rational-number computations and judge the reasonableness of the results.[2]

---

[1] © Copyright 2010. National Governors Association Center for Best Practices and Council of Chief State School Officers. All rights reserved.

[2] Standards for the English Language Arts, by the International Reading Association and the National Council of Teachers of English, Copyright 1996 by the International Reading Association and the National Council of Teachers of English. Reprinted with permission.

For a complete list of the standards, go to www.ncte.org/standards.

ISTE NETS for Students 2007: #3 and #4.[3]

OBJECTIVE(S): Given two boxes of raisins from different brands, students will determine which box of raisins is a better value by comparing their analyses/results with that of their peers.

ESTIMATED TIME: Approximately 30 minutes

MATERIALS NEEDED:

- Two different brands of raisins (enough small boxes for each student)
- Paper for recording data
- Inquiry lesson PowerPoint (PPT)

PREREQUISITE SKILLS: Students should have experience estimating, averaging, creating bar graphs, and finding mean, median, and mode. Also, they should have experience recording data and working using the scientific method.

LESSON PROCEDURES (Text in italics is suggested teacher dialogue.)

Anticipatory Set (Introduction): [1 minute]

- Ask students if generic/store-brand items are better than name-brand items (e.g., is a Polo-brand shirt better than a regular sport shirt from Target or Walmart?). [motivation]
- Display the question on PPT while asking students:, *How do you know you're really getting what you pay for with brand-name items? How about generic/store-brand items?* [Connection]

Present the Problem or Question: [1 minute]

Explain to class that today they will conduct an investigation, an inquiry, to learn which brand of raisins is the better buy. The question they will need to answer is "What factors make a brand of raisins the better value?" (Display question in PPT)

Form Hypotheses: [5 minutes]

Ask students to brainstorm what factors help determine whether a brand of raisins is a better value. Also ask them to form hypotheses about why these factors indicate a better value. As they brainstorm these hypotheses, ask them to also figure out ways in which they might test their hypotheses. Use PPT instructions to guide them in this process.

- Divide class into groups of four. Ask students to share their hypotheses with one another.
- Ask students in each group to select one of these hypotheses to test.
- Ask a member from each group to share these hypotheses and record them in PowerPoint.

Gather Data (and Display Data): [10 minutes]

Ask students to gather their data by representing the data on a sheet of paper—display instructions on PPT. (One way is to count the number of raisins in each box and share the

---

[3] National Educational Technology Standards for Students (NETS•S), Second Edition © 2007 ISTE® (International Society for Technology in Education), www.iste.org. All rights reserved.

results in the prepared spreadsheet.) Students may also determine other ways to analyze data; if so, they should incorporate this into the lesson. [$1.89 for Sun Maid, $1.59 for Grocery brand.] Some students might benefit from scaffolding, such as a data analysis worksheet that prompts them to count up the number of raisins per box and then add these for all boxes and divide by the number of boxes—to compute the average number of raisins per box (e.g., see Worksheet 10-2 in Appendix C).

Assess Hypotheses (Analyze Data): [5 minutes]
Once students have recorded their data, they may analyze and explain their findings to determine whether their hypothesis was correct. Use the following questions to prompt students' thinking: *Was your hypothesis correct? Why or why not? Do you need to test another hypothesis?*

Generalize (Closure): [3 minutes]

- Based on their data gathering and analysis, ask students what conclusions they have about the factors that make a brand of raisins the better value: *Do you believe your findings can be generalized to other brands of raisins (e.g., Dole, other generic/store brands?) Can you make any generalizations about generic/store-versus name-brand items based on your findings?* (Display these questions in PPT.)

Analysis of the inquiry process: [5 minutes]
Ask students to jot down their ideas about the process, why it was used, and how else they think it might be used.

ASSESSMENT
Formative assessment Collect students' brainstorms, hypotheses, and data spreadsheets

Summative assessment Give students another problem (generic/store versus brand name) to see how they analyze it

LESSON EXTENSIONS
Students could do the following:

1. Estimate how many raisins are in the boxes.
2. Investigate the nutritional aspects of raisins (e.g., calculate how much fructose or fiber is in a box of raisins).
3. Use scales for weighing raisins.
4. Examine the history of raisins. (Raisins were probably "discovered" by ancient people the first time they found them dried on the vine. The Phoenicians planted vineyards around Malaga and Valencia [Spain] and in Corinth [Greece] between 120 and 900 B.C. Around the same time, the Armenians were starting their vineyards in Persia.)
5. To make more informed decisions, students could conduct research about raisins by examining the following two sites:

   a) www.sunmaid.com (for additional info about SunMaid raisins)
   b) www.national-raisin.com/raisins (National Raisin Company raisin facts)

Differentiation Strategies for the Inquiry Model Lesson

In the sections that follow are some suggestions one might apply to differentiate instruction in the Inquiry Model Lesson.

Content

In the Inquiry model, the skills and knowledge (related to curriculum standards) that students will gain while participating in the inquiry process is the content that might be differentiated. Because the teacher will want all students to achieve this standard, efforts to differentiate content will involve (1) considering the nature of the materials that provide the data for the inquiry and (2) challenging high-achieving students to stretch their understandings further.

In this lesson, students are expected to develop strategies for estimating the results of the computation of rational numbers and judge the reasonableness of the results of this estimation. Although these standards might be taught without the use of actual boxes of raisins, using them as props is an excellent way to support the varying needs of students in this classroom. Students will be more engaged in the learning task because they get to manipulate their own boxes of raisins. Additionally, they will understand how to calculate the average number of raisins per box better if they count their own raisins and then use their experience to estimate the average number or raisins per box. The use of physical manipulatives and personal experience make the goal of estimation more concrete and less abstract. They provide powerful support for students who would typically struggle doing mental math or problems that do not seem to have a real purpose. Students who are highachieving might need more challenges than estimating the box of raisins. These students might be effectively grouped together, asked to complete the activity, and then challenged further. The best value of other items that might be included in a trail mix with the raisins might be explored including peanuts, dried fruit, and so on. Students would need to consider whether the same strategy for estimating quality in raisins could apply to items packaged differently. Or these students might be asked to extend their learning beyond the content standards in math by being asked to consider the qualitative as well as the quantitative aspects of value.

Process

Differentiating the process of instruction in this lesson can be performed in numerous ways. Varying the amount of structure according to the levels of inquiry is one such way. Some students might perform best if they are given detailed step-by-step instructions for how to proceed. For example, the teacher might meet with students in the group and say, "Today you will analyze the value of boxes of raisins based on the average number of raisins per box. You will first determine the number of raisins in your own boxes and then calculate the average across the class. You will complete your examination based on the different steps outlined, record your results, and answer questions related to this investigation."

Other students may excel with less prescribed methods for accomplishing their discovery and exploration. Students might also benefit from different levels of support during the inquiry process. For example, Worksheet 10-2 (Appendix C) could be used to support a group of students who need help recording the data for their investigation. Other groups might not need this support or find it limiting. Special care might be taken to increase the level of challenge presented by each step in the Inquiry model by sequencing of activities (from easy to harder). The amount of direct supervision and teacher support provided might also be varied from learner to learner depending on need. Flexible grouping might also be helpful. For example, ELL students could be paired to work with students who have stronger English skills, or the teacher could work more closely with ELL groups.

Product

The product of learning can also be differentiated. Students could be asked to report their findings in a variety of ways, such as in a group or individually, and to choose from a variety of reporting mechanisms, including (1) giving a multimedia presentation, (2) completing a worksheet, (3) making a podcast, or (4) completing a lab report. Also, the level of inquiry employed will likely result in differentiated products, too. For instance, in an Inquiry model lesson that incorporates open inquiry, students decide how they will solve the problem or question; therefore, the end product will vary individually or by group.

Chapter Summary

This chapter introduced the Inquiry model—a process-oriented instructional model that aims to teach students the skills, knowledge, and dispositions required for thinking systematically to answer important questions. Through their active involvement in the Inquiry model, students gain an understanding of content area knowledge while simultaneously participating in a process that introduces them to the skills and methods used to acquire knowledge in various academic disciplines. There are four different levels of inquiry that might be incorporated within the design of an Inquiry model lesson, including confirmation/verification, structured inquiry, guided inquiry, and open inquiry. Each level varies in the amount of information, structure, and direction

provided by the teacher. Teachers incorporate different levels of inquiry based on the specific goals for a lesson. The steps of the Inquiry model consists of six major steps: (1) identify or present/pose question, (2) make hypotheses, (3) gather data, (4) assess hypothesis, (5) generalize, and (6) analyze inquiry process. Use of the Inquiry Model accomplishes numerous goals. It can help students gain factual, conceptual, procedural, and metacognitive knowledge; promotes active, engaged learning; develops cognitive processes; facilitates student understanding; encourages students to serve as partners in the learning process; fosters student appreciation of "intellectual property"; and supports lifelong and lifewide learning.

Review Questions

1. What is the history of the Inquiry model?

2. What are the steps in the Inquiry model?

3. What type of content is best to teach when applying the Inquiry model? Provide and explain examples of content that would be appropriate and inappropriate.

4. What are the benefits of applying the Inquiry model? What are some of the challenges?

5. How can the Inquiry model be used to differentiate instruction and support diverse learners' needs?

6. How can technology be used to implement the Inquiry model?

Application Exercises

To promote your ability to apply the learning you gained in studying this chapter, complete the following exercises that challenge you to analyze a lesson plan you have written using the Inquiry model or using the lesson plan example included in this chapter.

TECHNOLOGY INTEGRATION ACTIVITY

1. Consider the following questions and discuss with a partner or reflect independently:
   a) In the lesson plan you are analyzing, how does (or could) the integration of technology tools make learning more efficient, effective, and engaging? Can you explain and indicate how you will measure its impact on student learning?
   b) Will all learners be aided through the integration of technology? Are there some who might need special support to gain full benefit from technology tools? How might you support this? Is there a way to build on strengths students bring to this lesson related to technology? How?
   c) What plans could you put in place to promote a more successful use of technology and minimize (or eliminate) risk of failure? What proactive plan could a teacher put in place ahead of lesson implementation to ensure that technology works smoothly and for all learners? What reactive approach could you take to ensure that desired learning still occurs if technology malfunctions during the lesson?

TEACHER PERFORMANCE ACTIVITIES

2. **Academic Vocabulary and Language Demands:** Academic vocabulary is the vocabulary that students must be able to understand to be successful performing content area learning. Language demands involve the ways language is used in speaking, writing, listening, and reading in the learning tasks of a lesson and in the expressions of student learning. For the lesson plan you are working with (your own or the one provided in the chapter), consider the following questions and discuss them with a partner or reflect on them alone:
   a) What academic vocabulary and language demands should teachers consider when planning and implementing Inquiry model lessons, particularly those that incorporate open-ended inquiry? What academic vocabulary must students comprehend prior to and during the Inquiry model lesson?
   b) How you would determine whether and which students have mastery of the academic language before the lesson begins?
   c) How might teachers scaffold students' proficiency with academic language throughout the various steps of the Inquiry model no matter the level of inquiry?

3. **Planning:** In the context of the lesson plan that you are analyzing, discuss the following with a partner or reflect independently:
   a) Explain how the steps of the Inquiry model build on each other to lead students to make clear and meaningful connections between identified learning goals or objectives.
   b) Consider how you have addressed or how you might address a variety of learning needs, interests, learning styles, real-world problems, and levels of inquiry in the Inquiry model lesson.
   c) What research or theory supports the use of the Inquiry model for instruction in your learning context?

4. **Implementation:** In the context of the lesson plan that you are analyzing, discuss the following questions with a partner or consider independently:
   a) Explain how the steps of the Inquiry model and the activities that students will perform in the lesson you are reviewing will result in learning that engages students in higher-order thinking and inquiry.
   b) What indicators would you look for during the implementation of your lesson to measure who is engaged, how students are working through the Inquiry model lesson using various levels of inquiry, and how much scaffolding is needed for them to achieve optimal learning?
   c) How well does your lesson challenge learners to apply their learning in real-world contexts? Explain.

5. **Assessment:** Consider the following questions and discuss with a partner or reflect independently:

a) How might you use pre-assessment to inform the design and implementation of the lesson? How might consideration of students' backgrounds, prior learning, and experiences—as they relate to learning goals and objectives—help you design a more effective Inquiry model lesson? Explain.

b) How does or could the lesson plan you are reviewing use formative assessment and student reflection of their own learning to direct the more successful implementation of instruction and different levels of inquiry? Is there a way to make instruction more intentional or improve it to address students' strengths, metacognition, or learning needs?

c) How does the plan you are reviewing support students' expression of learning, metacognition, and different levels of inquiry? Are there multiple forms of evidence of student learning, metacognition, and inquiry? How might students learn through an analysis of their performance and reflection on their own learning (metacognition)?

6. **Analyzing Teaching:** Consider the following questions and discuss with a partner or reflect independently:

a) Now that you have created and/or analyzed a lesson plan using the Inquiry model, consider how the model supports effective teaching, data analysis, and inquiry. Can you cite specific evidence or references that support your claim? Be specific in expressing your ideas.

b) What did you learn from this activity that might inform your future practice?

Discussion Questions

Review Figure 10-6 and the section in this chapter titled "What Are the Levels of Inquiry?" Then discuss with a partner or small group the following questions: (1) What are the advantages and disadvantages of teaching using these different inquiry levels? (2) When and why would you choose to teach at these different levels? (3) How you would structure the Inquiry model lesson to address the different levels of inquiry?

Journal Entry

Questions are a central feature of the Inquiry model. Can the same question be used for confirmatory, structured, and guided inquiry? Explain why or why not in a journal entry.

Resources

- Center for Inquiry-Based Learning Inquiry Exercises (CIBIL)—Created by a cooperative project involving North Carolina Schools and Duke University, the CIBIL site presents science and math exercises for students in grades 4 through 12 to encourage the use of inquiry-based learning in the classroom: www.ciblearning.org/resource.exercise.php

- EDC Center for Science Education: Publications and Other Resources Resulting from a Synthesis of Research on the Impact of Inquiry Science Instruction—This site presents synthesized research conducted on the use of inquiry-based learning and its impact on science instruction: http://cse.edc.org/products/inquirysynth/technicalReports.asp

- Historical Inquiry—This website is devoted to "doing history" and the art of historical inquiry. Definitions of historical inquiry, tutorials, publications, and other support are provided: www.historicalinquiry.com

- National Science Foundation. *Inquiry: Thoughts, views, and strategies for the K-5 classroom*: *Volume 2 of Foundations: A monograph for professionals in science, mathematics, and technology education*—This publication presents support for teachers attempting to do inquiry-based learning in grades K through 5: www.nsf.gov/pubs/2000/nsf99148

- National Science Teacher's Association Position Statement on Scientific Inquiry—This is the official position statement from the NTSA on

what inquiry is and why it is important: www
.nsta.org/about/positions/inquiry.aspx

- Inquiry and the National Science Education
Standards: A Guide for Teaching and
Learning—This site provides a link to a
valuable publication authored by Olson and
Loucks-Horsley in 2000 and published by
the National Academies Press explaining
in depth the connection between education
standards and inquiry: www.nap.edu/catalog.
php?record_id=9596

- Women and the British Empire: A Talking
DBQ—This website presents a quality lesson
using the Suchman Inquiry Model: http://
chnm.gmu.edu/wwh/modules/lesson8/
lesson8.php?c=plans&s=0

- Thirteen.org's Workshop Inquiry-Based
Learning—This site presents a well-rounded
resource that answers FAQs (frequently asked
questions) addressing everything from what
inquiry is to how it can benefit learners: www
.thirteen.org/edonline/concept2class/inquiry/
index.html

- Valley of the Shadow Project—This site provides
rich primary source documents for student viewing and inquiry: http://valley.vcdh.virginia.edu

- WebQuests—This website is devoted to explaining and showcasing examples of the WebQuest
inquiry model: www.webquest.org/index.php

Model	Problem-Based Learning Model
Knowledge Supported	• Factual Knowledge
	• Procedural Knowledge
	• Conceptual Knowledge
	• Metacognitive Knowledge
Added Value	• Develops 21st century skills, such as cognitive process skills (critical thinking and problem solving), as well as cooperative, social, and metacognitive skills using a structured approach
	• Often incorporates or mimics real-world problems
Technologies to Integrate	• Search tools to locate resources and/or make problems and their solutions more meaningful
	• Data analysis tools such as spreadsheets and databases to analyze data
	• Presentation tools or blogs, wikis, or websites to organize, share, and document implementation plans

The Problem-Based Learning Model

ajt/Shutterstock

Genevieve Washington had difficulty getting her sixth-grade students to take learning in her classroom seriously, especially in math. She remembered having the same problem as a student herself. Math had been meaningless until she got her first job—and paycheck. Abstract numbers quickly became relevant when they represented music downloads, milkshakes, and new clothes. Genevieve wanted her students to know the relevance in math as children, so she used Problem-Based learning in her teaching. Today she planned to ask her students to help her solve a real problem to help them understand the importance of their learning.

After her students filed into her classroom, Genevieve began explaining the lesson by saying, "The school is planning to replace the carpet in the aftercare room that many of you use after school each day. However, the school has only a small budget to purchase new carpet. Our principal heard we are studying area and thought we might be able to help. So she has challenged our class to come up with a plan and budget to replace the carpet."

Genevieve's students looked interested. Many nodded their heads acknowledging that the current aftercare room carpet was, indeed, worn. Genevieve continued, "We have a budget of $600. There are two big challenges involved in carpeting any space. The first is the fact that the width of carpets is finite. Carpets are made on standard looms that tend to be 12, 13, or 15 feet wide. Two pieces can be put next to each other, but that makes a seam—which, depending on the carpet texture, might be more or less noticeable and also come apart with lots of wear and tear. The length of a carpet is variable."

One hand shot up, "Do you mean that the rugs are made on looms like we used in art class last year?" Genevieve smiled, happy that students were making some connections with past learning. She replied, "Yes. Rugs are made in giant factories where the looms are specific sizes. Different kinds of carpets are made on different kinds of looms and those looms have different widths. Even though the loom restricts the width of the carpet, it can be cut in different lengths. Get it?"

Heads nodded. She continued, "The second challenge is that room measurements are finite, as well. We could also express that idea by saying, 'the room's dimensions are fixed.' They cannot be made bigger or smaller without construction. A third challenge is that rooms often have irregular shapes. Think about entryways and closets. When you buy carpet, you purchase a rectangular piece of a fixed width but a variable length that is priced by the square foot."

Genevieve then shared a couple of examples she had prepared using an interactive whiteboard. "For example, if I bought a carpet that was 8 feet wide by 10 feet long but I only needed to carpet a space that was 5 feet by 7 feet, I would waste a lot of carpet. I might not mind if the carpet was free, but if I were paying by the square foot, I would definitely care about wasted carpet!"

One student chimed in and said, "Yeah! That's a lot of money you could spend on something else."

Genevieve smiled. They understood her—she was encouraged that this real-life problem could be solved by her students!

She continued, "Our challenge is to figure out what size carpet we need and then what carpet makes the most sense to buy with our budget. We can choose from new or remnant carpet, carpet of different widths and lengths, and carpet with different colors and textures. We will need to determine which of these choices is most important. One of our goals will be to avoid wasting carpet and money. We also want to determine whether we will need more than one piece of carpet so that we can put the seams toward the side of the space to ensure they are invisible and remain intact."

One girl in the front row raised her hand and excitedly said, "Where do we start? This seems really complicated to me! I can do area on a worksheet, but I do not know how to figure this out—as much as I would like to have new carpet in the aftercare room."

Genevieve responded reassuringly, "You will get some help working on this problem. Now, let's get started." ∎

CHAPTER OBJECTIVES

After reading this chapter, you will be able to:

- Describe the Problem-Based Learning model, including its history and steps.
- Communicate applications and benefits of the Problem-Based Learning model and learn what it might look like in a classroom.
- List ways to implement and plan for teaching with the Problem-Based Learning model.

- Articulate how the Problem-Based Learning model might enable differentiated instruction and support diverse learners.
- Describe how technology can enhance teaching with the Problem-Based Learning model.

Introduction

Solving problems is a part of everyday life. Whether we are trying to find our way to a new classroom, figuring out how to adjust to a new diet recommended by a doctor, or selecting the best option for carpeting a room, our quality of life is influenced by our ability to solve problems. Although we may not be aware of it, we learn while trying to solve problems. We might find out that room numbers starting with two are on the second floor, that gluten-free foods can be purchased at certain grocery stores, or that a certain width of carpet will work better in a room because it can be installed so the seam does not show. We may not anticipate such learning, yet our motivation to solve the problem can necessitate and inspire it. In the opening scenario, the allure of new carpet for the aftercare room is enough to motivate learners willing to apply themselves in Genevieve Washington's sixth-grade class. Such is the case with most Problem-Based Learning—a powerful and useful learning model that is the subject of this chapter.

Problem-Based Learning motivates students to apply what they already know and inspires them to acquire new knowledge by presenting them with a problem they have an interest in solving. In addition to promoting learning related to academic content standards, Problem-Based Learning provides students opportunities to develop different problem-solving competencies, including how to devise strategies for identifying problems (analysis), framing problems (organization), and addressing problems (application, synthesis). As the opening scenario suggests, the Problem-Based Learning model allows students to apply knowledge in purposeful ways and see the relevance of what goes on in school to the world outside of it.

This chapter presents the Problem-Based Learning model with an overview of its history and the learning processes with which it is associated. It distinguishes between Problem-Based Learning and another learning model, Project-Based Learning. The chapter shares the advantages of Problem-Based Learning, including suggestions for when and how teachers should use it. Illustrations of how the model might look in practice are provided along with suggestions for how technology might support learning in the model. Tips for supporting the needs of diverse learners in this model are also presented along with a Problem-Based Learning model lesson example.

What Is the Problem-Based Learning Model?

The Problem-Based Learning model is an active learning model that allows students to learn and hone problem-solving skills, develop competence with academic content standards, and realize the relevance of applying content area learning for practical purposes. Unlike in other learning experiences where students gradually develop skills and knowledge that can be applied to solving a problem later on, in the Problem-Based Learning model, students start with a problem. A problem is a question or issue that has one or more solutions. Through a process of solving the problem, students develop content knowledge and skills, including many 21st century skills. The model emphasizes real-world applications for academic knowledge and thereby bridges classroom and real-world learning. It also supports students' development of problem-solving capabilities that are transferable within and outside the classroom. The model is highly motivational for students, provided that the problem is meaningful to them. Authentic problems—those that are real, important to students (not just their teachers), and appropriate in size and scope and that foster student curiosity—are best to use in Problem-Based Learning model lessons. Students might work to address practical classroom problems with a connection to academic standards (as in the opening scenario, where students are tasked with figuring out the best size of carpet for a school's aftercare room), or they might extend their learning to even more powerful levels (as in Scenario 11-2, which describes how science students are challenged to develop plans for an Earth Day competition). Figure 11-1 provides examples of topics one might explore using the Problem-Based Learning model.

What Are the History and Origins of the Problem-Based Learning Model?

The Problem-Based Learning model has its roots in medical education. It was first introduced in the 1950s at Case Western Reserve University. Faculty preparing doctors needed a way to support students' ability to apply professional skills and knowledge in real-world contexts. Problem-Based Learning influenced the instructional approaches and curriculum used in medical schools by challenging medical professionals to help their students apply their content knowledge to real medical cases. This methodology, eventually called Problem-Based Learning, was officially adopted as a pedagogical approach at Canada's

Figure 11-1   Examples of Topics to Explore with the Problem-Based Learning Model

Subject	Topic
Art	• What factors should be considered by a community making decisions about installing a 9-11 memorial? • What accounts for individual "taste" in art?
Language Arts	• Why do we ban books? • What factors contribute to Shakespeare's popularity?
Mathematics	• What strategies are used to increase a retailer's quarterly revenues? • How much would it cost to fly our class to Egypt to study the pyramids?
Music	• What could be done to improve the acoustics in a room and produce better sound? • How does the size of an object affect its pitch?
Health/Physical Education	• What factors influence personal wellness? • What are some ways teamwork can be enhanced?
Social Studies	• Consider the Japanese internment camps during World War II. When, if ever, should the Bill of Rights be violated? • What is the best form of government?
Science	• How can we safely store chemicals in the classroom storage closet? • What materials provide the most structural support for an egg dropped off the school roof?

McMaster University to promote students' ability to apply their scientific knowledge to clinical situations (Neufeld & Barrows, 1974). The model spread to academic programs in law, business, and also education. Currently, Problem-Based Learning is used as the predominant approach to learning at various institutions of higher education around the world, including the University of Delaware, Maastricht University in the Netherlands, Gadjah Mada University in Indonesia, and the University of Limerick in Ireland.

The Problem-Based Learning model harnesses the power of the larger Problem-Based Learning methodology in a more focused, condensed manner. Problem-Based Learning leverages many of the essential ingredients of Problem-Based Learning methodology to support student learning in educational environments that might not be able to adopt the methodology in its entirety. Use of the Problem-Based Learning model does not require an implementation of Problem-Based Learning methodology across an institution or for a long period of time. Also, it does not require a complete curriculum overhaul. It can be used in more limited, sporadic, and shorter-term ways. Lessons planned with the Problem-Based Learning model can be used as a part of a typical classroom that utilizes a larger repertoire of instructional approaches alongside other models, such as direct instruction, lecture, and Socratic Seminar.

Recently, another model, with the same acronym, Project-Based Learning, has gained popularity in K–12 educational settings. Project-Based Learning is a method to promote students' engagement in the learning process through the structuring of learning around the accomplishment of projects or tasks that have meaning and relevance for the learner. In this type of learning, students have a great deal of say about the projects they will work on and how they will do so.

Although Project-Based Learning shares much in common with Problem-Based Learning, they are two distinct models of learning. Both models represent a departure from the "learning as listening" mode of traditional instruction. They motivate students by centering learning on the accomplishment of a meaningful goal. In Problem-Based learning, that goal is solving a problem. In Project-Based Learning, that goal is completion of a project. Figure 11-2 compares these two powerful and popular learning models.

There is some overlap between the two models both in concept and in practice. Teachers who are looking to motivate their students, help them develop 21st century skills (such as critical-thinking and problem-solving skills), and challenge them to learn in real-world

Figure 11-2 Problem-Based Learning versus Project-Based Learning

Problem-Based learning	Project-Based Learning
Problem-Based Learning emphasizes applying existing skills and knowledge.	Project-Based Learning emphasizes developing new skills and knowledge.
Problem-Based Learning's main motivation is solving a problem.	The main motivation for Project-Based Learning is completing a project.
Problem-Based Learning may or may not involve completing a project.	Project-Based Learning may or may not involve solving a problem.
The teacher develops the problem, but students get control over how to solve it.	Students have a great deal of control over developing the project and the process for accomplishing it.
Problem-Based Learning provides opportunities for students to develop problem-solving skills.	Project-Based Learning can provide opportunities for students to develop problem-solving skills but always provides students opportunities to learn to manage the tasks involved in completing a project.
The interdisciplinary nature of problems is stressed.	The project can be interdisciplinary.
Students may work alone or in groups.	Students may work alone or in groups.
Teachers develop the tools used for assessment.	Students have a great deal of control over the development of tools for assessment.
An important by-product is learning to solve problems.	An important by-product is learning to manage complicated tasks and maintain focus.
Students are provided with resources rather than answers.	Students are supported with resources.
Problem-Based Learning is meaningful to the learners.	The project is meaningful to the learners.
Problem-Based Learning can vary in duration depending on the problem.	The project can vary in duration depending on the project.
Problem-Based Learning can be accomplished in groups, cooperative groups, or alone.	The project can be accomplished in groups, cooperative groups, or alone.

contexts may wish to use both of these models in their classrooms at different times. For example, in Scenario 11-3, during one quarter Joanna might use Problem-Based Learning for students to develop a travel guide to San Andrés, Colombia, then during the following one, she might use Project-Based Learning for students to work on a series of activities or projects that further develop students' Spanish language skills and proficiency.

A Project-Based Learning experience might also involve solving a problem, in which case the lesson would involve Problem-Based Learning. WebQuests, introduced in Chapter 10 because of their connection to Inquiry learning, provide an excellent framework for the support of lessons designed with the Problem-Based Learning model. WebQuests (see www .webquest.org/index.php) can and often are designed as Problem-Based Learning lessons that challenge learners to solve a problem.

When Should the Problem-Based Learning Model Be Applied and Why?

Because the Problem-Based Learning model helps motivate students to learn as well as build and apply important 21st century skills, teachers might want to use it often; however, it can be time consuming and impractical for frequent, everyday learning. Therefore, teachers should examine their curricular goals and students' needs to determine when the Problem-Based Learning model might be best applied. The Problem-Based Learning model is most effective for teaching students how to solve authentic problems; developing critical-thinking, cooperative, and social skills; and fostering self-directed learning. The following sections discuss what teachers should use the Problem-Based Learning model to accomplish.

Solve Authentic Problems

Problem solving is an essential 21st century skill, yet it is not a skill that all students learn easily on their own. Many students need to be taught how to solve problems. Problem-Based Learning provides a structured, procedural approach for teaching students how to solve problems. By using Problem-Based Learning, students engage in a process of problem solving that involves identifying or examining the problem, determining a possible solution to the problem, implementing the solution, and evaluating the impact of actions taken. The steps involved in the Problem-Based Learning model require students to analyze the situation and devise potential solutions and then reflect on their plans and/or actions. For example, in Scenario 11-3, students have the challenge of developing travel guides for their teacher's family who will be visiting the remote island of San Andrés, Colombia, for a family wedding. Students need to figure out a plan for the challenge and also conduct research by communicating with a group of students who live in San Andrés. By progressing through all of the phases of the Problem-Based Learning model, students will not only solve the problem but also develop and apply problem-solving skills.

Develop Critical-Thinking, Cooperative, and Social Skills

A benefit of the Problem-Based Learning model is that it helps students develop their critical-thinking, cooperative, and social skills—all of which are necessary for lifelong learning in the 21st century. Problem-Based Learning helps students cultivate these skills because it focuses on solving problems though examination of a problem, development of a strategy to solve the problem, implementation of the proposed strategy, and analysis of the implementation of the strategy through discussion and evaluation of its outcome. This is evident in the opening scenario, where students are tasked with developing a plan for replacing carpet in their school's aftercare room. Such activities force students to think critically about their learning, work collaboratively with other students, and thereby cultivate social skills.

Although the Problem-Based Learning model does not require that students work cooperatively toward solving a problem, most teachers structure Problem-Based Learning lessons so that students can learn from and with one another. Therefore, students who complete Problem-Based Learning lessons typically work together, which requires the development and use of cooperative and social skills. For instance, in Scenario 11-3, high school Spanish students collaborate on travel guides to San Andrés, Colombia. Therefore, they must agree on how to divide up responsibilities, develop a plan for creating the travel guide, and implement that plan. Each of those tasks in the Problem-Based Learning model requires cooperation. In this scenario, students also have to communicate with a buddy class in San Andrés—and in Spanish—so that students also develop cross-cultural communication skills.

Teach Students to Be Self-Directed Learners

What goes on in schools is supposed to prepare students for life outside of them. One important characteristic needed for successful living in the "real world" is the ability to work independently—without the help of one's teachers, other adults, and peers. Working independently requires many competencies, including the ability to (1) define one's tasks, (2) see oneself as capable of working independently, (3) stay on task, (4) be resourceful, (5) advocate for oneself, and (6) self-motivate and regulate one's progress and work. Problem-Based Learning can be an excellent method for providing opportunities for students to learn skills needed for working independently. For example, in Scenario 11-2, students learn how to frame problems and think systematically about ways in which their school might "go green." Because the problem is open ended, students have the freedom to work independently—either as individuals or in small groups—to devise solutions to the challenge.

Connect Curriculum to the Real World

Most of us are more motivated to learn when we see direct connections between the content we are learning *in* classrooms and what happens in the real world *outside* of them. Problem-Based Learning allows students to apply their prior knowledge and experiences to acquiring new knowledge and in a meaningful context. This connection to real-world problems is evident in all of the scenarios presented in this chapter. By employing the Problem-Based Learning model, teachers can make situations outside the classroom both relevant and meaningful to the learning that takes place inside of it.

What Are the Steps in the Problem-Based Learning Model?

The Problem-Based Learning model consists of four major phases or steps: (1) present or identify the problem, (2) develop a plan for solving the problem, (3) implement the plan for solving the problem, and (4) evaluate the implementation plan results. These steps are described below. Figure 11-3 provides a description of the teacher's and students' roles in this model; essentially, the teacher facilitates students' analysis of the content.

Figure 11-3 Teacher and Student Roles in the Problem-Based Learning Model

Problem-Based Learning Model Steps	Teacher Role	Student Role
Present or identify the problem	The teacher presents a "good" problem for students to explore or asks students to identify a problem. In either case, the teacher determines how to divide students into groups. During this phase, the teacher should also provide students with an outline of the tasks they will need to complete and a timeline for completing them.	The students examine the problem the teacher presents. In some cases, the students may identify the problem.
Develop plan for solving problem	The teacher asks students to develop a plan for solving the problem. He or she may need to ask probing questions to help students analyze the problem carefully and devise a plan for solving it. The teacher assigns or asks students to create their own groups to tackle the problem. The teacher will need to scaffold student learning and structure how students develop their plans.	The students develop a reasonable plan for solving the problem. Ideally, this occurs in groups, so students deliberate and determine the plan for tackling the problem.
Implement the plan	The teacher asks students to implement their plan. The teacher may need to provide additional scaffolding, such as helping students document or record the implementation of their plans so they can evaluate them in the subsequent phase.	The students test out or implement their plans. They should document what happens (the outcome) with their plans.
Evaluate the implementation	The teacher asks students to evaluate and reflect on their implementation plans and outcomes. The teacher should also require students to reflect on their individual and group contributions to solving the problem as well as what they might or should have done differently. The teacher can also help students examine the benefits and challenges of different approaches to solving the same problem.	Students evaluate and reflect on the implementation of their plans and their outcomes. They should also reflect on their individual and group contributions to solving the problem. Students should weigh the benefits and challenges of different approaches to solving the same problem.

Even if students have used Problem-Based Learning before, the teacher should fully introduce the model in its entirety and monitor student progress, learning, and interaction over the course of its use. Worksheet 11-1 in Appendix C is an example of a worksheet teachers might want students or groups to maintain as they progress through the Problem-Based Learning lesson. Moreover, teachers should develop some type of checkpoints or benchmarks that describe expectations and ways in which students will be assessed both formatively and summatively. Worksheet 11-2 provides a group processing activity for students to examine how their groups are working in the Problem-Based Learning lesson as well as how their interactions could be improved.

Step One—Present or Identify the Problem

The goal of the first step in the Problem-Based Learning model is for students to learn about and examine the problem. Either the teacher presents the problem or students identify it based on information introduced by the teacher. For instance, in the opening scenario, Genevieve Washington presents the problem to students by describing the principal's challenge for them to determine how much and what kind of carpet to choose to carpet the aftercare room. In Scenario 11-2, although students are presented with the general problem of developing a plan to help the school "go green," students must identify specific problems related to the school not yet using green practices.

Whether a teacher presents the problem or students identify it, teachers employing the Problem-Based Learning model will also need to complete several logistical steps before proceeding to the subsequent phases of the model. These logistical steps include establishing student groups (or deciding that students will work independently for all of the Problem-Based Learning lesson or only parts of it) and providing students with an outline of the various tasks they will need to complete and a timeline for completing them. The teacher should be prepared to ask questions that help students build on their prior knowledge about the topic as they examine the problem. Teachers should also develop activities to scaffold the development of a plan to solve the problem.

Step Two—Develop a Plan for Solving the Problem

In this phase, the students use the information examined in the previous phase or gathered elsewhere to form a plan of action for solving the problem. As students develop this plan, teachers need to scaffold students' progress, review their progress, and monitor their interactions to ensure that the groups work together towards the common goal of developing a plan to solve the problem. How teachers accomplish that is not deliberately defined in the Problem-Based Learning model because it is an open-ended model of teaching. Therefore, teachers should carefully gauge their students' individual needs and their ability to work independently or in small groups towards solving the problem.

Depending on the students, the teacher may need to work very closely with the group to scaffold the Problem-Based Learning lesson. Such is the case with the kindergarten students in Scenario 11-1. The kindergarteners must devise a plan—with support from their teacher—for figuring out how many pizzas to order for a pizza party. Older students might be able to do this independently, but, developmentally, it would likely be very difficult for kindergarteners to solve this kind of problem on their own. Therefore, in this scenario, the teacher works with a small group by walking them through the various steps of the Problem-Based Learning model and helping them develop a plan together. The situation described in Scenario 11-3, however, is quite different. The teacher in that scenario gives her students a lot of leeway for developing their travel guides to San Andrés, Colombia. Nonetheless, in both cases, the development of a plan requires data gathering and deliberation among group members.

Step Three—Implement the Plan for Solving the Problem

During the implementation phase of the Problem-Based Learning model, students test out the plan developed in the previous phase. In some cases, they will actually implement the plan proposed, as in Scenario 11-1, where the plan for ordering pizza for a pizza party is implemented. In other cases, such as in Scenarios 11-2 and 11-3, the actual implementation of the plan may not take place for a while, as it might involve other stakeholders or because the problem is a hypothetical one. For instance, in Scenario 11-2, students work toward the challenge of helping a middle school develop plans for "going green" as part of an Earth Day competition. In Scenario 11-3, students develop travel guides for a trip to San Andrés, Colombia.

The travel guides that contain information on airfares and hotel reservations might be implemented before the end of the school year, but those that provide sightseeing and dining recommendations will not be implemented until the teacher's brother's wedding.

Step Four—Evaluate the Implementation Plan Results

The final phase of the Problem-Based Learning model involves evaluation of the implementation plan developed to solve the problem. Here, students examine the plan they devised and its implementation to determine its effectiveness and/or accuracy. The evaluation should take into account that the nature of the Problem-Based Learning model is for students to examine problems that have multiple possible solutions. Therefore, teachers should allow sufficient time for students to reflect on, discuss, and assess the outcome. For example, in Scenario 11-1, the kindergarten students could reflect on their plans for how many pizzas to order based on their investigations of how many pieces each student in the class might eat and how many pieces of pizza are in a pizza from the restaurant where the pizza was ordered. They could also reflect on the plan, its implementation, and its outcome. Students might find that, even though they planned to order enough pizzas on the actual day of the pizza party, a student was absent, so they ended up with too much. (That, in turn, poses another problem—what to do with the extra pizza or how to divide up the pizza fairly.) Conversely, if more parents than planned came to help, there would be insufficient pizza for everyone.

In this phase, teachers might find their students need scaffolding and questioning to help them evaluate the effectiveness of the solution they developed. Students also may need support in thinking reflectively on their learning, the decisions made, and the plan implemented. For instance, after the pizza party, the teacher in Scenario 11-1 might ask students to share their thoughts about whether they ordered enough pizza. Before even ordering the pizza, the teacher might ask her students to consider what would happen if there is not enough pizza. Students could be asked during the implementation and, afterward, how well the plan they devised worked out. This could be done in an informal manner where the teacher verbally asks them to examine this question, or it could be a formal examination and reflection where they must justify their decisions, plan, and actions individually, in small groups, or even among the whole class.

What Does the Problem-Based Learning Model Look Like in the Classroom?

There are many different ways in which the Problem-Based Learning model might be implemented. The scenarios in this section provide three different ways in which the model might be employed in different grade levels and contexts.

Scenario 11-1

The marble jar for good behavior in Vanessa Wong's kindergarten class was full, so her students were going to be planning a pizza party. Vanessa knew that managing a Problem-Based Learning model lesson as a whole group would be difficult to orchestrate with a class of 24 very enthusiastic kindergarteners. However, she knew they would be motivated and could work hard to devise a reasonable plan for ordering pizza with her help. She would be estimating the number of pizzas to buy any-way—why not involve students in this real-world problem? Plus, it coincided with the year's goal to teach them problem solving in mathematics. Therefore, Vanessa divided the students into small, heterogeneous groups that would rotate through the different centers that week. One center would be the pizza party center in which students would work with her to plan how many pizzas to order. As one small group of students rotated through the pizza party center, the other students would work in other centers.

When Vanessa's first group arrived, she asked them if they liked to eat pizza, how many slices they usually ate and what kinds, and if they had ever had pizza at a party (e.g., birthday party). All of the students responded affirmatively, so she then introduced the "problem" (i.e., they are having a pizza party

Kindergarteners Eating Pizza
© Stockbroker/SuperStock

and need to order enough pizza for everyone). The kindergarteners were tasked with figuring out how many pizzas they would have to order for their class party later that month. To help them devise their plan for how many pizzas to order, Vanessa shared that the pizzas they would order had eight slices each. She asked them to use the pizza fraction manipulatives (fake pizza slices) to determine how many pizzas to order. She also encouraged them to discuss and draw out how they could solve this real-world problem. After discussion, Group #1 still needed more scaffolding, so Vanessa gave each of its members a checklist to help them come up with a plan. The checklist included a class list so they could query each member of the class about how many slices of pizza they usually eat—and also which kind (e.g., pepperoni, plain cheese, and so on). Group #2 decided to limit the pizza options (i.e., students had to choose from two different op-tions: cheese pizza or pepperoni pizza) since ordering several different kinds of pizzas would likely lead to waste of pizza.

In Group #3, the students were too overwhelmed figuring out how many pizzas were needed for the whole class, so Vanessa asked them to focus only on the four students in their own group. In this way, she scaled down the problem to enable this group to help solve it. She also asked students in the third group to draw or use the math fraction ma-nipulatives to determine how many slices of pizza the four of them would eat. Then she prompted them to decide how many pizzas total would be needed. The students deliber-ated among themselves about how to figure this out. One student suggested keeping a tally sheet of the different kinds of pizzas each student liked. Another drew each person and the number of slices estimated that the four of them would like to eat. Vanessa did not try to redirect their efforts; she let the team members deliberate on their own. She did, however, ask them questions like "How can we figure out how many pizzas to order? What kind of information should we ask your classmates to figure this out?"

The next step involved implementing the strategy based on the plans already devised. This would entail estimating the number of pieces of pizza and then calculating the total number of pizzas to order. Only one plan could be implemented (how many pizzas to order), so the students voted on the plan to employ. Then Vanessa implemented the plan by ordering the pizzas for the party. The party was a success. There was enough pizza for all of the students. After the party, students reviewed the results of their plans.

Scenario 11-2

Nada Kumar, principal of Rachel Carson Middle School, knew the school could do a better job with recycling and conserving energy—with "going green." The school's efforts to recycle paper were not enough. The school had to do more, so, at the next school wide assembly, she announced the "going green" Problem-Based Learning challenge. Teams of students from each grade level would compete as they worked together to figure out ways the school could "go green." She had already asked several people from the community to judge the competition. Winners would be announced on Earth Day.

Before introducing the Problem-Based Learning competition to the students at the assembly, Nada had already discussed the competition at several faculty meetings. During these meetings, it was decided students would have two weeks to work on the Problem-Based Learning challenge in their science courses. Students would develop plans for solving the "going green" challenge. For each step of the Problem-Based Learning challenge, students would get feedback from their teachers. They would test their ideas and evaluate their plans. Then a panel would announce one winner of the Problem-Based Learning competition for each grade level. Finally, Nada would determine which of the winners' ideas could realistically be implemented in the school.

Nada stopped into one sixth-grade science class and was impressed with what she saw. Students were conducting research online in small groups of four. The teacher shared that part of her students' plan for solving this problem was to do research. To start, students were researching ways other schools were "going green." Groups were also contacting the local power company to come to the school to conduct an energy audit and a solar energy expert who was also one of the student's parents for an interview. Nada was very excited about the efforts of this one class and was excited to see how students in other classes and grade levels were approaching the challenge.

Scenario 11-3

For weeks, Joanna Middleton's eleventh-grade Spanish III class had been conferencing, e-mailing, and even texting with a group of students in San Andrés, Colombia. The wonderful cultural exchange had all started with her brother's girlfriend (and now fiancée), Lucero, an English teacher at the local high school. Lucero thought it would be a great idea for her students to communicate with Joanna's students to practice English and learn about what it is like to be a teen in the United States. In turn, Joanna's students would practice speaking Spanish and learn about teens' lives on the small Colombian island.

When Joanna learned that her brother, a visiting professor at the National University of Colombia at San Andrés, had proposed to Lucero and was going to be married in San Andrés the following summer, she knew she could turn this exciting turn of events into a fun and real challenge for her students. This Problem-Based Learning unit would help her students develop not only their Spanish communication skills but also their technology, interpersonal, and problem-solving skills—all essential 21st century skills. After conferencing with Lucero about what might be helpful to her, Joanna announced the "problem" to the class. She wanted her students to develop travel guides for family and friends traveling to San Andrés from the United States. The students would get help from their friends in San Andrés who could be their on-the-ground cultural guides and provide first hand research and recommendations.

Joanna let her students group themselves by interest, but she limited the number of students in each group to a maximum of five. One group would research airfares and flight routes from major U.S. cities. Those students needed to determine the best bargains and routes for getting to San Andrés, which is in a remote location. Getting there would take some planning. Another group would explore places to stay in San Andrés and research packages for wedding guests. A third group decided to develop a things-to-do guide. Their guide would include what to do about tips, sightseeing, activities not to be missed, and some interesting history and facts about San Andrés. The fourth group decided to create a guide on local food and restaurants.

The next step was for each group to figure out a strategy for solving its challenge. Each would be responsible for developing a plan that would explain its objectives, procedures for addressing the objectives, and the deliverable their group would be responsible for creating. As a class, the students brainstormed how long this project would take and how they would be evaluated. Before beginning work on their deliverables, Joanna would need to approve their plan for finding and synthesizing their information. Once a group's plan was approved, the members would implement their strategy and develop their deliverable. When that was completed, they would evaluate the results and ultimately get feedback from Joanna's family and friends who used the students' San Andrés travel guides.

What Do These Scenarios Illustrate?

These scenarios share three different ways in which the Problem-Based Learning model might be implemented with students from different grade levels and using different real-world problems. Although the problems the students tackle are unique, they show how the different steps of the Problem-Based Learning model might be implemented in a variety of ways. These scenarios also demonstrate the roles of both students and teachers as they work through the Problem-Based Learning model lesson.

REFLECT: Consider how the different phases of the Problem-Based Learning model were implemented in these three scenarios. How might you incorporate some of these approaches in your current or future classroom? What scaffolding and support would you have to provide your students?

Planning for Teaching with the Problem-Based Learning Model

As with any other model of teaching, effective planning for teaching a Problem-Based Learning lesson involves preparation—no matter how open ended the problem. First and foremost, teachers need to identify a "good" problem (or help students discover one). Then they should determine how students will be grouped, how much time students will have to work on the Problem-Based Learning lesson, how they will scaffold student learning, and how they will monitor and assess group and individual progress, interactions, and learning. The following sections discuss what educational designers do when teaching with the Problem-Based Learning model.

Identify a "Good" Problem

One of the first steps in planning to teach Problem-Based Learning involves identifying a "good" problem. Problems are chosen or developed by the teacher to correspond with learning goals that he or she identifies for his or her students and with required curriculum. According to Schmidt, Rotgans, and Yew (2011), good problems to select as the basis of a Problem-Based Learning lesson are those that are

- ill-defined—the problem has multiple solutions or ways to solve it (there is no single, obvious answer or solution);
- authentic—the problem might be encountered in real life, such as figuring out how to carpet a room on a budget or how many pizzas to order for a class party; and
- engaging and interesting—the problem is engaging and interesting, involves students in the learning process, and motivates them to want to learn more, such as creating travel guides for a target location and audience.

The problems in all of the scenarios included in this chapter incorporate these characteristics.

Determine Grouping of Students

It is possible yet unusual for students to work independently while working through a Problem-Based Learning model lesson. Usually, it is not recommended because a rationale for using this model is that students learn from and with one another by sharing and exchanging ideas. Therefore, teachers should determine how they want to divide students into groups (e.g., heterogeneous or homogeneous groups, teacher or student selected, and so on) and the size of the groups themselves. For instance, in Scenario 11-1, the teacher has students work with her in small groups to determine how many pizzas to order for the pizza party; the teacher in Scenario 11-3, however, allows students to self-select their groups based on their interests.

Figure Out Time Allocation

Use of the Problem-Based Learning model often takes time not only for students to learn about the problem but also , more important, for them to conduct research to develop a plan, implement the plan, and finally evaluate it. Therefore, students must have sufficient time to think, exchange ideas, critique ideas, develop a solution to a problem, and evaluate its success. The teacher will need to allot an adequate amount of time for completing all of the phases of the model no matter how short or long the Problem-Based Learning lesson. It is also critical that students know this time frame at the beginning of the lesson so that they can allocate their time accordingly.

Problem-Based Learning lessons might take one class period or several days, as in Scenario 11-2, in which students will have as much as two weeks to develop their plans for "going green." How much time a teacher allocates to the integration of the Problem-Based Learning model depends on the teacher's goals and students' needs, abilities, and interests. Regardless, some flexibility will be important.

Develop Activities to Scaffold Learning

Scaffolding of student learning and analysis while working through a Problem-Based Learning lesson is vital to its success. Teachers should craft questions to foster student thinking while working through the various stages of the Problem-Based Learning model, and they should also create activities that will help students complete the phases and document their progress towards the goal of solving or addressing the problem. Activities should incorporate checkpoints for groups to share about their progress and report on how their groups are working together.

For instance, in Scenario 11-1, the teacher works with a small group of kindergarten students to help them figure out how many pizzas to order for a pizza party. Clearly, many kindergarteners would have difficulty deliberating this problem on their own, but with small-group discussion and support, the teacher helps each group determine how many pizzas to order. She scaffolds the problem by breaking it into smaller, more manageable parts for each group to tackle. Teachers might also wish to develop planning or problem-solving and reflection worksheets, such as those available in Worksheets 11-1 and 11-2.

Monitor and Assess Group and Individual Progress, Interactions, and Learning

When planning to teach a Problem-Based Learning lesson, teachers should develop strategies for monitoring and assessing group and individual student progress, interactions, and learning. As noted previously, one reason for using the Problem-Based Learning model is to teach students how to solve problems and to provide them practice doing so. Teachers should not take for granted that all students know how to solve problems, even if they have completed a Problem-Based Learning lesson previously. Therefore, to support students throughout this engaging yet open-ended learning process, teachers should either provide students with formative and summative assignments and due dates for completion or work with students in developing them. In Scenario 11-3 when Joanna presents the problem to her class about the need to develop travel guides, she could also share how much time (e.g., exact number of class periods and days) they will have to work on the Problem-Based Learning lesson as well as the expectations for the finished travel guides. She might also develop several formative assignments for the groups to complete and review with her as they progress. She could also meet with them periodically to review these assignments as well as to provide feedback and guidance and determine how they are getting along, including how roles are shared.

Differentiating Instruction with the Problem-Based Learning Model

The Problem-Based Learning model is thoroughly suited for differentiation. Problem-Based Learning can be very open ended, structured in different ways for different students, and incorporate more or less teacher scaffolding and assistance. How teachers differentiate the content, process, and/or product(s) of a Problem-Based Learning lesson will depend a great deal on their curricular goals and objectives; their students' needs, abilities, and interests; and the resources and time available for implementing a Problem-Based Learning lesson.

Content

Differentiation of the content in the Problem-Based Learning model can be achieved in three major ways. First, students could have different problems to address. In Scenario 11-3, students try to solve different problems (i.e., develop different travel guides), meaning that the content will vary from group to group. Second, the content students examine can be different. Third, the extent to which they examine this content can be different. This is particularly true for problems with multiple solutions. In Scenario 11-2, the content that students will investigate on "going green" depends entirely on what each group decides to explore. One group of students might want to interview a solar energy expert as well as to ask the local power company to conduct an energy audit, whereas another group might decide to research possibilities to "go green" on the Internet. The content students examine clearly varies between these examples although students have the same problem. Furthermore, each group will delve into the content at different depths. This is one of the advantages of Problem-Based Learning—it shows students that real problems do not require the same routes of discovery and learning.

Students might also access content in a variety of ways, and how they do so will be determined largely by the plan they aim to devise and the time and resources they will have to complete the Problem-Based Learning lesson. Students can work in groups or pairs to research information on the Internet (e.g., Scenario 11-3), examine the physical layout of a room to take measurements (e.g., opening scenario), work in a small group directly with the teacher (Scenario 11-1), and more.

Process

Teachers can differentiate the process of a Problem-Based Learning lesson by varying the makeup of groups in which students work to progress through the different phases of the lesson. One method is having students start out working individually for the first phase of the Problem-Based Learning model and then switch to working in small groups for the second, third, and fourth phases.

Scaffolding of students' individual and group progress and learning is an important aspect of differentiating the process. Teachers should develop supports for monitoring two aspects of students' work: what students do and how they do it. That is, teachers need to determine if students actually developed a plan to solve a problem and if they implemented it. Additionally, teachers need to gauge how well the students' groups got along and worked toward the problem they need to address. Some groups will be able to work independently in one or both areas, and others might need extra support. How teachers approach scaffolding in the Problem-Based Learning model will depend on their students, the problem itself, and the time allowed for solving the problem.

Teachers need to gauge how students are doing as they develop and implement their solutions because they may need to intervene at some point during the lesson. There are three main reasons a teacher may need to intervene. First, the teacher may need to direct students to appropriate resources and facilitate decision making. Second, the teacher may need to guide students in developing realistic plans for solving the problem. The final reason for intervention is to manage group dynamics. The teacher may need to support groups whose members do not get along; have difficulty contributing, listening to their peers, or delegating work; or are absent.

Product

The focus of Problem-Based Learning is on problems with varied and multiple outcomes, so the products of Problem-Based Learning lessons are naturally differentiated. For instance, it is feasible that in Scenario 11-1, which describes kindergarteners working with the teacher to determine how many pizzas to order, different groups will likely devise different procedures for figuring this out. Similarly, in the opening scenario, different groups might choose different types of carpet, get pricing from different carpet manufacturers and vendors, and establish varying priorities for their decisions.

The products or deliverables students create in these scenarios will probably vary in their substance and form, too. For instance, although Scenario 11-3 does not elaborate on the format of the travel guides the four groups will develop, the groups could create different travel guide products, such as a multimedia presentation, a website, a podcast, a wiki, a brochure, or even a short video.

What Are the Benefits of Applying the Problem-Based Learning Model?

Teaching with the Problem-Based Learning model fosters critical-thinking, problem-solving, and metacognitive skills. It also fosters student understanding of the complexity of real problems, promotes long-term retention, motivates students to learn, and activates prior knowledge. The following sections discuss what the Problem-Based Learning model does.

Promotes 21st Century Skills

Learning in the 21st century is characterized by using information and thinking to solve problems. In the Problem-Based Learning model, students do both, resulting in their development of 21st century skills. Problem-Based Learning requires students to learn how to focus on a problem and devise a plan to solve it. Critical thinking is developed as learners work to create, implement, and analyze the success of their efforts. Students analyze as they work to frame a problem, reason as they develop a problem-solving plan, self-monitor as they execute their plan, and evaluate their implementation. These critical-thinking skills are quite evident in all of the chapter scenarios as students address meaningful problems. The model also fosters metacognition a skill that enables self-awareness and future learning. In the final phase of the model, students must evaluate their plans for solving the problem. They must reflect on, examine, and evaluate their plans, actions, and justifications. By reflecting on their plans, students are also forced to examine their learning, their progress, and their contributions.

Fosters Student Understanding of the Complexity of Real-World Problems

As most of us know, successful living requires the ability to deal with complicated problems. Real-world problems are complex, multifaceted, and confusing. Many of the problems students are asked to solve at school fail to resemble these real-world problems. As explained in previous sections, the Problem-Based Learning model focuses on solving problems that are ill defined, authentic, and engaging—much like those encountered in life outside of school. Hence, the problems presented in the Problem-Based Learning model expose students to the complexity of real-world problems. Often, Problem-Based Learning experience even allows students to analyze and grapple with the same problems they might really encounter and to develop solutions to these problems that might also really be implemented.

Promotes Long-Term Retention

The Problem-Based Learning model has been shown to promote long-term retention of students' comprehension, understanding, and application of concepts (Wirkala & Kuhn, 2011). This is most likely due to the fact that the model focuses on actual problems, and that focus makes the issue real, contextual, and meaningful for students. The problem provides a context for student learning, and that context supports the understanding of the content and the formulation of a solution. The context also provides support for building on prior knowledge, making connections to other content knowledge, and seeing relationships between content. All of the scenarios in this chapter illustrate the power of context.

Motivates Students to Learn

The performance of many learners would improve if educational experiences were more motivational for them. The Problem-Based Learning model helps with student motivation in several ways. First, designing learning experiences around solving a problem is mentally stimulating. The challenge of solving a problem often ignites students' curiosity. Second, the problem itself can act as a "hook." Because of the real-world nature of the problem, students often see a relevance in a Problem-Based Learning experience because it has practical applications to life that are often missing in a textbook problem.

Activates Prior Knowledge

During the first phase of the Problem-Based Learning model in particular, students must activate (Wirkala & Kuhn, 2011) their prior knowledge and experience to help them determine how they will solve the problem at hand. In some instances, students will have had some experience with the problem, as in Scenario 11-1—it is highly likely that at least some of the students have been to parties where someone ordered pizza. If not, it is even more likely that students will have experienced their parents ordering pizza for the family dinner or when friends come over. In other instances, however, the activation of prior knowledge might require making connections to other content or experiences that are indirectly related. For example, in the opening scenario, students probably have not had to figure out how to recarpet an aftercare room before, but it is highly likely they have explored how to find area.

What Value Does Technology Add to the Problem-Based Learning Model?

Technology can play an integral role in the planning, implementation, and assessment of lessons that incorporate Problem-Based Learning. Numerous technology tools can help teachers plan to use and assess student learning in the Problem-Based Learning model as well as assist teachers in implementing the model. Technology tools can also be helpful to students as they work through the model's phases. There are so many useful technology tools and applications that we can describe only a few in this chapter. Figure 11-4 provides a list of the tools introduced in this section.

Planning

RESEARCH POTENTIAL PROBLEMS AND RESOURCES. To generate ideas for potential problems that focus learning in Problem-Based Learning, teachers could conduct research using search engines or directories such as Google. Web searches also help uncover information related to the problem, which helps teachers better assist students in developing their plans for solving the problem. In Scenario 11-3, the teacher might research information about the travel destination to discover ways to frame the problem

Figure 11-4 Technology Tools for the Problem-Based Learning Model

Use	Tools
Planning	
	Search engines • Dogpile: www.dogpile.com • Google: www.google.com • Yahoo!: www.yahoo.com
Implementing	
	Audio recording • Digital audio recorder, tape recorder Blogs • Blogger: www.blogger.com • Wordpress: http://wordpress.com Data analysis • InspireData: www.inspiration.com/InspireData • Microsoft Office (Access, Excel): http://office.microsoft.com/en-us/word • OpenOffice: www.openoffice.org Digital video • Digital video recorder or camera on computer Graphic organizers or tools • Bubbl: https://bubbl.us • Gliffy: www.gliffy.com • Inspiration: www.inspiration.com • Kidspiration: www.inspiration.com/Kidspiration • Popplet: http://popplet.com Web development: • Google sites: https://accounts.google.com • Posterous Spaces: https://posterous.com • Weebly: www.weebly.com Word-processing tools: • Microsoft Office (Word): http://office.microsoft.com/en-us/word • OpenOffice: www.openoffice.org
Assessing	
	Forms • Adobe Acrobat: www.adobe.com/products/acrobat.html • Google docs: www.google.com/google-d-s/documents Presentation tools • Keynote: www.apple.com/iwork/keynote • Microsoft Office (PowerPoint): http://office.microsoft.com/en-us/powerpoint • OpenOffice: www.openoffice.org • Prezi: http://prezi.com • Zoho Creator: www.zoho.com Student response tools • Turningpoint "clickers": www.turningpoint.com Other tools • Glogster: www.glogster.com • VoiceThread: http://voicethread.com

for students. Alternatively, the teacher might use a search engine to review some travel sites in advance. That way, if students struggle to find such information, the teacher will have a list of good sites at the ready. By researching in advance, the teacher is also able to ensure accuracy of content and identify ways he or she might need to frame the students' research for better results.

Using the Internet to prepare for Problem-Based Learning can yield a richer set of resources for the lesson. For example, teachers might find experts or video resources for students to examine as they work to solve the problem. In addition to using the Internet to locate resources for use during the lesson, teachers might also find interesting Problem-Based Learning lesson plans online that they may wish to implement or modify.

CREATE MATERIALS TO SCAFFOLD LEARNING. Before they can scaffold student learning in the Problem-Based Learning model, teachers must think thoughtfully and carefully about how they will support students in the four major phases of the model. Such thinking can be facilitated using various technology tools. Teachers can use word-processing and concept-mapping tools to develop materials for questioning and supporting students as they work through the different phases of the Problem-Based Learning model. The teachers in any of the scenarios presented in this chapter might create a flowchart that shows the major steps of the model (see Figure 11-5) to share with their students. After reviewing the chart, students could create a concept map that describes briefly what they did for each step in the process. Alternatively, the teacher could share such a flowchart that includes the expected steps and a timeline for completing them.

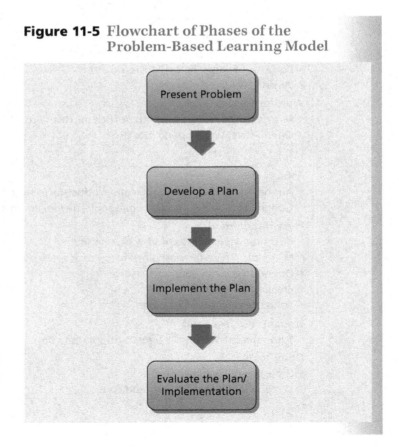

Figure 11-5 Flowchart of Phases of the Problem-Based Learning Model

Implementation

ORGANIZE, DOCUMENT, AND SHARE RESOURCES. There are many different tools teachers might ask students to use to organize, document, and share resources related to developing a plan to solve the problem of the Problem-Based Learning lesson. For instance, teachers could require students to use a blog, database, spreadsheet, word-processing software, website, or wiki. For instance, the teacher in Scenario 11-2 could ask students to develop a wiki that organizes, documents, and provides a mechanism for students to share their research with other students. Regardless of the tool(s), teachers should carefully select technology to ensure that it is compatible with current software and hardware used by students. It is also important to make certain that it will support the implementation plan.

ANALYZE DATA. Analyzing data is not an explicit phase or aspect of the Problem-Based Learning model because not all problems require data analysis for their solution. Most problems do, however, require some data gathering and/or analysis, and in those cases students will benefit from using technology to conduct the analysis. For instance, in Scenario 11-3, the high school student group working on airfares to and from San Andrés and U.S. locations could use spreadsheet tools to analyze and compare airfares for different routes and airlines and a database program to track departure cities and the best routes from those cities to San Andrés. The group researching places to stay and vacation packages could also use a spreadsheet or database program to keep track of the hotels and resorts they find, including their prices and amenities. Another group might use an online translator to conduct an initial review of their grammar and syntax in Spanish before sharing their guide with their native peers in San Andrés.

Assessment

CONDUCT FORMATIVE AND SUMMATIVE ASSESSMENT. Providing both formative and summative feedback is important to the success of the Problem-Based Learning model. Teachers might use blogs for students to document and share their learning-in-progress and as a reflection tool. As always, survey tools are useful for formative assessment. In the Problem-Based Learning model, teachers could use them to create forms on which students indicate how things are working in their groups, their success with various tasks, or other items important to the Problem-Based Learning lesson. Students can use technology tools to create a podcast or other type of text-based or video summary of the project that the teacher could use as a summative assessment.

DOCUMENT STUDENTS' UNDERSTANDINGS USING DIGITAL AUDIO AND VIDEO RECORDERS: Digital audio and video recorders can be used for capturing students' understandings during any phase of the Problem-Based Learning model. In fact, many teachers might want students to record their learning during each stage. They can use audio and video or even word-processing tools to document their learning, explanations (rationales), and plans. For example, teachers might ask students in Scenario 11-2 to create a short video "pitch" describing their ideas for their school to "go green."

PROVIDE INDIVIDUAL, PEER, AND GROUP EVALUATION. There are many different tools teachers can use for providing students the opportunity to conduct individual, peer, and group evaluations. For example, teachers could use Google docs (or online survey tools) to create a form rubric on which students enter their feedback. Again, students could record feedback in audio, video, or word-processed format. Audience response systems (i.e., clickers) allow students to vote anonymously on the best plans implemented to solve the problems.

Problem-Based Learning Model Lesson Plan Example

LESSON SAMPLE

The lesson plan that follows is an example of the Problem-Based Learning model. Figure 11-6 provides an outline of the lesson's different steps.

LESSON CONTEXT

GRADE LEVEL(S): Sixth

CONTENT AREA: Math

PHYSICAL TEACHING ENVIRONMENT: This lesson will be taught in a regular classroom.

APPLICATION OF REVISED BLOOM'S TAXONOMY: Students move from the lower levels of the revised Bloom's taxonomy (i.e., *remembering* the formula for area) to the higher levels (i.e., *analyzing* the problem in the lesson or *evaluating* when they are asked to consider the quality of their problem-solving plan and its implementation).

Figure 11-6 Outline of the Problem-Based Learning Model Lesson Steps

Problem-Based Learning Model Steps	Problem-Based Learning Model Lesson
Present or Identify the Problem	The teacher presents the problem—the need to replace the carpet in the aftercare room.
Develop Plan for Solving Problem	The teacher randomly assigns students to groups. She tasks them with developing a plan to solve the "problem."
Implement the Plan	The groups present their plans to the school principal, treasurer, teacher, and class. They vote on the "best plan" to implement and then implement it, if possible.
Evaluate the Implementation	The teacher asks students to evaluate each group's plans in addition to their cooperative and individual contributions.

Lesson Plan

GOAL(S): Students will be able to calculate the area of a rectangular space and use this information to solve the problem of carpeting a space.

Standard(s) Addressed:

Common Core Math Standard(s) Addressed—Sixth-Grade:[1] Solve real-world and mathematical problems involving area, surface area, and volume.

---

[1] © Copyright 2010. National Governors Association Center for Best Practices and Council of Chief State School Officers. All rights reserved.

OBJECTIVES: During the course of the lesson, students will do the following:

1. Identify the "problem" in a real-world situation involving area.
2. Successfully implement a plan for solving area problems independently.
3. Use data to make decisions to solve real-world problems.

ESTIMATED TIME: Three 50-minute periods

MATERIALS NEEDED:
- Tape measures
- Pencil/paper
- Calculator
- Spreadsheet program
- Graph paper

PREREQUISITE SKILLS: Students must understand the concept of area, how to measure area to the nearest foot, and how to calculate the area of real objects. They must also be able to frame story problems and develop plans for solving them.

LESSON PROCEDURES (Text in italics is suggested teacher dialogue.)
Anticipatory Set (Introduction): [4 minutes]

Motivation: Explain the "problem" (i.e., the school wants to order new carpet for a room and has a budget to work with). Explain further that knowledge of area can be applied to solve the problem of how much carpet is needed and then used to make a decision about the "best" carpet for the targeted room.

Information: Inform students that for three class periods they will work to solve a real-world problem related to area by applying the Problem-Based Learning model of teaching. The four major steps of the model will help them create and implement a plan to solve the problem and also help them practice problem solving.

Connection: Teacher states, *We have been learning to calculate area using two-dimensional shapes in our math unit. Now we are going to apply what we've learned to a real-world situation. We are going to calculate the area of a room and then make a decision about how much carpet we need to cover its floor. To develop a plan, we will use the Problem-Based Learning model in four major steps. It will take at least three class periods.*

1. **Step 1: Identify the problem**—In this step, the teacher shares the challenge: the need to figure out how much and what type of carpet to buy to recarpet the aftercare room. The teacher explains that students will have three class periods to develop a plan for replacing the carpet. Their plans will then be judged by the principal and treasurer of the school. Students will also have the opportunity to vote on the plan they believe should be implemented.
2. **Step 2: Develop a plan for solving the problem**—The teacher randomly assigns students to different groups to develop a plan. The teacher then assigns roles to each group member: for example, in a group of five, there is a data gatherer, a synthesizer, a leader, an encourager, and a reporter. The teacher provides a timeline for completing the major task of developing a plan for recarpeting the room and smaller assignments that will help them reach that deadline. The teacher also outlines a series of smaller tasks and responsibilities to be divided by the different group members. The groups take turns

going to the aftercare room to measure it, while the rest of the groups remain in their class to figure out what information is needed, where to find it, and what to do with it once they get it. Each group develops a plan for solving the problem. The teacher meets with each group individually to discuss their plans, which they record in a word-processing or presentation program. The teacher lets students know if their plans require revision and, if so, what revisions are needed and why. Students research different kinds of carpets, find prices, debate the merits of different materials and colors, and so on. Each group shares its plan for replacing the carpet in the aftercare room.

3. **Step 3: Implement the plan**—Since it is not feasible for every group's plan to be implemented, the principal, treasurer, teacher, and students all vote on the best plan to implement to replace the carpet in the aftercare room. The groups present their plans to the class, principal, and treasurer for the school. After all of the votes are in, the teacher announces the group whose plan will be used to replace the carpet in the aftercare room.

4. **Step 4: Evaluate the plan**—For this stage, the teacher asks students to evaluate their contributions, effectiveness of the plans, and group work. Although only one plan can be implemented, students also have the opportunity to evaluate all of the plans and to give and receive feedback. The teacher also asks students to reflect on their contributions as individuals and as a group to solving the problem: what worked well and what could be improved.

Closure: [2 minutes]

Now that we have calculated the area of the room in question, we can make a final decision about the carpet that will be best to use to cover the floor in this space. Please vote on the best plan—then we will invite the principal back to the classroom to share the best plan as well as all the great things you learned in the process.

ASSESSMENT

Formative assessment One method of formative assessment in this lesson would be to ask students to submit their problem-solving plans for review. By collecting these materials and then reviewing them, the teacher would have an opportunity to intervene and provide supportive feedback, if necessary, before students proceed with implementing their problem-solving plan. If no intervention is needed, students would then be able to receive encouragement and the teacher's endorsement to proceed with their plan.

Summative assessment Because there are several learning goals for this lesson, there would need to be measures for each goal included in the lesson assessment. To assess students' ability to solve the real-world area problem, the teacher would want to measure students' ability to identify the problem, develop a plan for solving it, and implement the plan effectively. As such, the teacher will want to collect and assess information submitted with students' plans and also their final solutions for the problem.

LESSON EXTENSIONS

Once students learn how to calculate the area of a room, they might be challenged to work on a room with more complicated area measurements. Later on, students might be asked to calculate the area of rooms that have highly irregular shapes as well as other areas, such as the surface area of a large body of water, a city block, and so on. Students might be further challenged by being given more difficult scenarios to apply problem-solving skills too. For example, students might be given a smaller or larger budget to work with when making decisions about carpet choices.

Differentiation Strategies for the Problem-Based Learning Model Lesson

The following sections have suggestions that could be applied to differentiate instruction in the Problem-Based Learning Model Lesson.

Content

One method of differentiating in this lesson will be to use media tools to communicate the problem that must be solved. Using a tool like a digital whiteboard will support communication of the problem in a visual format. Interior design software could help students visualize the room and its dimensions and show how different pieces and cuttings of carpet would fit in the room. When the teacher presents the challenge of calculating the area of the room in question and demonstrating how carpets come in specific widths and variable lengths, it will be helpful to use visual materials to illustrate this problem more clearly.

Another method of differentiating this lesson would be to challenge some learners to work with area at varying levels of difficulty. Some students could calculate area to the nearest foot and others to the nearest inch. These differences will involve more difficult computation and problem solving. Moreover, some learners could be challenged to use only carpet remnants. Remnants require greater problem-solving skills because they vary in size and shape more so than new carpet.

Process

One way to differentiate the learning process in this lesson would be to give students different tools to work with while calculating area. Depending on their readiness, some students might use calculators or spreadsheets, and others might still compute by hand. Another way to differentiate the learning process would be to provide different levels of support for students as they work through the various steps of the lesson. Whereas some students might need to confer with the teacher in greater depth, others will be able to work independently. Access to materials that provide scaffolding during the problem identification, planning, implementation, and evaluation steps might also be differentiated. For example, struggling students might be given the option of using a worksheet that walks them through the process of calculating area in a step-by-step manner.

Product

Differentiating the learning product in this lesson might be done by giving students a choice for how they will develop and present their plans. Completion of a worksheet might make sense for some learners who need structure. Open-ended methods like using a concept-mapping tool to display problem-solving steps could be a good option for other learners. Students might also be encouraged to choose their own best method for displaying the decision they made with regard to their plans.

Chapter Summary

This chapter introduced the Problem-Based Learning model, a problem-solving model that allows students to learn and hone problem-solving skills, develop competence with academic content standards, and realize the relevance of applying content area learning for practical purposes. It consists of four major steps, or phases: (1) presenting the problem, (2) developing a plan for solving the problem, (3) implementing the plan, and (4) evaluating the implementation of the plan. The model originated in medical education and has grown in popularity because of its effectiveness in teaching skills required for life and learning in the 21st century. Problem-Based Learning works best when the problems upon which learning focuses are ill defined, authentic, and engaging. The benefits of this model include that it promotes 21st skills, fosters understanding the complexity of real-world problems, fosters long-term retention, motivates students to learn, and activates students' prior knowledge.

Review Questions

1. What is the history of the Problem-Based Learning model?

2. What are the steps in the Problem-Based Learning model?

3. What type of content is best to teach when applying the Problem-Based Learning model? Provide and explain examples of content that would be appropriate and inappropriate.

4. What are the benefits of applying the Problem-Based Learning model? What are some of its challenges?

5. How can the Problem-Based Learning model be used to differentiate instruction and support diverse learners' needs?

6. How can technology be used to implement the Problem-Based Learning model?

Application Exercises

To promote your ability to apply the learning you gained in studying this chapter, complete the following exercises that challenge you to analyze a lesson plan you have written using the Problem-Based Learning model *or* using the lesson plan example included in this chapter.

TECHNOLOGY INTEGRATION ACTIVITY

1. Consider the following questions and discuss with a partner or reflect independently:
   a) In the lesson plan you are analyzing, how does (or could) the integration of technology tools make learning more efficient, effective, and engaging? Can you explain and indicate how you will measure the impact on student learning?
   b) Will all learners be aided through the integration of technology? Are there some who might need special support to gain full benefit from technology tools? How might you support this? Is there a way to build on strengths students bring to this lesson related to technology? How?
   c) What plans could you put in place to promote a more successful use of technology and minimize (or eliminate) risk of failure? What proactive plan could a teacher put in place ahead of lesson implementation to ensure that technology works smoothly and for all learners? What reactive approach could you take to ensure that desired learning still occurs if technology malfunctions during the lesson?

TEACHER PERFORMANCE ACTIVITIES

2. **Academic Vocabulary and Language Demands:** Academic vocabulary is the vocabulary that students must be able to understand to be successful performing content area learning. Language demands involve the ways language is used in speaking, writing, listening, and reading

in the learning tasks of a lesson and in the expressions of student learning. For the lesson plan you are working with (your own or the one provided in the chapter), consider the following questions and discuss them with a partner or reflect on them alone:

a) What academic vocabulary and language demands exist in the Problem-Based Learning model lesson? Make a list of the academic vocabulary students must comprehend and language demands of the model or learning experiences in the lesson plan.

b) How would you determine whether and which students have mastery of academic language before the lesson begins?

c) How might students be supported in developing proficiency with academic language in this lesson context?

3. **Planning:** In the context of the lesson plan that you are analyzing, discuss the following with a partner or reflect independently:

a) Explain how the steps of the Problem-Based Learning model build on each other to lead students to make clear and meaningful connections among identified learning goals or objectives and identify possible solutions to the problem presented in the lesson.

b) Consider how you have addressed or how you might address a variety of learning needs and approaches to addressing or solving the problem identified in the lesson.

c) What research or theory supports the use of this model for instruction in your learning context?

4. **Implementation:** In the context of the lesson plan that you are analyzing, discuss the following with a partner or consider independently:

a) Explain how the steps of the Problem-Based Learning model and the activities that students will perform in the lesson you are reviewing will result in engaged learning and hypothesis generation.

b) What indicators would you look for during the implementation of your lesson to measure who is engaged and how much?

c) How well does your lesson challenge learners to apply their learning in other related and meaningful contexts? Explain.

5. **Assessment:** Consider the following questions and discuss with a partner or reflect independently:

a) Does the plan you are reviewing make use of information gained through pre-assessment to inform the design of the lesson? Would consideration of students' backgrounds, prior learning, and experiences—as they relate to learning goals/objectives—help you design a more effective lesson? How?

b) How does or could the lesson plan you are reviewing use formative assessment to direct the more successful implementation of instruction and scaffold student learning in terms of the problem? Is there a way to make formative assessment more intentional or improve it to address students' strengths, learning needs, or problem-solving skills?

c) How does the plan you are reviewing support students' expression of learning, especially their problem-solving abilities? Are there multiple forms of evidence of student learning? How might students learn through an analysis of their performance throughout the various steps of the Problem-Based Learning model?

6. **Analyzing Teaching:** Consider the following questions and discuss with a partner or reflect independently:

a) Now that you have created and/or analyzed a lesson plan using the Problem-Based Learning model, consider how the model supports effective teaching and explicit instruction of problem solving. Can you cite specific evidence or references that support your claim? Be specific in expressing your ideas.

b) What did you learn from this activity that might inform your future practice?

Discussion Question

Problem-Based Learning model lessons are based on the study of problems. Discuss some problems you would like your current or future students to explore. Describe how you could apply the Problem-Based Learning model in those instances. What are the benefits and challenges of using this model in your academic content area?

Journal Entry

Explain why Problem-Based Learning is important to incorporate as a model of teaching in 21st century classrooms. What types of skills does it cultivate? Why are these skills important?

Resources

- Active Learning/Problem-Based Learning: This website is maintained by the University of Medicine and Dentistry of New Jersey—The site houses a list of excellent resources on Problem-Based Learning: http://cte.umdnj.edu/active_learning/active_pbl.cfm
- Problem-Based Learning Maastricht University—This site provides a short description of Problem-Based Learning: www.maastrichtuniversity.nl/web/faculties/fhml/targetgroup/exchangestudents/practicalinformation/teachingmethodpbl.htm
- QuestGarden—This site allows registered users to create and host WebQuests easily: www.questgarden.com
- WebQuest.org—This official WebQuest site houses many resources and examples of WebQuests: www.webquest.org/index.php
- Zunal WebQuest Maker—This site provides an easy, template-driven way to create WebQuests: www.zunal.com

Model	Cooperative Learning Models
Knowledge Supported	• Factual Knowledge
	• Conceptual Knowledge
	• Procedural Knowledge
	• Metacognitive Knowledge
Added Value	• Provides students opportunities to develop social skills
	• Helps students build positive relationships with peers
Technologies to Integrate	• Task management tools to present learning activities and organize resources
	• Graphic organizer tools to conceptualize steps and tasks in learning activities
	• Communication tools to support cooperation and sharing within and across groups
	• Survey, testing, and presentation tools for expression of learning

The Cooperative Learning Models

ajt/Shutterstock

Jeannette McDonald was encouraged by her new student's progress. Lydia, a spunky 12-year-old with cerebral palsy, had been in her eighth-grade social studies class for one month now she was performing very well academically. Using assistive devices to adapt tasks such as writing, Lydia had little difficulty fitting in academically. However, Jeannette longed for her to fit in socially as well. Admittedly, Lydia's confinement to a wheelchair made it more challenging for her to share all of the same experiences as her classmates and engage with friends outside of school. Yet in school, kids spent most of the day sitting. Jeannette thought that it should be easier to help her foster friendships.

At the end of one class period early in the semester, Jeanette noticed that Lydia—who was usually upbeat and positive—looked discouraged. When asked why, Lydia revealed to Jeannette that she missed her old school because she had had more friends there. She did not feel confident she could make new ones at Morraine Middle. After 17 years of teaching, Jeannette knew how hard it was for any middle school student to feel socially connected. She imagined it must be even harder for students with special needs. Jeannette was of the opinion that getting an "equitable educational experience in the least-restrictive environment" meant that special learners like Lydia must have positive relationships with peers as well as successful learning experiences. Jeannette made a silent vow to herself to help Lydia make social connections in her classroom in addition to academic ones.

Jeannette decided to plan a sequence of lessons with the Cooperative Learning model for the first time in 10 years. Sure, she had used this model quite regularly for many years, but she had gradually quit using because of pressures to teach to the standards and growing emphasis on individual student performance. Plus, in the teacher professional development workshops she participated in, her district emphasized using newer and more innovative teaching strategies instead.

Although helping to include students like Lydia was certainly reason enough to start using the Cooperative Learning model again, Jeannette knew it had potential to address other goals as well. It could enhance students' academic achievement, promote positive relationships between students, and improve everyone's self-esteem.

The first lesson Jeannette designed was one addressing the fragility of the Earth and how humans modify the Earth's physical form. She decided to use the Jigsaw Cooperative Learning model because it was well suited for covering large amounts of material. Students would have opportunities to master a topic working with other students in their "expert" group. Then, in "home" groups consisting of one student from each "expert" group, students would be challenged to teach other group members about their topic. Such structured and positive

Lydia
© Brian Mitchell

interactions would definitely get students connecting on a social level in meaningful ways and forming strong bonds. Yes, the Cooperative Learning model had great promise to help Lydia and all of Jeanette's other students, too. ■

CHAPTER OBJECTIVES

After reading this chapter, you will be able to:

- Describe three Cooperative Learning models, including their general history and steps.

- Communicate the applications and benefits of three Cooperative Learning models and learn what they might look like in a classroom.

- Explain how three Cooperative Learning models are implemented and how to plan for teaching with them.

- Articulate how three Cooperative Learning models might enable differentiated instruction and support diverse learners.

- Describe how technology can enhance teaching with three Cooperative Learning models.

Introduction

Most of us get excited when we are eligible for a "two for one" or "buy one, get one free" deal. If the deal is for something we need, like a cell phone, we are very excited. When what we need (e.g., a cell phone) also provides something we want (e.g., an integrated Web browser, camera, or games), we are overjoyed. The Cooperative Learning models presented in this chapter might be considered a *learning* "two for one deal" because these models provide students something they need and something they want. Students *need* to learn academic content, and most students *want* to interact with and have meaningful relationships with their peers. The Cooperative Learning models achieve both.

As the opening scenario suggests, Cooperative Learning models have a long history of successful use in preK-12 schools. However, today they have added relevance because they help students achieve academically, socially, and emotionally while simultaneously developing 21st century skills, such as critical-thinking, collaboration, communication, and creativity skills. Long valued for promoting positive relationships between students with diverse racial and ethnic backgrounds, these models are also helpful in fostering the inclusion of students with special needs. This chapter provides information about the General Cooperative Learning model and the Jigsaw and Graffiti Cooperative Learning models with more depth.

What Is the Cooperative Learning Model?

Several models of teaching fall under the Cooperative Learning models "umbrella." In this chapter, we introduce three Cooperative Learning models: the General Cooperative Learning model, the Jigsaw model, and the Graffiti model. Each of these models are considered Cooperative Learning models because they simultaneously promote students' development of social skills and mastery of academic content standards and reflect five critical attributes (addressed later in this chapter). These "social learning" models capitalize on students' natural inclination to construct knowledge socially while also developing students' ability to interact with peers productively.

What is unique about the Cooperative Learning models is that students' social interactions are structured, supported, and leveraged in ways that make academic learning more productive and powerful. The structured nature of the Cooperative Learning models is important because not all work that allows students to interact with each other promotes positive interactions or learning. However, the structured, organized opportunities to work and learn together—critical attributes of the Cooperative Learning models—do just that (Johnson, Johnson, & Roseth, 2010). In these models, teachers use planned activities to teach students behaviors required for working together and also challenge them to work together for both mutual and individual benefit.

The Cooperative Learning models take advantage of the untapped potential of using positively structured peer interactions to support student learning. Although it is far more common for teachers to acknowledge the negative influence students can have on one another's learning, the Cooperative Learning models accentuate the positive ways students can challenge one another to succeed. These models acknowledge that students' interactions during instruction can have three possible patterns. Students can (1) compete with one another to see who can be the "best," (2) work independently toward their own goals without acknowledging others, or (3) work together cooperatively with a vested interest in each other's learning, as well as their own (Johnson & Johnson, 1994). The Cooperative Learning models promote the third option by requiring students to work in small teams that are intentionally grouped using a variety of activities to learn content. Each team member is responsible for learning content and for helping his or her teammates learn. The atmosphere is one of shared learning and achievement.

Characteristics of Cooperative Learning

The Cooperative Learning models foster student learning in a variety of contexts. Likewise, these models work equally well at all grade levels and subject areas and in virtual and face-to-face learning environments as well. Cooperative Learning is also suitable for teaching factual, procedural, conceptual, and metacognitive knowledge. The models can be used alone or in conjunction with other instructional models addressed in this text. For example, a teacher might incorporate another model like the Inquiry model (Chapter 10) along with a Cooperative Learning model to teach an instructional unit.

Central to the Cooperative Learning models is that students work with each other in groups to accomplish individual and group learning goals. Although group work is a critical attribute of the Cooperative Learning models, cooperative learning is a special variety of group work characterized by five essential attributes: (1) positive interdependence, (2) individual accountability, (3) group processing, (4) promotive interaction, and (5) interpersonal and small-group skills (Johnson & Johnson, 1994). These are described in the following sections.

POSITIVE INTERDEPENDENCE. The practice of asking students to work together toward a common goal in ways that support the success of all students is called positive interdependence. In lessons using a Cooperative Learning model, the success of the group depends on the success of each individual participating in the group. Often this type of student-to-student relationship is described as "sink or swim"—meaning that everyone succeeds or fails together.

INDIVIDUAL ACCOUNTABILITY. In the Cooperative Learning models, group success results from the sum of individual efforts, so it requires that all members of the group perform their role to the best of their ability. For group members to work effectively with one another, they must feel that their individual efforts count and will be counted. Measures for individual accountability are built into the learning tasks and the assessment of lessons using the Cooperative Learning models to promote individual accountability. Such assessments include individual self-reports on participation as well as assessments of peer members' contributions. For example, in Scenario 12-3, students working on a project in a Cooperative Learning model lesson are asked to write a blog entry and reflect individually on (1) their greatest group accomplishment, (2) which member of the group was most instrumental in this accomplishment (if any), (3) their greatest individual contribution, (4) the role of these contributions in achieving the group's goals, and (5) how their work in the group was important for their own learning and that of their group. The instructor can read the entries by each member to determine each member's contribution.

GROUP PROCESSING. In Cooperative Learning model lessons, groups are asked to learn together not only side by side but also by engaging cognitively with other group members to develop new ideas, synthesize existing understandings, make decisions, and apply their knowledge in ways that represent the best of group thinking. Students also participate in evaluation of group processing. As a part of group processing activities, members are asked specifically to describe which member actions are helpful and unhelpful and to make decisions about which actions should continue and/or change (Johnson, Johnson, & Holubec, 1998). In this sense, accountability focuses on the individual contribution within the group and the contribution of the group as a whole, too. For example, in Scenario 12-1, students are asked to consider how their groups work together in a Graffiti lesson on sportsmanship.

PROMOTIVE INTERACTION. Promotive interaction involves interactions between students that are focused, positive, and benefit the individual and the group. Successful learning groups are fueled by positive social, emotional, and intellectual exchanges. Such interactions might include sharing of encouraging comments, explanations of how to solve problems, idea exchanges, and peer teaching. Often these interactions must be taught directly and modeled and practiced until they become a natural part of group interactions. Traditionally, these interactions have taken place in a face-to-face manner as students listen, talk, and share with one another in the classroom. However, with the advent of technology tools that support online and blended learning environments (e.g., online course management systems), promotive interactions can occur using Web conferencing, online discussion boards, shared documents, and even online chats. For example, in Scenario 12-3, a teacher might use an online tool like Google Docs to encourage students to post their ideas about research questions and survey items (and thereby engage in promotive interactions). Or, in an online calculus class, a teacher might use an asynchronous online discussion board and require students to post their individual strategies for how to solve one word problem in a larger series of problems (and thus engage in promotive interaction). The teacher might then encourage students to return to the discussion board, read the postings of their group members, and then (1) comment in a supportive way on the effort or thinking involved in their peers' postings, (2) ask clarification questions intended to help their peers better explain their thinking or idea, or (3) share an idea related to the strategy that might contribute to extending or refining the strategy.

In some cases, use of a discussion board functions to improve the quality of interactions. Because online discussions occur over a longer period of time—often delayed hours between postings—this type of promotive interaction can slow down and formalize the group's interactions because it allows more time for reflection on their learning. Learners who require more time for processing find this attribute increases the quality of their participation. The fact that discussion board postings are written also increases the quality of student interaction. These postings provide a rich record that allows group members and/ or their teacher the opportunity to track and analyze group exchanges.

INTERPERSONAL AND SMALL GROUP SOCIAL SKILLS. Because the success of a group and the learning performed by the group depend on each member's ability to communicate and work with others, social skills are essential to high-quality cooperative learning. As such, students' competence with social skills is too important to leave to chance. The positive interdependence of the group requires formal efforts to build teamwork and form community in these groups. The teaching, modeling, development, and practice of social skills (including active listening, trust building, conflict resolution, agreeing to disagree, and leadership) are ongoing activities and should be reinforced within the structure of the learning task. As such, the teacher will need to plan several opportunities for students to learn about and practice various social skills as well as reflect on them and assess them.

What Are the History and Origin of the Cooperative Learning Models?

Although learning that is characterized by supportive and structured interactions among peers has been a part of the informal learning process in many different cultures for centuries, the use of the Cooperative Learning models represents an innovation that is relatively new to formalized schooling. Learning activities that encourage collaboration among students in structured groups have a history stretching back to John Dewey's involvement in the progressive movement, but the formal introduction of the Cooperative Learning models in preK-12 classrooms did not occur until the 1960s. Popular awareness of the theory of group dynamics and a desire to promote successful racial integration led to the widespread use of these models in academic contexts. Research revealing the efficacy of Cooperative Learning models gave their use more traction. Over the last 50 years, these models have become some of the most popular with teachers in the United States. In fact, a study by Puma, Jones, Rock, and Fernandez (1993) investigating the educational opportunity of 3 million third-graders, revealed that 79% of teachers used Cooperative Learning in math and that 74% used it in language arts. The model has become a part of the fabric (Puma et al., 1993) of teaching and a regular component of published textbook series, trade books, district curriculum guides, and individual teacher lesson plans.

The factors that led to the models' initial development—awareness of the power of group dynamics, the goal of building positive relationships among a diverse student population, and their impact on student learning and development—continue to be important facets of learning in the 21st century. Schools and teachers still need ways to promote the development of positive classroom communities. Today's teachers, however, also need strategies that do this for face-to-face, virtual, and blended learning environments. Scenario 12-3, presented later in this chapter, demonstrates how the General Cooperative Learning model can be used in an online high school class. Although the model is useful for promoting improved relationships among students of different backgrounds, it also supports the inclusion of students with special needs, and the needs of all kinds of learners. For example, in the introductory scenario for this chapter, a middle school teacher decides to use the Jigsaw model to support a student with cerebral palsy in making social connections with her peers.

The Cooperative Learning models also address new challenges facing schools and society in the 21st century. The models prepare students to live, learn, and work in the 21st century as the Partnership for 21st Century Skills (P21, 2011a) suggests. The P21, a group of government, business, and education leaders, names the "4Cs"—creativity, communication, collaboration, and critical thinking—as essential "superskills" for citizens and workers in the 21st century. The group suggests that "to successfully face rigorous higher education coursework, career challenges, and a globally competitive workforce, U.S. schools must align classroom environments with real world environments by fusing the three Rs and four Cs" (P21, 2011b). Cooperative Learning models can promote collaboration and communication, and, depending on the academic standards addressed and learning processes utilized, they may also help students develop creativity and critical thinking.

When Should the Cooperative Learning Models Be Applied and Why?

The Cooperative Learning models are some of the most extensively implemented and researched models of teaching. These models have consistently demonstrated the ability to foster students' positive development in the following areas: (1) relationships among diverse student populations, (2) student self-esteem, (3) 21st century skills, and (4) inclusive education. The sections that follow elaborate on these ideas, report some relevant research findings, and share general commonsense observations. The following sections discuss what teachers should use the Cooperative Learning models to do.

Promote Positive Relationships among Diverse Student Populations

Although the Cooperative Learning models were initially introduced to promote tolerance and positive racial integration in classrooms, research shows that they do more than encourage tolerance—they result in acceptance. The structured interactions experienced by students participating in Cooperative Learning model lessons promote the development of cross-racial friendships (Hansell & Slavin, 1981). Most significantly, interaction during a Cooperative Learning model lesson results in positive relationships or "liking." When compared with traditional instructional experiences, cooperative learning experiences promote higher "effect" sizes for peers "liking" one another (Johnson & Johnson, 1989a; Johnson, Johnson, & Maruyama, 1983). This outcome of cooperative learning appears to be true regardless of differences in ability level, sex, disability, ethnic membership, social class, or task orientation. Additionally, students who collaborate in academic learning also show evidence of developing considerable commitment and caring for each other no matter what their initial impressions of and attitudes toward each other were when they started. According to Johnson and Johnson (1994), students who participate in Cooperative Learning models also "like the teacher more and perceive the teacher as being more supportive and accepting academically and personally" (p. 7).

Encourage the Increase of Students' Self-Esteem

Research suggests that participation in the Cooperative Learning models helps to develop students' self-esteem and results in students having more positive feelings about themselves (Johnson et al., 2010; Slavin, 1991). This positive effect appears to be related to the way the model supports interdependence. The Jigsaw model seems to show a significantly strong effect in promoting students' self-esteem. This is probably due to the fact that the model gives each student a unique role in supporting the group. Self-esteem–promoting effects appear to stretch across students from various racial groups and seem to make students feel less competitive and more supportive of their classmates.

Foster the Development of Creative and Critical Thinking

Research on the Cooperative Learning models suggests that these models promote development of the creative- and critical-thinking skills called out by the Partnership for 21st Century Skills (P21, 2011). For instance, Johnson and Johnson (1994) suggest that creative thinking increases as students cooperate toward a common goal. It seems reasonable that creative thinking is stimulated through the interchange of ideas that occur in cooperative learning groups and because of the models' high correlation of being used with more complicated tasks and learning processes.

Depending on the learning goals selected and the nature of the learning task involved in attaining these goals, the Cooperative Learning models can also promote critical thinking. Many cooperative learning structures work well to enhance thinking skills at all levels of the revised Bloom's taxonomy.

Support Inclusive Education Practices

The Cooperative Learning models also benefit the goals of inclusion in numerous ways. First, they support the academic and social success of students with special needs by providing them with opportunities to work productively in academic learning situations. Because these models are highly structured, special accommodations can be designed directly into group tasks and processes and into individual student roles themselves. Students with special needs can benefit from the exposure to positive peer modeling of academic learning behaviors and social skills that comes through experiences with the Cooperative Learning models. Second, they promote the development of rich relationships between "typical" learners and those with disabilities. As the introductory scenario suggests, students with special needs require educational experiences on par with those of their peers. The rationale behind inclusion—to provide all students with the least-restrictive environment for their learning—intends to enable students with special needs to have as equitable an educational experience as possible. One cannot overestimate the importance of quality peer relationships and learning experiences when attempting to meet this goal. Full inclusion into both academic and social dimensions of learning benefits all students—not just those with special needs.

What Are the Steps in the General Cooperative Learning Model?

The steps of the General Cooperative Learning model include (1) introducing the task; (2) naming, teaching, and practicing targeted social skills; (3) implementing the lesson and monitoring student interactions; (4) summarizing learning; (5) measuring group and individual accountability; and (6) conducting assessment. These steps are explained in the following sections. Figure 12-1 shows an overview of the teacher and student roles when using the General Cooperative Learning model.

Step One—Introduce the Task

During this step, the teacher provides an overview of the lesson, outlines students' roles and responsibilities, and lists the tasks to be completed. This step may also include a

Figure 12-1   Teacher and Student Roles in the General Cooperative Learning Model

General Cooperative Learning Model Steps	Teacher Role	Student Role
Introduce the task	Teacher provides an overview of the lesson and explains the students' individual and group tasks. Teacher presents students with a timeline and any materials needed. Teacher makes connections between learning tasks and their relevance to students.	Students listen and ask clarifying questions about the task.
Name, teach, and practice targeted social skills	Teacher names social skills that will be the focus of the lesson. If necessary, the social skills are taught and practiced using strategies like role play.	Students listen and practice the social skills. They ask clarifying questions.
Implement the lesson and monitor student interactions	Teacher oversees group learning processes. Teacher responds to learner needs as they arise. Teacher might also reinforce rules and conduct formative evaluation.	Students engage in the learning tasks and practice targeted social skills. Students take advantage of the resources provided and seek assistance when needed.
Summarize learning	Teacher engages students in activities that enable them to process what they have learned related to social skills and academic standards.	Students respond to teacher invitations to think, synthesize, and evaluate both academic and social lessons.
Measure group and individual accountability	Teacher facilitates process of measuring individual and group accountability. This might involve asking students to complete a reflection or a questionnaire.	Students engage in self-analysis and reflection to determine and articulate details about the quality of their own participation and that of their peers.
Assess learning	Teacher implements assessment plans for the lesson's academic standards. The assessment might measure individual learning of standards as well as group performance.	Students participate in assessments administered by their teacher. Assessments might include formal assessments, such as quizzes or tests, as well as alternative assessments, such as projects.

timeline with major due dates and assignments. Teachers may choose to introduce this important information about the task using a graphic organizer or calendar tool. When possible, the teacher should make the effort to show connections between the learning goals, learning process, group interactions, and relevance of the lesson to the real world and future learning. Depending on the curricular goals and students' readiness, prior knowledge, and needs, teachers may have to develop highly structured approaches to incorporating the General Cooperative Learning model. For instance, in Scenario 12-3, Janelle utilizes a structured approach for students to work together on a research project. How much structure a teacher needs to incorporate depends on the content and students. Some students will need a lot of scaffolding and direction, whereas others, even within the same class, will not.

Step Two—Name, Teach, and Practice Targeted Social Skills

As previously mentioned, many teachers decide to plan Cooperative Learning model lessons because they want the opportunity to build their students' social skills at the same time they work toward attaining academic content standards. A teacher should not assume that students know what social skills are in general, what a specific one like "active listening" looks like in particular, or why such skills might be desirable at all. Therefore, teachers should name, teach, model, and ask students to practice these social skills before the lesson begins and also practice and review them throughout the Cooperative Learning models, as needed. Depending on the social skill targeted for students to develop and the students' level of readiness for practicing it, teachers may find it beneficial to use a model like the Direct Instruction model in Chapter 5 to teach it. Other approaches might start simply by having the teacher state the social skill that the students will work on developing and practicing and then model or teach the particular skill (e.g., the teacher could show videos of the social skill) before asking students to practice it themselves. Students might practice the targeted social skills by role-playing, videotaping good and bad examples of the social skills, or even just talking about it. Figure 12-2 lists possible social skills teachers might want to teach and/or review with their students when implementing any of the Cooperative Learning models.

Figure 12-2 Cooperative Social Skills

- Asks questions
- Assists group members
- Contributes ideas
- Gives and receives constructive feedback
- Has a positive attitude
- Is a good listener
- Is supportive
- Is respectful
- Shares ideas
- Shows sensitivity to the feelings of others
- Takes turns to speak/share ideas
- Works cooperatively with peers

Step Three—Implement the Lesson and Monitor Student Interactions

During this step, students are responsible for implementing the activities that make up the learning components of the General Cooperative Learning model. That is, learners actively take on the tasks set before them, use resources made available to them, and request help from their peers and teachers when they need it. The teacher's role is to observe and monitor students' progress and address any group needs as they arise. However, how teachers do this will vary. For instance, a teacher might (1) enforce rules established for exercising the targeted social skill(s), (2) provide just-in-time support for academic learning, (3) conduct formative assessment and observe student learning, and/or (4) respond to other problems as they arise (such as offer technical support, as in Scenario 12-3 when students work in Glogster or VoiceThread).

Step Four—Summarize Learning

During this step, the teacher engages students in activities that allow them to summarize or otherwise develop closure regarding what they have learned from the lesson. The goal is to challenge students to process what they learned related to learning goals (both academic and social) to make connections to prior knowledge and content studied. Essentially, this step exercises students' metacognition. Scenario 12-3 illustrates how teachers might have students use technology in the form of blogs or online journals to summarize and reflect on their learning.

Step Five—Measure Group and Individual Accountability

The goal of this step is to gauge individual and group progress related to the social learning goals for the lesson. Individual accountability measures the extent to which each individual student has done his or her fair share of the work required to accomplish the learning task. Individual accountability also involves measuring how well each student performed her or his role. Teachers need to assess how much effort each student puts into the group's work, provide feedback to groups and individual students about their individual and group contributions, help avoid redundant efforts, and ensure that every group member is invested in the final outcome. Group accountability seeks to measure how well the group members functioned together. A common measure such as a survey or narrative reflection might be used to gain information about both types of accountability simultaneously. For example, students in Scenario 12-3 are asked to blog about their own contributions to the research lesson as well as those of their group members.

Step Six—Assess Learning

The teacher measures learning goals related to academic performance with a summative assessment. At this point, a traditional assessment, such as a test or quiz, or an alternative assessment, such as an oral presentation or project, might be assigned to determine the number and degree of learning goals attained.

What Are the Steps in the Jigsaw Model?

The steps in the Jigsaw model are simple and straightforward. They are described in the sections that follow and in Figure 12-3, which also includes the teacher's and students' roles.

Figure 12-3　Teacher and Student Roles in the Jigsaw Cooperative Learning Model

Jigsaw Cooperative Learning Model Steps	Teacher Role	Student Role
Introduce Jigsaw model	The teacher explains to students what the Jigsaw model is, how its name illustrates the interdependence of students working together in the model, and the goals for using it. Steps to the learning process are described and explained.	Students listen and ask clarifying questions.
Name, teach, and practice targeted social skills	Teacher names a social skill that will be the focus of the lesson. A method for observing the social skill and assessing it is devised (possibly with input from students).	Students define and practice the social skill and contribute to making plans for assessing the skill.
Assign heterogeneously grouped students to expert and learning groups	The teacher forms expert groups (which focus on a topic) and home groups (which include one member from each expert group).	Students form assigned groups.
Assemble expert groups and set task	Teacher meets with the various expert groups and provides them specific instructions about their task nvestigating the topic. The teacher provides resources and materials students need to complete their task.	Students make sure they understand their task and their role in completing it in the expert group.
Experts teach in their learning groups	Teacher supports students completing their assigned expert group tasks.	Students complete assigned tasks to research, learn, and make materials for teaching home group.
Measure group and individual accountability	The teacher facilitates the process of measuring individual and group accountability. This might involve asking students to complete a reflection or questionnaire.	Students reflect on their own behaviors and contributions as well as those of their peers.
Evaluate and provide team recognition	Teacher implements assessment and identifies highest performing group. Recognition is provided.	Students conduct assessment of the different groups—in many cases, teachers use these actual scores as part of each team's score.

Step One—Introduce Jigsaw Model

The teacher introduces the Jigsaw model by explaining to students what it is, how its name illustrates the interdependence of students working together in the model (like a jigsaw puzzle), and what the goals are for using it. The teacher should review the critical attributes of cooperative learning and describe how these attributes factor into the steps of the model. During this step, the teacher explains that students will be part of two groups—an "expert" group (which will focus on learning and sharing ideas associated with a topic of study) and a "home" group (which will comprise one member of each expert group). The teacher further explains that students will meet in expert groups, learn about their assigned topic, and decide how to teach what they learn to their home group. Then students will return to their home group and share their knowledge with the other members of the home group. Thereafter, each person in the home group will take a quiz, and the scores of each group member will be averaged together. The group with the highest average score will be recognized.

Step Two—Name, Teach, and Practice Targeted Social Skills

At this time, the teacher describes a social skill that students will focus on during the lesson. Such social skills should be those which facilitate learning in home and expert groups. Active listening, providing constructive criticism, or another appropriate skill might be selected (see Figure 12-2 for examples of other social skills a teacher might want to target in the Jigsaw model lesson). If necessary, the skill is taught, modeled, and practiced.

Step Three—Assign Heterogeneously Grouped Students to Expert and Home Groups

The third step is for the teacher to assign students to heterogeneous groups while also ensuring that students know who is in each of the expert and home groups. Teachers may assign membership to the expert groups to scaffold weaknesses or build on students' strengths.

Step Four—Assemble Expert Groups and Set Task

Once the students have been assigned to their groups, they meet in these groups and start to address the task. Each group should have access to the resources needed to research the particular topic. Within these groups, students should create a teaching handout or some other product to use to teach their home group members the topic mastered in their expert groups. To scaffold the development of such a teaching handout or other resource that can be shared, the teacher might ask that students answer particular questions in their expert groups, as in Scenario 12-2.

Step Five—Experts Teach in Their Home Groups

During this step, the teacher reviews student materials prepared in the expert groups to make sure they are complete, appropriate, and accurate. The teacher may also make copies of any materials for all of the students in the class or help students share their materials (e.g., e-mail the whole class a multimedia presentation). After reviewing these materials, the teacher assesses student learning related to these teaching product(s).

Then students assemble in their home groups. Each expert has an allotted amount of time to report on his or her topic, share the teaching product(s), and teach home group members about what he or she learned in the expert group. Careful attention is paid to each member's teaching time to ensure that all have an opportunity to share their learning with others in the home group. This also gives individual student experts the opportunity to develop important presentation skills.

Step Six—Measure Group and Individual Accountability

During this step, the teacher facilitates the process of assessing individual and group accountability. This might involve asking students to complete a reflection or questionnaire that gauges individual and group performance based on specific criteria. Often, teachers develop rubrics, with or without student input, to measure group and individual accountability.

Step Seven—Evaluate and Provide Team Recognition

After students use their allotted teaching time, the teacher distributes the assessment he or she has created to evaluate students. The assessment could be an objective, open-ended, or short answer quiz. Students take the quiz, and the teacher computes and averages scores by group. The group with the highest average score is recognized.

What Are the Steps in the Graffiti Model?

The Graffiti model's steps are similar to the General and Jigsaw Cooperative Learning models, but it has some distinct features (e.g., questions are the foundation of this model). Figure 12-4 outlines the model's major steps as well as the teacher's and students' roles.

Step One—Prepare Graffiti Questions

The first step of the Graffiti model involves developing questions that will lead students to achieve the learning goals for the lesson. The questions themselves might actually be the learning goals as in Scenario 12-1. In this scenario, Henry wants students to be able to define teamwork, describe what it looks like, understand why it is important, learn ways to build it, and comprehend how teamwork affects teams. As a result, he writes questions that will lead to the development of these understandings.

Step Two—Divide Students into Groups

The second step of the Graffiti model involves grouping students. The number of student groups should correspond with the number of questions being asked (e.g., for four questions, use four groups). Groups should not be so large that students can avoid participating. Groups of three to five students tend to work best. Strategies for grouping may be used to support the unique needs of the learners in the groups. In some instances, homogeneous groups may be a better grouping strategy. In others, the use of heterogeneous groups would be more supportive of learners' attainment of learning goals. Planning for groups is addressed in future sections of this chapter.

Figure 12-4   Teacher and Student Roles in the Graffiti Cooperative Learning Model

Graffiti Cooperative Learning Model Steps	Teacher Role	Student Role
Prepare Graffiti questions	Teacher develops questions that will enable students to attain learning goals. Teacher might choose to have the questions respond to varying levels of the revised Bloom's taxonomy.	
Divide students into groups	Teacher divides students into groups that will support learning goals and intended social interaction goals. The number of groups responds to the number of questions. Groups should include three to five students.	Students form groups as requested by their teacher.
Explain the process to the groups	Teacher explains the Graffiti process to students and names academic goals.	Students listen and ask clarifying questions.
A social skill is identified, explained, and practiced	Teacher explains the social skill and facilitates defining and practicing of this skill. Teacher facilitates development of social skills.	Students provide input on suitable accountability measures.
Distribute materials	Teacher passes out markers, questions, and any other necessary materials.	Student groups receive materials and prepare for learning.
Groups answer questions	Teacher monitors group activities and provides support when needed. Teacher keeps track of time and asks groups to switch questions when the allotted time is completed.	Student groups respond to each question in the time allotted to them and then move on to the next question when prompted by the teacher. They are careful not to look at the responses of other groups.
Groups process responses to questions	Teacher monitors student group interactions. Teacher provides supportive feedback as needed.	Groups return to the question they started with and synthesize or process the responses from all groups.
Share information	The teacher facilitates the sharing of responses from each group.	The groups report on their synthesis of the responses to the questions.
Measure group and individual accountability	Teacher facilitates the process of measuring individual and group accountability. This might involve asking students to complete a reflection or questionnaire.	Students engage in self-analysis and reflection to determine and articulate details and quality of their own participation and that of their peers.
Assess learning	Teacher implements assessment plans for the lesson's academic standards. The assessment might measure individual learning of standards as well as group performance.	Students participate in assessments administered by their teacher. Assessments might include formal assessments, such as quizzes or tests, as well as alternative assessments, such as projects.

Step Three—Explain the Process to the Groups

During this step, students are told that they will be asked to work with other students in a group to answer several questions. The teacher provides the students an explanation of why these questions are important and how they will help students meet learning goals for the lesson. The teacher explains that the activity is called "Graffiti" because the students will write their answers on chart paper affixed to the wall (like graffiti). If available, one group can also use a computer projected onto an interactive whiteboard or write their graffiti on a transparency projected onto the wall or whiteboard.

The teacher informs students that each group will start the activity by responding to the question that corresponds with its group number (e.g., group 1 will answer question 1) in an allotted amount of time. Then after answering this question, the group members will cover their answers and proceed to the next question (e.g., group 1 will move to question 2 and so on). The activity will continue until all of the groups have responded to all of the questions. The teacher also explains that once each group has responded to all of the questions, each group will be responsible for processing the answers from all groups for the first question answered (e.g., group 1 will summarize answers to question 1) and then sharing the information with the class. The types of processing activities groups are asked to engage in vary. They might be asked to summarize all of the group responses, generate new ideas from these responses, or identify similarities and differences among the responses.

Step Four—Identify, Explain, and Practice Social Skill

Appropriate use of social skills is necessary for the Graffiti model to work well. The teacher or the students should target one skill on which to focus—one that they need to be successful working together as a group. Once the skill is identified, the teacher ensures that students understand what the skill is, why it is important, and what it looks like (perhaps by providing instructions for doing it, modeling it, or showing video examples of it). During this step, the method of making students accountable for practicing the skill is also shared. The approach for accountability might be determined by the teacher or the students.

Step Five—Distribute Materials

The teacher gives the groups crayons or markers needed for sharing their ideas on the chart paper (or computer if one group is projecting its answers). The teacher then posts the chart paper with questions on the wall in different areas. The teacher is careful to ensure that there is enough space for groups to work without disturbing one another. If groups are going to be asked to take notes about their performance and those of their peers, they use the available tools to do so, which can range from paper and pencil to the use of digital tools, such as online questionnaires.

Step Six—Groups Answer Questions

Working together in the method they deem most appropriate, the group responds to the questions that have been asked on the chart paper (or computer if using one). The group is careful to make sure that their answers are shared but that they do not look at the responses previously written by other groups. When time is up, each group covers their responses, moves to another question, and responds to it. This step is complete when all groups have responded to all of the questions.

Step Seven—Groups Process Responses to Questions

During this step, each group goes back to the question they answered first. Following instructions from their teacher, the group members read and review all of the answers written by all of the groups. Then they process the responses by summarizing, analyzing, or synthesizing.

Step Eight—Share Information

Once each group has processed the responses to their assigned question, the groups share the results of their work. Students might share their results out loud, face-to-face in a presentation, or through other material they create (e.g., multimedia presentation, Web page, or online poster).

Step Nine—Measure Group and Individual Accountability

During this step, the teacher facilitates the process of measuring individual and group accountability that was determined at the outset. This might involve asking students to complete a reflection or questionnaire. Students engage in self-analysis and reflection to determine and articulate details of the quantity and quality of their own participation and that of their peers.

Step Ten—Assess Learning

During this step, the teacher implements assessment plans to measure attainment of the lesson's academic standards. The assessment might measure individual learning of standards, as well as group performance with standards. Students participate in the assessments administered by their teacher, which may be formal, traditional assessments, such as quizzes or tests, or alternative assessments, such as podcasts or multimedia presentations.

What Does the Cooperative Learning Model Look Like in the Classroom?

The Cooperative Learning models may be implemented in a variety of teaching and learning contexts. Although there are different Cooperative Learning models, each embodies the same critical attributes but uses different structured approaches to accomplish learning goals. The following scenarios illustrate the three different Cooperative Learning models introduced in this chapter and demonstrate ways each of them supports the critical attributes of cooperative learning.

Scenario 12-1

Physical education (PE) teacher Henry Kincaide knew that his fifth-grade students needed to learn more about teamwork both on the field and in the classroom—teamwork was a curriculum standard! So Henry decided to use a model he had experienced as a student himself in the 1980s—the Graffiti model of cooperative learning—in his PE classes. Henry started planning by typing learning goals in his online lesson planner. He then wrote questions for each goal on sheets of large-sized chart paper and stuck them on the walls in different areas of the gym. The questions were formulated to challenge learners at different cognitive levels and included the following:

- Remembering: What is teamwork?
- Understanding: What does teamwork look like?
- Applying: What are some ways to build teamwork?
- Analyzing: Why is it important to learn about teamwork?
- Evaluating: How would a team with teamwork function differently over the course of a season than one without it?

Once students arrived for class, Henry explained the lesson. He told the students he was looking for all of the students to provide supportive feedback as they learned about the concept of teamwork. Henry and his students discussed what supportive feedback might look like. He asked a couple of students to demonstrate good and bad examples of supportive feedback, which he videotaped so he could review it with students if they started to display negative feedback in their groups. Henry then handed out a rubric and explained that, at the end of the lesson, he would ask students to use it to rate themselves on their ability to provide supportive feedback and their group's contributions. Then he asked the students to divide up into the five groups he had assigned.

Henry told the groups that they would have time to answer each question on the chart paper but that each group should cover or turn over the answers when finished so other groups would not see their ideas (just yet). Groups would then take turns responding to each question. When all of the questions had been responded to, students would return to the paper where they began to review and analyze all of the answers on that paper. Their goal would be to summarize the various group responses—finding concepts that overlapped—and share their findings with the class as a whole. After all groups had shared their results, Henry would give them a quiz to ensure that everyone understood the concept. Group members would rate themselves and each of their group members on their practice of providing supportive feedback.

Scenario 12-2

Margot Singer was excited to introduce the new unit to her middle school Arabic I class. The goal was to push students beyond basic comprehension of vocabulary in Arabic. She wanted to help students understand the variety of cultures that speak Arabic. From her experiences, she had learned that too often students relied on stereotypes when interpreting culture and failed to understand the richness of the cultures that are Arabic speaking. If her students were really going to learn Arabic in her classroom, they needed to appreciate the culture connected with the language and its many contributions to other languages. So, Margot planned a lesson using the Jigsaw Cooperative Learning model to encourage students to become experts on one particular aspect of Arabic culture and develop a basic knowledge about several of its characteristics.

Margot divided her students into five expert groups and assigned each group a particular aspect of Arab culture to study: geography (where Arabic is spoken in the world), dress, traditions, foods, and religions. To support group processing, Margot provided each of the expert groups a list of questions to consider individually and as a group. These questions would help the expert group members develop materials they would use to teach their peers. The students were also challenged to take on a variety of different roles within their expert groups, including facilitator, recorder, encourager, summarizer, materials collector, and timekeeper. As a class, they developed the method of assessment that would be used to evaluate their group work at the end of the lesson—a questionnaire that would challenge them to share (1) their greatest group accomplishment, (2) which member of the group was most instrumental in this accomplishment (if any), (3) their greatest individual contribution, (4) the role of this contribution in the accomplishment of the group, and (5) the ways in which their work in the group was important for their own learning and that of their group.

Students spent four class periods working together to expand their knowledge and develop materials for teaching their peers in their home groups. Some groups developed simple handouts; other groups' products were more elaborate and took the form of social bookmark lists that compiled and summarized many useful resources. After becoming experts in their areas of study, students were reorganized into home groups. These groups consisted of five students each, with one student representing each expert group and dimension of Arabic culture. Once in their home groups, each expert was responsible for teaching fellow group members about his or her assigned topic.

In the home groups, students also practiced listening as a social skill. Without it, students would not understand the topics or be able to succeed on the exam that Margot would give after they completed peer teaching. Students competed to see which home group could get the highest combined score. The winner would earn the honor of being class representatives at the Arabic Culture booth for the school's world culture fair.

Scenario 12-3

Janelle DiGiorno enjoyed teaching her online students. She wanted her students to develop socially as well as intellectually in their virtual environment, so she used online communication and social networking tools to promote positive interactions.

In one English lesson, she had used the General Cooperative Learning model to promote students' attainment of the Common Core State Standards in this subject—specifically students' ability to do research, present their ideas, and make strategic use of digital tools. They would be assigned to heterogeneous cooperative learning groups and asked to work together on a research project. Collectively, they would develop a biography on an author whose work they would be studying during the following term. By the end of the lesson, students in all of the groups would be able to say, "I can identify good research questions. I can conduct research that answers my questions. I can analyze what I learn from my research. I can effectively present my ideas to others using digital tools. I know what a biography is."

To ensure the success of her students, Janelle used online tools to structure learning experiences as best she could. The lesson would have numerous requirements, including brainstorming, researching, documenting and referencing their research, synthesizing findings, writing the biography, checking their work, and taking on specific roles and responsibilities. Janelle created a handout explaining the roles she wanted students to take, which were as follows:

- Leader—This student would ensure that all of the group members knew what they needed to do and by when (a major task was updating the task management tool).
- Summarizer—This student summarized major points and research.

- Reporter—This student compiled the group's findings in the "wiki-biography".
- Proofreader—This student proofread all work to ensure that it addressed all requirements.

Janelle ensured that students' learning and collaborative work would be structured—students would know what they needed to do to research and write the biography and also when each assignment was due.

Janelle also planned the lesson to take full advantage of the collaboration tools available in the course management system. She encouraged students to use the group feature for asynchronous discussions, synchronous conferences to discuss and critique ideas, and file sharing. She also reminded them of the wiki tool built into the course management system and mentioned a few other free online tools. For instance, she planned to require the use of a task management tool, Zoho Task Management software (www.zoho.com/projects/task-management-software.html), for students to keep track of their work and progress. Also, in addition to having them create a wiki-biography for each author biography, she also wanted her students to demonstrate their learning in creative ways, as through the creation of a Glogster poster (www.glogster.com), VoiceThread (voicethread.com), or some other tool to share their biographies.

Janelle first introduced the biography research project by creating a short screencast explaining that students would use the group collaboration feature of the course management system to brainstorm research questions about the author they had chosen to research. Then, they would compile a list of the top five questions they thought each group should research and compile those in a document to share with the whole class. Janelle would then review their questions and provide feedback. After receiving her feedback, each group would be tasked with conducting research about the author, documenting their research strategy, and, finally, writing up their biography in a wiki.

To promote accountability while working together, Janelle asked students to identify two social skills important for good teamwork that each group would work on. Each student in the group would blog about their personal experiences and the group's interactions and keep track of the shared responsibility of participants. Finally, at the end of the lesson, she would give all of the students an open-ended exam that would assess what they learned about the different authors and, most important, the research skills practiced.

What Do These Scenarios Illustrate?

These scenarios are only three examples of the various learning goals, grade levels, and unique contexts in which the Cooperative Learning models can be used. Although the teachers applied different strategies in each example, all of the students were asked to work together for individual and group benefits and to take on different roles and responsibilities. Moreover, the students practiced helpful social skills that would promote their learning in each scenario, which are critical attributes of all of the Cooperative Learning models.

REFLECT: Consider how the Cooperative Learning model applied in each of the different scenarios supported students in achieving content area standards. Also, review how the different Cooperative Learning models demonstrate the critical attributes of positive interdependence, individual accountability, group processing, promotive interaction, and social skills development. How might you modify any of these Cooperative Learning models? How might this modification benefit your students? Also, consider the types of content that might be taught using each of these models.

Planning for Teaching with the Cooperative Learning Models

As noted previously, students need to be taught how to work together and what types of social skills are expected of them when working in groups. Teachers need to structure students' learning of content and social skills through appropriate scaffolding and facilitation; they should not take for granted, no matter the age or level of students, that they already know how to function effectively in groups. Working in cooperative groups can be very challenging if appropriate supports are not in place before and during instruction. Therefore, it is critical for teachers to complete the following two major tasks (each consisting of subtasks) before using any of these models of teaching: (1) planning goals, objectives, lesson implementation, and assessments and (2) planning for the critical attributes of cooperative learning. The following sections discuss what educational designers do when teaching with the Cooperative Learning models.

Plan Goals, Objectives, Grouping, Lesson Implementation, and Assessments

Advanced planning for any Cooperative Learning model is important because so much of student learning takes place without direct oversight from the teacher. Therefore, planning for the implementation of any of the Cooperative Learning models involves several important tasks: specifying the goals and objectives of the lesson, determining the group size and makeup, planning lesson implementation, and developing assessment measures.

SPECIFY GOALS AND OBJECTIVES. Specifying goals and objectives is a critical first step when planning to teach any of the Cooperative Learning models. The teacher establishes the goals for the learning experience based on the academic standards and social skills to be addressed. Often, the goals for social skills development also reflect an academic standard in a subject area. For example, in Scenario 12-1, the PE standards address effective teamwork directly in the subject area standards. Students must learn about teamwork because it is included in course content. It is equally likely that the targeted social skill for a Cooperative Learning model lesson may simply be chosen as a focus in the lesson because students need to learn and use a particular skill to make the lesson work productively. In Scenario 12-2, for instance, students must practice active listening in the Arabic culture lesson if they are going to work effectively together to learn about cultures that speak the language.

DETERMINE GROUP SIZE AND MAKEUP. Because student groups are so important in the Cooperative Learning model, it is critical for teachers to determine how students will be divided into groups. There are several different types of groups teachers might use when using a Cooperative Learning model (see Figure 12-5 for a variety of ways in which students can be grouped). Choices teachers make about grouping affect the number of students in a group, the ways in which students are grouped, the period of time the group works together, the degree of intentionality behind the formulation of groups, and the rationale for the composition of groups.

Figure 12-5 Types of Cooperative Learning Groups

Type of Group	Description of Group
Informal Groups	Informal groups are temporary and arbitrarily composed. Their composition might be based on the proximity of students to one another—grouping students together in "convenience groups"—or made to build or extend social bonds between students. When a teacher makes a group by saying, "Turn to your neighbor and discuss with one another," he or she is using informal grouping.
Formal Groups	Formal groups are designed in a purposeful way to achieve a particular academic or social goal. Factors to be considered in grouping students are whether students in a group might (1) complement one another and/or (2) challenge each other in some type of way. There are different types of formal groups that are composed to respond to these considerations for grouping.
Cooperative Base Groups	Cooperative base groups are a specialized type of formal group. Base groups are assigned and work together for more than one cooperative learning experience over a longer period of time (e.g., one or more academic terms). Using base groups (1) promotes commitment of group members through permanence, (2) saves time getting to know new group members, and (3) allows students to get to know one another well enough to become skilled in working together more effectively.
Heterogeneous Groups	Heterogeneous groups are formal groups that are designed to bring learners with different characteristics together. The intent is that bringing learners together help them form bonds and promote learning due to their differences in a complementary manner. The qualities that a teacher might consider mixing in this type of grouping include but are not limited to (1) ability level; (2) gender; (3) racial, cultural, or ethnic background; (4) socioeconomic status; and (5) learning style.
Homogeneous Groups	Homogeneous groups are formal groups that are designed to bring learners with similar characteristics together. The intent is to help them form bonds and promote learning due to their similarities in a productive and intentional manner. The qualities that might be considered in this type of grouping include but are not limited to (1) ability level; (2) gender; (3) racial, cultural, or ethnic background; (4) socioeconomic status; and (5) learning style.

Although Johnson et al., (2010) recommend that groups should range in size from two to four students, teachers need to decide exactly how many students will make up a group as well as how students will be grouped and what accommodations might be made for uneven group sizes, absences, and attrition. Likewise, they will need to determine whether all groups should be the same size. Any decisions made about grouping should be made based on (1) knowledge of the students and their needs, (2) the learning goals, (3) methods used to support their learning, and (4) physical space. Also, teachers should consider how well students might work together. Students who are very close friends might benefit from being separated and working in other groups to build friendships with and appreciation for other classmates.

PLAN LESSON IMPLEMENTATION. Although each of the Cooperative Learning models described in this chapter provides specific steps to follow, in all cases the teacher will need to determine how the lesson is to be implemented in terms of these steps and establish supports to scaffold student learning and interaction. Therefore, within these various steps, the teacher should plan step-by-step instructions to foster student learning, create materials that provide differentiated support for students based on their individual needs, decide which tools might be used, and outline time frames for completing major tasks and assignments. Teachers should share the lesson procedures in a format that can be distributed to all of the students (e.g., using a word-processed document, multimedia presentation tool, or a chart that shares assignment deadlines). The Cooperative Learning models provide many possible combinations of activities that students might perform in each model's steps. Therefore, for each phase, teachers should carefully consider what students should do and how they can support students. Clearly teachers' roles should be more facilitative; however, they might have to intervene if groups are not getting along, working productively, meeting deadlines, supporting one another, or understanding the goals, objectives, and tasks they need to address.

DEVELOP FORMATIVE AND SUMMATIVE ASSESSMENT MEASURES. To ensure that groups are working productively to address the lesson goals and objectives, teachers should create formative and summative assessments that assess student learning, application of the targeted social skill(s), and progress toward meeting these goals and objectives. Even though formative assessments can be developed spontaneously and as needed, it is nonetheless important for students to know they will be assessed at various stages. This helps keep students on target and scaffolds their learning. For example, in any of the scenarios presented in this chapter, a teacher could create an informal pop quiz on the content being learned to gauge student comprehension. This could be in the form of a survey, one-minute paper, or concept map—and it could be done individually, in small groups, or both (e.g., first students might work on it individually and then in their groups). Teachers could also incorporate planned formative assessments—even at the beginning of the Cooperative Learning model lesson.

Teachers should have a clear idea, before implementing a Cooperative Learning model lesson, of the summative assessment they will require for students to demonstrate their learning. This is very important because students need to know what is expected of them and their group members and how they will be assessed. Having a clear idea of the final assessment will not only help students understand the expectations for the Cooperative Learning model lesson but also assist them in working toward a common goal. For instance, in Scenario 12-3, the summative assessment is the development of a wiki-biography and another alternative product (e.g., a VoiceThread) about an author researched by each group. Explanation of the expectations of the requirements of this summative assignment will help students work more efficiently and effectively toward that common goal. Development of specific grading criteria (e.g., a rubric) will also enhance students' work and understanding of expectations.

Plan for the Critical Attributes of Cooperative Learning

To ensure effective implementation of the Cooperative Learning models, teachers must carefully plan how they will incorporate the critical attributes of Cooperative Learning. This involves determining which interpersonal skills to teach and how, establishing procedures for group processing and promotive interaction, and developing individual and group accountability measures.

DETERMINE THE INTERPERSONAL AND SMALL-GROUP SOCIAL SKILLS TO TEACH—AND HOW. Research shows that too often teachers implement Cooperative Learning model lessons without providing sufficient instruction or scaffolding that teaches students the necessary social skills for working together—even though research consistently shows that this is a universal need for successful implementation of these models (Sharan, 2010). As such, it is imperative that, before utilizing a Cooperative Learning model, teachers determine which social skills need to be targeted, defined, and practiced in the lesson itself (e.g., supportive feedback was the social skill targeted in Scenario 12-1). Note that this does not mean that only the teacher is involved in making such decisions. Students can and should be involved. For instance, in Scenario 12-3, the teacher asks each group to determine which two teamwork skills the group will work on. There are many different social skills that students can develop, no matter their age, ability level, or interest.

In addition to determining which social skills to teach, it is also important for teachers to determine how they will teach them. In other words, how will teachers engage students in learning about and practicing these skills? Teachers should not take for granted that students know how to work cooperatively, even if they have done so previously. Instead, they need to teach the targeted social skill(s) explicitly and give students the opportunity to practice it intentionally.

Scenario 12-1 shows how a teacher might make the teaching of such skills the focus of an entire lesson using the Graffiti model. It is also helpful if the teacher can illustrate the connection between the targeted social skill and academic learning goals. Doing so affords students the opportunity to ask clarifying questions about the targeted social skill and practice it. For example, in Scenario 12-1, students realize that to learn about teamwork, they need to work as a team. To foster the students' learning of teamwork, the teacher asks students to demonstrate and practice providing supportive feedback. In many cases, it will be useful to list the skills required for successful practice (e.g., see Figure 12-2) or develop a rubric that will be used to measure students' success performing this skill.

ESTABLISH PROCEDURES FOR GROUP PROCESSING AND PROMOTIVE INTERACTION. To ensure effective and efficient group processing and promotive interaction, teachers need to plan how they will scaffold and structure activities to foster these important aspects of the Cooperative Learning models. Sometimes this involves requiring completion of activities such as developing a step-by-step activity to use in a lesson, as suggested in Scenario 12-1, or providing a list of questions students can respond to individually and then share with one another, such as in Scenario 12-2. Other times, plans to support group processing involve using a variety of technology tools that foster reflection about the groups' progress, as in Scenario 12-3, where students maintain a blog. Simply put, teachers need to plan activities that allow for the groups to discuss, share, and reflect on their work as well as examine how effectively they are functioning and working together toward meeting the goals and objectives of the lesson. Group processing should involve examinations of both individual and group contributions.

Planning for promotive interaction is important. It is equally important to plan opportunities for students to discuss, share, and reflect on their work and practice of social skills. Although originally established to promote face-to-face interaction, promotive interaction can also occur in online environments, as Scenario 12-3 shows. In this scenario, students have group space to share ideas and interact in the course management system. Moreover, they have opportunities, via their blogs, to reflect on their progress.

DEVELOP ASSESSMENT FOR INDIVIDUAL AND GROUP ACCOUNTABILITY. Individual accountability refers to the responsibility each student has to contribute in a unique and productive way to the accomplishment of shared learning goals. Strategies for individual accountability seek to understand and measure the nature and level of contributions made by individual students. Johnson and Johnson (1994) explain that common ways to control individual accountability include the following:

- Keeping the size of the group small. The smaller the size of the group, the greater the individual accountability may be.
- Giving an individual test to each student.
- Randomly examining students orally by calling on one student to present his or her group's work to the teacher in the presence of the group or to the entire class.
- Observing each group and recording the frequency with which each member contributes to the group's work.
- Assigning one student in each group to serve in the role of checker. The checker asks other group members to explain the reasoning and rationale underlying group answers.
- Requiring that students teach what they learned to someone else. When all students do this, it is called *simultaneous explaining*.

Group accountability indicates how well the group has functioned together to accomplish the learning task. The emphasis of group accountability measures is to discover whether and to which degree the group has accomplished the desired goals together. Often efforts to measure group accountability uncover whether the group members supported all individuals in effectively practicing the targeted social skills.

Teachers should establish measures for monitoring both individual and group accountability throughout a lesson. For instance, a teacher might survey students to ask them to share information about individual contributions that influenced the group. The teacher may be interested in finding out if all of the students had a chance to contribute and "be heard," or whether all members participated to accomplish group goals—and, if not, what got in the way. If individuals have not participated effectively or if the groups are dysfunctional, teachers can then address problems to promote more positive, productive interactions in the future.

Johnson and Johnson (1994) suggest that measures for accountability should include information about whether individuals are providing each other with efficient and effective help and assistance; exchanging needed resources, such as information and materials, *and* processing information more efficiently and successfully; providing each other with feedback in order to improve their subsequent performance; challenging each other's conclusions and reasoning in order to promote higher-quality decision making and greater insight into the problems being considered; advocating the exertion of effort to achieve mutual goals; influencing each other's efforts to achieve the group's goals; acting in trusting and trustworthy ways; being motivated to strive for mutual benefit; and maintaining a moderate level of interest characterized by low anxiety and stress.

One way to foster better individual and group accountability is to establish clearly defined roles and responsibilities for individual group members. For instance, in Scenario 12-2, students in the Jigsaw model lesson must serve as individual experts who work with an expert team focused on the same goal and objective, and then they in turn teach their home groups the information gleaned in the expert groups.

Teachers might want to assign specific roles, as is the case in Scenario 12-3, where students must serve as leaders, summarizers, and proofreaders for their Cooperative Learning model lesson.

Differentiating Instruction with the Cooperative Learning Models

Content, process, and product can all be differentiated in a variety of meaningful ways when implementing any of the three Cooperative Learning models introduced in this chapter. This section describes some ways in which differentiated instruction might be incorporated in the Cooperative Learning models.

Content

The level of difficulty of content that is explored in a lesson applying a Cooperative Learning model can be matched optimally with the students' readiness, interests, and/ or learning styles. For example, the topic explored by a learner's expert group might be matched to correspond with a student's interests or readiness, as demonstrated in the Jigsaw Model Lesson at the end of this chapter. Likewise, questions asked in the Graffiti model can be developed to support the interests, readiness, and learning styles of students. The teacher can intentionally choose to use questions at each level of the revised Bloom's taxonomy (as in Scenario 12-1) or focus on questions from just one level of the taxonomy.

Process

Since grouping is an essential feature of all three of the Cooperative Learning models introduced in this chapter, teachers can easily differentiate the learning process by determining the composition of groups. Cooperative groups can be formed to bring students together in homogeneous or heterogeneous combinations that support their learning. This can allow a teacher to match students in ways that can support or challenge them. For example, students in the Jigsaw Model Lesson at the end of this chapter are grouped in homogeneous groups so that learners can work with others at their readiness level and tackle topics of differing levels of challenge. Students who are English language learners might be grouped to support their participation. When grouped with sympathetic and supportive classmates, they can get help translating their ideas verbally and in writing.

Within the different Cooperative Learning models, there is also room for differentiation support within the various steps. For example, in lessons using the Graffiti model, the type of processing activity students perform after questions are answered can also be assigned to groups based on their interest or their ability to perform a particular task. Different processing activities that challenge students to review and consider all of the group's responses to the Graffiti questions can vary in degree of difficulty and complexity. Summarizing, synthesizing, classifying, and comparing are all ways groups can process their group responses.

Teachers can also provide aids, such as written instructions, or allow students to respond to questions "open book" or using Internet resources. Students can be asked to focus on processing questions that are suited to their ability level. This can be done in an online format using a discussion group or a blog. Instead of writing answers on chart paper, students might record their responses on digital audio or video recorders. Differentiation of the learning process can also be performed by giving students access to different tools that support their learning.

Product

The product of a Cooperative Learning model lesson can also be differentiated in a variety of ways. Groups might have the opportunity to choose the type of product they want to create to demonstrate their learning, among several suggested by the teachers (as is the case in Scenario 12-3, where students can choose to demonstrate their biographies using a creative technology tool such as Glogster or VoiceThread). Different groups might be required to produce different products, and, in turn, they might be assessed using tools that support this variability but provide structured requirements (e.g., rubrics). Alternative assessments, such as a performance, a website, or even an oral presentation, are all options for students to demonstrate their learning in creative ways.

What Are the Benefits of Applying the Cooperative Learning Models?

Clearly, the Cooperative Learning models are powerful in that they couple rich and meaningful academic learning experiences with opportunities for students to build social skills. In addition to increasing students' academic learning and achievement and building their social skills, Cooperative Learning model lessons help students learn about and value cooperation in the classroom community. The following sections discuss what the Cooperative Learning models do.

Influence Student Learning and Achievement Positively

The Cooperative Learning models positively influence student achievement, as demonstrated in a synthesis of research conducted by Robert Slavin (1988), a noteworthy educational researcher and developer of the "Success for All" program. His research analyzing the collective knowledge gained from individual studies conducted over a 40-year period in various teaching and learning contexts concluded several key findings related to the implementation of the Cooperative Learning models. First, positive student achievement "effects" have been found to the same degree across all grade levels (2–12) and subject areas and in suburban, rural, and urban schools. Second, studies show equally positive effects on student achievement for high-, average-, and low-achieving students. Third, group goals and individual accountability for learning seem to be the important elements for promoting success across the Cooperative Learning models studied. Common sense would suggest that there are other reasons that these models improve student achievement, such as increased motivation, positive peer pressure, and a desire to help the team.

Another explanation for why Cooperative Learning models work to promote academic achievement is that student interactions with one another result in a greater variety of support for individual learning needs. Rather than being exposed to explanations only from their teacher, students also gain exposure to those from their peers. This can result in a greater number and variety of explanations that in turn foster increased understanding of the material as well. Because presentation of content is conducted by classmates (who are peers and also novices) rather than the teacher (who is not a peer and is typically considered an expert), students might be more patient and supportive of struggling students than they would be during teacher-centered lessons.

Help Students Learn about Cooperation and Value It

We all know that knowledge of a concept is deepened through personal experience. The same is true with the concept of "cooperation." Students can probably define what cooperation is, but many do not fully understand what it entails until they experience it and its benefits and reflect on it intentionally. The attributes of the Cooperative Learning models help ensure that students do, indeed, cooperate with one another. Therefore, students' experiences teach them powerful lessons about cooperation and provide them a way of learning how it can impact individuals and the group for the best.

Build Students' Social Skills

The Cooperative Learning models have long been recognized for being supportive of students' development of social skills. The power of these models derives from the fact that they target specific skills, provide students opportunities to learn them, and then embed their use and practice within a context that is meaningful to students. For instance, the focus of Scenario 12-1 is that students learn about teamwork. Teamwork is an important 21st century skill that all students must develop and foster throughout their life as learners and contributors to society.

Enhance Classroom Community

When students learn about the power of cooperation and develop social skills for interacting with one another, they also experience the resultant positive impact on the classroom community. The relationships students form with their peers while engaging in supportive learning experiences help them see the best in one another and, in some cases, work out their differences. This fosters a rich, open learning environment where students learn with and from one another. Learning is seen as a collective endeavor and not a competitive, stressful one.

What Value Does Technology Add to the Cooperative Learning Models?

Technology can be a valuable tool at every stage of teaching with the Cooperative Learning models. It makes planning, implementation, and assessment more efficient, effective, and engaging for the teacher and students alike. We describe just a few strategies in the sections that follow. Figure 12-6 provides a summary of some of these suggested technology applications, tools, and their purposes.

Planning

SHARE GOALS, OBJECTIVES, TIME-LINES, AND FORM GROUPS. A variety of technology tools can be used when teachers plan a lesson that incorporates a Cooperative Learning model. Graphic organizer tools, such as Gliffy or Inspiration, are helpful for developing flowcharts or other visual representations of the tasks students are to complete, as are timelines for their completion. Similarly, teachers might want to choose a task management tool, such as Backpack or Toodledo®, to help students manage the various major and minor tasks they will need to do on their own and in collaboration with other

Figure 12-6   Technology Tools for the Cooperative Learning Models

Use	Tools
Planning	
	Task management tools • 42 tasks: http://42tasks.com • Backpack: http://backpackit.com/?source=applist • Basecamp: http://basecamphq.com • Pegby: www.pegby.com/home/view • RemindPost: www.remindpost.com • Soshiku: http://soshiku.com • Thoughtboxes: www.thoughtbox.es • Toodledo: www.toodledo.com • Zoho online project management and planning software: www.zoho.com/projects Graphic organizers or tools • Bubbl: https://bubbl.us • Creately: http://creately.com • Gliffy: www.gliffy.com • Inspiration: www.inspiration.com • Kidspiration: www.inspiration.com/Kidspiration • Popplet: http://popplet.com • SpicyNodes: www.spicynodes.org/index.html
Implementing	
	Chat • Google talk: www.google.com/talk • tinychat: http://tinychat.com Blogs • Blogger: www.blogger.com • Edmodo: www.edmodo.com • Wordpress: http://wordpress.com Collaboration • ConceptShare: www.conceptshare.com • Delicious: www.delicious.com • Flikr: www.flickr.com • Google docs: www.docs.google.com • PbWorks: http://pbworks.com

continued

Figure 12-6 Technology Tools for the Cooperative Learning Models
continued

Use	Tools
Implementing (continued)	
	• Skype: www.skype.com/intl/en-us/home
	• SlideShare: www.slideshare.net
	• Wikispaces: www.wikispaces.com
	• Wridea: http://wridea.com
	• Zoho (collaboration applications): www.zoho.com
	File sharing
	• Dropbox: www.dropbox.com
	• YouSendIt: www.yousendit.com
	Video/Web conferencing
	• Anymeeting: www.anymeeting.com
	• GoToMeeting: www.gotomeeting.com/fec
	• Mikogo: www.mikogo.com
	• Skype: www.skype.com
	• Vyew: http://vyew.com
	• Yugma: www.yugma.com
Assessing	
	Online survey tools
	• Flisti: http://flisti.com
	• Google Forms: www.google.com/google-d-s/forms
	• Surveymonkey: www.surveymonkey.com
	Presentation tools
	• Keynote: www.apple.com/iwork/keynote
	• Microsoft Office (PowerPoint): http://office.microsoft.com/en-us/powerpoint
	• OpenOffice: www.openoffice.org
	• Prezi: http://prezi.com
	• Zoho Creator: www.zoho.com
	Student response tools
	• Turningpoint "Clickers": www.turningpoint.com
	Test creation tools
	• Quibblo: www.quibblo.com
	• QuizStar: http://quizstar.4teachers.org
	Other tools
	• Glogster: www.glogster.com
	• VoiceThread: http://voicethread.com

group members. Course management systems such as Blackboard and Moodle typically include task management and calendar features. Moreover, these systems often have excellent group tools that can be used to assign groups randomly or intentionally (e.g., by allowing the teacher to tailor the combination of students in each group and the total number of groups desired).

Implementation

COMMUNICATE ORGANIZE, CREATE, AND SHARE RESOURCES COLLABORATIVELY.
Collaborating and working toward shared learning and social skill(s) goals are at the heart of the Cooperative Learning models. There are numerous tools students can use to communicate ideas, share various products they create (e.g., audio, text-based, or video files), and house or store the different assignments they develop. For instance, to chat with their peers, students might use chat or video conferencing tools available within a course management system such as Blackboard or Moodle, or they might use tools such as Edmodo, tinychat, or Skype—even if they live in the same area. Wikis, Google docs, and the suite of collaboration tools available for free in Zoho allow students to develop their assignments collaboratively. Technology can help with sharing and storing of files as well. Again, the course management system can serve as a place to store and share files, or students can use tools such as Dropbox and YouSendIt.

Using audio and video recording of role-playing of social skills and behaviors can be very effective when teaching and modeling positive social skills and behaviors. For instance, in Scenario 12-1, teachers might video record students role-playing how to be supportive when working in small groups. They could ask students to model positive and negative examples of supportive feedback and then later use these videos to reflect on and compare how they actually practiced these skills in reality.

Assessment

CONDUCT FORMATIVE AND SUMMATIVE ASSESSMENT. Teachers should determine if they want to use these tools for individual and/or group assessment. For instance, teachers might use online surveys and quiz creation tools for individual or group assessment and supplement those with more creative outlets for assessing student learning, such as Glogster or VoiceThread. For formative assessment, teachers might require students to maintain individual or group blogs focused on the learning content and/or targeted social skills to be practiced and mastered. Having students record their learning via podcasts or video is another way to integrate technology with assessment.

PROVIDE INDIVIDUAL, PEER, AND GROUP EVALUATION. Individual, peer, and group evaluation are important to the success of the Cooperative Learning models. Audience-response systems can be effective tools, particularly for gauging anonymously how well groups are working together. Individual, peer, and group evaluations can be checklists, forms, or narratives created using word-processing tools.

Cooperative Learning Model Lesson Plan Example

The following lesson plan is an example of the Jigsaw Cooperative Learning model. Figure 12-7 provides an outline of the lesson's different steps, including the role of the teacher and students.

LESSON CONTEXT

GRADE LEVEL: Eighth

CONTENT AREA: Social studies

PHYSICAL TEACHING ENVIRONMENT: This lesson will be taught in a regular classroom.

TIME REQUIRED: This lesson will require two class periods, one for explanation and research and the other for peer teaching and evaluation.

APPLICATION OF REVISED BLOOM'S TAXONOMY: This lesson involves various stages of the revised Bloom's taxonomy.

Figure 12-7 Outline of Jigsaw Cooperative Learning Model Lesson Steps

Jigsaw Cooperative Learning Model Steps	Jigsaw Cooperative Learning Model Lesson
Introduce Jigsaw model	The teacher explains to students what the Jigsaw model is, how its name illustrates the interdependence of students working together in the model, and the goals for using it—to learn about the fragility of the Earth, the reasons humans modify it, and how it is changed by human activity. The teacher explains steps in the learning process and the tasks that will help the class achieve its academic and social learning goals.
Name, teach, and practice targeted social skills	The teacher explains that she will be looking for students to support one another by contributing equally and teaching one another effectively. The teacher will award groups for this.
Assign heterogeneously grouped students to expert and learning groups	The teacher forms expert groups that focus on one of the following topics: *Air, Land, Water, Ozone Layer, Combined effects.* The teacher also forms home groups that consist of one expert from each group.
Assemble expert groups and set task	The teacher meets with the various expert groups and provides them with specific instructions about their task in investigating the topic. The teacher provides resources and materials that students need to complete their task.
Experts teach in their learning groups	Students work together in expert groups to create materials that can be used to teach their peers. The teacher reviews expert group materials for accuracy and quality. These materials must include (1) a description of the human processes they researched that modify the Earth's physical environment; (2) pictures of these modifications (if applicable); (3) the reasons for the human modifications (i.e., commerce, survival, and so on; (4) the positive and negative impact of the modifications on the Earth, communities, and individuals; (5) alternatives to these modifications that might have more positive or less negative effects on the Earth; and (6) why the modification of the Earth studied should be of concern to the students in the class. The teacher monitors student work and provides support and assistance when needed.
Measure group and individual accountability	The teacher facilitates the process of measuring individual and group accountability. The teacher watches students and collects information so that she can identify two award-winning groups.
Evaluate and provide team recognition	The teacher implements assessment with a quiz and identifies the highest-. performing group. She recognizes the expert group that does the best job of sharing work responsibilities evenly and the home group whose members have done the best job teaching one another.

Lesson Plan

GOAL(S): Students will understand the fragility of the Earth and be able to understand how humans modify the physical environment and why.

Standard(s) Addressed (English Language Arts):

NATIONAL COUNCIL FOR GEOGRAPHIC EDUCATION/ENVIRONMENT AND SOCIETY:
Students will understand how human actions modify the physical environment.

OBJECTIVE(S):

1. Students will be able to identify some of the different ways that humans modify the physical environment.
2. Students will understand the reasons and necessity for human modifications to the Earth's physical environment.
3. Students will understand fragility of the Earth's physical environment and be able to identify some of the positive and negative impacts of human modifications to the physical environment.
4. Students will value careful use of the Earth's resources and efforts to protect the environment.

ESTIMATED TIME: Approximately 1 hour 15 minutes over two class periods

MATERIALS NEEDED:

- Adequate desktop or laptop computers for students working alone or in pairs
- Internet Web browser and other reference materials (encyclopedias, nonfiction books, and so on)
- Pencil and paper

PREREQUISITE SKILLS: Students will need to understand how to do research and create simple handouts to use in teaching their peers.

LESSON PROCEDURES (Text in italics is suggested teacher dialogue.)

Planning Stage: [30 minutes]

The teacher will consider how cooperative groups will be used and the composition of these groups. In this lesson, the teacher will create five heterogeneously grouped (by readiness) teams that will serve as "home" groups. The teacher will also create five "expert" groups that will be homogeneously grouped (also by readiness). Each of the expert groups will be matched with a task that is appropriate to their readiness for learning. During the planning stage, the teacher will also develop a research plan for each group. These plans will vary in their level of detail and scaffolding and be appropriate to the group and its topic.

Introduce Jigsaw Model: [7 minutes]

Teacher explains to students the Jigsaw model and its purpose in the class. The teacher says, *Class, for this next lesson we will participate in a cooperative learning experience called a Jigsaw. This model of instruction gets its name from a jigsaw puzzle. In a jigsaw puzzle, each piece is essential to the whole puzzle. In this lesson, each group member doing his or her job is essential to the whole class learning.*

In this lesson, you will work in two different groups to learn about the ways humans modify the physical environment of our planet. You will be part of a home group and an expert group.

I have given you a handout with your group assignments on it. You will notice that home groups are our normal work groupings, so the names next to this group should be familiar to you. The expert group will be a temporary group you will be a part of for this lesson. You will start this lesson in the expert group.

Each expert group will be assigned a different topic related to how humans modify the Earth's physical environment. In this group, you must research the topic and work together to prepare materials that you will use to teach other students what you learn about the topic. Each group will turn in a copy of its finished work to me. Next, you will meet with your home group. In this group, you will share what you have learned with the other group members, and they will share what they have learned with you. At the end of this sharing time, you will have an opportunity to discuss your group interactions and decide whether there are any that need to change or be applauded.

After that, I will evaluate you on what you have learned and taught each other. I will make my quiz using the materials you have created to teach each other—from the same materials your expert group will turn in. I will be making two awards at the end of this lesson. I will recognize the expert group that does the best job of sharing work responsibilities evenly, and I will recognize the home group in which members have done the best job teaching one another. As you work, be aware that I am looking for even sharing of responsibility and productive group work. As you may have noticed in my explanation, the success of this learning experience relies on everyone doing their own job the best that they can. I will oversee your work and help you when questions or problems arise. I will now answer any questions you may have.

Assign heterogeneously grouped students to expert and learning groups.

The teacher now makes sure that students know who is in each of the expert and home groups and explains, *Please look at the handout that lists your two different groups. In the expert group, you will research a topic and prepare materials to teach others about your topic. In the home group, you will teach others what you learned in your expert groups and then be assessed on what you learned together. Each person in the group will take a quiz, and the scores will be combined and then averaged together. The group with the highest average score will be recognized. Here are the expert group topics.*

The teacher then shares the expert groupings and their topics:

Expert Group #1: Air—Modifications to the ozone layer and air by pollution
Expert Group #2: Land—Landform modifications from mining and quarrying
Expert Group #3: Land—Modifications to the land from farming
Expert Group #4: Water—Effects on the Earth from pollution
Expert Group #5: Combined effects on the Earth's air, water/sea from global warming.
Note: These topics vary in level of complexity from easiest (group #1) to hardest (group #5).

Name, Teach, and Practice Targeted Social Skills: [10 minutes]

In this lesson, the teacher will ask students to practice two social skills. The first is equal contributions. The second is effective teaching (which involves effort, listening, and checking for understanding). The teacher will name these skills and initiate practicing these skills with students saying, *Our effective work in this lesson depends on everyone doing his or her best. One way you will do this is to monitor your contributions so that everyone in your group is able to contribute the same effort and amount of information during the research task. How can your groups monitor this?* Then the teacher may take suggestions from and then name the traits of effective teaching and ask students to monitor this by saying, *To be successful in this lesson, everyone will need to teach effectively. What are characteristics of good teaching?* The students might respond with ideas such as being prepared to teach (having materials ready), observing your students to make sure they understand, asking questions, and providing clarification. Then the teacher might continue, saying, *In your groups, you will be asked to consider these traits and practice them. You will be asked to evaluate one another's teaching informally, but we will measure how well you teach each other by seeing which group performs best on our quiz over the learning objectives for the lesson.*

Assemble Expert Groups and Set Task: [45 minutes]

Students meet in their expert groups and start the task. Each group has access to the resources it needs to research its topic. Within these groups, students are asked to create a teaching handout with information they will later use to teach their home group. The content of this teaching handout should include (1) a description of the human processes they researched that modify the Earth's physical environment; (2) pictures of these modifications (if applicable); (3) the reasons for modifications (i.e., commerce, survival, and so on); (4) the positive and negative impact of the modifications on the Earth, communities, and individuals; (5) alternatives to these modifications that might have more positive or less negative effects on the Earth; and (6) why the modification of the Earth studied should be of concern to the students in the class. By the end of the 45 minutes, students will have created their teaching handouts and turned them in to their teacher. The first class period ends.

Experts Teach in Their Learning Groups: [30 minutes]

Before the next class period begins, the teacher reviews these handouts and makes sure they are complete, appropriate, and accurate. She also makes copies of these handouts for all of the students in the class so that each will have a copy of all five for their notebook. After reviewing these materials, the teacher creates an assessment that measures student learning related to these teaching handouts. Students assemble in their home groups. Each expert reports on his or her topic and shares the teaching handout with all of the group members. Students will have 5 to 7 minutes to teach the other group members about what he or she learned in the expert group. Each member gets the same amount of teaching time to share his or her learning with their home group.

Measure Group and Individual Accountability: [5 minutes]

Students rate their peers and themselves in expert and home group activity.

Evaluate and Provide Team Recognition: [20 minutes]

After the allotted teaching time is up, the teacher distributes the assessment she created, and students take it. Their scores are computed and averaged by group. The group with the highest average score is recognized.

LESSON EXTENSIONS

Students could do any of the following:

- Create a persuasive speech expressing the need to preserve the Earth's physical environment
- Write a RAFT (Role, Audience, Framework, Topic) paper to express their learning in this lesson
- Meet again in their expert groups and discuss how their peer teaching went and critique their research and preparation of the teaching handout
- Meet again in their expert groups to create a multimedia presentation to share what they have learned with the home group members or a presentation for other groups of students/community members

Differentiation Strategies for the Cooperative Learning Model Lesson

In the sections that follow are some suggestions one might apply to differentiate instruction in the Jigsaw Cooperative Learning Model Lesson.

Content

The topics that students research to learn about the fragility of the Earth in this lesson vary in how concrete they are (whether they are visible) and also in their level of complexity. For example, the topic of modifications to the Earth's physical environment through farming is easier to see and understand than the topic of global warming. Likewise, the kinds of information available about each vary, so the related research also varies in difficulty. There is a great deal of information available about global warming. Information about this topic is likely to represent various agendas and biases, so students assigned to study this topic will need to focus on the kind of information they need without getting overwhelmed or distracted. They will also need to discern bias in the perspectives presented by the material. By contrast, students researching farming are likely to find fewer and more straightforward, less biased presentations of information.

One method for differentiating the degree of challenge associated with learning the content would be for the teacher to assign research topics intentionally based on students' ability to handle them. Therefore, expert groups would be homogeneously grouped so that students with demonstrated high achievement and learning readiness might be assigned more challenging topics related to the standards. Home groups would then be heterogeneously grouped with members who have varying academic achievement and readiness levels working together. Another method for differentiating content in this lesson would be to provide students with access to information in a different medium. Some students might be provided books at appropriate reading levels and more focused in their presentation of facts and concepts. Other groups might be provided books but also be allowed to use online resources from news sources, scientific experts, and the government to learn more about their topic.

Process

To differentiate the learning process, students might be offered varying degrees of structure or resources to support the separate activities of their work, such as (1) researching their topic and understanding it, (2) recording information about their topic, (3) making materials to teach their peers, and (4) teaching their peers. A written set of steps for the lesson might be provided to those who need it to stay on task with researching or recording information. A handout with clear suggestions for how to spend time during the researching/learning process might also benefit students and help them stay on track. Materials that help students focus on important details or make sense of their learning (concept-mapping tools) might be valuable aids in the learning phase (step five). During the teaching phase, support for learner differences might be provided by allowing students to work in different environments. For example, students who need quiet might benefit from a space where their group can learn without auditory distraction from others.

Product

A powerful way to differentiate the learning process would be to provide students with a broad array of options for producing their teaching materials that share the breadth and depth of their learning. Some groups might be satisfied by being asked to create a word-processed handout, as the lesson suggests. Paper, markers, and chart paper are simple options to provide. Other groups might need the motivation and/or creative power of a digital tool that would allow them to present their understanding to peers. Teachers who provide students with multiple options for how to create materials (products) that teach their expert information need to be careful to support the use of multiple formats during the teaching phase of this model, including sharing clear expectations for how students will be assessed.

Chapter Summary

This chapter provides an introduction to three Cooperative Learning models. In addition to introducing the General Cooperative Learning model, it describes two more structured Cooperative Learning models: the Graffiti and Jigsaw models. Although Cooperative Learning models differ in how students interact, all three of these Cooperative Learning models address five critical attributes. These attributes include (1) positive interdependence—that students succeed or fail together; (2) individual accountability—a measure for understanding student effort and attainment of academic and social learning goals; (3) group processing—an emphasis on the creation of learning that synergizes individual contributions within groups; (4) promotive interaction—intellectual, social, and emotional exchanges between students; and (5) development of interpersonal, small-group social skills—opportunities to practice behaviors that foster collaboration between individuals in productive ways.

The Cooperative Learning models were first developed and introduced in the 1960s to promote successful racial integration. Although they still support integration of students with varying backgrounds, they have gained new relevance as models that help students achieve academically, build self-esteem, develop 21st century skills, and encourage classroom community. The Cooperative Learning models embed strategies that support diverse learners but may also be appropriate for intentional differentiation of content, process, and learning products. Technology can be used in myriad ways that aid the planning process, implementation, and assessment of learning in differentiated settings.

Review Questions

1. What is the history of the Cooperative Learning models?

2. What are the steps in the Cooperative Learning models?

3. What type of content is best to teach when applying the Cooperative Learning models? Provide and explain examples of content that would be appropriate and inappropriate.

4. What are the benefits of applying the Cooperative Learning models? What are some of the challenges?

5. How can the Cooperative Learning models be used to differentiate instruction and support diverse learners' needs?

6. How can technology be used to implement the Cooperative Learning models?

Application Exercises

To promote your ability to apply the learning you gained in studying this chapter, complete the following exercises that challenge you to analyze a lesson plan you have written using a Cooperative Learning model *or* using the lesson plan example included in this chapter.

TECHNOLOGY INTEGRATION ACTIVITY

1. Consider the following questions and discuss with a partner or reflect independently:

   a) In the lesson plan you are analyzing, how does (or could) the integration of technology tools make learning more efficient, effective, and engaging? Can you explain and indicate how you will measure the impact on student learning?

   b) Will all learners be aided through the integration of technology? Are there some who might need special support to gain full benefit from technology tools? How might you support this? Is there a way to build on strengths students bring to this lesson related to technology? How?

   c) What plans could you put in place to promote a more successful use of technology and minimize (or eliminate) risk of failure? What proactive plan could a teacher put in place ahead of lesson implementation to ensure that technology works smoothly and for all learners? What reactive approach could you take to ensure that desired learning still occurs even if technology malfunctions during the lesson?

TEACHER PERFORMANCE ACTIVITIES

2. **Academic Vocabulary and Language Demands:** Academic vocabulary is the vocabulary that students must be able to understand to be successful performing content area learning. Language demands involve the ways language is used in speaking, writing, listening, and reading in the learning tasks of a lesson and in the expressions of student learning. For the lesson plan you are working with (your own or the one provided in the chapter), consider the following questions and discuss them with a partner or reflect on them alone:

   a) What academic vocabulary and language demands exist in the lesson? Make a list of the academic vocabulary students must comprehend and language demands of the Cooperative Learning model or learning experiences in the lesson plan.

   b) How would you determine whether and which students have mastery of the academic language in the Cooperative Learning model before the lesson begins?

   c) How might students be supported in developing proficiency with academic language in this Cooperative Learning model lesson?

3. **Planning:** In the context of the lesson plan that you are analyzing, discuss the following with a partner or reflect independently:

   a) Explain how the steps of the Cooperative Learning model build on each other to lead students to work cooperatively toward identified learning goals or objectives.

   b) Consider how you have addressed or how you might address a variety of learning needs and cooperative learning group configurations.

   c) What research or theory supports the use of this model for instruction in your learning context?

4. **Implementation:** In the context of the lesson plan that you are analyzing, discuss the following questions with a partner or consider independently:

   a) Explain how the steps of the Cooperative Learning model and the activities that students will perform in the lesson will ensure that all learners are engaged. What indicators would you look for during the implementation of your lesson to gauge who is engaged and how much?

   b) How well does your lesson challenge learners to apply their learning in meaningful and cooperative contexts? Explain.

5. **Assessment:** Consider the following questions and discuss them with a partner or reflect independently:

   a) How does the plan you are reviewing make use of information gained through pre-assessment to inform the design of the lesson and group responsibilities? Would consideration of students' learning needs, backgrounds, prior learning interests, and experiences as they relate to learning goals/objectives help you design a more effective lesson? How?

b) How does or could the lesson plan you are reviewing use formative assessment to direct the successful implementation of the Cooperative Learning model lesson? Is there a way to make the lesson more intentional or improve it to address students' strengths, ability to work with and learn from one another, and their learning needs?

c) How does the plan you are reviewing support students' expression and documentation of learning? Are there multiple forms of evidence of student learning? How might students learn through an analysis of their performance? How might you assess each student's contribution?

6. **Analyzing Teaching:** Consider the following questions and discuss them with a partner or reflect independently:

a) Now that you have created and/or analyzed a lesson plan using the Cooperative Learning model, consider how the model supports effective teaching and cooperative learning. Can you cite specific evidence or references that

support your claim? Be specific in expressing your ideas.

b) What did you learn from this activity that might inform your future practice?

Discussion Questions

What are some of the problems a teacher might encounter when using any of the Cooperative Learning models introduced in this chapter with his or her students? How might a teacher plan proactively to deal with those problems? What might appropriate solutions to those problems be? How might students from various ethnic and cultural backgrounds view cooperative learning?

Journal Entry

Working with others is an important part of many occupations. Reflect on the types of skills you need in your work as a teacher. Which of these skills would you consider to be cooperative ones? Explain why. Also describe how you might teach these in a Cooperative Learning model lesson.

Resources

- Cooperative Learning Institute—This institute, led by brothers David and Roger Johnson, houses a great deal of resources about cooperative learning, including references to research and materials that provide a general introduction to cooperative learning: www.co-operation.org

- International Association for the Study of Cooperative Learning in the Classroom—This is a professional association for those interested in joining a community engaged in studying and using cooperative learning: www.iasce.net
- Jigsaw Classroom—This site provides an overview and resources dealing with the Jigsaw Cooperative Learning model: www.jigsaw.org

Model	Integrative Model
Knowledge Supported	• Factual Knowledge
	• Conceptual Knowledge
	• Metacognitive Knowledge
Added Value	• Provides students with scaffolds for learning about large bodies of knowledge
	• Promotes critical-thinking and 21st century skills
Technologies to Integrate	• Databases that organize and filter content in organized bodies of knowledge
	• Multimedia materials that facilitate presenting and organizing content
	• Concept-mapping tools that enable exploration of content
	• Multimedia discussion tools to facilitate analysis and present learning
	• Communication tools that demonstrate student learning

The Integrative Model

ajt/Shutterstock

The room was silent. If truth be told, Ralph would love to have heard that sound 30 minutes earlier when he was transitioning from science centers to this math lesson. However, it was not welcome now, two minutes after he had asked his class, "Can anyone read this graph we have just made and tell me what conclusions we can draw from it?" It was not uncommon for him to receive silent, blank stares in response to a question that required deep thinking. In fact, it happened often in his second-grade classroom and, without bias, across all subject areas. However common they were, Ralph refused to get accustomed to them. He would get his students thinking for themselves if he had to work at it all year!

In the lunchroom later that morning, Ralph commiserated with Anju, an experienced kindergarten teacher. "Do your students have trouble thinking independently and answering analysis-type questions?"

"What do you mean?" Anju asked.

Ralph replied, "My students are having trouble thinking for themselves. They especially seem to have difficulty interpreting data, analyzing what they learn, and drawing conclusions. This is a consistent problem in all subject areas—today it was in math. We made a bar graph together based on information they shared with me about media viewing from a survey we designed and had their family members complete. When I asked them to form conclusions and generalizations about it, they looked at me with blank stares. They have no problem comprehending simple facts and answering basic questions about their learning, but when it comes to deeper analysis and learning independently—you know, generating new ideas and understandings from information they experience themselves—they struggle. They seem incapable of taking learning to the higher level."

"Well Ralph," Anju replied, "I think I know just what you mean. Yesterday we made a 'real graph' of what drinks we had at snack time. I had students stick their milk cartons, juice boxes, and water cups on chart paper; tallied each one; and asked them to tell me which drink was most popular. They could tell me what drinks everyone had and knew that each container represented one drink, but they could not interpret the graph to answer which drink was most popular *or* tell me what I would need to buy if I wanted to buy everyone their 'typical' drinks for a picnic. They do have trouble analyzing data, seeing patterns, thinking for themselves, and verbalizing their ideas."

"That is exactly what I mean, Anju, and I am not sure what to do about it. I am planning a unit on American Indians. I love history and thought I could get students thinking like historians—but they cannot be historians if they do not think and learn from data independently. After all, historians make a practice of using the very skills my students lack—they look at information presented through historical resources, examine it to find patterns and anomalies, interpret materials based on prior knowledge, and draw conclusions."

Shayla Roberts, the school mentor teacher listening from the other end of the table, shook her head with a grimace and interjected, "Welcome to Thomas Jefferson Elementary School. I hope you do not mind my listening to your conversation." Ralph and Anju shook their heads. "What you are experiencing is not unusual—at least here at TJ. Based on last year's proficiency test results, the whole school scored poorly on items that were related to data analysis and interpretation, specifically finding patterns, making generalizations, and drawing conclusions."

Ralph and Anju listened intently, not at all surprised. "Maybe you two would be willing to be my guinea pigs? I am planning a schoolwide in-service on approaches for scaffolding students' ability to learn from and synthesize information. Maybe you have seen the notice in our staff newsletter? The workshop is called, 'Drowning in Data: Scaffolding Students' Learning through the Integrative Model.' At any rate, I am looking for some teachers to work with me. Together we will develop some 'model' lessons using the Integrative model to share with the faculty during the workshop. Are you up for it? I think your plans to help your students think and act like historians are perfect. They need to develop, practice, and apply these skills—especially in the 21st century! Are you game?"

Ralph responded eagerly, "Yes, but what is the Integrative model?"

Shayla responded, "It is a model that capitalizes on teaching units that cover a lot of material, what we might call 'organized bodies of information.' It is also very useful for scaffolding students' understanding, analysis, and synthesis of organized bodies of information—and it will definitely help your students analyze material more critically and form generalizations and conclusions."

Shayla continued to explain how the model worked, and then she asked, "So, are you willing?" Both Ralph and Anju nodded enthusiastically. The Integrative model might be just what they and their students needed! ■

CHAPTER OBJECTIVES

After reading this chapter, you will be able to:

- Describe the Integrative model, including its history and steps.
- Communicate the applications and benefits of the Integrative model and learn what it might look like in a classroom.
- Explain how to implement and plan for teaching with the Integrative model.
- Articulate how the Integrative model might enable differentiated instruction and support diverse learners.
- Describe how technology can enhance teaching with the Integrative model.

Introduction

People from previous generations needed to know how to use machines to live well. People living in the 21st century need to know how to understand and use information to live well. Being able to find, collect, organize, compare, analyze, and synthesize information about innumerable topics in many media formats is essential 21st century skills. Today's citizens also need to be able to make connections, understand relationships, and develop inferences based on content. Ironically, these skills are as challenging to develop as they are important for successful living. New modes of teaching are required to teach these essential skills for learning. As the opening scenario illustrates, Ralph's second-grade students (and Anju's kindergarteners) have difficulty thinking independently and gaining new insights from information with which they are presented. They do not innately know how to analyze and synthesize information—they must be taught how.

One model of teaching that is well suited for guiding students as they work to learn from "organized [bodies] of knowledge . . . a combination of facts, concepts, generalizations, principles and rules, integrated with one another" (Kauchak & Eggen, 2012, p. 283) is the Integrative model. The Integrative model provides a structure that helps teachers guide students in a process of describing, comparing, categorizing, analyzing, examining relationships, and making generalizations about organized bodies of knowledge. It also scaffolds student learning through a series of four different phases during which students analyze the content-based materials presented in text and other formats.

This chapter provides an overview of the history of the Integrative model and its different phases. It also provides suggestions for when teachers should use the model, how they might plan to implement it, and what it looks like in practice. Later, the chapter discusses which technologies might be used for implementing the model and how teachers might effectively support diverse learners through the use of differentiation techniques. The chapter concludes with an Integrative Model Lesson.

What Is the Integrative Model?

The Integrative model is a purpose-driven instructional model that supports students as they work to develop the ability to learn independently using various thinking skills. In this model, the teacher facilitates students' analysis of information about a topic communicated in an organized collection of materials. Successful implementation of the model results in students processing information and ideas from rich content materials into new ideas and understandings. In the process, students grow in their ability to think, analyze, and draw conclusions independently. This model relies on formal strategies that teach students how to analyze and interpret information they might encounter in school and beyond. Through engagement in the Integrative model, students acquire and develop skills they can use regularly to make meaning from experiences in school and daily living. The model supports students' learning across the academic subject areas while also empowering them to become independent learners.

The Integrative model provides a practical structure for teaching learners to explore **organized bodies of knowledge**, which is content that consists of a combination of facts, concepts, generalizations, and their relationships. The phrase "organized body of knowledge" is one that varies depending on context, but we use the phrase to refer to a collection of information that is (1) so large that it cannot be easily understood without intentional analysis, (2) presented in some type of structured or ordered manner, and (3) not already analyzed, processed, or understood by a learner. Some sources that are typically considered organized bodies of knowledge include textbooks, databases, and spreadsheets. Students in Scenario 13-2 use a typical organized body of knowledge when they explore a government database about drugs. Nontypical organized bodies of knowledge can also be used, as is noted in Scenarios 13-2 and 13-3. In Scenario 13-2, students refer to their knowledge of three different works of literature. In Scenario 13-3, the organized body of knowledge is assembled by art students using graphic organizers.

Note that a great deal of the content that students learn in schools might be considered organized bodies of knowledge. Students must do more than just comprehend information presented in organized bodies of knowledge. They must also be able to make connections between this knowledge and other understandings and be able to formulate broad generalizations based on the content learned and examined.

During the Integrative model, students are guided by teachers as they (1) learn to explore, analyze, and interpret information in these materials; (2) process what the materials

Figure 13-1 Examples of Topics That Can Be Taught with the Integrative Model

Subject	Topics	
Art	Influence of politics on art	Different art movements
Language Arts	Literary genres	Themes in works about surviving life's challenges
Mathematics	Mathematics of art	Geometry postulates and theorems
Music	Families of instruments	Beat and rhythm in different types of music
Health/Physical Education	Human body systems	Food groups
Social Studies	Population changes	Revolutions
Science	Habitats	Animal classification

communicate; and (3) draw their own conclusions to generate new understandings and ideas. Examples of topics within the different academic content areas that might be taught using the Integrative model are outlined in Figure 13-1.

The Integrative model consists of four phases. Each phase purposefully focuses students in different cognitive processes that progress to drawing meaningful conclusions about information explored. In the first phase, students describe, compare, and search for patterns in the content that represents an organized body of knowledge. In the second phase, students explain the identified similarities and differences by examining the content more closely. That is, students must go beyond simple identification to explain why similarities and differences exist. During the third phase, students form hypotheses based on their examination of the content. Finally, in the fourth phase, students make broad generalizations about the content. They form conclusions that synthesize their understanding and also demonstrate how their understanding might be considered in a larger context.

The duration of lessons using the Integrative model varies. Their implementation may take one class period (as in Scenario 13-3), or it might take a longer period of time, ranging from days (as in Scenario 13-2, which takes several class periods) to even months (as in Scenario 13-1, which describes a lesson that occurs over the course of an entire quarter).

The Integrative model is timely for contemporary learners because it focuses on building skills for processing information resources (Partnership for 21st Century Skills, 2004). Students engage in comparing, categorizing, analyzing, organizing, and synthesizing. It also requires students to organize their ideas visually using graphic organizers to categorize information and see relationships (see Figures 13-4, 13-6, and 13-7 for examples of graphic organizers). These materials are developed by the teacher, by the students, or by the teacher together with the students. Graphic organizers help students to integrate their comprehension of the content being learned and later to substantiate their generalizations. For instance, in Scenario 13-3, students use graphic organizers (see Figure 13-7) to document facts learned about some of the major modern art movements (e.g., Cubism, Dadaism, and Impressionism).

What Are the History and Origins of the Integrative Model?

The Integrative model, developed by teacher educators Don Kauchak and Paul Eggen (Kauchak & Eggen, 2012), builds on the important work of Hilda Taba. Taba, a highly influential teacher and scholar in the field of education, authored the Taba Curriculum Development Project and several teaching models addressed previously in this text, including the Concept Attainment model (see Chapter 6), the Concept Development model (see Chapter 7), and the Inductive model (see Chapter 8). All of these models are designed to promote students' ability to think and reason—a major goal for all of Taba's work. In the Integrative model, as in the Taba models, the teacher plays a crucial role in supporting students' thinking. He or she acts as a facilitator whose questions assist students as they examine evidence, analyze patterns, make sense of relationships, and draw conclusions from an organized body of knowledge. The Integrative model complements the existing Taba models by promoting students' ability to think and make generalizations about data from organized bodies of knowledge.

The learning theory undergirding all of these models is that of constructivism. Constructivism asserts that learning is an active process in which the learner uses sensory input to construct meaning out of experiences. Important principles in constructivism reflected in the Integrative model are that (1) learners need to "do" something or engage in what is called "active learning" (Dewey, 1916), (2) people learn to learn as they learn (Resnick, 1987), (3) the crucial action of constructing meaning is mental (Vygotsky, 1962), (4) learning involves language (Vygotsky, 1962), and (5) learning is social (Vygotsky, 1962). For more on constructivism, refer to the resources at the end of this chapter.

When Should the Integrative Model Be Applied and Why?

First and foremost, the Integrative model is best utilized when teaching organized bodies of knowledge. It can be used with any grade level, but primary-grade teachers will need to provide considerable scaffolding through guided questioning, collection and analysis of data, and categorization of information. The model is also best applied for teaching units of instruction that incorporate conceptual knowledge, foster critical thinking, and involve making connections between information learned. The following sections discuss what teachers should use the Integrative model to do.

Teach about Organized Bodies of Knowledge

A great deal of content taught at all academic levels involves learning about organized bodies of knowledge. Organized bodies of knowledge represent a combination of facts, concepts, generalizations, and their relationships. Note that organized bodies of knowledge are not just concepts, although concepts are building blocks that support them and even form the basis for their organized structure. Figure 13-1 provides several examples of topics that would be considered organized bodies of knowledge in different content areas. Another example of an organized body of knowledge is in Scenario 13-2, where a group of eighth-graders are studying the different types of drugs and their effects on the body. The study of drug types involves learning about numerous facts, concepts, and ways in which these relate to one another. The Integrative model provides teachers with an effective method for teaching students how to analyze and learn from large amounts of related content and make connections between the content explored.

Support Students' Development of Conceptual Knowledge

The Integrative model is one of the best models for teaching conceptual knowledge—the interrelationship of facts, concepts, and generalizations that is at the heart of the model. It is an ideal model for teaching conceptual knowledge because the purpose of the model is to foster students' conceptual understanding of the content being learned based on facts, concepts, and generalizations. Students start by learning factual knowledge and then continue to use that knowledge to make larger connections between facts and concepts and, ultimately, to make informed inferences about the content studied. Scenario 13-3 provides an example of how the Integrative model promotes conceptual knowledge through a study of the smaller movements that make up modern art. Clearly, understanding of modern art requires comprehension of many facts, but it also entails tying together many ideas and concepts (e.g., see Figure 13-7).

Develop Critical-Thinking Skills

Teachers should use the Integrative model to promote critical-thinking skills, which involve thinking at the higher cognitive process levels of the revised Bloom's taxonomy (Anderson et al., 2001). In the first two phases of the Integrative model, students work at the lower stages of the revised Bloom's taxonomy, which emphasize factual knowledge, and then, in the last two phases, teachers gradually lead students in the application of higher-level cognitive process skills. For example, in the first phase of the model as illustrated in Scenario 13-2, students examine the similarities and differences between different types of drugs (see Figure 13-4 for an example). In the second phase, they examine the data collected to explain the identified similarities and differences between the different types of drugs (e.g., certain drugs are classified as hallucinogens because they can make people hallucinate, and certain drugs are more addictive than others). This involves scrutiny of the data by students to compare the facts they are learning. Students would then explain why particular similarities and differences might exist. Then, in the third phase, students are asked to form hypotheses based on the content reviewed. Students might hypothesize why certain drugs are more addictive than others or at which age one might become more addicted to a drug. Finally, in the fourth phase, students form broad generalizations about the content. Another example of how to support students' gradual progress through more difficult thinking skills is presented in the Integrative Model Lesson at the end of this chapter.

Make Connections between Content That Is Learned

One of the purposes of the Integrative model is for students to synthesize the content they are learning to make connections and inferences based on their analysis. (This occurs in the fourth and final stage of the model.) Finding relationships between content materials and the ideas presented in them is a 21st century problem-solving and critical-thinking skill. It involves analyzing how discrete parts of information (e.g., facts) make up a whole (e.g., concepts or principles), how these might relate, and what this means (i.e., what conclusions might be made from the content). The Integrative model allows students to learn, develop, and practice this lifelong learning competence in a school environment, and use it to enhance their content area learning and general academic performance. For example, in the Integrative Model Lesson at the end of this chapter, second-graders enter data in a graphic organizer to record some of the characteristics of different American Indian tribes. They analyze this information by comparing the different categories, making connections between them, and drawing broad conclusions about them.

What Are the Steps in the Integrative Model?

The Integrative model consists of four major phases: (1) Describe, compare, and search for patterns, (2) explain similarities and differences, (3) hypothesize outcomes for different conditions, and (4) generalize to form broad relationships. These phases are described below. Figure 13-2 provides a description of the teacher's and students' roles in this model; essentially, the teacher is a facilitator of students' analysis of the content.

Figure 13-2 Teacher and Student Roles in the Integrative Model

Integrative Model Phases	Teacher Role	Student Role
Describe, compare, and search for patterns	Teacher asks students to describe, compare, and search for patterns in the content examined by students. Teacher guides students through this phase by creating (or co-creating or asking students to create) graphic organizers to scaffold students' understanding and recording of information.	Students analyze the content by describing, comparing, and searching for patterns in the content studied. They (or the teacher) enter data/information into graphic organizers developed by the teacher or students, or co-developed by the teacher and students. (Note: Either the teacher or students record data in graphic organizer.)
Explain similarities and differences	Teacher asks students to explain similarities and differences.	Students explain similarities and differences in the content studied and substantiate their ideas using data from the graphic organizer.
Hypothesize outcomes for different conditions	Teacher asks students to hypothesize outcomes based on different conditions.	Students form hypotheses of possible outcomes related to the content studied and based on different conditions.
Generalize to form broad relationships	Teacher asks students to generalize their conclusions.	Students generalize their understanding to demonstrate understanding of the broad relationship between content studied.

Phase One—Describe, Compare, and Search for Patterns

The goal of the first phase of the Integrative model is multifaceted. It challenges learners to (1) conduct a preliminary exploration of an organized body of knowledge, (2) develop a basic understanding of what information is contained within, (3) gain an appreciation of how all of the "pieces" of the organized body of knowledge relate to one another and (if applicable) to other previously explored bodies of knowledge, and (4) consider connections to students' existing mental schema. Initial encounters with organized bodies of knowledge can be overwhelming for students because the information is often new, voluminous, and organized by structures students may not yet comprehend.

To help students manage information overload during this phase, the teacher can introduce students to the information in the body of knowledge gradually. Varying approaches for providing guidance are possible. Teachers can work with students in the classroom setting to provide real-time guidance, or teachers might provide guidance through instructions communicated in written (e.g., worksheets, multimedia presentations, or websites) or other formats (e.g., audio, visual, or multimedia materials). Teachers can also ask many questions to guide students' learning.

Regardless of the approach to guidance, the teacher should first ask students to describe their basic observations and impressions of the information they are exploring. Depending on the format of the information, students might click or scroll through an electronic database (e.g., see Scenario 13-2), flip through the pages in a collection of books (e.g., see Scenario 13-1), walk around the classroom examining photographs or paintings, listen to an audio collage of sounds, or view a collection of three-dimensional shapes. Teachers are encouraged to present the large bodies of knowledge in creative, nontext formats, so they should provide appropriate support for helping students make sense of them. Teachers must guide initial explorations of information in the body of knowledge with general and open-ended questions. For example, in Scenario 13-1 the teacher asks her fifth-grade students, "What did you record in your graphic organizers about the books you read by Beverly Cleary?" In Scenario 13-2, the teacher asks his eighth-graders, "Can you describe what you are looking at in the database provided?"

At this stage, teachers should also ask students to compare the information they are exploring. Although students may be ready to make other observations, the teacher should try to focus students only on these two cognitive activities. In Scenario 13-1, the teacher focuses discussion by providing a handout listing discussion questions such as "Can you tell me how the books you read are similar? Can you tell me how they are different?"

Finally, the teacher asks students to search for patterns in the information they are exploring. Students are encouraged to make observations that identify the recognition of repetition, recurrence with variations, larger trends, and internal connections. For example, in Scenario 13-1, a teacher might ask, "Students, can you identify some patterns in the works you read by Beverly Cleary?" Students might respond, "The author's main characters are all under the age of 12" or "The books are written in third person." In Scenario 13-2, the teacher might ask, "Can you identify some patterns about drugs from the database you explored?" Students might respond, "Some drugs are man-made." During this exploration for patterns, students might uncover the organizational structure beneath the information being explored. For example, students might identify that drugs are categorized into stimulants and depressants or natural, semisynthetic, synthetic, and designer drugs.

Students who record their learning in some manner as they progress through this phase find that it supports their mental processing of information while enabling them to record their thinking for future reference. Graphic organizers can be particularly useful in this first phase. Because students build their understanding of concepts and ideas of the organized body of knowledge gradually during this model, a graphic organizer can provide helpful insights to both the teacher and learners about the process involved in creating meaning and understanding. The content being explored and the learning goals requiring this exploration will determine what type of graphic organizer is most appropriate to use. Graphic organizers might be generic and come from a professional source (e.g., researchers, other teachers, and so on), or they might be created by the teacher from scratch specifically for the lesson. In some cases, it is beneficial to encourage students to create an appropriate graphic organizer for their exploration in the Integrative model. For instance, in Scenario 13-3, the teacher introduces students to a variety of resources and information representing some of modern art's major art movements. As the introduction of the lesson shows, the teacher notes that students will be learning many factual details about modern art movements and recording what they learn in a graphic organizer (see Figure 13-7).

Although the teacher asks students to enter information in the graphic organizer, the teacher also needs to scaffold students' learning by asking them general questions, such as "What do you see here?" or "What do you notice in these works of art?" or "Compare the characteristics recorded in our graphic organizer." In many cases, the teacher will need to ask more specific questions, such as "What similarities and differences are there among the art movements of this period? Be specific—tell me how Dadaism is the same or different from Impressionism?" and so on. Students become familiar with the information more easily when they have to describe it, search for patterns within it, and compare the facts, concepts, and details presented within it.

Phase Two—Explain Similarities and Differences

The goal of the second phase of the model is to explain similarities and differences in the organized body of knowledge being explored. That means students must first identify similarities and differences. The teacher may need to prompt students to examine the content being studied more closely.

Often, contributions shared in the first phase are revisited. For example, in Scenario 13-1, students might be asked to consider the fact that Beverly Cleary wrote books with main characters under the age of 12. The teacher might challenge students to consider how the main characters in the three different books are similar and different. As much as a graphic organizer helps students see what is common and uncommon among the content being studied, students should also be able to explain in words these commonalities and differences. For example, in the Integrative Model Lesson at the end of this chapter, students might explain that the geographic location of where different American Indians lived greatly influenced their way of living, the crops they grew, and more. Teachers may need to craft questions that elicit specific explanations of the similarities and differences. The Integrative Model Lesson provides a series of questions as examples.

Phase Three—Hypothesize Outcomes for Different Conditions

In this phase, the goal is to generate additional and different insights about the information being explored. During this phase of the Integrative model, students make hypotheses about the information presented in the body of knowledge as a means of stimulating deeper thought about the ideas contained within it. Some teachers describe this phase as one that catalyzes the mind to manipulate data playfully and view it from different angles.

Regardless of the explanation, in this phase, students use existing knowledge constructed in the first two phases to hypothesize outcomes for different conditions related to the data and achieve deeper meaning and understanding. In this phase, teachers ask students to examine the similarities and differences noted and then consider what the outcomes might have been if circumstances (e.g., history) had been different. Teachers will likely need to help students form hypotheses through questioning and sharing of example hypotheses. One way to have students form hypotheses is to ask them to brainstorm explanations for what they are studying under different conditions—in many cases, teachers will need to provide hypothetical conditions for them to form their educated guesses. Teachers can ask questions such as "What if the English had not settled in America in Jamestown or later Plymouth Rock?" or "Where might different American Indians have settled if there was no river?" Asking questions like these encourages a flexibility of thinking that is critical to the overall success of the model.

Phase Four—Generalize to Form Broad Relationships

The goal of the fourth phase is to help students synthesize their understanding by forming a broad generalization about the organized body of knowledge being studied. During this phase, the teacher may need to define what a generalization is and model how to develop one with students. When the teacher introduces the concept is not as important as the students' full comprehension of what it means.

The purpose of students' generalizations is for them to demonstrate their learning and comprehension of the organized body of knowledge. By making such inferences, students show they completely grasp the content at higher cognitive process levels, such as the "evaluate" level of the revised Bloom's taxonomy. Their conceptual knowledge is evident not only through the generalization(s) developed but also by their substantiation of the inference. When students can substantiate an inference, they are demonstrating their understanding at a conceptual—not just factual—level.

As with previous phases, it might be necessary for the teacher to ask questions to help students formulate these inferences. For instance, the teacher in Scenario 13-1 might ask, "What were some of the things that have made Beverly Cleary's books so popular with young readers of yesterday and today?" The teacher in Scenario 13-2 might ask, "What is an essential understanding about drugs you gained from exploring this database?" The teacher using the Integrative Model Lesson at the end of the chapter might ask, "What 'big' conclusion can you make about American Indians based on your exploration of this content."

Some examples of generalizations based on these questions might be "Beverly Cleary's books explore themes, feelings, and experiences that are important to children growing up in America" (Scenario 13-1), "The way of life of American Indians was largely influenced by the geography of where they lived" (see the Integrative Model Lesson at the end of the chapter), or "Different types of drugs are more addictive than others, depending on their pharmacological composition" (Scenario 13-2).

What Does the Integrative Model Look Like in the Classroom?

The Integrative model can have a significant amount of variation in its implementation, as there are many ways one might teach organized bodies of knowledge. For instance, specific phases can be implemented (with their intended cognitive activities supported) using real-time direction or recorded directions from the teacher. Variation also occurs because organized bodies of knowledge that might be explored using the Integrative model may vary extensively in format, size, and organization. The time required for an Integrative model lesson (or unit) can also vary significantly. If organized bodies of knowledge need to be created by students to implement the model, academic learning time will be required. In these instances it is best to view the Integrative model as a series of lessons or a unit of instruction rather than one lesson.

The scenarios in this chapter illustrate three different audiences and just a few ways in which the Integrative model might be implemented. The Integrative model, like others in this textbook, is flexible and can be modified in numerous ways to work better within various teaching and learning contexts provided the four basic phases are carried out in order.

Scenario 13-1

Claire Meyers' fifth-grade reading groups have been working on author studies this quarter. Claire is hoping her students will explore the work of popular, contemporary writers and gain a better understanding of their individual books, writing techniques, common themes, and the reasons for their perennial popularity. Each of her reading groups will be asked to focus on the works of a different author—Beverly Cleary, Andrew Clements, Roald Dahl, Kate DiCamillo, or Lois Lowry—and read three books by this author over the 10-week term.

Before starting the author study, Claire explains the model's major phases and her implementation plan. She explains that students will first read the books and create an organized body of knowledge about their author. Then they will use this information to understand each book, their assigned author, and all the authors. She further explains that, because students will work in numerous small groups, she will not be able to support them all at the same time.

To adjust for this, she has done some advanced planning and put together numerous documents to share with students, all available for download on the course website, explaining the process and guiding them gradually through it. This advanced planning will free Claire up to float around the room during author study time and respond to students' needs as they emerge. The documents on the website include the following:

a) The Project Description and Instructions—A handout explaining learning goals, the rationale for the author study, and specific

Working with Students in the Integrative Model
© Monkey Business Images/Shutterstock

Figure 13-3 Book Matrix Form—Story Map for One Book

Book One Title:	
Description of the main character:	
Important characters and brief descriptions:	
Other characters:	
Setting:	
Point of view (first person, third person, and so on):	
Literary techniques used by the author that are noteworthy (foreshadowing, story within a story, imagery, plot twist, side story, symbolism, humor, anthropomorphism, irony, flashback, dialogue):	
Problems the main character experiences:	
Lessons learned in the book:	
What I thought about the book:	

activities students will perform during the two class periods they will devote to the author study each week over the 10-week term

b) Book Discussion Questions—A handout with questions to be used to discuss the book and combine individual Book Matrices in each author group after individual books are completed,

c) Book Matrix Forms (Figure 13-3)—A handout to be completed with specific information about each book and then combined across the groups

d) An Author Study Synthesis—A four-page handout (one page of questions/activities for each phase of the model) to guide students as they analyze their completed Book Matrix forms

e) A Venn Diagram—Useful when comparing and contrasting main characters during the Integrative model phase 1

f) An Author Study Comparison Chart—Helpful in the second phase of the Integrative model, looking for patterns in the information

Over the next few weeks, students will be divided into groups, read, and record important information about their chosen books. They will collect information about each of their three books and organize it into a knowledge base. This work will take them through the four Integrative model phases. They will use a Venn diagram in the first phase (Figure 13-4) to compare prompts for the Author Study Comparison Chart (Figure 13-5) and then again in the second phase to explain the similarities and differences. Students will form hypotheses about the authors during the third phase. Finally, they use the Author Study Synthesis forms in the fourth phase to devise generalizations they will discuss as a class at the end of the unit.

Figure 13-4 Venn Diagram of Main Characters

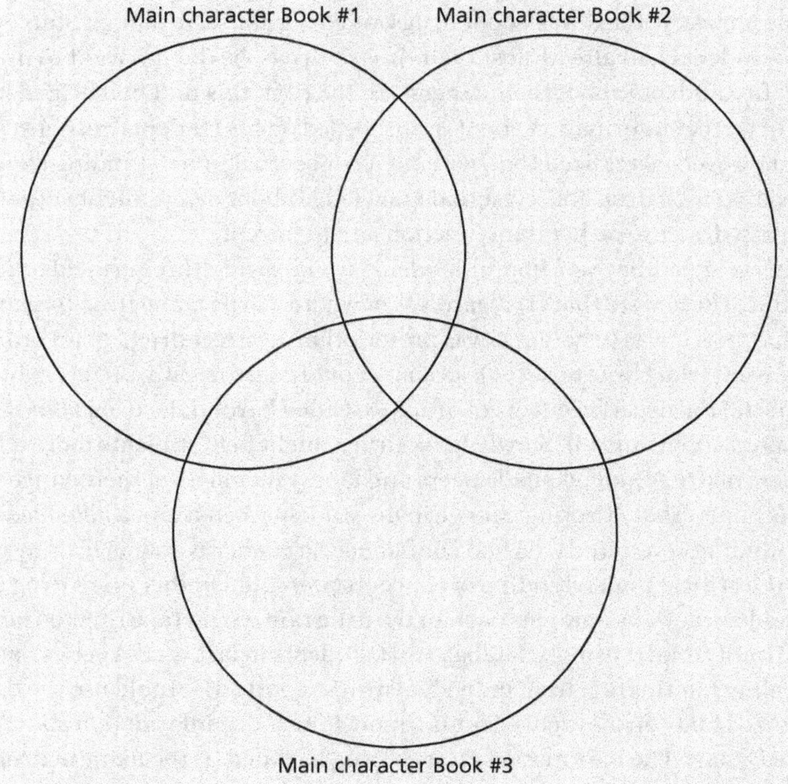

Main character Book #1   Main character Book #2

Main character Book #3

Figure 13-5 Author Study Comparison Chart

Book Title	Setting (when and where)	Main Characters (who)	Secondary Characters (who else)	Problem (what)	Conclusion
1.					
2.					
3.					

Scenario 13-2

One of the most important units the students in Stanley Cerevelli's eighth-grade health and wellness class studied was about drugs and drug abuse. Although Stanley's sister and two of his students had already lost their lives to drugs, he did not want to use scare tactics to teach his students about their dangers. In the past, this unit had helped his students learn a lot of factual information about drugs. Based on his students' responses at the end of the unit, however, he realized that, without a conceptual understanding about the problems associated with drug abuse, factual knowledge about drugs might actually facilitate his students' drug use rather than function as a deterrent.

This year, Stanley was hoping students would attain three critical understandings in the unit. These were that (1) regardless of where a drug came from (organic or man-made) or what type it was (whether it was prescription, a "street drug," or an ordinary product like spray paint which was misused), its abuse could cause negative, irreversible, and far-reaching effects; (2) the negative effects of drugs extended beyond the drug abuser to those he or she cared about; and (3) knowledge of drugs might help students more effectively avoid the dangers of drugs and persuade peers and family members of their dangers. Even though Stanley knew that effecting change in his students' behaviors challenged the odds in the surrounding community, he had confidence he could save some lives by getting students to gain the critical understanding of concepts presented in this year's drug unit.

Stanley knew his new approach to the drug unit would take time, so he decided to save significant time by using a database that students in last year's classes had created by compiling information from individual drugs reports. He would use the database as the organized body of knowledge for his lesson. It included information about 66 commonly abused drugs. The information on each drug included (1) the name of drug, (2) nicknames, (3) intended use, (4) source (where it comes from), (5) method of administration, (6) cost, (7) "typical" abuser profile, (8) abuse culture surrounding the drug, (9) level of addiction, (10) health risks, (11) negative effects of use, (12) legal penalties for taking/selling the drug, and (13) two URLs containing a testimonial about a story of personal experience related to this drug. With help from the technology teacher, Stanley created a Web-based version of the database so that this year's students could gradually add more information over a two-week period.

Stanley reserved the school's laptop cart for three class periods so that students could access the drug database for the lesson. Because Stanley did not want to leave his students' critical understandings to chance, he directed students through these resources very carefully with thoughtfully crafted questions. After explaining the procedure for the lesson, he asked students to look at the database he shared with them. Students were intrigued by the presentation of data and the various views the database let them have while examining the data. They could examine it through individual entries (showing information about just one drug at a time) or in a table view to see different categories of information. Students comfortable with advanced database features could query the data and also sort it by the various categories or fields. Using the different views, students were able to manipulate and describe the data more accurately. There was not a bored student in the room.

Once students described the data, Stanley told them where the database came from and asked them to search for patterns in it. As they worked, Stanley guided students through this phase by encouraging them to create (and in some cases helping students co-create) graphic organizers that would scaffold their understanding and recording of information (see Figure 13-6 for an example). He asked them, "What patterns do you see about where

Figure 13-6 Example of Types of Drugs Concept Map

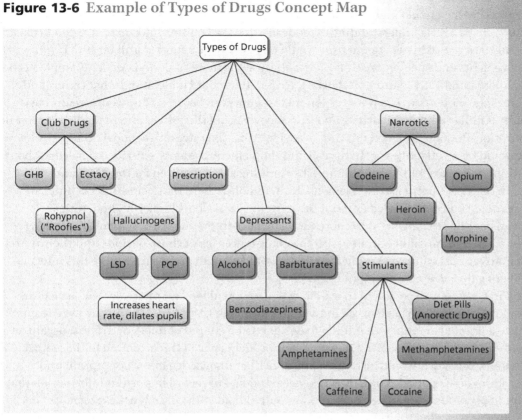

drugs come from, how they are abused, and what are their effects?" Next, he asked students to explain the similarities and differences in the drugs. He asked many questions, including "How are the different types of drugs similar and different in their cost? In their patterns of abuse? In their different effects?" After students had thoroughly examined the similarities and differences, Stanley asked them to hypothesize about the different individuals in general and people they know in particular who might be more likely to abuse certain types of drugs. He challenged them to make assertions about (and then discuss in a group) the effects of certain drugs, the possible succession of problems, and effects arising from the abuse of individual drugs in particular and drugs in general. Finally, he challenged students to make some broad generalizations about drugs and drug abuse—based on the data—and then summarize those generalizations in the form of a short three-minute video, multimedia presentation, song, or paper about what they learned about drugs. In reviewing his students' work, Stanley was thrilled to discover that they had arrived at the critical understandings he had anticipated and even gone beyond his expectations. At the end of the drug unit, he knew he had figured out a better way to teach his students this critical and potentially lifesaving understanding of the topic.

Scenario 13-3

Rudolfo's high school advanced placement (AP) art history course consisted of students in grades 10 through 12 from all over the state. His was one of several AP courses students could take 100% online through the state's virtual online high school. Pre-assessment data gathered using the virtual high school's course management system indicated that Rudolfo's students had little understanding of modern art. Based on this information, Rudolfo decided his best use of instructional time would be to conduct a shorter unit on 19th century art movements and spend more time on the study of the modern period. Students would need to understand 19th century art, however, before they could understand what trends and forces the modern artists were responding to. However, because they were already basically familiar with major artists and works, coverage of the 19th century could be shorter in duration. Rudolfo designed this unit overview using the Integrative model because he knew it would be an effective way to refresh and supplement students' existing knowledge about this period in art while also building the thinking skills required for the AP exam.

In the 19th Century Art Movements Unit, Rudolfo would first help students build an organized body of knowledge about the movements of Neo-Classicism, Romanticism, Realism, Impressionism, Neo-Impressionism, Post-Impressionism, Symbolism, and Art Nouveau and introduce students to the characteristics of those periods and their representative artists and works. Then students would work in groups to explore this information to gain a deeper understanding of it.

First, students were asked to watch, listen, or download and read a screencast lecture Rudolfo prepared on each of the individual movements. While doing so, they were to complete a graphic organizer that Rudolfo designed and shared online. The graphic organizer had a threefold purpose. First, it would help students pay better attention to the lecture content. Second, it would help them organize their knowledge into a conceptual understanding of the period. Third, it would help students to record important information that would become an organized body of knowledge about 19th century art movements.

Students posted their draft graphic organizers in Google Docs after listening to and reading the lectures with the other members of their learning group. Using this online tool, students could freely collaborate and revise their graphic organizers (see Figure 13-7 for an example of an incomplete graphic organizer). Next, Rudolfo reviewed the graphic organizers for accuracy, making sure that the collective knowledge pooled together by

Figure 13-7 19th Century Art Movements

Movement	Major Characteristics	Time	Influences	Artist	Example
Romanticism					
Realism					
Impressionism					
Post-Impressionism					
Symbolism					
Art Nouveau					

his students would generate correct understandings. Then students were asked to work together in groups to tackle the different phases of the Integrative model: One group would need to post a short video, audio, or text-based presentation describing the similarities and differences among the movements; another group would need to create and post a multi-media presentation explaining the noted similarities and differences; and a third group would work on a multimedia presentation titled "What if, then," which was a series of hypotheses about what might have transpired under different conditions. Finally, Rudolfo would bring the students together in the online discussion asking each group to review all of the presentations to form a generalization about 19th century art movements. They would need to post their inferences as the culminating activity for their study.

What Do These Scenarios Illustrate?

These three scenarios present the implementation of the Integrative model at different grade levels by different teachers and within different time spans. Each teacher has unique learning goals, methods for facilitation, and use of grouping, timing, and pacing, yet all of the teachers challenge students to develop critical-thinking skills while also learning about important content area standards at the same time.

REFLECT: Consider your own content area and some of the organized bodies of knowledge you have to teach. How might you use the Integrative model for teaching your students this content? Would you break it out over a long period of time as in Scenarios 13-1 and 13-2, or would you use it to introduce an entire unit, as in Scenario 13-3? Explain your decisions.

Planning for Teaching with the Integrative Model

As the scenarios show, there are many different ways to implement the Integrative model. Certain steps should be taken by teachers in the planning stages to ensure the best odds for success. These are (1) ensuring learning goals are compatible with the Integrative model, (2) identifying critical understandings that students should acquire in the lesson, (3) developing graphic organizers that scaffold students' comprehension and analysis, (4) creating questions to promote thinking at all levels of the revised Bloom's taxonomy, and (5) selecting resources for analysis. The following sections discuss what educational designers do when teaching with the Integrative model.

Ensure Compatibility of Learning Goals with the Integrative Model

As mentioned previously, the Integrative model is highly effective when addressing learning goals that are related to students' development of conceptual understanding of ideas presented within organized bodies of knowledge—these learning goals are considered "critical understandings." **Critical understandings** might be concepts (e.g., prescription drugs) or generalizations (e.g., 19th century art movements occurred simultaneously and influenced one another)—they are the most important ideas that must be learned.

The model is equally effective addressing learning goals related to students' development of critical-thinking skills required to understand information presented in organized bodies of knowledge. Therefore, when teaching with the Integrative model, teachers must first engage in reflection and self-questioning to determine if the learning goals they have identified can be addressed through use of the Integrative model. For example, in Scenario 13-2, Stanley might ask, "Can my students really learn the potential impact of drug abuse on themselves and those they care about by exploring the resources about drugs I have directed them to? Can students draw appropriate understandings about the impact of drug abuse through the phases of the Integrative model lesson I have planned?" In Scenario 13-3, Rudolfo might ask himself, "Will using the Integrative model familiarize students with the major characteristics, artists, and works of the 19th century art movements?" and "Will students' completion of this Integrative model lesson support their development of the foundational knowledge necessary for understanding the characteristics of modern art we will study in our next unit?"

Review of content standards can certainly help in determining these critical understandings. Teachers using the Integrative model often teach above and beyond the standards because wording of standards is often too narrowly focused on facts or concepts and not generalizations.

Identify Critical Understandings about the Organized Bodies of Knowledge

Identification of critical understandings about the organized bodies of knowledge will improve teachers' ability to plan the Integrative model lesson, scaffold student learning, and select appropriate resources. Of course, as with most inductive curricula, students will likely determine additional understandings, but it is important for teachers to have some ideas of the most critical understandings students should attain during the Integrative model lesson(s).

According to Wiggins and McTighe (2005), understanding has the following characteristics:

1. An understanding is an important inference, drawn from the experience of experts, stated as a specific and useful generalization.
2. An understanding refers to transferable, big ideas having enduring value beyond a specific topic.
3. An understanding involves abstract, counterintuitive, and easily misunderstood ideas.
4. An understanding is best acquired by "uncovering" (i.e., it must be developed inductively, co-constructed by learners) and "doing" the subject (i.e., using the ideas in realistic settings and with real-world problems).
5. An understanding summarizes important strategic principles in skill areas. (pp. 128–129).

These ideas about the characteristics of understanding apply to generalizations as well. Teachers should strive to devise generalizations that incorporate the characteristics of Wiggins and McTighe's notion of understanding. See Chapter 7 for more about generalizations.

Develop Graphic Organizers to Scaffold Students' Learning

The Integrative model works so well because it scaffolds students' learning of organized bodies of knowledge. One effective way for teachers to support students' learning throughout all of the phases of the model, is by requiring students to record their learning using graphic organizers (see Chapter 5 for a lesson on graphic organizers).

Graphic organizers can be useful as tools to support studying a large body of knowledge (e.g., Scenario 13-1 when students record information about books they have read), as tools supporting the analysis of a body of knowledge (e.g., Scenario 13-1 when students use a Venn diagram to compare characters in books they have read), or for both purposes (e.g., in Scenario 13-3, students use Rudolfo's organizer to record their learning about 19th century art movements). In these scenarios, graphic organizers are tools for prompting certain types of thinking, such as comparison and pattern recognition. They are practical because they allow students to record information in a way that facilitates information processing. Such organizers also fill a role in communicating student thinking and documenting their learning. This information can assist teachers in correcting misunderstandings and directing intervention in their efforts to ensure all students understand the content. Finally, graphic organizers can be used to communicate accountability and assessment information.

Although graphic organizers are not necessary when using the Integrative model, they support and promote its success. Because the scope of some organized bodies of knowledge is so great, teachers may need to review carefully student-created graphic organizers to ensure that they address the major concepts students will need to comprehend to form generalizations. There are several examples of graphic organizers throughout this text and several in this chapter (e.g., see Figures 13-3, 13-4, 13-5, 13-6, and 13-7).

Create Questions Based on the Revised Bloom's Taxonomy

The advanced formulation of questions based on the revised Bloom's taxonomy (see Chapter 1, Figure 1-2) can contribute to increased success with the Integrative model when the questions foster students' critical-thinking skills related to their analysis of the organized body of knowledge being studied. The revised Bloom's taxonomy serves as an appropriate schema for developing the questions because the phases in the Integrative model require students to examine material on a continuum of increasing difficulty and challenge with regard to cognitive processes (see Figure 13-8 for sample questions teachers might ask aligned with the phases of the Integrative model and revised Bloom's taxonomy cognitive process skills levels).

Select Resources for Analysis

Although the quality of instruction is associated with its design (see Chapter 2 for more about instructional design), what students learn during instruction also has a lot to do with the quality of resources and materials they encounter while learning. Poor resource choices often lead to misconceptions and rudimentary or tangential learning. Low-quality resources can also promote the formation of stereotypes, inaccuracies, and/or biases, as would likely be the case if inappropriate resources were chosen for a unit like the one in the opening scenario on American Indians. It is, therefore, imperative that teachers choose resources that will best enhance their students' learning and analysis of the organized body of knowledge they will study—or that they guide students in this process if they are selecting resources themselves.

Clearly, there are many types of resources teachers (or students) might choose. Selected resources must help students attain the ultimate goal of the Integrative model: forming

Figure 13-8 Sample Questions Using the Revised Bloom's Taxonomy with the Integrative Model

Integrative Model Phase	Revised Bloom's Taxonomy Cognitive Process Level	Sample Questions
1. Describe, compare, and search for patterns	Remember	What do you notice/see? What similarities do you see? What differences do you notice?
2. Explain similarities and differences	Understand	How do you account for the similarities identified? How do you explain the differences noted?
3. Hypothesize outcomes for different conditions	Apply Analyze	How might the outcome have been different if *x* happened (or did not happen)? What might have happened if circumstances had been different?
4. Generalize to form broad relationships	Evaluate	What is the "So what?" idea of what you have studied? What broad generalization can you make based on the material examined?

generalizations about the content. To that end, the resources chosen should be age and developmentally appropriate and have enough depth and breadth for students to be able to describe, compare, hypothesize, and develop generalizations. Moreover, teachers should provide or guide students in finding resources that provide multiple ways to learn about the organized body of knowledge—from books, magazines, primary sources, secondary sources, video, audio, and so on. In Integrative model lessons where students develop the organized body of knowledge, such as in Scenarios 13-1 and 13-3, the teacher should examine the information for accuracy, validity, and overall quality throughout the Integrative model lesson.

Differentiating Instruction with the Integrative Model

As the scenarios in this chapter illustrate, there are a variety of ways in which the Integrative model might be implemented and differentiated. Although phases in this model are clearly outlined, what teachers plan for students to do during each of these phases may be differentiated in a variety of ways. Whereas younger students and those with less experience applying cognitive process skills, especially critical-thinking skills, will require more teacher direction and support, older students accustomed to rigorous analysis of material may need less. As educational designers, teachers need to design instruction using the Integrative model in ways that best fit students' needs, interests, and developmental level.

Content

Teachers have a great deal of leeway in differentiating the content (the organized body of knowledge) studied in the Integrative model. The teacher might consider the group composition as a whole or look at individual students' readiness, learning style or profile, and interest. Alternatively, the teacher might consider the content to be the source of the organized body of knowledge (i.e., who creates this body of knowledge and where it comes from) or the nature of the organized body of knowledge (i.e., the content presented and its level of difficulty).

The source of the organized body of knowledge used in the Integrative model lesson is the first consideration teachers must make when differentiating content. Teachers must decide whether to challenge students to create their own organized body of knowledge, use one that is already constructed, or co-construct one with students. In some cases, it will be a better fit for students to explore a body of knowledge they have created independently, such as in Scenarios 13-1 and 13-3. In some cases, the process of finding and organizing information benefits students who need this intellectual challenge. In other cases, students will need to explore an organized body of knowledge provided by their teacher. This option is often easier for students, especially for those without the independence to collect and organize new knowledge. An option that supports learners of multiple levels is the co-creation of an organized body of knowledge with their teacher's assistance. In the Integrative Model Lesson at the end of this chapter, the teacher models how to organize ideas and information in a teacher-created graphic organizer and then supports some students in its completion by working with them while others work independently.

The nature of the information in the collective body of knowledge might also be differentiated. For example, groups of learners who are proficient readers might be asked to explore an online database during an Integrative model lesson while another group composed of students with less proficiency are asked to examine a simpler interpretation, prepared by their teacher, of the information in the database.

In some instances, teachers can allow students to select for themselves the materials presenting the body of knowledge based on their own unique interests and readiness level. Such is the case in Scenario 13-1, in which the teacher allows students to choose which books to read by the author their group will study. Use of materials presented in alternative formats (e.g., multimedia, video, or audio formats) can also allow students to select the resources that support differentiation. For example, in Scenario 13-2, the teacher invites learners to explore a body of knowledge created by the previous year's students containing access to information in multimedia formats. In this Web-based resource, students whose needs might be better met experiencing information in nontextual formats can do so.

Process

The most important consideration for teachers who hope to differentiate the process of the Integrative model is to consider carefully how they will scaffold students' learning during the model's four phases. This involves carefully designing in each of the phases learning experiences that help students describe, compare, hypothesize, and generalize about the organized body of knowledge. Knowing the needs of the different learners will help teachers gauge what types of supports students will need and when. For instance, teachers can differentiate the degree of support students receive when completing the graphic organizers documenting their learning. In the Integrative Model Lesson at the end of this chapter, the teacher records information on the graphic organizer rather than having the students enter their own information.

Another method of differentiating the learning process is to vary the types of questions used during the implementation of the model. Teachers can use the revised Bloom's taxonomy as a structure for developing questions that support differentiating and increasing degrees of challenge throughout the lesson. Choices made about grouping and consideration paid to students' readiness, interest, and/or learning style can also support efforts to differentiate in the Integrative model.

Product

Differentiation of the learning product will allow students to use the most effective method for demonstrating their attainment of learning goals. Learning goals for an Integrative model lesson will include (1) critical understandings about the organized body of knowledge and (2) the ability to engage in thinking skills required for comprehension of information resources. There are many possible products students might create to demonstrate that learning goals have been met. Some products include graphic organizers developed before, during, or after the Integrative model lesson (as in Scenarios 13-1 and 13-2) or multimedia presentations documenting and explaining their understanding in the different phases of the Integrative model (as in Scenario 13-3). In some cases, support for differentiation can be offered by allowing students to choose the best product that demonstrates their learning. In other cases, differentiation occurs by using tools students select (as in Scenario 13-2, where students can choose to create a video, multimedia presentation, song, or paper that summarizes their generalizations about what they have learned about drugs).

■ What Are the Benefits of Applying the Integrative Model?

The most obvious benefit of the Integrative model is that it supports students' development of critical understanding of content. The model also promotes development of critical-thinking skills, supports awareness of relationships between concepts, and develops students' ability to synthesize information from various resources. The following sections discuss what the Integrative model does.

Develops Students' Critical Understanding of Content

The four phases of the Integrative model lead to students' formulation of broad generalizations about the organized body of knowledge studied. The thinking processes involved in these phases foster students' understanding of the big picture, the "So what?" of learning, because the model requires students to synthesize all of the information they have studied to make inferences. The model requires students to evaluate their understanding by describing the essential understandings gleaned from the study of the organized body of knowledge. In Scenario 13-1, for example, students need to reflect on their learning after reading three books by the same author and share what they think is the big idea—the major inference that applies about the three books.

Promotes Development of Critical-Thinking Skills

Generally, the Integrative model promotes students' development of 21st century skills—particularly critical-thinking skills—by engaging students in four phases of analysis, starting with the first phase, where students describe and compare their learning, and then finishing in the fourth phase, during which they develop inferences about the organized body of knowledge studied. Comparing parts of organized bodies of knowledge and their whole, as well as hypothesizing and synthesizing learning into inferences, are all critical-thinking skills. Each of the scenarios in this chapter and the Integrative Model Lesson at the end of this chapter demonstrate ways in which the Integrative model cultivates students' application of critical-thinking skills.

Supports Awareness of Relationships between Concepts

Students required to examine the "big picture" of the organized body of knowledge must also examine the smaller parts that make up the larger concept (body of knowledge) and how the smaller parts relate or not. For instance, in the Integrative Model Lesson, students are asked to examine the characteristics of the different American Indian tribes studied to determine their relationships and differences. The use of graphic organizers and questioning based on the revised Bloom's taxonomy help students analyze the relationships that exist between facts and concepts that make up the organized body of knowledge and also analyze any generalizations that emerge.

Synthesizes Learning from a Variety of Resources

The nature of the Integrative model involves selecting the best materials from a variety of resources—relying only on a text, for instance, to learn about American Indians (as in the Integrative Model Lesson at the end of the chapter) or the types of drugs and their effects (see Scenario 13-2) would limit students' understanding of the organized body of knowledge. Students can have multiple, rich opportunities to cull their understanding of the organized body of knowledge through analysis of a myriad of resources, including text, audio, video, photos, drawings, and more.

What Value Does Technology Add to the Integrative Model?

Teachers can capitalize on the use of technology for the planning, implementation, and assessment of learning when teaching with the Integrative model. Although some tools can be used in all three areas (e.g., use of survey tools), technology provides teachers with some unique ways for planning, implementing, and assessing students' learning when using the Integrative model. Figure 13-9 provides a list of the technology tools introduced in this section.

Planning

Both teachers and students can locate resources using various technology tools such as online databases (e.g., library databases), collections/repositories (e.g., Library of Congress American Memory), search engines (e.g., Google), or directories. Resource materials should include a variety of sources ranging from print—textbooks, fiction, nonfiction books, and magazines—to multimedia sources that incorporate video, graphics, and audio. Moreover, resources can also be people. Teachers might wish to connect students with individuals in other parts of the

Figure 13-9 Technology Tools for the Integrative Model

Use	Technology Tools
Planning	
	Search engines • Google: www.google.com Online repositories/databases • Library of Congress American Memory: http://memory.loc.gov/ammem/index.html Resources organizing access to content materials and/or presenting assignments • Google Sites: www.google.com/sites/overview.html • Weebly: www.weebly.com Graphic organizers or tools supporting analysis • Bubbl: https://bubbl.us • Gliffy: www.gliffy.com • Inspiration: www.inspiration.com • Kidspiration: www.inspiration.com/Kidspiration • Popplet: http://popplet.com • SpicyNodes: www.spicynodes.org/index.html Timeline creation tools • timetoast: www.timetoast.com • Timeliner: www.tomsnyder.com/timelinerxe
Implementing	
	Visual presentation of questions • Keynote: www.apple.com/iwork/keynote • Google docs: www.google.com/google-d-s/documents • SMART Notebook: www.smarttech.com • PowerPoint: www.microsoft.com • Prezi: http://prezi.com Reference list creation tools • EasyBib: www.easybib.com • Zotero: www.zotero.org Social bookmarking • Delicious: www.delicious.com • Diigo: www.diigo.com Audio recording • Digital audio recorder, tape recorder Digital video • Digital video recorder or camera on computer
Assessing	
	Online survey tools • SurveyMonkey: www.surveymonkey.com SMS Polling • Poll Everywhere: www.polleverywhere.com Test creation tools • Quibblo: www.quibblo.com • QuizStar: http://quizstar.4teachers.org

continued

Figure 13-9 Technology Tools for the Integrative Model
continued

Use	Technology Tools
Assessing	
	Audio and digital video recording • Digital audio recorder, tape recorder • Digital video recorder or camera on computer Other tools • Glogster: www.glogster.com • VoiceThread: http://voicethread.com

world involved in some way with the organized body of knowledge under study. For example, a teacher might invite and schedule a videoconference interview with a scientist who studies addiction.

Many useful technology tools are available for the development of graphic organizers by both teachers and students. Several are available for free online, such as Bubbl, Gliffy, Popplet, and Spicynodes. Inspiration and Kidspiration software programs are not free, but they do not require an Internet connection. Teachers might also want students to develop timelines to further their understanding of the organized body of knowledge. Some useful tools for creating timelines are timetoast and TimeLiner software. Timelines can also be created using word-processing tools (e.g., Microsoft Word or OpenOffice) or any of the graphic organizer tools shared previously. Many course management systems, such as Blackboard or Moodle, and collaborative tools, such as Google docs, allow students to create and share files, which can include graphic organizers that their peers can also access.

Technology tools are also a great support for questioning and creating materials for questioning. Word-processing software is an obvious tool for this purpose, but other tools can be used for creating questions and then collecting and evaluating students' answers to them. For instance, online survey tools such as SurveyMonkey offer free access, albeit with limited features (more features are available with a paid subscription), to tools that teachers and students can use to develop questions in many styles, including multiple-choice, ranked, and open-ended short-answer and essay questions. Other tools teachers might use for creation of questions to show and share with students are: Keynote, Notebook, PowerPoint, or Prezi, among many other options. Audience response systems can be utilized for this same purpose.

Implementation

Technology is a powerful ally for teachers needing to organize the numerous materials required to make teaching using the Integrative model a success. Teachers can use technology tools to organize, document, and share resources in a variety of ways ranging from developing a bibliography or reference list (e.g., EasyBib) to creating a resource list in Word to using an online tool (e.g., Delicious or Diigo) to keep track of and share links. Also, teachers might use research tools (e.g., Zotero) and website creation tools (like Weebly) to organize different resources to be examined both in print and online.

Assessment

As with other models, technology tools can be used in the Integrative model to con-duct pre-assessment, formative assessment, and summative assessment. Online survey and test creation tools allow teachers to assess students' understanding at all stages of the assessment continuum. Teachers can use online surveys, test creation tools, or graphic organizers to pre-assess students' prior knowledge, to assess their learning as they pro-gress (formatively), or as they form broad generalizations (summatively). Some tools, such as Quibblo and QuizStar, are designed specifically for creating tests and quizzes. If teachers have access to a course management system, they should also be able to develop quizzes and tests using those tools. Tools such as VoiceThread and Glogster can be used for assessment purposes as well (e.g., requiring students to cre-ate an interactive poster). Audience response systems can also help students compare aspects of the organized body of knowledge being learned by examining their factual knowledge about them.

Digital audio and video recorders can capture students' understandings during any phase of the Integrative model. In fact, many teachers might want students to record or at least document their learning during each stage and especially at the fourth phase, when students develop broad generalizations about the organized body of knowledge studied.

■ How Is the Integrative Model Implemented?

The following is a lesson plan that incorporates the Integrative model. Figure 13-10 provides an outline of the lesson's different steps.

Figure 13-10 Outline of the Integrative Model Lesson Steps

Integrative Model Steps	Integrative Model Lesson
Describe, compare, and search for patterns	After engaging with a variety of materials to learn about various American Indian tribes and recording their learning in a graphic orga-nizer, students describe, compare, and search for patterns among all of the data in the graphic organizer that was co-developed by the class and teacher.
Explain similarities and differences	The teacher asks students to work with partners and then the whole class to explain the similarities and differences identified.
Hypothesize outcomes for different conditions	The teacher asks students to make educated guesses about how things might have been different under different conditions. Tip: The teacher should craft questions before the lesson in the event that students have a tough time formulating hypotheses.
Generalize to form broad relationships	The teacher asks students to share their big ideas about American Indians. Students share their inferences regarding American Indians first with their partners and then with the class as a whole. They work together to do a radio show about American Indians.

Integrative Model Lesson Plan Example

LESSON CONTEXT

GRADE LEVEL(S): Second

CONTENT AREA: Social Studies

PHYSICAL TEACHING ENVIRONMENT: This lesson will be taught in a regular classroom.

APPLICATION OF REVISED BLOOM'S TAXONOMY: Students move from the lower levels of the revised Bloom's taxonomy (i.e., *remember*, by describing the different characteristics of the American Indian tribes studied) to the higher levels (i.e., *evaluate*, by forming generalizations about American Indians).

Lesson Plan

GOAL(S): Students will gain an understanding of American Indian tribes and culture in the United States.

Standard(s) Addressed:

National Curriculum Standards for Social Studies:

Learners will understand the following:

- Culture: "Culture" refers to the behaviors, beliefs, values, traditions, institutions, and ways of living together of a group of people. (p. 27)
- Culture: Concepts such as: similarities, differences, beliefs, values, cohesion, diversity. (p. 27)
- Time, Continuity, and Change: The study of the past is the story of communities, nations, and the world. (p. 31)
- Time, Continuity, and Change: That historical events occurred in times that differed from our own but often have lasting consequences for the present and future. (p. 31)
- People, Places, and Environments: The theme of people, places, and environments involves the study of location, place, and the interactions of people with their surroundings. (p. 35)
- People, Places, and Environments: Factors that contribute to similarities and differences among peoples locally and in places across the world, including ethnicity, language, and religious beliefs. (p. 35)
- Individuals, Groups, and Institutions: The theme helps us know that people belong to groups and institutions that influence them and by which they are influenced. (p. 42)

ISTE NETS for Students 2007 #3 and #4.

OBJECTIVE(S):

1. Students will describe and compare at least four American Indian tribes from different regions of the United States by completing a graphic organizer. (See Worksheet 13-1 in Appendix C.)
2. Students will explain the identified similarities and differences between American Indians from different regions of the United States.

3. Students will hypothesize and substantiate outcomes about American Indians from different regions of the United States.
4. Students will make generalizations about American Indians from different regions of the United States.

ESTIMATED TIME: Three to five class periods

MATERIALS NEEDED:

- Books about American Indians for research
- Graphic organizer handout (Worksheet 13-1 in Appendix C)
- Computer and projector

PREREQUISITE SKILLS: Students should be able to read and comprehend text at the second-grade level as well as understand major vocabulary, know how to read a basic map, understand directions on a map, and comprehend how to form hypotheses and generalizations.

LESSON PROCEDURES (Text in italics is suggested teacher dialogue.)

Anticipatory Set (Introduction): [4 minutes]

Motivation: Ask students to draw (individually) what they believe American Indians look like and the type of home they might live in. Ensure that they do not share their drawings with anyone until after they are done.

Information: Inform students that for several class periods they will be learning about American Indians, often also called Native Americans. They will be doing a special lesson that helps them organize all the information they will learn so that they can compare the different tribes, explain the similarities and differences, make guesses about how things might have been different, and, finally, make some conclusions about American Indians.

Connection: Ask students to share and discuss their drawings. Ask them to explain why they depicted the American Indians as they did. Tell students that they will be studying several American Indian tribes and learning about how interesting and different they were. Each student will receive a notebook for keeping track of their learning and reflections on it.

A. Phase 1: Describe, compare, and search for patterns

Together with students, the teacher examines a variety of resources—books, websites, videos, and journal transcriptions—to gather information about different Indian tribes. As students engage with these materials, the teacher asks them to complete a graphic organizer (see Worksheet 13-1) about American Indian tribes that he also completes on a computer and simultaneously projects for all to see.

As a class, the teacher models how to complete the graphic organizer. Some students fill out sections on their own, and others need help by seeing the teacher model it.

The teacher hands out a sheet with several questions. Students are asked to describe and compare the information collected in the graphic organizer by answering the following questions in pairs:

1. What are some of the major American Indian tribes that reside in the United States?
2. Where do or did they live?
3. From which language family did their language originate?
4. What was their lifestyle?

As students discuss their answers, the teacher asks them to refer back to the graphic organizer they created together. As they answer, he records their ideas under each question using multimedia presentation slides. On each slide, the teacher types the details of their answers while also noting who answered the question.

Phase 2: Explain similarities and differences

The teacher asks students to examine the matrix and verbalize some comparisons and patterns between the different American Indian tribes, such as where they lived in the United States, what type of home they had, and so on. Then, the teacher asks students to explain the similarities and differences by asking questions like "How can you explain their lifestyle (e.g., of hunting and gathering)? In what ways are they different? Alike? Explain."

Phase 3: Hypothesize outcomes for different conditions

After this discussion, the teacher asks the students to devise hypotheses of what might have been different if conditions were different. For instance, the teacher might ask students to think about their way of life: "How would a Chinook's way of life be different if he or she lived in the Southeast or the Plains? Explain." (Ask students to provide support for their hypotheses by writing them down.) As students reply, the teacher should type students' responses on the computer (or overhead).

Phase 4: Generalize to form broad relationships

Ask students to form broad generalizations or big ideas that summarize their learning about American Indians. Be sure to ask them to substantiate their inferences by referring back to the graphic organizer they completed together as a class. Examples of possible student responses are the following: Not all American Indians are the same, and American Indians' lives depended on where they lived—if they lived near the water, they were usually fishermen.

Closure: The teacher asks students to summarize in small groups what they have learned about American Indians by (1) discussing what they have learned, (2) writing a short summary of their learning about American Indians, and (3) sharing with the class the group summary.

ASSESSMENT

Formative assessment   Teachers could check students' understanding of the concepts about American Indians as they study the unit. The creation of a graphic organizer on their own with certain facts is a low-key way to conduct formative assessment of students' comprehension.

Summative assessment   Students could create a recorded podcast educational segment to teach their families (and possibly also students in other grades) about what they learned about American Indians.

LESSON EXTENSIONS

1. American Indians of the Chesapeake: www.smithtrail.net/native-americans
2. America in 1607: Jamestown and the Powhatan:
   http://ngm.nationalgeographic.com/2007/05/jamestown/jamestown-standalone
3. John Smith's Journal: www.johnsmith400.org/journal.htm
4. Virginia's First People: http://virginiaindians.pwnet.org
5. National Museum of the American Indian: www.nmai.si.edu
6. Native Americans resource list for teaching to or about Native Americans:
   http://comminfo.rutgers.edu/professional-development/childlit/ChildrenLit/nalist.html

7. NOVA: Pocahontas Revealed: www.pbs.org/wgbh/nova/pocahontas
8. U.S. Department of the Interior Indian Affairs Tribal Directory: www.bia.gov/WhoWeAre/BIA/OIS/TribalGovernmentServices/TribalDirectory/index.htm
9. Visit your library and locate as many fiction and nonfiction books as possible about American Indians. Ask students to create other charts for other American Indian tribes.

Differentiation Strategies for the Integrative Model Lesson Plan

In the sections that follow are some suggestions one might apply to differentiate instruction in the Integrative Model Lesson.

Content

Content might be differentiated by presenting or asking students to choose/vote on the American Indian tribes to study. Moreover, reading materials of different levels of complexity could be chosen. For instance, a beginning reader series might be selected for struggling readers and an encyclopedia for advanced ones. The teacher might include photos of the different types of dress, homes, and geographic location and textual firsthand accounts by Europeans of their encounters with American Indians (e.g., Lewis and Clark expedition journal: www.pbs.org/lewisandclark/archive/idx_jou.html).

Process

One way to differentiate the process for this lesson is to have different groups of students work on only one American Indian tribe, then all of the groups "teach" one another. Another possibility involves grouping students into pairs or individually for the different phases of the Integrative model.

Product

The final phase of the Integrative model requires students to develop a broad generalization about the organized body of knowledge studied—in this case, it is American Indians. Teachers could ask students simply to devise a general conclusion about American Indians based on the information studied. This might be in the form of a short essay, video or audio recording explanation, or a radio show where students share their conclusions.

Chapter Summary

In this chapter, you learned about the Integrative model. This model is a purpose-driven instructional model that supports students as they work to develop the ability to learn independently using various thinking skills. In this model, the teacher facilitates students' analysis of information about a topic communicated in an organized body of knowledge. Successful implementation of the model results in students processing information and ideas from rich content materials into new ideas and understandings. Some sources that are typically considered organized bodies of knowledge include textbooks, databases, and spreadsheets. The Integrative model consists of four phases. Each purposefully focuses students in different cognitive processes that progress to drawing meaningful conclusions about information explored. First, students describe, compare, and search for patterns in the content that represents an organized body of knowledge. Then students explain the identified similarities and differences by examining the content more closely. Next, students form hypotheses based on their examination of the content. Finally, in the fourth phase, students make broad generalizations about the content by forming conclusions that synthesize their understanding and demonstrate how it might be considered in a larger context.

The Integrative model was developed by teacher educators Don Kauchak and Paul Eggen (Kauchak & Eggen, 2012) and builds on the important work of Hilda Taba. When participating in lessons designed with the model, students learn and practice critical-thinking skills when analyzing and using data for subjectarea learning. The model can be used with any grade level, but primary-grade teachers will need to provide considerable scaffolding through guided questioning, collection and analysis of data, and categorization of information. The model is also best applied for teaching units of instruction that incorporate conceptual knowledge, foster critical thinking, and involve making connections between information learned.

Review Questions

1. What is the history of the Integrative model?

2. What are the steps in the Integrative model?

3. What type of content is best to teach when applying the Integrative model? Provide and explain examples of content that would be appropriate and inappropriate.

4. What are the benefits of applying the Integrative model? What are some of its challenges?

5. How can the Integrative model be used to differentiate instruction and support diverse learners' needs?

6. How can technology be used to implement the Integrative model?

Application Exercises

To promote your ability to apply the learning you gained in studying this chapter, complete the following exercises that challenge you to analyze a lesson plan you have written using the Integrative model *or* using the lesson plan example included in this chapter.

TECHNOLOGY INTEGRATION ACTIVITY

1. Consider the following questions and discuss with a partner or reflect independently:
   a) In the lesson plan you are analyzing, how does (or could) the integration of technology tools make learning more efficient, effective, and engaging? Can you explain and indicate how you will measure the impact on student learning?

   b) Will all learners be aided through the integration of technology? Are there some who might need special support to gain full benefit from technology tools? How might you support this? Is there a way to build on strengths students bring to this lesson related to technology? How?

   c) What plans could you put in place to promote a more successful use of technology and minimize (or eliminate) risk of failure? What proactive plan could a teacher put in place ahead of lesson implementation to ensure that technology works smoothly and for all learners? What reactive approach could you take to ensure that desired learning still occurs even if technology malfunctions during the lesson?

TEACHER PERFORMANCE ACTIVITIES

2. **Academic Vocabulary and Language Demands:** Academic vocabulary is the vocabulary that students must be able to understand to be successful performing content area learning. Language demands involve the ways language is used in speaking, writing, listening, and reading in the learning tasks of a lesson and in the expressions of student learning. For the lesson plan you are working with (your own or the one provided in the chapter), consider the following questions and discuss them with a partner or reflect on them alone:

   a) What academic vocabulary and language demands exist related to the organized body of knowledge which is the focus of the Integrative model lesson? Make a list of the academic vocabulary that students must comprehend and language demands to participate successfully in the Integrative model lesson.

   b) How would you determine whether and which students have mastery of the academic language before, during, and after the lesson?

   c) How might students be supported in developing proficiency with academic language throughout the entire Integrative model lesson?

3. **Planning:** In the context of the lesson plan that you are analyzing, discuss the following with a partner or reflect independently:

   a) Explain how the steps of the Integrative model build on each other to lead students to make clear and meaningful connections among identified learning goals or objectives.

   b) Consider how you have addressed or how you might develop a variety of questions to address different learning needs at multiple levels of the revised Bloom's taxonomy.

   c) What research or theory supports the use of the Integrative model for instruction in your learning context?

4. **Implementation:** In the context of the lesson plan that you are analyzing, discuss the following with a partner or consider independently:

   a) Explain how the phases of the Integrative model lesson will result in sustained student engagement throughout lesson. What indicators would you look for during the implementation of your lesson to measure who is engaged and how much? What questioning and supports will be necessary to help students learn about the organized body of knowledge studied in the Integrative model lesson?

   b) How well does the lesson overall challenge learners to develop hypotheses for different, hypothetical outcomes and to form a broad generalization regarding the organized body of knowledge? Explain.

5. **Assessment:** Consider the following questions and discuss them with a partner or reflect independently:

   a) How does the plan you are reviewing make use of information gained through pre-assessment to inform the design of the Integrative model lesson? Would consideration of students' backgrounds, prior learning, and experiences as they relate to learning goals/objectives help you design a more effective lesson? How?

   b) How does or could the lesson plan you are reviewing use formative assessment to improve the delivery of the lesson?

   c) How does the plan you are reviewing support students' expression of and reflection on their learning? Are there multiple forms of evidence of student learning? How might students learn through an analysis of their performance and reflection on their learning (metacognition)?

6. **Analyzing Teaching:** Consider the following and discuss with a partner or reflect independently:

   a) Now that you have created and/or analyzed a lesson plan using Integrative model, consider how the model supports effective teaching, questioning, and comprehension of the organized body of knowledge. Can you cite specific evidence or references that support your claim? Be specific in expressing your ideas.

b) What did you learn from this activity that might inform your future practice?

Discussion Questions

Select an organized body of knowledge that you might teach. Discuss with a partner the different relationships you see in the content. What similarities and differences exist? Can you explain them? What if conditions were different? What is the "big idea" you would want students to "take home" regarding this organized body of knowledge? Explain.

Journal Entry

The Integrative model is best used for teaching organized bodies of knowledge. Consider those in your content area. Reflect on your own experiences as a student and consider how you learned to navigate the structure and ideas contained in these organized bodies of knowledge. Did you receive guidance from others or work independently? Explain. Consider the value of providing your own students guidance as they learn to identify patterns, observe details, and draw conclusions. Describe what you will do to guide them.

Resources

- Constructivism: www.thirteen.org/edonline/concept2class/constructivism/index.html
- Constructivism: http://carbon.ucdenver.edu/~mryder/itc/constructivism.html

- The Application of the Integrative Model to Teach the Formation of American Political Parties: www.societyforhistoryeducation.org/pdfs/Mitchell.pdf

Model	Socratic Seminar Model
Knowledge Supported	• Factual Knowledge
	• Conceptual Knowledge
	• Metacognitive Knowledge
Added Value	• Provides an accountability measure for students' preparedness for class
	• Provides students opportunities to learn to listen and communicate more effectively
Technologies to Integrate	• Search engines to find rich resources for exploration and analysis
	• Graphic organizers to support analysis
	• Multimedia materials that present content for exploration and analysis
	• Microblogging or other communication tools to facilitate questioning during dialogue
	• Audio/video recording of dialogue for later analysis
	• Online assessment or audience response system tools to facilitate summative assessment

The Socratic Seminar Model

ajt/Shutterstock

Jasmina Kovac was a teacher with a mission. She had immigrated to the United States years earlier when she and several other family members had been offered asylum after the Bosnian War. At first, she found the midsize midwestern college town strange. As time passed, however, and thanks to her experience as a teacher, she found that her affection for her adopted nation and its democratic ideals grew profound.

Because of her experiences during the war, and out of a desire to serve her new homeland, Jasmina decided to become a social studies teacher. Simply helping her middle school classes meet "adequate yearly progress" was not enough for Jasmina. She taught with a mission—to inspire her students to become active participants in democracy. She wanted them to value their rights as American citizens and care about democratic ideals—not just remember them to get a good grade on a test. This was not an easy task, however. Drawing from her own experiences in Bosnia to illustrate the importance of citizenship was somewhat helpful, but she needed more than this. She knew she needed additional methods to engage learners in these "big ideas" related to her subject and passion.

Fortunately Jasmina was surrounded by talented colleagues, and great teaching ideas could be found by simply walking through the hallway in her building. One day, inspiration came from Hugh Oberfield's language arts classroom, where students seemed unusually engaged. Peering in Hugh's room, Jasmina saw 25 seventh-graders leaning forward and listening attentively. A skinny, fair-haired girl talked animatedly about a reading she had done for homework. As soon as she finished, a boy wearing glasses jumped in with excitement responding to the ideas she had shared. Hugh sat back watching with satisfaction, nodding his head and taking notes on the students' interaction. Jasmina made a note to ask Hugh what was going on—maybe he could help her find ways to get her students more engaged in history!

"Hugh, what was that technique you were using during fourth period?" she asked him later that day.

"Did you like it?" he responded.

"It seemed to be working to get your students interested in their readings," she said. "I'm 'fishing' for new ways to help my social studies students to share their opinions, care for, and value the content I am teaching."

"The technique is called the 'Socratic Seminar model' Jasmina," Hugh told her. "It is a common approach for teaching English and language arts because it works well as a strategy for promoting dialogue about what students are asked to read. I like it because it allows students to express their views about what they have read, and I find that they often share new insights that resonate with peers. I lead the dialogue with questions designed to promote critical thinking among the group so it challenges them intellectually."

"Sounds like it might be really helpful," Jasmina interjected.

"But practically," Hugh continued, "the strategy works better than any other method to get students to do their homework. It makes them accountable to their peers and that is a powerful motivator, even more than a pop quiz!"

"Sounds great," Jasmina interjected, "tell me more about why it works."

"Well, it works well to address other standards in language arts like listening and speaking," Hugh responded. "Today, active listening was our goal—did you notice how they were using their body language to listen? I thought they looked really 'cute' leaning in. One student actually tipped his chair over at the beginning of class! Something else that

I like is that it builds students' comprehension. If they did not understand a reading the first time, they can listen and learn from their peers during the Socratic Seminar model."

"Yes, I can see how that might be useful. Would you give me some materials about this 'Socratic Seminar'?" asked Jasmina.

"Sure," Hugh replied.

Three weeks later, Jasmina's students sat in a circle in her classroom leaning over a copy of the *Pledge of Allegiance*. Jasmina, a bit apprehensive but excited, explained how the Socratic Seminar model lesson would work. First students would read the *Pledge of Allegiance* paying attention to its wording. Then they would reread it, focusing on the big ideas. Then she would open with a question that established a basic understanding of the *Pledge of Allegiance*. Throughout the process, she would ask them questions that would gradually increase in difficulty. At the end of the lesson, students would be asked to write a brief essay explaining what they would do if they were the teacher of a student who refused to say the *Pledge of Allegiance*. Students looked at Jasmina with curiosity. She knew that was a good sign and after a deep breath asked, "Do you have any questions?" She had a good feeling when four hands energetically shot in the air. ■

CHAPTER OBJECTIVES

After reading this chapter, you will be able to:

- Describe the Socratic Seminar model, including its history and steps.
- Communicate the applications and benefits of the Socratic Seminar model and learn what it might look like in a classroom.
- Explain how to implement and plan for teaching with the Socratic Seminar model.
- Articulate how the Socratic Seminar model might enable differentiated instruction and support diverse learners.
- Describe how technology can enhance teaching with the Socratic Seminar model.

Introduction

Education in classical Athens—one of the world's first democratic societies—promoted learners' ability to gain deep understanding of important topics through questioning and dialogue. Today, the Socratic Seminar model, which captures this tradition, provides modern-day educators and their students the same support for the development of these important skills.

In the opening scenario, Jasmina Kovac wants to engage her students in the important concepts associated with social studies. She wants them to develop deep understandings—those that affect both the affective and cognitive learning dimensions. Rote knowledge is not enough for Jasmina. To be successful, her students must care about, value, and practice their democratic rights—not just understand them. She intends to use the Socratic

Seminar model to promote students' deep understanding of and emotional and intellectual engagement with the broad concepts of liberty and freedom. At the same time, she will promote their exercise of critical thinking and metacognitive knowledge.

This chapter provides an overview of the Socratic Seminar model, an introduction to its steps, and the type of content that is best taught using the model. Also, the chapter explores the value of this model in contemporary 21st century classrooms to promote students' development of critical thinking and communication skills. The chapter introduces technology for enhancing the model's efficacy and closes with a discussion of the benefits of the Socratic Seminar model, suggestions for implementing it, and possible differentiation strategies.

What Is the Socratic Seminar Model?

The Socratic Seminar model is an instructional model that uses structured questioning with debate or dialogue to promote learners' development of critical-thinking skills and exploration of ideas. Traditionally, the model has been used in conjunction with the study of articles, poetry, stories, essays, speeches, and historical documents in printed format. However, it can also be used with content materials presented in multimedia formats, including audio and video. After allowing students to experience the materials, the teacher facilitates an intentionally planned dialogue that supports students as they explore, compare, contrast, relate, synthesize, and analyze ideas. Working together with the guidance from their teacher, learners who participate in a Socratic Seminar model lesson co-construct meaning from facts, information, and concepts based on materials they have read or otherwise experienced. During shared dialogue, learners gain greater understanding of the curriculum content, connect with one another on an intellectual level, and develop communication skills of value in life and future learning. Although use of the Socratic Seminar model involves dialogue and debate, the methodology takes a highly structured and disciplined approach to these interchanges. All Socratic Seminar model lessons involve dialogue, but not all discussions and debates are Socratic Seminar model lessons.

The Socratic Seminar model is a powerful learning tool for many reasons. It provides both a structure and a purpose for students' analysis of content-based materials and an authentic accountability measure. Figure 14-1 lists several lesson topics that might incorporate the Socratic Seminar model in different content areas.

Embedded within the steps of the model is a supportive structure for students' learning about content and development of critical-thinking skills. These steps progress gradually in difficulty and the degree of critical thinking required. First, the students read or explore content-based materials independently, in pairs, or in small groups. During this activity, students' consideration of content materials might be supported through the use of various graphic organizers or other analysis tools. After performing this initial work, students gather and discuss the ideas gleaned from these materials with the supportive guidance of their teacher, who gradually asks students to respond to more challenging and open-ended questions as the dialogue progresses. Peers also offer each other support throughout the dialogue, as they share insights and opinions, as well as tips, tricks, and other learning strategies with one another. Students work collaboratively to make meaning as a group in ways that are complementary to the efforts of their teacher.

Lessons designed using the Socratic Seminar model give a meaningful purpose to the exploration of ideas presented using traditional (e.g., print-based) and digital

Figure 14-1 Sample Lesson Topics That Explore Content-Based Materials with the Socratic Seminar Model

Subject	Lesson Topic
Art	"The themes in the work of the Hudson River School artists"—Students review artistic work of Thomas Cole, Albert Bierstadt, and Asher Brown Durand and then explore the themes that influenced their work.
Language Arts	"*To Kill a Mockingbird* book discussion"—Students read *To Kill a Mockingbird* and engage in dialogue about the literary elements of the book and their personal reactions.
Mathematics	"Media bias and statistics"—Students analyze graphs from *USA Today* and consider how media bias might contribute to the communication of statistical data.
Music	"Exploring traditional music across two cultures"—Students listen to traditional music from Ireland and New Guinea and discuss similarities, differences, compositional purposes, and emotional responses.
Health/Physical Education	"Bullying"—Students read a blog written by a student being bullied and explore how students can be proactive and reactive to bullying using verbal and nonverbal communication.
Social Studies	"Human rights during World War II"—Students read *Farewell to Manzanar* by Jeanne Wakatsuki Houston and the *Diary of Anne Frank* to compare and contrast the violation of human rights by the Axis and Allied powers during World War II.
Science	"Pros and cons of space exploration"—Students read works presenting the pros and cons of space exploration and then engage in dialogue about issues associated with scientific progress.

(e.g., video) formats. Often students have difficulty understanding the reason for exploring content materials when the teacher uses a traditional lesson that relies on lecture or broad discussion. Because the Socratic Seminar model is focused and purposeful in its design, students learn about the relevance of the content being explored. They are also able to put into better perspective comprehensive concepts, such as human rights, poverty, and democracy, elucidated in newspaper articles, musical compositions, movies, podcasts, and other media.

Scenario 14-1 provides an example of relevancy and perspective in action. Students are asked to experience and think about traditional music from Ireland before coming to a weekly music class where they will discuss the music through a Socratic Seminar model lesson. What might seem unnecessary becomes relevant in this example when the teacher requires students to listen for the purpose of comparing the music to that of other cultures and discussing personal reactions to it. In addition to providing supportive structure and purpose, the Socratic Seminar model provides students needed motivation and accountability for their learning. Students who are not usually motivated to learn for learning's sake might become engaged during a Socratic Seminar model lesson because they want to look good in front of their peers. The Socratic Seminar model allows students to showcase their learning and effort in front of an audience. Drawing from content materials they have read, viewed, or listened to, students can compare, discuss, debate, explore, and elucidate with each other. Because this dialogue is performed in a public forum, it is difficult—if not impossible—for students to hide behind their desks. As a result, students often perform at higher levels of the revised Bloom's taxonomy (Anderson et al., 2001) during Socratic Seminar model lessons. Whether accountability is audited through a formal measure, such as with a formal written peer review as demonstrated in Scenario 14-3, or simply an informal one, such as in Scenario 14-1, the extent to which students have done their homework and contributed orally is easily noted. Teachers often appreciate the shared accountability afforded by this model.

What Are the History and Origins of the Socratic Seminar Model?

The Socratic Seminar model is named after the Greek philosopher Socrates (469 BC–399 BC). The model itself reflects Socrates' teaching tradition and the instructional pedagogies he was known to utilize. Having left no written legacy himself, what we know about Socrates, his life, and teaching approaches come from secondhand sources (May, 2000). The dialogues recorded by his students, Plato and Xenophon, share specifics about how he taught. The plays written about his life by his contemporary Aristophanes provide information about what and whom he taught. It is interesting to consider that these ancient works might constitute the first recorded evidence of a teacher's curriculum plans and instructional approaches in human history!

What kind of a teacher was Socrates? What, whom, why, and how did he teach? From these writings, we know that Socrates' pedagogy relied on questioning and dialogue to promote critical thinking and the illumination of ideas. **Dialogue** is an open-ended, flexible, reciprocal interchange in which individuals think about, question, discuss, and interrogate ideas to gain different perspectives on a topic while also temporarily suspending their own beliefs. Throughout Socrates' dialogues, the participants display the behaviors of being open-minded listeners who are respectful of others' views and work together to form a common understanding.

Discussion is not the equivalent of Socratic dialogue, however. Discussions tend to be less regimented and structured than dialogues. That more fluid format means that discussions often meander to bring out the perspectives of students and appreciation for the diverse ideas and opinions of the group. By comparison, Socratic Seminar model dialogues are more purposeful and structured. In fact, that structure is a critical attribute of any Socratic Seminar model dialogue—whether it be constructed to generate consensus and shared understanding or to develop individual ones. The degree and nature of structure in a Socratic Seminar model lesson is determined largely by the type of questioning structure teachers use. Questions might be developed using the various levels of the revised Bloom's taxonomy with increasing levels of difficulty, or questions might be clustered around a central topic of exploration.

To foster meaningful, deep dialogue, Socrates used a special type of questioning called **Socratic questioning**, the purpose of which is to elicit answers from the students. Exploration of Socrates' dialogues suggests that he relied on six types of questions. Paul (1995) identified them as follows:

1. Questions for clarification
2. Questions that probe assumptions

3. Questions that probe reasons and evidence
4. Questions about viewpoints and perspectives
5. Questions that probe implications and consequences
6. Questions about questions

In the Socratic Seminar model, teachers develop questions falling within these six question types to elicit thoughtful, reflective, dialogue among students. Regardless of the type of question being posed, however, Socratic questioning assumes that learners already possess knowledge and have the ability to become aware of and further this understanding. In practice, therefore, the teacher often feigns ignorance and asks students to answer questions that will help them attain deeper comprehension and mastery of concepts.

What distinguishes the Socratic Seminar model is that Socratic questioning is used in a systematic manner in conjunction with a structured dialectic—a dialogue, argument, or debate—to explore important curriculum content. Much like Socrates used his method to explore broad Athenian virtues such as piety, wisdom, temperance, courage, and justice, today's teachers can use the method to address broad conceptual ideas in a range of academic content areas.

Today, the benefits of learning with the Socratic Seminar model are highly relevant. In fact, Cookson (2009) contends that Socratic inquiry is essential considering the plethora of material available at our fingertips. Moreover, the skills the model promotes align well with those advocated by the Partnership for 21st Century Skills (2011).

Socratic questioning and questioning that involves discussion and dialogue are techniques practiced in medical, legal, and scientific education as well as in the education of students at all educational levels. In modern K–12 school settings, Mortimer Adler was the primary advocate of Socrates' pedagogies. An American philosopher, educator, and author, Adler was among the first to promote the use of Socratic pedagogies to support democratic schooling. In his books *The Paideia Proposal* (1982) and *Paideia Problems and Possibilities* (1983), Adler argued that education should be rooted in three goals: (1) the acquisition of knowledge, (2) the development of intellectual skills, and (3) the enlarged understanding of ideas and values. The use of the Socratic Seminar model supports teaching and learning within American schools by doing all three.

When Should the Socratic Seminar Model Be Applied and Why?

The Socratic Seminar model may be used when teaching content from any of the academic disciplines. It is suitable for learners after they begin to reason at higher levels, often around age seven. This model has long been used in language arts and social studies, but it is an incredibly valuable tool in all subject areas. The Socratic Seminar model appears to be particularly useful in (1) supporting students' development of factual, conceptual, and metacognitive knowledge, (2) developing students' ability to use cognitive processes, (3) facilitating students' ability to learn from content-based materials, and (4) teaching students effective communication skills. The following sections elaborate on these ideas. The following sections discuss what teachers should use the Socratic Seminar model to do.

Support Students' Development of Factual, Conceptual, and Metacognitive Knowledge

For learning experiences to be truly effective, they must provide students opportunities to use what they learn. The Socratic Seminar model provides students practical ways to use factual, conceptual, and metacognitive knowledge. Students gain factual knowledge completing assigned readings, doing other activities that involve exploration of content materials, and examining the facts surrounding a topic. Comprehension and mastery of basic facts is essential to the conversations and exchange of ideas that students will experience with their peers in the Socratic Seminar model. For example, in the opening scenario, students in Jasmina's social studies class need factual knowledge about democratic rights gained from a close read of the *Pledge of Allegiance* before engaging in meaningful dialogue with their classmates. These facts provide the foundation for discussing bigger conceptual ideas about the topic.

The Socratic Seminar model also promotes the development of conceptual knowledge. The conversational interchange in which students engage ideally supports learners as they develop their ideas. Moreover, the interchange allows students to work together as a group to expand its collective knowledge. For example, engaging in questions that stimulate thinking on various levels of the revised Bloom's taxonomy may cause students' ideas to expand. As in Scenario 14-3, Jeremy begins to see the value of space exploration because of what his classmate Colleen has shared. Such exchanges can result in the reconceptualization of existing ideas. Dialogue may also promote the evolution of collective knowledge. In Scenario 14-2, students discuss bullying in general and offer individual contributions about the personal impact of bullying in particular. The resultant dialogue leads to a refinement of existing notions about the concepts being explored.

The Socratic Seminar model also promotes students' metacognitive knowledge because it requires students to suspend their own views, be open to those of others, and reflect on their own ideas and thoughts—both as individuals and as part of a group tackling a concept. Through the Socratic Seminar model, students analyze their own and others' thinking, compare their thinking to that of others, and decide if they ultimately agree or disagree. Scenario 14-1 shows how Rowena prompts her students to examine their ideas about the musical pieces they listened to and the thought processes involved in their analysis.

Develop Students' Cognitive Processes

A growing trend in curriculum development across the academic disciplines in 21st century classrooms is the increasing emphasis on the development of students' cognitive processes. Cognitive processes are skills required for developing understanding and constructing knowledge in the various academic disciplines. As noted in Chapter 1, Anderson et al. (2001) categorize these skills using the following verbs: (1) remember, (2) understand, (3) apply, (4) analyze, (5) evaluate, and (6) create. Generally, all disciplines apply cognitive processes in some way, such as comparing, classifying, predicting, and the like. These skills are necessary no matter the age or content area, but some organizations consider cognitive process skills to be particularly relevant for their academic disciplines, such as those addressed in the National Science Standards: observing, inferring, and measuring (Padilla, 1990). Many of these skills might also be called critical-thinking skills because they require higher-level thinking. Regardless of what we call these intellectual skills, the Socratic Seminar model supports students' development of them through purposeful communication, dialogue, and debate about facts, concepts, and occurrences addressed in content materials.

Help Students Learn from Content Materials

Use of rich content materials informs, educates, and stimulates students' thinking as they prepare for participation in a Socratic Seminar model lesson. The choices teachers have for content materials are broad and varied. Materials selected for use in the Socratic Seminar model can be print and/or digital or represent primary or secondary sources. **Primary sources** provide firsthand testimony or direct evidence concerning a topic under investigation. Individuals, witnesses, or recorders who experienced the events or conditions being documented created these original materials. Often these sources are created at the time when the events or conditions are occurring, but primary sources can also include autobiographies, memoirs, and oral histories developed later. Primary sources are characterized by their content, not by their format. That is, materials in original format, on microfilm or microfiche, in digital format, or in some type of published format can all be primary sources. **Secondary source materials** present an interpreted account of events or conditions being documented, and as such they might also be used for the Socratic Seminar model. Both types of resources provide learners access to ideas, concepts, principles, and occurrences related to content in the academic content areas. It is important for students to explore both types of resources as preparation for the Socratic Seminar model.

Teach Effective Listening and Communication

Students communicate a great deal with one another, but not all of it is effective or meaningful to learning content. Just as the Cooperative Learning model (see Chapter 12) provides a structure for the direct teaching of social skills, so does the Socratic Seminar model. Because successful implementation of this model depends on students doing their part, many teachers use the Socratic Seminar model as a vehicle for teaching students how to listen actively and communicate effectively. The dialogue in a Socratic Seminar model lesson becomes a tool for learners to explore content, listen to multiple perspectives, and develop the ability to express their own points of view tactfully, assertively, and perhaps even persuasively. In Scenario 14-3, Jeremy has a tough time accepting another student's argument regarding space until he listens more attentively to the evidence provided by the peer.

Help Students Develop Cooperative and Social Skills

During a lesson using the Socratic Seminar model, learners work together as a team to come to a shared understanding about a topic—even if they do not agree. Arriving at that shared understanding requires that students learn how to work together cooperatively. The skills needed to work cooperatively involve social skills such as listening, waiting one's turn, supporting one another, being careful about body language, and more. (We discuss cooperative skills with more depth in Chapter 12.) Throughout the phases of the Socratic Seminar model, students have the opportunity to practice developing these skills.

What Are the Steps in the Socratic Seminar Model?

The Socratic Seminar model consists of four basic steps: (1) introducing the Socratic Seminar model, (2) facilitating the Socratic Seminar model dialogue, (3) reviewing and summarizing the dialogue, and (4) evaluating the dialogue. Figure 14-2 describes the roles of teachers and students in this model.

Step One—Introduce the Socratic Seminar Model

The first step in implementing the Socratic Seminar model is a crucial one. In this step, teachers should explain the purpose of the Socratic Seminar model in general and the intended learning goals for the lesson in particular. In this explanation, teachers should carefully and explicitly state the expectations for curricular learning (e.g., to understand better the *Pledge of Allegiance*) as well as any secondary goals for student achievement (e.g., developing students' listening skills). Secondary goals might include opportunities to practice effective communication, experience decoding, interpret and analyze selected content

Figure 14-2   Teacher and Student Roles in the Socratic Seminar Model

Socratic Seminar Model Steps	Teacher Role	Student Role
Introduce the Socratic Seminar Model	Teacher explains the goals for student participation in the dialogue. Ground rules and procedures are also shared.	Students listen and ask questions if any occur.
Facilitate the Socratic Seminar Model	Teacher asks opening question and follows up with additional questions corresponding to the flow of the dialogue. The teacher also monitors student progress and observes student behavior. Teacher may take notes to record important points and discoveries. Teacher continues to generate questions to extend and deepen student learning.	Students respond to questions posed by the teacher by addressing one another. They acknowledge one another's contributions, react to peers' ideas, and build on what is explored to co-construct meaning of the content materials. Students adhere to ground rules.
Review and Summarize the Dialogue	Teacher assists students in reviewing major points in the dialogue and facilitates students' summary of main ideas and discoveries pertaining to what was explored by the class. If needed, the teacher may provide points that are overlooked.	Students respond to teacher questions and participate in reviewing and summarizing the main points of the Socratic Seminar model dialogue.
Evaluate the Dialogue	Teacher facilitates evaluation of general discussion and student performance.	Students share ideas and input. Students reflect on and assess their contributions to the Socratic Seminar model.

Figure 14-3 Tips for Student Success in the Socratic Seminar Model

- Base opinions and other statements on the source materials (substantiate with points from the source materials).
- Wait for your turn.
- Refrain from raising your hands or interrupting others.
- Listen carefully—with your ears and your body.
- Address one another in a respectful manner.
- Take turns when discussing.
- Work to open your minds to others' ideas and suspend judgment.
- Communicate precisely and concisely.
- Reflect on your ideas and those of your peers.
- Understand the difference between a Socratic Seminar model dialogue and a class discussion.
- Know your responsibilities in participating in the Socratic Seminar model.

materials, and work together as a class community. This is the time to introduce students to the steps they must complete to prepare for participation in the Socratic Seminar model.

It is wise to document in writing (e.g., via a handout or other tangible notes students can review) what students are expected to do outside of class to prepare for the Socratic Seminar model. To promote better student preparation and participation, consider creating a checklist of which materials you want students to explore, where they can find them, how they are to interact with them (read, listen to, or watch), and any initial ideas you want them to consider related to them. Students should receive the source materials in hardcopy format and/or have digital access to them.

At this point, it is also a good time to teach students the norms for the Socratic Seminar model dialogue. Some teachers develop a set of ground rules—with or without student input—for participation in the dialogue. See Figure 14-3 for tips to share with students for how they can be successful when participating in the Socratic Seminar model. For a Declaration of Student Responsibilities when teaching with the Socratic Seminar model, see Chapter 2 of Ball and Brewer's (2000) book *Socratic Seminar in the Block*.

After introducing the model, move students into a seating arrangement that allows them to view one another. Such a seating arrangement promotes communication and feelings of inclusion in the Socratic Seminar model. A circular, square, or rectangular arrangement usually works best. During the Socratic Seminar model, the teacher should be seated at the same level as his or her students rather than seated apart from or standing above students.

Step Two—Facilitate the Socratic Seminar Model

During the seminar phase of the Socratic Seminar model, the teacher has several roles: (1) ask questions, (2) direct and encourage the exploration of ideas, (3) promote equitable and universal participation, (4) enforce respectful communication, (5) listen to students, and (6) prepare to review and summarize the dialogue. To begin the seminar, the teacher poses an opening question. Depending on the questioning strategy being used (see the section "Planning for Teaching with the Socratic Seminar Model" for information about two major questioning strategies in this chapter), the question might be basic or broad. During the dialogue, the students should address one another and not the teacher, even when the teacher asks the questions. Students should always respond by addressing their comments to one another. It is important to note that during the dialogue, the teacher's main role is to facilitate but not participate in the dialogue.

As the dialogue unfolds, the teacher will need to monitor and keep track of student contributions as a way to promote universal and equitable participation. Depending on the character of the class, it may be wise to use some mechanism that students already know. For example, the use of "talking tokens" is a useful technique for ensuring that all of the students have an opportunity and a motivation to contribute to the dialogue. Tokens may be something as simple as tongue depressors or strips of paper. Each student receives the same number of tokens (e.g., five for a 50-minute class period), and every time a student participates, he or she offers up a token. Once a student uses all of his or her tokens, the student must remain silent until all of the students are without tokens. Teachers can vary the rules for "spending" tokens. For instance, teachers might require that only after each student has given up at least two tokens can a student use a third (i.e., until all students have used two tokens, the student will need to refrain from speaking). This tip is especially helpful for evening out participation in large classes and making sure everyone has an equal opportunity to speak.

During the dialogue the teacher may want to take notes of important student comments (these may be useful during the next step) or ask for student volunteers to be responsible for this task. Even though recording comments is not directly related to facilitating the dialogue as it happens, having a written record of comments and ideas will help the teacher to facilitate the next step of the Socratic Seminar model—summarizing and providing highlights of the dialogue during the Socratic Seminar model's wrap-up, review, or closure.

If necessary, the teacher may need to enforce the ground rules that have been determined for the Socratic Seminar model and perhaps even remind students verbally of their responsibilities. If no ground rules were established before the start of the Socratic Seminar model, the teacher may need to invoke the typical classroom rules.

Step Three—Review and Summarize the Dialogue

During this step, the goal is to reexamine and summarize the exploration that occurred during the dialogue. The teacher's role is to facilitate students' review and summary of the dialogue and to archive it for future reference. Teachers should ask questions such as the following:

- What did we learn during this dialogue?
- How has this dialogue challenged the understanding of the concept you held before the Socratic Seminar model?
- What can we do with what we have learned?
- How does what we have learned in the process change our understanding of our subject or influence future actions?

Students should be asked to share their reactions to these types of questions, and they should also be invited to ask their own review or summary questions. If necessary, the teacher may interject details that were absent from student contributions.

The accomplishments of the Socratic Seminar model should be connected to the learning goals that were set for the lesson. As a group, the teacher and students should consider whether and how well the class addressed the learning goals. Often, the teacher also shares his or her experiences as the Socratic Seminar model facilitator.

Step Four—Evaluate the Dialogue

In the last step of the Socratic Seminar model, the evaluation step, students and their teacher have the opportunity to consider the quality of the total Socratic Seminar model dialogue and each student's individual contribution and participation in it. The goal of this step is to determine how well the class performed and generate useful information for improving future dialogues. When analyzing the dialogue, many teachers benefit from giving students an active role in its evaluation. The teacher may ask questions such as the following:

- How well did our class accomplish the learning goals during this dialogue? How did you contribute individually?
- What can we use from this experience to improve future Socratic Seminar model lessons?

The specific student behaviors targeted for assessment may include the quality and quantity of participation, the nature of participation (e.g., effectiveness of communication and use of source materials to substantiate arguments), and level of preparation. Different individuals might evaluate individual students. Sometimes students are asked to reflect and self-evaluate, as in Scenario 14-2. In other cases, such as in Scenario 14-3, students do peer evaluations. Occasionally, the teacher will make an observation and judgment about student contributions in the Socratic Seminar model. Figure 14-4 provides an example of a rubric a teacher might use to assess students' contribution and participation. Figures 14-5 and 14-6 are sample assessments teachers might use to learn about the success of the Socratic Seminar model from the students' point of view. Depending on the Socratic Seminar model's goals, it may be appropriate to ask students to demonstrate learning through a test, project, or some other method of assessment. With the opening scenario of this chapter, for example, Jasmina might ask her students to write a position paper explaining whether they agree with the Supreme Court decision that allows students to decide whether to recite the *Pledge of Allegiance*.

Figure 14-4 Rubric for Assessing Students' Participation in and Contributions to a Socratic Seminar Model

	Excellent	Good	Fair	Unsatisfactory
Conduct	Demonstrates respect for learning the process, has patience with different opinions and complexity, shows initiative by asking others for clarification, brings others into the conversation, moves conversation forward, speaks to all participants, avoids talking too much.	Generally shows composure but may display impatience with contradictory or confusing ideas, comments but does not necessarily encourage others to participate, may tend to address only the teacher or get into debates.	Participates and expresses a belief that one's ideas are important in understanding the source, may make insightful comments but is either too forceful or too shy and does not contribute to the progress of conversation, tends to debate not discuss.	Displays little respect for the learning process, is argumentative, takes advantage of minor distractions, uses inappropriate language, speaks to individuals rather than ideas, arrives unprepared.

Figure 14-4
continued

Rubric for Assessing Students' Participation in and Contributions to a Socratic Seminar Model

	Excellent	Good	Fair	Unsatisfactory
Speaking/ Reasoning	Understands question before answering, cites evidence from source, expresses thoughts in complete sentences, is logical and insightful, moves conversation forward, makes connections between ideas, resolves apparent contradictory ideas, considers others' viewpoints, avoids faulty logic.	Responds to questions voluntarily, comments show an appreciation for the source but not for the subtler points within it, makes logical comments but does not connect them to other speakers' comments, advances ideas interesting enough that others respond to them.	Responds to questions but may have to be called on, has read the source but not put much effort into preparing questions and ideas for the seminar, makes detailed comments but may not connect them to the logical flow of the conversation.	Extremely reluctant to participate even when called on, makes illogical and meaningless comments, may mumble or express incomplete ideas, takes little or no account of previous comments or important ideas in the source.
Listening	Pays attention to details, writes down questions, takes into account all participants when responding, demonstrates that he or she has kept up, points out faulty logic, overcomes distractions.	Generally pays attention and responds thoughtfully to ideas and questions of other participants and the teacher, may become distracted or absorbed in own ideas such that becomes unable to focus on the ideas of others.	Appears to find some ideas unimportant while responding to others, may have to have questions repeated, takes few notes during the seminar.	Appears uninvolved in the seminar, makes comments that display complete misinterpretation of questions or comments of other participants.
Analysis	Thoroughly familiar with source; has notations and questions in the margins; has underlined key words, phrases, and ideas; has identified possible contradictions; pronounces words correctly.	Has read the source and comes with some ideas from it but these may not be written out in advance, understands the vocabulary but may mispronounce some new or foreign words.	Appears to have read or skimmed the source but has not marked the source or made meaningful notes or questions, shows difficulty with vocabulary, mispronounces important words, misunderstands key concepts, shows little evidence of serious reflection prior to the seminar.	Student is unprepared for the seminar; is unfamiliar with important words, phrases, and ideas in the source; has made no notes or marked any questions in the source; makes no attempt to get help with difficult material.

Source: Copyright N. Lynn Schofield. Used with permission.

Figure 14-5 Sample Socratic Seminar Model Student Assessment

1. How would you rate the Socratic Seminar model?
   _____ Excellent (All class members participated, listened, had good ideas, did not interrupt.)
   _____ Good (Class members generally participated, but the students could have shared better ideas and had better behavior.)
   _____ Fair (There were side conversations and interruptions and students were distracted.)
   _____ Poor (There were lots of interruptions, side conversations, and rude behavior.)
2. What should we do differently next time as a class/group?
3. What should the facilitator do differently next time?
4. What should you do differently next time as an individual?

Figure 14-6 Sample Socratic Seminar Model Student Self-Assessment

Instructions: Check off the behaviors that you demonstrated during the Socratic Seminar Model Lesson.

Positive Behaviors

_____ 1. I came prepared for the Socratic Seminar model lesson.
_____ 2. I was courteous to the other students.
_____ 3. I paused and thought before speaking.
_____ 4. I listened to others share their opinions.
_____ 5. I kept an open mind for opinions different from my own.
_____ 6. I acted as a positive role model for other students.
_____ 7. I built on what was said before I shared my opinion.
_____ 8. I used specific examples from the source to support my opinion and statements.
_____ 9. I felt comfortable speaking in the Socratic Seminar model lesson.
_____ 10. I expressed my opinions clearly.

Negative Behaviors

_____ 11. I interrupted others.
_____ 12. I acted silly.
_____ 13. I did not look at the person who was speaking.
_____ 14. I talked off the topic.
_____ 15. I talked too much or not at all.
_____ 16. I did not pay attention.
_____ 15. I was not a good listener.

What Does the Socratic Seminar Model Look Like in the Classroom?

In many ways, the implementation of the Socratic Seminar model will look similar from class to class and grade to grade, particularly if teachers are employing the steps articulated in the previous section. Yet there are unique ways to implement the model, with varying degrees of emphasis on teacher or student direction and participation. The specifics of how the model is taught will depend on the teacher and the target audience, as the following three scenarios demonstrate.

Scenario 14-1

"You really cannot learn about music without listening to it," Rowena Walczuk said, as students shuffled out of the classroom groaning. The first lesson would focus on the standard that stated, "Students will be able to compare and contrast music from various cultural traditions." Rowena asked her students to go online and listen to two pieces of Irish folk music that captured the experiences and concerns of common people and that used inexpensive or homemade instruments. This exploration would serve as a stark contrast to their last unit of study focusing on classical music.

When students returned to class the following week, Rowena determined whether students (1) had listened to the music, (2) could name the musical instruments used in the music, and (3) had a sense of the lyrics' meaning. Students whose understanding seemed to be lacking were brought up to speed by those better prepared, and all were now set to communicate at a higher level of dialogue. After explaining the rules for the dialogue and moving students' chairs into a circle, Rowena began with a general question: "What did you notice about the music I asked you to listen to?"

Students looked around uneasily—they rarely were asked to talk about music. Sensing their hesitation, Rowena followed up with a prompting question: "What were the lyrics of the songs about?" The students received this question better, and they retold the stories behind the songs and their impressions of them. Rowena then asked, "What type of people wrote these songs? Where would they have lived? What would they have done for a living? What were their joys, cares, and concerns?" She made sure to leave enough wait time after each question so that students had time to think and respond thoughtfully. The students jumped in with their ideas about the song's authors—Rowena corrected inaccurate information when necessary. As the dialogue continued, more and more students participated. Students seemed to be eager to prove that they understood the music, even though it was very different from what they usually listened to.

"Okay so now that we have outlined basic information, we are ready to compare the two songs," Rowena said. Warmed up, students readily shared their ideas. Rowena started to type ideas quickly on her laptop so students could refer back to them later. Next, Rowena said, "Now that we have compared them, let's think about the significance of these two pieces as representations of 'traditional' music. Based on what we already talked about, what *is* traditional music?" The dialogue continued as students proposed various definitions and built on each others' ideas. Finally, before reviewing and summarizing the dialogue, Rowena said, "My last question for you is, 'How did you initially react to the music you heard? What did it make you feel? Think about? Did you like it?' Reflect on your own thinking." The students' reactions made Rowena think that they might agree that listening to different kinds of music was not as bad as they thought. It should be easy for them to write a brief reflection in their music response journal expressing their own evaluation of their participation in the dialogue.

Scenario 14-2

Bullying was a big problem in fifth grade. It was a great topic to engage students' interest in practicing "communication skills to enhance health" as the National Health Education Standards suggested. Joel Strausbaugh figured this might help his sometimes apathetic students to get on board with his learning goals. To motivate students, he would ask them to read excerpts from a blog he had found online. The blog had been written by a middle school student who had used this online journal to record details about a bullying experience and his feelings related to it. Students seemed reluctant to talk about bullying at first, but being able to talk about someone else's experiences helped take the pressure off of them. Joel had helped his students discuss an important classroom issue and addressed the learning standard related to communication as well.

Students came to class prepared and excited. "Hey, I really liked reading that kid's blog Mr. S." said one student. "Yeah, it was like reading my sister's diary . . . very juicy!" said another. After running through the plans for the dialogue with the class, the conversation got off to a fast-paced start. Joel started by asking, "How could the blogger have used what we have learned about effective communication to change his year in fifth grade?" The dialogue opened up with suggestions from five students. Joel made sure they addressed and looked at each other and not him. The dialogue was flowing so well that he even had to remind them that only one conversation was supposed to take place at a time. As students shared their ideas, other topics arose, such as behaviors that the blogger had done that made him an easy victim, opportunities for turning around the situation, and suggestions for resources and supports the blogger might have sought out. Peppered throughout the dialogue were expressions of understanding, empathy, and solidarity with the bullied blogger. Joel was blown away by how knowledgeable his students were about bullying—especially cyberbullying. He was amazed as his students taught each other—and him—a thing or two about the topic. They knew more than he did and helped him refine what he had thought cyberbullying was and how it was different and worse than traditional bullying.

The class period flew. The resounding theme was that more effective communication might have changed bullying outcomes for the blogger. At the end of the dialogue, the students summarized their conversation by making a list of suggested ways communication would help in a bullying situation. After students completed a formal, graded evaluation of their individual participation using a rubric he had given out earlier, Joel explained that their grasp of what they had learned would be assessed with a "RAFT" assignment due in one week. They would choose from one of three combinations of writing assignments that varied the **R**OLE, **A**UDIENCE, **F**ORMAT, or **T**OPIC of the piece to express their learning—this was a differentiation technique he had used with success in the past. Students could choose to write an e-mail to the blogger giving him advice about what to do the next time he was bullied, make up a cartoon or comic for other middle schoolers about the characteristics of effective communication, or write a song explaining to their teacher what they had learned from the Socratic Seminar model. The lesson had been a great success.

Scenario 14-3

Inspiring students to care about debate in science was a challenge during the "Special Topics in Science" course that Janette's seniors took during their last semester before graduating. It was hard enough to interest them in January, but by April it was nearly impossible. Still, it was Janette's job to try, and she had been teaching seniors for several years. She had learned through experience that if she required students to talk about what they had read for homework, they were more likely to do it because they cared about what their peers thought. She had also learned that they seemed to be more interested when materials came from real sources, such as magazines, journals, and websites, as opposed to their textbook. So it was with optimism that she planned to use the Socratic Seminar model to stimulate their interest in addressing the standard "Students will understand the controversies involved in scientific progress." The idea of "controversy" might interest them even if the topic does not.

Janette had chosen to assign students to read four of a set of eight readings previously selected on space exploration. They were organized in an ascending order of difficulty. This provided students the opportunity to read the articles that interested them and work to rise to the challenge of more advanced writing styles if needed, or choose simpler takes on the topic. To help learners, she also provided them with a graphic organizer that contained a table with two columns—one for the "pros" and the other for the "cons" of space exploration. After students arranged their desks, reviewed the rules for the Socratic Seminar model, and started working, Janette was shocked to see how they engaged with the questions she had prepared.

Students seemed to be listening and interacting, contradicting, interjecting, caring, and learning, What surprised her most, though, was how attentive they were in their listening, Could it really be? At one point, Janette almost ended up doing some direct teaching when a student named Jeremy could not see the benefit of space exploration introduced by another classmate. However, another classmate, Colleen, set him straight with her explanation, which referred to supportive arguments shared in two of the assigned sources: a magazine article and a NASA video. Although Rebecca had shared a similar argument, Jeremy listened more carefully when Colleen talked, perhaps because she articulated her position so well, and substantiated it with direct references to the sources. By the time Janette summarized

High School Students Participating in a Socratic Seminar Model Lesson
© Andresr/Shutterstock

the dialogue and asked students to choose another student to provide them with supportive feedback for their next Socratic Seminar model lesson, she was flabbergasted by what had happened. The Socratic Seminar model would become a standard part of her teaching repertoire with all her classes, not just this one at the end of the academic year.

What Do These Scenarios Illustrate?

The scenarios illustrate different ways in which the Socratic Seminar model might be implemented in practice, even with younger students. The teachers each use different techniques for questioning and pacing, in addition to the content that is the focus of the lesson, all to promote engaging dialogues throughout the lesson.

REFLECT: Take a moment to examine each of these scenarios and the variations of the Socratic Seminar model. What other variations were noted (e.g., How were students' participation and attainment of learning goals assessed? How did the different teachers go through the four major steps of the Socratic Seminar model?). Examine how you might modify the Socratic Seminar model and how it might benefit your current or future students. Also, consider the types of content that you teach or would like to teach that might be a good match for this model.

Planning for Teaching with the Socratic Seminar Model

Careful planning makes or breaks most instructional models; the Socratic Seminar model is no different. Work done to prepare for the facilitation of the Socratic Seminar model will pay dividends in student learning and create a more satisfying Socratic Seminar model. There are two essential steps that teachers must do before using the Socratic Seminar model: select the source materials to serve as the center of dialogue and develop the questions to promote active, thoughtful dialogue among students. The following sections discuss what educational designers do when teaching with the Socratic Seminar model.

Select the Source Materials

Traditionally, the sources for using the Socratic Seminar model have been textual in nature; however, teachers should not feel limited to using only print-based materials. There are many primary and secondary source materials in the form of video, audio, and media that teachers might wish to select. Teachers might also choose a mix of materials that are historic or contemporary and/or presented in a variety of media formats. Whatever the resource chosen, it is important that teachers choose materials that stimulate students' critical thinking about content related to targeted learning goals. Effort should be made to ensure that source materials are (1) closely linked to learning goals/standards, (2) rich and stimulating, (3) developmentally appropriate for learners, (4) easily accessible by all students, and (5) able to foster dialogue for a specified time period.

Once teachers identify the learning goals, the specific resource materials can be chosen. For example, in Scenario 14-2, the target health education learning goal selected is Standard 4.5.1 from the National Health Education Standards (National Center for Chronic Disease Prevention and Health Promotion, Division of Adolescent and School Health, 2008), which requires that students "demonstrate effective verbal and nonverbal communication skills to enhance health" (para. 3). Therefore, blog entries communicating students' experiences with bullying might be an appropriate source material to choose. Reading these materials might provide additional information and a context for developing students' ability to ask for help, self-advocate, and respond to bullying. Similarly, as is illustrated in Scenario 14-1, the music learning objective is that "students will be able to compare music from various cultural traditions." Consequently, listening to musical compositions from different cultural traditions would be appropriate.

When selecting source materials, teachers should also make certain that materials are appropriate for learners. For example, reading materials, whether they are print based or located on the Internet, should be chosen at an appropriate reading level for students. Teachers might also wish to differentiate the content by giving students the opportunity to choose which materials they will explore from a list of options. Other differentiation strategies for content materials are provided later in this chapter. In cases when materials might be difficult for students to comprehend easily, teachers should provide supportive materials or activities that scaffold their comprehension to aid students' understanding and comprehension. Such materials might include questions to consider, an analysis worksheet, a graphic organizer, or an anticipation guide.

Materials selected should also be accessible to all, and not just some, students. If multimedia materials are chosen, as is the case in Scenario 14-2 where the teacher asks students to listen to music online, the teacher needs to consider whether students have access to the Internet, as well as their computer skills. Because the success of the Socratic Seminar model depends on students being able to prepare and participate, teachers should do what they can to set students up for success.

Finally, teachers should choose materials that are provocative enough to sustain a Socratic Seminar model dialogue for a certain period of time. In some schools, students might have a 90-minute block period compared to others that meet for only 45 minutes. Although it might be tough to gauge exactly which sources will provoke more dialogue, careful selection of source materials that engage students in dialogue and promote multiple perspectives and interpretations work best when making choices for sources for the Socratic Seminar model. Choosing a simple, straightforward source will not foster the kind of questions and dialogue that are at the heart of the Socratic Seminar model.

Develop Questions for the Socratic Seminar Model Dialogue

Another critical planning step for teachers is the development of questions for the dialogue. This step serves as the mechanism for Socratic questioning (presented earlier in this chapter) that is the foundation of the Socratic Seminar model dialogue and will determine how challenging and successful the dialogue will be for learners. The planning and clustering of questions should be performed with learning goals in mind and related to the needs of the learners. There are two different strategies for developing and asking questions in the Socratic Seminar model: (1) developing questions using the revised Bloom's taxonomy and (2) creating questions by "clustering questions." We describe each of these in the following section.

DEVELOP QUESTIONS USING THE REVISED BLOOM'S TAXONOMY. One strategy for developing questions involves creating a series of questions that gradually increase in cognitive challenge. The revised Bloom's taxonomy has a similarly escalating series of cognitive process dimensions, and as such the taxonomy provides a useful framework for developing questions to be used in the Socratic Seminar model.

To use this strategy, a teacher would first examine the cognitive process dimension of the revised Bloom's taxonomy table (see Chapter 1, Figure 1-3) to develop a series of questions that address each category in the cognitive process dimension. For example, looking at Figure 14-7, the lowest level is "remembering." In this category, a teacher would craft a question that helps students demonstrate what they recognize or recall about the source material chosen for the Socratic Seminar model. Then the teacher would examine the next category up in the continuum—"understanding." To help students demonstrate their understanding, the teacher would construct a question that asks students to interpret, exemplify, classify, summarize, infer, compare, or explain their comprehension of the source material. The teacher would continue forming questions throughout all of the categories until he or she reached the highest level of "creating." For two different sets of questions

Figure 14-7 Examples of Socratic Seminar Model Questions Using the Revised Bloom's Taxonomy

Cognitive Process Skill Dimension	*Pledge of Allegiance*	Bullying Online
Remembering	What rights does the *Pledge of Allegiance* specifically name?	What problem does the blog author write about?
Understanding	What does the *Pledge of Allegiance* mean?	How does being bullied make the blog author feel?
Applying	What are some other real-world examples of "liberty" as defined in the *Pledge of Allegiance*?	What have we learned about effective verbal communication that might have been useful to the bullying victim?
Analyzing	Should students be required to say the *Pledge of Allegiance*? Why or why not?	What behaviors made the blog author an easy target for the bully? How could he have used his communication skills to shape a different outcome?
Evaluating	Do you say the *Pledge of Allegiance*? Why or why not?	How would you have dealt with the bullying situation if it were you? Your friend? A stranger? Your student? Your child?
Creating	How might you teach the *Pledge of Allegiance* and what it means to someone new to the United States?	Can you explain how verbal and nonverbal communication might be used to write a different story than is recorded in the blog entries we read about bullying?

using this strategy, review Figure 14-7. Working through the cognitive process dimension in a gradual order offers teachers the opportunity to create questions using an increasing level of challenge and requiring deeper, more flexible levels of thinking. The progression also provides students with a form of scaffolding, as it supports learners and allows them to build confidence as they engage in dialogue about the source material in the Socratic Seminar model.

DEVELOP QUESTIONS BY CLUSTERING QUESTIONS. Clustering questions is another strategy used by teachers facilitating Socratic Seminar model lessons. Clustering questions allows teachers more flexibility in responding to the emergent nature of the dialogue they are leading. When clustering questions, the teacher develops a broad question that promotes exploration by students. Then he or she develops other questions that might be asked depending on the direction that the dialogue takes. Clustering questions should lead participants into the core ideas and values of the source material and challenge students to substantiate their answers with illustrative points or instances found in the source material. Questions that incorporate this strategy must be open ended and reflect genuine curiosity—they should not have only one right answer. Some generic questions that teachers might ask to promote exploration of source materials and the content within are included in Figure 14-8.

Figure 14-8   Sample Clustering Questions to Ask in a Socratic Seminar Model

1. **Sample key questions for examining the source:**

   a. What is the main idea or underlying value in the source?
   b. What is the author's purpose or perspective?
   c. What does (a particular phrase) mean?
   d. What might be a good title for the source?
   e. What is the most important word/sentence/paragraph?

2. **Sample questions to move the discussion along:**

   a. Who has a different perspective?
   b. Who has not yet had a chance to speak?
   c. Where do you find evidence for that in the source?
   d. Can you clarify what you mean by that?
   e. How does that relate to what (someone else) said?
   f. Is there something in the source that is unclear to you?
   g. Has anyone changed their mind?

3. **Sample questions to bring the discussion back to students in closing:**

   a. How do the ideas in the source relate to our lives? What do they mean for us personally?
   b. Why is this material important?
   c. Is it right that . . . ? Do you agree with the author?

4. **Sample debriefing questions:**

   a. Do you feel like you understand the source at a deeper level?
   b. How was the process for us? Did we adhere to our norms?
   c. Did you achieve your goals to participate?
   d. What was one thing you noticed about the seminar?

Source: Modified from Chowning and Fraser (2007, p. 107).

Differentiating Instruction with the Socratic Seminar Model

The Socratic Seminar model challenges students to gain deep understanding of ideas using strategies that already have some differentiation. The model supports students who struggle by allowing them to interact with and learn from their peers collaboratively as they all work together to make meaning related to investigated materials. The model also helps learners who require auditory support for their learning. However, other strategies exist that can allow a teacher to meet diverse student needs during the Socratic Seminar model. These are explained in the sections that follow.

Content

Content materials selected for the Socratic Seminar model should provide learners with opportunities to explore the source materials selected for the Socratic Seminar model. When print materials are used, one simple differentiation strategy that can support learners is to choose items that are compatible with the students' varying reading levels. The readability tool contained in Microsoft Word (and explained in Figure 10-9, Chapter 10) helps teachers determine the readability of a text in digital format. If a text is too difficult for students to read, a "text reader" program like "Jaws" (see www.freedomscientific.com/products/fs/jaws-product-page.asp) might be useful to employ. In some cases, students can make choices to support their own differentiated experiences. When possible, a selection of readings might be offered with the option that students read the two that work best for them. In other cases, effective differentiation can be practiced by providing students access to content materials in alternative media formats (e.g., audio or video). Alternative textual formats, such as scripts, cartoons, newspaper articles, videos, songs, photos, and works of art, can provide students experiences that let them engage with ideas in ways that work for them. For instance, in the Socratic Seminar Model Lesson at the end of this chapter, students can listen to the *Pledge of Allegiance* instead of or in addition to only reading it in print.

Process

The learning process in the Socratic Seminar model can be differentiated to support student learning in a number of ways. First, teachers can provide students tools to support their work investigating, exploring, and analyzing source materials. Graphic organizers, prediction guides, and questions can offer different students a variety of ways to understand and analyze the source materials chosen for the Socratic Seminar model. For example, in the Socratic Seminar Model Lesson at the end of this chapter, students who might need help focusing on the important details of the *Pledge of Allegiance* can use the analysis worksheet (see Worksheet 14-1 in Appendix C) to prepare for the dialogue. Similarly, the graphic organizer in Scenario 14-3 also supports the science students who might need organizational help listing the pros and cons of space exploration so that they can later compare them.

Second, partnering strategies such as think-pair-share can also provide additional ways for students' formulation and refinement of their ideas. Students can engage in dialogue and answer more challenging questions in pairs before sharing their final answers with the whole group. Another strategy to differentiate is to use inner and outer circles for the Socratic Seminar model (Copeland, 2005). Some call this a "fishbowl" activity because the inner circle is like a goldfish in a fishbowl viewed by those sitting around it. The inner circle is a group of students, usually half the class, who will participate in the Socratic Seminar model dialogue. Students in the outer circle observe and take notes but do not participate in the dialogue. Often, teachers then ask students to switch participation in the different circles so that they experience what it is like to examine a topic as a participant in the inner and outer circles and to analyze the same or similar source material and then discuss their ideas as a whole.

Product

Differentiating the learning product is another way to support differentiation. In the Socratic Seminar model, the product of learning might be considered student contributions to the dialogue. However, in some lessons, a demonstration of the extent to which a learning goal has been met is another important measure. When this is the case, teachers can provide students with a variety of options for communicating their learning. Scenario 14-3 offers the example of a teacher using a RAFT strategy to demonstrate students' comprehension of controversy surrounding scientific progress. The product might also be differentiated by providing options for reviewing and summarizing the dialogue. This might be in the form of an audio podcast, a multimedia presentation, or a concept map using a graphic organizer. In Scenario 14-2, students have three different options for demonstrating their learning: writing a blog entry, creating a cartoon or comic, or writing a song.

What Are the Benefits of Applying the Socratic Seminar Model?

There are many benefits to using the Socratic Seminar model in one's teaching. Teachers seeking to develop several types of knowledge, build on students' prior knowledge, foster students' communication skills, promote exploration of important and complex topics, empower students, and cultivate 21st century skills should consider designing lessons that use the Socratic Seminar model. The following sections discuss what the Socratic Seminar model does.

Develops Factual, Conceptual, Procedural, and Metacognitive Knowledge

The Socratic Seminar model provides a meaningful context for developing students' factual, conceptual, metacognitive, and, in some cases, even procedural knowledge. In this model, students articulate their thoughts and analysis based on facts (i.e., factual knowledge) to build a foundational understanding of the content under study. As students progress through the model's steps, they also examine their ideas and those of their peers, examine the facts and concepts presented and argued (i.e., conceptual knowledge), substantiate their ideas, and reflect on their own learning (i.e., metacognitive knowledge).

Builds on Prior Knowledge

This model helps students examine their prior knowledge and relate their prior learning to the new materials examined. For example, students might relate their own conceptions of freedom with the concept of freedom as expressed in the *Pledge of Allegiance*, as in the Socratic Seminar Model Lesson at the end of this chapter.

Fosters Communication among and with Peers

How many times a day does a classroom teacher ask her students to stop talking with each other so that they can learn about the content being studied? Many! Yet students love interacting with one another. Why not capitalize on this love and promote learning about content at the same time? In the Socratic Seminar model, teachers give students an opportunity to communicate with peers for a positive purpose: to learn. Providing students structure and purpose for their communication allows students to take advantage of their conversations, nurturing the development of communication skills that can enhance their daily interactions in the classroom.

Promotes Student Exploration of Important and Complex Ideas

The Socratic Seminar model provides deep and rich opportunities to investigate, question, and analyze the information and ideas presented in curriculum materials. The Socratic Seminar model dialogue allows students to work together to co-construct meaning from what they read or experience.

Empowers Students

The Socratic Seminar model encourages students to take ownership of their learning by giving them responsibilities for creating a beneficial learning experience. The feedback they receive from their teacher and seeing themselves as creators of ideas allows them to acknowledge themselves as smart and capable of further learning.

Develops 21st Century Skills

Today's students need to be able to work cooperatively, communicate effectively, inter-rogate and synthesize ideas concisely, and solve problems efficiently, among many other important life skills. All of these skills are 21st century skills (see Chapter 1 for a thorough description) that students can cultivate when learning with the Socratic Seminar model.

What Value Does Technology Add to the Socratic Seminar Model?

This section describes several novel ways in which technology might be utilized for the planning, implementation, and assessment of learning when using the Socratic Seminar model. Although technology has not traditionally been used when teaching with this model, there are numerous ways in which technology might be incorporated into aspects of the model or the planning, implementation, and assessment of student learning. Figure 14-9 provides numerous technologies introduced in this chapter for supporting the teach-ing of this model.

Planning

FIND CONTENT MATERIALS TO EXPLORE. Search engines and online databases are excellent tools for identifying rich, meaningful content materials in print and multimedia format. Resources such as the U.S. National Archives and Research Administration, Project Gutenberg, and museum websites (e.g., Smithsonian's American Art Museum) are clear-inghouses easily accessed online for locating primary source materials that are not only authentic but also motivational for students.

ORGANIZE MATERIALS AND PROVIDE STUDENTS WITH ACCESS TO THEM. Technology tools give teachers an effective means for organizing and sharing source materials chosen as the centerpiece for the dialogue in the Socratic Seminar model. For instance, if relying on materials found online, teachers can create a simple website using a tool like Weebly. Teachers might also benefit from using a social bookmarking tool such as Delicious or StumbleUpon to organize and share materials for student exploration. If visually rich mate-rials are used, perhaps Pinterest would be a useful tool. These tools can be of particular importance when students are allowed to make a choice of materials to explore from a larger number.

CREATE MATERIALS THAT WILL HELP STUDENTS PREPARE FOR DIALOGUE OF SOURCE MATERIALS. Word cloud creation tools like Tagxedo or Wordle allow students or teachers

Figure 14-9 Technology Tools for the Socratic Seminar Model

Use	Tools
Planning	
	Electronic sources for content materials
	• Search engines, online databases
	• U.S. National Archives & Records Administration (historical documents): www.archives.gov/historical-docs
	• Project Gutenburg (free e-books): www.gutenberg.org/wiki/Main_Page
	Resources for organizing access to content materials and/or presenting assignments
	• Pinterest: http://pinterest.com
	• StumbleUpon: www.stumbleupon.com
	• Weebly: www.weebly.com
	Graphic organizers or tools supporting analysis
	• Bubbl: https://bubbl.us
	• Inspiration: www.inspiration.com
	• Kidspiration: www.inspiration.com/Kidspiration
	Word clouds
	• Tagxedo: www.tagxedo.com
	• Wordle: www.wordle.net
Implementing	
Asking questions	"Real-time" sharing of contributions
	• Twitter: www.twitter.com
	Visual presentation of questions
	• Keynote: www.apple.com/iwork/keynote
	• SMART Notebook: www.smarttech.com
	• PowerPoint: www.microsoft.com
	• Prezi: http://prezi.com
	Audio recording
	• Digital audio recorder, tape recorder
Assessing	
Evaluating the discussion	Online survey tool
	• Surveymonkey: www.surveymonkey.com
	Audience response tools
	• TurningPoint "Clickers": www.turningtechnologies.com

to create innovative, visual representations of the source materials and/or dialogue that aid and stimulate student comprehension. These tools can also be used to capture and display the major ideas in a written piece of work.

CONDUCT PRE-ASSESSMENT. The lesson will go more smoothly if students master any prerequisite knowledge before the Socratic Seminar model dialogue begins. Using audience response systems like clickers to learn what students know and how well prepared they are for the Socratic Seminar model lesson will make it much more effective.

Implementation

Technology tools are not required during a traditional Socratic Seminar model, but they can be useful and supportive of learning goals and student growth.

DIALOGUE ONLINE. To extend the classroom outside the walls of a brick-and-mortar classroom, teachers might utilize an online discussion tool to conduct a virtual Socratic Seminar model dialogue. Most course management systems (e.g., Blackboard) have discussion boards and live chat features that teachers can set up asynchronously or synchronously. These tools give students the opportunity to engage in the Socratic Seminar model without ever having to set foot in a physical classroom. Although this is not a traditional implementation of the Socratic Seminar model, the tool is used more or less in the same way with students writing their responses to questions or saving an audio response. In turn, peers can read or listen to their responses and make their own, too, expanding the dialogue. Also, just as a teacher might facilitate a face-to-face Socratic Seminar model lesson, he or she might facilitate one online or using a blended teaching approach as well.

PRESENT QUESTIONS IN VISUAL FORMAT. For visual learners and those with learning challenges (e.g., difficulty focusing), it is helpful to provide students with a visual representation of questions during the Socratic Seminar model dialogue. Presentation software such as Keynote, PowerPoint, and SMART Notebook are very useful tools for displaying the Socratic Seminar model questions on a projector for all of the students to see. Some teachers even create and share concept maps of all the questions they will ask during a dialogue for all of the students to see and review.

RECORD AND ARCHIVE STUDENT CONTRIBUTIONS AND THE DIALOGUE ITSELF USING DIGITAL AUDIO RECORDERS. Digital audio recorders or recording apps on smartphones can be used for capturing the dialogue (or portions of it) for students to review or reflect on later. If students are absent or wish to review any portion of the dialogue, the recording provides these students with the ability to do so. Moreover, they might benefit from an archive of the dialogue.

SUPPORT STUDENT CONTRIBUTIONS USING MICROBLOGGING. Microblogging tools, online tools (e.g., Twitter) that allow individuals to share their ideas in bits and pieces (e.g., up to 140 characters at a time), and often using a cell phone can provide a real-time channel for students who might want to voice opinions during a Socratic Seminar model but might be reluctant to do so face-to-face. The teacher might monitor students' feeds during the dialogue and interject with ideas shared. Students could have the option of using their cell phones or computer to contribute their ideas to the group. This tool might help students gain confidence and improve their likelihood of participating more fully in future Socratic Seminar model lessons. Such a tool might also be useful for students who are English language learners by providing them the opportunity to communicate in written instead of verbal format.

INTRODUCE AND EXAMINE CONTROVERSIAL TOPICS USING AUDIENCE RESPONSE SYSTEMS. Audience response systems can be used to ascertain students' identified or anonymous opinions on a variety of source materials, including controversial ones. There are many sensitive topics in which students may not feel comfortable voicing an opinion; clickers might provide a risk-free way for students to share their ideas.

Assessment

RECORD AND REPLAY THE SOCRATIC SEMINAR MODEL DIALOGUE. Audio and video capture technology tools might be used for assessing the different skills students cultivate when working through the Socratic Seminar model. For instance, teachers might use audio recorders or video cameras to record students' communications, interactions, and engagement during a Socratic Seminar model dialogue. Students could then review the audio or video recording to critique their argument and communication skills, their body language, and more. Moreover, they might assess their own contributions to the dialogue and that of their peers.

ASSESS STUDENT LEARNING USING AUDIENCE RESPONSE SYSTEMS. Audience response systems are excellent tools for monitoring students' understanding, particularly at the lower levels of the revised Bloom's taxonomy, which focuses on recalling facts. To ensure that students comprehend the material, teachers might incorporate the use of audience response systems to determine quickly who and how many students can answer important facts correctly during any stage of a Socratic Seminar model lesson.

Socratic Seminar Model Lesson Plan Example

The following is a lesson plan that incorporates the Socratic Seminar model. Figure 14-10 provides an outline of the lesson's different steps.

Figure 14-10   Outline of the Socratic Seminar Model Lesson Steps

Socratic Seminar Model Steps	Socratic Seminar Model Lesson
Introduce the model	Teacher explains goals for student participation in the dialogue. Ground rules and procedures are shared.
Conduct the seminar	Teacher begins with the opening question: "What are the major ideas in the *Pledge of Allegiance*?" Students respond to the various questions posed by their teacher while also acknowledging one another's contributions and reacting to peers. Teacher monitors their behavior by asking questions to extend and deepen student learning.
Review and summarize the seminar	Teacher assists students in reviewing the major points of the dialogue about the *Pledge of Allegiance* and facilitates students' summary of the dialogue. If needed, the teacher may highlight points that were overlooked.
Evaluate the dialogue	Teacher facilitates evaluation of the general discussion, student performance, and students' reflection on their own learning.

LESSON CONTEXT

GRADE LEVEL(S): Sixth

CONTENT AREA: Social studies

PHYSICAL TEACHING ENVIRONMENT: This lesson will be taught in a regular classroom with students seated in a circular or rectangular formation. They must be able to see one another.

APPLICATION OF THE REVISED BLOOM'S TAXONOMY: This lesson requires students to exercise thinking skills on every level of the revised Bloom's taxonomy. Teacher questions challenge students at gradually higher order levels of thinking.

Lesson Plan

GOAL: Students will explore the democratic ideals of liberty and justice while considering the challenges of providing these rights "for all."

Standard(s) Addressed:

Common Core State Standard for English Language Arts & Literacy in Social Studies[1]—Grade 6
- Determine a theme or central idea of a text and how it is conveyed through particular details; provide a summary of the text distinct from personal opinions or judgments.
- Determine the meaning of words and phrases as they are used in a text, including figurative and connotative meanings; analyze the impact of a specific word choice on meaning and tone.

National Council of Teachers of English/International Reading Association Standards for Language Arts[2]
- Standard 1: Students read a wide range of print and non-print texts to build an understanding of texts, of themselves, and of the cultures of the United States and the world; to acquire new information; to respond to the needs and demands of society and the workplace; and for personal fulfillment. Among these texts are fiction and nonfiction, classic and contemporary works.
- Standard 3: Students apply a wide range of strategies to comprehend, interpret, evaluate, and appreciate texts. They draw on their prior experience, their interactions with other readers and writers, their knowledge of word meaning and of other texts, their word identification strategies, and their understanding of textual features (e.g., sound-letter correspondence, sentence structure, context, graphics).
- Standard 4: Students adjust their use of spoken, written, and visual language (e.g., conventions, style, vocabulary) to communicate effectively with a variety of audiences and for different purposes.

---

[1] Standards for the English Language Arts, by the International Reading Association and the National Council of Teachers of English, Copyright 1996 by the International Reading Association and the National Council of Teachers of English. Reprinted with permission.

[2] Standards for the English Language Arts, by the International Reading Association and the National Council of Teachers of English, Copyright 1996 by the International Reading Association and the National Council of Teachers of English. Reprinted with permission.

- Standard 6: Students apply knowledge of language structure, language conventions (e.g., spelling and punctuation), media techniques, figurative language, and genre to create, critique, and discuss print and non-print texts.
- Standard 11: Students participate as knowledgeable, reflective, creative, and critical members of a variety of literacy communities.
- Standard 12: Students use spoken, written, and visual language to accomplish their own purposes (e.g., for learning, enjoyment, persuasion, and the exchange of information).

For a complete list of the standards, go to www.ncte.org/standards.

NATIONAL COUNCIL FOR SOCIAL STUDIES

Theme 10: An understanding of civic ideals and practices is critical to full participation in society and is an essential component of education for citizenship, which is the central purpose of social studies.

OBJECTIVES:

1. Students will review the rights articulated in the *Pledge of Allegiance.*
2. Students will examine some of the contradictions in the practice of saying the *Pledge of Allegiance.*
3. Students will articulate some of the challenges of democracy.

ESTIMATED TIME: Approximately 45 minutes

MATERIALS NEEDED:

- Copy of the *Pledge of Allegiance*
- Graphic organizer for analysis of the *Pledge of Allegiance*
- Clickers (audience response system)
- Socratic Seminar model evaluation questions on a presentation for use with clickers

PREREQUISITE SKILLS/KNOWLEDGE: Students should have previous experiences saying the *Pledge of Allegiance.*

LESSON PREPARATION

Selecting text or other content materials: The teacher provides copies of the *Pledge of Allegiance* to all of the students. Because this reading is short, students do not need to prepare for the Socratic Seminar model in advance. The teacher may also want to prepare an analysis worksheet that will be useful in helping students examine the *Pledge of Allegiance* in an in-depth manner. This will prepare them for more active participation in the dialogue. (See Worksheet 14-1 in Appendix C for an example.)

Planning the dialogue/evaluation questions: The teacher will prepare questions from each level of the revised Bloom's taxonomy to ask during the Socratic Seminar model. These questions will provide gradually increasing challenges for learners and help them explore both the concepts in the *Pledge of Allegiance* and the concepts associated with the act of saying the *Pledge of Allegiance.* This in-depth understanding will in turn promote students' consideration of the ideals and challenges of American democracy.

LESSON PROCEDURES (Text in italics is suggested teacher dialogue.)

Anticipatory Set (Introduction): [4 minutes]

Motivation: *Many of you have said the "Pledge of Allegiance" every day that you have attended school in the United States. Have you ever thought about what it means? Have you ever wondered if you had to say it? We are going to discuss these questions today.*

Information: *The "Pledge of Allegiance" was composed by a man named Francis Bellamy in 1892. It has been modified since then four times, most recently in 1954, when the phrase "under God" was added. In 1943, the U.S. Supreme Court ruled that it was unconstitutional to require students to say the "Pledge of Allegiance." However, most schools across the United States recite the "Pledge of Allegiance" on a daily basis. In our Socratic Seminar model lesson, we are going to consider what the words of the "Pledge of Allegiance" mean and what the act of saying the Pledge of Allegiance means within the context of American democracy.*

Connection: *How do you feel when you say the Pledge of Allegiance? What would/does it feel like to stand silent while others say the "Pledge of Allegiance?" What would it feel like if you were told you could no longer say the "Pledge of Allegiance" at school? During our dialogue we will consider these ideas and more.*

Introduce the Model: [5 minutes]

The teacher will explain the purpose of the Socratic Seminar model and its reason for use in this lesson. The teacher will set ground rules for learners and establish procedures that will provide for an effective dialogue. The teacher will orchestrate students' arrangement of desks in a circle.

Class, in our lesson we are going to use a learning model called the Socratic Seminar model. The Socratic Seminar model lesson will provide our class a structured method for talking about important ideas presented in the source materials we will explore: the "Pledge of Allegiance." By using this model, we will investigate important concepts in our civics unit in social studies. You will also get a chance to work on your listening, communication, and critical-thinking skills.

In our lesson today, everyone will be expected to participate because everyone has important ideas to share. The success of our dialogue will rely in large part on how well we communicate with and listen to one another. So there are some ground rules for participation. First, everyone will be asked to share their ideas three times. You have been given three "talking tokens." You will offer one up each time you talk. Once you have used all your tokens, you will be asked to be silent until everyone's tokens are used. By the end of the lesson, everyone should have used his or her tokens. Second, everyone will be expected to respond to the questions that are asked. It is requested that you stay on topic as much as possible and address the class when you respond—not your teacher (even though I will be asking the questions). Third, you will review and summarize the dialogue. Fourth, you will be asked to determine how well the class examined the topic and make recommendations for future dialogues.

The questions I ask will get more difficult throughout the lesson. They will challenge you to think in different ways about the ideas associated with our lesson. Toward the end of the lesson, you will be asked to review the major ideas in the dialogue and summarize what we have learned. Then we will evaluate how well we met our learning goals and performed individually in this Socratic Seminar model lesson.

Are there any questions? Let's begin. Please start by reading the "Pledge of Allegiance" and completing the Analysis Worksheet that you downloaded.

Students read the *Pledge of Allegiance* and complete the worksheet (Worksheet 14-1 in Appendix C). [10 minutes]

Conduct the Seminar: [20 minutes]

The teacher might ask the following questions to lead the dialogue:

- *What are the major ideas in the "Pledge of Allegiance"?*
- *Why do we say the "Pledge of Allegiance"?*
- *What specific rights does the "Pledge of Allegiance" refer to?*
- *What are liberty and justice? How are these rights enforced? Can you give examples of ways you exercise your liberty? Can you give examples of ways that justice is served?*
- *How do you feel when you say the "Pledge of Allegiance"?*
- *Are there reasons why people might not want to say the "Pledge of Allegiance"? Do they have to?*
- *Can you think of any other ideas you would add to the "Pledge of Allegiance" if you had the power to do so? What other ideas are important to our democracy and nation?*
- *What would happen if you decided not to say the "Pledge of Allegiance" at school? Why might you decide you did not want to say the "Pledge of Allegiance"?*
- *What contradictions are there in the "Pledge of Allegiance"? How can the needs of the democracy and the rights of individuals be balanced?*
- *If you were president, would you require school children to say the "Pledge of Allegiance"? Why or why not?*
- *If you were a school principal and a student decided not to say the "Pledge of Allegiance," what would you do?*
- *If your friend decided not to say the "Pledge of Allegiance," what would you say to him or her?*

Review and Summarize the Dialogue: [10 minutes]

The teacher facilitates a review of major topics and asks the class to summarize what they learned:

- *So now that we have explored the "Pledge of Allegiance" and what it means to say it, let's consider what we learned from our dialogue and about democracy.*
- *What did we learn about the concepts in the "Pledge of Allegiance"? How do we see these concepts supported and contradicted in requiring students to say the "Pledge of Allegiance"?*
- *What are some important practices in democracy? How can these practices be done in a way that supports the goals of democracy?*
- *What did you learn that you did not know before this dialogue?*
- *Will you do, say, or believe anything differently because of this lesson?*

Evaluate the Dialogue: [5 minutes]

The teacher will facilitate students' analysis of the dialogue as a whole and the individual evaluation of each student's participation in it. In advance, the teacher will have created a "clicker" presentation that asks students to rate the dialogue on its ability to (1) make students think carefully, (2) make students think about new ideas, (3) challenge students' existing ideas and beliefs, (4) help students better understand the concepts associated with the *Pledge of Allegiance*, and (5) articulate the ideals and challenges of democracy.

The teacher will also ask students to rate their participation in terms of the quality and significance of their comments, the frequency of their comments, their performance listening actively, and their adherence to established ground rules.

LESSON EXTENSIONS

After the lesson is completed, it may be desirable to provide students with an opportunity to apply what they have learned and take a personal position related to the concepts discussed. If appropriate for meeting learning goals, students might be required to write a position paper describing whether they agree with the Supreme Court decision allowing citizens not to say the *Pledge of Allegiance*.

Differentiation Strategies for the Socratic Seminar Model Lesson

In the sections that follow are some suggestions one might apply to differentiate instruction in the Socratic Seminar Model Lesson.

Content

Although the content of instruction will not be differentiated, students' access to it might be. Students might either read or listen to the *Pledge of Allegiance* as a means for stimulating their thinking about its words and the concepts it communicates. Students who are new to the United States may lack understanding of what the *Pledge of Allegiance* is and how it is used in different contexts throughout the United States. For these students, it may be helpful to provide experiences that would enrich their understanding in advance of this lesson.

Process

The Socratic Seminar Model Lesson provides learners with many opportunities to share ideas and interact. However, interacting face-to-face is difficult for many learners. Some teachers find it useful to open a microblog feed during dialogues in class. By doing so, students can use computers, tablet computers, or cell phones to interject questions and ideas in real time without having to actually speak aloud. In cases when it is less important for students to work on and refine communication skills, this alternative mode for participating in the learning process may support learners who are shy or introverted or who lack confidence in their contributions.

Product

The measurement of student performance might be varied given students' individual capabilities. Students might be held to different expectations regarding their frequency and quality of comments. Likewise, various tools could be used to differentiate the method for evaluation. Students might measure their performance using a Likert rating scale or write an open-ended reflection. They might also develop a play summarizing their learning.

Chapter Summary

In this chapter, you learned about the Socratic Seminar model. This model is a useful method for facilitating students' exploration of source materials and the bigger concepts associated with the academic content areas. The primary purpose of the Socratic Seminar model is to achieve a deeper understanding about the ideas and values of those source materials. The secondary purpose is to promote students' ability to communicate effectively with one another about intellectual ideas. Socratic Seminar model lessons are related to the pedagogies used by Socrates to prepare citizens for democracy in classical Athens. Comprehension of important ideas, as well as the ability to communicate, ask, and answer questions, are all competencies embedded within the model. Students develop these competencies while interacting with their peers in a structured dialogue led by their teacher. The Socratic Seminar model allows students to learn and practice behaviors needed to continue learning in students' future lives and schooling. It can be employed at all educational levels, in any subject areas, and with all learners who are able to communicate, reason, and engage in dialogue with their peers.

Review Questions

1. What is the history of the Socratic Seminar model?

2. What are the steps in the Socratic Seminar model?

3. What type of content is best to teach when applying the Socratic Seminar model? Provide and explain examples of content that would be appropriate and inappropriate.

4. What are the benefits of applying the Socratic Seminar model? What are some of the challenges?

5. How can the Socratic Seminar model be used to differentiate instruction and support diverse learners' needs?

6. How can technology be used to implement the Socratic Seminar model?

Application Exercises

To promote your ability to apply the learning you gained in studying this chapter, complete the following exercises that challenge you to analyze a lesson plan you have written using the Socratic Seminar model *or* using the lesson plan example included in this chapter.

TECHNOLOGY INTEGRATION ACTIVITY

1. Consider the following questions and discuss with a partner or reflect independently:
   a) In the lesson plan you are analyzing, how does (or could) the integration of technology tools make learning more efficient, effective, and engaging? Can you explain and indicate how you will measure the impact on student learning?
   b) Will all learners be aided through the integration of technology? Are there some who might need special support to gain full benefit from technology tools? How might you support this? Is there a way to build on students' technology skills and strengths in this lesson? If so, explain how.
   c) What plans could you put in place to promote the successful use of technology and minimize (or eliminate) risk of failure? What proactive plan could a teacher put in place ahead of lesson implementation to ensure that technology works smoothly and for all learners? What reactive approach could you take to ensure that desired learning still occurs even if technology malfunctions during the lesson?

TEACHER PERFORMANCE ACTIVITIES

2. **Academic Vocabulary and Language Demands:** Academic vocabulary is the vocabulary that students must be able to understand to be successful performing content area learning. Language demands involve the ways language is used in speaking, writing, listening, and reading in the learning tasks of a lesson and in the expressions of student learning. For the lesson plan you are working with (your own or the one provided in the chapter), consider the following questions and discuss them with a partner or reflect on them alone:

   a) What academic vocabulary and language demands exist in the lesson related to the dialogue of the Socratic Seminar model? Make a list of the academic vocabulary students must comprehend and language demands to participate successfully in the Socratic Seminar model dialogue.

   b) How would you determine whether and which students have mastery of the academic language before, during, and after the lesson?

   c) How might students be supported in developing proficiency with academic language throughout the entire Socratic Seminar model dialogue?

3. **Planning:** In the context of the lesson plan that you are analyzing, discuss the following with a partner or reflect independently:

   a) Explain how the steps of the Socratic Seminar model build on each other to lead students to make clear and meaningful connections among identified learning goals or objectives.

   b) Consider how you have addressed or how you might develop a variety of questions to address different learning needs at multiple levels of the revised Bloom's taxonomy.

   c) What research or theory supports the use of this model for instruction in your learning context?

4. **Implementation:** In the contenxt of the lesson plan that you are analyzing, discuss the following with a partner or consider independently:

   a) Explain how the steps of the Socratic Seminar model and the questions that students will examine in the lesson will result in sustained student engagement throughout the Socratic Seminar model. What indicators would you look for during the implementation of your lesson to measure who is engaged and how much? How will you monitor which questions prompt the deepest thinking and dialogue?

   b) How well does your questioning and the lesson overall challenge learners to apply their learning in meaningful contexts, including hypothetical situations? Explain.

5. **Assessment:** Consider the following questions and discuss them with a partner or reflect independently:

   a) How does the plan you are reviewing make use of information gained through pre-assessment to inform the design of the lesson and questions devised for the Socratic Seminar model dialogue? Would consideration of students' backgrounds, prior learning, and experiences as they relate to learning goals/objectives help you design a more effective lesson and questions? How?

   b) How does or could the lesson plan you are reviewing use formative assessment to improve the delivery of the lesson as well as foster dialogue?

   c) How does the plan you are reviewing support students' expression of and reflection on their learning? Are there multiple forms of evidence of student learning? How might students learn through an analysis of their performance and reflection on their learning (metacognition)?

6. **Analyzing Teaching:** Consider the following and discuss with a partner or reflect independently:

   a) Now that you have created and/or analyzed a lesson plan using the Socratic Seminar model, consider how the model supports effective teaching, questioning, and dialogue. Can you cite specific evidence or references that support your claim? Be specific in expressing your ideas.

   b) What did you learn from this activity that might inform your future practice?

Discussion Question

Socrates prepared citizens for participation in Athenian democracy using pedagogies characterized by questioning and dialogue. Today, these methods are still useful in preparing citizens for democracy. What specific skills, knowledge, and competencies can participation in the Socratic Seminar model help students develop?

Journal Entry

Write about the compatibility of the Socratic Seminar model with your personal teaching style. How comfortable do you feel facilitating open-ended dialogues with your students? What challenges do you foresee using the Socratic Seminar model with your students? How will you plan to address these?

Resources

Socratic Seminar Model

- Socratic Lesson Plans—Contains 95 lessons that incorporate the Socratic Seminar: www.lessonplanet.com/search?keywords=socratic+seminar&media=lesson
- National Paideia Center—This website, supporting the Paideia movement, provides excellent materials on the Socratic Seminar model approach, including lesson plans that cover all disciplines that can be downloaded and used: www.paideia.org
- Strategy Guide: Socratic Seminars—This guide, developed by the International Reading Association and the National Council of Teachers of English, provides information about implementing the Socratic Seminar: www.readwritethink.org/professional-development/strategy-guides/socratic-seminars-30600.html
- Books on the Socratic Seminar in Middle and High School Settings—The following two books are excellent resources for incorporating Socratic Seminar model lessons in middle and high school classrooms. Each has scenarios and rubrics for these populations:
  - Copeland, M. (2005). *Socratic circles: Fostering critical and creative thinking in middle and high school*. Portland, ME: Stenhouse.
  - Moeller, V., & Moeller, M. (2001). *Socratic Seminars and literature circles for middle and high school English*. Larchmont, NY: Eye on Education.

Socratic Questioning and Dialogue

- Socratic Seminar and Levels of Questioning—This article provides an explanation of one way to conceptualize the different levels of questioning needed to foster an effective Socratic Seminar: http://gallery.carnegiefoundation.org/collections/castl_k12/yhutchinson/media/socraticseminar.html
- Questioning in a Socratic Seminar—This is a video of a group of fourth-graders and a teacher demonstrating Socratic questioning: www.youtube.com/watch?v=6k4PyHwFja0
- Authenticity: Is It Possible to Be Authentic?—This is an example of a Socratic dialogue: www.philodialogue.com/Authenticity.htm
- Critical Thinking—This site, developed by a professor and his son to provide a rigorous source of information on critical thinking, houses a lot of resources on critical thinking: www.criticalthinking.net/index.html
- Foundation and Center for Critical Thinking—This site hosts many resources and videos on critical thinking: www.criticalthinking.org
- Engaging Students in Conducting Socratic Dialogues: Suggestions for Science Teachers—This article provides information about how science teachers can engage their students in Socratic dialogue and questioning. *Journal of Physics Teacher Education:* www.phy.ilstu.edu/pte/publications/engaging_students.pdf

Appendix A

The ADDIE Model in Practice

Teachers can use the phases of ADDIE in whole or in part to help them develop more effective lessons, units, and instructional materials. The focused, organized thinking guided by the various ADDIE phases can increase instructional effectiveness when addressing large instructional challenges, such as determining the best way to address curriculum standards in a unit of instruction, or small ones, such as selecting the best model of teaching to address a standard dealing with conceptual knowledge. Teachers can use just one ADDIE phase—such as the analysis phase to help them better understand the learning context—or apply them all when the situation warrants.

The following scenario explains how Rich, the ninth-grade teacher in the opening scenario of Chapter 2, implements the ADDIE model when leading an interdisciplinary team in redesigning a ninth-grade research paper unit. With instructions from his principal to "rework the research paper unit to make it more relevant to 21st century learners," Rich applies the entire ADDIE model he learned from the NASA instructional designers. He also uses the revised Bloom's taxonomy (Anderson et al., 2001) explained in Chapter 1 and integrates Understanding by Design (UbD) (Wiggins & McTighe, 2005) within ADDIE's phases.

ANALYSIS. During this first stage of the ADDIE model, Rich and his colleagues first examine the standards they need to address with their learners in the unit. Because the school district has been using UbD, the team uses portions of this approach within this phase of ADDIE to help them explore in depth the content standards that are the focus of the unit. During the UbD process, the group brainstorms the "essential questions" related to the standards and identifies the "enduring understandings" they want students to have when leaving the unit's instructional experiences.

Once they have achieved full understanding of the unit content, the team writes objectives to break what students should know and be able to do at the end of instruction into more focused and more easily assessed learning goals. They relate these objectives to the revised Bloom's taxonomy by distinguishing between the factual, procedural, conceptual, and metacognitive knowledge the individual objectives address. For example, they take the academic standard in their course of study, "Students will be able to develop open-ended research questions that are focused and can be extended," and then break it down into the following objectives that are mapped with the revised Bloom's taxonomy knowledge dimensions and cognitive processing categories:

- **Learning Goal #1:** Students will understand what a high-quality research question is. (conceptual knowledge/comprehension)
- **Learning Goal #2:** Students can name the critical attributes/characteristics of research questions in general and high-quality research questions in particular. (factual knowledge/application)
- **Learning Goal #3:** Students will be able to identify some areas that interest them that they might want to learn more about. (procedural knowledge/synthesis)
- **Learning Goal #4:** Students will be able to apply a set of criteria to evaluate the quality of a research question. (procedural knowledge/evaluation)

- **Learning Goal #5:** Students will be able to develop a research question based on their own interests and refine this question to make it a high-quality one. (metacognitive knowledge/ creation).

The mapping of objectives within the revised Bloom's taxonomy allows the teachers to consider more carefully the different types of knowledge students are expected to gain in the unit and to make better matches between the cognitive processing category and the different types of knowledge. Later in the ADDIE phases, this foundational understanding about their content will help the interdisciplinary team decide if a model of teaching will be required to address specific learning goals and, if so, which model of teaching might be most appropriate.

At this time, the team also creates "I CAN" statements for the various learning goals. These statements express the intended student learning outcomes in "student-friendly" language that ninth-graders can understand. Sharing these statements with the students will enable students to be more aware of the purposes for instruction. It will also empower students to be more invested in their learning.

After clarifying the content of instruction, the team considers the needs of the audience—that is, their ninth-grade students—as they relate to these standards. One of the first characteristics the team considers is students' experiences as digital-age learners. Because the primary reason for reworking the research paper unit is to make it more relevant to students, the teachers must take into account that students are growing up in a technology-rich world. Rich and his colleagues consider how information about the needs of their ninth-graders might be made factual rather than speculative. They want to ground decisions about how to meet student needs in real data, so Rich helps the team develop a needs assessment.

In the needs assessment, the team makes plans to identify technology competencies along two parameters. First, they want to identify the students' existing competencies so they can capitalize on them. Second, they want to identify areas of technological competency the students might need support in developing. The team also makes plans to use the needs assessment to investigate which tools their students have access to in their homes and to identify other information related to student readiness that might be helpful to know. In discussion with one another, the team brainstorms ways that the strategic use of instructional technologies might support student learning about research while also improving student engagement.

Working with the interdisciplinary team, Rich inventories the relevant technologies students will have access to in the school building as well as some of the issues and barriers associated with using them. As the team examines the learning goals for its unit, a clearer picture emerges of the resources they have available and those they need to obtain to support the research paper unit.

DESIGN. In the design phase, Rich and his colleagues examine the learning goals and consider which instructional models might be most appropriate to use when developing the lessons to address the specific learning goals they have identified. After much discussion, the team decides that Learning Goal #1 will be most effectively addressed with a concept model (the idea of a "high-quality research question" is a concept). They decide that a good research question is one that (1) is worth asking and (2) can be answered with available resources. Because their concept has clearly defined attributes, the team chooses to employ the Concept Attainment model for Learning Goal #1. (The Concept Attainment model is a specialized tool that is compatible with this particular type of concept.) They cross-check their decision by referring back to how they mapped this objective to the revised Bloom's taxonomy (see Figure 1-3 in Chapter 1). They confirm that this model of teaching will promote the development of this conceptual knowledge.

Meeting Learning Goal #4 will require students to learn and apply a process for evaluating a research question and determining its quality. Because the Direct Instruction model is useful when teaching procedures, the team decides to use it in conjunction with Learning Goal #4. Applying the Direct Instruction model will allow teachers to model for students the process of evaluating research questions and then help students gradually gain the independence to develop and evaluate research questions on their own.

A shorter discussion leads the group to select the Direct Instruction model for use with Learning Goal #4 because this goal promotes students' ability to evaluate a research question and determine its quality. Because attainment of this learning goal will require students to learn and apply a process for evaluating the quality of research questions, Direct Instruction will be an appropriate model. The Direct Instruction model, which is useful when teaching procedures, will allow the teachers implementing the research paper unit to model the evaluation process for students. Then the model will allow the students to gradually gain independence so they can develop and evaluate research questions on their own.

Along with these plans, the team considers how formative evaluation can be conducted on the quality of the lessons they create for each learning goal. Information gained from formative evaluation will be used to improve instruction as it is delivered when the unit is tested or "piloted." It will also guide revisions of the lessons and direct future implementation of the unit. The quality of the unit is not the only thing that will need to be evaluated, however. At this time, the interdisciplinary team also considers how student learning will be assessed using traditional and alternative assessments.

DEVELOP. In the development phase, Rich puts plans for the needs assessment into action by creating a survey that can be administered using an online survey tool. Other teachers on his team create the lesson plans and materials for the Concept Attainment lesson, the Direct Instruction lesson, and other lessons in the unit. During this phase, each of the teachers on the team administers the needs assessment developed by Rich. Once the group obtains data about student needs, it works to refine the unit to address those needs. For example, all students reported that they have access to the Internet at home or at a library within walking distance. Therefore, one revision the group makes is to incorporate online research tools to support students during the research process. These tools will help students take notes and keep track of references during the research process. Based on needs assessment data, the team also decides to allow students the option of presenting research paper content in either traditional style (print) or an alternative manner (e.g., via a website or podcast).

During the develop phase, the team also creates summative assessment tools. These include a rubric for evaluating students' research papers and other assessments that will help the ninth-grade teachers measure student attainment of the various learning goals.

IMPLEMENT. Later in the school year, Rich and a colleague named Portia implement a pilot, or test, of the plan for the new research paper unit. They are excited to put the team's plans in place, give students high-tech tools to support their work, and provide students with different options for showcasing their learning in the unit. During the formative assessment of their implementation, Rich and Portia note more excitement, motivation, and interest in the research unit among students. They realize they do not need to work as hard to encourage motivation and engagement in their students. Rich and Portia implement the lessons the team developed and find that the various instructional models they have chosen support students' development of different kinds of knowledge related to their success with the unit.

EVALUATE. After Rich and Portia implement the research paper unit with their classes, they collect feedback from this first implementation to determine the success of the unit redesign. As they conduct a summative evaluation of the students' effort, achievement, and growth, they also gain information that helps them refine the unit for use with all ninth-grade students the following year. The responses from the students involved in the pilot suggest that while a great deal of the unit is successful, additional support materials should be created for learners who struggle with evaluating the quality of the Web-based resources they find. Rich and Portia collaborate on a plan for adding a new lesson to the unit on how to evaluate Web-based resources. They share the new lesson with other members of the unit redesign team so that it can be incorporated in the research paper unit that will implemented throughout the ninth-grade next year.

What Does This Scenario Illustrate?

The ADDIE model provides Rich and his colleagues with a systematic way to approach the redesign of the research paper unit. It gives them focus, direction, and structure as they work to make the research paper unit more relevant to their learners. The scenario demonstrates that the benefits of following the ADDIE approach are numerous. First, Rich and his colleagues can be confident that the unit will continue to support learners in the same ways and at the same levels as it has in the past. In addition, using ADDIE allows them to extend the positive impact of the research paper experience to a larger group of learners and increase student motivation, growth, and achievement across the ninth grade. Use of the ADDIE model also enables the interdisciplinary team of teachers to ground instructional decisions in the needs of their current students rather than in the needs of those they have taught in the past—and make the best possible use of the resources available to address the academic content. Furthermore, the model also provides a structure for facilitating the cooperative work among members of the interdisciplinary team. Finally, the ADDIE phases (sometimes referred to as steps) keep the teachers on track and focused on their tasks.

Concept Teaching Advanced Materials

Before a teacher can be expected to teach a specific concept, he or she must have a foundational understanding of what concepts are in general. Once a mastery of concepts and concept vocabulary is gained, a teacher is more effective in understanding and teaching them. Vocabulary associated with teaching concepts is shared in Appendix Figure B-1. Concepts in general and particular can be better understood by examining a combination of characteristics. These are as unique as the concept itself. Such characteristics allow concepts to be categorized. These characteristics are explored in the following sections and materials.

Appendix Figure B-1 Concept Vocabulary and Examples

Vocabulary	Example
A **concept** is a mental construct, label, or "an abstract or generic idea generalized from particular instances." More specifically, a concept is "a category or set of objects, conditions, events, or processes that can be grouped together based on similarities and represented by a word or other symbol or image."	Dog, pet, companion, and service animal
Attribute is "a special name used to refer to the characteristics that determine whether a particular symbol or object is a member of a particular class" (Merrill & Tennyson, 1977, p. 24).	Some attributes of dogs include that they walk on four legs, have ears, are domesticated canines, and have canine teeth. These are all characteristics that describe how we identify dogs. Some of these attributes are critical and others are not.
Critical attributes are common, essential, nonvarying, and specific characteristics unique to a concept. It is an essential feature that is "necessary for determining class membership" (Merrill & Tennyson, 1977, p. 24).	Critical attributes of dogs are that they have canine teeth and are domesticated canines. These are critical attributes because a canine cannot be considered a dog without these attributes.
Noncritical or variable attributes are any varying features of a concept that are not necessary characteristics of the concept; they are "not necessary for determining class membership" (Merrill & Tennyson, 1977, p. 24).	A dog might have ears and walk on four legs, but these are not critical attributes of dogs. If a dog only had one ear because of a birth defect or walked on three legs because of an accident, it would still be a dog.
Generalizations consist of several related concepts that form a larger one. Lang and Evans (2006) define generalizations as "rules, regulations, principles, laws, conclusions, inferences, axioms, proverbs, mottoes, propositions, and hypotheses" (p. 279). An example of a generalization is the "rule" for rounding numbers.	A canine that has been domesticated is a dog.
Conjunctive concepts have a single set of critical attributes or "unchanging rule structures" (Lang & Evans, 2006, p. 282) that must all be present (Merrill & Tennyson, 1977).	A female dog is a bitch. Bitches give birth to live young.

Appendix Figure B-1   Concept Vocabulary and Examples

continued

Vocabulary	Example
A **disjunctive concept** is "one in which any of several critical attributes can be present but all need not be present" (Merrill & Tennyson, 1977, p. 26).	A Canid is a wolf, dog, fox, or jackal.
Relational concepts are concepts whose meanings depend on comparisons or relationships.	The concept of "domestication" can be understood only when related to the concept of undomesticated or "wild."
Concrete concepts are those that one can see, touch, hear, smell, or feel in some way.	A puppy is a dog in its first six months of life. Puppies are smaller than adult dogs and make different noises. Physical differences between puppies and adult dogs can be observed via the five senses. One can see, touch, feel, hear, and taste a puppy (and be licked by one!).
Abstract concepts exist only in the mind.	The concept of "bonding," which implies the connection dogs have with each other or their human companions, is not visible in itself, but behaviors that demonstrate it are visible.
Specific concepts are very precise.	A toy dog is a dog that was bred to be a companion animal.
General concepts are not precise.	The concept of a "juvenile" Canidae is a general one that suggests an immature animal of the biological family Canidae. But it will refer to different ages depending on which species and breed one is referring to.
Formal concepts are learned in formal settings (e.g., at school or church).	We learn in school that a dog is a mammal and has certain characteristics that make it able to be classified as such—fur, nurses its young, and so on.
Informal concepts are learned in informal settings (e.g., at play or in free time).	A child might learn about appropriate behavior with a dog through his or her informal interactions with a family dog or neighborhood dog.
Superordinate concepts are overarching concepts.	A working dog (according to the American Kennel Club) is a purebred dog from stock that was bred to perform such jobs as guarding property, pulling sleds, and carrying out water rescues.
Subordinate concepts are concepts that fall under a superordinate concept.	A Saint Bernard is a working dog. They were originally bred to locate freezing and helpless travelers during snowstorms.

Understanding Concepts

Lang and Evans (2006) suggest categorizing concepts by (1) kind of concept, (2) the relationships that exist between a concept's critical attributes, and (3) the hierarchy demonstrated by a concept (Lang & Evans, 2006). The kind of concept refers to the level of concreteness/abstractness, specificity/generality, and formality/informality of the concept. The nature and degree of relationships between a concept's critical attributes also vary, allowing them to be categorized as conjunctive, disjunctive, or relational. A concept's hierarchy conveys the superordinate, subordinate, and coordinate relationships of a concept to other concepts. Examining these taxonomical features of concepts enhances concept instruction (Merrill & Tennyson, 1977) because concepts do not exist in a vacuum—they are part of a complex, interconnected schema (Piaget, 1926) representing comprehension of our world. The following section describes these categories in more detail.

Kinds of Concepts

Concrete concepts are those that one can see, touch, hear, smell, or feel in some way. Examples of concrete concepts include apples, books, and computers. On the other hand, **abstract concepts** exist only in the mind. They cannot be experienced using any of the five senses. Examples of abstract concepts are envy, success, and community. The primary differences between concrete and abstract concepts are that (1) abstract concepts lack the direct sensory referents of concrete concepts (Paivio, 1986, as cited in Crutch & Warrington, 2005), (2) concrete concepts provide greater contextual information in a person's knowledge base (Schwanenflugel & Shoben, 1983, as cited in Crutch & Warrington, 2005), and (3) abstract concepts lack the semantic features of concrete ones (Plaut & Shallice, 1993, as cited in Crutch & Warrington, 2005). In other words, concrete concepts provide more information for processing—including sensory information, contextual information, and semantic information—than abstract concepts.

Specific concepts signify very precise, detailed ideas such as π, a quotation mark, or a fjord. Often they are the building blocks of general concepts that are called "generalizations." **Generalizations** consist of several related concepts that form a larger one. Lang and Evans (2006) define generalizations as "rules, regulations, principles, laws, conclusions, inferences, axioms, proverbs, mottoes, propositions, and hypotheses" (p. 279). An example of a generalization is the "rule" for rounding numbers. The rule involves rounding up to a predesignated digit if the number is followed by a 5, 6, 7, 8, or 9 (e.g., 33.75 is rounded up to 34). If a 0, 1, 2, 3, or 4 follows the number, then one rounds down (e.g., 33.21 is rounded down to 33). In both of these cases, an individual must understand the specific value of a number to be able to round up or down.

The context in which individuals learn and experience concepts provides another means for classifying concepts. **Formal concepts** are those that one learns in formal situations, such as in schools or workshops or via other structured or prescribed relationships (e.g., parent–child relationship). The concepts introduced in this text are formal ones, as are those learned in elementary, middle, and high school. The concepts learned in a cooking class (e.g., special terminology of cooking utensils or techniques) are also formal ones. Alternatively, individuals learn **informal concepts** through informal contexts and relationships. Examples would include the concepts a child learns while playing games with friends, either face-to-face or online, or those a teenager learns by "hanging out, messing around, and geeking out" (Horst, Herr-Stephenson, & Robinson, n.d.) in a social networking community (e.g., Facebook or MySpace).

Relationship of a Concept's Critical Attributes

Concepts can be classified by the relationship between the concept's critical attributes that define it, which are conjunctive, disjunctive, or relational. **Conjunctive concepts** have a single set of critical attributes that must all be present (Merrill & Tennyson, 1977). An example of a conjunctive concept is a "bitch"—a bitch is a female dog. Both of these attributes—female and dog—are necessary for a dog to be a bitch. A **disjunctive concept** "is one in which any of several critical attributes can be present but all need not be present" (Merrill & Tennyson, 1977, p. 26). A disjunctive concept would be a "Canid," which is a wolf, dog, fox, or jackal. The concept is disjunctive because a Canid may be any of these different animals. **Relational concepts** are concepts whose meanings depend on comparisons or relationships. They do not have special attributes but must have a fixed relationship between or among attributes. A dog can be considered domesticated only if it is compared to "wild" or undomesticated dogs.

Hierarchy of a Concept

Concepts may also be defined and therefore understood in part by their hierarchy. Their hierarchy refers to the relationships between the concepts and subconcepts. The **superordinate concept** is the overarching concept. **Coordinate concepts** are subconcepts that share the same critical attributes as the superordinate concept, but they have unique attributes that distinguish them from other coordinate concepts within the same hierarchical level. The **subordinate concepts** are concepts categorized under the different coordinate concepts. They too share critical attributes of the superordinate concept, but they also have distinctive attributes that fall under each one's corresponding coordinate concept. A graphic presenting ideas for understanding a concept's hierarchy is included in Appendix Figure B-2.

Appendix Figure B-2   Hierarchy of a Concept

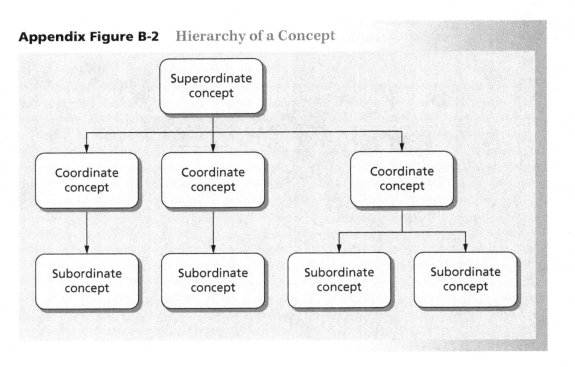

Other resources that are useful for teaching concepts are shown in Appendix Figure B-3 and B-4.

Appendix Figure B-3   Concept Map of Concept Ideas

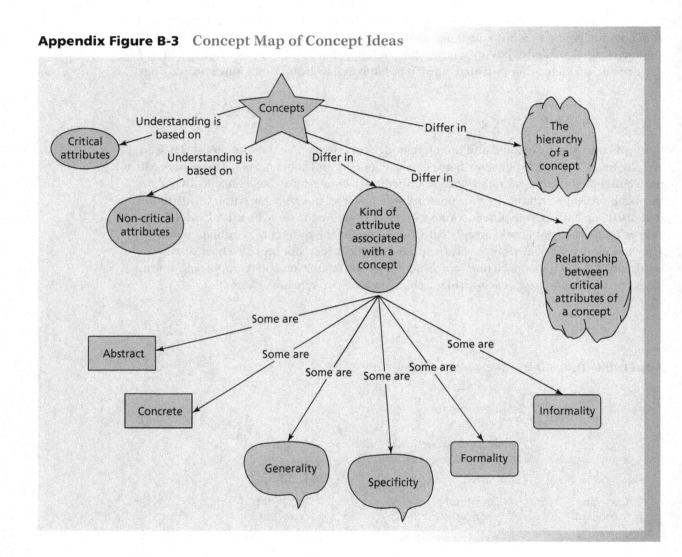

Appendix Figure B-4   Black-Line Master for Concepts

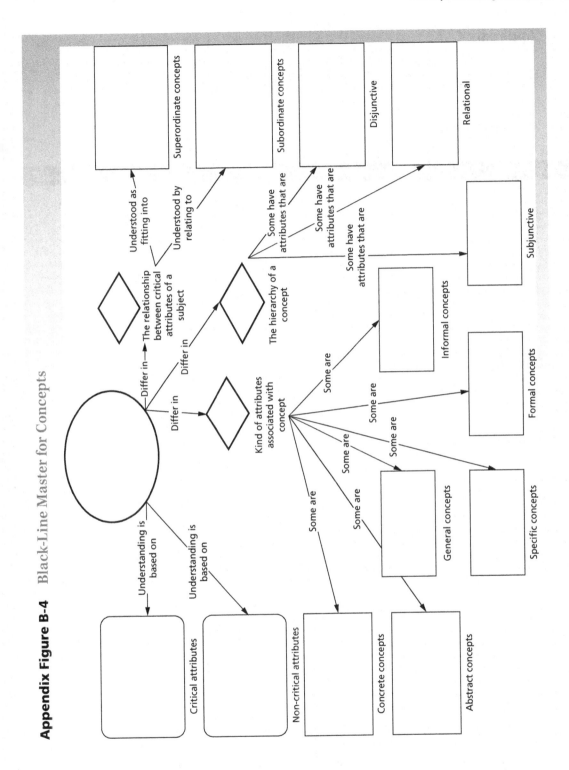

Worksheets

Worksheet 5-1 KWLH Chart

K "What I know"	W "What I want to know"	L "What I learned"	H "How I can learn more"

Worksheet 5-2 Empty Bucket

DUMP EVERYTHING YOU KNOW ABOUT _____
INTO THE BUCKET. USE THE SPACE ON THE BUCKET FOR "OVERFLOW."

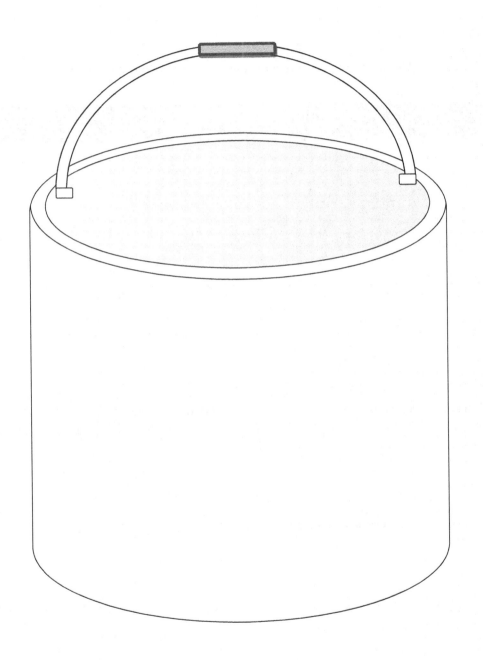

Worksheet 6-1 Concept Attainment Model Planning

SUBJECT: **GRADE LEVEL:**

CONCEPT DEFINITION:

CRITICAL ATTRIBUTES:

NONCRITICAL ATTRIBUTES:

PRESENT EXAMPLES: Data Set (List the examples and nonexamples and then number them in the order in which you will present them.)

Examples	Nonexamples	

FORM AND ANALYZE HYPOTHESES: (Describe how you will help students analyze the examples and non-examples and form hypotheses about the concept. Be specific—list the questions you will ask students and what you will expect students to do.)

CLOSURE: What will you or the students do or say to ensure that they understand the concept? Explain.

APPLICATION: What specific activity will students do to apply what they learned? (Describe what students will do.)

OTHER NOTES:

Worksheet 6-2 Concept Attainment Model Planning Example

SUBJECT: Art   **GRADE LEVEL:** 7

CONCEPT DEFINITION: Symmetry is when an object, image, or thing has the same shape, size, and corresponding parts on either side of at least one line of symmetry.

CRITICAL ATTRIBUTES: 1) has the same size, shape, and corresponding parts on both sides of a line of symmetry, 2) when at least two sides of an object or thing are exactly the same

NON-CRITICAL ATTRIBUTES: More than one line of symmetry, different types of symmetry (e.g., reflection, rotation)

PRESENT EXAMPLES: Data Set (List the examples and nonexamples and then number them in the order in which you will present them.)

Examples	Nonexamples
1.	2.
3.	4.
5.	6.
7. **H**	8. **R**
9.	10.
11.	12.

FORM AND ANALYZE HYPOTHESES: (Describe how you will help students analyze the examples and non-examples and form hypotheses about the concept. Be specific—list the questions you will ask students and what you will expect students to do.)

To help students analyze the examples and nonexamples, I will ask them the following questions, probing with additional questions when/if necessary:

1. What attributes does "X" example have that is similar to "Y" example?
2. How are the attributes different from those presented in the nonexamples? Explain and justify your reply with data from the examples/nonexamples.
3. What similarities and differences have you noticed between the examples and nonexamples? Explain and justify your reply with data from the examples/nonexamples.

To help students form hypotheses, I will ask the following questions, probing with additional questions when/if necessary:

1. What is your hypothesis about what this concept is?
2. What is your definition of the concept? Write it down.
3. How do data presented (examples and nonexamples) support your hypothesis?
4. Why do you believe you are correct?
5. Share your hypothesis with a partner. Discuss why you believe your definition of the concept is correct.

CLOSURE: What will you or the students do or say to ensure they understand the concept? Explain.

I will ask students to work with a partner to co-develop a definition of the concept, which will then be shared with the whole class. Then each pair will share its definition, and the class will vote on the most accurate definition of the concept. Also, I will ask students to reflect on the process by asking them to answer the following questions: "What did you learn?" "How did you learn it?" "What did you learn about "symmetry"? "What did you learn about analyzing the examples and nonexamples?" Were you surprised at your initial hypotheses?" "How long did it take to comprehend what" "symmetry" is? *Please write down your ideas on a blank sheet of paper.*

APPLICATION: What specific activity (or activities) will students do to apply what they learned? (Describe what students will do.)

Students will complete Worksheet 6.4: Concept Attainment—Application and answer: "Are there any nonexamples that can be changed into examples?" "Why or why not?"

OTHER NOTES: Students who need extra help may examine this online lesson: www.linkslearning.org/Kids/1_Math/2_Illustrated_Lessons/4_Line_Symmetry/index.html

---

Worksheet 6-3 Concept Attainment Model—Scaffolding Student Thinking

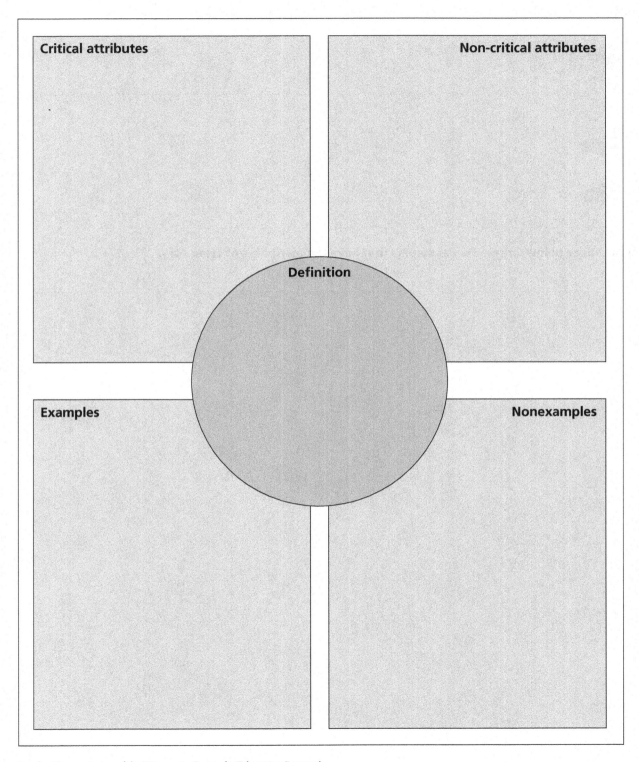

Critical attributes

Non-critical attributes

Definition

Examples

Nonexamples

Used with permission of the Wisconsin Center for Education Research.

Worksheet 6-4 Concept Attainment Model—Application

How could you change these nonexamples into examples of symmetry? (Draw and explain.)

_____

_____

_____

In the space below, create two examples that have the attributes of symmetry.

Frayer, D., Frederick, W. C., & Klausmeier, H. J. (1969). A schema for testing the level of cognitive mastery. Madison, WI: Wisconsin Center for Education.

Worksheet 7-1 Concept Development Model Example

1. **List:** List as many items related to the concept as possible. As you list items, consider "What do you know about this concept?"

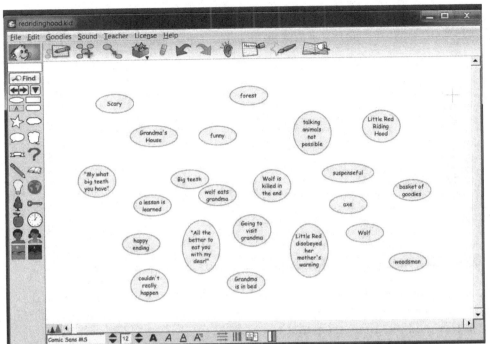

2. **Group:** Group these items and consider "Which items belong together?"

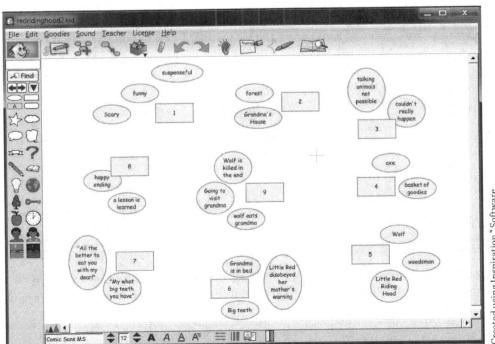

3. **Label:** Create labels, words, or phrases that describe the contents of each group by asking yourself, "What would you call these groups you have formed?"

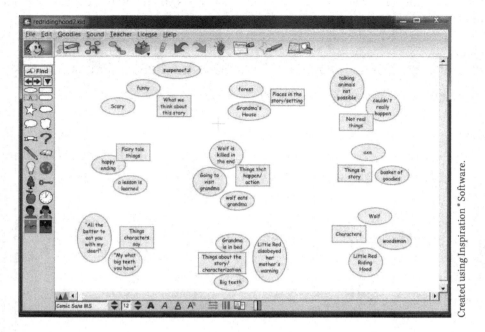

Created using Inspiration® Software.

4. **Regroup:** Review how items have been grouped and examine how you might regroup these items by answering, "Could some of these belong in more than one group? Can we put these same items in different groups? Why would you group them that way?"

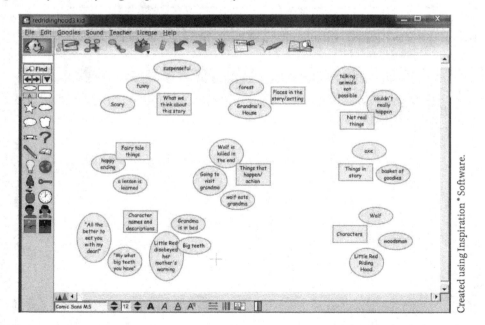

Created using Inspiration® Software.

5. **Synthesize:** Think of one sentence that summarizes these groupings by answering, "What is one sentence that summarizes the relationship between the items you listed in groups with different labels?"

Fiction stories are enjoyable, make-believe stories that tell things that happen to characters in certain settings using dialogue.

Worksheet 7-2 Concept Development Model Lesson

1. List: List as many items related to the concept as possible. As you list items, consider "What do you know about this concept?"

2. Group: Group these items and consider "Which items belong together?"

3. Label: Create labels, words, or phrases that describe the contents of each group by asking yourself, "What would you call these groups you have formed?"

4. Regroup: Review how items have been grouped and examine how you might regroup these items by answering, "Could some of these belong in more than one group? Can we put these same items in different groups? Why would you group them that way?"

5. Synthesize: Think of one sentence that summarizes these groupings by answering, "What is one sentence that summarizes the relationship between the items you listed in groups with different labels?"

Worksheet 9-1 Vocabulary Acquisition Model WordMap

Root:

Prefix:

Suffix:

Sentence:

Vocabulary Word Definition

Synonym:

Antonym:

Related Words:

Worksheet 9-2

My Spelling of Vocabulary	What I Think It Means	Actual Spelling	Actual Definition	Synonym	Antonym	Drawing / Graphic

Worksheet 9-3 Venn Diagram

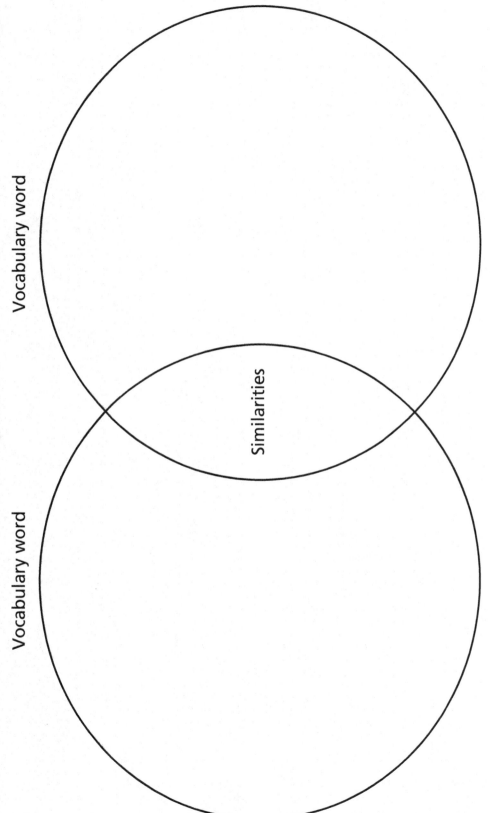

Vocabulary word

Vocabulary word

Similarities

Worksheet 9-4 American versus French Revolution

	Type of Government	Characteristics of People	Reasons for Conflict	Actions and Events Leading to Revolution
American				
French				

Worksheet 10-1 Reflection before Planning an Inquiry Lesson

1. What goals do I have for students' content area learning using this inquiry? (specific curriculum standards)

2. What goals do I have for student learning as it relates to understanding and participating in the discovery process? (collecting, interpreting, and so on)

3. How will I share these goals with my students? How can I empower them to be partners in the learning process?

4. In what ways will the students be actively involved in the inquiry process? How can I motivate them to care about the learning?

5. What prerequisite skills and knowledge do students need to have before participating in this inquiry lesson?

6. What are the ways I can differentiate the materials with which students work, the support provided during the learning process, and the product of learning?

Worksheet 10-2 Inquiry Model Lesson—Data Analysis

STEP 1: Make your hypothesis by deciding which brand of raisins you think is the better value. (HINT: For this inquiry, the "best value" has the most raisins for the price you paid per unit.) The store-brand raisins were $1.75 for six 1.5-ounce boxes, and the name-brand raisins were $2.50 for eight 1.5-ounce boxes. Write down your hypothesis by filling in the statement below:

I believe that the _____ will be the better value because _____.

STEP 2: Individually count your own raisins in the store-brand and in the name-brand boxes. Record how many raisins are in each box below.

_____ How many raisins I had in my box—Store Brand
_____ How many raisins I had in my box—Name Brand

STEP 3: Write down the names of your group members and the number of raisins they have in each box of raisins.

Name of Group Member	Number of Raisins Per Box—Store Brand	Number of Raisins Per Box—Name Brand

STEP 4: Average the total number of raisins in each box for the name brand of raisins and the store brand of raisins. You can calculate the average by adding the total number or raisins of each type (adding all the results going down the column) and then dividing this number by the number of people in your group.

_____ Average number of raisins—Store Brand   _____ Average number of raisins—Name Brand

STEP 5: Determine the price per unit (1.5-ounce box of raisins). This is known as the "unit price." To calculate the unit price, you will first need to figure out the price per 1.5-ounce box of raisins. Do this by dividing the cost of the raisins by the number of boxes (find this in Step 1).

_____ Price per unit of raisins—Store Brand   _____ Price per unit of raisins—Name Brand

STEP 6: Determine which brand, the store brand or name brand, provides more raisins for the price.

How many raisins do you get for the price per unit? _____

One way to do this might be to divide the unit price by the number of raisins you get for this price and calculate the per-raisin cost.
What did you find out? _____

STEP 7: Which raisins were less expensive? _____ How does this finding compare with your hypothesis? _____

STEP 8: After you are finished, consider these questions: Are there any problems with the method of calculating the "best value" based on the number of raisins per box? _____

Is there another way you might find the "best value" of raisins besides the number of raisins for the price paid per unit? Explain. _____

Worksheet 11-1 Problem-Based Learning Model Process

1. In your own words, describe the problem.

2. Brainstorm what information or materials you will need to solve the problem.

3. Brainstorm a plan for solving the problem.

4. What is your plan to solve the problem?

5. Describe the outcome of your problem after you implemented it.

Worksheet 11-2 Problem-Based Learning Model Group Checkpoint

1. Describe how your team is working together to solve the problem.

2. How might your work toward solving the problem be improved?

3. What is your contribution to solving the problem?

Worksheet 13-1 American Indian Tribes

	Chinook	Cheyenne	Comanche	Mohawk	Navajo	Seminole
Name Means	—	Red talkers, or people of different speech	The people	Eaters of men	Cultivated fields	Derived from the Spanish word *cimarrón*, which means "wild"
Call Themselves	Chinook	Dzi tsi stas (beautiful people or our people)	Nuumu	Kaniengehage (people of the flint)	Dineh (the people)	Sim A No Le Unconquered people
Geographic Location	Northwest Washington and Oregon along the Columbia River	Plains Near Great Lakes (Minnesota)	Plains Oklahoma	Northeast Lived along St. Lawrence River in Canada and Mohawk Valley in central New York	Southwest Northeastern Arizona, northwestern New Mexico, and southeastern Utah	Southeast Florida and Oklahoma
Lifestyle	Fishing and trading	Planting and hunting	Hunting	Hunting, gathering, and farming	Hunting and farming	Fishing and hunting
Language Family	Chinookan	Algonquian	Uto-Aztecan Numic	Iroquoian	Athapaskan	Muskogean
Homes	Large rectangular wood plank houses	Tipis	Tipis	Longhouses	Hogans (traditional)	Chickees

Worksheet 14-1 *Pledge of Allegiance* Analysis

1. What are the major ideas expressed in the words of the *Pledge of Allegiance*? (HINT: It might be helpful to consider the key words.)

2. Take two of those ideas and explain what they mean to you. Explain how and why they are important to the people of the United States of America.

3. What are the major reasons for saying the *Pledge of Allegiance*? Why is it recited in schools and other events?

4. What does the *Pledge of Allegiance* mean to you personally? Explain.

Appendix D

Instructional Model Matrix

Chapter/Name of Model	Major Steps or Phases	Description	Origins of the Model	Types of Knowledge the Model Is Best Suited to Teach	Support for 21st Century Learning
Chapter 5 Direct Instruction	1. Introduction 2. Presentation 3. Guided practice 4. Independent practice	A teacher-led instructional model that is useful for promoting understanding of procedures among students who gradually develop independence using new learning.	Emerged from behavioral approaches such as Skinner's theory of operant conditioning and Vygotsky's social development theory.	Procedural knowledge/ procedures or content that can be broken down into discrete segments	• Fosters logical, organized thinking • Fosters independent learning of procedures • Provides practice in and application of existing knowledge
Chapter 6 Concept Attainment	1. Presentation of examples 2. Formation and analysis of hypotheses 3. Closure 4. Application	A teacher-guided instructional model through which students develop an understanding of a concept by examining examples and nonexamples and by analyzing their critical and noncritical attributes.	Based on the work of Hilda Taba (1967), which advocated the importance of teaching students to develop, understand, and make generalizations about concepts. Also related to the work of cognitive psychologist Jerome Bruner, who espouses that learning is an active, social process in which students construct new ideas or concepts based on their current knowledge.	Conceptual knowledge/ especially concepts with clearly defined attributes	• Promotes discrimination and generalization • Fosters inquisitiveness
Chapter 7 Concept Development	1. Listing 2. Grouping 3. Labeling 4. Regrouping 5. Synthesizing	A student-centered model that promotes understanding of concepts through inductive reasoning about examples for the purpose of grouping and classifying them.	Created by Hilda Taba in 1971 to support students' learning and practice of thinking skills.	Concepts and conceptual knowledge Also good for teaching facts related to the concept	• Supports ability to classify, think flexibly, and make generalizations • Fosters development of organizational skills • Encourages recognition of relationships and understanding of concepts

Chapter/Name of Model	Major Steps or Phases	Description	Origins of the Model	Types of Knowledge the Model Is Best Suited to Teach	Support for 21st Century Learning
Chapter 8 Inductive Model	1. Lesson introduction 2. Divergent phase 3. Convergent phase 4. Closure 5. Application	A teacher-guided model that challenges students to recognize patterns and details in content under investigation.	Directly influenced by Hilda Taba. The model promotes and requires inductive reasoning, which traces its roots to Sir Francis Bacon.	Factual Knowledge Conceptual Knowledge	• Promotes inductive reasoning, skills of observation, and recognition of patterns and details • Allows practice with convergent and divergent thinking • Fosters interaction with and skills for making sense of content materials • Cultivates strategies for deep learning of content
Chapter 9 Vocabulary Acquisition Model	1. Pretest knowledge of words critical to content 2. Elaborate on and discuss invented spellings and hypothesized meanings 3. Explore patterns of meaning 4. Read and study 5. Evaluate and posttest	A teacher-guided model for teaching vocabulary in a procedural and inductive manner. The model helps students develop their own understanding of the meaning of a word(s) through analysis of the parts of the word and their meanings.	Thomas Estes was the first to coin the model's title and formalize its steps for exploring the meanings and patterns inherent in words.	Factual knowledge of vocabulary words Also supports development of conceptual knowledge of language and vocabulary	• Develops recognition of details, making of connections with prior knowledge, and creative thinking • Encourages development of skills for independent vocabulary learning

Chapter/Name of Model	Major Steps or Phases	Description	Origins of the Model	Types of Knowledge the Model Is Best Suited to Teach	Support for 21st Century Learning
Chapter 10 Inquiry Model	1. Present/pose question 2. Make hypothesis 3. Gather data 4. Assess hypothesis 5. Generalize 6. Analysis of inquiry process	A process-oriented instructional model that teaches students the skills, knowledge, and dispositions required for thinking systematically to answer important questions.	Stems from the idea of the use of the scientific method as a way of teaching "scientific ways of knowing." The most recent variations of the model were developed in response to the modern need to teach students to effectively use and manage a multitude of informational sources.	Procedural knowledge Conceptual knowledge Metacognitive knowledge	• Promotes problem-solving skills • Introduces students to scientific ways of knowing • Fosters skills and dispositions for learning to learn
Chapter 11 Problem-Based Learning	1. Present or identify the problem 2. Develop a plan for solving the problem 3. Implement the plan for solving the problem 4. Evaluate the implementation plan results	An active learning model that challenges students to learn and apply knowledge of content with problem-solving skills to meaningful problems in the academic disciplines.	Developed in medical education settings and first used in the 1950s to prepare doctors to apply professional skills and knowledge in real-world contexts.	Factual knowledge Procedural knowledge Conceptual knowledge Metacognitive knowledge	• Cultivates application of knowledge to real-world contexts • Encourages learning of useful processes to solve problems
Chapter 12 Cooperative Learning (General Cooperative Learning Model)	1. Introduce the task 2. Name, teach, and practice targeted social skills	A model that capitalizes on students' inclination to learn socially and promotes students' development of social skills and understanding of content.	Developed in early 1970s by social scientists at John Hopkins University to help schools in Baltimore, Maryland, manage newly integrated classrooms.	Factual knowledge Procedural knowledge Conceptual Knowledge Metacognitive knowledge	• Promotes skills for productive collaboration and communication (listening, taking turns) • Teaches benefits of teamwork and cooperation

Chapter/Name of Model	Major Steps or Phases	Description	Origins of the Model	Types of Knowledge the Model Is Best Suited to Teach	Support for 21st Century Learning
	3. Implement the lesson and monitoring student interactions 4. Summarize learning 5. Measure group and individual accountability 6. Conduct assessment				
Chapter 13 Integrative Model	1. Describe, compare, and search for patterns 2. Explain similarities and differences 3. Hypothesize outcomes for different conditions 4. Generalize to form broad relationships	A teacher-guided model that supports students as they work to develop the ability to learn independently using various critical thinking skills. Students analyze an organized body of knowledge to develop new ideas and understandings while learning to think, analyze, and draw conclusions independently.	Developed by Hilda Taba as a part of the Taba Curriculum Development Project.	Factual knowledge Procedural knowledge Metacognitive knowledge	• Supports ability to draw conclusions and make connections and generalizations • Encourages ability to examine, analyze, and make sense of large amounts of materials
Chapter 14 Socratic Seminar	1. Introduce the Socratic Seminar model 2. Facilitate the Socratic Seminar dialogue 3. Review and summarizing the dialogue 4. Evaluate the dialogue	A teacher-guided model that encourages development of thinking skills and exploration of ideas through the use of structured questioning with debate or dialogue.	Greek philosopher and teacher Socrates developed the general method of teaching through questioning.	Factual knowledge Procedural knowledge Metacognitive knowledge	• Fosters communication and collaboration skills (listening and questioning) • Develops thinking skills, including questioning, synthesis, and analysis

Lesson Plan Framework

Lesson Plan

Completion of this in-depth lesson plan framework supports a systematic approach to instructional decision making. The framework reflects major ideas in the text and is intended to promote more intentional practice and successful teaching.

1. **Subject(s):**
2. **Grade Level(s):**
3. **Summary:** A short description of the lesson for your reference or to share with others.
4. **Standards Addressed:** Reference the curriculum and technology standards that are addressed in this lesson. You may want to use "shorthand" to reference specific standards. For example: subject, strand, grade, learning standard.
5. **Objectives/Learning Goals:** Write the objectives that express what students will know and be able to do at the end of the lesson. Remember that it is easiest to work with objectives that are (1) focused, or deal with only one type of knowledge that will be targeted through instruction (i.e., factual, procedural, conceptual, or metacognitive); (2) stated as learning outcomes; and (3) clear. Consider writing objectives as "I CAN statements" that express the objectives in simple language appropriate for sharing with students.
6. **Instructional Model:** Explain why you have chosen the specific instructional model utilized.
7. **Cognitive Process Dimension(s) addressed (according to the revised Bloom's taxonomy):** Consider what cognitive processes might be required for fully understanding of the objectives.
8. **Types of Knowledge:** Consider the types of knowledge covered in the various objectives. Note what types of knowledge are addressed in this model. Explain how you will stimulate activities that promote them.

Learning Context

Situate what will be learned and performed within the specific and general context.

9. **General Rationale:** Include a brief statement about why the learning goals are important in the school curriculum. Try to include information that expresses how learning is relevant to students in *life and future learning.*
10. **Specific Rationale:** Provide a brief statement with information about why learning goals are important within the specific subject or unit. Include information about how learning is relevant to students *now.*
11. **Learner Characteristics:** Document your thoughts about the needs of diverse learners involved in the lesson. Consider what data you have to substantiate your thoughts (e.g., individualized education plan, beginning of year survey, and so on) and how individual backgrounds, lived experiences, interests, and learning style might influence readiness for learning. Include what you will need to evaluate these needs and what you will do to address them.

Methodology

Explain in detail what must happen to implement the lesson. Include enough detail so that someone else could use your plan if they want to.

   a. Preparation: Describe any thinking or activities you would need to perform to be ready for the lesson.

    i. Materials

    ii. Leading questions

    iii. Plans for grouping

    iv. Location for where the lesson will take place

    v. Time required for the lesson (break this down in the procedure if necessary)

    vi. Instructional materials (include samples if available)

12. **Procedures:** Describe step-by-step procedures for how the lesson will take place. Provide as much detail as would be required for someone else to teach the lesson. Include the steps of the specific model you have chosen.

13. **Plans for Differentiation:** Include detailed information about how you will differentiate instruction and why.

14. **Plans for Technology:** Explain how technology will make the lesson more efficient, effective, or engaging. Write down any specific skills you will need to learn to be successful. Make note of any details that might need to be attended to in order to promote the successful integration of technology tools or techniques.

15. **Anticipation of Difficulties:** Anticipate unexpected events that might happen and influence the success of the lesson, including those related to technology. In this section, include proactive plans that will minimize anticipated difficulties and reactive plans for dealing with them if they occur.

Assessment

Explain how you will evaluate the students' performance *as well as* the design and implementation of the lesson.

16. **Student Assessment:** Explain how you will measure to what extent your students meet each of the objectives stated in this lesson plan. Include plans for measuring achievement. Also consider how you will measure effort and growth if applicable.

17. **Lesson Assessment:** Include how you will determine whether the design and implementation of the lesson are successful.

18. **Rationale:** Reflect on why you have chosen the particular method(s) for student and lesson assessments.

19. **Assessment Plan and Tools:** Describe your plans for assessing student learning and attainment of objectives. Be sure to include an example of the pre-assessment, formative assessment, or summative assessment tools you plan to utilize to assess student learning.

References

CHAPTER ONE

Anderson, L. W., Krathwohl, D. R., Airasian, P. W., Cruikshank, K. A., Mayer, R. E., Pintrich, P. R., Raths, J., & Wittrock, M. C. (2001). *A taxonomy for learning, teaching, and assessing.* New York: Longman.

Aud, S., Hussar, W., Planty, M., Snyder, T., Bianco, K., Fox, M., Frohlich, L., Kemp, J., & Drake, L. (2010). *The condition of education 2010* (NCES 2010–028). National Center for Education Statistics, Institute of Education Sciences, U.S. Department of Education. Washington, DC.

Bloom, B. S. (1956). *Taxonomy of educational objectives, handbook I: The cognitive domain.* New York: David McKay Co Inc.

Gay, G. (2010). *Culturally responsive teaching: Theory, research, & practice* (2nd ed.). New York: Teachers College Press.

Gray, T., & Fleischman, S. (2004). Educating Language Learners. *Educational Leadership, 62*(4), 84–85.

Hilbert, M., & Lopez, P. (2011). The world's technological capacity to store, communicate, and compute information. *Science, 332*, 60–65.

Hoffman, L., & Sable, J. (2006). *Public elementary and secondary students, staff, schools, and school districts: School year 2003–04.* U.S. Department of Education Institutes of Education Statistics (NCES 2006–307). Retrieved from http://nces.ed.gov/pubs2006/2006307.pdf

International Society for Technology in Education. (2007). NETS-S for students 2007. Retrieved from http://www.iste.org/standards/nets-for-students.aspx

Jansen, J. (2010). Use of the Internet in higher income households. Retrieved from http://pewinternet.org/~/media//Files/Reports/2010/PIP-Better-off-households-final.pdf

Joyce, B., Weil, M., & Calhoun, E. (2009). *Models of teaching* (8th ed.). Boston, MA: Allyn & Bacon.

National Center for Education Statistics. (2005). *The condition of education 2005.* Washington, DC: U.S. Government Printing Office.

Partnership for 21st Century Skills. (2004). *Framework for 21st century learning.* Retrieved from http://www.p21.org/index.php?option=com_content&task=view&id=254&Itemid=119

Prensky, M. (2001). Digital natives, digital immigrants. *On the Horizon, 9*(5), 1–6. Retrieved from http://www.marcprensky.com/writing/Prensky%20-%20Digital%20Natives,%20Digital%20Immigrants%20-%20Part1.pdf

Tomlinson, C. (1999). *The differentiated classroom: Responding to the needs of all learners.* Alexandria, VA: Association for Supervision and Curriculum Development.

Tomlinson, C. (2003). Differentiating instruction for academic diversity. In J. M. Cooper (Ed.), *Classroom teaching skills* (pp. 149–180). Boston: Houghton Mifflin Company.

CHAPTER TWO

Anderson, L. W., Krathwohl, D. R., Airasian, P. W., Cruikshank, K. A., Mayer, R. E., Pintrich, P. R., Raths, J., & Wittrock, M. C. (2001). *A taxonomy for learning, teaching, and assessing.* New York: Longman.

Day, C., Calderhead, J., & Denicolo, P. (Eds.) (1993). *Research on teacher thinking: Understanding professional development.* Washington D.C.: The Falmer Press.

Dick, W. (1987). A history of instructional design and its impact on educational psychology. In J. Glover & R. Roning (Eds.), *Historical foundations of educational psychology.* New York: Plenum.

Dick, W., Carey, L., & Carey, J. O. (2008). *The systematic design of instruction* (7th ed.). Boston: Allyn & Bacon.

Gagné, R. M. (1965). *The conditions of learning* (1st ed.). New York: Holt, Rinehart and Winston.

Gustafson, K. (2002). What is instructional design? In R. A. Rieser & J. V. Dempsey (Eds.), *Trends and issues in instructional design and technology.* Upper Saddle River, NJ: Pearson Education.

Harris, J., & Hofer, M. (2009a). Instructional planning activity types as vehicles for curriculum-based TPACK development. In C. D. Maddux, (Ed.). *Research highlights in technology and teacher education 2009* (pp. 99–108). Chesapeake, VA: Society for Information Technology in Teacher Education (SITE).

Harris, J. & Hofer, M. (2009b). Instructional planning activity types as vehicles for curriculum-based TPACK development. In Proceedings of Society for Information Technology and Teacher Education International Conference. Norfolk, VA: AACE.

Harris, J., Mishra, P. & Koehler, M. J. (2009). Teachers' technological pedagogical content knowledge and learning activity types: Curriculum-based technology integration reframed. *Journal of Research on Technology in Education, 41*(3), 393–416.

Heinich, R., Molenda, M., Russell, J. D., & Smaldino, S. E. (1999). *Instructional media and technologies for learning* (6th ed.) Upper Saddle River, NJ: Merrill.

Joyce, B., Weil, M., & Calhoun, E. (2009). *Models of teaching* (8th ed.). Boston, MA: Pearson.

Wiggins, G., & McTighe, J. (2005). *Understanding by Design.* Expanded 2nd Edition. Alexandria, VA: ASCD.

Willis, J. (2000). The maturing of constructivist instructional design: Some basic principles that can guide practice. *Educational Technology, 40*(1), 5–16.

Yinger, R. T. (1980). A study of teacher planning. *The Elementary School Journal, 80*(3), 107–127.

Yinger, R. T., & Clark, R. J. (1979). Three studies of teacher planning. Paper presented at the annual meeting of the American Educational Research Association.

Zahorik, J. A. (1982). Learning activities: Nature, Function and practice. *The Elementary School Journal, 82*(4), 309–317.

CHAPTER THREE

Koehler, M., & Mishra, P. (2008). Introducing TPCK. In AACTE Committee on Innovation and Technology (Ed.). *Handbook of technological pedagogical content knowledge (TPCK) for educators.* New York: Routledge/Taylor & Francis Group for the American Association of Colleges of Teacher Education.

Mishra, P. (2009). *TPACK newsletter #2: Feb09 edition.* Retrieved from http://punya.educ.msu.edu/2009/02/27/tpack-newsletter-2-feb09-edition/

Mishra, P., & Koehler, M. J. (2006). Technological pedagogical content knowledge: A new framework for teacher knowledge. *Teachers College Record, 108*(6), 1017–1054.

Shulman, L. S. (1986). Those who understand: Knowledge growth in teaching. *Educational Researcher, 15*(2), 4–14.

Shulman, L. S. (1987). Knowledge and teaching: Foundations of the new reform. *Harvard Educational Review, 57*(1), 1–22.

Technological pedagogical content knowledge. (n.d.). [image]. Retrieved from http://tpack.org/

CHAPTER FOUR

Anderson, L. W., Krathwohl, D. R., Airasian, P. W., Cruikshank, K. A., Mayer, R. E., Pintrich, P. R., Raths, J., & Wittrock, M. C. (2001). *A taxonomy for learning, teaching, and assessing.* New York: Longman.

Black, P., & Wiliam, D. (1998a). Assessment and classroom learning. *Assessment in Education, 5*(1), 7–74.

Black, P., & Wiliam, D. (1998b). Inside the black box: Raising standards through classroom assessment. *Phi Delta Kappan, 80*(2), 139–148.

Stiggins, R. J. (2005). *Student-involved assessment for learning.* Upper Saddle River, NJ: Pearson Prentice Hall.

Wiggins, G. (1998). *Educative assessment: Designing assessments to inform and improve student performance.* San Francisco: Jossey-Bass.

Wiggins, G., & McTighe, J. (2005). *Understanding by design* (2nd ed.). Alexandria, VA: ASCD.

CHAPTER FIVE

Huitt, W. (2008). Direct Instruction: A transactional model. *Educational Psychology Interactive.* Valdosta, GA: Valdosta State University.

Hunter, M. C. (1982). *Increasing instructional effectiveness in elementary and secondary schools.* Thousand Oaks, CA: Corwin Press.

Kauchak, D., & Eggen, P. (2012). *Learning and teaching: Research-based methods* (6th ed.). Boston: Allyn & Bacon.

Skinner, B. F. (1953). *Science and human behavior.* New York: Macmillan.

Slavin, R. (2006). *Educational psychology* (8th ed.). Boston: Pearson/Allyn & Bacon.

CHAPTER SIX

Anderson, L. W., Krathwohl, D. R., Airasian, P. W., Cruikshank, K. A., Mayer, R. E., Pintrich, P. R., Raths, J., & Wittrock, M. C. (2001). *A taxonomy for learning, teaching, and assessing.* New York: Longman.

Bruner, J. S., Goodnow, J. J., & Austin, G. A. (1956). *A study of thinking.* New York: John Wiley & Sons.

Driscoll, M., & Tessmer, M. (1985). The rational set generator: A method for creating concept examples for teaching and testing. *Educational Technology, 25*(2), 29–32.

Frayer, D., Frederick, W. C., & Klausmeier, H. J. (1969). *A schema for testing the level of cognitive mastery.* Madison, WI: Wisconsin Center for Education Research.

Markle, S. M., & Tiemann, P. W. (1970). *Really understanding concepts: Or, In frumious pursuit of the Jabberwock* (3rd ed.). Champaign, IL: Stipes Publishing.

Merrill, M. D., & Tennyson, R. D. (1977). *Teaching concepts: An instructional design guide.* Englewood Cliffs, NJ: Educational Technology Publications.

Taba, H. (1967). *Teacher's handbook for elementary social studies: An inductive approach.* Reading, MA: Addison-Wesley.

Taba, H., & Elkins, D. (1966). *Teaching strategies for the culturally disadvantaged.* Chicago: Rand McNally & Company.

Tennyson, R. D., & Cocchiarella, M. J. (1986). An empirically based instructional design theory for teaching concepts. *Review of Educational Research, 56*(1), 40–71.

Tennyson, R. D., & Park, O-C. (1980). The teaching of concepts: A review of instructional design research literature. *Review of Educational Research, 50*(1), 55–70.

CHAPTER SEVEN

Bredderman, T. (1978). *Elementary school process curricula: A meta-analysis.* ERIC reproduction service 170333.

Bransford, J., Brown, A. L., & Cocking. R. R. (1999). *How people learn.* Washington, D.C.: National Academy Press.

Fraenkel, J. R. (1992). Hilda Taba's contribution to social studies education. *Social Education, 56*(3), 172–178.

Jonassen, D. H. (2000). *Computers as mindtools for schools: Engaging critical thinking* (2nd ed). Upper Saddle River, NJ: Prentice Hall.

Taba, H. (1967). *Teacher's handbook for elementary social studies: An inductive approach.* Reading, MA: Addison-Wesley.

Taba, H., Durkin, M. C., Fraenkel, J. R., & McNaughton, A. H. (1971). *A teacher's handbook to elementary social studies: An inductive approach* (2nd ed.). Reading, MA: Addison-Wesley.

Worthen, B. R. (1968). Discovery and expository task presentation in elementary mathematics. *Journal of Educational Psychology Monograph, 59*(1).

CHAPTER EIGHT

Bacon, F. (1620/1855). *The Novum organum, or a true guide to the interpretation of nature,* trans. (G. W. Kitchin, Trans.). Oxford: Oxford University Press.

Bereiter, C. (2002). *Education and mind in the knowledge age.* Mahwah, NJ: Laurence Erlbaum.

Bruner, J. (1960). *The process of education.* Cambridge, MA: Harvard University Press.

convergent. (n.d.). In *Merriam-Webster online dictionary.* Retrieved from www.merriam-webster.com/dictionary/convergent

divergent. (n.d.). In *Merriam-Webster online dictionary.* Retrieved from www.merriam-webster.com/dictionary/divergent

Fraenkel, J. R. (1992). Hilda Taba's contribution to social studies education. *Social Education, 56*(3), 172–178.

Glover, J. A., Ronning, R. R., & Reynolds, C. R. (Eds.). (1989). *Handbook of creativity*. New York, NY: Plenum.

Guilford, J. P. (1950). Creativity. *American Psychologist, 5,* 444–454.

Taba, H. (1967). *Teacher's handbook for elementary social studies: An inductive approach*. Reading, MA: Addison-Wesley.

Wiggins, G., & McTighe, J. (2005). *Understanding by design* (2nd ed.). Alexandria, VA: Association for Supervision and Curriculum Development.

CHAPTER NINE

Anderson, L. W., Krathwohl, D. R., Airasian, P. W., Cruikshank, K. A., Mayer, R. E., Pintrich, P. R., Raths, J., & Wittrock, M. C. (2001). *A taxonomy for learning, teaching, and assessing*. New York, NY: Longman.

Anstrom, K., DiCerba, P., Butler, F., Katz, A., Millet, J., & Rivera, C. (2010). *A review of the literature on academic English: Implications for K-12 English language learners*. Washington, DC: George Washington University Center for Equity and Excellence in Education. Retrieved from: ceee.gwu.edu/Academic%20Lit%20Review_FINAL.pdf

Baker, S. K., Simmons, D. C., & Kameenui, E. J. (1995). *Vocabulary acquisition: Synthesis of the research*. Technical Report No. 13. Eugene, OR: National Center to Improve the Tools of Educators, University of Oregon. Retrieved November 11, 2008, from: idea.uoregon.edu/~ncite/documents/techrep/tech13.html

Beck, I. L., McKeown, M. G., & Kucan, L. (2008). *Creating robust vocabulary: Frequently asked questions and extended examples*. New York: Guilford.

Bereiter, C. (2002). *Education and mind in the knowledge age*. Mahwah, NJ: Laurence Erlbaum.

Bloom B. S. (1956). *Taxonomy of educational objectives, Handbook I: The cognitive domain*. New York, NY: David McKay Co.

Carlo, M., August, D., McLaughlin, B., Snow, C., Dressler, C. Lippman, D., et al. (2004). Closing the gap: Addressing the vocabulary needs of English Language Learners in bilingual and mainstream classrooms. *Reading Research Quarterly, 39,* 188–215.

Cassiday, J., & Weinrich, J. (1997). What's hot and what's not for 1997. *Reading Today, 14*(4), 34.

Cassiday, J., & Weinrich, J. (1998). What's hot and what's not for 1997. *Reading Today, 15*(4), 1–28.

conductor. (2012). In *Merriam-Webster online dictionary*. Retrieved from www.merriam-webster.com/dictionary/conductor

equilibrium. (2012). In *Merriam-Webster online dictionary*. Retrieved from www.merriam-webster.com/dictionary/equilibrium

etymology. (2012). In *Merriam-Webster online dictionary*. Retrieved from www.merriam-webster.com/dictionary/etymology

Francis, D. J., Rivera, M., Lesaux, N., Kieffer, M., & and Rivera, H. (2006). *Practical guidelines for the education of English Language Learners: Research-based recommendations for instruction and academic interventions* (No. 2). Portsmouth, NH: Center on Instruction.

Gunter, M. A., Estes, T. H., & Schwab, J. (2007). *Instruction: A models approach* (5th ed.). Boston, MA: Allyn & Bacon.

Jonassen, D., Beissner, K., & Yacci, M. (1993). *Structural knowledge: Techniques for representing, conveying, and acquiring structural knowledge*. Englewood Cliffs, NJ: Lawrence Erlbaum Associates.

Marzano, R. J. (2004). *Building background knowledge for academic achievement*. Alexandria, VA: Association for Supervision and Curriculum Development.

morphology. (2012). In *Merriam-Webster online dictionary*. Retrieved from www.merriam-webster.com/dictionary/morphology

Nagy, W. E., & Scott, J. A. (2000). Vocabulary processes. In M. L. Kamil, P. Mosenthal, P. D. Pearson, & R. Barr (Eds.), *Handbook of reading research* (Vol. 3, pp. 269–284). Mahwah, NJ: Erlbaum.

National Reading Panel. (2000). *Report of the National Reading Panel: Teaching children to read—an evidence-based assessment of the scientific research literature on reading and its implications for reading instruction. Reports of the subgroups*. Rockville, MD: NICHD Clearinghouse [online]. Available: www.nichd.nih.gov/publications/nrp/upload/smallbook_pdf.pdf

Piaget, J. (1923/1926). *The language and thought of the child*. London: Routledge and Kegan Paul.

Scarcella, R. (2008). Academic language: Clarifying terms. *AccELLerate! The Quarterly Newsletter of the National Clearinghouse for English Language Acquisition (NCELA), 1*(1), 5–6.

Stahl, S. A., & Fairbanks, M. M. (1986). The effects of vocabulary instruction: A model-based meta-analysis. *Review of Educational Research, 56,* 72–110.

CHAPTER TEN

Anderson, L. W., Krathwohl, D. R., Airasian, P. W., Cruikshank, K. A., Mayer, R. E., Pintrich, P. R., Raths, J., & Wittrock, M. C. (2001). *A taxonomy for learning, teaching, and assessing*. New York, NY: Longman.

Banchi, H., & Bell, R. (2008). The many levels of inquiry. *Science and Children, 46*(2), 26–29.

Bell, R. L., Smetana, L, & Binns, I. (2005). Simplifying inquiry instruction: Assessing the inquiry level of classroom activities. *The Science Teacher, 72*(7), 30–33.

Bransford, J. D., Brown, A. L., & Cocking, R. R. (1999). *How people learn: Brain, mind, experience, and school*. Washington, DC: National Academy Press.

BSCS. (1989). *New designs for elementary school science and health*. Dubuque, IA: Kendall/Hunt Publishing.

BSCS. (2008). BSCS 5E Instructional Model. BSCS website. Retrieved from www.bscs.org/curriculumdevelopment/features/bscs5es.html

Dodge, B. (1995, 1997). *Some thoughts about WebQuests*. Retrieved from webquest.sdsu.edu/about_webquests.html

Dodge, B. (2007). *What is a WebQuest?* In WebQuest website. Retrieved from www.webquest.org/index.php

Friedman, A. M., & Heafner, T. L. (2007). You think for me, so I don't have to. *Contemporary Issues in Technology and Teacher Education [Online serial], 7*(3). Available: www.citejournal.org/vol7/iss3/socialstudies/article1.cfm

Hansler, D. D. (1985). *Studies on the effectiveness of the cognition enhancement techniques for teaching thinking skills.* (ERIC Document Reproduction Service No. 266 432).

Herron, M. D. 1971. The nature of scientific inquiry. *School Review 79*(2), 171–212.

inquiry. (2012). In *Merriam-Webster online dictionary.* Retrieved from www.merriam-webster.com/dictionary/inquiry

Karplus, R. (1977). *Teaching and the development of reasoning.* Berkeley, CA: University of California Press.

Levstik, L. S., & Barton, K. C. (2001). *Doing history: Investigating with children in elementary and middle schools.* Mahwah, NJ: Lawrence Erlbaum Associates.

National Council of Teachers of English. (2009). *NCTE framework for 21st century curriculum and assessment.* Retrieved from *National Council of Teachers of English:* www.ncte.org/governance/21stcenturyframework

Olson, S., & Loucks-Horsley, S. (2000). *Inquiry and the National Science Education Standards: A guide for teaching and learning.* Washington, DC: National Academies Press. Retrieved from www.nap.edu/catalog.php?record_id=9596

Rezba, R. J., Auldridge, T., & Rhea, L. (1999). *Teaching and learning the basic science skills.* Retrieved from www.doe.virginia.gov/VDOE/Instruction/TLBSSGuide.doc

Saud, M. (1990). *The scientific method of Ibn Al-Haytham.* Islamabad: Islamic Research Institute, International Islamic University.

Schwab, J. (1963). *Biological sciences curriculum study: Biology teachers' handbook.* New York, NY: Wiley.

scientific method flowchart. (n.d.). Retrieved from scifiles.larc.nasa.gov/text/kids/Research_Rack/tools/scientific_method.html

Suchman, J. R. (1962). *The elementary school training program in scientific inquiry. Report to the U.S. Office of Education, Project Title VII.* Urbana, IL: University of Illinois.

CHAPTER ELEVEN

Neufeld, V. R., & Barrows, H. S. (1974). The "McMaster Philosophy": An approach to medical education. *Journal of Medical Education, 49*(11), 1040–1050.

Schmidt, H. G., Rotgans, J. I., & Yew, E. H. (2011). The process of problem-based learning: What works and why. *Medical Education, 45,* 792–806.

Wirkala, C., & Kuhn, D. (2011). Problem-based learning in K-12 education: Is it effective and how does it achieve its effects? *American Educational Research Journal, 48*(5), 1157–1186.

CHAPTER TWELVE

Hansell, S., & Slavin, R. E. (1981). Cooperative learning and the structure of interracial friendships. *Sociology of Education, 54,* 98–106.

Johnson D. W., & Johnson, R. (1989). *Cooperation and competition: Theory and research.* Edina, MN: Interaction Book Company.

Johnson, D. W., & Johnson, R. T. (2009). An educational psychology success story: Social interdependence theory and cooperative learning. *Educational Researcher, 38*(5), 365–379.

Johnson, D.W., Johnson, R., & Holubec, E. (1998). *Cooperation in the classroom.* Boston, MA: Allyn and Bacon.

Johnson, D. W., Johnson, R. T., & Maruyama, G. (1983). Interdependence and interpersonal attraction among heterogeneous and homogeneous individuals: A theoretical formulation and a meta-analysis of the research. *Review of Educational Research, 53*(1), 5–54.

Johnson, D. W., Johnson, R. T., & Roseth, C. (2010). Cooperative learning in middle schools: Interrelationship of relationships and achievement. *Middle Grades Research Journal, 5*(1), 1–18.

Johnson, R. T., & Johnson, D. W. (1994). An overview of cooperative learning. In J. Thousand, A. Villa, and A. Nevin (Eds.), *Creativity and collaborative Learning.* Baltimore, MD: Brookes Press.

Partnership for 21st Century Skills. (2011a). Framework for 21st century learning. Retrieved from: www.p21.org/index.php?option=com_content&task=view&id=254&Itemid=119

Partnership for 21st Century Skills. (2011b). FAQ. Retrieved from: www.p21.org/index.php?option=com_content&task=view&id=195&Itemid=183#why_students

Puma, M. J., Jones, C. C., Rock, D., & Fernandez, R. (1993). Prospects: The congressionally mandated study of educational growth and opportunity. Interim Report. Bethesda, MD: Abt Associates.

Sharan, Y. (2010). Cooperative learning for academic and social gains: Valued pedagogy problematic practice. *European Journal of Education, 45*(2), 300–313.

Slavin, R. E. (1988). Cooperative learning and student achievement. *Educational Leadership, 46*(2), 31–33.

Slavin, R. E. (1991). Synthesis of research of cooperative learning. *Educational Leadership, 48*(5), 71–82.

Vygotsky, L. (1978). *Mind in society: The development of higher psychological processes.* Cambridge, MA: Harvard University Press.

CHAPTER THIRTEEN

Anderson, L. W., Krathwohl, D. R., Airasian, P. W., Cruikshank, K. A., Mayer, R. E., Pintrich, P. R., Raths, J., & Wittrock, M. C. (2001). *A taxonomy for learning, teaching, and assessing.* New York, NY: Longman.

Dewey, J. (1916) *Democracy and education. An introduction to the philosophy of education* (1966 edn.), New York: Free Press.

Kauchak, D. P., & Eggen, P. D. (2012). *Learning and teaching research-based methods* (6th ed.). Boston, MA: Pearson.

Partnership for 21st Century Skills. (2004). Framework for 21st century learning. Retrieved from: www.p21.org/index.php?option=com_content&task=view&id=254&Itemid=119

Resnick, L. B. 1987. *Education and learning to think.* Washington, DC: National Academy Press.

Vigotsky, L. V. (1962). *Thought and language.* Cambridge, MA: MIT Press.

Wiggins, G., & McTighe, J. (2005). *Understanding by design* (2nd ed.). Alexandria, VA: Association for Supervision and Curriculum Development.

CHAPTER FOURTEEN

Adler, M. J. (1982). *The Paideia proposal: An educational manifesto.* New York, NY: Collier.

Adler, M. J. (1983). *Paideia problems and possibilities: A consideration of questions raised by the Paideia proposal.* New York, NY: Macmillan.

Anderson, L. W., Krathwohl, D. R., Airasian, P. W., Cruikshank, K. A., Mayer, R. E., Pintrich, P. R., Raths, J., & Wittrock, M. C. (2001). *A taxonomy for learning, teaching, and assessing.* New York, NY: Longman.

Ball, W. H., & Brewer, P. (2000). *Socratic seminars in the block.* Larchmont, NY: Eye on Education.

Chowning, J. T., & Fraser, P. (2007). *An ethics primer.* Seattle, WA: Northwest Association of Biomedical Research.

Cookson, P. W. (2009). What would Socrates say? *Educational Leadership, 67*(1), 8–14. Retrieved from www.ascd.org/publications/educational-leadership/sept09/vol67/num01/What-Would-Socrates-Say%C2%A2.aspx

Copeland, M. (2005). *Socratic circles: Fostering critical and creative thinking in middle and high school.* Portland, ME: Stenhouse.

May, H. (2000). *On Socrates.* Belmont, CA: Wadsworth.

Moeller, V., & Moeller, M. (2001). *Socratic seminars and literature circles for middle and high school English.* Larchmont, NY: Eye on Education.

National Center for Chronic Disease Prevention and Health Promotion, Division of Adolescent and School Health. (2008). CDC's School Health Education Resources (SHER). NHES: Standard 4. *Centers for Disease Control and Prevention.* Retrieved from www.cdc.gov/HealthyYouth/SHER/standards/4.htm

Padilla, M. J. (1990). *The science process skills.* In National Association for Research in Science Teaching. Retrieved from www.narst.org/publications/research/skill.cfm

Partnership for 21st Century Skills. (2011). Framework for 21st century learning. Retrieved from www.p21.org/index.php?option=com_content&task=view&id=254&Itemid=119

Paul, R. W. (1995). *Critical thinking: How to prepare students for a rapidly changing world.* Tomales, CA: Foundation for Critical Thinking.

APPENDIX B

Crutch, S. J., & Warrington, E. K. (2005). Abstract and concrete concepts have structurally different representational frameworks. *Brain: A Journal of Neurology, 128*(3), 615–627.

Horst, H. A., Herr-Stephenson, B., & Robinson, R. (n.d.). Final report: Media ecologies. Retrieved February 14, 2009, from http://digitalyouth.ischool.berkeley.edu/book-mediaecologies

Lang, H. R., & Evans, D. N. (2006). *Models, strategies, and methods for effective teaching.* Boston: Pearson Education.

Merrill, M. D., & Tennyson, R. D. (1977). *Teaching concepts: An instructional design guide.* Englewood Cliffs, NJ: Educational Technology Publications.

Paivio, A. (1986). *Mental representations: A dual coding approach.* Oxford: Oxford University Press.

Piaget, J. (1923/1926). *The language and thought of the child.* London: Routledge and Kegan Paul.

Plaut, D. C., & Shallice, T. (1993). Deep dyslexia: A case study of connectionist neuropsychology. *Cognitive Neuropsychology, 10*, 377–500.

Schwanenflugel, P. J., & Shoben, E. J. (1983). Differential context effects in the comprehension of abstract and concrete verbal materials. *Journal of Experimental Psychology: Learning, Memory, and Cognition 9*, 82–102.

Name Index

Subject Index